Selective Serotonin Re-uptake Inhibitors

Second Edition

This series has been supported by an educational grant from
SmithKline Beecham Pharmaceuticals

PERSPECTIVES IN PSYCHIATRY VOLUME 5

Selective Serotonin Re-uptake Inhibitors

Second Edition

Advances in Basic Research and Clinical Practice

Edited by

J.P. Feighner
Feighner Research Institute, San Diego, California, USA

and

W.F. Boyer
Atlanta Veterans Administration Medical Center, USA

JOHN WILEY & SONS

Chichester · New York · Brisbane · Toronto · Singapore

Other Wiley Editorial Offices

John Wiley & Sons, Inc., 605 Third Avenue,
New York, NY 10158-0012, USA

Jacaranda Wiley Ltd, 33 Park Road, Milton,
Queensland 4064, Australia

John Wiley & Sons (Canada) Ltd, 22 Worcester Road,
Rexdale, Ontario M9W 1L1, Canada

John Wiley & Sons (Asia) Pte Ltd, 2 Clementi Loop #02-01,
Jing Xing Distripark, Singapore 0512

Library of Congress Cataloging-in-Publication Data

Selective serotonin re-uptake inhibitors : advances in basic research
and clinical practice / edited by J.P. Feighner and W.F. Boyer. —
2nd ed.
    p.   cm.—(Perspectives in psychiatry; v. 5)
    Rev. ed. of: Selective serotonin re-uptake inhibitors / J.P.
Feighner and W.F. Boyer. c1991.
    Includes bibliographical references and index.
    ISBN 0 471 95600 7 (alk. paper)
    1. Antidepressants. 2. Serotonin uptake inhibitors.
3. Serotoninergic mechanisms. I. Feighner, John Preston, 1937–
II. Boyer, W. F. III. Series: Perspectives in psychiatry
(Chichester, England): v.5
    [DNLM]: 1. Serotonin Antagonists—therapeutic use. 2. Mental
Disorders—drug therapy.   W1 PE871F v.5 1996 / QV 126 S463 1996]
RM332.F45 1996
616.85′ 27061—dc20
DNLM/DLC
for Library of Congress   95-39512
                                                                CIP

British Library Cataloguing in Publication Data

A catalogue record for this book is available from the British Library

ISBN 0 471 956007

Typeset in 10/12pt Garamond ITC by Vision Typesetting, Manchester
Printed and bound in Great Britain by Biddles Ltd, Guildford
This book is printed on acid-free paper responsibly manufactured from sustainable forestation,
for which at least two trees are planted for each one used for paper production.

Contents

Contributors

J.C. Ballanger

Director – Institute of Psychiatry, Medical University of South Carolina, 171 Ashley Avenue, Charleston, South Carolina, 29425-0742, USA

E.R. Berndt

Professor of Applied Economics, MIT Sloan School of Management, Analysis Group Inc., One Brattle Square, 5th Floor, Cambridge, MA 02138, USA

R.J. Boland

Assistant Professor, Department of Psychiatry and Human Behavior, Brown University, Department of Psychiatry, Miriam Hospital, USA

W.F. Boyer

Veterans Hospital, Psychiatric Department, 1670 Clairemont Drive, Decatur, Georgia, GA 30033, USA

K. Brøsen

Dept of Pharmacology, Institute of Medical Biology, Odense University, Winsløwparken 19, DK-5000, Odense, Denmark

P.J. Cowen

MRC Clinical Scientist, Department of Psychiatry, Littlemore Hospital, Oxford OX4 4XN

D.L. Dunner

Department of Psychiatry & Behavioural Sciences, Outpatient Psychiatry Centre, 4225 Roosevelt Way N.E., Suite 306, Seattle, WA 98105, USA

G.J. Emslie

Department of Psychiatry, University of Texas Southwestern Medical Centre at Dallas, 5323 Harry Hines Boulevard, Dallas, Texas, TX 75235-9070, USA

J.P. Feighner

Feighner Research Institute, 5375 Mira Sorrento Place, East Tower Building, 2nd Floor, Suite 210, San Diego, CA 92121, USA

S.N. Finkelstein

Executive Director, Pharmaceutical Indu, MIT Sloan School of Management, Analysis Group Inc., One Brattle Square, 5th Floor, Cambridge, MA 02138, USA

P.E. Greenberg

Vice-President and Director, Health Care Economics Practice, Analysis Group Inc., One Brattle Square, 5th Floor, Cambridge, MA 02138, USA

E. Hollander

Department of Psychiatry, Mount Sinai School of Medicine, One Gustave L Levy Place, New York, NY 10029, USA

C.L.E. Katona

Department of Psychiatry, UCL Medical School, Wolfson Building, Middlesex Site, Riding House Street, London W1N 8AA

M.B. Keller

Mary E. Zucker Professor and Chairman, Department of Psychiatry and Human Behavior, Brown University School of Medicine, Butler Hospital, 345 Blackstone Boulevard, Providence, Rhode Island, 02906, USA

R.C. Kessler

Institute for Social Research, Department of Sociology, University of Michigan, USA

B.E. Leonard

University College Galway, Department of Pharmacology, Galway, Eire

C.A. Marsden

Dept of Physiology & Pharmacology, University of Nottingham Medical School, Queen's Medical Centre, Nottingham NG7 2UH

S.A. Montgomery

St Mary's Hospital Medical School, Academic Psychiatry Department, Praed Street, London W2

T.L. Nells

Associate, Analysis Group Inc., One Brattle Square, 5th Floor, Cambridge, MA 02138, USA

B.B. Rasmussen

Dept of Clinical Pharmacology, Institute of Medical Biology, Odense University, Winsløwparken 19, DK-5000, Odense, Denmark

D.J. Stein

Department of Psychiatry, University of Stellen-bosch, PO Box 19063, Tygerberg 7505, South Africa

M.E. Zucker

Professor and Chairman, Dept of Psychiatry and Human Behaviour, Brown University, Miriam Hospital, 345 Blackstone Boulevard, Providence, Rhode Island, 02906, USA

In memoriam
Eli Robins, M.D.
February 22, 1921 – December 21, 1994
With admiration, respect and appreciation for a great thinker
and inspirational teacher

Preface to the second edition

The first edition to this book was published a mere five years ago. Since that time there has been an explosion of interest about and use of the selective serotonin re-uptake inhibitors in clinical medicine. During this time the SSRIs have established themselves as important medications in both medical and popular culture. The media have swung from regarding the SSRIs as panacea to poison and seem to be coming back to a reasonable middle ground. Fortunately, science works as it always does; with the collection of more data and more experience the true value of these compounds is easier to appreciate.

We have undertaken the second edition to update the reader on this wealth of data. We have again aimed the book at all those who take care of depressed patients, but especially at practising mental health professionals, primary care providers and trainees in these fields. There is sometimes a dichotomy in these disciplines between those who regard nothing as proven without a series of replicated, well-designed experiments and those who embrace therapies on the basis of little controlled data. This is a healthy tension, as it reflects the sometimes differing goals of scientists and clinicians. It is true that initial promising reports often do not stand up to further investigation, but is it also true that many important discoveries stem from the observations of clinicians.

In writing and editing this book we have tried to do justice to both sides. Controlled data, case series and even a few personal observations and communications from colleagues are included and duly referenced. We leave it to the intelligence and backgound of our readers to draw the appropriate conclusions. We hope that this book will prove to be both a good review and a resource document for those in the field of helping people with emotional disorders.

JP Feighner
WF Boyer

Preface to the first edition

Over the past ten years, we have had the opportunity to work with citalopram, fluoxetine, fluvoxamine, paroxetine, sertraline, and other selective serotonin re-uptake inhibitors. We are convinced that these drugs represent a significant addition in psychiatry because of their relative lack of side-effects, low toxicity in overdose, and broad range of potential clinical indications. Indeed, their widespread and increasing use in the United States and other countries underlines this importance. We therefore undertook the writing of this book to create a document that reflects the state of the art in terms of the clinical issues surrounding these medications.

The first chapter of the book reviews the evidence that points to the effects of these drugs on serotonergic function and the central role of serotonin in many psychiatric disorders, while the following chapter reviews the pharmacology of the selective serotonin re-uptake inhibitors. The remaining chapters contain reviews of clinical trials of the selective serotonin re-uptake inhibitors in many of the conditions previously mentioned, concluding with a chapter on important clinical issues in the use of these agents.

We have aimed this book at all those who take care of depressed patients, but especially at residents and clinicians in psychiatry and general medicine. Clinicians are confronted daily with human suffering and require knowledge of what is both safe and effective for their patients. This is a different stance from that of the pure scientist, who accepts nothing as fact until replicated experimental evidence is available. Hence the purpose of this book is to review the available evidence from a clinical standpoint. We have offered conclusions based on considerable data and conjectures based on more limited evidence and have tried to indicate which is which. We have made use of our own experience, controlled studies, case series, and case reports, as well as studies from the animal literature. We have also included an extensive bibliography to allow the reader to delve into subjects at greater depth. It is our sincere hope that the reader will find this book not only an introduction to an important and rapidly growing area but also a useful reference work.

JP Feighner
WF Boyer

1

The neuropharmacology of serotonin in the central nervous system

Charles A. Marsden

INTRODUCTION

Serotonin (5-hydroxytryptamine, 5-HT) is an indoleamine with a wide distribution in plants, animals, and man. In mammals it is found in blood platelets, mast cells and the enterochromaffin cells of the gut. The peripheral actions of serotonin include vasoconstriction (and some vasodilatation) together with a role in the control of gut tone and motility due to smooth muscle contraction. Platelet serotonin has an important role in platelet aggregation involving 5-HT_2 receptor activation. Within the brain and spinal cord serotonin acts as an important neurotransmitter involved in a variety of physiological and behavioural functions ranging from the control of sleep and wakefulness, feeding, thermoregulation, cardiovascular function, emesis, sexual behaviour, spinal regulation of motor function, emotional and psychotic behaviour, and drug-induced hallucinatory states.

Our knowledge of the basic plan of the serotonin-containing pathways in the central nervous system (CNS) dates back from the pioneering work of the Swedish school of histochemists established by Falck and Hillarp (Falck *et al.*, 1962) who used the fluorescence histochemical method to visualize catechol and indoleamines *in situ* in the brain. These studies showed that serotonin was localized within specific neuronal pathways, the cell bodies being found in discrete brain nuclei—the midbrain and brain stem raphe nuclei (Dahlström and Fuxe, 1964). During the following 15–20 years, information about the role of serotonin pathways in the

Selective Serotonin Re-uptake Inhibitors: Advances in Basic Research and Clinical Practice, Second Edition, Edited by J.P. Feighner and W.F. Boyer
© 1996 John Wiley & Sons Ltd

control of physiological and behavioural functions has expanded, largely based on a growing understanding of the control of serotonin metabolism in the nerve endings and on the development of drugs that interfered with this process. One of the major events in this process was the development of compounds that prevented the enzymatic inactivation, or the re-uptake of serotonin released from nerve endings and the finding that such drugs possessed antidepressant effects.

It was not until the late 1970s and the early 1980s that the great explosion occurred in our understanding of the receptor systems involved in serotonergic function. It is now clear that there is not a single 5-HT receptor, but a family of receptors subserving specific functions at pre- and postsynaptic sites. The identification of these receptor subtypes and the development of relatively selective agonists and antagonists has and will continue to increase our understanding of the functional role of serotonin and our awareness of the large clinical potential of drugs that alter serotonergic function.

The aim of the present article is to provide a general overview of the current state of knowledge of the neuroanatomy, neurochemistry, and neuropharmacology of the serotonergic neurones in the CNS and to review their possible role in behaviour and mental disease.

SEROTONERGIC PATHWAYS IN THE CNS

Early studies demonstrated that serotonin was found in substantial amounts in cat and dog brain but with regional variations (Twarog and Page, 1953; Amin et al., 1954): the limbic regions showed especially high serotonin levels, indicating an involvement in emotional behaviour. It was the systematic studies of the Swedish group, using fluorescence histochemistry, that led to the detailed mapping of the serotonin-containing neurones in the raphe nuclei and their forebrain and spinal projections (Dahlström and Fuxe, 1964; Fuxe, 1965; Fuxe et al., 1968). Later Steinbusch and colleagues in Holland developed an antibody to serotonin and refined the earlier maps of the serotonergic pathways in the rat brain using immunohistochemistry (Steinbusch et al., 1978; Steinbusch, 1981). More recently, further immunocytochemical studies have revealed a structural heterogeneity in the axon terminals that arise from the dorsal and median raphe (Kosofsky and Molliver, 1987). Such morphological diversity, linked with the receptor diversity described later, may be important in understanding the role of serotonin in the control of emotional behaviour.

Serotonin pathways to the forebrain

Numerous studies have shown that the serotonergic projections to the forebrain arise from cell bodies within the raphe nuclei of the rostral brainstem: principally the dorsal and median raphe nuclei (Figure 1). The projections of these two nuclei do

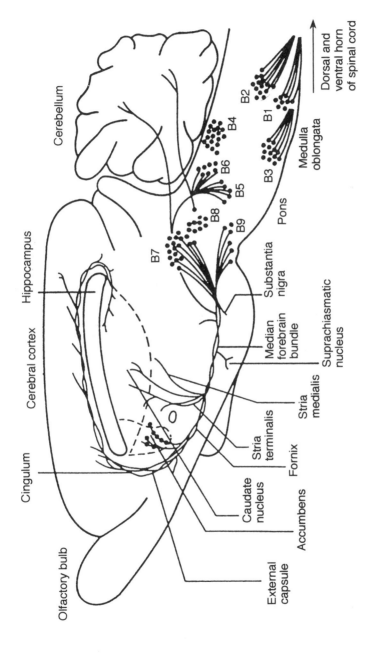

Figure 1. Schematic diagram showing the distribution of the main serotonin-containing pathways in the rat brain. B4–B9 = midbrain raphe nuclei serotonin neuronal cell bodies. B1–B3 = brain stem raphe serotonin cell bodies. (Adapted from Cooper *et al*, 1982.)

not fully overlap with a relatively specific innervation of some forebrain areas by one of the nuclei. While the projections to the hippocampus come mainly from the median raphe, those to the striatum are from the dorsal raphe, but both nuclei send serotonergic projections to the cortex. Thus, the rostral part of the dorsal raphe projects to the striatum and cortex while the caudal portion, along with neurones in the median raphe, projects to the hippocampus (Jacobs *et al.*, 1974). Furthermore, the cortical pathways from the different parts of the dorsal raphe may use separate routes (Tohyama *et al.*, 1980). Hence the innervation of the forebrain by serotonergic fibres is widespread (cortex, hippocampus, striatum, amygdala, accumbens, substantia nigra, hypothalamus) but arises from neurones within two discrete raphe nuclei. However, within the various brain regions, the serotonergic innervation is organized so that identifiable cell groups within the two raphe nuclei send projections to multiple, but functionally related, cortical regions.

Further diversification occurs at the level of axons and their terminals, with regional specialization in the pattern of the cortical serotonergic innervation. There are differences within the various cortical areas in the morphology, density, and orientation of the serotonin terminals (Molliver, 1987). Their density is very high in the frontal cortex and decreases in more caudal areas, while in the cingulate cortex, outer areas of the parietal cortex, and the hippocampus, there is a clear laminated arrangement of coarse beaded fibres. In other areas of the cortex the fibres are very fine.

Interestingly, this morphological heterogeneity of the fibres appears to be linked to their origins in the two raphe nuclei, the coarse beaded fibres coming from serotonergic neurones in the median raphe and fine fibres from the dorsal raphe (Kosofsky and Molliver, 1987; Mamoumas *et al.*, 1992).

The morphological diversity of the serotonergic innervation of the cortical and hippocampal (limbic) regions raises several intriguing questions:

1. Do the two types of fibres have different sensitivities to drugs that modify serotonin function?
2. Are the different fibre types associated with specific functional roles and what is the distinction between the functions of the dorsal versus the median raphe serotonergic neurones?
3. Are there mechanisms (receptors?) that allow selective activation or inhibition of specific serotonergic cell groups within the two raphe nuclei and thus differential control of the serotonergic innervation of specific cortical areas?

With regard to the first question, there is some debate at present. Molliver and his co-workers, using immunohistochemistry, have demonstrated a selective neurotoxic action of a range of amphetamine-derived neurotoxins (e.g. parachloroamphetamine, fenfluramine, 3,4-methylenedioxyamphetamine (MDA), 3,4-methylenedioxymethamphetamine (MDMA) and methamphetamine) on the fine serotonergic terminals while the beaded terminals are spared (Mamoumas *et al.*, 1992, Molliver and Molliver, 1990). These data suggest that the dorsal raphe neurones are selectively vulnerable to the neurotoxins and, in particular, the dorsal raphe cortical innervation as this is one of the major locations of the fine terminals. Recent studies, however, using *in vivo* microdialysis to measure changes in extracellular serotonin have shown that fenfluramine can release serotonin from dorsal and median raphe derived nerve terminals in the frontal cortex (dorsal raphe) and the dorsal hippocampus (median raphe) (McQuade *et al.*, 1995). The microdialysis studies are, however, looking at the acute pharmacological effects of the drugs and these findings do not exclude the possibility that although the pharmacological effects are similar on dorsal and median raphe neurones, there might also be a longer term selective vulnerability of the dorsal raphe neurones to the neurotoxic effects of these amphetamine-based drugs.

The second question concerns the functional diversity of fine (dorsal raphe) versus beaded (median raphe) terminals. It remains to be determined whether the auto- and heteroreceptor regulation of these two types of neurones differ both at the cell body and terminal level, and whether fine and beaded terminals are associated with different postsynaptic serotonergic receptor subtypes. A greater understanding of the physiological functional diversity of these two types of terminals will help determine whether it is possible to distinguish between them at a behavioural level and thus their relevance to antidepressant drug action.

Serotonergic innervation of the spinal cord

Both the dorsal and ventral horns and the intermediolateral column of the spinal cord receive a serotonergic innervation from cell bodies located within the raphe nuclei of the caudal brain stem (raphe magnus, pallidus, and obscurus, Figure 1). The innervation of the dorsal horn comes mainly from neurones situated in the raphe magnus and is principally concerned with modulation of sensory (pain) information. In contrast, the ventral horn innervation comes from serotonergic cells in the raphe pallidus and obscurus and plays an important role in the regulation of motor function, while the serotonergic fibres in the intermediolateral column come from the same raphe nuclei and are involved in the regulation of sympathetic activity.

An important feature of the spinal serotonergic system is the coexistence of various neuropeptides with serotonin. Specific examples of this are the coexistence of substance P, thyrotrophin-releasing hormone, a proctolin-like peptide, and galanin within serotonin in the neurones projecting to the ventral horn (Johanssen *et al.*, 1981; Gilbert *et al.*, 1982). The relationship between the indoleamine and peptides is not simple. Firstly, not all the peptides are found in all serotonergic neurones: some contain only serotonin, while others contain serotonin plus one or more of the peptides (Hökfelt *et al.*, 1991). Secondly, some peptides (e.g. substance P, thyrotrophin-releasing hormone) enhance the 5-HT$_2$ postsynaptic receptor-mediated responses (e.g. back muscle contractions, Fone *et al.*, 1991), while proctolin has inhibitory effects on the same responses. In some cases, the peptide interaction may be via direct modulation of serotonergic receptor function at the postsynaptic level, while in others the peptide may act at a presynaptic site to modulate the release of serotonin. An improved understanding of these mechanisms will increase our knowledge of the control of spinal motor function and aid the treatment of motor disorders (e.g. amylolateral sclerosis).

It should be borne in mind that drugs that act on serotonergic systems, such as selective serotonin re-uptake inhibitors, will potentiate 5-HT receptor-mediated events in the spinal cord as well as in the brain; thus spinal effects may have a role in the clinical profile of these drugs. For example, re-uptake inhibitors are known to alter reproductive activity in female animals (Everitt, 1977), and such effects may involve a spinal serotonergic motor component. A final point for consideration with regard to spinal serotonergic innervation is the need carefully to assign the correct serotonergic system (forebrain or spinal) to the behavioural effects observed with serotonergic drugs. Thus, many components of the classical serotonin syndrome (e.g. hindlimb abduction and forepaw treading) that are produced by systemic administration of serotonin agonists (for review see Heal *et al.*, 1992) also occur when the drugs are given intrathecally—i.e. directly into the lumbar region of the spinal cord, indicating that they are mediated by 5-HT receptors in the spinal cord and not in the brain (Fone *et al.*, 1991).

SYNTHESIS AND METABOLISM OF SEROTONIN IN THE CNS

The levels of serotonin in the CNS only represent about 1–2% of the total amount found in the body (Bradley, 1989). The indoleamine cannot cross the blood–brain barrier, and hence all the neuronal serotonin in the CNS is synthesized locally. Serotonin is formed by a two-step process involving the hydroxylation of the essential amino acid L-tryptophan to 5-hydroxytryptophan (5-HTP), which is then decarboxylated to serotonin (Figure 2).

L-tryptophan crosses the blood–brain and neuronal barriers using a competitive, facilitated transported carrier for neutral amino acids. Tryptophan is hydroxylated by tryptophan hydroxylase; this is the rate-limiting step in the synthesis of serotonin and as under normal physiological conditions the enzyme is not saturated, situations that lead to an increase in brain tryptophan and oral tryptophan stimulate synthesis and, on this basis, L-tryptophan preparations have been used in the treatment of depression. There is, however, still debate as to whether the increase in synthesis results in increased release; a controversy supported by the equivocal results obtained that tryptophan potentiates the antidepressant effects of monoamine oxidase inhibitors (Coppen and Swade, 1988). There are also several studies illustrating the successful use of L-tryptophan challenges to investigate neuroendocrine function (prolactin release) in normal and depressed patients (Siever *et al.*, 1986; Cowen *et al.*, 1988; Goodwin *et al.*, 1987; Deakin *et al.*, 1990). Various other factors have been shown to influence the availability of tryptophan to the CNS, including the

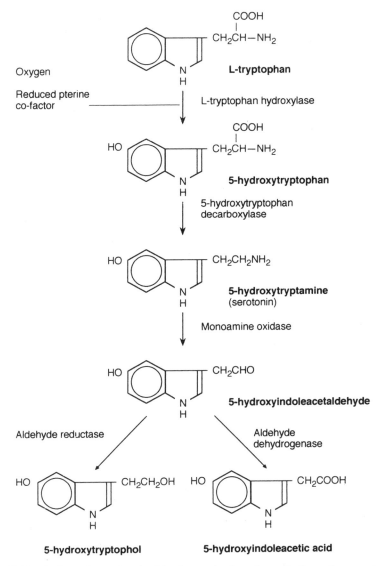

Figure 2. Metabolic pathways involved in the synthesis and metabolism of serotonin.

state of the liver with respect to tryptophan metabolism (hepatic encephalopathy is characterized by very high levels of tryptophan in the brain) and the degree of plasma protein binding.

Serotonin can be synthesized in both the cell bodies (raphe nuclei) and the terminals, although the latter site is probably more important for the short-term regulation of serotonin synthesis. Serotonin formed in the cell body is transported to the terminals of the dendrites and axon, release taking place by a Ca^{++}-dependent process from the readily releasable pool of serotonin stored in vesicles to protect it from metabolism by mitochondrial monoamine oxidase (MAO). There is evidence that newly synthesized serotonin is preferentially released (Kuhn *et al.*, 1986), but it is not clear whether release takes place exclusively from the vesicles: there may be two pools of serotonin in the terminals, cytoplasmic and vesicular, which release sero — tonin under different physiological conditions (Grahame-Smith, 1974; Elks *et al.*, 1979).

Following its release, serotonin is inactivated principally by re-uptake into sertonergic nerve terminals using a Na^+/K^+ ATPase-dependent carrier (Shaskan and Snyder, 1970). Once back inside the serotonergic neurone the transmitter is either re-stored in the vesicles (Slotkin *et al.*, 1978) or metabolized by MAO, an enzyme widely distributed throughout the body and primarily located within the brain on the outer mitochondrial membrane. Not only does MAO metabolize serotonin, it also deaminates amines with the general formula R-CH_2-NH_2, where R is a substituted aryl or alkyl group. The amines that fall into this category include serotonin, dopamine, noradrenaline, adrenaline, tyramine, and tryptamine. It is now evident that there are two forms of MAO: A and B—the preferred substrates for A being noradrenaline and serotonin, while tyramine, tryptamine, and dopamine are the preferred substrates from type B although they can also be deaminated by type A. This recognition of the A and B isoenzymes has led to the development of MAO inhibitors with selectivity for either.

SITES FOR DRUG ACTION

Within this scheme of the synthesis and metabolism of serotonin there are several steps at which drugs can either increase or decrease the neuronal function of serotonin (Figure 3, Fuller, 1985).

Changes in the availability of tryptophan due to tryptophan administration or a low-tryptophan diet will increase or decrease, respectively, the metabolism of serotonin although this will not necessarily alter the neuronal release of serotonin.

Decreased synthesis of serotonin follows the inhibition of tryptophan hydroxylase by parachlorophenylalanine. As tryptophan hydroxylase is the rate-limiting step in the production of serotonin, inhibition of this enzyme leads to a profound decrease in the levels of serotonin in the brain. There are other compounds that decrease tryptophan hydroxylase activity, including various tryptophan analogues (e.g. 6-fluorotryptophan) and halogenated analogues of amphetamine (e.g. p-chloroamphetamine and fenfluramine). The full mechanism of action of the latter group of compounds on serotonergic neurones is not fully understood but involves several actions apart from inhibition of tryptophan hydroxylase (Fuller, 1985), including non-Ca^{++}-dependent release of serotonin (see below), re-uptake inhibition, and a possible neurotoxic action on selected serotonergic neurones as already discussed. Inhibitors of tryptophan hydroxylase have had considerable

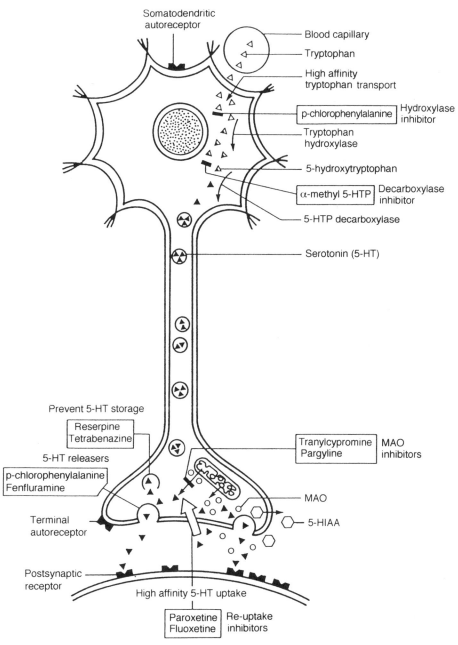

Figure 3. Diagram of a serotonin nerve terminal showing the main events in the life cycle of serotonin and the sites at which drugs may influence serotonergic function. For clarity, examples of drugs acting at serotonergic receptors have been omitted. (Adapted from Cooper *et al.*, 1982.)

impact on experimental work to investigate the function of serotonin, but have no clinical value.

Inhibition of 5-HTP decarboxylase has little effect on serotonin levels as this enzyme is normally saturated. Furthermore, this enzyme also decarboxylates DOPA so that inhibitors will influence the synthesis of both serotonin and dopamine. The basal levels of 5-HTP (and DOPA) are normally too low to be measured by existing methodology. However, decarboxylase inhibition leads to a rapid accumulation of these precursors, and this can be used as an index of the rate of serotonin synthesis.

Reserpine—which produced long-term depletion of serotonin (and catecholamines), and tetrabenazine—which causes short-term depletion of serotonin, prevent the intraneuronal storage of serotonin. By preventing storage, these drugs expose newly synthesized serotonin to MAO, leading to amine depletion and increased tissue levels of the metabolites (5-HIAA in the case of serotonin). The behavioural effects of amine depletion by reserpine constituted a landmark in the early understanding of the possible involvement of serotonin and noradrenaline in depression, but the universal effect of the drug on intraneuronal amine storage systems and the consequent general depletion of all amines limit the use of reserpine in studies that wish to investigate specifically the function of serotonin.

Drugs that increase serotonin release (p-chloroamphetamine, fenfluramine) act by causing Ca^{++}-independent release and have relatively specific effects because they enter serotonergic nerve terminals using the selective uptake system. A long established *in vivo* test for novel uptake inhibitors has been their ability to prevent the effects of serotonin released by p-chloroamphetamine. Both p-chloroamphetamine and fenfluramine increase serotonin release *in vitro* (Garattini *et al.*, 1975) and *in vivo* (Marsden *et al.*, 1979; Crespi *et al.*, 1990), resulting acutely in behaviours induced by stimulation of the serotonin receptor (Trulson and Jacobs, 1976). The usefulness of these drugs for the investigation of serotonergic function has been limited by their long-term effects on tryptophan hydroxylase and by possible neurotoxicity towards serotonergic neurons, resulting in decreased neuronal serotonin.

The irreversible monoamine oxidase inhibitors such as tranylcypromine, pargyline and, more recently the selective MAO A (clorgyline) and MAO B (selegiline) inhibitors, reduce serotonin metabolism. These drugs will principally increase intraneuronal cytoplasmic serotonin as it will not be metabolized following re-uptake from the synaptic cleft. This results in an increase in the amount of serotonin available for release, and consequently in an increase in extracellular serotonin and a decrease in 5-HIAA *in vivo* (Sleight *et al.*, 1988a; Crespi *et al.*, 1990).

The antidepressant properties of the non-selective (i.e. A and B) MAO inhibitors (for review see Murphy *et al.*, 1986) have played an important role in the development of the amine theory of depression. The potential advantage of the selective MAO B inhibitors as antidepressants was that they would have the clinical effects of the non-selective inhibitors without the adverse effects caused by the inhibition of the tyramine metabolism, as this amine is metabolized by MAO A, however, selegiline is not antidepressant. More recently, interest has focused on the reversible inhibitors of MAO A (RIMAs) such as moclobemide as these have antidepressant properties but are relatively free of side-effects.

Drugs that inhibit the neuronal re-uptake of serotonin range from compounds that inhibit both noradrenaline and serotonin re-uptake (amitriptyline, imipramine) to those that are selective for either noradrenaline (maprotiline) or serotonin (paroxetine, fluoxetine) re-uptake. Over many years these drugs have been conspicuously the most successful antidepressants, although possessing certain disadvantages in the case of the non-selective tricyclics (notably antimuscarinic side-effects) and the common problem of a slow onset of antidepressant action (2–3 weeks). The delay in onset of action provides a challenge to supporters of the amine theory in terms of explaining why the delay occurs when inhibition of re-uptake is immediate. This has led to the concept that adaptive changes are involved in the clinical effects of the re-uptake and MAO inhibitors as well as those in lithium. Thus the most relevant experimental work involves chronic treatment with antidepressants, combined with a detailed investigation of the functional status of serotonergic neurones. In recent years, this work has made considerable advances due to the marked increase in our understanding of the 5-HT receptor and, in particular, the emergence of a variety of 5-HT receptor subtypes and increased knowledge about their specific functional roles in the control of serotonergic function (see below).

SEROTONIN RECEPTORS

As already mentioned, there has been a rapid increase in our understanding of the receptors associated with serotonergic function in the periphery and in central neurones. It is now well established that there are multiple 5-HT receptors (Hoyer *et al.*, 1994): currently the number is about 14 (Figure 4) and there has been a consequent development of numerous compounds with relative specificity for one or more of those receptor subtypes. The initial classification of 5-HT receptors was based on ligand binding studies, any functional identification being based largely on investigations using peripheral preparations (Bradley *et al.*, 1986). In recent years the explosion of information about receptor diversity has been fuelled by the application of molecular biology to identify the structure of the receptors which has made it possible to chart the structural interrelationships between the subtypes (Figure 4).

The neuropharmacology of serotonin receptors in the CNS

The question of physiological function in the brain is generally the least understood because of the lack of appropriate methodology with which to overcome the

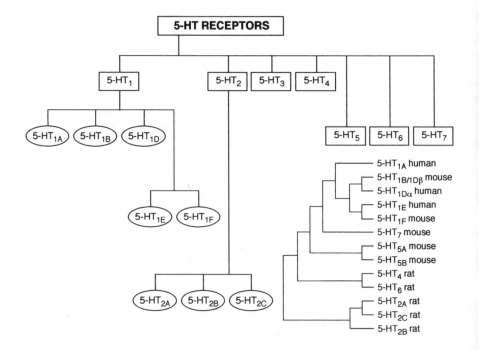

Figure 4. Serotonin receptor subtypes (inset: dendogram of the amino acid sequences to show the degree of homology between the different subtypes).

problems of studying CNS mechanisms. Despite these limitations, there is now substantial information to indicate the possible role of specific 5-HT receptors in the regulation of serotonergic function in the brain (Aghajanian, 1992; Marsden and Kendall, 1992). The present discussion will concentrate on the functional role of the 5-HT receptor subtypes and on their possible involvement in the antidepressant action of inhibitors of serotonin re-uptake (e.g. paroxetine). There is a vast selection of drugs (agonists, antagonists, partial agonists) with affinity for one or more of the serotonin receptors (e.g. see Hoyer $et\ al.$, 1994 for a comprehensive review of the available compounds).

It should be noted, however, that very few drugs are really selective for one receptor subtype. The exceptions are few and include 8-OHDPAT, an agonist at the 5-HT$_{1A}$ receptor (although even this drug has affinity for 5-HT$_7$ receptors) and some of the 5-HT$_{1A}$ partial agonists, ritanserin as an antagonist of 5-HT$_2$ receptors (but with affinity for both 5-HT$_{2A}$ and 5-HT$_{2C}$ receptors), and some of the 5-HT$_3$ antagonists (e.g. ondansetron). This lack of absolute selectivity for a specific receptor complicates investigations using these novel compounds to determine the functional role of the receptor subtypes but various approaches can be used.

Identification of the effector systems that link the receptor subtype with a physiological response such as release of Ca^{++}

The effector systems are either biochemical (coupled to adenylyl cyclase or phosphoinositide hydrolysis) or involve direct linkage to a cation membrane channel (K^{+}) (Figure 5, Conn and Sanders-Bush, 1987).

Adenylyl cyclase: 5-HT receptors are either negatively or positively coupled to adenylate cyclase. It is important, when trying to understand the physiological relevance of the 5-HT receptor-linked changes in adenylate cyclase or phosphoinositide hydrolysis, also to understand how information is transduced from the membrane recognition site (the receptor) through the receptor-coupled mechanisms. The receptors are coupled to the biochemical effect system by one of several G protein systems. The effector system influences the physiology of the neurone (or other cell type) by altering ion conductance across membrane, either directly or by producing second messengers inside the cell (cyclic AMP from ATP or inositol phosphates and diacylglycerol from polyphosphoinositides). These second messengers can then mobilize intracellular Ca^{++} or activate protein kinases (Berridge, 1984).

The cyclic AMP/adenylate cyclase-linked receptors work through the protein kinases, which lead to the phosphorylation of phosphoproteins inside the cells, which in turn regulate various aspects of cell function (including carbohydrate metabolism, neurotransmitter release, and ion conductance, Nestler and Greengard, 1983). Thus activation or inhibition of adenylyl cyclase and the subsequent change in the conversion of ATP to cyclic AMP can have a variety of effects of cellular function but, in the case of neuronal 5-HT receptors, the most important are the effects on cation conductance and neurotransmitter release.

One further complication should be considered when assessing the importance of observed changes in the accumulation of cyclic AMP (the normal way of measuring changes in adenylate cyclase activity). There are examples of receptors that activate more than one type of effector pathway; hence, although one might establish that a particular 5-HT receptor subtype is linked to adenylate cyclase, the same receptor may also be linked to another effector system through a different G protein. With these points in mind, one can consider the relevance of the linkage of 5-HT receptor subtypes to adenylyl cyclase (Figure 5).

All the existing 5-HT$_1$ subtypes are negatively linked to adenylyl cyclase. This effect is difficult to show experimentally as the reduction is small (20–30%), and the most effective studies have investigated the inhibition by 5-HT$_1$ agonists of the forskolin-induced increase in adenylyl cyclase in cultured (Bockaert *et al.*, 1987) and homogenate hippocampal preparations (De Vivo and Maayani, 1986). The pharmacological data indicate that such inhibition is associated with 5-HT$_{1A}$ receptor activation (De Vivo and Maayani, 1988; Sleight *et al.*, 1988b). Similar studies have shown that the 5-HT$_{1D}$ receptor in the substantia nigra of the guinea-pig is also negatively linked to adenylyl cyclase (Waeber *et al.*, 1989) as is the 5-HT$_{1B}$ receptor in cultures of hamster fibroblasts (Sevwen *et al.*, 1988).

Although there are no published accounts that 5-HT$_1$ receptors are positively

14

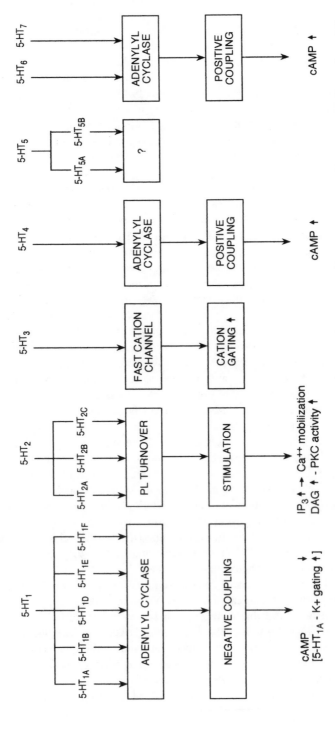

Figure 5. The main effector mechanisms involved in serotonin receptor mediated actions. Data compiled from reviews by Marsden and Kendall, 1992; Hoyer et al, 1994; Lucas and Hen, 1995.

cAMP = cyclic AMP; IP$_3$ = inositol 1,4,5-triphosphate; DAG = diacyglycerol; PKC = protein kinase C; PL = phospholipid.

*Some evidence for positive coupling with 5-HT$_{1A}$.

linked to adenylyl cyclase in membrane preparations, it has been shown that Xenopus oocytes injected with 5-HT_{1A} receptor, mRNA, demonstrate positive coupling (Uezeno *et al.*, 1993). The matter is further complicated by the observation that *in vivo* activation of putative 5-HT_{1A} receptors in the rat hippocampus using 8-OHDPAT produces an increase in extracellular cAMP measured using *in vivo* microdialysis (Cadogan *et al.*, 1994). Whether this increase in cAMP represents positive coupling of 5-HT_{1A} receptors or positive coupling of 5-HT_7 receptors for which 8-OHDPAT also has affinity remains to be determined. However, it is clear that the interpretation of *in vitro* data in terms of predicted *in vivo* responses may not be simple. In summary, there is evidence that 5-HT_{1A}, 5-HT_{1B} and 5-HT_{1D} receptors are all negatively linked to adenylyl cyclase *in vitro*, probably leading to increased K^+ conductance, thereby decreasing the entry of Ca^{++}. Whether 5-HT_{1A} receptors are positively linked to adenylyl cyclase *in vivo* remains to be determined.

The 5-HT_4, 5-HT_6 and 5-HT_7 receptors are also coupled to adenylyl cyclase but with all these receptors the coupling is positive, using receptors expressed in cell culture (e.g. Plasat *et al.*, 1993; Shenker *et al.*, 1987; Dumuis *et al.*, 1988).

Phosphoinositide hydrolysis
The phosphoinositide second messenger can, through the major products of its reactions (diacyglycerol and inositol triphosphate), either increase intracellular Ca^{++} or activate specific protein kinases in a similar manner to the adenylyl cyclase system. Extensive pharmacological studies have demonstrated that the 5-HT_2 family of receptors (5-HT_{2A}, 5-HT_{2B} and 5-HT_{2C}) are all linked to the phosphoinositide hydrolysis system (for review see Hoyer *et al.*, 1994). In blood platelets and the cerebral cortex, which are both rich in 5-HT_2 binding sites, serotonin stimulates the formation of inositol phosphate with a good correlation between the increase and its inhibition by known 5-HT_2 antagonists (Kendall and Nahorski, 1985; Conn and Sanders-Bush, 1985).

Within the choroid plexus, which regulates both the formation and composition of cerebrospinal fluid, the only 5-HT receptor subtype identified using radioligand binding studies is the 5-HT_{2C} site (Pazos *et al.*, 1985). This receptor, like the 5-HT_2 site in the cortex, is also linked to phosphoinositide hydrolysis, based on antagonist studies (Conn and Sanders-Bush, 1986; Conn *et al.*, 1986). 5-HT_{2C} receptors are not exclusively located within the choroid plexus, and behavioural effects following activation of 5-HT_{2C} receptors (e.g. administration of 1-(3-chlorophenyl) piperazine (mCPP)) have been reported which are not associated with choroid plexus function. Most interesting of these effects in the context of the present discussion is that mCPP tends to cause panic attacks in individuals susceptible to these attacks (Charney *et al.*, 1987; Kalus *et al.*, 1990) and that 5-HT_{2C} receptors have been identified in brain regions, such as the amygdala, associated with defence behaviour (Pompeiano *et al.*, 1994). Interestingly, the 5-HT_{2C} response in the choroid plexus is increased following serotonergic denervation with the neurotoxin 5,7-dihydroxy-tryptamine, indicating denervation supersensitivity and a postsynaptic location for the 5-HT$_{2C}$ receptor (Conn *et al.*, 1987). However, similar denervation had no effect on the 5-HT$_{2A}$-mediated cortical response (Conn and Sanders-Bush, 1986). More recently it has been shown that rearing rats in social isolation, which increases responsiveness to aversive situations, also leads to 5-HT$_{2C}$ receptor supersensitivity as measured by the behavioural effects of mCPP (Fone *et al.*, 1995).

The effector linkage mechanisms for the serotonin receptors are summarized in Figure 5.

Identification of serotonin receptors that regulate serotonin neuronal firing, release and metabolism

It is now established that negative feedback, autoreceptor control of neuronal function, is a common feature of amine neurones, the receptors being located on the dendrites and on the neuronal soma (somatodendritic autoreceptors), and on the nerve terminals (terminal autoreceptors). The interesting feature of the serotonergic system is that the somatodendritic and terminal autoreceptors are different subtypes, in contrast to the noradrenergic system where the function at both sites is served by the α_2-adrenoceptor.

Electrophysiological studies have shown that the 5-HT$_{1A}$ agonist 8-OHDPAT, whether applied systemically or iontophoretically, is a potent inhibitor of neuronal firing or raphe neurones. The 5-HT$_{1A}$ agonists mimic the effects of 5-HT (de Montigny *et al.*, 1984; Sprouse and Aghajanian, 1986, 1988). This inhibition of firing is associated with decreased release of cortical 5-HT *in vivo* (Crespi *et al.*, 1990) and is not produced by 5-HT$_{1B}$ agonists (Crespi *et al.*, 1990). The 5-HT$_{1A}$ partical agonists and potential anxiolytics (buspirone, gepirone, and ipsapirone) also inhibit the firing of raphe neurones and inhibit release as full agonists (Sharp *et al.*, 1990), but they act as partial agonists on the postsynaptic 5-HT$_{1A}$ receptor on hippocampal pyramidal cells (Martin and Mason, 1987; Sprouse and Aghajanian, 1988). Thus, there is evidence that the 5-HT$_{1A}$ receptor acts as the somatodendritic autoreceptor in the raphe nuclei as well as being a postsynaptic receptor in the hippocampus (reviewed by Marsden and Kendall, 1992).

Extensive *in vitro* and *in vivo* studies in the rat have shown that the pharmacology of the terminal autoreceptor differs from that of the 5-HT$_{1A}$ somatodentritic autoreceptor, as it has the profile of the 5-HT$_{1B}$ receptor. Activation of the receptor causes inhibition of serotonin release from the terminals (Brazell *et al.*, 1985; for review see Marsden and Kendall, 1992) (Figure 6). The story of the terminal autoreceptor is complicated by the finding that there is a molecular but not pharmacological distinction between this receptor in the rat (5-HT$_{1B}$) and man (5-HT$_{1D}$). The 5-HT$_{1D}$ receptor consists of two forms (5-HT$_{1D\beta}$ and 5-HT$_{1D\alpha}$) with the 5-HT$_{1D\beta}$ being the species homologue of the 5-HT$_{1B}$ receptor (see Hoyer *et al.*, 1994 for a review). There is both molecular and functional evidence that apart from terminal sites (striatum, accumbens, hippocampus), 5-HT$_{1D}$ receptors are also found in the dorsal raphe nucleus (Starkey and Skingle, 1994) where they inhibit 5-HT release. It remains to be determined whether it is possible to pharmacologically

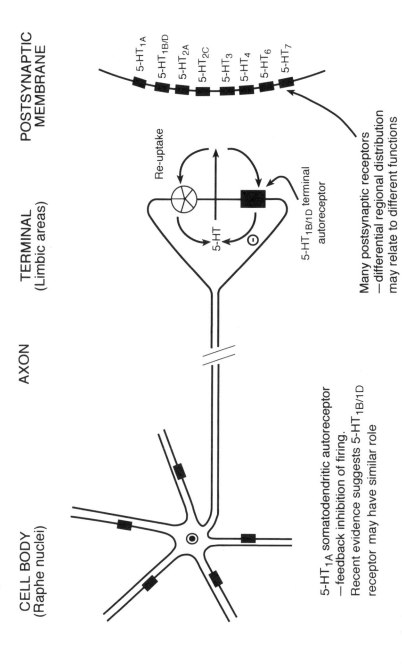

Figure 6. The suggested locations of serotonin receptor subtypes associated with pre- and postsynaptic sites of the serotonergic neurone.

distinguish between the terminal 5-HT$_{1D}$ autoreceptor and the 5-HT$_{1D}$ receptor in the raphe.

Identification of serotonin receptors that regulate the release of other neurotransmitters

Serotonin has been shown to be involved in the presynaptic regulation of the release of other transmitters and the role of 5-HT$_3$ receptors has attracted most attention in this respect. *In vitro* and *in vivo* studies have indicated that 5-HT$_3$ receptors inhibit the release of acetylcholine in the cortex but increase the release of dopamine in the striatal and mesolimbic systems (Barnes *et al.*, 1989; Hagan *et al.*, 1987). These effects may be relevant in terms of the reported improvement in cognitive function and the anti-schizophrenic effects seen in animals after administration of 5-HT$_3$ antagonists (e.g. ondansetron, zacopride, granisetron) although the clinical importance of these findings remains to be established.

More recently, Done and Sharp (1994) have demonstrated *in vivo* that a 5-HT$_2$ (possibly 5-HT$_{2A}$) receptor provides tonic inhibitory control over noradrenaline release in the rate hippocampus and that this tonic inhibition can be removed by 5-HT$_2$ receptor antagonists (e.g. ritanserin) or inhibition of serotonin release by activation of the 5-HT$_{1A}$ somatodendritic autoreceptor (i.e. administration of 5-HT$_{1A}$ agonists or partial agonists—buspirone). Such findings may help explain the relationship between noradrenergic and serotonergic mechanisms in depression and anxiety.

Dewey and colleagues (1995) examined the role of serotonin in modulating striatal dopamine. The 5-HT$_2$ receptor antagonists, altanserin and SR-46469B, increased extracellular striatal dopamine concentrations. Citalopram, which stimulates 5-HT$_2$ receptors acutely by making more serotonin available in the synapse, decreased striatal dopamine. This finding may help explain the efficacy of combined D$_2$/5-HT$_2$ receptor antagonists in refractory schizophrenia (Kane, 1992) as well as the induction or exacerbation of extrapyramidal symptoms rarely associated with SSRI treatment (Coulter and Pillans, 1995).

ASSESSMENT OF BEHAVIOUR IN ANIMALS AND MAN

This is a complex field and the present discussion will attempt to highlight some of the major findings and bring them together as a coherent hypothesis of the possible generalized function of brain serotonin in behaviour. Two points must be made at the start; firstly, most of the data are from animals and rather few from man and one always has to be careful in extrapolating ideas obtained in animal studies to man. Can one produce relevant animal models of anxiety, panic, and depression? Animal models of mental disease have two major uses; firstly as predictors of the clinical value of new drugs and secondly as a means of unravelling the possible neurobiology of the disease. The models used to detect potential anxiolytic drugs are either based on conditioned conflict tests, such as the Geller–Seifter conflict procedure or acute social situations involving aversion or fear, such as the elevated plus maze or social interaction test. Anxiety in humans, however, develops over time and is not just an acute state condition but may also involve trait characteristics. Thus most existing models fail to consider trait involvement and so may bear little relevance to the neurobiology of human generalized anxiety disorder (GAD) and, consequently, have limited value in the detection of potential drugs for the treatment of GAD. It will be important, in the future, to place more careful consideration on the design of our animal models incorporating features that model trait characteristics. The final problem concerns serotonin and our lack of understanding about how this neurotransmitter, which projects to many forebrain regions and has a multiplicity of receptor subtypes, is controlled so that it can be involved in a range of behavioural responses. For example, one can postulate that serotonin is important in both GAD and panic but that different regional serotonin pathways are involved in each condition; how is one subset of serotonin pathways activated but not another? This could occur through differential control of subgroups of serotonin neurones within the raphe nuclei or differential control at the terminal sites by terminal auto- or heteroceptors. Secondly, many of the results are derived from studies using drugs with reported relative selectivity for one receptor subtype over another. However, the truly receptor selective drug in a very rare breed; for example mCPP which has been used extensively in animals and man as a 5-HT_{2C} agonist also has appreciable activity at 5-HT_{1B}, 5-HT_{2A} and 5-HT_{2B} receptors (Hoyer *et al.*, 1994). Thus with such studies the conclusions always need to be qualified.

Aversive behaviour

This is a complex area of research as aversive situations bring in many aspects of behaviour in animals. These include response to novelty, cognition, unconditional response to fear (panic), exploratory behaviour, vigilance, and response to external stimuli. The preponderance of these various factors will depend upon the nature of the test employed. However, some generalizations can be made with reference to specific models. For example using models investigating the natural response of rats to aversive situations (novel environments (elevated plus maze and the black–white box) in which the animal has the choice of entering a novel but "safe" area compared to a novel but "unsafe" area), 5-HT_{1A} partial agonists (e.g. buspirone) decrease the aversiveness of the unsafe area (i.e. an anxiolytic effect). This has been explained by an agonist action at 5-HT_{1A} presynaptic receptors inhibiting 5-HT function indicating that increased 5-HT function causes anxiety (Chopin and Briley, 1987; Marsden, 1989). In contrast activation of *post*synaptic 5-HT_{1A} receptors in the periaqueductal grey area (PAG), which is considered important in human panic, markedly reduces the escape response produced by activation of the PAG (Beckett *et al.*, 1992; Graeff *et al.*, 1993). Furthermore, a similar anti-aversive effect is produced by local injection of the serotonin re-uptake inhibitor zimelidine into the PAG which supports the view that this brain area contains postsynaptic 5-HT receptors involved in the restraint of defence behaviour (Schutz *et al.*, 1985). Both stimulation of the PAG and exposure of rats to novelty (elevated plus maze) results in the appearance of immediate early gene expression (c-fos and c-jun) in certain common brain areas including the PAG, the amygdala, ventral hippocampus, and the paraventricular (Graeff *et al.*, 1993; Sandner *et al.*, 1993; Beckett *et al.*, 1995). Similarly there is release of serotonin in the hippocampus and the frontal cortex in the rat and guinea-pig on exposure to novelty or aversive conditions but no simple relationship between inhibition of this release and anti-anxiety behaviour (for review see Marsden *et al.*, 1995). Such findings support the proposal put forward by Fanselow (1991) and Deakin and Graeff (1991) for a role of the amygdala in the evaluation of the degree of danger before activation of both the PAG and serotonergic function in the dorsal raphe nucleus increases restraint until the threat becomes too great at which point the serotonergic excitatory input to the amygdala (possibly mediated by 5-HT_{2C} receptors) results in the expression of panic. Thus it would appear that the serotonin involvement in anxiety/panic may involve a complex interaction between an anti-aversive or restraining role for postsynaptic 5-HT_{1A} and possible 5-HT_{2A} receptors in the PAG and a pro-aversive role for 5-HT_{2C} receptors in the amygdala–hippocampal complex (Figure 7). Thus, 5-HT_{1A} receptor activation may have apparently opposite effects depending upon the type of behavioural model used, indicating that serotonergic pathways may subserve more than one functional role in aversive responses. 5-HT_{2C} receptor activation, mainly using mCPP, has been implicated in pro-aversive (anxiogenic) behaviour in both animals and man. But again closer investigation would suggest that the behaviours associated with 5-HT_{2C} activation in rodents are more closely related to human panic than anxiety.

Feeding behaviour

An increase in serotonergic function (i.e. increased 5-HT release (fenfluramine) or re-uptake inhibition (fluoxetine)) has an anorexic effect in man and animals. In contrast, activation of presynaptic 5-HT_{1A} receptors in the raphe nuclei causing decreased serotonergic function causes increased intake in freely feeding rats (for review see Cooper, 1992). At present the best evidence available for the postsynaptic 5-HT receptor involved in the anorexic effects of increased 5-HT release indicates that 5-HT_{2C} receptor activation is important. Bulimia may involve a deficiency in CCK-satiety mechanisms and as there appears to be a reciprocal relationship between 5-HT and CCK in satiety, increasing serotonergic tone in bulimics may help overcome the CCK deficiency although it remains to be determined whether this

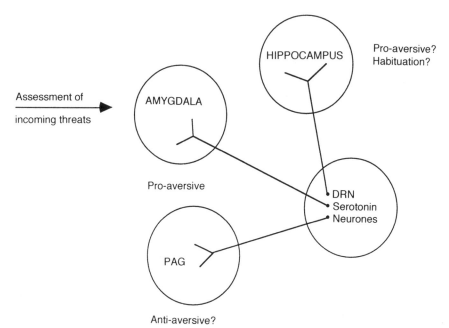

Figure 7. Diagram showing that dorsal raphe serotonergic neurones can produce either anti-aversive (PAG) or pro-aversive behaviours (amygdala–hippocampus). The amygdala is concerned with the assessment of incoming threats and itself sends projections to both the dorsal raphe and the PAG in which glutamate may be the neurotransmitter.

involves postsynaptic 5-HT$_{1A}$ (Voigt *et al.*, 1995) or 5-HT$_{2C}$ receptors (Poeschla *et al.*, 1993).

Sexual behaviour

In summary 5-HT agonists or increased serotonergic function are inhibitory on sexual function in male rats. This may not be a change in purposeful sexual behaviour but rather a change in impulsivity and restraint as will be discussed later.

Sleep

There is no sound evidence linking specific 5-HT receptor subtypes to specific aspects of sleep although 5-HT$_2$ antagonists (e.g. ritanserin) are reported to increase the quality of sleep (amount of slow wave sleep). It is well established that serotonergic mechanisms, via the suprachiasmatic nucleus, are involved in the control of diurnal rhythms and the sleep–wake cycle in rodents. Thus the overall role of serotonin in sleep may be through a change in alertness and vigilance.

Reward behaviour

There is increasing evidence for an involvement of serotonin in behaviour associated with reward mechanisms. While the role of serotonin in reward is not fully understood there is substantial evidence from animal studies to indicate that SSRIs, such as fluoxetine, decrease the consumption of drugs of abuse and craving during withdrawal although the 5-HT receptors involved have not been identified. Such an effect fits in with the idea that one function of brain serotonin is the control of impulsivity possibly by the inhibition of dopaminergic pathways involved in reward. There are also reports that 5-HT$_3$ antagonists have marked effects in animal studies on both the rewarding effect of drugs of abuse and withdrawal syndromes that follow cessation of treatment; again the results of clinical trials are awaited (for review see Tyers and Hayes, 1992). The localization of serotonin receptors and their putative functions are summarized in Table 1.

WHAT ROLE HAS SEROTONIN IN BEHAVIOUR AND MENTAL DISEASE?

From the data present it is clear that it is difficult to either describe serotonergic function by one single behavioural function or ascribe specific behaviours to an action at a single 5-HT receptor. It should also be remembered we have no information yet about the role of 5-HT$_{4-7}$ receptors in behaviour. It would however appear that many of the 5-HT pathways in the brain have complementary roles; a principal function is to inhibit behaviour and decrease impulsivity. Dysfunction of this role may underlie impulsive suicidal behaviour as well as aspects of panic, anxiety and depression.

The final section will look at how this idea of serotonergic function may help predict the clinical use of drugs acting on 5-HT mechanisms and receptors, bearing in mind that the final response may depend upon the balance between these two roles for serotonin and the symptomatology of the disease. There is substantial overlap in symptoms between anxiety and depression, and again between depression and the negative symptoms of schizophrenia. Similarly, there is overlap between panic disorders and OCD. This opens the question as to whether drugs should be tested on very circumscribed symptomatic groups or wider spectrum groups. Similarly, drugs acting on very specific receptors may be effective within a narrow symptomatic range while less selective drugs or drugs with a wider effect on serotonergic function may have a greater treatment range (i.e. combined dopamine/5-HT receptor antagonists for schizophrenia, SSRIs for anxiety/panic/OCD/depression).

Depression

The best evidence suggests that depression, particularly when linked with suicidal behaviour, is associated with reduced serotonergic function in limbic areas,

Table 1. Localization and function of serotonin receptor subtypes in brain.

Receptor	Regional localization	Subcellular localization	Functions
5-HT$_{1A}$	Amygdala, hippocampus, PAG, raphe nuclei	Somatodendritic postsynaptic	Autoreceptor (raphe), adaptive responses to aversion, ingestive behaviours, neuroendocrine control
5-HT$_{1B/D\beta}$	S. nigra, globus pallidus, superior colliculus	Terminals, somatodendritic (raphe)	Autoreceptor (terminals) autoreceptor (raphe?)
5-HT$_{1E}$	Amygdala, caudate	NK	NK
5-HT$_{1F}$	Hippocampus, spinal cord	NK	NK
5-HT$_{2A}$	Cortex, hippocampus, striatum, spinal cord	Postsynaptic terminals?	Control of noradrenaline release, hallucinogenic behaviours, sleep, aversion
5-HT$_{2B}$	Unknown at present	NK	NK
5-HT$_{2C}$	Choroid plexus, brain stem, amygdala, hippocampus, striatum	Postsynaptic	Aversive behaviours, hypoactivity, ingestive behaviours, anti-convulsive (Tecott *et al*, 1995)
5-HT$_3$	Area postrema, nucleus tractus solitarius, lower brain stem, limbic regions	Terminals postsynaptic	Sensory function, emesis, control of neurotransmitter release, anxiety?, cognition?, psychosis?
5-HT$_4$	Striatum, hippocampus, thalamus, olfactory, bulb	NK	Affective disorders? motor co-ordination? arousal, visual perception?
5-HT$_5$	Cortex, hippocampus, habenula	NK	NK
5-HT$_6$	Cortex, accumbens, caudate, hippocampus	NK	Motor function? affective behaviour?
5-HT$_7$	Hippocampus, hypothalamus, raphe nuclei	NK	Similar to 5-HT$_6$?

Data compiled from Hoyer *et al*, 1994 and Lucas and Hen, 1995.
NK = Not known.
The list of brain regions is not exhaustive for each receptor but contains the main areas relevant to possible involvement in the antidepressant/anxiolytic actions of SSRIs.

although it is far from clear which specific 5-HT receptor subtypes are involved. The most effective drug treatment is the use of tricyclic re-uptake inhibitors or SSRIs and the most important information will come from chronic studies with these drugs. At present, results indicate that long-term treatment with fluoxetine or paroxetine decreases the sensitivity of the somatodendritic autoreceptor (5-HT_{1A}) and may increase the number of postsynaptic 5-HT_{1A} receptors (see below). Clearly, further studies are required to understand the effects of SSRIs on different 5-HT receptor subtypes and the possible functional interaction between the subtypes particularly at the level of the receptor coupling mechanisms. In general, SSRIs in depression appear to reset the level of serotonergic function resulting in increased basal serotonergic tone.

Anxiety

The working hypothesis has been that anxiety is associated with increased 5-HT release and function and that drugs which reduced 5-HT release (autoreceptor agonists, appropriate postsynaptic receptor antagonists) will be anxiolytic. Indeed, in animal models of anxiety there is evidence that 5-HT release is increased as already discussed but these are all state (acute) models and the increase in 5-HT release may not be the cause of the symptoms but rather a response to the situation. This may be supported by findings that rats reared from weaning in isolation show increased response to an aversive situation (i.e. increased anxiety compared to group-reared rats) but no increase in 5-HT release on exposure to an aversive situation (Bickerdike *et al* 1993) suggesting the increase in serotonin release may be involved with coping or habituation stress. Clinical results with buspirone (Buspar), a 5-HT_{1A} partial agonist, provide some support for the excess 5-HT theory of anxiety but clinical results are mixed. In contrast, SSRIs appear to have anxiolytic as well as antidepressant effects after chronic treatment. This group of drugs increase serotonin function and so may potentiate the disinhibitory effects of serotonin decreasing the awareness of the anxiety state and so improve habituation to aversive situations.

There are reports of 5-HT_2 receptor antagonists being anxiolytic in the clinical setting although such effects may relate to an action at 5-HT_{2C} receptors and an anti-panic effect (see below). The interesting animal data with 5-HT_3 antagonists using animal models of anxiety still need to be matched with appropriate clinical studies.

Panic and OCD

As already mentioned, studies with 5-HT_{1A} agonists implicate these receptors in the PAG in a restraining role in panic. In contrast, activation of 5-HT_{2C} receptors can induce panic attacks in man. These results suggest that panic, as well as OCD, may involve conflicting serotonergic pathways; one being pro-aversive and the other anti-aversive. The most important data relating to observations that more than one 5-HT receptor subtype is involved in panic is the apparent effectiveness of SSRIs in the treatment of panic and OCD. As with their use in anxiety and depression, prolonged treatment is required, indicating that a change in receptor sensitivity is involved in the mechanism of action resulting in the "retuning" or resetting of serotonergic function. Another clinical approach may be the development of selective antagonists of the 5-HT$_{2C}$ receptor.

Craving and addiction

Craving may represent increasing impulsivity—a feature associated with low serotonergic function. Again, there is evidence that SSRIs may be useful in the treatment of addiction but the precise mechanisms involved need to be established although again the essential action may be to increase serotonergic function.

What adaptive changes occur with chronic SSRI treatment?

Inhibitors of re-uptake increase the synaptic concentration of serotonin (and noradrenaline), probably by binding to the modulatory site identified using [^{3}H]-imipramine or paroxetine. From what has been described about serotonin autoreceptors, one immediate consequence of the increased synaptic concentration of serotonin will be activation of the 5-HT$_{1A}$ and 5-HT$_{1B/1D}$ receptors, leading to decreased neuronal firing and terminal release (for review see Blier and de Montigny, 1994). This suggests that after chronic treatment, the net effect of the change in synaptic serotonin and the activation of the autoreceptors will determine the pharmacological actions that are important for the antidepressant properties of the re-uptake inhibitors. Such studies have utilized the various tests available to investigate the function of the serotonin receptor subtypes.

One of the most consistent changes observed after tricyclic antidepressant treatment is down-regulation of 5-HT$_2$ receptors, both using measurement of [^{3}H]-ligand binding and functional tests (Bowery *et al.*, 1995). However, if the change in binding is used as a measure, not all selective serotonin re-uptake inhibitors appear to down-regulate the 5-HT$_2$ site (Fraser *et al.*, 1988; Nelson *et al.*, 1989; Cadogan *et al.*, 1993). Interestingly, 5-HT$_2$ agonists (ketanserin and ritanserin) as well as 5-HT$_2$ agonists (DOM, DOI), against conventional wisdom also down-regulate the responsiveness of 5-HT$_2$ receptors. Neither 5-HT$_2$ antagonists nor agonists are established antidepressants, indicating that the down-regulation of 5-HT$_2$ receptors is not essential for an antidepressant effect. Indeed, electroconvulsive shock treatment increases the responsiveness of 5-HT$_2$ receptors in rats (Grahame-Smith, 1988).

The effects of antidepressant drugs on 5-HT$_1$ receptor binding are inconclusive—another example of the problems encountered with interpretation of such data. In contrast, functional studies on the 5-HT$_{1A}$ receptor indicate that chronic uptake inhibition decreases the functional state of the 5-HT$_{1A}$ somatodendritic autoreceptor, i.e. the ability of this receptor to reduce serotonin neuronal firing is attenuated (de Montigny *et al.*, 1984; Grahame-Smith, 1988). In contrast, there is no detectable change in the terminal autoreceptor (5-HT$_{1B}$) in the rat (Sleight *et al.*, 1989). A consequence of the somatodendritic autoreceptor down-regulation after chronic SSRI administration is an increase in the release of serotonin from terminals in forebrain regions (Bel and Artigas, 1993), an effect not observed with acute SSRI administration (Bel and Artigas, 1992). Thus the major effect of chronic SSRI treatment is to increase presynaptic release of serotonin which is then available to act on postsynaptic 5-HT$_{1A}$ receptors and in this respect the postsynaptic 5-HT$_{1A}$ receptor may be of importance as electrophysiological studies have shown these may exhibit enhanced responsiveness after chronic SSRI (Blier and de Montigny, 1994) (Table 2). What happens with the many other postsynaptic 5-HT receptors is unclear as is their role in depression/anxiety but the introduction of molecular techniques to knock out the expression of specific receptors or produce animals with the genes for specific receptors deleted should provide exciting new information in the immediate future (Tecott *et al.*, 1995; Lucas and Hen, 1995).

From a clinical viewpoint, one way to increase the onset of the antidepressant action of re-uptake inhibitors may be to prevent the initial 5-HT$_{1A}$ autoreceptor inhibition of serotonin release by giving the uptake inhibitor in combination with a 5-HT$_{1A}$ receptor antagonist. early experimental work in animals has shown this approach to work with a more rapid onset in the increase in terminal serotonin release when pindolol (a 5-HT$_{1A/\beta}$ adrenoceptor antagonist) is given with an SSRI (Hjorth, 1993). Furthermore, preliminary clinical studies have also produced promising results with remission of symptoms within days rather than weeks (Artigas *et al.*, 1994). With the development of selective 5-HA$_{1A}$ receptor antagonists (e.g. WAY-100635) it is hoped that such combination treatment will receive full consideration in the future. Please also see chapter 2 of this volume (The biochemical specificity of action of the SSRIs)

CONCLUSIONS

Serotonin appears to play a major role in the control of impulsivity and restraint. There are numerous 5-HT receptor subtypes but, as yet, there is little information about the role of specific subtypes in the control of behaviour. Major advances in our understanding of the role of serotonin in mental disease will come from improved information about the mechanisms involved in the clinical effectiveness of selective serotonin re-uptake inhibitors in depression, anxiety, panic, OCD and drug abuse.

Table 2. Serotonin receptors and release: effects of chronic antidepressant treatments.

Treatment	5-HT$_{1A}$ somatodendritic autoreceptor	5-HT$_{1B/1D}$ terminal autoreceptor	5-HT release	5-HT$_{1A}$ postsynaptic receptor	5-HT$_{2A}$ postsynaptic receptor
Tricyclics	↓	↓?	↑	↑ or NC	↓ or NC
SSRIs	↓	NC	↑	↑ or NC	↓ or NC
Lithium	↓	NC	↑	↑	?
Electroconvulsive shocks	↓	NC	↑	↑	↑

Data compiled from Grahame-Smith, 1988; Fraser et al, 1988 and Blier and de Montigny, 1994.
NC = No change

REFERENCES

Aghajanian GK (1992) Central 5-HT receptor subtypes: Physiological responses and signal transduction mechanisms. In: Marsden CA and Heal DJ (eds) *Central Serotonin Receptors and Psychotropic Drugs*, pp 39–55. Blackwell Scientific Publications, Oxford.

Amin AH, Crawford TBB and Gaddum JH (1954). The distribution of substance P and 5-hydroxytryptamine in the central nervous system of the dog. *J Physiol* **126**, 596–618.

Artigas F, Perez V and Alvarez E (1994) Pindolol induces a rapid improvement of depressed patients treated with serotonin re-uptake inhibitors. *Arch Gen Psychiatry* **51**, 248–251.

Barnes JM, Barnes NM, Costall B *et al.* (1989) 5-HT₃ receptors mediate inhibition of acetylcholine release in cortical tissue. *Nature* **338**, 762–763.

Beckett SRG, Aspley S, Duxon MS, *et al.* (1995) Ultrasound induced aversion in the rat. *J Psychopharmacol* **9** (suppl.), A33 (129).

Beckett SRG, Lawrence AJ, Marsden CA and Marshall PW (1992) Attenuation of chemically induced defence response by 5-HT₁ receptor antagonists administered into the periaqueductal grey. *Psychopharmacology* **108**, 110–114.

Bel N and Artigas F (1992) Fluvoxamine preferentially increases extracellular 5-HT in the raphe nuclei: an *in vivo* microdialysis study. *Eur J Pharmacol* **229**, 243–245.

Bel N and Artigas F (1993) Chronic treatment with fluvoxamine increases extracellular 5-HT in frontal cortex but not in raphe nuclei. *Synapse* **15**, 243–245.

Berridge MJ (1984) Inositol triphosphate and diacyglycerol as second messengers. *Biochem J* **220**, 345.

Bickerdike MJ, Wright IK and Marsden CA (1993) Social isolation attenuates rat forebrain 5-HT release induced by KCL stimulation and exposure to a novel environment. *Behav Pharmacol* **4**, 231–236.

Blier P and de Montigny C (1994) Current advances and trends in the treatment of depression. *Trends Pharmacol Sci* **15**, 220–226.

Bockaert J, Dumuis A, Bonhelal R, *et al.* (1987) Piperazine derivatives including the anxiolytic drugs, byspirone and buspirone are agonists at 5-HT₁A receptors negatively coupled with adenylate cyclase in hippocampal neurons. *Naunyn Schmiedebergs Arch Pharmacol* **335**, 588–592

Bowery *et al.* (1995) *An Autoradiographic Comparison of ³H-paroxetine and ³H-imipramine in Human whole Brain Sections.* Presented at the ECNP Congress, 1–4 October, Venice.

Bradley PB (1989) *Introduction to Neuropharmacology*, p 351. Butterworth & Co.

Bradley PB, Engel G, Fennik W *et al.* (1986) Proposals for the classification and nomenclature of functional receptors for 5-hydroxytryptamine. *Neuropharmacology* **25**, 563–567.

Brazell MP, Marsden CA, Nisbet AP *et al.* (1985) The HT-₁ receptor agonist RU24969 decreases 5-hydroxytryptamine (5-HT) release and metabolism in the rat frontal cortex *in vitro* and *in vivo*. *Br J Pharmacol* **86**, 209–216.

Cadogan AK, Kendall DA and Marsden CA (1994) Serotonin 5-HT₁A receptor activation increases cyclic-AMP formation in rat hippocampus *in vivo*. *J Neurochem* **62**, 1816–1821.

Cadogan AK, Marsden CA, Tulloch I and Kendall DA (1993) Evidence that administration of paroxetine or fluoxetine enhances 5-HT₂ receptor function in the brain of the guinea-pig. *Neuropharmacology* **32**, 249–256.

Charney DS, Woods, SW, Goodman WK and Heninger GR (1987) Serotonin function in anxiety. II. Effects of the serotonin agonist mCPP in panic disorder patients and healthy subjects. *Psychopharmacology* **92**, 14–24.

Chopin P and Briley M (1987) Animal models of anxiety the effects of compounds that modify 5-HT neurotransmission. *Trends Pharmacol Sci* **8**, 383–388.

Clarke DE, Craig DA and Fozard JR (1989) The 5-HT₄ receptor naughty, but nice. *Trends Pharmacol Sci* **10**, 385–386.

Conn PJ and Sanders-Bush E (1985) Serotonin-stimulated phosphoinositide turnover. Mediated by the S2 binding site in rate cerebral cortex but not in subcortical regions. *J Pharmacol Exp Ther* **234**, 195–203.

Conn PJ and Sanders-Bush E (1986) Regulation of serotonin-stimulated phosphoinositide hydrolysis: Relation to serotonin 5-HT$_2$ binding site. *J Neurosci* **6**, 3669–3675.

Conn PJ and Sanders-Bush E (1987) Central serotonin receptors: effector systems, physiological roles and regulation. *Psychopharmacology* **92**, 267–277.

Conn PJ, Janowsky A and Sanders-Bush E (1987) Denervation supersensitivity of 5-HT$_{1C}$ receptors in rat choroid plexus. *Brain Res* **400**, 396–398.

Conn PJ, Sanders-Bush E, Hoffman BJ, *et al.* (1986) A unique serotonin receptor in choroid plexus is linked to phosphatidylinositol turnover. *Proc Natl Acad Sci* **83**, 4086–4088.

Cooper JR, Bloom FE and Roth RH (1982) *The Biochemical Basis of Neuropharmacology:* 4th edition. Oxford University Press.

Cooper SJ (1992) 5-HT and ingestive behaviour. In: Marsden CA and Heal DJ (eds) *Central Serotonin Receptors and Psychotropic Drugs,* pp 260–291. Blackwell Scientific Publications, Oxford.

Coppen A and Swade C (1988) 5-HT and depression: The present position. In: Briley M and Fillion G (eds) *New Concepts in Depression,* pp. 120–136. Macmillan Press, London.

Coulter DM and Pillans PI (1995) Fluoxetine and extrapyramidal side effects. *Am J Psychiatry* **152(1)**, 122–125.

Cowen PJ, Charig EM, McCance SL, *et al.* (1988) The effect of amitriptyline and mianserin on the prolactin response to intravenous tryptophan. *J Psychopharmacol* **2**, 2.

Crespi F, Garratt JC, Sleight AJ, *et al.* (1990) *In vivo* evidence that 5-hydroxytryptamine (5-HT) neuronal firing and release are not necessarily correlated with 5-HT metabolism. *Neuroscience* **35**, 139–144.

Dahlström A and Fuxe K (1964) Evidence for the existence of monoamine-containing neurons in the central nervous system. I. Demonstration of monoamines in cell bodies of brain neurons. *Acta Physiol Scand* **62** (Suppl 232), 1–55.

De Vivo M and Maayani S (1986) Characterisation of the 5-HT$_{1A}$ receptor mediated inhibition of forskolin-stimulated adenylate cyclase activity in guinea-pig and rat hippocampal membranes. *J Pharmacol Exp Ther* **238**, 248–253.

De Vivo M and Maayani S (1988) 5-HT receptors coupled to adenylate cyclase. In: Sanders-Bush E (ed) *The Serotonin Receptors,* pp 141–179. Humana Press, New Jersey.

de Montigny C, Blier P and Chaput Y (1984) Electrophysiologically identified serotonin receptors in the rat CNS. *Neuropharmacology* **23**, 1511–1520.

Deakin JFW and Graeff FG (1991) 5-HT and mechanisms of defence. *J Psychopharmacol* **5**, 305–315.

Deakin JFW, Pennell I, Upadhyada AJ, *et al.* (1990) A neuroendocrine study of 5-HT function in depression: evidence for biological mechanisms of endogenons and psychosocial causation. *Psychopharmacology* **101**, 85–92.

Dewey SL, Smith GS, Logan J, *et al.* (1995) Serotonergic modulation of striatal dopamine measured with positron emission tomography (PET) and *in vivo* microdialysis. *J Neurosci* **15**, 821–829.

Done CJG and Sharp T (1994) Biochemical evidence for the regulation of central noradrenergic activity by 5-HT$_{1A}$ and 5-HT$_2$ receptors: microdialysis studies in the awake and anaesthetized rat. *Neuropharmacology* **33**, 411–422.

Dumuis A, Bonhelal R, Sebben M, *et al.* (1988) A 5-HT receptor in the central nervous system, positively coupled with adenylate cyclase antagonised by ICS 20593C. *Eur J Pharmacol* **146**, 187–188.

Elks ML, Youngblood WW and Kizer JS (1979) Serotonin synthesis and release in brain slices, independence of tryptophan. *Brain Res* **172**, 471–486.

30   C.A. Marsden

Everitt BJ (1977) Effects of clomipramine and other inhibitors of monoamine uptake on the sexual behaviour of female rats and rhesus monkeys. *Postgrad Med J* **53** (Suppl 4), 202–210.

Falck B, Hillarp N-A, Thieme G, *et al.* (1962) Fluorescence of catecholamines and related compounds condensed with formaldehyde. *J Histochem Cytochem* **10**, 348–354.

Fanselow MS (1991) The midbrain periaqueductal grey as a coordinator of action in response to fear and anxiety. In: Depaulis A and Bandler R (eds) *The Midbrain Periaqueductal Grey Matter: Functional, Anatomical and Neurochemical Organisation*, pp. 151–174. Plenum Press, New York.

Fone KCF, Johnson JV, Bennett GW, *et al.* (1989) Involvement of 5-HT$_2$ receptors in the behaviours produced by intrathecal administration of selected 5-HT agonists and the TRH analogue (CG3509) to rats. *Br J Pharmacol* **96**, 599–608.

Fone KCF, Robinson J and Marsden CA (1991) Characterization of the spinal motor behaviours produced by intrathecal administration of 5-HT agonists in the rats. *Br J Pharmacol* **104**, 1547–1555.

Fone KCF, Shalders, K, Fox Z, *et al.* (1995) 5HT$_{2C}$ receptor supersensitivity following isolation rearing in rats. *J Psychopharmacol* **9** (suppl.) A56, (223).

Fraser A, Offord SJ and Lucki I (1988) Regulation of serotonin receptors and responsiveness in the brain. In: Sanders-Bush E (ed) *The Serotonin Receptors*, pp 319–362. Humana Press, New Jersey.

Fuller RW (1985) Drugs altering serotonin synthesis and metabolism. In: Green AR (ed) *Neuropharmacology of Serotonin*, pp 1–20. Oxford University Press.

Fuxe K (1965) Evidence for the existence of monoamine neurons in the central nervous system. IV. Distribution of monoamine nerve terminals in the central nervous system. *Acta Physiol Scand* **64** (Suppl 247), 39–85.

Fuxe, K, Hökfelt T and Ungerstedt U (1968) Localization of indolealkylamine in the CNS. *Adv Pharmacol* **6**, 235–251.

Garattini S, Buczko W, Jori A *et al.* (1975) The mechanism of action of fenfluramine. *Postgrad Med J* **51** (Suppl 1), 27–35.

Gilbert RFT, Emson PC, Hunt SP, *et al.* The effects of monoamine neurotoxins on peptides in rat spinal cord. *Neuroscience* **7**, 69–88.

Goodwin GM, Fairburn CG and Cowen PJ (1987) The effects of dieting and weight loss on neuroendocrine responses to L-tryptophan, clonidine and apomorphine in volunteers: important implications for neuroendocrine investigation in depression. *Arch Gen Psychiatry* **44**, 952–955.

Graeff FG, Silveira MCL, Nogueira RL, *et al.* (1993) Role of the amygdala and periaqueductal gray in anxiety and panic. *Behav Brain Res* **58**, 123–131.

Grahame-Smith DG (1974) How important is the synthesis of brain 5-HT in the physiological control of its central function? *Adv Biochem Psychopharmacol* **10**, 83–91.

Grahame-Smith DG (1988) Neuropharmacological adaptive effects in the actions of antidepressant drugs ECT and Lithium. In: Briley M and Fillion G (eds) *New Concepts in Depression*, pp 1–14. Macmillan Press, London.

Hagan RM, Butler A, Hill JM, *et al.* (1987) Effect of the 5-HT$_3$ receptor antagonist GR38032F on responses to injection of a neurokinin agonist into the ventral tegmental area of the rat brain. *Eur J Pharmacol* **138**, 303–305.

Heal DJ, Luscombe GP and Martin KF (1992) Pharmacological identification of 5-HT receptor subtypes using behavioural models. In: Marsden CA and Heal DJ (eds) *Central Serotonin Receptors and Psychotropic Drugs*, pp 56–99. Blackwell Scientific Publications, Oxford.

Hökfelt, T. Tsuruo Y, Ulfhake B *et al.* (1989) Distribution of TRH-like immunoreactivity with special reference to coexistence with other neuroactive compounds. *Ann NY Acad Sci* **553**, 76–105.

Hoyer D, Clarke DE, Fozard JR, *et al.* (1994) VII International Union of Pharmacology Classification of Receptors for 5-hydroxytryptamine (Serotonin). *Pharmacol Rev* **46**, 157–203.

Jacobs BL, Wise WD and Taylor KM (1974) Differential behavioural and neurochemical effects following lesons of the dorsal or median raphe nuclei in rats. *Brain Res* **79**, 353–361.

Johanssen O, Hökfelt T, Pernow B, *et al.* (1981) Immunohistochemical support for three putative transmitters in one neuron: Co-existence of 5-hydroxytryptamine substance P and thyrotropin releasing hormone-like immunoreactivity in medullary neurons projecting to the spinal cord. *Neuroscience* **6**, 1857–1881.

Kalus O, Kahn RS, Wetzler S, *et al.* (1990) Behavioural hypersensitivity to m-chlorophenylpiperazine in a subject with subclinical panic attacks. *Biol Psychiatry* **28**, 1053–1057.

Kane JM (1992) Clinical efficacy of clozapine in treatment-refractory schizophrenia: an overview. *Br J Psychiatry* **Suppl (17, May)**, 41–45.

Kendall DA and Nahorski SR (1985) 5-hydroxytryptamine-stimulated inositol phospholipid hydrolysis in rat cerebral cortex slices. Pharmacological characterization and effects of antidepressants. *J Pharmacol Exp Ther* **233**, 473–479.

Kosofsky BE and Molliver ME (1987) The serotonergic innervation of the cerebral cortex: Different classes of axon terminals arise from dorsal and median raphe nuclei. *Synapse* **1**, 153–168.

Kuhn DM, Wolf WA and Yondim MBN (1986) Serotonin neurochemistry revisited: A new look at some old axioms. *Neurochem Int* **8**, 141–154.

Lucas JJ and Hen R (1995) New players in the 5-HT receptor field: genes and knockouts. *Trend Pharmacol Sci* **16**, 246–252.

Mamoumas LA, Wilson MA, Axt KH and Molliver ME (1992) Morphological aspects of serotonergic innervation. In: Bradley PB, Handley SL, Cooper SJ, Key BJ, Barnes NM and Coote JH (eds) *Serotonin, CNS Receptors and Brain Function. Advances in Biosciences* **85**, 97–118. Pergamon Press.

Marsden CA (1989) 5-hydroxytryptamine receptor subtypes and new anxiolytic drugs: an appraisal. In: Tyrer PJ (ed) *Psychopharmacology of Anxiety*, pp. 3–27. Oxford University Press.

Marsden CA and Kendall DA (1992) Neurochemical identification of 5-HT receptor subtypes. In: Marsden CA and Heal DJ (eds) *Central Serotonin Receptors and Psychotropic Drugs*, pp. 16–38. Blackwell Scientific Publications, Oxford.

Marsden CA, Beckett SRG, Wilson W, *et al.* (1995) Serotonin involvement in animal models of anxiety and panic. In: Takada A and Curzon G (eds) *Serotonin and Related Monoamines in the CNS and Periphery*, pp 135–143. Elsevier Science.

Marsden CA, Conti J, Strope E, *et al.* (1979) Monitoring 5-hydroxytryptamine release in the brain of the freely moving unanaesthetised rat using *in vivo* voltammetry. *Brain Res* **171**, 85–99.

Martin KF and Mason F (1987) Ipsapirone is a partial agonist at 5-hydroxytryptamine$_{1A}$ receptors in the rat hippocampus: electrophysiological evidence. *Eur J Pharmacol* **141**, 479–483.

McQuade R, Cowen PJ and Sharp T (1995) *In vivo* evidence that d-fenfluramine releases 5-HT from nerve terminals of both the dorsal and median raphe nuclei. *Br J Pharmacol* **116**, 220P.

Molliver DC and Molliver ME (1990) Anatomic evidence for a neurotoxic effect of (I) fenfluramine upon serotonergic projections in the rat. *Brain Res* **511**, 165–168.

Molliver MR (1987) Serotonergic neuronal systems: What their anatomic organisation tells us about function. *J Clin Psychopharmacol* **7** (Suppl 6), 3S–23S.

Murphy DL, Aulakh CS and Garrick NA (1986) How antidepressants work: cautionary conclusions based on clinical and laboratory studies of the longer term consequences of antidepressant drug treatment. In: Antidepressants and receptor function. *Ciba Found Symp* **123**, 106–125.

Nelson DR, Thomas DR and Johnson AM (1989) Pharmacological effects of paroxetine after repeated administration to animals. *Acta Psychiatr Scand* **80** (Suppl 350), 21–23.

Nestler EJ and Greengard P (1983) Protein phosphorylation in the brain. *Nature* **305**, 583–588.

Pazos A, Hoyer D and Palacios JM (1985) The binding of serotoninergic ligands to the choroid plexus: characterization of a new type of serotonin recognition site. *Eur J Pharmacol* **106**, 539–546.

Plassat JL, Amlaiky N and Hen R (1993) Molecular-cloning of a mammalian serotonin receptor that activates adenylyl cyclase. *Mol Pharmacol* **44**, 229–236.

Poeschla B, Gibbs J. Samansky KJ, *et al.* (1993) Cholecystokinin-induced satiety depends on activation of $5HT_{1C}$ receptors. *Am J Physiol* **264**, R62–R64.

Pompeiano M, Palacios JM and Mengod G (1994) Distribution of the $5\text{-}HT_2$ receptor family mRNAs: comparison between $5\text{-}HT_{2A}$ and $5\text{-}HT_{2C}$ receptors. *Mol Brain Res* **23**, 163–176.

Sandner G, Oberling P, Silveira MC, *et al.* (1993) What brain structures are active during emotions? Effect of brain stimulation elicited by aversion on c-fos immunoreactivity and behaviour. *Behav Brain Res* **58**, 9–18.

Schutz MTB, de Aguiar JC and Graeff FG (1985) Anti-aversive role of serotonin on the dorsal periaqueductal grey matter. *Psychopharmacology* **35**, 240–345.

Sevwen K, Magnaldo I and Pouyssegur J (1988) Serotonin stimulates DNA synthesis in firboblasts acting through $5\text{-}HT_{1B}$ receptors coupled to a G_1-protein. *Nature* **335**, 254–256.

Sharp T, Buckus LI, Hjorth S, *et al.* (1990) Further investigations of the *in vivo* pharmacological properties of the putative $5\text{-}HT_{1A}$ antagonist, BMY7278. *Eur J Pharmacol* **176**, 331–340.

Shaskan EG and Snyder SH (1970) Kinetics of serotonin accumulation into slices from rat brain: Relationship to catecholamine uptake. *J Pharmacol Exp Ther* **163**, 425.

Shenker A, Maayani S and Weinstein H (1987) Pharmacological characterization of two 5-hydroxytryptamine receptors coupled to adenylate cyclase in guinea-pig hippocampal membranes. *Mol Pharmacol* **31**, 357–367.

Siever LJ, Coccaro EF, Benjamin E, *et al.* (1986) Adrenergic and serotonergic receptor responsiveness in depression. In: Antidepressants and receptor function. *Ciba Found Symp* **123**, 148–163.

Sleight AJ, Marsden CA, Martin KF, *et al.* (1988a) Relationship between extracellular 5-hydroxytryptamine and behaviour following monoamine oxidase inhibition and L-tryptophan. *Br J Pharmacol* **93**, 303–310.

Sleight AJ, Marsden CA, Palfreyman MG, *et al.* (1988b) Chronic MAO A and MAO B inhibition decreases the $5\text{-}HT_{1A}$ receptor-mediated inhibition of forskolin-stimulated adenylate cyclase. *Eur J Pharmacol* **154**, 225–261.

Sleight AJ, Smith RJ, Marsden CA, *et al.* (1989) The effects of chronic treatment with amitriptyline and MDL72394 on the control of 5-HT release *in vitro*. *Neuropharmacology* **28**, 477–480.

Slotkin TA, Seidler FJ, Withmore WL, *et al.* (1978) Rat brain synaptic vesicles. Uptake and specification of [^{3}H] norepinephrine and [^{3}H] serotonin in preparations from the whole brain and brain regions. *J Neurochem* **31**, 961–962.

Sprouse JS and Aghajanian GK (1986) (-)-Propranolol blocks the inhibition of serotonergic dorsal raphe cell firing by $5\text{-}HT_{1A}$ selective agonists. *Eur J Pharmacol* **128**, 295–298.

Sprouse JS and Aghajanian GK (1988) Responses of hippocampal pyramidal cells to putative serotonin $5\text{-}HT_{1A}$ and $5\text{-}HT_{1B}$ agonists: A comparative study with dorsal raphe neurones. *Neuropharmacology* **27**, 707–715.

Starkey SJ and Skingle M (1994) $5\text{-}HT_{1D}$ as well as $5\text{-}HT_{1A}$ autoreceptors modulate 5-HT release in the guinea-pig dorsal raphe. *Neuropharmacology* **33**, 393–402.

Steinbusch HWM (1981) Distribution of serotonin-immunoreactivity in the central nervous system of the rat: cell bodies and terminals. *Neuroscience* **6**, 557–618.

Steinbusch HWM, Verhofstad AAJ and Joosten HWJ (1978) Localization of serotonin in the central nervous system by immunohistochemistry: description of a specific and sensitive technique and some applications. *Neuroscience* **3**, 81.

Tecott LH, Sun LM, Akana SF, *et al.* (1995) Eating disorder and epilepsy in mice lacking 5-HT$_{2C}$ serotonin receptors. *Nature* **374**, 542–546.

Tohyama M, Shiosaka S, Sakanaka M, *et al.* (1980) Detailed pathways of the raphe dorsalis neuron to the cerebral cortex with use of horseradish peroxidase-3,3',5,5' tetramethylbenzidine reaction as a tool for the fibre tracing technique. *Brain Res* **181**, 433–439.

Trulson ME and Jacobs BL (1976) Behavioural evidence for the rapid release of CNS serotonin by PCA and fenfluramine. *Eur J Pharmocal* **36**, 149–154.

Twarog BM and Page IH (1953) Serotonin content of some mammalian tissues and urine and method for its determination. *Am J Physiol* **175**, 157–161.

Tyers MB and Hayes AG (1992) 5-HT receptors and addiction. In: Marsden CA and Heal DJ (eds) *Central Serotonin Receptors and Psychotropic Drugs*, pp. 292–305. Blackwell Scientific Publications, Oxford.

Uezono Y, Bradley J, Min C, *et al.* (1993) Receptors that couple to two classes of G-proteins increase cAMP and activate GFTR expressed in *Xenopus* oocytes. *Receptor Channels* **1**, 233–241.

Voight J-P, Fink H and Marsden CA (1995) Evidence for the involvement of the 5-HT$_{1A}$ receptor in CCK induced satiety in rats. *Naunyn Schmiedebergs Arch Pharmacol* **351**, 217–220.

Waeber C, Schoeffter P, Palacios JM, *et al.* (1989) 5-HT$_{1D}$ receptors in guinea-pig and pigeon brain. *Naunyn Schmiedebergs Arch Pharmacol* **340**, 479–485.

2

The comparative pharmacological properties of selective serotonin re-uptake inhibitors in animals

B.E. Leonard

INTRODUCTION

The accidental discovery of imipramine and iproniazid as effective antidepressants some 30 years ago, and the subsequent finding that these drugs changed the functional activity of biogenic amines in the rat brain, served to focus research onto the role of noradrenaline (NA) and 5-hydroxytryptamine (serotonin, 5-HT) as a possible basis for the mode of action of antidepressants (see Ayd and Blackwell, 1970). Coincidentally with the discovery of the antidepressant properties of imipramine and iproniazid, the antihypertensive alkaloid reserpine was shown to cause depression in a minority of patients with hypertension. This effect was attributed to the ability of the drug to deplete central neuronal stores of biogenic amines (Everett and Toman, 1959).

Detailed experimental studies of drugs that could either alleviate or cause depression showed that they either prevented the intraneuronal degradation of NA and 5-HT (the monoamine oxidase inhibitors—MAOIs), reduced the rate of removal of biogenic amines from the synaptic cleft (the tricyclic antidepressants—TCAs), facilitated the re-uptake of NA and/or 5-HT thereby reducing the duration of action of the transmitter at the postsynaptic receptor site (e.g. lithium salts that enhance NA uptake) or enhanced the intraneuronal catabolism of NA and

Selective Serotonin Re-uptake Inhibitors: Advances in Basic Research and Clinical Practice, Second Edition, Edited by J.P. Feighner and W.F. Boyer
© 1996 John Wiley & Sons Ltd

5-HT by decreasing their vesicular storage (reserpine). The results of such experimental studies formed the basis for the biogenic amine theory of depression which, despite its modification in recent years, still forms the biochemical basis of depression. This theory is based on the seminal studies of Schildkraut (1965), Coppen (1967), and Lapin and Oxenkrug (1969) and proposes that depression occurs as a result of the reduced availability of NA and/or 5-HT in the synaptic cleft.

Whereas the biogenic amines may play a pivotal role in the aetiology or depression, it is now apparent that many other neurotransmitters and neuromodulators such as the neuropeptides and prostaglandins may play a role (see Emrich *et al.*, 1979). Furthermore, despite the primacy of theories concerning the role of 5-HT and NA in the aetiology of depression, 20 years of experimental and clinical studies have provided little in the way of unequivocal evidence.

In the last 20 years, antidepressants have been developed that show a high degree of selectivity for the noradrenergic, serotonergic or dopaminergic systems. In addition, other drugs with antidepressant properties have been developed that show selectivity for subpopulations of 5-HT receptors, or that modulate the GABAergic system either directly or indirectly via the benzodiazepine receptor. Table 1 identifies some of the novel antidepressants that have been developed in the last two decades. Such drugs are often referred to as second generation antidepressants. While there is no evidence that the second generation antidepressants are therapeutically more effective that the TCAs and MAOIs, there is ample clinical evidence that they are better tolerated and have fewer adverse effects (particularly cardiovascular effects). This raises the question of whether all antidepressants have a

Table 1. Some second generation antidepressants.

Drug class	Examples
Selective monoamine oxidase A inhibitors	Brofaromine, cimoxatone, moclobemide
Alpha 2-adrenoceptor antagonists	Idazoxan[b], mianserin, mirtazapine (mepirzapin)
Selective serotonin (5-hydroxytryptamine; 5-HT) re-uptake inhibitors	Citalopram, fluoxetine, fluvoxamine, paroxetine, sertraline, zimelidine[a]
Noradrenaline (norepinephrine) re-uptake inhibitors	Levoprotiline[b], nomifensine[a], oxaprotiline
Serotonin re-uptake enhancer	Tianeptine
5-TIA partial agonists	Gepirone[b], ipsapirone[b]
Benzodiazepine analogues	Alprazolam, adinazolam, zometapine[b]
Drugs modulating dopaminergic function	Amfebutamone (bupropion)
γ-aminobutyric acid (GABA-mimetics)	Fengabine, progabide
Nontricyclic antidepressants	Lofepramine

[a]Drugs withdrawn because of serious adverse effects.
[b]Clinical efficacy uncertain.

common mechanism of action. If so, is this action related to adaptational changes in NA or 5-HT receptors as has been postulated by Charney and coworkers (1990), Leonard (1994a), and Richelson (1990).

PHARMACOLOGICAL PROPERTIES OF THE SSRIs

The undoubted success of the TCAs in the treatment of depression stimulated research into ways in which their efficacy and speed of onset of action could be improved. To date, despite the numerous different types of antidepressants that are now available, there is no convincing evidence that any are more efficacious or quicker in onset than the TCAs that were introduced some 30 years ago. It is certain however that the second generation antidepressants have fewer adverse effects (particularly cardiovascular side-effects) and are better tolerated than the TCAs (see Leonard, 1993). These advantages are attributable to the relative specificity of action of the newer antidepressants for the serotonergic and/or noradrenergic system and lack of effect on the α_1- and α_2-adrenoceptors, histamine receptors, muscarinic receptors and dopamine receptors. This evidence can be shown in *in vitro* studies in which cortical membranes from rat brain, and other tissues, is incubated with the appropriate ^{3}H-labelled ligand for the appropriate receptor in the presence of different concentrations of the antidepressant (see Table 2).

Structure–activity studies of the TCAs showed that the potency of a drug to inhibit either NA or 5-HT re-uptake *in vitro* was related to the structure of the aliphatic side-chain. Thus the classical studies of the effects of amitriptyline and imipramine on the uptake of ^{3}H-NA and ^{3}H-5-HT into rat brain slices *in vitro* clearly demonstrated that both drugs were approximately equipotent in inhibiting NA and 5-HT uptake. However, the slight changes in the structure of the aliphatic side-chains of these drugs, as occurs *in vivo* in the liver by a process of N-demethylation, led to a great affinity of the resulting desmethylated metabolite for the NA transport site. As these metabolites of amitriptyline and imipramine (nortriptyline and desipramine respectively) were subsequently found to be as clinically effective as their parent compounds, it was assumed that their antidepressant activities were related to their abilities to inhibit 5-HT and/or NA. The potency and selectivity of the TCAs for the 5-HT uptake site was found to be enhanced by substitution of the chloro or cyano group in the tricyclic ring. Thus clomipramine and cyanopramine were shown to be the most potent 5-HT re-uptake inhibitors in the tricyclic antidepressant series. Unfortunately, all the TCAs with the tertiary amine structure in the aliphatic side-chain are demethylated in the liver *in vivo* to form active metabolites that are relatively selective for the NA uptake site. More importantly, all of the tertiary and secondary TCAs were found to have similar adverse side-effects which limited any therapeutic advantage which they might have over the older TCAs, imipramine and amitriptyline. The structures of some of the TCAs are shown in Figure 1 and their relative selectivity for NA, 5-HT and dopamine (DA) uptake sites shown in Table 3.

Table 2. Inhibition of radioligand binding *in vitro* to rat brain synaptosomal membranes by some SSRI and TCA antidepressants.

^{3}H Ligand	D_2 (spiperone)	5-HT$_{1A}$ (8-OH-DPAT)	5-HT$_{2A}$ (ketanserin)	Alpha^1 (prazosin)	Alpha^2 (idazoxan)	Beta (dihydroalprenalol)
Paroxetine	52 000	>100 000	18 000	19 000	8900	35 000
Citalopram	33 000	15 000	5600	1600	18 000	>100 000
Sertraline	24 000	100 000	8500	2800	1800	14 000
Fluvoxamine	66 000	>100 000	12 000	4800	1900	89 000
Fluoxetine	32 000	79 000	710	14 000	2800	18 000
Clomipramine	430	28 000	54	60	1800	22 000
Imipramine	2400	8900	120	440	2500	>5000
Desipramine	3800	2500	160	1300	5500	>5000

Data abridged from Hyttel (1994) and Johnson (1991).
All values expressed as the inhibitory constants (Ki) in nM. Pharmacological activity is unlikely to occur *in vitro* when the Ki values exceed 1000 nM. Thus, none of the SSRIs is likely to have a direct effect on any of the receptors shown, (nor on histamine, or muscarinic receptors) at pharmacological doses *in vivo*.

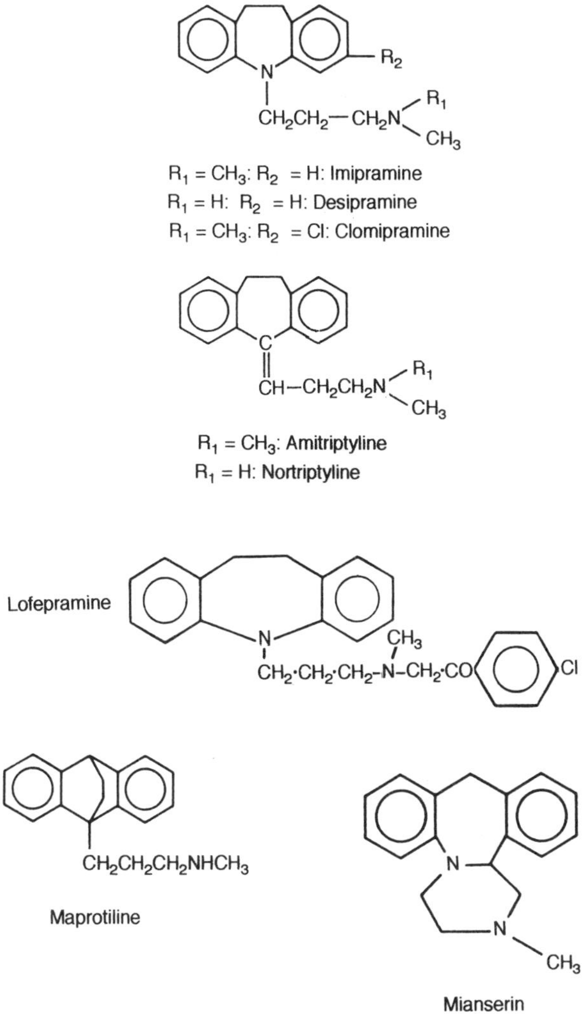

R₁ = CH₃: R₂ = H: Imipramine
R₁ = H: R₂ = H: Desipramine
R₁ = CH₃: R₂ = Cl: Clomipramine

R₁ = CH₃: Amitriptyline
R₁ = H: Nortriptyline

Lofepramine

Maprotiline

Mianserin

Figure 1. Structure of some tricyclic antidepressants.

Attempts to eliminate the action of putative antidepressants on adrenoceptors, muscarinic receptors and histamine 1 receptors, and to enhance the selectivity of the compound for one of the monoamine transport sites, necessitated the abandoning of the tricyclic or pseudo tricyclic structure; maprotiline is an example of a pseudo tricyclic antidepressant that combines specificity in inhibiting NA uptake with similar cardiovascular side-effects to those seen with the conventional TCAs. The only novel tricyclic antidepressant to be developed that combined selectivity for inhibiting NA

Table 3. Effect of some SSRIs and TCAs on the uptake of ^{3}H-biogenic amines into rat brain slices *in vitro.*

	5-HT uptake	NA uptake	DA uptake	Na: 5-HT ratio	DA: 5-HT ratio
Paroxetine	0.29	81	5100	280	17 590
Citalopram	1.80	61 000	40 000	3400	22 222
Sertraline	0.19	160	48	840	253
Fluvoxamine	3.8	620	42 000	160	11 053
Fluoxetine	6.8	370	5000	54	735
Clomipramine	1.5	21	4300	14	28 667
Imipramine	35	14	17 000	0.4	486
Desipramine	200	0.83	9100	0.004	0.2×10^{-4}

Data expressed as IC_{50} values (nM) (abridged from Hyttel, 1994).

re-uptake with reduced anticholinergic and cardiovascular side-effects was lofepramine, a compound in which the side-chain ends in a chlorophenyl acyl ring.

An important breakthrough in the development of antidepressants that combined selectivity in inhibiting 5-HT re-uptake with minimal effects on adrenergic, histaminergic and cholinergic receptors came with the synthesis of the tricyclic antidepressant zimelidine, even though there was evidence that its metabolite norzimelidine did inhibit the re-uptake of NA (Ross and Renyi, 1977). Following the world-wide withdrawal of this antidepressant in 1983 because its use was associated with an increased incidence of Guillain–Barré syndrome, five other SSRIs were soon introduced for clinical use and these have dominated the antidepressant market in recent years. The structures of fluvoxamine, fluoxetine, paroxetine, sertraline and citalopram are shown in Figure 2 and their potency (*in vitro* and *ex vivo*) in inhibiting the re-uptake of ^{3}H-NA, 5-HT and DA is summarized in Table 3.

It can be seen from Table 4 that these SSRIs differ in their relative potency in inhibiting ^{3}H-5-HT and ^{3}H-NA uptake into rat cortical synaptosomes *in vitro*, sertraline and paroxetine being the most potent 5-HT uptake inhibitors while fluoxetine is the least potent. However, in comparison to clomipramine, none of these SSRIs appreciably inhibits NA uptake *in vitro*. This may be illustrated by the data in which the ratio of the IC_{50} values (the concentration required to inhibit the uptake of NA or 5-HT by 50%) for NA and 5-HT is correlated.

A number of questions arise regarding the relevance of data obtained from rat brain synaptosomes *in vitro* to the affinity of these SSRIs for the 5-HT transporter in the human brain. Recently, the 5-HT transporter for the human brain has been cloned and its chromosomal location determined (Ramamoorthy *et al.*, 1993). The cloned rat 5-HT transporter is more closely related to the human NA transporter rather than the human 5-HT transporter. This may account for the fact that inhibition of the human 5-HT transporter by the SSRIs shows differences in potency to the inhibition of the rat 5-HT transporters. Thus Hoffman *et al.* (1991) have reported that the inhibitory constants (Ki values in nM) for paroxetine, citalopram, fluoxetine,

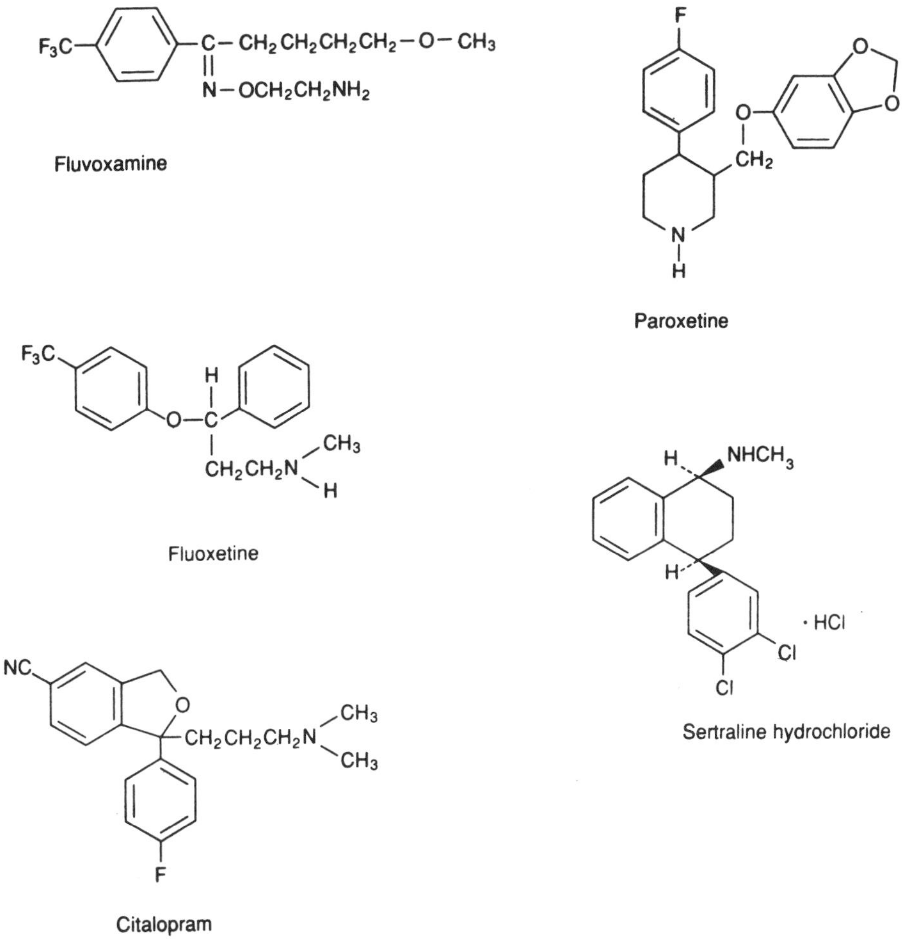

Fluvoxamine

Paroxetine

Fluoxetine

Sertraline hydrochloride

Citalopram

Figure 2. Structural formulae of SSRIs.

clomipramine, imipramine and amitriptyline were 3.1, 6.1, 33, 7.1, 209, and 262 respectively. Another explanation for the differences in the relative potencies of the SSRIs in the rat and human 5-HT transporter may be related to the differences in the precise location of the binding of the different drugs to the 5-HT transporter site. It has been shown that imipramine, paroxetine and citalopram bind to different areas of the 5-HT transporter with citalopram only binding to the 5-HT specific portion of the transporter. It is presently unclear whether the location of the SSRI binding sites on the human 5-HT transporter differs from that of the rat brain transporter.

The main difference between the five SSRIs that arises from the *in vitro* uptake studies is seen in the effects on ^{3}H-DA uptake; only sertraline appears to inhibit the re-uptake of this amine. Whether the inhibition of dopamine re-uptake by sertraline has any relevance to its therapeutic effects (or side-effects) is unknown. Sertraline also significantly inhibits sigma receptor sites (Tulloch 1993; Tulloch 1995; Tulloch *et al.*, 1995). The dosage range for the five SSRIs used to treat depression is shown in Table 4. It can be seen that there is no apparent correlation between the potency of

Table 4. Comparison of the effects of some SSRIs on the uptake of ^{3}H-biogenic amines *ex vivo* and their average daily therapeutic doses.

	Inhibition of ^{3}H-5-HT uptake *ex vivo*	Inhibition of ^{3}H-NA- uptake *ex vivo*	Average daily dose (mg)
Paroxetine	1.9	>30	20–50
Citalopram	5.9	>30	20–40
Sertraline	2.9	>30	50–200
Fluvoxamine	23	>30	100–200
Fluoxetine	7.0	>30	20–40

Potency of the inhibition of ^{3}H-5-HT or ^{3}H-NA uptake expressed as the ED_{50} values in mg/kg following oral administration of the antidepressant. (After Nelson *et al.*, 1989.)

the drugs in inhibiting 5-HT uptake *ex vivo* and the daily dose which is required effectively to treat depression. This suggests that the inhibition of 5-HT re-uptake may be a necessary condition for the antidepressant activity, but it is not by itself a sufficient explanation.

Pharmacological properties of the metabolites of the SSRIs

All five of the well-established SSRIs undergo metabolism in the liver and the resulting metabolites may differ slightly in their pharmacological properties from the apparent compound. The main difference between the five SSRIs lies in the activity of their metabolites. Thus paroxetine and fluvoxamine do not produce any metabolites that, at least at therapeutic doses, are likely to make a significant contribution to their pharmacological effects. By contrast, fluvoxetine and citalopram both produce pharmacologically active metabolites whose actions probably contribute to the antidepressant effects of the parent compounds. Citalopram is desmethylated in the liver to desmethyl citalopram which is less potent that the parent drug in inhibiting 5-HT re-uptake but is much more potent than citalopram in inhibiting NA re-uptake, at least *in vitro* (Hyttel, 1982). The second metabolite of citalopram is didesmethyl citalopram and this also shows weak 5-HT uptake inhibitory properties. Considerable attention has been paid to norfluoxetine, the active metabolite of fluoxetine. This metabolite is some four times more potent than fluoxetine in inhibiting 5-HT re-uptake; at steady state the plasma concentration of norfluoxetine exceeds that of the parent drug (Lemberger *et al.*, 1985). Fluoxetine is therefore unique among the five SSRIs that have been extensively studied in that it produces a pharmacologically more active metabolite which also has a much longer half-life than the parent drug. Paroxetine, sertraline, fluvoxamine and citalopram all have elimination half-lives in the range of 15–26 hours whereas the elimination half-life of fluoxetine is 84 hours and that of its metabolite approximates to 146 hours (see Leonard, 1993). The long half-life of fluoxetine may be advantageous should the depressed patient miss taking the drug for one or two days. However, such a long half-life can be disadvantageous should it be desirable to switch the patient to an MAOI. Under these circumstances hyperpyrexia and symptoms that characterize the "serotonin syndrome" may occur which may be life-threatening to the patient. A washout period of 4–5 weeks is therefore recommended before a patient on fluoxetine is given an MAOI; in the case of the other four SSRIs that have half-lives of the order of one day the washout period recommended is one to two weeks (see Leonard, 1993).

The effects of a number of SSRIs and their metabolites on the uptake of ^{3}H-5-HT, NA and DA into synaptosomes from rat brain is shown in Table 5.

Table 5. Comparison of the effects of the metabolites of some SSRIs on the uptake of ^{3}H-biogenic amines *in vitro*.

	^{3}H-5-HT	^{3}H-NA	^{3}H-DA	NA : 5-HT ratio
Citalopram	1.8	6100	40 000	3388
Desmethyl citalopram	14	740	28 000	53
Didesmethyl citalopram	22	1400	11 000	64
Fluoxetine	6.8	370	5000	54
Norfluoxetine	3.8	580	4300	153
Clomipramine	1.5	21	4300	14
Desmethyl clomipramine	40	0.45	2100	0.01

Data expressed as IC_{50} values (nM). Abridged and amended from Hyttel (1994).

Another pharmacokinetic parameter that needs consideration when SSRIs are used concerns the interaction of concurrently administered drugs with the plasma binding site to which the SSRIs are attached. Fluoxetine, paroxetine and sertraline are over 90% bound to serum proteins whereas fluvoxamine and citalopram are about 80% serum protein bound. While these slight differences in plasma protein binding are of theoretical interest, there is to date little evidence that such factors are of practical relevance.

In the liver, the cytochrome P450 isoenzyme system (CYP450) catalyses the oxidation of many endogenous substances and lipophilic drugs. There are 4 CYP450 isoenzymes of importance in the metabolism of antidepressant drugs namely CYP450–1A2, 2C, 3A4 and 2D6 of which the latter isoenzyme is responsible for the oxidation of many tricyclic antidepressants, some neuroleptics (eg.

haloperidol, thioridazine, perphenazine), β-blockers and type 1C antiarrhythmics (eg. flecainide). The 3A4 isoenzyme also oxidizes some tricyclic antidepressants, some benzodiazepines and terfenadine while the 1A2 isoenzyme oxidizes warfarin, theophylline and some tricyclic antidepressants. The SSRI's differentially inhibit the CYP450 isoenzymes and therefore drug – drug interactions may arise if a drug which is usually metabolised by this isoenzyme is given concurrently with a SSRI. For example, fluoxetine and norfluoxetine inhibit CYP450 2C, 2D6 and 3A4 and may therefore interact with TCAs, some antipsychotic drugs, some antiarrhythimics and carbamazepine whereas fluvoxamine, which preferentially inhibits the 1A2 isoenzyme, could interact with warfarin, propranolol, theophylline and to a small extent TCAs. This subject has been extensively reviewed by De Vane (1994), Zussman (1995) and Brosen (1990).

The biochemical specificity of action of the SSRIs

One of the first experimental studies to show convincingly that TCAs, MAOIs and ECS caused similar adaptational changes in neurotransmission arose from the observation that the density and functional activity of β-adrenoceptors in the rat frontal cortex was decreased following chronic (but not acute) treatment (Vetulani *et al.*, 1976; Bannerjee *et al.*, 1977). As the duration of treatment necessary to produce a decrease in β-adrenoceptor density and function approximately coincided with the time of onset of the antidepressant response in man, it was postulated that this could be the common biochemical mechanism whereby all antidepressant treatments produce their beneficial effects (Vetulani *et al.*, 1976). Unfortunately, it was soon discovered that a substantial proportion of the second generation antidepressants either have inconsistent effects on cortical β-adrenoceptor density (for example fluvoxamine: Brunello *et al.*, 1986) or have no effect (for example, paroxetine, citalopram, fluoxetine and mianserin, see Johnson, 1991). Changes in the density of cortical β-adrenoceptors may not necessarily reflect the functional activity of these receptors however. Fluoxetine, for example, has been shown to decrease the activity of noradrenaline- or isoprenaline-stimulated adenylate cyclase, the second messenger system which is linked to the cortical β-receptor and which initiates the biological function of the receptor (Baron *et al.*, 1988). It is also interesting to note that co-administration of fluoxetine with mianserin or the selective NA re-uptake inhibitor maprotiline accentuates the reduction in β-receptor-linked adenylate cyclase activity (Askura *et al.*, 1987). One possible explanation for these findings is that a pharmacokinetic interaction occurs between these antidepressants, a possibility that has not been critically assessed. It is also possible that a pharmacodynamic interaction occurs as a consequence of the adaptive changes in the noradrenergic and serotonergic systems that result from the chronic administration of these antidepressants. Thus Brunello and coworkers (1985) have shown that lesions of serotonergic tracts prevent the reduction in the density of cortical β-adrenoceptors caused by chronic desipramine treatment. Norman and

Leonard (1994) have critically reviewed the limitations and prospects for increasing the speed of onset of antidepressant response. There is preliminary evidence that pindolol potentiates the effect of paroxetine both clinically and pre-clinically with enhanced onset of action (Artigas *et al.*, 1994; Davidson and Stamford, 1995). Further controlled trials, must be done to explore this potentiation.

So far emphasis has been placed on the interconnection between 5-HT receptors

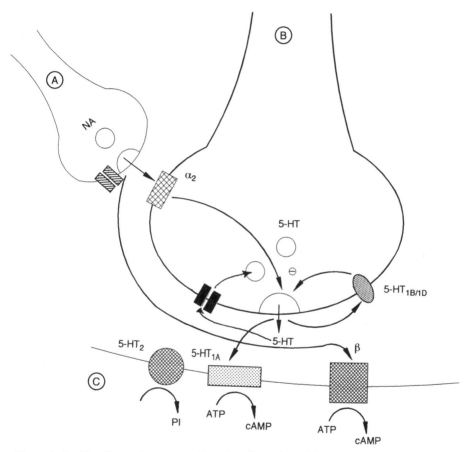

Figure 3. **A** Noradrenergic neurone. Noradrenaline released from terminal activates both the alpha$_2$ heteroceptor on the 5-HT terminal (B) and the postsynaptic beta adrenoceptor. The alpha$_2$ heteroceptor inhibits the release of 5-HT from the 5-HT terminal.
B Serotonergic neurone. The release of 5-HT is modulated by the alpha$_2$ heteroceptor and the inhibitory 5-HT$_{1B}$ (rat) or 5-HT$_{1D}$ (human, guinea-pig) presynaptic receptor.
C Postsynaptic site. In addition to the 5-HT$_{1A}$, 5-HT$_{2A}$ and beta adrenoceptors, alpha$_1$ receptors are also located at some central postsynaptic sites. The second messenger systems which are linked to the postsynaptic receptors produce phosphatidyl inositols or cyclic nucleotides that, by phosphorylating membrane proteins, cellular enzymes etc., initiate the biological responses of the postsynaptic cell.

and β-adrenoceptors as a possible explanation of the antidepressant effects of the SSRIs and other antidepressants. There is unequivocal evidence however that α_2-adrenoceptors located on 5-HT terminals may modulate the release of 5-HT and therefore contribute to the antidepressant effects of such drugs (Raiteri et al., 1990). Such α_2-adrenoceptors act as inhibitory heteroceptors on serotonergic terminals (Blier et al., 1990). Thus the possibility arises that antidepressants which increase the intersynaptic concentration of NA desensitize the α_2-heteroceptors on serotonergic terminals and thereby indirectly facilitate the release of 5-HT (Blier et al., 1993). Such an occurrence could account for the synergistic effect of fluoxetine and desipramine in the treatment of depression (Nelson et al., 1991) although the possibility remains that a pharmacokinetic interaction that results from an inhibition of desipramine metabolism by fluoxetine could be responsible for its effect. A diagrammatic representation of the possible interrelationship between the cortical α_2, β and 5-HT receptors that may be of relevance to the long-term adaptive changes in serotonergic and adrenergic transmission following the chronic administration of antidepressants is illustrated in Figure 3.

The results of such studies, and those of others in which the effects of the MAOI pargyline and the selective catecholamine re-uptake inhibitor nomifensin were found to have qualitatively similar effects to the SSRIs and TCAs on cortical β-adrenoceptor function and 5-HT$_2$ receptor density (Paul et al., 1988). It may be concluded that chronically administered antidepressants cause interdependent adaptive changes in 5-HT$_2$, and α_2- and β-adrenoceptors in the rat cortex which may be of relevance to the antidepressant actions of these drugs. It seems unlikely that such changes in adrenoceptors and serotonin receptors are sufficient to explain the common mechanism of action of all antidepressants, particularly as it has been shown that some antidepressants may alter neuronal structure (Wong et al., 1991), influence the coupling mechanism between the receptor and the second messenger system (see Leonard, 1994a), and elicit changes in the phosphorylation of microtubules within the nerve cell (Perez et al., 1989). Such changes in the plasticity of the nervous system that occur following the chronic administration of different types of antidepressants may represent the biochemical changes that are necessary for antidepressant activity to occur.

CHANGES IN NEUROTRANSMITTER RECEPTORS IN THE MAMMALIAN BRAIN AFTER CHRONIC ANTIDEPRESSANT TREATMENT

Antidepressant therapy is usually associated with a delay of 2–3 weeks before the onset of beneficial effect (Oswald et al., 1972). Much of the improvement seen early in the treatment with antidepressants is probably associated with a reduction in anxiety that often occurs in the depressed patient, and improvement in sleep caused by the sedative action of many of these drugs. The delay in the onset of the therapeutic response cannot be easily explained by the pharmacokinetic profile of the drugs since peak plasma and therefore brain concentrations are usually reached in 7–10 days. Furthermore, the 2–3 week delay is also seen in many, although not all, patients given ECT. Thus the amine hypothesis, which was based on the acute effects of antidepressants on the re-uptake of biogenic amines or on the inhibition of monoamine oxidase activity, has undergone drastic revision in recent years to account for the disparity between the immediate effects of antidepressants and the onset of their clinical effects. Researchers have therefore switched their attention from the actions of antidepressants on presynaptic mechanisms that govern neurotransmitter synthesis, re-uptake, and metabolism, to the changes in receptor function. Table 6 summarizes some of the changes in neurotransmitter receptors that occur in the cortex of rat brain following ECT or the chronic administration of antidepressants. It can be seen that irrespective of the nature of the treatment, adaptational changes occur in adrenoceptors, serotonin, dopamine, and GABA-B receptors.

Table 6. Changes in neurotransmitter receptors that occur in the cortex of rat brain following chronic antidepressant treatment.

Cortical beta-adrenoceptors	Decreased functional activity and density
Cortical alpha$_1$-adrenoceptors	Increased density
Cortical alpha$_2$-autoreceptors	Decreased functional activity
Dopamine autoreceptors	Decreased functional activity
Cortical GABA$_B$ receptors	Decreased density
Limbic 5-HT$_{1A}$ receptors	Increased density and decreased functional activity
Cortical 5-HT$_2$ receptors	Decreased density and functional activity

(See Leonard, 1993.)

In addition to these changes in GABA-B and biogenic amine receptors, recent evidence by Earley *et al.* (1990) has shown that a decrease in cortical muscarinic receptors occurs in the bulbectomized rat model of depression but, like most of the changes in biogenic amine receptors, returns to control values following treatment with both typical and atypical antidepressants. Thus, irrespective of the specificity of the antidepressants following their acute administration, it would appear that a common feature of all these drugs is to correct the abnormality in neurotransmitter receptor function. Such an effect of chronic antidepressant treatment largely parallels the time of onset of the therapeutic response and forms the basis of the receptor sensitivity hypothesis of depression and the common mode of action of antidepressants.

.   The mechanisms whereby chronic antidepressant treatment causes changes in such diverse neurotransmitter receptors is unknown. Considerable attention has recently been focused on the interaction between serotonergic and beta-adrenergic receptors, which may be of particular relevance to our understanding of the therapeutic effect of antidepressants. Thus the chronic administration of antidepressants enhances inhibitory response of forebrain neurones to microiontophoretically applied 5-HT (Aghajanian and de Montigny, 1978). This enhanced response is blocked by lesions of the noradrenergic projections to the cortex (Gravel and de Montigny, 1987). This dual effect could help to explain enhanced serotonergic function that arises after chronic administration of antidepressants or ECT. Thus most antidepressants decrease the functional activity of the β-adrenoceptors that normally have an inhibitory role on the cortical 5-HT system. This decrease results in a disinhibition or facilitation of serotonergic and dopaminergic-mediated behaviours.

Conversely, impairment of the serotonergic system by means of selective neurotoxins or 5-HT synthesis inhibitors largely prevents the decrease in functional activity of cortical β-adrenoceptors that usually arises following chronic antidepressant treatment (Brunello *et al.*, 1985). Experimental evidence suggests that these apparent changes in β-adrenoceptors that occur following chronic antidepressant treatment are more likely to be due to an increase in the density of 5-HT$_{IB}$ receptor sites, which are also labelled by the β-adrenoceptor antagonist dihydroalprenolol, a ligand conventionally used to identify β-adrenoceptors (Stockmeier and Keller, 1986).

Both clinical and experimental studies have provided evidence that 5-HT can regulate dopamine turnover. Thus, several investigators have shown that a positive correlation exists in depressed patients between the homovanillic acid (HVA) and 5-HIAA concentrations in the CSF (Agren *et al.*, 1986). In experimental studies, stimulation of the 5-HT cell bodies in the median raphe causes reduced firing of the substantia nigra where dopamine is the main neurotransmitter (Dray *et al.*, 1976). Agren *et al.* (1986) have provided convincing evidence that 5-HT plays an important role in modulating dopaminergic function in many regions of the brain, including the mesolimbic system. Such findings imply that the effects of antidepressants that show an apparent selectivity for the serotonergic system could be equally ascribed to a change in dopaminergic function in mesolimbic and mesocortical regions of the brain.

The net result of the activation of the secondary messenger systems is to increase the activity of the various protein kinases that phosphorylate membrane-bound proteins to produce a physiological response (Nestler *et al.*, 1984). Racagni and coworkers (1991) have investigated the effect of chronic antidepressant treatment on the phosphorylation of proteins associated with the cytoskeletal structure of the nerve cell. These investigators suggest that antidepressants could affect the function of the cytoskeleton by changing the components of the associated protein phosphorylation system. In support of their hypothesis, these researchers showed that both typical (e.g. desipramine) and atypical (e.g. ($\pm$) oxaprotiline, a specific noradrenaline re-uptake inhibitor and fluoxetine, a selective 5-HT uptake inhibitor) antidepressants increased the synthesis of a microtubule fraction possibly by affecting the regulatory subunit of protein kinase type II. These changes in cytoskeletal protein synthesis occurred only after chronic antidepressant treatments and suggest that antidepressants, besides their well-established effects on pre- and postsynaptic receptors, amine uptake systems, and amine systems, might change neuronal signal transduction processes distal to the receptor.

Another possible mechanism whereby antidepressants may change the physical relationship between neurones in the brain is by inhibiting neurite outgrowths from nerve cells. Thus Wong and coworkers (1991) showed that the tricyclic antidepressant amitriptyline, at therapeuticaly relevant concentrations, inhibited neurite outgrowth from chick embryonic cerebral explants *in vivo*. These investigators postulate that the reduction in the rate of synthesis of cyclic AMP caused by amitriptyline is responsible for the reduced neurite growth. While the relevance of such findings to the therapeutic effects of amitriptyline in man is unclear, they do suggest that a common mode of action of all antidepressants could be to modify the actual structure of nerve cells and possibly eliminate inappropriate synaptic contacts that are responsible for behavioural and psychological changes associated with depression.

Hypercortisolism occurs commonly in depression, and the relative insensitivity of the pituitary–adrenal axis to the inhibitory feedback effect of the glucocorticoid dexamethasone is used as a biochemical marker of the disease. One possible explanation for this insensitivity to dexamethasone may lie in the hypersensitivity of central glucocorticoid receptors.

Interest in the possible association of central glucocorticoid receptors with altered central neurotransmitter function arose from the observation that such receptors have been identified in the nuclei of catecholamine and 5-HT containing cell bodies in the brain (Harfstand *et al.*, 1986). Burnstein and Cidlowski (1989) have shown that glucocorticoid receptors function as DNA binding protein which can modify the transcription of genes. Chronic imipramine treatment increases glucocorticoid receptor immunoreactivity in rat brain, the changes being particularly pronounced in the noradrenergic and serotonergic cell body regions (Kitayama *et al.*, 1988). Preliminary clinical studies have also shown that lymphocyte glucocorticoid receptors are abnormal in depressed patients (Giller *et al.*, 1988). Such findings lend support to the hypothesis that the changes in central neurotransmission occurring in depression are a reflection of the effects of chronic glucocorticoids on the transcription of proteins that play a crucial role in neuronal structure and function. Sulser and Sanders-Bush (1987) have formulated a 5-HT/noradrenaline glucocorticoid link hypothesis of affective disorders based on such findings. If the pituitary–adrenal axis plays such an important role in central neurotransmission, it may be speculated that glucocorticoid synthesis inhibitors (e.g. metyrapone) could reduce the abnormality in neurotransmitter function by decreasing the cortisol concentration.

The adaptation of central glucocorticoid type 2 receptors to the decrease in the concentration of corticoid caused by antidepressants would appear to require chronic drug treatment. Recent *in vitro* hybridization studies in the rat have demonstrated that typical antidepressants increase the density of glucocorticoid receptors (Pepin *et al.*, 1989). Such an effect could increase the negative feedback mechanism and thereby reduce the synthesis and release of cortisol. There is preliminary clinical evidence that metyrapone may produce a beneficial effect in depressed patients more rapidly than typical antidepressants (Dinan, 1994).

Role of 5-HT in depression: relevance to the mode of action of antidepressants

5-HT is believed to play a multifunctional role in depression. This view arises from the clinical and experimental evidence that 5-HT is involved in the regulation of mood, sleep, vigilance, memory and learning, feeding and sexual behaviour, all of which are deranged to varying extent in severe depression (see Leonard, 1994b). It is well established that 5-HT produces its physiological effects by activating one or more of the 14 or more subtypes of 5-HT receptor (Leonard, 1994b), but which of these receptor subtypes is primarily involved in the action of antidepressants is uncertain. One approach to unravelling the changes in 5-HT receptors in depression has been to study the effects of chronically administered antidepressants on 5-HT receptor subtypes in the rat brain. Despite the low affinity of most antidepressants for the 5-HT receptors *in vitro* (see Table 6), there is experimental evidence to show that chronic antidepressant treatment results in a hypersensitivity of postsynaptic 5-HT$_{1A}$ receptors and a hyposensitivity of the presynaptic 5-HT$_{1A}$ receptors (De Montigny *et al.*, 1990; Hamon *et al.*, 1987).

This conclusion supports the earlier findings of Goodwin and coworkers (1985) who reported that the hypothermic effect of the 5-HT$_{1A}$ receptor agonist 8-hydroxy-dipropyl amino tetrahydronaphthylene (8-OHDPAT) is reduced following the chronic administration of desipramine, zimeldine and mianserin. Such an observation is consistent with the view that the 5-HT$_{1A}$ somodendritic receptors are desensitized, and made functionally hypoactive, by chronic antidepressant treatment. Earlier studies by Aghajanian and de Montigny (1978) had shown that different TCAs enhanced the responsiveness of postsynaptic 5-HT receptors to iontophoretically applied 5-HT. This increased sensitivity of the postsynaptic 5-HT receptors only occurred following the chronic administration of the antidepressant and was independent of the effects of the antidepressants inhibiting the monoamine re-uptake. Similar results have been obtained following the chronic administration of the selective serotonin re-uptake inhibitors such as paroxetine, sertraline and citalopram (Blier *et al.*, 1990).

There are a number of possible explanations for these findings. In addition to the changes in the functional activity of the 5-HT$_{1A}$ receptors, Chaput *et al.* (1986) have shown that the 5-HT autoreceptors (of the 5-HT$_{1B/1D}$ subtype) in the rat hippocampus are desensitized following chronic treatment with citalopram. Similar results have been obtained following chronic treatment with fluoxetine (Blier *et al.*, 1988) and paroxetine (de Montigny *et al.*, 1989). As the 5-HT autoreceptors have an inhibitory function on 5-HT release, it seems possible that the increase in serotonergic neurotransmission that follows chronic (but not acute) treatment with the SSRIs is particularly due to the desensitization of 5-HT autoreceptors.

Such experimental findings are important in that they unify the mechanism whereby both the TCAs and many of the second generation antidepressants enhance central serotonergic function following their chronic administration. Thus

TCAs and electroconvulsive shocks act by sensitizing the postsynaptic $5\text{-}HT_{1A}$ receptors whereas the SSRIs and MAOIs increase serotonergic transmission by desensitizing the inhibitory somatodendritic and terminal 5-HT autoreceptors. Mianserin, and probably other second generation antidepressants that do not inhibit 5-HT re-uptake, probably act in a similar manner to the TCAs. De Montigny, Chaput and Blier (1993) have recently summarized the electrophysiological evidence that supports the hypothesis that all types of antidepressants facilitate central serotonergic transmission by changing the sensitivity of different populations of $5\text{-}HT_{1A}$ receptors and have shown that such changes are correlated with the time of onset of the antidepressant response when the drugs are given to depressed patients.

The $5\text{-}HT_{2A}$ receptors also appear to be involved both in the aetiology of depression and in the mode of action of antidepressants. There is evidence from studies of the chronic effects of TCAs and SSRIs on the density of $5\text{-}HT_2$ receptors in the rat forebrain that most antidepressants decrease the number of receptors (Peroutka and Snyder, 1980; Stolz *et al.*, 1983; Nelson *et al.*, 1989). Both amitriptyline and sertraline have also been shown to decrease the activity of the phosphatidyl-inositol linked second messenger system following their chronic administration (Sanders-Bush *et al.*, 1989). However, electroconvulsive shock treatment (ECT) increases the densities of these receptors in the frontal cortex. As ECT is probably one of the most effective treatments for severe depression, the results of such studies make it improbable that changes in the density of cortical $5\text{-}HT_{2A}$ receptors are causally connected to the antidepressant effects of these treatments. Furthermore, despite the observation that most types of antidepressants have a moderate affinity for $5\text{-}HT_{2A}$ receptors *in vitro*, there is no apparent correlation between their affinity for their receptors and their antidepressant potency (Ogren and Fuxe, 1985). Nevertheless, Deakin and Graeff (1991) have argued that depression could arise from a pathological increase in $5\text{-}HT_{2A}$ receptor function in limbic regions of the brain. This view would concur with our studies of 5-HT induced platelet aggregation studies in depressed patients before and following effective antidepressant treatment with both TCAs and with various second generation antidepressants including theSSRI, sertraline (Healy *et al.*, 1983; 1985; Butler and Leonard, 1988; Butler *et al.*, 1988). The $5\text{-}HT_{2A}$ receptor on the human platelet membrane appears to be structurally similar to that located in limbic regions of the brain (Leysen *et al.*, 1981), and therefore changes in the functional activity of the platelet membrane receptor may be relevant to the changes occurring centrally.

There is experimental evidence to show chronic (but not acute) administration of paroxetine and fluoxetine to rats attenuates the hypoactivity induced by the $5\text{-}HT_{2B/2C}$ agonist (1-(3-chlorophenyl) piperazine (mCPP) (Kennett *et al.*, 1994a). mCPP is known to be anxiogenic in both man and rodents (Kennett, 1993), and its effects can be antagonized in man by the non-selective $5\text{-}HT_2$ antagonist ritanserin (Kennett, 1993). Other clinical studies have shown that the responsiveness of patients with panic disorder to mCPP is enhanced which suggests that the $5\text{-}HT_{2B/2C}$

receptors are supersensitive in this disorder. Thus the efficacy of SSRIs such as paroxetine and fluoxetine is attenuating the symptoms of panic disorder, and anxiety disorders such as obsessive–compulsive disorder, may be attributed to a desensitization of 5-HT$_{2B/2C}$ receptors (Kennett *et al.*, 1994b). This suggests that such a desensitization may contribute to the anxiolytic effects of the SSRIs, although experimental evidence suggests that such a change in 5-HT $_2$ receptor function may not be sufficient to explain the complete therapeutic action of the SSRIs.

Clinical studies have shown that the number of 5-HT$_{2A}$ receptor sites on the platelet membrane of untreated depressives is significantly elevated but normalizes following effective antidepressant treatment (Butler *et al.*, 1988). However, the functional activity of these receptors, as shown by 5-HT induced aggregation, is markedly reduced in the untreated depressed patient but normalizes following effective antidepressant treatment. It is interesting to note that the density of 5-HT$_{2A}$ receptors is also increased in the frontal cortex of the brain of suicide victims (Stanley and Mann, 1983; Arora and Meltzer, 1989). One must conclude that there is a disparity between the effects of chronic administration of antidepressants on the 5-HT$_{2A}$ receptor function in rats, as exhibited by the decreased activity of the phosphatidyl-inositol system which reflects the receptor activity (Sanders-Bush *et al.*, 1989; Kendall and Nahorski, 1985), and the increase in platelet 5-HT$_{2A}$ receptor function in the response of depressed patients to effective antidepressant treatment.

Such findings also emphasize the difficulties that arise when trying to interpret the action of antidepressants for their chronic effects in animals. From the clinical studies that have already been summarized it can be speculated that a fundamental biochemical abnormality in depression may lie in the G-protein transducer mechanism which links the 5-HT$_{2A}$ receptor to the second messenger system (Kendall and Nahorski, 1985; Leonard, 1994b). Effective antidepressant treatment would appear to correct this defective coupling system and thereby return 5-HT$_{2A}$ receptor function to its normal state.

It is self-evident that changes in the dynamics of 5-HT caused either by a genetically based pathological process that underlines depression, or that follows the chronic administration of an antidepressant, is unlikely to be restricted to one 5-HT receptor subtype. There is evidence from both clinical and experimental studies that both 5-HT$_{1A}$ and 5-HT$_{2A}$ receptors are somewhat involved in the aetiology of depression. Deakin *et al.* (1991) have hypothesized that the 5-HT$_{1A}$ and 5-HT$_{2A}$ receptors are primarily involved in the depressive and anxiety symptoms of depression respectively. It is not without interest that 5-HT$_{1A}$ partial agonists such as ipsapirone, gepirone and zalospirone have been shown to have both anxiolytic and antidepressant activity in some rodent models of depression (Pinder and Wieringa, 1993). However, flesinoxan would appear to be potentially an even more interesting compound as it combines 5-HT$_{1A}$ agonist properties with a 5-HT$_2$ receptor antagonist (Pinder and Wieringa, 1993). Preliminary clinical studies show that flesinoxan has antidepressant properties but its therapeutic efficacy will depend on the outcome of detailed double-blind studies. Clearly more experimental and clinical studies are needed in

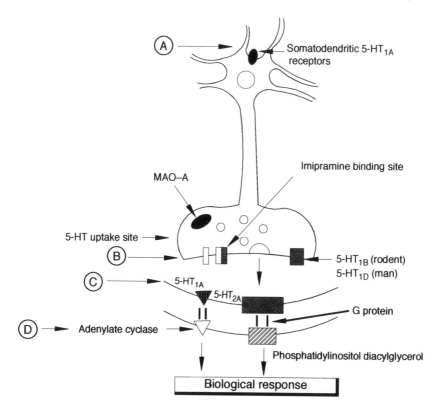

Figure 4. Changes that occur following the chronic administration of antidepressants.
A SSRIs and MAOIs desensitize the inhibitory 5-HT$_{1A}$ somatodendritic receptors.
B SSRIs and MAOIs desensitize the inhibitory 5-HT$_{1B}$/5-HT$_{1D}$ inhibitory auto receptor on the presynaptic terminal. After acute administration, the TCAs and the SSRIs inhibit the uptake of 5-HT into the nerve terminal by binding to the imipramine binding site (or its equivalent). 5-HT transport sites are also found on the cell body and axonal projection but their precise role in serotonergic transmission is unclear. Presumably they change in 5-HT in the vicinity of the receptors. 5-HT$_{1B}$ and $_{1D}$ receptors appear to have a similar function but are structurally slightly different according to the species in which they are found.
C TCAs, ECT and most non-SSRI second generation antidepressants sensitize the postsynaptic 5-HT$_{1A}$ receptors thereby increasing serotonergic function. The density of 5-HT$_{2A}$ receptors is decreased by TCAs and SSRIs in rat brain following chronic treatment; in the depressed patient however the number of 5-HT$_{2A}$ receptors is increased and normalizes following effective treatment.
D There is experimental evidence that the activity of the second messenger system associated with the 5-HT$_{2A}$ receptor is decreased following chronic antidepressant treatment. There is also circumstantial evidence that the G-protein coupling mechanism between the 5-HT$_{2A}$ receptor and its second messenger is hypofunctional in depressed patients but normalizes following effective treatment. This suggests that some antidepressants may improve the receptor–second messenger G-protein coupling mechanism.

order to determine the role of 5-HT$_{1A}$ and 5-HT$_{2A}$ receptors (and possibly other 5-HT receptor subtypes) in depression and the mode of action of antidepressants.

In conclusion, although the precise mechanism whereby antidepressants produce their therapeutic effects is incompletely understood, there is a growing body of evidence to suggest that 5-HT$_{1A}$ and 5-HT$_{2A}$ receptors play an important role. It is unlikely that the 5-HT receptors only are involved in bringing about the therapeutic response to antidepressant treatments (see Table 6).

Nevertheless, 5-HT would appear to be crucially involved in the action of these drugs and the possible changes elicited by the different types of antidepressants that ultimately result in enhanced serotonergic function in the brain are shown diagrammatically in Figure 4.

EFFECTS OF THE SSRIS ON ANIMAL BEHAVIOUR

Despite the pronounced effects of the SSRIs on brain serotonergic function there is no evidence that any of these drugs has any effect on the gross behaviour of rodents (Koe et al., 1983; Stark et al., 1985). All the SSRIs will potentiate the pharmacological effects of 5-hydroxytryptophan (5-HTP, the precursor of 5-HT) and tryptophan which produces a characteristic behavioural profile of forelimb movements and head shakes at non-toxic doses. At high doses agitation and hyperthermia occur. These symptoms are characteristic of the "serotonin syndrome". The characteristic movements initiated in rodents by the combination of a SSRI with 5-HTP or tryptophan is unique for this class of antidepressant and has been used to detect potential SSRI antidepressants in screening tests. Unlike the TCAs, none of the SSRIs antagonizes the hypothermic or ptosis-inducing effects of tetrabenazine or reserpine in mice. Such tests are frequently used as screening tests for antidepressants but have largely been superseded by more sophisticated and reliable tests (such as the learned helplessness test of Porsolt et al., 1979) because of the large number of false positive and negative compounds selected by the reserpine or tetrabenazine antagonism tests. The median effective doses of the SSRIs in potentiating the effects of 5-HTP or tryptophan reflect the potency of these drugs in inhibiting 5-HT re-uptake (see Hyttel, 1994).

Immobility induced in rodents by placing them in a large container of warm water from which they cannot escape has become widely used as a test for potential antidepressant activity. Most TCAs and second generation antidepressants suppress the immobility (Porsolt et al., 1979; Porsolt, 1981), but it would appear that the SSRIs are less active than the TCAs in this test. Because antihistaminic and anticholinergic drugs are active in this Porsolt test, while many therapeutically effective antidepressants are inactive, the usefulness of this behavioural test as a predictor of antidepressant activity has been questioned. Nevertheless, the Porsolt test is of value as an initial screening method for antidepressant activity because the activity of the drug is often apparent after acute administration. A more laborious, but undoubtedly more reliable, test for antidepressant activity is the olfactory bulbectomized rat model of depression. This has been extensively studied by Leonard and coworkers (see Leonard and Tuite, 1981; Van Riezen and Leonard, 1990) who have shown that TCAs, MAO-A inhibitors and the SSRIs which have been tested are active in attenuating the hyperactivity of bulbectomized rats in a stressful novel environment (the open field apparatus). The important feature of this rodent model is that activity is only apparent after chronic treatment with antidepressants; psychotropic drugs which lack antidepressant activity are inactive in this model.

Effect of SSRIs on feeding behaviour

There is good experimental evidence to show that 5-HT is crucially involved in food intake and food selection. For example, ($\pm$) fenfluramine which releases 5-HT and fluoxetine are known to be effective anorexic agents in both animals and man. Clinically these drugs reduce the frequency of binge eating in patients with bulimia. The experimental and clinical involvement of 5-HT in feeding behaviour has been extensively reviewed by Dourish (1992).

Initial studies of the effect of fluoxetine on the food intake of rats suggested that there was a close association between the inhibition of 5-HT re-uptake and the anorexic effect of the antidepressant (Goudie *et al.*, 1976). More recently, however, it has been shown that the doses of fluoxetine and norfluoxetine required to inhibit food intake were several times those required to inhibit 5-HT uptake (Caccia *et al.*, 1992; Wong *et al.*, 1988), but were equivalent to those required to inhibit the uptake of catecholamines. Further studies on the effects of fluoxetine on feeding behaviour showed that the drug increased the latency to eat and decreased the eating rate. This action of fluoxetine could be blocked by the non-specific 5-HT_1 receptor antagonist metergoline which suggests that one or more of the 5-HT_1 receptor subtypes was involved in the anorexic action of fluoxetine (Lee and Clifton, 1992). Of the SSRIs investigated for their effect on rodent feeding behaviour, zimelidine, alaproclate, sertraline, indalpine and paroxetine have been shown to have a qualitatively similar effect to fluxoetine in reducing the food intake.

In addition to the SSRIs, there is also experimental evidence to suggest that 5-HT_{1A} agonists, and possibly 5-HT_2 agonists, inhibit feeding in a dose-dependent manner (see Leonard, 1994b). As such receptors would be functionally activated by any of the SSRIs *in vivo*, it would appear that 5-HT plays a necessary (if not sufficient) role in modulating food intake. The effects of the SSRIs on the microstructure of feeding behaviour in the rat may be of relevance in explaining the clinical usefulness of those drugs in the treatment of bulimia.

Anxiolytic activity of SSRIs

There is increasing evidence that the SSRIs in clinical use are effective in the treatment of anxiety disorders in addition to their well established role in the treatment of depression. However, the experimental data supporting the clinical observations has been largely lacking until Lightowler *et al.* (1994) showed that the long term administration of paroxetine increased the interaction of rats in a social interaction test. Such findings support the clinical evidence that the SSRIs (as exemplified by paroxetine) have an anxiolytic, in addition to an antidepressant action, following their chronic administration.

Effect of the selective SSRIs on extrapyramidal function

The anecdotal reports in the clinical literature suggesting that some SSRIs may exacerbate extrapyramidal symptoms in patients with Parkinson's disease (see Bouchard *et al.*, 1989) suggest that 5-HT may have an inhibitory effect on striatal dopaminergic function. Indeed experimental studies by Baldessarini and Marsh (1990) showed that fluoxetine inhibited the function in the striatum, an effect which was maintained following the chronic administration of the drug. Other studies had previously shown that paroxetine could induce oral hyperkinesias in the monkey (Korsgaard *et al.*, 1985) which would support the hypothesis that SSRIs as a class may precipitate extrapyramidal symptoms particularly in those patients whose striatal dopaminergic system is compromised as would occur in Parkinson's disease. Also, sigma ligands (fluoxetine, sertraline, fluvoxamine) can produce temporary dystonias with intrarubral injections (Leonard *et al.*, 1995).

Of the other movement disorders in which 5-HT has been implicated, the tic disorders (for example, Tourette's syndrome) has recently achieved attention. Tic-like movements in animals (defined as involuntary, sudden, rapid, recurrent, arrhythmic, stereotyped movements) can be induced by 5-HT, NA, GABA and glutamate receptor stimulation (Handley and Singh, 1986). The SSRIs have been investigated in the treatment of tic disorders because of the high frequency of such disorders in patients with obsessive–compulsive disorder. In a rodent model of tic disorder citalopram has been shown to both improve and exacerbate the condition. Overall results for the treatment of such movement disorders have been disappointing however (see Handley and Dursun, 1992).

Effect of SSRIs on pain perception

The presence of 5-HT terminals in the dorsal and ventral horns of the spinal cord has long been associated with pain modulation. The dorsal and ventral horns are innervated from cell bodies located in the raphe magnus, pallidus and obscurus located within the caudal brain stem. It would appear that the serotonergic terminals treated in the dorsal horn are primarily concerned in the modulation of pain perception. Clearly drugs that increase the functional activity of the serotonergic system such as the SSRIs may be expected to have an effect on pain perception. However, experimental studies have failed to show that SSRIs such as citalopram, zimelidine and femoxetine alter pain perception in rodents as measured by the hot plate test (Sugrue, 1979). Nevertheless such drugs will potentiate morphine-induced antinociception. Whether such an event is due to a pharmacokinetic interaction between morphine and the SSRIs, or involves changes in neuropeptides such as substance P which also play a role in modulating pain perception in the spinal cord, is unknown. Nevertheless, it does seem possible that the SSRIs can have antinociceptive activity if given in high enough doses (Fasmer *et al.*, 1989).

CONCLUSIONS

The SSRIs are a chemically diverse group of drugs whose clinical use in depression has recently been extended to the treatment of pain disorder, obsessive–compulsive disorder and bulimia. Such a broad pharmacological profile is a reflection of the physiological role that 5-HT plays in the brain. An increasing knowledge of the distribution and function of the dozen or so 5-HT receptor subtypes is assisting our understanding of the mechanism whereby the SSRIs can bring about their effects at the cellular level. The differences between the five main SSRIs in animals relate primarily to their pharmacokinetics and potency in inhibiting 5-HT re-uptake *in vitro* and *ex vivo*. There is little evidence from animal studies that any of these SSRIs can be significantly distinguished from one another. This is not to suggest that differences between these drugs do not occur in man. To quote Werner Von Heisenberg: "What we observe is not nature itself, but nature exposed to our method of questioning". Perhaps we have been asking the wrong questions about how the SSRIs work and if it is possible to distinguish between them.

REFERENCES

Aghajanian GK and de Montigny C (1978) Tricyclic antidepressants: Long term treatment increases responsivity of rat forebrain neurons to serotonin. *Science* **202**, 1303–1306.

Agren H, Mefford IN, Rudorfer MV, *et al.* (1986) Interacting neurotransmitter systems. *J Psychiatr Res* **20**, 175–193.

Arora RC and Meltzer HY (1989) Serotonergic measures in brains of suicide victims: 5HT2 binding sites in the frontal cortex of suicide victims and control subjects. *Am J Psychiatry* **146**, 730–736.

Askura M, Tsukamoto T, Kubota H, *et al.* (1987) Role of serotonin in regulation of beta adrenoceptors by antidepressants. *Eur J Pharmacol* **141**, 95–100.

Ayd FJ and Blackwell B (1970) *Discoveries in Biological Psychiatry.* Lippincott, Philadelphia.

Artigas F, Perez V, Alurez E (1994) Pindolol induces a rapid improvement of depressed patients treated with serotonin reuptake inhibitors. *Arch Gen Psychiatry* **51**, 248–51.

Baldessarini RJ and Marsh E (1990) Fluoxetine and side effects. *Arch Gen Psychiatry* **47**, 191–192.

Bannerjee SP, King, LS, Riggi SJ, *et al.* (1977) Development of beta-adrenoceptor subsensitivity by antidepressants. *Nature* **268**, 455–456.

Baron BM, Ogden AM, Siegel BW, *et al.* (1988) Rapid down regulation of beta adrenoceptors by co-administration of desipramine and fluoxetine. *Eur J Pharmacol* **154**, 125–134.

Blier P, Chaput Y and de Montigny C (1978) Long term 5HT reuptake blockade but not monoamine oxidase inhibition decreases the function of terminal 5HT autoreceptors: an electrophysiological study in the rat brain. *Naunyn Schmiedebergs Arch Pharmacol* **337**, 246–254.

Blier P, Chaput Y and De Montigny C (1988) Long-term 5-HT reuptake blockade but not monoamine oxidase inhibition decreases the function of terminal 5-HT autoreceptors: an electrophysiological study in the rat brain. Naunyn–Schmiedeberg *Arch Pharmacol* **337**, 246–254.

Blier P, De Montigny C and Chaput Y (1990) A role for the serotonin systems in the mechanism of action of antidepressants. *J Clin Psychiatry* **51 (Suppl. 4)**, 14–20.

Blier P, Mongeau R, Weiss M and de Montigny C (1993) Modulation of serotonin neurotransmission by presynaptic alpha2 adrenergic receptors: a target for antidepressant pharmacotherapy? In: Mendlewicz J, Brunello N, Langer SZ and Racagni G (eds) *New Pharmacological Approaches to the Therapy of Depressive Disorders*, pp 74–82. Karger, Basel.

Bouchard RH, Pourcher E and Vincent P (1989) Fluoxetine and extrapyramidal side effects. *Am J Psychiatry* **146**, 1352–1353.

Brosen K (1990) Recent developments in hepatic drug oxidation: implications for clinical pharmacokinetics. *Clin Pharmacokinet* **18**, 220–239.

Burnstein KL and Cidalowski JA (1989) Regulation of gene expression by glucocorticoids. *Annu Rev Physiol* **51**, 683–699.

Brunello N, Riva M, Voltera A, *et al.* (1986) Biochemical changes in rat brain after acute and chronic administration of fluvoxamine, a selective 5HT uptake blocker: comparison with desmethyl imipramine. *Adv Pharmacother* **2**, 186–196.

Brunello N, Voltera A, Cagiano R, *et al.* (1985) Biochemical and behavioral changes in rats after prolonged treatment with desipramine: interaction with p-chlorophenylalanine. *Naunyn Schmiedebergs Arch Pharmacol* **331**, 20–22.

Butler J and Leonard BE (1988) The platelet serotonergic system in depression and following sertraline treatment. *Int Clin Psychopharmacol* **3**, 343–347.

Butler J, Tannian M and Leonard BE (1988) The chronic effects of desipramine and sertraline on platelet and synaptosomal 5HT uptake in olfactory bulbectomized rats. *Prog Neuropsychopharmacol Biol Psychiatry* **12**, 585–594.

Caccia S, Bizzi A, Coltro G, *et al.* (1992) Anorectic activity of fluoxetine and norfluoxetine in rats—relationship between brain concentrations and *in vitro* potencies on monoaminergic mechanisms. *J Pharm Pharmacol* **44**, 250–254.

Chaput Y, de Montigny C and Blier P (1986) Effects of a selective 5-HT reuptake blocker, citalopram, on the sensitivity of 5HT autoreceptors: electrophysiological studies in the rat. Naunyn–Schmiedebergs *Arch Pharmacol* **330**, 342–349.

Charney DS, Southwick SM, Delgado PL, *et al.* (1990) Current status of the receptor sensitivity hypothesis of antidepressant action. In: Amsterdam JD (ed) *Pharmacotherapy of Depression*, pp 13–17. Marcel Dekker, New York.

Coppen A (1967) The biochemistry of affective disorders. *Br J Psychiatry* **133**, 1237–1264.

Davidson C and Stamford JA (1995) Pindolol potentiates the effect of paroxetine on 5-HT efflux in the rat dorsal raphe nucleus. *Eur Neuropsychopharmacology* **5(3)**, P278.

Deakin JFW, Guimaraes FS, Wang M and Hensman R (1991) Experimental tests of the 5HT receptor imbalance theory of affective disorders. In: Sandler M, Coppen A and Harnetts S (eds) *5-Hydroxytryptamine in Psychiatry*, pp. 143–154. Oxford Medical Publications, Oxford.

Deakin JFW and Graeff FG (1991) 5-HT and mechanims of defence, *J Psychopharmacol* **5**, 305–315.

de Montigny C, Chaput Y and Blier P (1989) Long term tricyclic and electroconvulsive treatment increases responsiveness of dorsal hippocampus $5HT_{1A}$ receptors: an electrophysiological study. *Soc Neuroscience Abstracts* **15**, 854.

de Montigny C, Chaput Y and Blier P (1990) Modification of serotonergic neuron properties by long-term treatment with serotonin reuptake blockers. *J Clin Psychiatry* **51 (Suppl B)**, 4–8.

de Montigny C, Chaput Y and Blier P (1993) Classical and novel targets of antidepressant drugs. In: Mendlewicz J, Brunello N, Langer SZ and Racagni G (eds) *New Pharmacological Approaches to the Therapy of Depressive Disorders*, pp. 8–17. Karger, Basel.

De Vane CL (1994) Pharmacokinetics of the newer antidepressants: clinical relevance, *Am J Med* **97** (Suppl. 6A), 13S–23S.

Dinan TG (1994) Glucocorticoids and the genesis of depressive illness: a psychobiological model. *Br J Psychiat* **164**, 365–371

Dourish CT (1987) Brain 5HT$_{1A}$ receptors and anxiety. In: Dourish CT, Ahlenius S and Hutson PH (eds) *Brain 5HT$_{1A}$ receptors*, pp 261–277. Ellis Horwood, Chichester.

Dourish CT (1992) 5HT receptor sub-types and feeding behaviour. In: Bradley PB, Handley SL, Cooper SJ, Key BJ, Barnes NM and Coote JH (eds) *Serotonin, CNS Receptors and Brain Function*, pp 179–202. Pergamon Press, Oxford.

Dray A, Gonge TJ and Oakley NR (1976) Evidence for the existence of a raphe projection to the substantia nigra in rat. *Brain Res* **113**, 45–57.

Earley B, Glennon M, Lally M, *et al.* (1990) Autoradiographic distribution of cholinergic muscarinic receptors in olfactory bulbectomized rat after chronic treatment with mianserin and desipramine. *Proceedings of the Society for Neuroscience Abstracts* No. 1.

Emrich HM, Hollt V, Kissling W, *et al.* (1979) Beta endorphin-like immunoreactivity in cerebrospinal fluid and plasma of patients with schizophrenia and other neuropsychiatric disorders. *Pharmacopsychiatry* **2**, 269–276.

Eriksson E *et al.* (1995) The serotonin reuptake inhibitor paroxetine is superior to the noradrenaline reuptake inhibitor maprotiline in the treatment of premenstrual syndrome. *Neuropsychopharmacology* **12**, 167–176.

Everett GM and Toman TEO (1959) Mode of action of *Rauwolfia serpentina* alkaloids and motor activity. In: Masseiman J (ed) *Biological Psychiatry*, pp 75–87. Grune and Stratton, New York.

Fasmer OB, Hunskaar S and Hole K (1989) Antinociceptive effect of serotonergic reuptake inhibitors in mice. *Neuropharmacology* **28**, 1363–1366.

Giller GL, Yehuda R and O'Loughlin M (1988) Lymphocyte glucocorticoid receptors in PTSD, major depression, panic and schizophrenia. *Proceedings of the American College of Neuropsychopharmacology*, San Juan, p. 179.

Goodwin GM, De Sousa RJ and Green AR (1985) Presynaptic serotonin receptor mediated response in mice attenuated by antidepressant drugs and electroconvulsive shock. *Nature* **317**, 531–533.

Goudie AJ, Thornton EW and Wheeler TJ (1976) Effects of Lilly 110140, a selective inhibitor of 5-hydroxytryptamine uptake on food intake and on 5-hydroxytryptamine induced anorexia: Evidence for serotonergic inhibition of feeding. *J Pharm Pharmacol* **28**, 318–320.

Gravel P and de Montigny C (1987) Noradrenergic denervation prevents sensitization of rats forebrain neurons to serotonin by tricyclic antidepressant treatment. *Synapse* **1**, 237–239.

Hamon M, Emerit MB, Mestikaws S, *et al.* (1987) Pharmacological, biochemical and functional properties of 5HT$_{1A}$ binding sites labelled by 8-OH-DPAT in the rat brain. In: Dourish CT, Ahlenius S and Hudson PH (eds) *Brain 5HT1A Receptors*, pp 34–51. Ellis Horwood, Chichester.

Handley SL and Singh L (1986) Involvement of the locus coeruleus in the potentiation of the quipazine induced head-twitch response by diazepam and beta adrenoceptor agonists. *Neuropharmacology* **27**, 1315–1321.

Handley SL and Dursum SM (1992) Serotonin and Tourette's syndrome: movements such as head-shakes and wet-dog shakes may model human ticks. In: Bradley PB, Handley SL,

Cooper SJ, Key BT, Barney NM and Coote JH (eds) *Serotonin, CNS Receptors and Brain Function*, pp 235–254. Pergamon Press, Oxford.

Harfstrand A, Fuxe K and Cintra A (1986) Glucocorticoid receptor immunoreactivity in monoamine neurons of rat brain. *Proc Natl Acad Sci USA* **83**, 9779–9783.

Healy D, Carney PA and Leonard BE (1983) Monoamine related markers of depression. *J Psychiatr Res* **17**, 251–258.

Healy D, Carney PA, O'Halloran A and Leonard BE (1985) Peripheral adrenoceptors and serotonin receptors in depression. *J Affective Disord* **17**, 285–292.

Hoffman BJ, Mezey E and Brownstein MJ (1991) Cloning of a serotonin transporter affected by antidepressants. *Science* **254**, 579–580.

Hyttel J (1982) Citalopram—pharmacological profile of a specific serotonin uptake inhibitor with antidepressant activity. *Prog Neuropsychopharmac Biol Psychiatry* **6**, 277–295.

Hyttel J (1994) Pharmacological characterization of selective serotonin reuptake inhibitors. *Int Clin Psychopharmacol* **9 (Suppl 1)**, 19–26.

Johnson AM (1991) The comparative pharmacological properties of selective serotonin re-uptake inhibitors in animals. In: Feighner JP and Boyer WF (eds) *Selective Serotonin Re-uptake Inhibitors*, pp 37–70. John Wiley & Sons, Chichester.

Kendall DA and Nahorski SR (1985) 5-Hydroxytryptamine stimulates inositol phospholipid hydrolysis in rat cerebral cortex slices: Pharmacological characterization and effects of antidepressants. *J Pharmacol Exp Ther* **23**, 473–484.

Kennett GA (1993) 5HTIC receptors and their therapeutic relevance. *Curr Opin Invest Drugs* **2**, 313–326.

Kennett GA, Bailey F, Piper DC, *et al.* (1994) Effect of SB 200646A, a $5HT_{2C}$ receptor antagonist, on two conflict models of anxiety. *Br J Pharmac* **112**, 303P.

Kennett GA, Lightowler S, De Biasi V *et al.* (1994) Effect of chronic administration of selective 5-hydroxytryptamine and noradrenaline uptake inhibitors on a putative index of $5HT_{2C/2B}$ receptor function. *Neuropharmac* **33**, 1581–1588.

Kitayami I, Cintra AM, Fuxe K, *et al.* (1988) Effects of chronic imipramine treatment on glucocorticoid receptor immunoreactivity in various regions of the rat brain. *J Neural Transm*, **73**, 191–203.

Koe BK, Weissman A, Welch WM, *et al.* (1983) Sertraline, a new uptake inhibitor with selectivity for serotonin. *J Pharmacol Exp Ther* **226**, 686–700.

Korsgaard S, Gerlach J and Christensson E (1985) Behavioural aspects of serotonin-dopamine interaction in the monkey. *Eur J Pharmacol* **118**, 245–252.

Lapin IP and Oxenkrug GF (1969) Intensification of central serotonergic processes as a possible determinant of the thymoleptic effect. *Lancet* **I**, 132–136.

Lee MD and Clifton PG (1992) Partial reversal of fluoxetine anorexia by the 5HT antagonist metergoline. *Psychopharmacol* **107**, 359–364.

Lemberger L, Bergstrom RF, Walen RL, *et al.* (1985) Fluoxetine: clinical pharmacology and physiological disposition. *J Clin Psychiatry* **46**, 14–19.

Leonard BE (1993) Comparative pharmacology of new antidepressants. *J Clin Psychiatry* **54 (Suppl)**, 6–15.

Leonard BE (1994a) Second generation antidepressants: chemical diversity but unity of action? In: Montgomery SA and Corn TH (eds) *Psychopharmacology of Depression*, pp 19–31. Oxford University Press, Oxford.

Leonard BE (1994b) Serotonin receptors—where are they going? *Int Clin Psychopharmacol* **9 (Suppl 1)**, 7–18.

Leonard BE and Tuite M (1981) Anatomical, physiological and behavioural aspects of olfactory bulbectomy in the rat. *Int Rev Neurobiol* **22**, 251–286.

Leonard *et al.* (1995) *Motor Effects of some Selective Serotonin Reuptake Inhibitors Following Direct Injection into the Red Nucleus of the Rat: Evidence for Involvement of Sigma*

Receptors. Presented at the ECNP Congress, 1–4 October, Venice.

Leysen JE, Awontere F, Kennis L, *et al.* (1981) Receptor binding profile of R 414681, a novel antagonist at 5HT$_2$ receptors. *Life Sci* **20**, 1015–1018.

Lightowler S, Kennett GA, Williamson JR, *et al.* (1994) Anxiolytic-like effects of paroxetine in the rat social interaction test. *Pharmac Biochem Behav* **49**, 281–285.

Nelson DR, Palmer KJ and Johnson AM (1989) Pharmacological effects of paroxetine after repeated administration to animals. *Acta Psychiatr Scand* **80 (Suppl 350)**, 21–23.

Nelson JC, Mazura CM, Bowen MB and Jatlow PI (1991) A preliminary open study of the combination of fluoxetine and desipramine for rapid treatment of major depression. *Arch Gen Psychiatry* **48**, 303–307.

Nestler EJ, Walaas ST and Greengard P (1984) Neuronal phosphoproteins: physiological and clinical implications. *Science* **225**, 1357–1364.

Norman TR and Leonard BE (1994) Fast acting antidepressants—can the need be met? *CNS Drugs* **2**, 120–131.

Ogren SO and Fuxe K (1985) Effects of antidepressant drugs on cerebral serotonin receptors. In: Green AR (ed) *Neuropharmacology of Serotonin*, pp 131–180. Oxford University Press, Oxford.

Oswald I, Brezinova V and Funleavy DL (1972) On the slowness of action of tricyclic antidepressants. *Br J Psychiatry* **120**, 673–677.

Paul IA, Duncan GE, Powell KR, *et al.* (1988) Regionally specific neuronal adaptation of beta adrenoceptors and 5HT$_2$ receptors after antidepressant administration in the forced swim test and after chronic antidepressant treatment. *J Pharmacol Exp Ther* **246**, 956–1001.

Pepin MC, Beaulieu S and Barden N (1989) Antidepressants regulate glucocorticoid receptor messenger RNA concentrations in primary neuronal cultures. *Mol Brain Res* **6**, 77–83.

Perez J, Tinelli D, Brunello N and Racagi G (1989) cAMP-dependent phosphorylation of soluble and crude microtubule fractions of rat cerebral cortex after prolonged desmethylimipramine treatment. *Eur J Pharmacol* **172**, 305–316.

Peroutka SJ and Snyder SH (1980) Long-term antidepressant treatment decreases spiroperidol-labelled serotonin receptor binding. *Science* **210**, 88–90.

Pinder RM and Wieringa JH (1993) Third-generation antidepressants. *Med Res Rev* **13**, 259–325.

Porsolt RD (1981) Behavioral despair. In: Enna SJ, Malick JB and Richardson E (eds) *Antidepressants, Neurochemical, Behavioural and Clinical Perspective*, pp 121–139. Raven Press, New York.

Porsolt RD, Berlin A, Blavet N, Deniel M and Jalfre M (1979) Immobility induced by forced swimming in rats: effects of agents which modify central catecholamine and serotonin activity. *Eur J Pharmacol* **57**, 201–210.

Racagni G, Tinelli D, Bianchi E, Brunello N and Percy J (1991) cAMP-dependent binding proteins and endogenous phosphorylation after antidepressant treatment. In: Sandler M, Copper, A and Harnet S (eds) *5-Hydroxytryptamine in Psychiatry*, pp 116–123. Oxford Medical Publications, Oxford.

Raiteri M, Maura G, Folghera S, *et al.* (1990) Modulation of 5HT release by presynaptic inhibitory alpha2-adrenoceptors in the human cerebral cortex. *Naunyn Schmiedebergs Arch Pharmacol* **342**, 508–512.

Ramamoorthy S, Bauman AL, Moore KR, *et al.* (1993) Antidepressant and cocaine sensitive human serotonin transporter: molecular cloning, expression and chromosomal localization. *Proc Natl Acad Sci USA* **90**, 2542–2546.

Richelson E (1990) Antidepressants and brain neurochemistry. *Mayo Clin Proc* **65**, 1227–1236.

Ross SB and Renyi AL (1969) Inhibition of the uptake of tritiated 5-hydroxytryptamine in brain tissue. *Eur J Pharmacol* **7**, 270–277.

Sanders-Bush E, Breeding M, Knoth K, *et al.* (1989) Sertraline-induced desensitization of the serotonin 5-HT$_2$ receptors transmembrane signalling system. *Psychopharmacology* **99**, 64–69.

Schildkraut JJ (1965) The catecholamine hypothesis of affective disorders, a review of supporting evidence. *Am J Psychiatry* **122**, 413–418.

Stanley M and Mann JJ (1983) Increased serotonin 2 binding sites in frontal cortex of suicide victims. *Lancet* **i**, 214–216.

Stark P, Fuller RW and Wong DT (1985) The pharmacological profile of fluoxetine. *J Clin Psychiatry* **46**, 7–13.

Stockmeier CA and Keller KJ (1986) *In vivo* regulation of the serotonin 2 receptor in rat brain. *Life Sci* **38**, 117–127.

Stolz JF, Marsden CA and Middlemiss DM (1983) Effect of chronic antidepressant treatment and subsequent withdrawal on 3H-5HT and 3H-spiperone binding in rat frontal cortex and serotonin mediated behaviour. *Psychopharmacology* **80**, 150–155.

Sugrue MF (1979) On the role of 5-hydroxytryptamine in drug induced antinociception. *Br J Pharmacol* **65**, 677–681.

Sulser F and Sanders-Bush E (1976) The serotonin norepinephrine link hypothesis of affective disorders: receptor interactions in the brain. In: Erlich RH, Lennox E, Kornecki E, *et al.* (eds) *Molecular Basis of Neuronal Responsiveness*, pp 489–502. Plenum, New York, NY.

Tulloch IF, (1993) The pharmacological selectivity of serotonin reuptake inhibitors. *Eur Psychiatry* **8 (Suppl 1)**, 55–85

Tulloch IF, *et al.* (1995) *Pharmacological Differences between Selective Serotonin Reuptake Inhibitors: Interaction with 5-HT$_2$ and Sigma Binding Sites in Human Brain in vitro.* Presented at the ECNP Congress, 1–4 October, Venice.

Van Riezen H and Leonard BE (1990) Effects of psychotropic drugs on the behaviour and neurochemistry of olfactory bulbectomized rats. *Pharmacol Ther* **47**, 21–34.

Vetulani J, Schwartz RJ, Dingell JV, *et al.* (1976) A possible common mechanism of action of antidepressant treatments: reduction in the sensitivity of the noradrenergic-cyclic AMP generating system in rat limbic forebrain. *Naunyn Schmiedebergs Arch Pharmacol* **293**, 109–114.

Wong DT, Reid LR and Threlkeld PG (1988) Suppression of food intake in rats by fluoxetine: comparison with enantiomers and effects of serotonin antagonists. *Pharmacol Biochem Behav* **31**, 475–479.

Wong KL, Bruck RC and Farabman IA (1991) Amitriptyline mediated inhibition of neurite outgrowth from chick embryonic cerebral explants involves a reduction in adenylate cyclase activity. *J Neurochem* **57**, 1223–1330.

Zussman BD, Davie CC, Fowles SE, Kumar R, Long U, Wargenau M and Sourgens H (1995) Sertraline, like other SSRIs is a significant inhibitor of desipramine metabolism in vivo. *British Journal of Clinical Pharmacology* **39**, 550–551 (P).

3

The serotonin hypothesis: Necessary but not sufficient

Philip J. Cowen

INTRODUCTION

Almost 30 years ago, Coppen (1967) proposed that depressive illness is caused by decreased brain serotonin (5-HT) function. It is now widely accepted that brain 5-HT function is diminished in depressed patients and that this abnormality is somehow causally associated with the depressed state. The fact that selective serotonin re-uptake inhibitors (SSRIs) are effective antidepressants has added further support to the 5-HT hypothesis, because it suggests that pharmacological reversal of impaired brain 5-HT function in depressed patients is sufficient to ameliorate the depressed state (Cowen, 1990).

Despite the attractions of the 5-HT hypothesis, closer inspection of the evidence reveals a number of problems which were summarized by Boyer and Feighner (1991) in the previous edition of this volume:

1. Biochemical evidence of altered 5-HT function in depression is often indirect and the data are inconsistent.
2. Decreased brain 5-HT function has been proposed to underlie a wide range of disorders, including obsessive–compulsive disorder, eating disorders, alcoholism, premenstrual syndrome, and impulse control disorders. How can the same biochemical abnormality plausibly cause all these conditions?

Selective Serotonin Re-uptake Inhibitors: Advances in Basic Research and Clinical Practice, Second Edition, Edited by J.P. Feighner and W.F. Boyer
© 1996 John Wiley & Sons Ltd

3. 5-HT neurones in the brain cannot be considered in isolation because they have important interconnections with other neurotransmitter pathways (for example, the catecholamines), whose function may also be abnormal in depression.
4. The fact that a disorder can be treated with a drug that increases brain 5-HT function, does not mean that the disorder is caused by 5-HT deficiency. The utility of anticholinergic drugs in Parkinson's disease provides a simple example of this phenomenon.

These cogent objections still remain. A major problem for research in this area is that while we know much about the clinical phenomenology of depression, and the neuropharmacology of SSRIs, at present we have little idea of how decreases in brain 5-HT function could result in the clinical depressive syndrome or by what neuropsychological mechanism an increase in brain 5-HT function might attenuate it. Much of this uncertainty comes about through our lack of knowledge of the role of brain 5-HT pathways in normal behaviour.

This chapter begins with a brief account of what is known about 5-HT and behaviour, particularly in humans. Following this, it considers the evidence that brain 5-HT function is decreased in depression, focusing on findings where there have been a reasonable number of attempts at replication. Finally, it reviews the effect of antidepressant drugs on aspects of brain 5-HT in humans and concludes by discussing how far changes in brain 5-HT function may contribute to the therapeutic effects of antidepressant drugs.

5-HT AND BEHAVIOUR

Studies in animals

5-HT fibres have an extremely widespread distribution, innervating virtually all regions of the central nervous system, but particularly cortex, limbic regions, basal ganglia and hypothalamus (Tork, 1990). This widespread distribution probably explains why alterations in 5-HT function in animals can modify so many behaviours, including motor output, learning, sleep, circadian pattern, food intake and sexual activity. In common with other monoamines it appears that the role of 5-HT is to modify on-going activity in widely distributed neuronal circuits. Some have proposed that 5-HT pathways have a general neuromodulatory role across diverse brain regions, for example, to constrain the flow of information through neural systems (Spoont, 1992) or to facilitate disengagement of non-rewarding behavioural responses (Handley and McBlane, 1991).

With regard to depression, Deakin and Graeff (1991) have suggested that a particular subset of 5-HT neurones that link the 5-HT cell bodies in the median raphe nuclei with postsynaptic 5-HT$_{1A}$ receptors in the hippocampus have the function of maintaining adaptive behaviours in the face of aversive stimuli. Failure of this neuronal response leads to helplessness in animals and depression in humans. The same authors have proposed that effective antidepressant treatments have in common the ability to enhance postsynaptic 5-HT$_{1A}$ receptor function. This has the effect of increasing resilience and coping behaviour.

Studies in humans

5-HT and mood

There is little direct evidence that acute alterations in brain 5-HT function alter mood in healthy humans. Some mood lowering effects, however, have been noted following acute reduction of brain 5-HT function by dietary manipulation. The latter has been accomplished by administering a drink of amino acids which lack the 5-HT precursor, tryptophan (TRP).

The TRP-free amino acid drink is believed to decrease brain 5-HT neurotransmission by lowering the amount of TRP available for brain 5-HT synthesis. Two mechanisms might account for this reduction in TRP availability. First, a TRP-free amino acid drink decreases plasma TRP via stimulation of protein synthesis in the liver. Because TRP is an essential amino acid, this process of protein synthesis must utilize endogenous TRP which results in a lowering of plasma TRP levels. A second mechanism by which a TRP-free amino acid drink might lower brain TRP is that the neutral amino acids present in the drink could compete with endogenous plasma TRP for transport across the blood–brain barrier (see Young *et al.*, 1985).

Using a 100 g TRP-free amino acid drink, Young *et al.* (1985) reported a small but significant lowering of mood in healthy male subjects, which was detectable on adjective check-lists. Subsequent studies have not always found this effect (Abbott *et al.*, 1992; Oldman *et al.*, 1994) and more recently it has been proposed that the effect of TRP depletion to lower mood might be apparent only in those who have a vulnerability to depression or who have some depressive symptoms prior to the procedure. Confirmation for the former proposal has come from a study of Benkelfat *et al.* (1994) where TRP depletion significantly lowered mood in healthy male subjects with a strong family history of depression, but not in those who lacked this vulnerability factor. This suggests that the effect of decreased brain 5-HT function to lower mood might be manifest only in those with a predisposition to develop depression. At what level this predisposition interacts with the procedure of TRP depletion is unclear.

5-HT and cognition

It is possible, of course, that the effect of 5-HT on mood is mediated indirectly, through other neuropsychological processes. Psychological formulations of depression have focused on the importance of learning and memory, particularly for affect-laden material. Recent studies in our laboratory have shown that TRP depletion produces impairments in learning and retrieval (Park *et al.*, 1994). It is possible, therefore, that decreased brain 5-HT function may play a part in the cognitive impairments seen in depression, although it is not clear how the latter phenomena could be related to typical depressive symptomatology, such as low self-esteem and anhedonia. Presumably, cognitive impairment might result in poor problem-solving skills which could be a maintaining factor in the depressive disorder.

5-HT and impulse control

Although there is little evidence from investigations in healthy humans, data from both patient studies and animal experimental work suggest that low brain 5-HT function is linked with impulsivity and irritable aggressive behaviour (Coccaro *et al.*, 1989; Linnoila and Virkkunen, 1992; Higley *et al.*, 1992). In depressed patients, such behaviours are often associated with attempted or completed suicide. The proposed behavioural association between impaired brain 5-HT function and suicidal behaviour (Mann *et al.*, 1990) is mentioned here because studies of depressed patients often include subjects who have exhibited suicidal thinking and behaviour and, conversely, studies of suicide and attempted suicide will usually include patients suffering from major depression.

5-HT FUNCTION IN DEPRESSION

One of the major problems in assessing brain 5-HT function in depressed patients is the technical difficulty of measuring 5-HT metabolism and function in the living human brain. For this reason many of the methods employed have been indirect, for example measurement of 5-HT and its metabolites in peripheral fluids, and 5-HT receptors on blood platelets. How far such measures reflect brain 5-HT function is unclear.

An important confounding factor in studies of depressed patients is the use of previous psychotropic drug treatment, which can have effects on measures of 5-HT function that outlast standard wash-out periods. For example, treatment of healthy subjects with clomipramine can produce a rapid decrease in platelet imipramine binding which may persist for several weeks following treatment (Poirier *et al.*, 1985). While it is possible to study untreated depressed patients from primary care sources, the severity of illness of such subjects is often less than populations of psychiatric patients. This can lead to another important confounding factor between studies, namely differing composition of patient groups, a problem not always overcome by the use of standardized diagnostic criteria.

Plasma tryptophan (TRP)

As mentioned above, the synthesis of 5-HT in the brain is dependent on the availability of TRP from plasma. Several recent studies have found that plasma TRP concentration is decreased in drug-free depressed patients (see Anderson *et al.*, 1990a). However, the decrease is small and would be unlikely by itself to have much consequence for brain 5-HT neurotransmission. Diminished plasma TRP levels are more likely to be found in depressed patients with melancholic features (Maes *et al.*, 1987; Anderson *et al.*, 1990a). A possible explanation for this is that lowered plasma TRP levels are found in healthy volunteers who lose weight by dieting (Anderson *et al.*, 1990b), and weight loss is a diagnostic feature of melancholic depression. Concomitant weight loss, therefore, may contribute to the decline in plasma TRP in depressed patients.

Platelet 5-HT measures

Platelet 5-HT uptake
Numerous studies have investigated the uptake of 5-HT into blood platelets in depression, with the majority showing a decrease in uptake compared to controls (see Meltzer and Arora, 1991). The decrease in 5-HT uptake appears to be attributable to a reduction in the maximum rate of 5-HT uptake (V_{max}) rather than in a change in the affinity of the uptake sites for 5-HT (Km). This suggests that the reduction in platelet 5-HT uptake in depression is caused by non-competitive inhibition. The decrease in 5-HT uptake in the platelet does not seem to be caused by a reduction in the number of 5-HT uptake sites (see below).

Platelet imipramine binding
Tritiated imipramine binds to a specific site on the platelet which is thought to be part of the 5-HT uptake site. Early studies suggested that large reductions in the binding of tritiated imipramine to platelets existed in drug-free depressed patients (Briley *et al.*, 1980), but several more recent investigations have failed to confirm this effect (see Mellerup and Langer, 1990). A recent meta-analysis of the published investigations suggested that platelet imipramine binding probably is decreased to some extent in depressed patients compared to healthy controls (Ellis and Salmond, 1994). However, in any meta-analysis, it is difficult to discount the effect of publication bias, and the results are not weighted according to the methodological quality of the studies analysed.

More recent investigations that have measured the binding of tritiated paroxetine to platelets have found no consistent differences between depressed patients and controls (see D'Hondt *et al.*, 1994). Paroxetine is a more selective ligand for the 5-HT uptake site than imipramine. This suggests that if platelet imipramine binding is indeed lower in depressed patients, it is probably not due to alterations in the number of 5-HT uptake sites.

Platelet 5-HT$_2$ receptors
Human platelets possess receptors of the 5-HT$_2$ subtype, whose function is to promote aggregation. There has been much interest in platelet 5-HT$_2$ receptors

because of the findings from some post-mortem studies that suggest an increase in number of 5-HT_2 receptors in the frontal cortex of depressed patients, particularly suicide victims (see below). The platelet studies have been contradictory (Table 1). An important confounding factor is that tricyclic antidepressant treatment increases the number (B_{max}) of platelet 5-HT_2 receptors, as detected by tritiated or iodinated lysergic acid diethylamide (LSD), and it is not known for how long this effect may persist (Cowen *et al.*, 1987; McBride *et al.*, 1994). Previous antidepressant treatment, therefore, may contribute to the increase of 5-HT_2 receptors seen in some studies of depressed patients.

Table 1. Platelet 5-HT_2 receptor binding in depression.

Study	Ligand	Depression vs Controls (B_{max})
Cowen *et al.* (1987)	^{125}I-LSD	No change
Arora and Meltzer (1989a)	^{3}H-LSD	Increase*
Biegon *et al.* (1990)	^{3}H-Ketanserin	Increase
Pandey *et al.* (1990)	^{125}I-LSD	Increase
McBride *et al.* (1994)	^{125}I-LSD	No change

*Increases in females only.

Cerebrospinal fluid 5-HIAA

Cerebrospinal fluid (CSF) levels of the 5-HT metabolite, 5-hydroxyindoleacetic acid (5-HIAA), have been used to provide an index of brain 5-HT turnover but there is disagreement about how far lumbar CSF 5-HIAA levels correlated with 5-HIAA concentrations in the brain (Stanley *et al.*, 1985; Gjerris, 1988). Studies in depressed patients have given rather inconsistent findings, but overall it can be concluded that depressed patients as a group do not have reliably lowered levels of CSF 5-HIAA (see for example, Koslow *et al.*, 1983).

There is more consistent evidence that CSF 5-HIAA levels are lower in depressed patients who have made suicide attempts (see Brown *et al.*, 1992) and follow-up studies have shown that depressed patients with low CSF 5-HIAA levels may be at greater risk of suicidal behaviour in the future (Asberg *et al.*, 1976; Roy *et al.*, 1989; Brown and Linnoila, 1990). Generally, the abnormalities in 5-HIAA are more apparent in those who have made violent suicide attempts (Traskman *et al.*, 1981). Other studies of the association between low CSF 5-HIAA and suicidal behaviour have suggested that this relationship is not confined to depressed patients but is seen in other conditions such as personality disorders and schizophrenia (see Roy *et al.*, 1990). Furthermore, low CSF 5-HIAA levels are also found in subjects with personality disorder who exhibit impulsive aggressive behaviour towards others (see Linnoila and Virkkunen, 1992).

Recent formulations of the relationship between low CSF 5-HIAA, suicide and aggression have suggested that low CSF 5-HIAA (and presumptively low brain 5-HT function) may correlate with a cluster of personality traits such as irritability, aggression and impulsivity (Coccaro *et al.*, 1989; Roy *et al.*, 1990). Thus in subjects with long-standing difficulties in impulse control, low CSF 5-HIAA may be a trait marker which correlates with the presence of these personality characteristics. It seems plausible that when individuals with such characterological traits become depressed they may be more likely to engage in impulsive acts of self-harm.

Brain neurochemistry

Most post-mortem studies of brain 5-HT neurochemistry use material collected from suicide victims. While a considerable proportion of these subjects will have been depressed, suicide victims have often suffered from considerable psychiatric comorbidity, particularly substance abuse. In addition, post-mortem studies face formidable methodological problems in terms of appropriate matching with control samples. Important issues include the delay before post-mortem examination, consequences of tissue storage, effects of previous drug treatment, and mode of death (see Horton, 1992).

Brain 5-HIAA
Early studies suggested that levels of CSF 5-HIAA in hind brain were decreased in suicide victims. However, in more recent investigations the results have been contradictory and the issue remains undecided. There is no consistent evidence that brain 5-HIAA levels are altered in cortical areas in suicide (see Horton, 1992).

Imipramine binding sites
Two early studies suggested that imipramine binding in cortex was lowered in suicide victims (Stanley *et al.*, 1982; Perry *et al.*, 1983), but subsequent investigations have not confirmed this (see Horton, 1992). Similarly, use of the more selective tritiated paroxetine to identify 5-HT uptake sites has not revealed any differences between suicide victims and controls (Lawrence *et al.*, 1990; Andersson *et al.*, 1992). It therefore seems unlikely that suicide is associated with a decrease in 5-HT uptake sites in cortex.

Brain 5-HT$_2$ receptors
The initial description of increased numbers (B_{max}) of brain 5-HT$_2$ receptors in suicide victims aroused much interest (Mann *et al.*, 1986). However, the subsequent findings have been contradictory (Table 2). In general, studies that have found increased 5-HT$_2$ receptor binding have used rather less selective ligands for the 5-HT$_2$ receptor (such as spiperone or LSD), but there are exceptions to this (see Hrdina *et al.*, 1993). It is possible that the increase in receptor numbers is more apparent in those who have used violent means of suicide (Arora and Meltzer, 1989b). However, in the large and carefully controlled study of Lowther *et al.* (1994),

Table 2. 5-HT$_2$ receptors in frontal cortex in suicide victims.

Study	Ligand	Suicide vs Controls (B$_{max}$)
Owen *et al.* (1986)	^{3}H-Ketanserin	No change
Mann *et al.* (1986)	^{3}H-Spiperone	Increase
Cheetham *et al.* (1988)	^{3}H-Ketanserin	No change
Arora and Meltzer (1989b)	^{3}H-Spiperone	Increase
Arango *et al.* (1990)	^{125}I-LSD	Increase
Hrdina *et al.* (1993)	^{3}H-Ketanserin	Increase
Arranz *et al.* (1994)	^{3}H-Ketanserin	No change
Lowther *et al.* (1994)	^{3}H-Ketanserin	No change

violent suicide was not associated with an increase in 5-HT$_2$ receptor numbers. In this connection, it is worth noting that an autoradiographic investigation of patients with major depression who died of natural causes also reported an increase in ^{3}H-ketanserin binding in frontal cortex (Yates *et al.*, 1990).

Where workers have found increases in brain 5-HT$_2$ receptors in post-mortem studies of suicide victims, they have usually concluded that this change represents an adaptive up-regulation of 5-HT$_2$ receptors due to decreased presynaptic release of 5-HT. It is possible that this kind of adaptive change might become apparent only when 5-HT output from nerve terminals is very substantially reduced. It is conceivable that reductions of this magnitude might be seen only in certain subgroups of suicide victims, perhaps where additional factors, such as substance abuse or malnutrition, contribute to the decline in brain 5-HT activity.

Other 5-HT receptors
Other 5-HT receptor subtypes have been less studied in suicide victims. There is interest in the role of 5-HT$_{1A}$ receptors in the aetiology of depression (see below), but post-mortem studies do not suggest consistent changes in postsynaptic 5-HT$_{1A}$ receptor binding in suicide (Horton, 1992; Arranz *et al.*, 1994).

5-HT neuroendocrine tests

5-HT neuroendocrine challenge tests have an advantage over the methods described above in that they provide a functional assessment of brain 5-HT neurotransmission. The hypothalamus receives a dense innervation from the raphe nuclei and activation of brain 5-HT pathways produces reliable increases in plasma concentrations of various anterior pituitary hormone, notably prolactin (PRL), growth hormone (GH), and corticotrophin (ACTH). The increase in ACTH leads to elevated plasma levels of cortisol which can also be used as a marker of 5-HT neuroendocrine response. The increase in plasma level of a particular hormone that follows a selective 5-HT challenge provides a measure of the functional activity of brain 5-HT pathways (see Power and Cowen, 1992a).

5-HT neuroendocrine tests presumably measure the functional activity of 5-HT pathways in the hypothalamus. This may not be the equivalent of determining brain 5-HT function in cortical or limbic regions. However, both the clinical symptomatology and neuroendocrine abnormalities seen in depressed patients suggest that changes in hypothalamic function are present in depressive disorders. This means, however, that where there is evidence in depressed patients that a particular 5-HT-mediated endocrine response is abnormal, it is important to exclude a primary abnormality in the hypothalamic–pituitary regulation of the hormone concerned.

5-HT neuroendocrine probes
The choice of drug challenge is a critical factor in the design of neuroendocrine challenge tests. Clearly specificity of action and good tolerance are vital aspects. Available 5-HT probes are usually classified into those that increase brain 5-HT function by facilitating presynaptic 5-HT function and those that act directly on 5-HT receptors (Table 3). Direct receptor agonists of increasing specificity are now becoming available. This should enable the sensitivity of specific 5-HT receptor subtypes to be assessed.

Table 3. 5-HT neuroendocrine challenges in depression.

Presynaptic	L-tryptophan (precursor)
	5-hydroxytryptophan (precursor)
	clomipramine (uptake inhibitor)
	fenfluramine (releaser)
Postsynaptic	buspirone ($5\text{-}HT_{1A}$ agonist)
	ipsapirone ($5\text{-}HT_{1A}$ agonist)
	mCPP ($5\text{-}HT_2$ agonist)
	MK-212 ($5\text{-}HT_2$ agonist)

In both animal and human studies, there is evidence that the release of certain anterior pituitary hormones is regulated by multiple postsynaptic 5-HT receptor subtypes. In the male rat, for example, ACTH release can be provoked by selective activation of $5\text{-}HT_{1A}$, $5\text{-}HT_{2A}$, and $5\text{-}HT_{2C}$ receptors (see van de Kar, 1991). From this it would be predicted that the effect of 5-HT precursors, such as 5-hydroxytryptophan (5-HTP), to increase ACTH levels would be mediated via indirect activation of several different subtypes of postsynaptic 5-HT receptors. This, however, does not seem to be the case. In the rat, studies with selective 5-HT receptor antagonists have shown that 5-HTP-induced ACTH release appears to be mediated solely via indirect activation of $5\text{-}HT_{2A}$ receptors, despite the undoubted ability of $5\text{-}HT_{1A}$ and $5\text{-}HT_{2C}$ receptors to stimulate ACTH release (Gartside and Cowen, 1990). The reason for this surprising selectivity in postsynaptic receptor responses to precursor loading is not known.

Endocrine responses to tryptophan (TRP)

Intravenous TRP, in doses of 5 g or greater, reliably increases plasma concentrations of PRL and GH in humans. It is presumed that the neuroendocrine responses to TRP result from increased 5-HT release as a consequence of enhanced brain 5-HT synthesis. Acute pretreatment of healthy subjects with the 5-HT re-uptake inhibitor, clomipramine, increases TRP-induced PRL and GH release, indicating that these endocrine responses are likely to be mediated by brain 5-HT pathways (Anderson and Cowen, 1986). Further studies with selective 5-HT receptor antagonists suggest that both the PRL and GH response to TRP are mediated via indirect activation of postsynaptic 5-HT$_{1A}$ receptors (Smith *et al.*, 1991).

Five studies of drug-free depressed patients have reported blunted PRL and GH responses to intravenous TRP compared to healthy controls (see Power and Cowen, 1992a). In one study, however, the difference in PRL response in depressives could be accounted for by decreased TRP levels following infusion (Koyama and Meltzer, 1986), while in two others, diminished PRL responses could only be demonstrated when patients with recent acute weight loss were excluded (Cowen and Charig, 1987; Deakin *et al.*, 1990). Such exclusions are reasonable because in healthy volunteers who lose weight by dieting, there is an increase in the PRL response to TRP (Anderson *et al.*, 1990b). Accordingly, concomitant weight loss in depressed patients may obscure blunted PRL responses to TRP.

Upadhyaya *et al.* (1991) studied a group of depressed patients with TRP before and following recovery from major depression. They found that following recovery and a drug-free period of at least 3 months, the PRL and GH responses of the patients had returned to normal. This suggests that the blunted endocrine responses to TRP in depressed patients are a state rather than a trait abnormality.

Endocrine responses to clomipramine

Given intravenously, clomipramine produces increases in plasma PRL but there is little difference in the dose that causes PRL release and that which induces nausea, making this test a difficult one to use. Clomipramine is a selective 5-HT re-uptake inhibitor but is metabolized *in vivo* to desmethylclomipramine, a noradrenaline re-uptake inhibitor. However, during the time period of an acute clomipramine neuroendocrine challenge, plasma levels of desmethylclomipramine are not detectable (Anderson *et al.*, 1992).

Three studies in depressed patients have found that the PRL responses to clomipramine are blunted compared to the responses of healthy controls (see Power and Cowen, 1992a). There is no information at present concerning the identity of the postsynaptic 5-HT receptor subtype(s) that may mediate the PRL response to clomipramine in humans.

Endocrine responses to fenfluramine

Fenfluramine is a 5-HT releasing and uptake inhibiting agent, which has been used both as the racemate, dl-fenfluramine and the d-isomer, d-fenfluramine. Of the two compounds, d-fenfluramine is the more selective probe of 5-HT pathways (see McTavish and Heel, 1992). In both animals and humans, the PRL response to d-fenfluramine is abolished by the 5-HT$_2$ receptor antagonist, ritanserin, indicating that this endocrine response is mediated by indirect activation of 5-HT$_{2A}$ or 5-HT$_{2C}$ receptors, or both subtypes acting together (Goodall *et al.*, 1993). Studies using pindolol, as a 5-HT$_{1A}$ receptor antagonist, suggest that 5-HT$_{1A}$ receptors do not play a significant role in d-fenfluramine-induced PRL release (Park and Cowen, 1995).

Blunted PRL responses to fenfluramine have been found in six of 10 studies of drug-free depressed patients (see Power and Cowen, 1992a; Maes *et al.*, 1991; Lichtenberg *et al.*, 1992), so this abnormality does not seem to be as consistent as the finding of impaired PRL response to TRP. Blunting of responses to fenfluramine appears to be associated with two major, but rather different, groups of features:

1. More severe depressive symptoms, particularly patients with melancholic (or endogenous) depression and cortisol hypersecretion (Mitchell *et al.*, 1990; Lichtenberg *et al.*, 1992).
2. Patients with aggressive and impulsive traits and a history of suicide attempts, who often have additional diagnoses of personality disorder (Coccaro *et al.*, 1989).

It is worth while noting that subjects in the latter group may manifest blunted PRL responses to fenfluramine in the absence of a current depressive disorder (Coccaro *et al.*, 1989). Presumably, here the blunted PRL responses may represent a trait marker of 5-HT dysfunction and could, perhaps, correspond with the abnormalities in CSF 5-HIAA that have been reported in subjects who tend to behave in an aggressive and impulsive way (see above). In the first group, however, where blunted PRL responses to fenfluramine are associated with severe depression and cortisol hypersecretion, the impaired endocrine response appears to be a state marker of depression which remits with clinical recovery (Shapira *et al.*, 1993).

Endocrine responses to 5-HTP
Administration of the 5-HT precursor, 5-HTP, increases plasma cortisol in humans, but the response to oral 5-HTP is somewhat modest. As noted above, the ACTH response to 5-HTP in animals is mediated by indirect activation of 5-HT$_{2A}$ receptors (Gartside and Cowen, 1990). In healthy volunteers, the cortisol response to 5-HTP is attenuated by ritanserin but not by pindolol, suggesting that 5-HTP-induced cortisol release is mediated via 5-HT$_2$ receptors (Lee *et al.*, 1991; Meltzer and Maes, 1994a).

Studies of 5-HTP in depressed patients have yielded rather inconsistent findings. Where abnormalities have been reported, they have indicated an enhanced cortisol reponse to 5-HTP, particularly in females (see Power and Cowen, 1992a). Why the endocrine responses to 5-HTP should be enhanced in depression, while those to TRP and other presynaptic 5-HT probes are blunted, is unclear. The enhanced responses to 5-HTP have been attributed to a supersensitivity of postsynaptic 5-HT$_2$ receptors secondary to decreased 5-HT release. It is possible that weight loss, with accompanying reductions in plasma TRP, may play a part in the production of the enhanced responses; a similar effect seems to occur in a subgroup of patients tested with TRP (see above).

Endocrine responses to 5-HT$_{1A}$ receptor agonists

A number of selective 5-HT$_{1A}$ receptor ligands are now becoming available for clinical study. The endocrine responses of depressed patients to these agents is of considerable interest in view of the blunted PRL and GH responses to TRP found in depression (see above). The diminished endocrine responses to TRP in depressed subjects implicate abnormalities in neurotransmission at postsynaptic 5-HT$_{1A}$ synapses. Accordingly, use of a directly acting, postsynaptic 5-HT$_{1A}$ receptor agonist should help localize this defect in 5-HT neurotransmission to the presynaptic neurone or the postsynaptic 5-HT$_{1A}$ receptor.

Administration of 5-HT$_{1A}$ receptor agonists to humans produces a characteristic profile of endocrine and thermic effects. The most reliable changes are an increase in plasma GH and a decrease in body temperature (see Cowen, 1993). Given in sufficient doses, most 5-HT$_{1A}$ receptor agonists also increase plasma ACTH and cortisol. Studies with pindolol suggest that the ACTH, GH and hypothermic responses to 5-HT$_{1A}$ receptor agonists are mediated by activation of 5-HT$_{1A}$ receptors (Lesch, 1992; Cowen, 1993). Some currently employed 5-HT$_{1A}$ receptor agonists, notably buspirone, also increase plasma PRL levels. However, the role of 5-HT$_{1A}$ receptors in buspirone-induced PRL release is unclear, and blockade of dopamine D$_2$ receptors may be the more important mechanism (Meltzer *et al.*, 1991).

Studies in animals suggest that endocrine responses to 5-HT$_{1A}$ receptor challenge are mediated by activation of postsynaptic 5-HT$_{1A}$ receptors (see Cowen, 1993). Whether the 5-HT$_{1A}$ receptors involved in the hypothermic response are located presynaptically on raphe cell bodies, or at postsynaptic sites, is controversial and shows important species differences (Bill *et al.*, 1991).

Results of studies with 5-HT$_{1A}$ receptor agonists in drug-free depressed patients have yielded inconsistent findings (Table 4). Considering the various investigations, Lesch (1992) used ipsapirone, which is a more selective probe than buspirone, but studied only 12 patients. Meltzer and Maes (1994b) studied the greatest number of patients but measured only PRL and cortisol responses to buspirone. Of the endocrine responses produced by the buspirone, the increase in plasma GH is the most likely to be mediated by 5-HT$_{1A}$ receptors (Anderson and Cowen, 1992).

Both the studies that reported hypothermic responses to 5-HT$_{1A}$ receptor challenge in depressed patients found the responses to be impaired (Table 4). Interpretation of this finding is made difficult by uncertainty as to whether these receptors are located pre- or postsynaptically (see above). Our group also studied the GH response to buspirone in depressed subjects and found them very similar to those of healthy controls (Cowen *et al.*, 1994). This is of interest because buspirone-induced GH release is a consequence of direct activation of postsynaptic 5-HT$_{1A}$ receptors, while the GH response to TRP, which is reliably blunted in

Table 4. Neuroendocrine studies of 5-HT$_{1A}$ receptor agonists in depressed patients.

Study	Drug	Number of patients	Response in depressed patients vs controls
Lesch (1992)	ipsapirone	12	cortisol ↓, ACTH ↓, temp ↓
Cowen *et al.* (1994)	buspirone	20	growth hormone NC, ACTH NC, temp ↓
Meltzer and Maes (1994b)	buspirone	45	cortisol NC, prolactin NC
Moeller *et al.* (1994)	buspirone	13	prolactin ↓

NC = no change; temp = hypothermic response.

depressed patients, involves indirect activation of these receptors (via increased 5-HT release). Taken together, the data suggest that the impairment in TRP-induced GH release in depression is due to abnormal function of presynaptic 5-HT neurones and not to impaired sensitivity of postsynaptic 5-HT$_{1A}$ receptors.

Endocrine responses to other 5-HT receptor challenges
Few studies have been reported of other 5-HT receptor challenges in depressed patients. The endocrine and thermic responses to m-chlorophenylpiperazine (mCPP) and 6-chloro-2-(1-piperazinyl)-pyrazine (MK-212) differ from those of the 5-HT$_{1A}$ receptor agonists. Neither of these drugs is a highly selective ligand, but their endocrine responses probably involve activation of 5-HT$_2$ receptors, most likely the 5-HT$_{2C}$ subtype in the case of mCPP (see Cowen, 1993). At present, there is no consistent evidence that depressed patients have altered endocrine responses to either of these drugs (see Power and Cowen, 1992a).

Cortisol hypersecretion and 5-HT neuroendocrine function
It was mentioned above that the presence of blunted responses to fenfluramine in depression correlated with cortisol hypersecretion. One study also found that cortisol hypersecretion was associated with blunted PRL responses to TRP (Deakin *et al.*, 1990), but another did not (Cowen and Charig, 1987). These findings have given rise to suggestions that changes in brain 5-HT function in depression may be secondary to cortisol hypersecretion (see Deakin *et al.*, 1990; Dinan, 1994).

This proposal is supported by data from animal studies indicating that the expression of 5-HT$_{1A}$ receptors is modulated by cortisol. There are also data showing that increased cortisol secretion diminishes 5-HT$_{1A}$-mediated behavioural responses (see Deakin and Graeff, 1991). Taken together the findings suggest that the primary pathogenesis of depression may lie in abnormal cortisol secretion (or perhaps an unusual sensitivity of 5-HT pathways to cortisol). The fact that cortisol-lowering agents, such as ketoconazole, may relieve depressive symptoms offers some support for this hypothesis (Wolkowitz *et al.*, 1993).

Conclusions

5-HT neuroendocrine tests provide a reasonably consistent body of evidence that brain 5-HT function is impaired in depressed patients. The most reliable abnormality is a lowered PRL response to drugs that enhance 5-HT function through actions on presynaptic 5-HT neurones. At this point, it is worth noting that neither the PRL response to the pituitary lactotroph stimulant, thyrotropin releasing hormone (TRH), nor that to the dopamine D_2 receptor antagonist, metoclopramide, is decreased in depressed patients (Rubin *et al.*, 1989; Anderson and Cowen, 1991). These data suggest that the impairment in 5HT-mediated PRL release in depression is due to abnormalities in 5-HT pathways, and not to alterations in the pituitary regulation of PRL secretion.

Studies to date suggest that in patients with major depression, decreased 5-HT-mediated PRL release is a state marker of the disorder; this implies that depressive disorders are associated with a reversible impairment of brain 5-HT function. A limited amount of evidence suggests that the changes in 5-HT neuroendocrine function in depression are due to a dysfunction in presynaptic 5-HT neurones rather than alterations in postsynaptic 5-HT receptors.

At present we can say little about the effect of depression on specific 5-HT receptor subtypes and their associated pathways. However, endocrine responses to TRP are consistently decreased in depression, and if these responses are indeed mediated via indirect activation of postsynaptic 5-HT_{1A} receptors, it suggests that impairments of postsynaptic 5-HT_{1A}-mediated responses may be a fairly common accompaniment of depressive disorders. This proposal receives support from the finding that in patients with bulimia nervosa, blunted PRL responses to TRP are found in subjects who suffer from coexisting major depression, but not in those who do not (Brewerton *et al.*, 1992). Overall the data are consistent with the hypothesis of Deakin and Graeff (1991) that 5-HT_{1A} pathways play an important role in mediating resilience to adversity, and that failure of this mechanism leads to depression (see above).

Abnormalities in the PRL responses to fenfluramine are found less consistently in depressed subjects but appear to be associated particularly with more severe forms of illness and cortisol hypersecretion. Fenfluramine-induced PRL release is probably mediated via indirect activation of 5-HT_2 receptors. This suggests that in some depressed patients, notably those with melancholic features and cortisol hypersecretion, both postsynaptic 5-HT_{1A} and 5-HT_2-mediated responses are decreased.

Among depressed patients there appear to be a subgroup with a long-standing propensity to behave in an impulsive aggressive way towards themselves or others. These subjects may be particularly likely to make impulsive suicide attempts when depressed. Current studies suggest that such individuals have low CSF 5-HIAA and a blunted PRL response to fenfluramine. These abnormalities are likely to be trait markers that persist in the absence of significant depressive symptomatology.

The impairment of the PRL response to fenfluramine in such subjects is of interest in view of the suggestion that 5-HT_2 receptors may be important in restraining unconditioned behaviours such as escape and aggression (Deakin and Graeff, 1991). The findings in major depression suggest how similar abnormalities in some aspects of 5-HT function may be found in diverse diagnostic groupings, particularly where the clinical psychopathology includes significant mood disturbance or disorders of impulse control (see van Praag *et al.*, 1990).

5-HT FUNCTION AND ANTIDEPRESSANT DRUGS

Studies in animals

There is much evidence from animal experimental studies that different classes of antidepressant drugs facilitate aspects of brain 5-HT function. For example, in a series of studies using *in vivo* electrophysiology, Blier and de Montigny have shown that repeated administration of tricyclic antidepressants (TCAs), monoamine oxidase inhibitors (MAOIs) and SSRIs increases overall neurotransmission at postsynaptic 5-HT_{1A} synapses in rat hippocampus (for a review of this work see Blier and de Montigny, 1994).

In contrast, acute antidepressant administration does not increase the electrophysiological effect of 5-HT in this model. Blier and de Montigny (1994) have proposed that repeated administration of antidepressant drugs results in a number of adaptive changes in 5-HT neurones and it is these adaptive changes that allow the increase in 5-HT neurotransmission to take place. The time needed for the adaptive changes to occur accounts for the delay in clinical response to antidepressant drugs.

In the case of SSRIs, for example, studies with microdialysis *in vivo* have shown that acute treatment has only a weak effect on extracellular 5-HT in terminal regions. This is probably because simultaneous activation of somatodendritic 5-HT_{1A} autoreceptors decreases 5-HT cell firing and hence 5-HT release from nerve terminals. If SSRI treatment is continued for several days, however, a sustained increase in extracellular 5-HT is apparent together with electrophysiological evidence of a desensitization of cell body 5-HT_{1A} autoreceptors (Bel and Artigas, 1992; Blier and de Montigny, 1994). The delay in onset of action of SSRIs can therefore be explained by the time needed for desensitization of 5-HT autoreceptors, for it is only when this has occurred, that the ability of SSRIs to enhance 5-HT neurotransmission is fully expressed (Artigas, 1993). A preliminary study in humans has lent some support to this proposal (see below).

Antidepressant drugs and 5-HT function in humans

Studies with blood platelets confirm that tricyclic antidepressants and SSRIs inhibit the uptake of 5-HT *in vivo* in both healthy volunteers and depressed patients (see Cowen, 1990). The effect of antidepressant drugs on brain 5-HT function can be assessed by the neuroendocrine tests that were described earlier. Of the various tests, studies with 5-HT precursors are of particular interest because they would be expected to reveal the effect of the antidepressant treatment on overall 5-HT neurotransmission.

Antidepressant drugs and PRL responses to TRP

TCAs, MAOIs and SSRIs all increase the PRL response to TRP in depressed patients (Charney *et al.*, 1984; Price *et al.*, 1985; 1989; Cowen *et al.*, 1990). However, drugs that lack significant 5-HT re-uptake inhibiting properties *in vivo*, such as mianserin or trazodone, do not produce this effect (Cowen, 1988; Price *et al.*, 1988). Interestingly, the size of the increase in TRP-induced PRL release appears to correlate with the potency of the antidepressant concerned to block the re-uptake of 5-HT. Thus, the SSRI, fluvoxamine, produces a very large increase in the PRL response to TRP, while the effect of the TCA, desipramine, is fairly modest (Figure 1).

From the work described above, increases in the PRL response to TRP following antidepressant treatment are likely to reflect facilitation of brain 5-HT$_{1A}$ neurotransmission, an interesting finding in view of the hypothesis of Deakin and Graeff (1991) that enhancement of postsynaptic 5-HT$_{1A}$ receptor function in the hippocampus

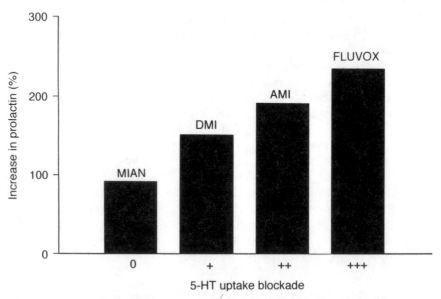

Figure 1. The mean per cent increase in prolactin response to intravenous L-tryptophan (TRP) following repeated treatment with mianserin (MIAN), desipramine (DMI), amitriptyline (AMI) and fluvoxamine (FLUVOX) in depressed patients. The increase in prolactin response correlates with the ability of the antidepressant to inhibit the uptake of 5-HT (reproduced from Power and Cowen, 1992b).

is an important mechanism in antidepressant action. This suggestion is consistent with the reported antidepressant effects of 5-HT_{1A} receptor agonists such as buspirone and gepirone (see Deakin, 1993).

Antidepressant drugs and cortisol responses to 5-HTP

Repeated treatment with SSRIs, such as fluoxetine, increases the cortisol response to 5-HTP suggesting that these drugs enhance 5-HT_2-mediated responses in the brain. However, this effect is not produced by TCAs, perhaps because they also possess 5-HT_2 receptor antagonist properties, or perhaps because they are less effective at blocking 5-HT re-uptake than SSRIs (Meltzer, 1990).

The differing effects of SSRIs and TCAs on 5-HT neuroendocrine responses have some interesting implications for the comparative clinical effects of these classes of antidepressants (see Power and Cowen, 1992). The data suggest that SSRIs facilitate 5-HT_{1A} neurotransmission to a greater extent than TCAs and, in addition, increase 5-HT_2 neurotransmission while TCAs do not. These differing effects may not be of particular consequence for the treatment of major depression where SSRIs and TCAs seem to be of about equal efficacy. In some conditions, however, such as obsessive–compulsive disorder, SSRIs are superior to TCAs, and it seems likely that this results from the ability of SSRIs to produce a more substantial increase in brain 5-HT neurotransmission.

5-HT and antidepressant response

While it is clear that certain antidepressant drugs increase brain 5-HT function, it is not established how this effect may relate to clinical antidepressant action. Perhaps the best evidence that increased brain 5-HT function is sufficient to produce an antidepressant response comes from the efficacy of SSRIs in the treatment of major depression. However, while SSRIs block the uptake of 5-HT within a few hours of administration, a significant clinical antidepressant effect may not be observed for several weeks. A number of reasons have been proposed to account for this delay in antidepressant action:

1. A sufficiently large increase in 5-HT neurotransmission can occur only after neuroadaptive changes in 5-HT neurones (see above).
2. Changes in 5-HT neurotransmission produce changes in other neurotransmitter pathways that are responsible for mediating the antidepressant action.
3. Changes in 5-HT neurotransmission do not alter mood directly but instead influence some other aspect of neuropsychological function, for example learning processes, which in turn leads to remission of the depressive syndrome.

If the reason for the delay in onset of antidepressant action with SSRIs is due to the development of neuroadaptive changes in 5-HT neurones, specifically the desensitization of $5\text{-}HT_{1A}$ autoreceptors (see above), the speed of onset of clinical antidepressant activity should be increased by co-administration of an SSRI with a $5\text{-}HT_{1A}$ autoreceptor antagonist (Artigas, 1993). In an open study of five depressed patients who were treated concomitantly with pindolol and paroxetine, Artigas *et al.* (1994) found a greater than 50% decline in ratings on Hamilton Depression Scale in less than one week. Clearly these findings are of great interest, but further controlled studies are needed. Pindolol is, of course, also a β-adrenoceptor antagonist, and it will be important to study the effect of selective $5\text{-}HT_{1A}$ receptor antagonists when these become available for clinical investigation.

It is also worth noting that $5\text{-}HT_{1A}$ receptor antagonists could block postsynaptic $5\text{-}HT_{1A}$ receptors as well as $5\text{-}HT_{1A}$ autoreceptors. If it is indeed correct that facilitation of postsynaptic $5\text{-}HT_{1A}$ receptor function is important in mediating antidepressant action, it is possible that $5\text{-}HT_{1A}$ receptor antagonism could actually undermine antidepressant efficacy (Deakin *et al.*, 1993). If, however, the findings of Artigas *et al.* (1994) are confirmed it suggests that a large enough increase in brain 5-HT function early in treatment can indeed produce a rapid antidepressant effect.

Reversal of antidepressant activity

If enhancements in 5-HT neurotransmission are important in mediating the therapeutic effects of antidepressant drug treatment, it would be predicted that measures inhibiting brain 5-HT function might reverse clinical antidepressant activity. In some early studies, Shopsin *et al.* (1975; 1976), found that administration of the 5-HT synthesis inhibitor, para-chloro-phenylalanine, to depressed patients who had recently recovered following treatment with either imipramine or tranycypromine led to a rapid return of depressive symptoms.

More recent studies of this effect have used the techniques of TRP depletion described earlier. Delgado *et al.* (1990) reported that 14 of 21 patients who had recently recovered with antidepressant drug treatment experienced significant clinical relapses a few hours after TRP depletion. The symptoms resolved after the subjects returned to a normal diet. When patients relapsed, the depressive symptoms and cognitions were very similar to those experienced during the acute depressive episode, suggesting that TRP depletion was reversing the actions of the antidepressant drugs rather than simply provoking dysphoric psychological effects.

Further studies from this group have shown that the liability to relapse is determined by the type of antidepressant a patient may be taking. For example, relapse rates are higher in patients maintained on drugs that have prominent acute effects on brain 5-HT function, such as MAOIs and SSRIs. In contrast, patients taking desipramine, whose principal pharmacological action is to block the re-uptake of noradrenaline, have a much lower risk of relapse after TRP depletion. Interestingly, the converse effect seems to occur if recovered depressed patients are challenged with the catecholamine synthesis inhibitor, α-methyl-para-tyrosine. Following this procedure, patients taking desipramine show frequent relapses but those maintained on SSRIs do not (see Salomon *et al.*, 1993).

Conclusions

The findings above suggest that acute facilitation of brain 5-HT function, for example by inhibiting 5-HT re-uptake, is sufficient to result in an antidepressant effect in depressed patients, although there is an obvious delay between initiation of this pharmacological effect and appearance of a clinical antidepressant response. As we have seen, a number of reasons for the delay in onset of antidepressant effect have been proposed. The work of Artigas *et al.* (1994) suggests that a sufficiently large increase in brain 5-HT function in the right place might produce an antidepressant effect after very short-term treatment. Even if this is the case, secondary changes in neurotransmitters other than 5-HT might still make an important contribution to the clinical antidepressant action.

The data from the TRP depletion and α-methyl-para-tyrosine studies suggest that antidepressant drugs work through different mechanisms to produce the same ultimate clinical response. It is hard to resist the conclusion that the antidepressant effect of desipramine is mediated through facilitation of brain noradrenaline function while that of SSRIs is enacted via enhanced brain 5-HT function. Whether different patients with differing biochemical forms of depression respond selectively to noradrenaline or 5-HT-promoting antidepressants is not clear at present. It seems at least as likely that clinical "responders" might do well following any one of a number of pharmacological interventions.

The TRP depletion data also suggest that intact 5-HT neurotransmission is necessary for the continued expression of the antidepressant effect of drugs such as SSRIs. Whatever the role of neuroadaptive changes in 5-HT and other neurones during the initiation of the antidepressant effect, clearly abrupt reduction of brain 5-HT function acutely reverses the antidepressant effect some antidepressant drugs have. With these antidepressants, it seems reasonable to conclude that increased brain 5-HT function is playing a direct role in maintaining the improvement in mood and other depressive symptoms.

The role of 5-HT pathways in mediating the other therapeutic effects of antidepressant drugs is less well established. For example, SSRIs are effective in the treatment of obsessive–compulsive disorder (OCD), but while acute TRP depletion causes relapse in coexisting depressive symptomatology in OCD patients, it does not cause a recrudescence of obsessive–compulsive phenomena (Barr *et al.*, 1994). While this supports the idea that a continued facilitation of brain 5-HT function is needed to maintain antidepressant efficacy, it raises the possibility that resolution of obsessive–compulsive symptoms is linked to a different mechanism. It is also, possible, however, that relapse of obsessional symptoms might not be detectable unless subjects were to be exposed to specific provoking stimuli. The use of TRP depletion to reverse, in a temporary way, the therapeutic effects of drugs that increase brain 5-HT function could lead to significant improvements in our knowledge of the neuropharmacological and neuropsychological actions of this class of compounds.

Acknowledgement

The studies of the author reported in this article were supported by the Medical Research Council.

REFERENCES

Abbott FV, Etienne P, Franklin KBJ, *et al.* (1992) Acute tryptophan depletion blocks morphine analgesia in the cold-presser test in humans. *Psychopharmacology* **108**, 60–66.

Anderson IM and Cowen PJ (1986) Clomipramine enhances prolactin and growth hormone responses to L-tryptophan. *Psychopharmacology* **89**, 131–133.

Anderson IM, Parry-Billings M, Newsholme EA, *et al.* (1990a) Decreased plasma tryptophan concentration in major depression: relationship to melancholia and weight loss. *J Affect Disord* **20**, 185–191.

Anderson IM, Parry-Billings M, Newsholme EA, *et al.* (1990b) Dieting reduces plasma tryptophan and alters brain 5-HT function in women. *Psychol Med* **20**, 785–791.

Anderson IM and Cowen PJ (1991) Prolactin response to the dopamine antagonist, metoclopramide, in depression. *Biol Psychiatry* **30**, 313–316.

Anderson IM and Cowen PJ (1992) Effect of pindolol on endocrine and temperature responses to buspirone in healthy volunteers. *Psychopharmacology* **106**, 428–432.

Anderson IM, Ware CJ, da Roza Davis JM, *et al.* (1992) Decreased 5-HT-mediated prolactin release in major depression. *Br J Psychiatry* **160**, 372–378.

Andersson A, Eriksson A and Marcusson J (1992) Unaltered number of brain serotonin uptake sites in suicide victims. *J Psychopharmacol* **6**, 509–513.

Arango V, Ernsberger P, Marzuk PM *et al.* (1990) Autoradiographic demonstration of increased serotonin 5-HT$_2$ and beta-adrenergic binding sites in the brain of suicide victims. *Arch Gen Psychiatry* **47**, 1038–1047.

Arora RC and Meltzer HY (1989a) Increased serotonin$_2$ (5-HT$_2$) receptor binding as measured by ^{3}H-lysergic acid diethylamide (^{3}H-LSD) in the blood platelets of depressed patients. *Life Sci* **44**, 725–734.

Arora RC and Meltzer HY (1989b) Serotonergic measures in the brains of suicide victims: 5-HT$_2$ binding sites in the frontal cortex of suicide victims and control subjects. *Am J Psychiatry* **146**, 730–736.

Arranz B, Eriksson A, Mellerup E, *et al.* (1994) Brain 5-HT$_{1A}$, 5-HT$_{1D}$ and 5-HT$_2$ receptors in suicide victims. *Biol Psychiatry* **35**, 457–463.

Artigas F (1993) 5-HT and antidepressants: new views from microdialysis studies. *Trends Pharmacol Sci* **14**, 262.

Artigas F, Perez V and Alvarez E (1994) Pindolol induces a rapid improvement of depressed patients treated with serotonin reuptake inhibitors. *Arch Gen Psychiatry* **51**, 248–251.

Asberg A, Traskman L and Thoren P (1976) 5-HIAA in cerebrospinal fluid: a biochemical suicide predictor. *Arch Gen Psychiatry* **33**, 1193–1197.

Barr LC, Goodman WK, McDougle CJ, *et al.* (1994) Tryptophan depletion in patients with obsessive–compulsive disorder who respond to serotonin reuptake inhibitors. *Arch Gen Psychiatry* **51**, 309–317.

Bel N and Artigas F (1992) Fluvoxamine preferentially increases extracellular 5-hydroxytryptamine in the raphe nuclei: an *in vivo* microdialysis study. *Eur J Pharmacol* **229**, 101–103.

Benkelfat C, Ellenborgen M, Dean P, *et al.* (1994) Enhanced susceptibility to the mood lowering effects of tryptophan depletion in young male adults at genetic risk for major affective disorders. *Arch Gen Psychiatry* **51**, 687–697.

Biegon A, Essar N, Israeli M, *et al.* (1990) Serotonin 5-HT_2 receptor binding on blood platelets as a state dependent marker in major affective disorder. *Psychopharmacology* **102**, 73–75.

Bill DJ, Knight M, Forster EA, *et al.* (1991) Direct evidence for an important species difference in the mechanism of 8-OH-DPAT-induced hypothermia. *Br J Pharmacol* **103**, 1857–1864.

Blier P and de Montigny C (1994) Current advances and trends in the treatment of depression. *Trends Pharmacol Sci* **15**, 220–226.

Boyer WF and Feighner JP (1991) The serotonin hypothesis: necessary but not sufficient. In: Feighner JP and Boyer WF (eds) *Selective Serotonin Reuptake Inhibitors*, pp. 71–80. John Wiley & Sons, Chichester.

Brewerton TD, Mueller EA, Lesen MD, *et al.* (1992) Neuroendocrine responses to m-chlorophenylpiperazine and L-tryptophan in bulimia. *Arch Gen Psychiatry* **49**, 852–861.

Briley MS, Langer SZ, Raisman R, *et al.* (1980) Tritiated imipramine binding sites are decreased in platelets of untreated depressed patients. *Science* **209**, 303–305.

Brown GL and Linnoila M (1990) CSF serotonin metabolite (5-HIAA) studies in depression, impulsivity and violence. *J Clin Psychiatry* **51 (Suppl 4)**, 31–41.

Brown SL, Botsis AJ and Van Praag HM (1992) Suicide: CSF and neuroendocrine challenge studies. *Int Rev Psychiatry* **4**, 141–148.

Charney DC, Heninger GR and Sternberg DE (1984) Serotonin function and the mechanism of action of antidepressant treatment: effects of amitriptyline and desipramine. *Arch Gen Psychiatry* **41**, 359–365.

Cheetham SC, Crompton MR, Katona CLE, *et al.* (1988) Brain 5-HT_2 receptor binding sites in depressed suicide victims. *Brain Res* **443**, 272–280.

Coccaro EF, Siever LJ, Klar HM, *et al.* (1989) Serotonergic studies in patients with affective and personality disorders. *Arch Gen Psychiatry* **46**, 587–599.

Coppen AJ (1967) The biochemistry of affective disorders. *Br J Psychiatry* **113**, 1237–1264.

Cowen PJ and Charig EM (1987) Neuroendocrine responses to intravenous tryptophan in major depression. *Arch Gen Psychiatry* **44**, 958–966.

Cowen PJ, Charig EM, Fraser S, *et al.* (1987) Platelet 5-HT receptor binding during depressive illness and tricyclic antidepressant treatment. *J Affect Disord* **13**, 45–50.

Cowen PJ (1988) Prolactin response to tryptophan during mianserin treatment. *Am J Psychiatry* **145**, 740–741.

Cowen PJ (1990) A role for 5-HT in the action of antidepressant drugs. *Pharmacol Ther* **46**, 43–51.

Cowen PJ, McCance SL, Gelder MG, *et al.* (1990) The effect of amitriptyline on endocrine responses to intravenous L-tryptophan. *Psychiatry Res* **31**, 201–208.

Cowen PJ (1993) Serotonin receptor subtypes in depression: evidence from studies in neuroendocrine regulation. *Clin Neuropharmacol* **16 (Suppl 3)**, S16–S18.

Cowen PJ, Power AC, Ware CJ, *et al.* (1994) 5-HT_{1A} receptor sensitivity in major depression: a neuroendocrine study with buspirone. *Br J Psychiatry* **164**, 372–379.

D'Hondt P, Maes M, Leysen JE, *et al.* (1994) Binding of [^{3}H]paroxetine to platelets of depressed patients: seasonal differences and effects of diagnostic classification. *J Affect Disord* **32**, 27–35.

Deakin JFW (1993) A review of clinical efficacy of 5-HT_{1A} agonists in anxiety and depression. *J Psychopharmacol* **7**, 283–289.

Deakin JFW, Pennell I, Upadhyaya AJ, *et al.* (1990) A neuroendocrine study of 5-HT function in depression: evidence for biological mechanisms of endogenous and psychosocial causation. *Psychopharmacology*, **101**, 85–92.

Deakin JFW and Graeff FG (1991) 5-HT and mechanisms of defence. *J Psychopharmacol* **5**, 305–315.

Deakin JFW, Graeff FG and Guimaraes FS (1993) Clinical implication of microdialysis findings. *Trends Pharmacol Sci* **14**, 263.

Delgado PL, Charney DS, Price LH, *et al* (1990) Serotonin function and the mechanism of antidepressant action: reversal of antidepressant-induced remission by rapid depletion of plasma tryptophan. *Arch Gen Psychiatry* **47**, 411–418.

Dinan TG (1994) Glucocorticoids and the genesis of depressive illness: a psychobiological model. *Br J Psychiatry* **164**, 365–371.

Ellis PM and Salmond CE (1994) Is platelet imipramine binding reduced in depression: a meta-analysis? *Biol Psychiatry* **36**, 292–299.

Gartside SE and Cowen PJ (1990) Mediation of ACTH and prolactin responses to 5-HTP by 5-HT$_2$ receptors. *Eur J Pharmacol* **179**, 103–109.

Gjerris A (1988) Do concentrations of neurotransmitters in lumbar CSF reflect cerebral dysfunction in depression? *Acta Psychiatr Scand* **345**, 21–24.

Goodall EM, Cowen PJ, Franklin M, *et al* (1993) Ritanserin attenuates anoretic, endocrine and thermic responses to d-fenfluramine in human volunteers. *Psychopharmacology* **112**, 461–466.

Handley SL and McBlane JW (1991) 5-HT—The disengaging transmitter? *J Psychopharmacol* **5**, 322–326.

Higley JD, Mehlman PT, Taub DM, *et al* (1992) Cerebrospinal fluid monoamine and adrenal correlates of aggression in free ranging rhesus monkeys. *Arch Gen Psychiatry* **49**, 436–441.

Horton RW (1992) The neurochemistry of depression: evidence derived from studies of post-mortem brain tissue. *Mol Aspects Med* **13**, 191–203.

Hrdina PD, Demeter E, Vu TB, *et al* (1993) 5-HT uptake sites and 5-HT$_2$ receptors in brain of antidepressant-free suicide victims/depressives: increase in 5-HT$_2$ sites in cortex and amygdala. *Brain Res* **614**, 37–44.

Koslow SH, Maas JW, Bowden CL, *et al* (1983) CSF and urinary biogenic amines and metabolites in depression and mania. *Arch Gen Psychiatry* **40**, 999–1010.

Koyama T and Meltzer HY (1986) A biochemical and neuroendocrine study of the serotonergic system in depression. In: Hippius H, Klerman GL and Matussek N (eds) *New Results in Depression*, pp 169–188. Springer, Berlin.

Lawrence KM, De Paermentier F, Cheetham SC, *et al* (1990) Brain 5-HT uptake sites labelled with [^{3}H] paroxetine, in antidepressant-free depressed suicides. *Brain Res* **526**, 17–22.

Lee MA, Nash JF, Barnes M, *et al* (1991) Inhibitory effect of ritanserin on the 5-hydroxytryptophan-mediated cortisol, ACTH and prolactin secretion in humans. *Psychopharmacology* **103**, 258–264.

Lesch KP (1992) 5-HT$_{1A}$ receptor responsivity in anxiety disorders and depression. *Prog Neuropsychopharmacol Biol Psychiatry* **15**, 723–733.

Lichtenberg P, Shapira B, Gillon D, *et al* (1992) Hormone responses to fenfluramine and placebo challenge in endogenous depression. *Psychiatry Res* **43**, 137–146.

Linnoila M and Virkkunen M (1992) Aggression, suicidality and serotonin. *J Clin Psychiatry* **53** **(Suppl 10)**, 46–51.

Lowther S, De Paermentier F, Crompton MR, *et al* (1994) Brain 5-HT$_2$ receptors in suicide victims: violence of death, depression and effects of antidepressant treatment. *Brain Res* **642**, 281–289.

Maes M, De Ruyter M, Hobin P, *et al* (1987) Relationship between the dexamethasone suppression test and the L-tryptophan/competing amino acid ratio in depression. *Psychiatry Res* **21**, 323–325.

Maes M, D'Hondt P, Suy E, *et al* (1991) HPA-axis hormones and prolactin responses to dextro-fenfluramine in depressed patients and healthy controls. *Prog Neuropsychopharmacol Biol Psychiatry* **15**, 781–790.

Mann JJ, Arango V and Underwood MD (1990) Serotonin and suicidal behaviour. *Ann NY Acad Sci* **600**, 476–485.

Mann JJ, Stanley M, McBride A, *et al.* (1986) Increased serotonin$_2$ and β-adrenergic receptor binding in the frontal cortices of suicide victims. *Arch Gen Psychiatry* **43**, 954–959.

McBride PA, Brown RP, De Meo M, *et al.* (1994). The relationship of platelet 5-HT$_2$ receptor indices to major depressive disorder, personality traits and suicidal behaviour. *Biol Psychiatry* **35**, 295–308.

McTavish D and Heel RC (1992) Dexfenfluramine. *Drugs* **43**, 713–733.

Mellerup E and Langer SZ (1990) Validity of imipramine platelet binding sites as a biological marker of endogenous depression. A World Health Organisation Collaborative Study. *Pharmacopsychiatry* **23**, 113–117.

Meltzer HY (1990) Role of serotonin in depression. *Ann NY Acad Sci* **600**, 486–500.

Meltzer HY and Arora RC (1991) Platelet serotonin studies in affective disorders: evidence for a serotonergic abnormality. In: Sandler M, Coppen A and Harnett S (eds) *5-Hydroxytryptamine in Psychiatry: a Spectrum of Ideas*, pp. 50–89. Oxford University Press, Oxford.

Meltzer HY, Gudelsky GA, Lowy MT *et al.* (1991) Neuroendocrine effects of buspirone: mediation by dopaminergic and serotonergic mechanisms. In: Tunnicliff G, Eison AS and Taylor OP (eds) *Buspirone: Mechanisms and the Clinical Aspects*, pp 117–192. Academic Press, San Diego.

Meltzer HY and Maes M (1994a) Effect of pindolol on the L-5-HTP-induced increase in plasma prolactin and cortisol concentrations in man. *Psychopharmacology* **114**, 635–643.

Meltzer HY and Maes M (2994b) Effects of buspirone on plasma prolactin and cortisol levels in major depressed and normal subjects. *Biol Psychiatry* **35**, 316–323.

Moeller FG, Steinberg JL, Fulton M, *et al.* (1994) A preliminary neuroendocrine study with buspirone in major depression. *Neuropsychopharmacology* **10**, 75–83.

Oldman AD, Walsh AES, Salkovskis P, *et al.* (1994) Effect of acute tryptophan depletion on mood and appetite in healthy female volunteers. *J Psychopharmacol* **8**, 8–13.

Owen F, Chambers DR, Cooper SJ, *et al.* (1986) Serotonergic mechanisms in brains of suicide victims. *Brain Res* **362**, 185–188.

Pandey GN, Pandey SC, Janicak PG, *et al.* (1990) Platelet serotonin-2 receptor binding sites in depression and suicide. *Biol Psychiatry* **28**, 215–222.

Park SB, Coull JT, McShane RH, *et al.* (1994) Tryptophan depletion in normal volunteers produces selective impairments in learning and memory. *Neuropharmacology* **33**, 575–588.

Park SBG and Cowen PJ (1995) Effect of pindolol on the prolactin response to d-fenfluramine. *Psychopharmacology* **118**, 471–474.

Perry EK, Marshall EF, Blessed G, Tomlinson BE and Perry RH (1983) Decreased imipramine binding in the brains of patients with depressive illness. *Brit J Psychiat* **142**, 188–192.

Poirier MF, Loo H, Benkelfat C, *et al.* (1985) [^{3}H]Imipramine binding and [^{3}H]5-HT uptake in human blood platelets: changes after one week chlorimipramine treatment. *Eur J Pharmacol* **106**, 629–633.

Power AC and Cowen PJ (1992a) Neuroendocrine challenge tests: assessment of 5-HT function in anxiety and depression. *Molec Aspects Med* **13**, 205–220.

Power AC and Cowen PJ (1992b) Fluoxetine and suicidal behaviour: some clinical and theoretical aspects of a controversy. *Br J Psychiatry* **161**, 735–741.

Price LH, Charney DS and Heninger GR (1985) Effects of tranylcypromine treatment on neuroendocrine, behavioural and autonomic responses to tryptophan in depressed patients. *Life Sci* **37**, 809–818.

Price LH, Charney DS and Heninger GR (1988) Effect of trazodone treatment on serotonergic function in depressed patients. *Psychiatry Res* **24**, 165–175.

Price LH, Charney DS, Delgado PL, *et al.* (1989) Effects of desipramine and fluvoxamine treatment on the prolactin response to tryptophan. *Arch Gen Psychiatry* **46**, 625–631.

Roy A, De Jong J and Linnoila M (1989) Cerebrospinal fluid monoamine metabolites and suicide behaviour in depressed patients: a five year follow-up study. *Arch Gen Psychiatry* **46**, 609–612.

Roy A, Virkkunen M and Linnoila M (1990) Serotonin in suicide, violence and alcoholism. In: Coccaro EF and Murphy DL (eds) *Serotonin in Major Psychiatric Disorders*, pp 187–208. American Psychiatric Press, Washington, DC.

Rubin RT, Poland RE, Lesser IM, *et al.* (1989) Neuroendocrine aspects of primary endogenous depression. V. Serum prolactin measures in patients and matched control subjects. *Biol Psychiatry* **25**, 4–21.

Salomon RM, Miller HL, Delgado PL, *et al.* (1993) The use of tryptophan depletion to evaluate central serotonin function in depression and other neuropsychiatric disorders. *Int Clin Psychopharmacol* **8 (Suppl 2)**, 41–46.

Shapira B, Cohen J, Newman ME, *et al.* (1993) Prolactin response to fenfluramine and placebo challenge following maintenance pharmacotherapy withdrawal in remitted depressed patients. *Biol Psychiatry* **33**, 531–535.

Shopsin B, Gershon S, Goldstein J, *et al.* (1975) Use of synthesis inhibitors in defining a role for biogenic amines during imipramine treatment in depressed patients. *Psychopharmacol Comm* **1**, 239–249.

Shopsin B, Freedman E and Gershon S (1976) Parachlorophenylalanine reversal of tranylcypromine effects in depressed patients. *Arch Gen Psychiatry* **33**, 811–819.

Smith CE, Ware CJ and Cowen PJ (1991) Pindolol decreases prolactin and growth hormone responses to intravenous L-tryptophan. *Psychopharmacology* **103**, 140–142.

Spoont MR (1992) Modulatory role of serotonin in neural information processing: implications for human psychopathology. *Psychol Bull* **112**, 330–350.

Stanley M, Virgilio J and Gershon S (1982) Tritiated imipramine binding sites are decreased in frontal cortex of suicides. *Science* **216**, 1337–1339.

Stanley M, Traskman-Bendz L and Dorovini-Zis K (1985) Correlations between aminergic metabolites simultaneously obtained from human CSF and brain. *Life Sci* **37**, 1279–1286.

Tork I (1990) Anatomy of the serotonergic system. *Ann NY Acad Sci* **600**, 9–35.

Traskman L, Asberg M, Bertilsson L, *et al.* (1981) Monoamine metabolites in CSF and suicidal behaviour. *Arch Gen Psychiatry* **38**, 631–636.

Upadhyaya AK, Pennell I, Cowen PJ, *et al.* (1991) Blunted growth hormone and prolactin responses to L-tryptopan in depression: a state dependent abnormality. *J Affect Disord* **21**, 213–218.

van der Kar LD (1991) Neuroendocrine pharmacology of serotonergic (5-HT) neurones. *Annu Rev Pharmacol Toxicol* **31**, 289–320.

van Praag HM, Asinis GM, Kahn RS, *et al.* (1990) Nosological tunnel vision in biological psychiatry: a plea for functional psychopathology. *Ann NY Acad Sci* **600**, 501–510.

Wolkowitz OM, Reus VI, Mandredi F, *et al.* (1993) Ketoconazole administration in hypercortisolemic depression. *Am J Psychiatry* **150**, 810–812.

Yates M, Leake A, Candy JM, *et al.* (1990) 5-HT$_2$ receptor changes in major depression. *Biol Psychiatry* **27**, 489–496.

Young SN, Smith SE, Phil RO, *et al.* (1985) Tryptophan depletion causes a rapid lowering of mood in normal males. *Psychopharmacology* **87**, 173–177.

4

Selective serotonin re-uptake inhibitors: Pharmacokinetics and drug interactions

Kim Brøsen and Birgitte Buur Rasmussen

The selective serotonin re-uptake inhibitors (SSRIs) are small lipophilic molecules which readily cross biological membranes. They are generally well absorbed via the gastrointestinal mucosa although the time to reach the maximal plasma concentration is relatively long, 4–8 hours. Fluoxetine, paroxetine and especially sertraline are extensively bound to plasma proteins (95–99% binding), but the protein binding for citalopram and fluvoxamine is relatively less pronounced (50–75%). The distribution to the tissues is extensive, and the volumes of distributions are in the range from 400–4000 l. Fluvoxamine, paroxetine and sertraline are high-clearance drugs with total clearances of 1–3 l/min. Citalopram and fluoxetine are intermediate clearance drugs with total clearances of about 0.5 l/min. Fluoxetine has a relatively low clearance and a very large volume of distribution (1500–3000 l). In combination this leads to a very long half-life: two days after a single dose and eight days after repeated dosing (Pato *et al.*, 1991). The corresponding values for the active metabolite norfluoxetine are seven days and 19 days. The prolongation in half-lives at steady-state suggests that fluoxetine and norfluoxetine saturate their own metabolism in the course of repeated dosing similar to what has been reported for paroxetine (Sindrup *et al.*, 1992a). The four other SSRIs have intermediate half-lives that range from 12 to 36 hours. All of the SSRIs are predominantly eliminated by cytochrome P450 catalysed oxidation in the liver. Citalopram and fluoxetine contain one chiral

Selective Serotonin Re-uptake Inhibitors: Advances in Basic Research and Clinical Practice, Second Edition, Edited by J.P. Feighner and W.F. Boyer
© 1996 John Wiley & Sons Ltd

centre (Figure 1) and are administered as racemates. Paroxetine and sertraline have two chiral centres (Figure 1) and are administered as the pure trans- and cis-isomers, respectively. The basic pharmacokinetics of the SSRIs has been detailed elsewhere (van Harten, 1993; Perucca et al., 1994a, Altamura et al., 1994).

The SSRIs are generally well tolerated and the therapeutic index is large. A concentration-effect relationship for the antidepressant effect has not been established. This means that the pharmacokinetic variability in the steady-state concentrations on a fixed dose is probably not important. Accordingly, pharmacokinetic interactions caused by a reduction in the absorption fraction, and the decrease in protein binding or induction or inhibition of the oxidation of the SSRIs are most likely of limited clinical relevance.

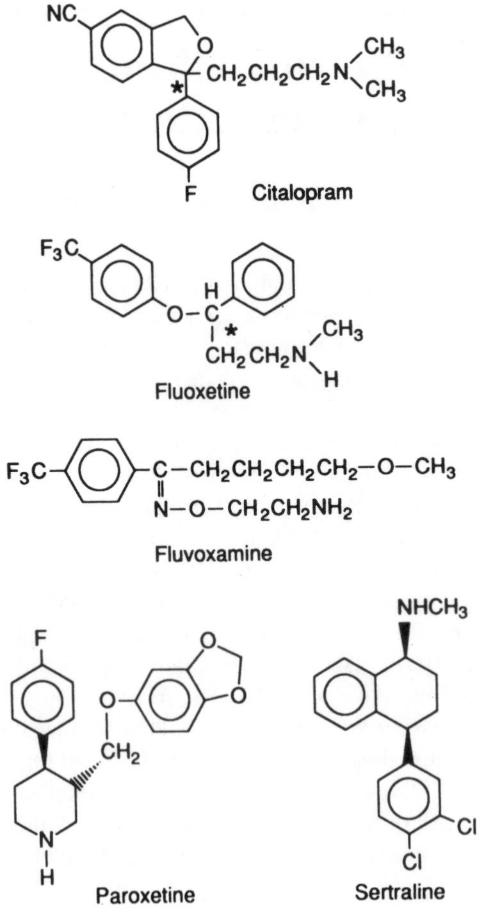

Figure 1. Structural formula of the selective serotonin reuptake inhibitors. (Brøsen et al., 1993b, reproduced with permission.)

However, it is very important that the SSRIs are inhibitors and indeed some of them very potent inhibitions of particular drug metabolizing P450s. Hence, some of the SSRIs have the potential for causing clinically important interactions due to inhibition of drug oxidation in the liver. There is no convincing evidence to support that the SSRIs differ from one another with regard to efficacy or adverse effects. Accordingly, the differences in terms of isozyme specific interactions is a major feature that differentiates the SSRIs (Brøsen, 1993). This chapter gives an updated review on the relationship between SSRIs and the cytochrome P450 system.

CYTOCHROME P450

Cytochrome P450 is a group of heme proteins and each consists of a single protein chain (MW 50–60 kd) and a heme molecule as prostetic group. Each P450 is encoded by a separate gene, and it is believed that 3.5 billion years ago there only existed one P450 gene (Nelson *et al.*, 1993). The ancestral gene underwent gene duplications and subsequent mutations in the course of the evolution to give rise to the present day gene super family. More than 100 mammalian P450 genes in 12 families have been identified. The P450 genes are grouped into families according to the degree of amino acid similarity of the encoded enzymes (Nelson *et al.*, 1993). The P450 gene is designated with the prefix CYP for *CY*tochrome and *P*eak. The latter is due to the fact that cytochrome P450 enzymes have a spectrophotometric absorption maximum at a wavelength of 450 nm. CYP is followed by an Arabic numeral for the family, a capital letter for the subfamily and an Arabic numeral for the individual species. The same designation is used for genes and enzymes, except that the genes are written in italics. The P450s can roughly be grouped into those which are involved in the biosynthesis of endogenous compounds such as steroids, prostaglandins and fatty acids and those which are involved in the oxidation of exogenous compounds such as plant toxins, environmental pollutants and drugs. To date, about 10 major drug metabolizing P450s have been identified in humans. The most important ones are listed in Table 1. It is possible that there are, in addition, some minor hepatic forms or major extrahepatic forms which have not yet been identified.

The CYP1A subfamily has two members. The CYP1A1 is expressed in the placenta and lungs of smokers, and minimally in the liver of non-smokers. The CYP1A2 is mainly expressed in the liver, and it is induced by tobacco smoking and by omeprazole. It as a major enzyme catalysing the oxidation of several clinically important drugs (Table 1). The CYP1A2 also plays a key role in the bioactivation of some procarcinogenic amines formed in meat during cooking (Boobis *et al.*, 1994), and according to a theory that now prevails subjects with a high CYP1A2 activity are at increased risk of developing certain cancers (Boobis *et al.*, 1994). The CYP1A2 activity can be determined *in vivo* by assessment of caffeine metabolism (Brock-möller and Roots, 1994).

Drug metabolizing enzymes in family 2 have been identified in the A, C, D and E subfamilies. The CYP2A6 catalyses the 7-hydroxylation of coumarin but a broader clinical relevance of this P450 has not yet been established.

The CYP2C subfamily consists of at least two important drug metabolizing P450s, the CYP2C9 and the CYP2C19 (Table 1). CYP2C9 oxidizes tolbutamide, S-warfarin, some nonsteroidal anti-inflammatory drugs and phenytoin. A broader clinical relevance of this enzyme for clinical psychopharmacology has not yet been established. It has recently been shown that the CYP2C19 is the source of the S-mephenytoin oxidation polymorphism and that the absence of the enzyme in poor metabolizers (PM) is due to a point mutation in the *CYP219* gene (de Morais *et al.*, 1994). The mephenytoin PM frequency is about 3% in whites and about 20% in orientals.

The CYP2D6 is the source of the sparteine/debrisoquine oxidation polymorphism and about 7% of whites are PM (Alván *et al.*, 1990). The PM frequency is only 1–2% in blacks and orientals. There are multiple inactivating mutations in the *CYP2D6* gene and that explains why no enzyme is formed in the PM. At the opposite extreme are the ultrarapid metabolizers with a multiplication of the *CYP2D6* gene (Johansson *et al.*, 1993). It is possible to genotype about 90% of the PM correctly by the polymerase chain reaction (PCR) (Heim and Meyer, 1990). The fact that CYP2D6 is not expressed in PM offers a unique experimental situation: the role of the enzyme in drug metabolism can be assessed by comparing the clearance in panels of extensive metabolizers (EM) and PM. The total clearance in EM is 2–5 times higher in EM compared with the PM for most of the substrates listed in Table 1. The very intensive study of the clinical pharmacokinetics of the CYP2D6 has resulted in the identification of more than 30 clinically important drugs as substrates for the enzyme. CYP2D6 phenotyping or genotyping is valuable in therapeutic drug monitoring of tricyclic antidepressants, neuroleptics and antiarrhythmics (Brøsen and Gram, 1989).

The CYP2E1 is a major enzyme catalysing the bioactivation of detrimental compounds such as benzene, chlorinated and flourinated hydrocarbons and nitrosamines. A catalytic activity towards the oxidation of some drugs has also been established (Table 1).

The four enzymes in the CYP3A subfamily make up 25–50% of the total content of P450 in the liver. The two major enzymes are CYP3A3 and CYP3A4 which have identical substrate specificities and which have 98% amino acid similarity. In fact, it is unclear whether CYP3A3 and CYP3A4 are encoded by separate genes or by the same gene and hence represent allelic variants (Watkins, 1994). The CYP3A4 is expressed in extra-hepatic tissues in particular in the mucosa of the small intestine. The abundance of CYP3A4 in the gut mucosa implies a substantial first-pass metabolism for many substrates. The CYP3A5 is not expressed in all livers and it seems to have a catalytic activity different from that of CYP3A/4. It is still uncertain whether the CYP3A7 is expressed in the human liver (Watkins, 1994).

The individual P450 oxidizes more than one drug and there is a considerable

Table 1 The characteristics of drug metabolising cytochrome P450s.

Isozyme	Substrates	Inhibitors	Inducers	Other characteristics
CYP1A2	Antipyrine Caffeine Clozapine Clomipramine Imipramine Paracetamol Phenacetin Propranolol Tacrine Theophylline	Fluvoxamine Furafylline Enoxacin	Polycyclic aromatic hydrocarbons Omeprazole	Makes up 5–10% of the total P450 in the liver. Not expressed at birth. Activates promutagens and procarcinogens
CYP2A6	Coumarin			A broader, clinical relevance of this isozyme for psychotropic drugs has not been established. Makes up 10–20% of the total P450 in the liver.
CYP2C9	Antipyrine Diclofenac Phenytoin S-warfarin Tolbutamide	Fluvastatin Sufaphenazole		
CYP2C19	Amitriptyline Citalopram Clomipramine Diazepam Imipramine Mephobarbital Moclobemide Omeprazole Proguanil Propranolol S-mephenytoin	Fluvoxamine Fluoxetine Ketoconazole Moclobemide	Rifampicin	Makes up about 5% of the total P450 in the liver. Source of the S-mephenytoin oxidation polymorphism. Absent from the liver in 3% of whites, 10% of West Greenlanders, and 20% of Orientals (poor metabolizers). Several inactivating mutations in the CYP2C19 gene. Genotyping of poor metabolizers is possible.
CYP2D6	Antiarrhythmics: Aprindine	Fluphenazine Moclobemide	None	Genetic polymorphism. (Sparteine/debrisoquine type.)

Table 1 cont. overleaf

Encainide
Flecainide*
Mexiletine
Propafenone
β-blockers:
Metroprolol
Propranolol
Neuroleptics:
Perphenazine*
Haloperidol*
Remoxipride
Risperidone
Thioridazine*
Zuclopenthixol
Opiates:
Codeine
Dextromethorphan
Dihydrocodeine
Ethylmorphine
Hydrocordone
Tramadol
SSRIs:
Fluoxetine*
Paroxetine*
Tricyclic antidepressants:
Amitriptyline
Clomipramine
Desipramine
Imipramine
N-desmethylclomipramine
Nortriptyline
Trimipramine
Miscellaneous:
Debrisoquine
Maprotiline
Methylenedioxymethamphetamine
("ecstasy")

Quinidine
Yohimbine
Substrates marked
with *

Dose-dependent kinetics.
Many potent inhibitors.
Stereo-selective metabolism.
Absent from the livers of 7–8% of whites
and 1–2% of blacks and Orientals (poor
metabolizers) due to multiple inactivating
mutations in the CYP2D6 gene.
Genotyping of extensive and poor
metabolizers is possible.

	Substrates	Inhibitors	Inducers	
	Sparteine Venlafaxine			
CYP2E1	Chlorzoxazone Enflurane Halothane Paracetamol	Disulfiram	Ethanol Isoniazid	Makes up about 5% of the cytochrome P450 in the liver. Activates certain procarcinogens.
CYP3A4	Antiarrhythmics: Lidocaine Propafenone Quinidine Anti-cancer drugs: Ifosfamide Tamoxifene Toremifene Benzodiazepines: Alprazolam Diazepam Midazolam Triazolam Calcium channel blockers: Diltiazem Felodipine Nifedipine Verapamil Hormones: Cortisol Ethinylestradiol Testosterone Miscellaneous: Carbamazepine Cyclosporine A Erythromycin Imipramine Omeprazole Proguanil Terfenadine	Ketoconazole Erythromycin Grapefruit juice Norfluoxetine Triacetyloleandomycin	Carbamazepine Dexamethasone Phenobarbital Prednisolone Rifampicine	Expressed in both the liver and the intestinal mucosa. Makes up about 25% of the total content of P450 in the liver. Pronounced first-pass metabolism for many substrates. Activates procarcinogens (Aflatoxin B)

overlapping in substrate specificities between different P450s. Therefore, many of the drugs in Table 1 are listed under more than one P450. The individual P450 is characterized by its substrates, inhibitors, inducers and by the influence of genetic and environmental factors. The finding that a particular P450 is a major catalyst of the oxidation of a drug has the implication that the functional characteristics of the enzyme will be a major source of the pharmacokinetic variability. This concept is particularly important for the rational prediction of drug–drug interactions. When two substrates of a particular P450 are co-administered there is the possibility of competitive inhibition. Some drugs are potent inhibitors without being substrates of a particular P450. One example is quinidine which is a very potent inhibitor of CYP2D6 without being metabolized by the enzyme (Table 1). An isozyme-specific interaction is only clinically relevant if the elimination of the substrate almost entirely depends on the P450, if the inhibitor is potent, if the therapeutic index of the substrate is small, and if clinical dose titration is not feasible (Brøsen and Gram, 1989; Brøsen, 1990).

PAROXETINE

Paroxetine is oxidized to inactive metabolites which are sulphated and glucuronated and subsequently excreted via the kidneys.

Paroxetine was the first SSRI shown to be a potent inhibitor of the CYP2D6 catalysed bufuralol metabolism by human liver microsomes (Brøsen et al., 1991). The early finding has subsequently been confirmed using imipramine, sparteine and dextromethorphan as test drugs (Skjelbo and Brøsen, 1992; Crewe et al., 1992; Otton et al., 1993). The potent inhibition in vitro was expressed in terms of the apparent inhibitor constant K_i that ranged from 0.15 to 0.80 μM (Brøsen et al., 1991; Skjelbo and Brøsen, 1992; Crewe et al., 1992). The apparent K_i is the concentration of the inhibitor which at low substrate concentrations reduces the rate of oxidation by 50%. Accordingly, the lower the K_i the more potent is the inhibitor. Paroxetine is also a potent inhibitor of CYP2D6 in vivo. EM subjects are converted to PM of sparteine (phenocopy) during intake of paroxetine 30 mg/day (Brøsen et al., 1991; Sindrup et al., 1992a). The potent inhibition was reversed within the first week after cessation of paroxetine (Sindrup et al., 1992a). The importance of the CYP2D6 inhibition by paroxetine in terms of plasma clearance was investigated using desipramine as a marker drug. The median clearance in 9 EM and 8 PM was 102 and 15 l/hour respectively before paroxetine. During paroxetine 20 mg/day the clearance values were 22 and 18 l/hour (Brøsen et al., 1993a). The drop in clearance in the EM but not in the PM confirmed that paroxetine is a potent and selective inhibitor of CYP2D6. The paroxetine–desipramine interaction has also been investigated during repeated dosing of desipramine 50 mg/day for 20 days. The average steady-state concentration of desipramine increased by about 400% (Alderman et al., 1994). Paroxetine also inhibits imipramine metabolism but to a lesser extent (Härtter et al.,

1994). The discrepancy between imipramine and desipramine in this regard is due to the fact that imipramine is predominantly eliminated by N-demethylation catalysed by CYP1A2, CYP2C19 and CYP3A4 (Table 1) and that paroxetine inhibition of these enzymes is minimal (Table 2).

Studies addressing the role of CYP2D6 for the oxidation of paroxetine itself have shown that CYP2D6 is a high-affinity saturable enzyme which becomes less important for paroxetine elimination at repeated or increasing doses (Sindrup *et al.*, 1992a, b). This means that the average steady-state concentration of paroxetine is less than two times higher in sparteine PM than in EM. In agreement with the *in vivo* studies it was subsequently shown with human liver microsomes that the potent CYP2D6 inhibitor, quinidine, only blocked about two thirds of paroxetine metabolism. The remaining one third reflects oxidation by other low affinity P450s (Bloomer *et al.*, 1992).

Thus, the relation between paroxetine and CYP2D6 illustrates three important features (Table 1): genetic polymorphism of the sparteine/debrisoquine type, saturation kinetics in EM and drug–drug interactions with other substrates due to potent and selective inhibition of the enzyme.

FLUVOXAMINE

Fluvoxamine is mainly demethylated at its methoxy group (Figure 1) to an inactive metabolite. Besides the main metabolite there are at least 10 minor inactive metabolites (van Harten, 1993). Nothing is known about which P450s catalyse the oxidation of fluvoxamine.

The steady-state plasma levels of amitriptyline, clomipramine, imipramine and trimipramine increased up to seven times during intake of fluvoxamine (Bertschy *et al.*, 1991; Spina *et al.*, 1992, 1993a; Härtter *et al.*, 1993; Seifritz *et al.*, 1994), whilst that of the corresponding secondary amines nortriptyline, N-desmethylclomipramine, desipramine and desmethyltrimipramine largely remained unchanged. The observations showed that fluvoxamine is a potent inhibitor of the N-demethylation of the parent compounds but only a moderate inhibitor of the CYP2D6 catalysed hydroxylation of the active metabolites. In keeping with this it was shown that fluvoxamine is a very potent inhibitor of the N-demethylation of imipramine in human liver microsome preparation *in vitro* (Skjelbo and Brøsen, 1992). The potent inhibition was expressed in terms of a very low apparent inhibitor constant K_i .of 0.14 μM. In comparison the apparent K_i for the CYP2D6 catalysed 2-hydroxylation of imipramine was 3.9 μM (Skjelbo and Brøsen, 1992). The moderate inhibition of CYP2D6 *in vitro* has later been confirmed using sparteine and dextromethorphan as probe drugs (Crewe *et al.*, 1992; Otton *et al.*, 1993).

CYP1A2 is one of the enzymes catalysing the N-demethylation of imipramine (Lemoine *et al.*, 1993) and probably also of amitriptyline, clomipramine and trimipramine, and it was therefore hypothesized that fluvoxamine is a potent

Table 2. Inhibitory effects of SSRIs on drug metabolizing P450 isozymes.

SSRI:	CYP1A2[a]	CYP2C9	CYP2C19[b]	CYP2D6[c]	CYP2E1[a]	CYP3A4[a]
Citalopram	Minimal	Not tested	Minimal	Moderate	Minimal	Minimal
N-desmethylcitalopram	Minimal	Not tested	—	Moderate	Minimal	Minimal
Fluoxetine	Minimal	Not tested	Moderate	Very potent	Minimal	Minimal
Norfluoxetine	Minimal	Not tested	—	Very potent	Minimal	Moderate
Fluvoxamine	Very potent	Not tested	Moderate	Moderate	Minimal	Minimal
Paroxetine	Moderate	Not tested	Minimal	Very potent	Minimal	Minimal
Sertraline	Minimal	Not tested	Not tested	Moderate	Minimal	Minimal

[a]Data from Brøsen et al., 1993b; Rasmussen et al., 1995; von Moltke et al., 1994.
[b]Only tested in vitro using S-mephenytoin as test drug.
[c]Data from Brøsen et al., 1991; Skjelbo and Brøsen, 1991; Crewe et al., 1992; Otton et al., 1993.

inhibitor of CYP1A2. This hypothesis was further supported by three case reports on a pharmacokinetic interaction between fluvoxamine and theophylline. Theophylline is N-demethylated and C-hydroxylated by CYP1A2 (Sarkar *et al.*, 1992). One case (Diot *et al.*, 1991) was an 83-year-old man who became intoxicated during treatment with theophylline 600 mg/day. The intoxication was due to an increase in theophylline levels from 9.4 mg/l without fluvoxamine to 39.8 mg/l during concomitant intake of fluvoxamine 100 mg/day. A 70-year-old man developed dizziness, blurred vision and an episode of ventricular tachycardia and tremor during combined treatment with fluvoxamine 100 mg/day and theophylline 800 mg/day. The plasma concentration of theophylline increased from about 80 μM to about 200 μM (Thomson *et al.*, 1992). The third case was an 11-year-old boy who complained of severe headaches, tiredness and vomiting due to an increase in theophylline levels from 14.2 mg/l to 27.4 mg/l during the combined intake of theophylline 600 mg and fluvoxamine 50 mg/day (Sperber, 1991).

In a subsequent experiment it was shown that fluvoxamine had an apparent K_i of 0.12–0.24 μM for inhibition of the phenacetin O-deethylation in human liver microsomes (Brøsen *et al.*, 1993b). This experiment confirmed that fluvoxamine is a very potent inhibitor of CYP1A2, and this was later confirmed using ethoxyresorufin as a marker reaction (Figure 2) (Rasmussen *et al.*, 1995). None of the other SSRIs is a potent inhibitor of CYP1A2 (Brøsen *et al.*, 1993b; Rasmussen *et al.*, 1995) (Figure 2). A dose-dependent increase in the mephenytoin S/R ratio has been observed in healthy volunteers and this suggests that fluvoxamine is a moderate inhibitor of CYP2C19 *in vivo* (data to be published).

It was recently confirmed that the mechanism of the interaction between fluvoxamine and theophylline is a potent inhibition of the three primary oxidative pathways of theophylline metabolism in the human liver (Rasmussen *et al.*, 1995). And, most certainly, this is due to inhibition of CYP1A2.

The potent inhibition of CYP1A2 has a number of implications for the use of fluvoxamine. First, as already discussed, fluvoxamine has the potential for causing drug–drug interactions with substrates of CYP1A2. Besides tricyclic antidepressants and theophylline this has been shown for propranolol (Benfield and Ward, 1986). Caffeine, which is present in coffee, tea and coca-cola, is eliminated almost entirely by the CYP1A2 and not surprisingly, caffeine metabolism is virtually abolished and hence the elimination half-life increased about eight times during fluvoxamine intake (data to be published).

Fluvoxamine may also become an important tool for the quantitative assessment of CYP1A2 in the metabolism of drugs and other xenobiotics, and this has recently been shown *in vitro* with theophylline as a test drug (Rasmussen *et al.*, 1995). Clozapine is another example serving to illustrate this. Two groups of researchers have recently independently discovered that clozapine plasma levels were increased up to 10 times during concomitant intake of fluvoxamine (Figure 3) (Hiemke *et al.*, 1994; Jerling *et al.*, 1994). In a subsequent study it was shown that the caffeine metabolic ratio as an index for CYP1A2 activity correlated excellently with the area

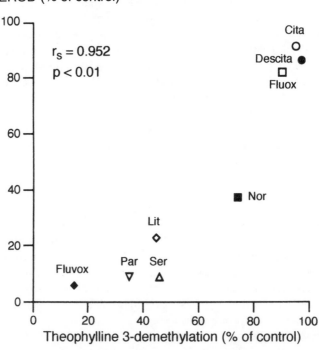

Figure 2.   *Above* A scatter plot of the correlation between two marker reactions for CYP1A2 activity in human liver microsomes: ethoxyresorutin 0-deethylation (EROD) and theophylline 3-demethylation. *Opposite* A scatter plot of the correlation between two marker reactions for CYP3A4 activity in human liver microsomes: the 6β-hydroxylation of testosterone and cortisol.

The oxidations were carried out during inhibition with SSRIs in a final concentration of 100 μM. The data are expressed in percent of the rates observed without inhibitor.

○ Citalopram, ● Desmethylcitalopram, □ Fluoxetine, ■ Norfluoxetine, ♦ Fluvoxamine, ◇ Litoxetin, ▽ Paroxetine, △ Sertraline.

under the plasma concentration curve after a single oral dose of clozapine (Bertilsson *et al.*, 1994). Thus, thanks to fluvoxamine, clozapine has been identified as a new substrate for CYP1A2. This is in very good agreement with earlier reports showing that smoking reduces the plasma levels of clozapine (Haring *et al.*, 1989). The fact that both clozapine and caffeine heavily depend on CYP1A2 for their elimination means that they are competitive inhibitors of each other's metabolism. Thus, the mechanism for the interaction between clozapine and caffeine (Vainer and Chouinard, 1994) could very well be pharmacokinetic rather than pharmacodynamic in nature. A 26-year-old woman suffering from obsessive–compulsive disorder treated with levomepromazine 400 mg/day and fluvoxamine 50 mg/day developed tonic–clonic seizures twice during two separate treatment periods (Grinspoon *et*

Inhibition of CYP3A by SSRI

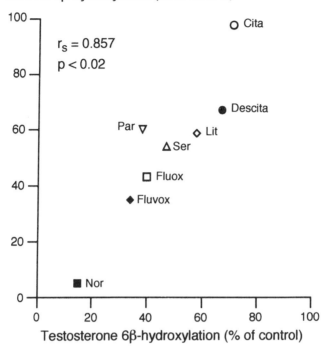

Cortisol 6β-hydroxylation (% of control)

$r_s = 0.857$
$p < 0.02$

○ Cita
● Descita
Par ▽
◇ Lit
△ Ser
□ Fluox
◆ Fluvox
■ Nor

Testosterone 6β-hydroxylation (% of control)

al., 1993). No seizures were observed during levomepromazine monotherapy 800 mg/day or fluvoxamine monotherapy 250 mg/day. Nothing is known about which P450s catalyse levomepromazine metabolism, but the possibility that CYP1A2 is responsible needs further study, and also that the interaction between levomepromazine and fluvoxamine has a pharmacokinetic background.

Carbamazepine is oxidized by CYP3A4 (Kerr *et al.*, 1994) and fluvoxamine inhibition of this isozyme *in vitro* is minimal (Rasmussen *et al.*, 1995) (Table 2, Figure 2). A pharmacokinetic interaction between the two drugs therefore seems unlikely. Nevertheless, a case report showed that the carbamazepine plasma level increased during fluvoxamine intake (Martinelli *et al.*, 1993). However, a formal pharmacokinetic study in healthy volunteers (Spina *et al.*, 1993b) failed to show any statistically significant increase in the carbamazepine steady-state plasma concentrations during fluvoxamine 100 mg/day. It is, nevertheless, advisable to check the carbamazepine plasma concentration if fluvoxamine is added.

Fluvoxamine prolongs the elimination half-life and decreases the total clearance of alprazolam and diazepam by a factor two to three (Fleishaker and Hulst, 1994; Perucca *et al.*, 1994b). Alprazolam is predominantly metabolized by CYP3A4 (von

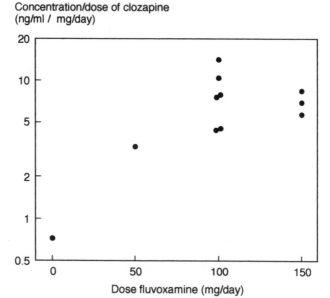

Figure 3. Relation between the ratio concentration/daily dose of clozapine and the daily dose of fluvoxamine in one patient who developed toxic symptoms when fluovoxamine was added to the clozapine treatment. From Jerling *et al.*, 1994, reproduced with permission.

Moltke *et al.*, 1994) and diazepam is oxidized in parallel via CYP2C19 and CYP3A4 (Andersson *et al.*, 1994).

The plasma warfarin concentration increased 65% during fluvoxamine intake and accordingly the prothrombin time also increased (Benfield and Ward, 1986). It is advisable to monitor the prothrombin time during combined warfarin and fluvoxamine treatment. The active enantiomer S-warfarin is oxidized by CYP2C9 (Table 1) but the effect of fluvoxamine on this enzyme has not been investigated (Table 2).

CITALOPRAM

Citalopram is N-demethylated to desmethylcitalopram and didesmethylcitalopram none of which is thought to contribute to the antidepressant effect. Citalopram is a racemic drug (Figure 1) but the serotonin re-uptake inhibitory properties reside in the S-enantiomer (Hyttel *et al.*, 1992). There are no published data on the stereoselective pharmacokinetics of citalopram.

Racemic citalopram and N-desmethylcitalopram exert minimal inhibition on all of the cytochrome P450 isozymes tested so far (Table 2). Citalopram and N-desmethylcitalopram as moderate inhibitors of CYP2D6 *in vitro* as judged from K_i

values that ranged from 1.3 to 19 μM (Skjelbo and Brøsen, 1992; Crewe *et al.*, 1992; Otton *et al.*, 1993). In agreement with this, the sparteine metabolic ratio was only slightly elevated and the desipramine plasma level was on average increased by 50% in healthy volunteers (Gram *et al.*, 1993; Sindrup *et al.*, 1993) during intake of citalopram 40 mg/day. Isozyme specific drug–drug interactions are unlikely to occur during citalopram treatment.

The role of CYP2C19 and CYP2D6 for the biotransformation of citalopram and its two N-demethylated metabolites were investigated in three panels of healthy EM for both sparteine and mephenytoin, sparteine PM and mephenytoin PM (Sindrup *et al.*, 1993). Thus, racemic citalopram is partially N-demethylated by CYP2C19, and N-desmethylcitalopram is further demethylated by CYP2D6.

SERTRALINE

Sertraline is N-demethylated to an inactive metabolite, and there are no data available on which P450s are involved in the biotransformation of sertraline.

Sertraline exerts moderate inhibition on the P450s tested so far *in vitro* (Table 2). In human liver microsome preparations sertraline had an apparent K_i for inhibition of sparteine of 0.70 μM (Crewe *et al.*, 1992) and a similar experiment with dextromethorphan gave a K_i of 1.5 μM (Otton *et al.*, 1993). The apparent K_i values for sertraline were about as low or slightly higher than those reported for fluoxetine and paroxetine, and it was therefore suspected that sertraline is nearly as potent an inhibitor of CYP2D6 catalysed drug oxidations *in vivo* as the two other SSRIs. This has turned out not to be the case. In two separate studies on healthy volunteers sertraline 50 mg/day produced a 30–40% increase in the steady-state plasma levels of desipramine also given in a dose of 50 mg/day (Preskorn *et al.*, 1994; Alderman *et al.*, 1994). In a third formal pharmacokinetic study, it was recently shown that the area under the plasma concentration curve of desipramine after a single dose of 100 mg, on average, was 1.74 times (range 1.12–3.19) higher during sertraline 150 mg/day (Zussmann *et al.*, 1994). This somewhat more pronounced effect may illustrate that the inhibition of the CYP2D6 mediated metabolism by sertraline is dose-dependent. In one patient a 60% increase in desipramine plasma concentration was observed during concomitant intake of sertraline 50 mg/day (Lydiard *et al.*, 1993). In another patient sertraline increased the desipramine levels by 250% (Barros and Asnis, 1993). In conclusion the available data show that sertraline is a moderate inhibitor of the CYP2D6 *in vivo*. The apparent *in vitro*/*in vivo* discrepancy in this regard serves to illustrate that inhibition studies with human liver microsome preparations can either be used to generate a hypothesis of something which ought to be studied *in vivo* or to confirm the mechanism of an observation already made *in vivo*. The *in vivo* studies showed that sertraline is a moderate inhibitor of CYP2D6. However in some patients, especially at high doses, sertraline may increase the plasma levels up to three times, and with some CYP2D6 substances, such as tricyclic antidepressants, this will cause a clinically important interaction. It is recommended to control the serum level of CYP2D6 substrates whenever possible if sertraline is added. Apart from that P450 specific interactions seem unlikely during sertraline treatment.

FLUOXETINE

Fluoxetine and its active metabolite norfluoxetine are racemates and R- and S-fluoxetine are almost equally potent SSRIs, but S-norfluoxetine is about 20 times more potent than R-norfluoxetine in this regard (Fuller *et al.*, 1992). Data on the stereoselective metabolism of fluoxetine are scanty. In one small study of seven depressed patients who took fluoxetine 20 mg/day the plasma levels of the two S-enantiomers were about two times higher than the plasma levels of the R-enantiomers (Torok-Both *et al.*, 1992). This suggests that the absorption fraction of the R-enantiomers is either lower than that of the S-enantiomers or that the total clearance of the R-enantiomers is higher than the total clearance of the S-enantiomers. The clinical significance of the stereoselective disposition of fluoxetine is not known.

The first reports that the plasma levels of nortriptyline and desipramine increased up to 500% during concomitant intake of fluoxetine appeared in 1988 less than one year after launching fluoxetine (Vaughan, 1988), and the initial observations have later been confirmed in numerous reports. Fluoxetine inhibits desipramine metabolism more than it does imipramine metabolism (Bergstrom *et al.*, 1992), suggesting that fluoxetine is a relatively selective inhibitor of CYP2D6. Indeed both racemic fluoxetine and racemic norfluoxetine are very potent inhibitors of CYP2D6 catalysed drug oxidations in human liver microsome preparations having apparent K_i values in the range 0.19–0.92 μM (Brøsen and Skjelbo, 1991; Skjelbo and Brøsen, 1992; Crewe *et al.*, 1992; Otton *et al.*, 1993). Accordingly, fluoxetine and norfluoxetine are as potent inhibitors as paroxetine *in vitro*. By use of the human liver microsomal bufuralol 1'-hydroxylase activity as a marker reaction for CYP2D6 (Stevens and Wrighton, 1993) it was shown that the K_i values were 0.22, 1.38, 0.31 and 1.48 μM for S-fluoxetine, R-fluoxetine, S-norfluoxetine and R-norfluoxetine respectively. Thus, both of the R-enantiomers are less potent inhibitors of CYP2D6 than the corresponding S-enantiomers. The apparent Michaelis constant K_m for oxidation of a substrate by a certain enzyme is the same as the substrate's K_i for inhibition of the enzyme. If CYP2D6 catalyses the N-demethylation of R- and S-fluoxetine then the expected K_m is about 1 μM. At R- and S-norfluoxetine concentrations of 50–100 μM, which are two orders of magnitude higher than the putative K_m, Stevens and Wrighton (1993) found that the rate of N-demethylation showed a weak but statistically significant correlation with the amount of immunodetectable CYP2D6 in microsomes from 14 human livers. Surprisingly, neither quinidine nor serum containing an anti-liver-kidney-microsome antibody against CYP2D6 inhibited the N-demethylations. This could be due to saturation of CYP2D6 at the very high substrate concentrations relative to the K_m. Thus the *in vitro* data suggest that the N-demethylation of R- and S-fluoxetine proceeds in parallel via the saturable CYP2D6 and via alternative low-affinity enzymes. Racemic fluoxetine and norfluoxetine have been screened for their ability to inhibit other P450s *in vitro*. Inhibition of CYP1A1, CYP1A2, CYP2A6 and CYP2E1 was minimal (Brøsen *et al.*, 1993b; Rasmussen *et al.*, 1995). Norfluoxetine was a relatively potent inhibitor of the 6-β-hydroxylation of cortisol and testosterone, two marker reactions for CYP3A4 (Figure 2) (Rasmussen *et al.*, 1995). In agreement with this, von Moltke *et al.* (1994) found that norfluoxetine had an apparent K_i for inhibition of alprazolam hydroxylation of 11 μM. A moderate dose dependent increase in mephenytoin S/R ratio has been observed in healthy volunteers who took fluoxetine (data to be published, this laboratory) and this suggests that either fluoxetine, norfluoxetine or both are moderate inhibitors of CYP2C19.

A moderate decrease in the clearance and a moderate increase in the elimination half-life of diazepam during fluoxetine 60 mg per day (Lemberger *et al.*, 1988) may reflect inhibition of both CYP2C19 and CYP3A4. Fluoxetine/norfluoxetine are also weak inhibitors of alprazolam metabolism *in vivo* (Greenblatt *et al.*, 1992) and this interaction is probably due to inhibition of CYP3A4. Although studies on an interaction between fluoxetine and carbamazepine have given contradictory results (Grimsley *et al.*, 1991; Spina *et al.*, 1993b) it is advisable to check the carbamazepine level if fluoxetine is added. An increase in the haloperidol plasma levels was reported in three out of 11 patients who took haloperidol 5–40 mg/day and fluoxetine 20 mg/day (Goff *et al.*, 1991), and this interaction could be due to inhibition of CYP2D6 (Table 1). An interaction between fluoxetine and clozapine was reported on the basis of six patients who took an average dose of clozapine 346 mg/day and an average dose of fluoxetine 36 mg/day and who had a mean clozapine serum level of 434 ng/ml (Centorrino *et al.*, 1994). In comparison, a control group of 17 patients who took an average dose of clozapine 300 mg/day and no fluoxetine had a mean level of 247 ng/ml. This could suggest that fluoxetine inhibits clozapine metabolism *in vivo* which is somewhat surprising in the light of the fact that neither fluoxetine nor norfluoxetine inhibits CYP1A2 *in vitro* (Brøsen *et al.*, 1993b; Rasmussen *et al.*, 1995) (Table 2, Figure 2). Bradycardia was observed in a 54-year-old man who was prescribed a combination of metoprolol 100 mg/day and fluoxetine 20 mg/day. The interaction was thought to arise from a combined inhibition of CYP2D6 and CYP3A4 since both enzymes are claimed to be involved in the biotransformation of metoprolol (Walley *et al.*, 1993).

Intermittent frequent sinus tachycardia occurred in a 41-year-old man with no previous history of disease (Swims, 1993). The patient took terfenadine 120 mg/day and fluoxetine 20 mg/day. The arrhythmia was thought to arise from an interaction between the two drugs. Terfenadine undergoes nearly 100% first-pass metablism via CYP3A4 to an active metabolite (Woosley *et al.*, 1993). Terfenadine itself is cardiotoxic, and serious proarrhythmias have been reported due to inhibition of CYP3A4. It is possible that the moderate CYP3A4 inhibition by norfluoxetine is sufficient to cause a dangerous interaction, and the combination of terfenadine and fluoxetine should be avoided.

CONCLUSIONS AND PERSPECTIVES

The presence of multiple drugs metabolizing P450s in the liver has been known for 20 years but the relevance of this for drug development has only been recognized during the last couple of years. With this new knowledge it will become possible in the future to predict many but not all of the pharmacokinetic interactions that otherwise would have been discovered during post-marketing surveillance.

All of the SSRIs inhibit CYP2D6. However paroxetine, fluoxetine and norfluoxetine are potent inhibitors of CYP2D6, whereas citalopram, fluvoxamine and sertraline inhibit CYP2D6 to a lesser extent. Hence fluoxetine and paroxetine have the potential for causing serious drug–drug interactions with some CYP2D6 substrates unless the dose of the CYP2D6 substrate is reduced by 50–75%. Fluvoxamine is a very potent inhibitor of CYP1A2 but the other SSRIs seem not to be. By analogy CYP1A2 substrates should be given in doses that are only 10–50% of the standard. During fluvoxamine treatment patients should be informed about the interaction with caffeine and advised either to reduce coffee drinking or drink decaffeinated coffee instead.

REFERENCES

Alderman J, Greenblatt DJ, Allison J, Preskorn SH, Chung M and Harrison W (1994) *Desipramine Pharmacokinetics with the Serotonin Reuptake Inhibitors, Paroxetine or Sertraline*, Abstract presented at the XIX CINP Congress, Washington, 26 June–1 July 1994.

Altamura AC, Moro AR and Percudani M (1994) Clinical pharmacokinetics of fluoxetine. *Clin Pharmacokinet* **26(3)**, 201–214.

Alván G, Bechtel P, Iselius L and Gundert-Remy U (1990) Hydroxylation polymorphisms of debrisoquine and mephenytoin in European populations. *Eur J Clin Pharmacol* **39**, 533–537.

Andersson T, Miners JO, Veronese M and Birkett D (1994) Diazepam metabolism by human liver microsomes is mediated by both S-mephenytoin hydroxylase and CYP3A isoforms. *Br J Clin Pharmacol* **38**, 131–137.

Barros J and Asnis G (1993) An interaction of sertraline and desipramine. *Am J Psychiatry* **150**, 1751–1752.

Benfield P and Ward A (1986) Fluvoxamine. A review of its pharmacodynamic and pharmacokinetic properties, and therapeutic efficacy in depressive illness. *Drugs* **32**, 313–334.

Bergstrom RF, Peyton AL and Lemberger L (1992) Quantification and mechanism of the fluoxetine and tricyclic antidepressant interaction. *Clin Pharmacol Ther* **51**, 239–248.

Bertilsson L, Carrillo JA, Dahl ML, LLerena A, Alm C, Bondesson U, Lindström L, de la Rubia IR, Ramos S and Benitez J (1994) Clozapine disposition covaries with the CYP1A2 activity determined by the caffeine test. *Br J Clin Pharmacol* **38**, 471–473.

Bertschy G, Vandel S, Allers G and Volmat R (1991) Fluvoxamine–tricyclic antidepressant interaction. An accidental finding. *Eur J Clin Pharmacol* **40**, 119–120.

Bloomer JC, Woods FR, Haddock RE, Lennard MS and Tucker GT (1992) The role of cytochrome P4502D6 in the metabolism of paroxetine by human liver microsomes. *Br J Clin Pharmol* **33**, 521–523.

Boobis AR, Lynch AM, Murray S, de le Torre R, Solans A, Farré M, Segura J, Gooderham NJ and Davies DS (1994) CYP1A2-catalyzed convertion of dietary heterocyclic amines to their proximate carcinogens is their major route of metabolism in humans. *Cancer Res* **54**, 89–94.

Brockmöller J and Roots I (1994) Assessment of liver metabolic function. Clinical implications. *Clin Pharmacokinet* **27(3)**, 216–248.

Brøsen K and Gram LF (1989) Clinical significance of the sparteine/debrisoquine oxidation polymorphism. *Eur J Clin Pharmacol* **36**, 537–547.

Brøsen K (1990) Recent developments in hepatic drug oxidation: implications for clinical pharmacokinetics. *Clin Pharmacokinet* **18**, 220–239.

Brøsen K, Gram LF and Kragh-Sørensen P (1991) Extremely slow metabolism of amitriptyline but normal metabolism of imipramine and desipramine in an extensive metabolizer of sparteine, debrisoquine, and mephenytoin. *Ther Drug Monit* **13**, 177–182.

Brøsen K and Skjelbo E (1991) Fluoxetine and norfluoxetine are potent inhibitors of P450IID6—the source of the sparteine/debrisoquine oxidation polymorphism. *Br J Clin Pharmacol* **32**, 136–137.

Brøsen K (1993) The pharmacogenetics of the selective serotonin reuptake inhibitors. *Clin Invest* **71**, 1002–1009.

Brøsen K, Hansen JG, Nielsen KK, Sindrup SH and Gram LF (1993a) Inhibition by paroxetine of desipramine metabolism in extensive but not in poor metabolizers of sparteine. *Eur J Clin Pharmacol* **44**, 349–355.

Brøsen K, Skjelbo E, Rasmussen BB, Poulsen HE and Loft S (1993b) Fluvoxamine is a potent inhibitor of cytochrome P4501A2. *Biochem Pharmacol* **45**, 1211–1214.

Centorrino F, Baldessarini RJ, Kando J, Frankenburg FR, Volpicelli SA, Poupolo PR and Flood JG (1994) Serum concentrations of clozapine and its major metabolites: effects of cotreatment with fluoxetine or valproate. *Am J Psychiatry* **151**, 123–125.

Crewe HK, Lennard MS, Tucker GT, Woods FR and Haddock RE (1992) The effect of selective serotonin re-uptake inhibitors on cytochrome P4502D6 (CYP2D6) activity in human liver microsomes. *Br J Clin Pharmacol* **34**, 262–265.

Diot P, Jonville AP, Gerard F, Bonnelle M, Autret E, Breteau M, Lemarie E and Lavandier M (1991) Possible interaction entre théophylline et fluvoxamine. *Therapie* **46(2)**, 170–171.

Fleishaker JC and Hulst LK (1994) A pharmacokinetic and pharmacodynamic evaluation of the combined administration of alprazolam and fluvoxamine. *Eur J Clin Pharmacol* **46**, 35–39.

Fuller RW, Snoddy HD, Krushinski JH and Robertson DW (1992) Comparison of norfluoxetine enantiomers as serotonin reuptake inhibitors *in vivo*. *Neuropharmacology* **31**, 997–1000.

Goff DC, Midha KK, Brotman AW, Waites M and Baldessarini RJ (1991) Elevation of plasma concentrations of haloperidol after the addition of fluoxetine. *Am J Psychiatry* **148**, 790–792.

Gram LF, Hansen MGJ, Sindrup SH, Brøsen K, Poulsen JH, Aaes-Jørgensen T and Overø KF (1993) Citalopram: interaction studies with levomepromazine, imipramine, and lithium. *Ther Drug Monit* **15**, 18–24.

Greenblatt DJ, Preskorn SH, Cotreau MM, Horst WD and Harmatz JS (1992) Fluoxetine impairs clearance of alprazolam but not of clonazepam. *Clin Pharmacol Ther* **52**, 479–486.

Grimsley SR, Jann MW, Carter G, D'Mello AP and D'Souza MJ (1991) Increased carbamazepine plasma concentrations after fluoxetine coadministration. *Clin Pharmacol Ther* **50**, 10–15.

Grinshpoon A, Berg Y, Mozes T, Mester R and Weizman A (1993) Seizures induced by combined levomepromazine-fluvoxamine treatment. *Int Clin Psychopharmacol* **8**, 61–62.

Haring C, Meise V, Hampel C, Saria A, Fleischhacker WW and Hinterhüber H (1989) Dose-related plasma levels of clozapine: Influence of smoking behaviour, sex and age. *Psychopharmacology* **99**, 538–540.

Härtter S, Wetzel H, Hammes E and Hiemke C (1993) Inhibition of antidepressant demethylation and hydroxylation by fluvoxamine in depressed patients. *Psychopharmacology* **110**, 302–308.

Härtter S, Hermes B, Szegedi A and Hiemke C (1994) Automated determination of paroxetine and its main metabolite by column switching and on-line high-performance liquid chromatography. *Ther Drug Monit* **16**, 400–406.

Heim M and Meyer UA (1990) Genotyping of poor metabolisers of debrisoquine by allele-specific PCR amplification. *Lancet* **336**, 529–532.

Hiemke C, Weighmann H, Dahmen N, Wetzel H and Müller H (1994) Elevated serum levels of clozapine after addition of fluvoxamine. *Clin Psychopharmacol* **14**, 279–281.

Hyttel J, Bøgesø KP, Perregaard J and Sánchez C (1992) The pharmacological effect of citalopram resides in the (S)-(+)-enantiomer. *J Neural Transm* **88**, 157–160.

Jerling M, Lindström L, Bondesson U and Bertilsson L (1994) Fluvoxamine inhibition and carbamazepine induction of the metabolism of clozapine: evidence from a therapeutic drug monitoring service. *Ther Drug Monit* **16**, 368–374.

Johansson I, Lundqvist E, Bertilsson L, Dahl ML, Sjöqvist F and Ingelman-Sundberg M (1993) Inherited amplification of an active gene in the cytochrome P450 CYP2D locus as a cause of ultrarapid metabolism of debrisoquine. *Proc Natl Acad Sci USA* **90**, 11 825–11 829.

Kerr BM, Thummel KE, Wurden CJ, Klein SM, Kroetz DL, Gonzales FJ and Levy RN (1994) Human liver carbamazepine metabolism. Role of CYP3A4 and CYP2C8 in 10,11-epoxide formation. *Biochem Pharmacol* **47**, 1969–1979.

Lemberger L, Rowe H, Bosomworth JC, Tenbarge JB and Bergstrom RF (1988) The effect of fluoxetine on the pharmacokinetics and psychomotor responses of diazepam. *Clin Pharmacol Ther* **43**, 412–419.

Lemoine A, Gautier JC, Azoulay D, Kiffel L, Belloc C, Guengerich FP, Maurel P, Beaune P and Leroux JP (1993) The major pathway of imipramine metabolism is catalyzed by cytochromes P-450 1A2 and P-450 3A4 in human liver. *Mol Pharmacol* **43**, 827–832.

Lydiard RB, Anton RF and Cunningham T (1993) Interactions between sertraline and tricyclic antidepressants. *Am J Psychiatry* **150**, 1125–1126.

Martinelli V, Bocchetta A, Palmas AM and del Zompo M (1993) An interaction between carbamazepine and fluvoxamine. *Br J Clin Pharmacol* **36**, 615–616.

von Moltke LL, Greenblatt DJ, Cotreau-Bibbo MM, Harmatz JS and Shader RI (1994) Inhibitors of alprazolam metabolism *in vitro*: effect of serotonin-reuptake-inhibitor antidepressants, ketoconazole and quinidine. *Br J Clin Pharmacol* **38**, 23–31.

de Morais SMF, Wilkinson GR, Blaisdell J, Nakamura K, Meyer UA and Goldstein JA (1994) The major genetic defect responsible for the polymorphism of S-mephenytoin metabolism in humans. *J Biol Chem* **269**, 15 419–15 422.

Nelson DR, Kamataki T, Waxman DJ, Guengerich FP, Estabrook RW, Feyereisen R, Gonzalez FJ, Coon MJ, Gunsalus IC, Gotoh O, Okuda K and Nebert DW (1993) The P450 superfamily: update on new sequences, gene mapping, accession numbers, early trivial names of enzymes, and nomenclature. *DNA and Cell Biology* **12**, 1–51.

Otton SV, Wu D, Joffe RT, Cheung SW and Sellers EM (1993) Inhibition by fluoxetine of cytochrome P450 2D6 activity. *Clin Pharmacol Ther* **53**, 401–409.

Pato MT, Murphy DL and DeVane CL (1991) Sustained plasma concentrations of fluoxetine and/or norfluoxetine four and eight weeks after fluoxetine discontinuation. *J Clin Psychopharmacol* **11**, 224–225.

Perucca E, Gatti G and Spina E (1994a) Clinical pharmacokinetics of fluvoxamine. *Clin Pharmacokinet* **27**, 175–190.

Perucca E, Gatti G, Cipollo G, Spina E, Barel S, Soback S, Gips M and Bialer M (1994b) Inhibition of diazepam metabolism by fluvoxamine: a pharmacokinetic study in normal volunteers. *Clin Pharmacol Ther* **56**, 471–476.

Preskorn SH, Alderman J, Chung M, Harrison W, Messig M and Harris S (1994) Pharmacokinetics of desipramine coadministered with sertraline or fluoxetine. *J Clin Psychopharmacol* **14**, 90–98.

Rasmussen BB, Mäenpää J, Pelkonen O, Loft S, Poulsen HE, Lykkesfeldt J and Brøsen K (1995) Selective serotonin reuptake inhibitors and theophylline metabolism in human liver microsomes: Potent inhibition by fluvoxamine. *Br J Clin Pharmacol* **39**, 151–159.

Sarkar MA, Hunt C, Guzelian PS and Karnes T (1992) Characterization of human liver cytochromes P450 involved in theophylline metabolism. *Drug Metab Dispos* **20**, 31–37.

Seifritz E, Holsboer-Trachsler E, Hemmeter U, Eap CB and Baumann P (1994) Increased trimipramine plasma levels during fluvoxamine comedication. *Eur Neuropsychopharmacol* **4**, 15–20.

Sindrup SH, Brøsen K, Gram LF, Hallas J, Skjelbo E, Allen A, Allen GD, Cooper SM, Mellows G, Tasker TGC and Zussman BD (1992a) The relationship between paroxetine and the sparteine oxidation polymorphism. *Clin Pharmacol Ther* **5**, 278–287.

Sindrup SH, Brøsen K and Gram LF (1992b) Pharmacokinetics of the selective serotonin reuptake inhibitor paroxetine oxidation polymorphism. *Clin Pharmacol Ther* **5**, 288–295.

Sindrup SH, Brøsen K, Hansen MGJ, Aaes-Jørgensen T, Overø KF and Gram LF (1993) Pharmacokinetics of citalopram in relation to the sparteine and the mephenytoin oxidation polymorphisms. *Ther Drug Monit* **15**, 11–17.

Skjelbo E and Brøsen K (1992) Inhibitors of imipramine metabolism by human liver microsomes. *Br J Clin Pharmacol* **34**, 256–261.

Sperber AD (1991) Toxic interaction between fluvoxamine and sustained release theophylline in an 11-year-old boy. *Drug Safety* **6**, 460–462.

Spina E, Campo GM, Avenso A, Pollicino MA and Caputi AP (1992) Internation between fluvoxamine and imipramine/desipramine in four patients. *Ther Drug Monit* **14**, 194–196.

Spina E, Pollicino AM, Avenso A, Campo GM, Perucca E and Caputi AP (1993a) Effect of fluvoxamine on the pharmacokinetics of imipramine and desipramine in healthy subjects. *Ther Drug Monit* **15**, 243–246.

Spina E, Avenoso A, Pollicino AM, Caputi AP, Fazio A and Pisani F (1993b) Carbamazepine coadministration with fluoxetine or fluvoxamine. *Ther Drug Monit* **15**, 247–250.

Stevens JC and Wrighton SA (1993) Interaction of the enantiomers of fluoxetine and norfluoxetine with human liver cytochromes P450. *J Pharmacol Exp Ther* **266**, 964–971.

Swims MP (1993) Potential terfenadine-fluoxetine interaction. *Ann Pharmacother* **27**, 1404–1405.

Thomson AH, McGovern EM, Bennie P, Caldwell G and Smith M (1992) Interaction between fluvoxamine and theophylline. *Pharmacol J* **137**, letter.

Torok-Both GA, Baker GB, Coutts RT, McKenna KF and Aspeslet LJ (1992) Simultaneous determination of fluoxetine and norfluoxetine enantiomers in biological samples by gas chromatography with electron capture detection. *J. Chromatogr* **579**, 99–106.

van Harten J (1993) Clinical pharmacokinetics of selective serotonin reuptake inhibitors. *Clin Pharmacokinet* **24**, 203–220.

Vainer JL and Chouinard G (1994) Interaction between caffeine and clozapine. *J Clin Psychopharmacol* **14**, 284–285.

Vaughan DA (1988) Interaction of fluoxetine with tricyclic antidepressants. *Am J Psychiatry* **145**, 1478.

Walley T, Pirmohamed M, Proudlove C and Maxwell D (1993) Interaction of metoprolol and fluoxetine. *Lancet* **341**, 967–968.

Watkins PB (1994) Noninvasive tests of CYP3A enzymes. *Pharmacogenetics* **4**, 171–184.

Woosley RL, Yiwang C, Freiman JP and Gillis RA (1993) Mechanism of the cardiotoxic actions of terfenadine. *JAMA* **269**, 1532–1536.

Zussman BD, Davie CC, Fowles SE, Kumar R, Lang U, Wargenau M and Sourgens H (1994) *Sertraline, like other SSRIs, is a Significant Inhibitor of Desipramine Metabolism* in vivo. Poster presented at the ACNP meeting in Puerto Rico, 12 December 1994.

5

Efficacy of selective serotonin re-uptake inhibitors in acute depression

William F. Boyer and John P. Feighner

Since the first edition of this book there have been a huge number of studies of the efficacy of SSRIs in various forms of depressive illness. In a few areas efficacy issues appear relatively well settled. In others the efficacy data is incomplete but provocative. This chapter briefly reviews this literature, in the hope of providing a sense of where this area of study has been and where it needs to go.

MAJOR DEPRESSION

A review of all SSRI efficacy studies in major depression would now require a book in itself. However a number of investigators have presented meta-analyses of these studies. Anderson and Tomenson (1994) conducted one such review. They examined 54 well-designed studies and were able to extract data which allowed comparison of the efficacy of SSRIs both individually and as a group, in inpatients and outpatients, with high or low severity of depression and versus TCAs with both serotonergic and noradrenergic activity or relatively "pure" noradrenergic TCAs. There were no significant differences in efficacy between SSRIs and TCAs whether SSRIs were considered individually or together. There were also no differences according to initial severity of depression. These findings correspond to other

Selective Serotonin Re-uptake Inhibitors: Advances in Basic Research and Clinical Practice, Second Edition, Edited by J.P. Feighner and W.F. Boyer
© 1996 John Wiley & Sons Ltd

meta-analyses of SSRI efficacy data (Bech *et al.*, 1994; Bech, 1989; Bech and Ciadella, 1992; Byrne, 1989; Kasper *et al.*, 1992).

In Anderson and Tomenson's (1994) meta-analysis, SSRIs as a group were slightly less effective than TCAs among inpatients. This was principally accounted for by the lower efficacy of paroxetine in this group. This in turn rested largely with a study done by the Danish University Antidepressant Group (DUAG) (1980) in which clomipramine was used as the control TCA. This may not have been a generalizable finding. Combined data from six double-blind comparisons of paroxetine and clomipramine ($N = 309$) show no significant differences in antidepressant efficacy (Link, 1992; Hunter, 1995). Others have noted that the relatively poor showing of several investigational antidepressants in DUAG studies was due to an unusually high response rate to clomipramine (Vestergaard *et al.*, 1993). Two additional studies of paroxetine in hospitalized depressed patients were published about the time that Anderson and Tomenson's review was presented. These studies showed no significant differences in antidepressant efficacy between paroxetine and either imipramine or amitriptyline (Aiminen *et al.*, 1994; Stuppaeck *et al.*, 1994).

This discussion has so far concentrated on comparisons between SSRIs and tri- or tetracyclic antidepressants. An equally important question is how the SSRIs compare to each other. Two large trials ($N = 108$ and $N = 250$) of fluoxetine versus sertraline have been reported. These two studies support equivalent antidepressant efficacy (Aguglia *et al.*, 1993; Martindale *et al.*, 1993). A number of trials of fluoxetine versus paroxetine have also been reported. They have included both variable dose and fixed dose comparisons (20 mg paroxetine versus 20 mg fluoxetine). These studies also show similar antidepressant efficacy for these two SSRIs. They also suggest there may be an earlier onset of action with paroxetine (De-Wilde *et al.*, 1993; Tignol, 1992; Shrivastava *et al.*, 1993; Garcia-Barriga, 1994; Geretsegger *et al.*, 1994).

SEVERE DEPRESSION AND MELANCHOLIA

There is an impression among some psychiatrists that SSRIs may not work as well as TCAs in severe depression and/or melancholia. Relatively few studies support this viewpoint. One of these was the paroxetine DUAG study just discussed. Roose and colleagues cited this study as consistent with the poor response rate they obtained with fluoxetine in medically ill elderly patients with melancholia (10%). This was considerably less than the 83% response rate they obtained in a nortriptyline-treated historical control group and lower than almost all reported fluoxetine trials (Roose *et al.*, 1994). In a third study Danjou (1994) reported that the atypical antidepressant venlafaxine (not a TCA) was significantly superior to fluoxetine in melancholia.

On the other hand there is considerable evidence to support the SSRIs' efficacy in melancholia and severe depression. Pande and Sayler (1993) compared the efficacy of fluoxetine, TCAs, and placebo in 3183 patients with mild (HAMD < 17), moderate (HAMD 18–24), or severe depression (HAMD > 25). Fluoxetine was significantly superior to placebo within all three severity subgroups. There were also no significant differences in improvement or response rates between fluoxetine and TCAs within all three subgroups (Pande and Sayler, 1993).

Another study which supports the efficacy of SSRIs in melancholia is an eight-week, multicentre, double-blind investigation of 89 outpatients with DSM III R major depression. Fifty-two of these patients also met criteria for melancholia. For the total group fluoxetine was significantly superior to placebo. When the diagnostic subgroups were examined fluoxetine remained significantly superior to placebo among the melancholic patients, but not those without melancholia (Heiligenstein *et al.*, 1994). In another study, Ginestet (1989) reports to no significant differences between fluoxetine and clomipramine in the treatment of 50 inpatients suffering from DSM III R melancholia.

Combined data from fluvoxamine trials indicate that the response rate to fluvoxamine is comparable to that seen with tri- and tetracyclic antidepressants (24%) and greater in severely depressed patients than in patients with mild or moderate illness (Mendlewicz, 1992). Fluvoxamine is also clearly effective in melancholia. Feighner and colleagues (1989) employed fluvoxamine in a six-week double-blind study among severely depressed inpatients. All but one patient also fulfilled DSM III criteria for melancholia. Fluvoxamine was superior to both imipramine and placebo on the Hamilton Depression Scale, CGI severity of illness and BPRS total score. Similarly, Svestka and colleagues (1992) reported that fluvoxamine was very effective in an open trial of 50 hospitalized depressed patients with DSM III R melancholia.

Bouchard and colleagues (1987) compared citalopram with maprotiline in a six-week double-blind trial of 96 depressed patients. There was a significant reduction in depression scores in both groups with no significant difference between active drugs, whether the patient groups were considered as a whole or as melancholic or non-melancholic groups.

Lapierre (1991) reported the results of three 6–8 week studies of sertraline versus amitriptyline in major depression. Sertraline was comparable to amitriptyline and efficacy was found in both moderately and severely depressed patients as well as those with and without melancholia.

Data concerning the efficacy of paroxetine in severe depression have already been discussed. Available data also suggest its efficacy in melancholia. A meta-analysis of paroxetine data ($N = 178$) showed that it was significantly superior to placebo ($N = 66$) in the treatment of melancholia. A meta-analysis of severely depressed hospitalized patients (HAMD $\geqslant 25$) included 109 paroxetine treated patients and 107 patients treated with a tricyclic or tetracyclic control antidepressant. Paroxetine and active controls showed comparable efficacy (Tignol *et al.*, 1992).

These studies found that SSRIs are as effective as TCAs in severe or melancholic depression. This is also supported by the meta-analysis of all major SSRI versus tricyclic studies conducted by Anderson and Tomenson (1994) discussed in the previous section.

BIPOLAR DEPRESSION

Relatively few studies of the treatment of bipolar depression have been performed. This is probably due to greater difficulty in recruiting patients as well as ethical concerns about precipitation of mania or rapid cycling. All of the SSRIs have been associated with precipitation of mania, although the risk of a manic reaction may be less than with TCAs (Settle and Settle, 1984; Lebegue, 1987; Rasmussen, 1991; Burrai *et al.*, 1991; Dorevitch *et al.*, 1993; Ghaziuddin, 1994; Bryois and Ferrero, 1994).

Cohn and colleagues (1989) conducted a six-week, double-blind comparison of fluoxetine, imipramine and placebo in 89 patients with bipolar depression. Endpoint analysis showed that 86% of the fluoxetine patients improved versus 57% of imipramine and 38% of placebo-treated patients. Only 7% of fluoxetine versus 30% of imipramine patients discontinued because of side-effects. In another series 42 of 60 (70%) patients with bipolar disorder in the depressive phase responded to 20–60 mg/day of fluoxetine for eight weeks (Ambrosio *et al.*, 1992).

Rasmussen (1991) compared the incidence of mania with paroxetine, placebo, and comparison drugs for unipolar patients and those with a history of mania. The results are shown in Table 1.

Table 1. Incidence of mania associated with paroxetine, placebo and active control.

Group	Unipolar	Bipolar
Paroxetine	0.9% (27/2829)	2% (3/134)
Active control	0.5% (4/776)	11% (10/86)
Placebo	0.4% (2/554)	

The difference between active control and paroxetine for bipolar patients was statistically significant ($p < 0.05$). It was conjectured that paroxetine may have a lower risk of precipitating mania than convenitional antidepressants (Rasmussen, 1991).

Peet (1994) calculated the rate of treatment-emergent switch into mania from all available clinical trial data on the selective serotonin re-uptake inhibitors: fluoxetine, fluvoxamine, paroxetine, and sertraline, relative to groups treated with TCAs or placebo. In predominantly unipolar depressives, the rate of manic switch was less than 1% and differences between drugs and placebo were statistically but not clinically significant. In bipolar depressives, manic switch occurred substantially more often with TCAs (11.2%) than with SSRIs (3.7%) or placebo (4.2%).

ATYPICAL DEPRESSION

Pande and colleagues (1992) reported that fluoxetine was as effective as, and better tolerated than phenelzine in patients with mood-reactive atypical depression as defined by the Quitkin *et al* criteria. They studied 40 patients, whom they treated with fluoxetine (20–60 mg/day) or phenelzine (45–90 mg/day). Beham and colleagues (1994) studied 40 patients with DSM III R atypical depression whom they randomly assigned to sertraline or clomipramine. The results showed a non-significant trend in favour of sertraline. In another study (Stratta *et al.*, 1991) imipramine and fluoxetine were comparable in the treatment of 32 randomly assigned patients with atypical depression as defined by Quitkin (Quitkin *et al.*, 1993). Fluoxetine however had a greater effect on atypical symptoms.

Simpson and DePaulo (1991) used fluoxetine to treat the chronic atypical depression in 16 bipolar II outpatients. These patients had been depressed for an average of 5.3 years prior to starting fluoxetine and had had poor responses to tricyclics, MAOIs, and lithium. Ten of the 13 patients who took fluoxetine for 10 or more months had a good or very good response. Only one patient discontinued fluoxetine because of side-effects.

DEPRESSION WITH PROMINENT ANXIETY

There may be concern about prescribing an SSRI for patients with prominent anxiety, since anxiety may itself be a side-effect of the medication. Systematically collected data do not support this concern, however. Filteau and colleagues (1992) analysed data from 10 studies of SSRIs (sertraline, zimelidine, fluvoxamine, fluoxetine), selective noradrenergic uptake inhibitors (desipramine, maprotiline, oxaprotiline), mixed uptake inhibitors (amitriptyline, imipramine) and partial 5-HT_2 antagonists (ritanserin, trazodone, nefazodone). The data showed no differences between these classes in their efficacy in agitated or retarded depressives. In a subsequent analysis the same investigators (1993) found that SSRI responders tended to be initially *more* anxious and agitated than non-responders.

Beasley and colleagues (1991) reviewed data from 706 outpatients with DSM III major depression treated with either high-dose fluoxetine (median 80 mg/day) or imipramine (median 200 mg/day). Imipramine and fluoxetine were comparable in overall antidepressant effect as well as in reduction of sleep disturbance and scores on the anxiety/somatization factor. Baseline psychomotor state predicted activation–sedation side-effects only for imipramine, which caused more sedation in patients with psychomotor retardation at baseline. Reduction in sleep disturbance and anxiety was independent of baseline psychomotor agitation or retardation. However there was a trend ($p = 0.092$) for more drug discontinuations due to activation for fluoxetine than imipramine.

Tollefson and colleagues (1994) conducted a similar meta-analysis to determine whether comorbid anxiety affected efficacy or predisposed patients to specific adverse events. Data were evaluated from 19 randomized, double-blind clinical trials comparing fluoxetine with placebo, a TCA or both in 3183 patients with major depression. Patients were characterized as initially anxious or non-anxious on the basis of the HAMD anxiety/somatization factor. Fluoxetine was significantly more effective than placebo in treating both anxious and non-anxious major depression. Fluoxetine was also significantly more effective than placebo in reducing the HAMD anxiety/somatization factor score. The overall efficacy of fluoxetine and TCAs was comparable in all subgroups.

Dunbar and Fuell (1992) assessed the effect of paroxetine on anxiety and agitation associated with depression. Data from short-term clinical trials of paroxetine ($N = 2963$), placebo ($N = 554$) and active control ($N = 1151$), were compared. Neither paroxetine nor active control caused new anxiety symptoms. Paroxetine had a more robust effect in reducing baseline symptoms of agitation compared to active control (Hunter, 1995). There was also no difference between the three groups in adverse events indicative of increased arousal. Furthermore the use of major and minor tranquillizers in the paroxetine and active control groups was similar.

DYSTHYMIA

Because of the similarities between the diagnostic criteria for major depression and dysthymia one of the difficulties in studying this area is to select patients without major depression, i.e. "pure" dysthymia. Nevertheless several such studies or case series utilizing SSRIs have been reported. Hellerstein and colleagues (1993) conducted a randomized double-blind study of fluoxetine versus placebo in the treatment of 35 patients with "pure" dysthymia. Fluoxetine was significantly superior to placebo in this sample.

Rosenthal and coworkers (1992) reported that 12 of 17 patients (71%) with "pure" dysthymia responded to fluoxetine or trazodone. Lapierre and colleagues (1994) found a 73% response rate among 52 dysthymic patients treated openly with fluoxetine. Nobler and colleagues (1994) reported very similar results (75% responders) in a sample of 12 elderly patients with dysthymia who were treated with fluoxetine.

Dunner and Schmaling (1954) reported an interim analysis of a trial of fluoxetine versus cognitive therapy in 21 patients with dysthymia. Both treatments appeared to be equally effective. Fluoxetine was also as effective as tianeptine, a selective promoter of serotonin uptake, in a mixed group of 206 outpatients with either DSM III R major depression or dysthymia (Delalleau *et al.*, 1994).

Little has been published on the use of other SSRIs in dysthymia. Lee and colleagues (1994) reported that sertraline and amitriptyline were equally effective in a sample of 29 patients with dysthymia, although the ability to detect a true difference with such a small sample is low. Phillip and colleagues (1994) compared paroxetine and maprotiline in a six-week double-blind study of 245 patients with RDC minor depression, which is related to dysthymia. Paroxetine was significantly or numerically superior on a number of outcome measures.

GERIATRIC DEPRESSION

There is a large literature concerning SSRIs in geriatric depression. Fluoxetine has been reported to be equivalent to amitriptyline (Altamura *et al.*, 1989a), doxepin (Feighner and Cohn, 1985) and mianserin (Tollefson *et al.*, 1993) and showed a trend toward superiority in a small study which compared it to trazodone (Owley and Flaherty, 1994).

Paroxetine was found to be equivalent to doxepin (Cohn *et al.*, 1992), clomipramine (Guillibert *et al.*, 1989; Pelicier and Schaeffer, 1993), amitriptyline (Hutchison *et al.*, 1992; Altamura *et al.*, 1989b) and mianserin (Dorman *et al.*, 1990) in depressed geriatric patients. Paroxetine was found to be superior to fluoxetine in one study of elderly depressives (Geretsegger *et al.*, 1994). Fluvoxamine was reported to be equivalent to mianserin (Phanjoo *et al.*, 1989) and dothiepin (Rahman *et al.*, 1991) and superior to fluoxetine (Owley and Flaherty, 1994). However in one study fluvoxamine did not perform as well as moclobemide had in another investigation (Bocksberger *et al.*, 1992). In light of the issue of the efficacy of SSRIs in severe depression it is worth noting that several of these studies were of depressed inpatients (Altamura *et al.*, 1989a, b; Dorman *et al.*, 1990; Phanjoo *et al.*, 1989; Rahman *et al.*, 1991; Bocksberger *et al.*, 1992).

Relatively little has been published concerning sertraline and citalopram in geriatric depression. Sertraline was found to be largely equivalent to amitriptyline in a large ($N = 241$) multi-centre study. Amitriptyline was significantly superior on one variable (Cohn *et al.*, 1990). Citalopram was significantly superior to placebo in another large ($N = 149$) multicentre study of depressed geriatric patients (Nyth *et al.*, 1992).

Only two case series reported essentially negative results with SSRIs in geriatric depression. The study by Roose and colleagues (1994) has already been described. These investigators published their experience with a group of medically ill depressed patients who were treated with fluoxetine. The response rate of fluoxetine-treated patients (10%) was significantly lower than that of a historical control group treated with nortriptyline (83%). Giakas and colleagues (1993) found only three of 11 fluoxetine-treated elderly depressed patients responded to fluoxetine versus none of the 13 who were treated with bupropion. Together these reports do not go far to contradict the positive results in the larger number of better-controlled studies.

CHILDHOOD AND ADOLESCENT DEPRESSION

Whether antidepressant medication is superior to placebo in childhood depression remains unsettled (Keller *et al.*, 1991). A significant reason for this may be the reluctance of pharmaceutical companies to fund large trials with depressed children and adolescents. The literature concerning SSRI use in children and adolescents reflects this state of affairs. Published studies are small, and do not have the advantage of the common methodology employed in multi-centre trials.

Simeon and colleagues (1990) enrolled 40 patients, aged 13–18, in an eight-week double-blind placebo controlled trial of fluoxetine, 40–60 mg per day. Approximately two-thirds showed moderate or marked improvement with both treatments. Fluoxetine was superior to placebo on all measures except sleep disorder, but none of the differences was significant. However, with a sample this size there would have to be approximately a 60% difference in efficacy to have even a 50% chance of detecting it!

Cohen and colleagues (1991) reviewed records of 40 adolescent inpatients, most of whom had a depressive disorder, who were treated with fluoxetine on an inpatient unit. There was a clinical and statistically significant decrease in CGI severity of illness ratings. Seventy-seven percent of patients manifested some side-effects, which were not connected to dose (5–60 mg/day).

Apter and colleagues (1994) treated 20 adolescent inpatients, aged 13–18 years, in an eight-week, open-label trial of fluvoxamine for patients with OCD ($N = 14$) or major depressive disorder (MDD) ($N = 6$) with daily doses in the range 100–300 mg. Fluvoxamine appeared effective in decreasing depression and bulimic symptoms.

A preliminary study, Rodriguez-Ramos *et al.* (1996) demonstrates that paroxetine is effective and well tolerated in adolescent patients with depression.

SEASONAL AFFECTIVE DISORDER

Seasonal affective disorder (SAD) is a relatively newly recognized variant of depressive illness. To date there has been only one published case series concerning SSRI use in SAD. In this study fluoxetine was as effective as light treatment in a sample of 40 SAD patients (Kasper *et al.*, 1994).

DISCUSSION

The SSRIs may be effective in a variety of depressive subtypes. In this they are similar to monoamine oxidase inhibitors but lack the safety concerns which limit the MAOIs' usefulness. It is not surprising that the best evidence for the efficacy of SSRIs exists for major depression since regulatory agencies approve antidepressants for the treatment of this disorder. There is also good evidence for their efficacy in melancholia and geriatric depression. The efficacy of SSRIs in depressed patients with prominent anxiety is worth emphasizing, because it runs counter to clinical intuition. In fact there is a suggestion that patients with prominent anxiety and/or agitation may respond better than those without.

Several areas, such as treatment of seasonal affective disorder and depression in children and adolescents, clearly require more study. The efficacy of SSRIs versus newer agents such as mixed serotonin-norepinephrine uptake inhibitors also deserves more attention. One may expect the literature concerning the proper place of SSRIs in depression to continue to grow and evolve.

REFERENCES

Aguglia E, Casacchia M, Cassano GB, Faravelli C, Ferrari G, Giordano P, *et al* (1993) Double-blind study of the efficacy and safety of sertraline versus fluoxetine in major depression. *Int Clin Psychopharmacol* **8**, 197–202.

Altamura AC, Percudani M, Guercetti G and Invernizzi G (1989a) Efficacy and tolerability of fluoxetine in the elderly: a double-blind study versus amitryptiline. *Int Clin Psychopharmacol* **4 (Suppl 1)**, 103–106.

Altamura AC, De-Novellis F, Guercetti G, Invernizzi G, Percudani M and Montgomery SA (1989b) Fluoxetine compared with amitriptyline in elderly depression: a controlled clinical trial. *Int J Clin Pharmacol Res* **9**, 391–396.

Ambrosio LA, Buccomino D, Filippo A, Filippo P, Marchese G, Barrese E, *et al* (1992) Bipolar disorder: clinical trials with fluoxetine. *Minerva Psichiatr* **33**, 305–312.

Anderson I and Tomenson B (1994) *A Meta-analysis of the Efficacy of Selective Serotonin Reuptake Inhibitors Compared to Tricyclic Antidepressants in Depression.* Presented at the XIX CINP meeting, Washington, DC, 1994.

Apter A, Ratzoni G, King RA, Weizman A, Iancu I, Binder M, *et al* (1994) Fluvoxamine open-label treatment of adolescent inpatients with obsessive–compulsive disorder or depression. *J Am Acad Child Adolesc Psychiatry* **33**, 342–348.

Arminen SL, Ikonen U, Pulkkinen P, Leinonen E, Mahlanen A, Koponen H, *et al* (1994) A 12-week double-blind multi-centre study of paroxetine and imipramine in hospitalized depressed patients. *Acta Psychiatr Scand* **89**, 382–389.

Beasley CM, Sayler MEU, Bosomworth JC and Wernicke JF (1991) High-dose fluoxetine: efficacy and activating-sedating effects in agitated and retarded depression. *J Clin Psychopharmacol* **11**, 166–174.

Bech P (1989) Clinical properties of citalopram in comparison with other antidepressants: a quantitative metanalysis. In: Montgomery S-A (ed) *Citalopram: the New Antidepressant from Lundbeck Research*, pp 56–68. Excerpta Medica, Amsterdam.

Bech P and Cialdella P (1992) Citalopram in depression—meta-analysis of intended and unintended effects. *Int Clin Psychopharmacol* **6 (Suppl 5)**, 45–54.

Bech P, Tollefson G, Cialdella P, Birkett M (1994) *A Meta-analysis of Controlled Fluoxetine Trials.* Presented at the XIX CINP meeting, Washington, DC, 1994.

Beham P, Berti C and Doogan DP (1994) *Sertraline and Clomipramine in Atypical Depression—A Double Blind Study.* Presented at the XIX CINP Meeting, Washington, DC, 1994.

Bocksberger PH, Gachoud JP, Richard J and Dick P (1992) Comparison of the efficacy and tolerability of moclobemide and fluvoxamine in elderly patients. *Clin Neuropharmacol* **15 (1 Suppl B)**, 146.

Bouchard JM, Delaunay J, Delisle JP, Grasset N, Mermberg PF, Molczadzki M, *et al* (1987) Citalopram versus maprotiline: a controlled, clinical multicentre trial in depressed patients. *Acta Psychiatr Scand* **76**, 583–592.

Bryois C and Ferrero F (1994) Mania induced by citalopram. *Arch Gen Psychiatry* **51**, 662–663.

Burrai C, Bocchetta A and del-Zompo M (1991) Mania and fluvoxamine [letter]. *Am J Psychiatry* **148**, 1263–1264.

Byrne MM (1989) Meta-analysis of early phase II studies with paroxetine in hospitalized depressed patients. *Acta Psychiatr Scand* **80 (Suppl 350)**, 138–139.

Cohen LS, Schneider O, Rubin L, Nandi D and Bonn D (1991) *Fluoxetine in Adolescent Psychiatric Inpatients*. Presented at the American Psychiatric Association Annual Meeting, 1991.

Cohn CK, Shrivastava R, Mendels J, Cohn JB, Fabre LF, Claghorn JL, *et al.* (1990) Double-blind multicenter comparison of sertraline and amitriptyline in elderly depressed patients. *J Clin Psychiatry* **51 (Suppl B)**, 28–33.

Cohn JB, Collins G, Ashbrook E and Wernicke JF (1989) A comparison of fluoxetine, imipramine and placebo in patients with bipolar depressive disorder. *Int Clin Psychopharmacol* **4**, 313–322.

Cohn J, Cohn C, Dunner D, Feighner JP, Feive RF, Halikas J, *et al.* (1992) Two combined, multicenter double-blind studies of paroxetine and doxepin in geriatric patients with major depression. *J Clin Psychiatry* **52 (Suppl 2)**, 57–60.

Danish University Antidepressant Group (1990) Paroxetine: a selective serotonin reuptake inhibitor showing better tolerance, but weaker antidepressant effect than clomipramine in a controlled multicenter study. *J Affect Disord* **18**, 289–299.

Danjou P (1994) *A Randomised, Double-blind, Comparison of Venlafaxine and Fluoxetine in Inpatients with Major Depression and Melancholia*. Presented at the XIX CINP meeting, Washington, DC, 1994.

Delalleau B, Alby JM, Cabane J and Ferreri M (1994) *Efficacy and Safety of Tianeptine (T) in Major Depressive Disorder and in Dysthymia with Somatic Complaints: Double-Blind Study vs Fluoxetine (F)*. Presented at the XIX CINP Meeting, Washington, DC, 1994.

De-Wilde J, Spiers R, Mertens C, Bartholome F, Schotte G and Leyman S (1993) A double-blind, comparative, multicentre study comparing paroxetine with fluoxetine in depressed patients. *Acta Psychiatr Scand* **87**, 141–145.

Dorman T, Clarke A and Vince MJ (1990) A double blind study comparing the efficacy, tolerability and effects on sleep of paroxetine and mianserin in elderly depressed hospital patients. *17th CINP Congress Abstracts* **1**, 78.

Dorevitch A, Frankel Y, Bar-Halperin A, Aronzon R and Zilberman L (1993) Fluvoxamine-associated manic behavior: a case series. *Ann Pharmacother* **27**, 1455–1457.

Dunbar GC and Fuell DL (1992) The anti-anxiety and anti-agitation effects of paroxetine in depressed patients. *Int Clin Psychopharmacol* **6 (Suppl 4)**, 81–90.

Dunner DL and Schmaling KB (1994) *Treatment of Dysthymia: Fluoxetine versus Cognitive Therapy*. Presented at the XIX CINP Meeting, Washington, DC, 1994.

Feighner JP, Boyer WF, Meredith CH and Hendrickson GG (1989) A placebo-controlled inpatient comparison of fluvoxamine maleate and imipramine in major depression. *Int Clin Psychopharmacol* **4**, 239–244.

Feighner JP and Cohn JB (1985) Double-blind comparative trials of fluoxetine and doxepin in geriatric patients with major depressive disorder. *J Clin Psychiatry* **46 (3 Pt 2)**, 20–25.

Filteau MJ, Lapierre YD, Bakish D and Blanchard B (1992) *Clinical Profiles of Antidepressants: A Meta-analysis on 400 Patients*. Presented at the American Psychiatric Association Annual Meeting, San Francisco, 1992.

Filteau M-J, Baruch P, Bakish D, Blanchard A, Pourcher E and Lapierre YD (1993) *Specific Serotonin Reuptake Inhibitors and Agitated Depression*. Presented at the American Psychiatric Association Annual Meeting, San Francisco, 1993.

Garcia-Barriga AOC (1994) *A Double-Blind Study With Paroxetine vs Fluoxetine in Depressive Patients*. Presented at the Society for Biological Psychiatry Annual Meeting, Phil, PA.

Geretsegger C, Bohmer F and Ludwig M (1994) Paroxetine in the elderly depressed patient: Randomized comparison with fluoxetine of efficacy, cognitive and behavioural effects. *Int Clin Psychopharmacol* **9**, 25–29.

Ghaziuddin M (1994) Mania induced by sertraline in a prepubertal child [letter]. *Am J Psychiatry* **151**, 944.

Giakas AUWJ, Miller HL, Hensala JD, Rohrbaugh R, Salomon RM, Licinio J, *et al.* (1993) *Fluoxetine versus Bupropion in Geriatric Depression.* Presented at the American Psychiatric Association Annual Meeting, San Francisco..

Ginestet D (1989) Fluoxetine in endogenous depression and melancholia versus clomipramine. *Int Clin Psychopharmacol* **4 (Suppl 1)**, 37–40.

Guillibert E, Pelicier Y, Archambault JP, Chabannes G, Clerc G, Desvilles M, *et al.* (1989) A double-blind, multicentre study of paroxetine versus clomipramine in depressed elderly patients. *Acta Psychiatr Scand* **80 (Suppl 350)**, 132–134.

Heiligenstein JH, Tollefson GD and Faries DE (1994) Response patterns of depressed outpatients with and without melancholia: A double-blind, placebo-controlled trial of fluoxetine versus placebo. *J Affect Disord* **30**, 163–173.

Hellerstein DJ, Yanowitch P, Rosenthal J, Samstag LW, Mauer M, Kasch K, *et al.* (1993) A randomized double-blind study of fluoxetine versus placebo in the treatment of dysthymia. *Am J Psychiatry* **150**, 1169–1175.

Hunter B (1995) *Paroxetine vs Clomipramine in Primary Care Patients with Depression and Associated Anxiety.* Presented at the ECNP Congress, 1–4 October, Venice.

Hutchinson DR, Tong S, Moon CA, Vince M and Clarke A (1992) Paroxetine in the treatment of elderly depressed patients in general practice: a double-blind comparison with amitriptyline. *Int Clin Psychopharmacol* **6 (Suppl 4)**, 43–51.

Kasper S, Fuger J and Moller HJ (1992) Comparative efficacy of antidepressants. *Drugs* **43 (Suppl 2)**, 11–22.

Kasper S, Ruhrmann S, Martinez B and Moller Hans-J (1994) *Comparative Effectivity of Light Therapy and Pharmaco-Therapy in Seasonal and Non-Seasonal Affective Disorder.* Presented at the XIX CINP Meeting, Washington, DC, 1994.

Keller MB, Lavori PW, Beardslee WR, Wunder J and Ryan N (1991) Depression in children and adolescents: new data on "undertreatment" and a literature review on the efficacy of available treatments. *J Affect Disord* **21**, 163–171.

Lapierre YD (1991) Controlling acute episodes of depression. *Int Clin Psychopharmacol* **6 (Suppl)**, 23–35.

Lapierre YD, Ravindran AV and Bakish D (1994) *Serotonergic Agents in Primary Dysthymia.* Presented at the XIX CINP Meeting, Washington, DC, 1994.

Lebegue B (1987) Mania precipitated by fluoxetine. *Am J Psychiatry* **144**, 1620.

Lee MS, Kim SH, Suh KY and Kwak DI (1994) *Efficacy of Sertraline in Dysthymia.* Presented at the XIX CINP Meeting, Washington, DC, 1994.

Link C (1992) Paroxetine vs clomipramine: an overview. *Clin Neuropharmacol* **15 (Suppl B)**, 176.

Martindale JJ and Bennie E (1993) *Double-blind Study of Sertraline and Fluoxetine in Outpatients with Major Depression.* Presented at the American Psychiatric Association Annual Meeting, San Francisco, 1993.

Mendlewicz J (1992) Efficacy of fluvoxamine in severe depression. *Drugs* **43 (Suppl 2)**, 32–39.

Nobler MS, Devanand DP, Singer TM, Roose SP and Sackeim HA (1994) *Fluoxetine Treatment for Elderly Patients with Dysthymic Disorder: A Pilot Study.* Presented at the American Psychiatric Association Annual Meeting, Philadelphia, 1994.

Nyth AL, Gottfries CG, Lyby K, Smedegaard-Andersen L, Gylding-Sabroe J, Kristensen M, *et al.* (1992). A controlled multicenter clinical study of citalopram and placebo in elderly depressed patients with and without concomitant dementia. *Acta Psychiatr Scand* **86**, 138–145.

Ottevanger EA (1993) A meta-analysis of published fluvoxamine studies in hospitalized depressed patients: A comparison with tri- and tetracyclic antidepressants. *Eur Neuropsychopharmacol* **3**, 327.

Owley T and Flaherty J (1994) New-onset narcolepsy and paroxetine. *Psychosomatics* **35**, 585.

Pande AC, Haskett RF and Greden JF (1992) Fluoxetine versus phenelzine in atypical depression. *Biol Psychiatry* **(Suppl) 31**.

Pande AC and Sayler ME (1993) Severity of depression and response to fluoxetine. *Int Clin Psychopharmacol* **8**, 243–245.

Peet M (1994) Induction of mania with selective serotonin re-uptake inhibitors and tricyclic antidepressants. *Br J Psychiatry* **164**, 549–550.

Pelicier Y and Schaeffer P (1993) Multicenter double-blind study comparing the efficacy and tolerance of paroxetine and clomipramine in reactive depression in the elderly patient. *Encephale* **19**, 257–261.

Phanjoo A, Wonnacott S, Hodgson A and Whitehead AM (1989) A study of fluvoxamine versus mianserin in elderly depressed patients. In: Stefanis CN, Soldatos CR and Rabavilas AD (eds) *Psychiatry Today: VIII World Congress of Psychiatry Abstracts*, p. 276. Elsevier, New York.

Philipp M, Benkert O, Schwarze H, Fickinger MP and Staab HJ (1994) *Comparison of Paroxetine and Maprotiline in Minor Depression.* Presented at the XIX CINP Meeting, Washington, DC, 1994.

Quitkin FM, Stewart JW, McGrath PJ, Tricamo E (1993) Columbia atypical depression: A subgroup of depressives with better response to MAOI than to tricyclic antidepressants or placebo. *Br J Psychiatry* **163** (Suppl 21, Sep), 30–34

Rahman MK, Akhtar MJ, Savla NC, Sharma RR, Kellett JM and Ashford JJ (1991) A double-blind, randomised comparison of fluvoxamine with dothiepin in the treatment of depression in elderly patients. *Br J Clin Pract* **45**, 255–258.

Rasmussen JGC (1991) *The Potential Role of Antidepressants in the Precipitation of Mania.* New Research Program and Abstracts, American Psychiatric Association Annual Meeting, New Orleans, 1991.

Rodriguez-Ramos P, de Dios Vega JL, San-Sebastián-Cabases J, Sordo-Sordo L, Mardomingo-Sanz MJ (1996) Effects of paroxetine in depressed adolescents. *Eur J Clin Res* (in press).

Roose SP, Glassman AH, Attia E and Woodring S (1994) Comparative efficacy of selective serotonin re-uptake inhibitors and tricyclics in the treatment of melancholia. *Am J Psychiatry* **151**, 1735–1739.

Rosenthal J, Hemlock C, Hellerstein DJ, Yanowitch P, Kasch K, Schupak C, *et al.* (1992) A preliminary study of serotonergic antidepressants in treatment of dysthymia. *Prog Neuropsychopharmacol Biol Psychiatry* **16**, 933–941.

Settle EC Jr and Settle GP (1984) A case of mania associated with fluoxetine. *Am J Psychiatry* **141**, 280–281.

Shrivastava RK, Shrivastava S and Overweg N (1993) *Efficacy Trial: Paroxetine and Fluoxetine in Depression.* Presented at the American Psychiatric Association Annual Meeting, San Francisco, 1993.

Simeon JG, Dinicola VF, Ferguson HB and Copping W (1990) Adolescent depression: a placebo-controlled fluoxetine treatment study and follow-up. *Prog Neuropsychopharmacol Biol Psychiatry* **14**, 791–795.

Simpson SG and DePaulo JR (1991) Fluoxetine treatment of bipolar II depression. *J Clin Psychopharmacol* **11**, 52–54.

Stratta P, Bolino F, Cupillari M and Casacchia M (1991) A double-blind parallel study comparing fluoxetine with imipramine in the treatment of atypical depression. *Int Clin Psychopharmacol* **16**, 193–196.

Stuppaeck CH, Geretsegger C, Whitworth AB, Schubert H, Platz T, Konig P, *et al.* (1994) A multicenter double-blind trial of paroxetine versus amitriptyline in depressed inpatients. *J Clin Psychopharmacol* **14**, 241–246.

Svestka J, Ceskova E, Rysanek R, Obrovska V and Kamenicka V (1992) The status of fluvoxamine among the antidepressive agents. *Cesk Psychiatr* **88**, 209–219.

Tignol J (1992) A double-blind, randomised, multicenter study comparing paroxetine 20 mg daily versus fluoxetine 20 mg daily in the treatment of adults with major depression. *Clin Neuropharmacol* **15 (1 Suppl B)**, 177.

Tignol J, Stoker MJ and Dunbar GC (1992) Paroxetine in the treatment of melancholia and severe depression. *Int Clin Psychopharmacol* **7**, 91–94.

Tollefson AUGD, Bosomworth JC, Heiligenstein JH, Schatz EJ and Albritton R (1993) *A Placebo-controlled Trial of Fluoxetine in Geriatric Major Depression.* Presented at the American Psychiatric Association Annual Meeting, San Francisco, 1993.

Tollefson GD, Holman SL, Sayler ME and Potvin JH (1994) Fluoxetine, placebo, and tricyclic antidepressants in major depression with and without anxious features. *J Clin Psychiatry* **55**, 50–59.

Vestergaard P, Gram LF, Kragh-Sorensen P, Bech P, Reisby N and Bolwig TG (1993) Therapeutic potentials of recently introduced antidepressants. Danish University Antidepressant Group. *Psychopharmacology Series* **10**, 190–198.

6

Selective serotonin re-uptake inhibitors in long-term treatment of depression

Stuart A. Montgomery

DEPRESSION AWARENESS AND THE NEED FOR TREATMENT

Successful treatment of depression depends on many different factors, including the willingness of the depressed person to seek help and the diagnostic skills and knowledge about treatment of the physician. Most important is a productive therapeutic relationship between patient and doctor which enables the patient not only to accept treatment but also to persist with it for the appropriate length of time. A variety of issues contribute to the failure to achieve successful treatment, not least of which is the stigma associated with psychiatric illness which often dissuades many individuals from seeking medical help, despite suffering major depression of a severity that clearly impairs their general functioning. Unfortunately depression is not recognized by the physician in many of those who do seek treatment, but even when depression is recognized the proportion of patients receiving treatment with pharmacotherapy in appropriate doses for an adequate period of time is very small (Keller *et al.*, 1986).

TOLERABILITY AND ACCEPTABILITY OF TREATMENT

Some patients are reluctant to accept medication because of a perception that antidepressants are associated with high levels of unpleasant side-effects. The

Selective Serotonin Re-uptake Inhibitors: Advances in Basic Research and Clinical Practice, Second Edition, Edited by J.P. Feighner and W.F. Boyer
© 1996 John Wiley & Sons Ltd

anticholinergic side-effects of the tricyclic antidepressants (TCAs) are well known and patients often find them difficult to tolerate. These side-effects are frequently cited as the reason for patients discontinuing treatment prematurely and it appears that in usual clinical practice as many as 60% of patients discontinue TCA treatment early (Johnson, 1981). These side-effects and consequent poor tolerability of TCAs also lead to subtherapeutic doses being given, particularly in primary care. Patients have difficulty tolerating the TCAs and it may be difficult or impossible in many sufferers to raise the dose to within the optimum therapeutic range.

One of the important recent advances in the treatment of depression has been the development of antidepressants that are safer than the older TCAs and that have an improved side-effect profile. The selective serotonin re-uptake inhibitors (SSRIs) were developed as antidepressants in response to the need to produce drugs that were more selective in their pharmacological effect in order to avoid the unnecessary effects on transmitter systems that do not contribute to the therapeutic response but which increase the side-effect burden.

The efficacy of the different SSRIs in the treatment of acute episodes of depression has been established in large independent clinical trial programmes that have demonstrated convincing efficacy compared with placebo and have shown efficacy of the same order as the reference TCAs used as comparators (Montgomery, 1995). The particular advantage of these antidepressants is therefore not that they demonstrate a significant increase in overall efficacy, although they may have increased efficacy in certain subgroups of depression such as obsessional depression, but that they represent a more efficient way of delivering effective treatment because of their benign side-effect profile. The direct benefit of the improved side-effect burden is that patients can be persuaded to persist with treatment at a full therapeutic dose for an adequate length of time to ensure sustained response. The advantage associated with the SSRIs compared with the TCAs has been reported in four meta-analyses of the published literature on comparisons of discontinuation from treatment because of side-effects with SSRIs compared with TCAs (Montgomery et al., 1994; Anderson and Tomenson, 1995; Montgomery and Kasper, 1995; Song et al., 1993). These show a significant improved compliance with treatment with the SSRIs compared with the TCAs despite the rather low doses of TCAs employed in the studies.

Poor compliance with medication is a serious problem as a patient who discontinues treatment because of side-effects may well lose confidence in treatment and be lost to care. The usefulness of the TCAs is limited by the difficulty in achieving good compliance with medication. Persuading patients to persist with treatment may be possible during the 4–6 weeks of the acute episode needed for the symptoms to resolve but it is likely to be a much greater problem in long-term treatment. Prolonged treatment is normally undertaken to prevent relapse of the currently treated episode or prevention of a new episode; however in this situation the patient will be even less likely to tolerate unwanted side-effects. The availability of well-tolerated antidepressants is therefore an important issue for long-term treatment.

IMPROVING THE STANDARDS FOR LONG-TERM EFFICACY

The introduction of a series of new antidepressants has been accompanied by an increase in the stringency in the standards according to which efficacy is established. Where formerly the efficacy of an antidepressant was usually demonstrated in studies lasting 4–6 weeks it is now required in the European Union that long-term efficacy is also demonstrated in placebo controlled studies. This development reflects the increasing recognition that depression is a long-term illness requiring long-term treatment and carries the advantage that long-term studies provide a more thorough test of the efficacy of a treatment. Clearly the most useful treatment is one that not only treats the acute episode of depression but which also keeps the patient well and prevents relapse. It cannot be taken for granted that an antidepressant that is effective in acute treatment is necessarily effective in long-term treatment. The remainder of this chapter will consider two aspects of long-term antidepressant therapy; continuation treatment (of the index episode) and prophylaxis against future episodes.

CONTINUATION TREATMENT WITH TCAs

Depression is not an illness that can be treated to produce a cure, at least with the antidepressants currently available. Even when the symptoms appear to have responded in acute treatment, a period of vulnerability appears to persist during which, if medication is discontinued, the symptoms of the inadequately treated episode are likely to reappear. This period of treatment needed to consolidate the response is referred to as the continuation treatment period and is thought to last for some 4–6 months. Two placebo controlled studies of imipramine and three of amitriptyline in long-term treatment carried out in the 1960s and 1970s established the efficacy of these antidepressants in preventing the relapse (Klerman *et al.*, 1974; Mindham *et al.*, 1973; Prien *et al.*, 1973; Seager and Bird, 1962; Stein *et al.*, 1980). These early studies tested efficacy in relapse prevention in discontinuation studies where responders to antidepressant treatment were randomized to placebo or antidepressant and then followed up for about six months. Not all of the studies were positive, for example one of these early studies which found amitriptyline to be effective was not able to demonstrate efficacy for imipramine. Most TCAs have not been properly tested for efficacy in proper continuation treatment studies.

In these and subsequent placebo controlled studies it has been shown that if antidepressants are discontinued early after apparent response, between 30% and 50% of patients may expect their depressive symptoms to return early in the following 4–6 months. More recently introduced antidepressants have been more thoroughly investigated in long-term treatment than was the case when the early TCAs were introduced. These long-term studies have strengthened our knowledge of the need for a period of continuation treatment to consolidate response.

SSRIs IN CONTINUATION TREATMENT

Two approaches have been taken in assessing the efficacy of SSRIs in relapse prevention, both using a discontinuation model. The efficacy of paroxetine and sertraline was assessed in long-term treatment in studies with a duration of one year (Montgomery and Dunbar, 1993; Doogan and Caillard, 1992). This study duration has the disadvantage of a potential confusion between the appearance of symptoms representing the relapse of the inadequately treated depressive episode and symptoms representing the occurrence of a new episode. The studies of continuation treatment have indicated that the majority of relapses occur relatively early in the months following discontinuation of antidepressant and that the period of consolidation of response is approximately 4–6 months. It could be expected therefore that the appearance of depressive symptoms in the latter months of a one-year study would represent a new episode of depression. The studies of paroxetine and sertraline were of sufficient size that it was possible to analyse the first four months of the study separately from the later months and therefore to assess efficacy in relapse prevention as distinct from recurrence prevention.

Paroxetine

In the study of paroxetine (Montgomery and Dunbar, 1993) 135 patients, who had at least two previous episodes of depression, responded in the acute open treatment phase of the study and were randomized to treatment with 20–30 mg paroxetine or placebo. The number of patients withdrawn from the study with a relapse of depression in the four months continuation treatment phase of the study was significantly greater in the placebo treated group than the paroxetine treated group, two of 68 compared with 13 of 67. Survival analysis, which provides a sensitive measure of efficacy, also showed a highly significant advantage for paroxetine.

Sertraline

A similar study compared sertraline with placebo in patients who had responded to acute treatment with sertraline. This study included both patients with a first episode of depression and patients with recurrent episodes. In this study of 295 patients who were randomized to sertraline or placebo the efficacy of sertraline in the prevention of relapse was demonstrated in the first four-month period of the study (Doogan and Caillard, 1992).

Citalopram

The efficacy of citalopram in long-term treatment was tested in two separate placebo controlled studies over the six-month period of continuation treatment following response of the acute episode (Montgomery *et al.*, 1993c; Robert and Montgomery, 1995). In the first of these, responders in a double-blind placebo controlled study of the efficacy of citalopram in the treatment of acute episodes of major depression (Montgomery *et al.*, 1992) were randomized to receive, double-blind, either the same dose of citalopram to which they had responded or placebo. Two doses of citalopram, 20 mg and 40 mg daily, were used in the acute treatment study so that it was possible to compare response on the different doses both in acute and in continuation treatment. A total of 147 patients who had responded to citalopram were randomized to active treatment or placebo. There were significantly fewer relapses on both citalopram 20 mg and citalopram 40 mg during the study compared with placebo. Survival analysis showed that patients receiving either the lower or the higher dose of citalopram had a significantly lower risk of relapse at 24 weeks compared with patients randomized to placebo, and there was no difference between the doses.

In the second study, a flexible dose of 20–60 mg of citalopram titrated to achieve the dose for response in the acute phase was found to sustain response significantly better than the responders randomized to placebo (Robert and Montgomery, 1995).

Fluvoxamine and fluoxetine

There are some data from continuation treatment of responders in acute treatment studies which suggest that fluvoxamine and fluoxetine are also effective in continuation treatment. The formal studies have not yet, however, been completed and it is therefore not possible to be sure of the efficacy of fluvoxamine in continuation treatment. The open treatment continuation phase of the prophylactic study of fluoxetine (Montgomery *et al.*, 1988) suggests efficacy for fluoxetine but again there is no formal placebo controlled study.

The efficacy of the SSRIs has been carefully investigated in continuation treatment relapse prevention designs. In general it seems that the efficacy of the SSRIs in relapse prevention is rather better established than the TCAs, few of which have been properly investigated.

LENGTH OF CONTINUATION TREATMENT

The reappearance of depressive symptoms in the months immediately following apparent response of an acute episode of depression if antidepressants are discontinued is a consistent finding in the early and later studies. The data provide robust evidence for the need for continuing antidepressant treatment to cover the vulnerable period following apparent response. It is now generally accepted that a period of continuation treatment is necessary and it is recommended in different consensus guidelines that all courses of antidepressant treatment continue for at least six months (Montgomery et al., 1993a, b; WHO Mental Health Collaborating Centres, 1995). Unfortunately the average length of antidepressant treatment is estimated, on the basis of prescription data, to be only six weeks and there is thus a wide discrepancy between the treatment patients receive and that which is generally considered necessary. Wider education on the benefits of adequate courses of treatment is clearly needed.

DOES THE COURSE OF PATIENTS WHO RESPOND TO PLACEBO DIFFER?

In any study of the efficacy of antidepressants in the acute treatment of depression there is an important proportion of patients who respond to placebo. The question arises whether these patients require any pharmacological treatment. The study of citalopram in relapse prevention provided some interesting information to help answer this question (Montgomery et al., 1993). In this study, to preserve blindness, the patients who responded to placebo in the acute placebo controlled study were continued double-blind on placebo in the six-month relapse prevention study and their outcome analysed separately from the other groups. This was the first blinded study of the outcome in the longer term of placebo responders.

In the follow-up period the relapse rate of the patients who had responded to placebo and continued to be treated with placebo was very similar to the patients whose treatment with citalopram was discontinued and replaced with placebo. The survival analysis of the relapse rate in the two groups showed similar rates of relapse and with a similar time course. In other words response to placebo in acute treatment in many patients tends not to be sustained. It seems likely that pharmacological treatment would be needed and would improve the later outcome. Patients who respond to placebo require careful follow up to intervene in the relapse which appears very likely to occur.

This finding is also interesting in that it answers the criticism that has been made of discontinuation studies in that a biased population may be produced by this design (Greenhouse et al., 1991). Concerns are sometimes expressed that the relapse seen in discontinuation studies may represent in some way a provocation of depression by the withdrawal of previous antidepressant treatment (Damluji and Ferguson, 1988). The finding of a similar relapse rate on placebo, whether prior response was to treatment with placebo or active drug, shows that the patients are not differentiated in this way and discontinuation studies therefore provide a valid test of efficacy.

PREVENTING NEW EPISODES OF DEPRESSION: PROPHYLAXIS OR MAINTENANCE TREATMENT

The recurrent nature of depression has tended in the past to be underestimated. It had been thought that many depressions occurred as a single episode but it seems that this optimistic view was due to a failure to follow up patients for an adequate period. More thorough studies have suggested that few depressions occur as a single episode and rates of around 80–90% are reported for recurrent depression (Angst, 1992; Lee and Murray, 1988). Depression is a serious illness and the disability and risks associated with each episode have provided the impetus to look for strategies of secondary prevention. Attention has increasingly focused on the appropriateness of long-term prophylactic treatment with antidepressants to prevent new episodes.

The advantages of safety and tolerability described for the SSRIs compared with the early TCAs which make them preferable for the continuation treatment period are even more important when very long-term, or even life-time, treatment is under consideration. As a group, the SSRIs have been very thoroughly investigated in prophylactic treatment unlike the TCAs, only one of which, imipramine, has been the subject of extensive studies. Not all TCAs that have been tested in prophylactic designs have shown efficacy and caution is therefore needed in extrapolating from efficacy in acute treatment to the longer term. For example, nortriptyline was not shown to be different from placebo in a small but well-conducted study in elderly patients (Georgotas *et al.*, 1989). The same study found that phenelzine was effective, which would suggest that the failure of nortriptyline was not just attributable to the small study size.

To be sure that an antidepressant is effective in preventing new episodes it must be tested in patients who have definitively recovered from an episode of depression. For this reason a period of continuation treatment to consolidate response should be included in studies of prophylaxis to ensure the patients included have recovered. It is unclear in an individual patient exactly how long the continuation treatment period should be but the studies that have led to the adoption of a minimum period of four months suggest that after this time very few of the appearances of depressive symptoms would be relapse of the original episode and a new episode would be more likely. An alternative method has been to analyse separately the early continuation treatment period of a study and the later period which represents the prophylactic phase of preventing new episodes. This technique, first adopted by Prien *et al.* (1984) in the NIMH imipramine studies, is now in wide use.

Fluoxetine

The long-term efficacy of fluoxetine has been tested in a group with recurrent depression with at least two episodes in five years (Montgomery *et al.*, 1988). A group of 456 patients with major depression were treated openly with fluoxetine and responders were continued for four and a half months to ensure continued response of the original episode. In the subsequent one year placebo controlled study 88 patients on fluoxetine in a dose of 40 mg, and 94 on placebo were analysed for recurrence of depression. There was a highly significant reduction in the number of new episodes of depression in the fluoxetine treated group compared with placebo where after one year more than one-half of the patients had already had a new episode of recurrent depression.

Paroxetine

The prophylactic efficacy of paroxetine was established by examining the recurrence of depression in the prophylactic phase of a one-year study separately from the continuation phase (Montgomery and Dunbar, 1993). There was a significant reduction in the rate of new episodes on paroxetine compared with placebo shown by the survival analysis over the eight-month prophylactic treatment period. The efficacy of paroxetine in prophylactic or maintenance treatment is established in this study.

Sertraline

The same approach was used to test the prophylactic efficacy of sertraline in Doogan and Caillard's (1992) long-term efficacy and safety study. In the prophylactic phase of this study there was a significant reduction in the rate of new episodes compared with placebo. This indicates that sertraline is associated with significant prophylactic or maintenance efficacy although this was a retrospective analysis.

RELATIVE EFFICACY IN PROPHYLAXIS

The studies of prophylactic treatment with SSRIs have been consistent in showing a significant advantage for the SSRI compared with placebo in reducing the risk of new episodes. There has however been some variation in the actual number of recurrences seen during the studies which could be expected from the variations in the methodology adopted. Some studies used a more demanding criterion before the recurrence of depressive symptoms was declared a new episode and this would reduce the expected recurrence rate (Montgomery et al., 1991). For this reason it is not possible to carry out a meta-analysis of studies to compare the relative efficacy of different antidepressants. Widely differing criteria for different patient populations, as well as substantial differences in the outcome criteria, make any conclusions on relative efficacy based on comparisons of different studies meaningless.

DOSE IN LONG-TERM TREATMENT

Most of the long-term treatment studies have used the full antidepressant dose and the estimate of efficacy has therefore been based on these doses. It has been the practice of some physicians to consider lowering the dose for long-term treatment when a patient has responded. In the continuation treatment period there is some evidence that lowered doses may be effective. For example in Mindham *et al.*'s (1973) study of continuation treatment with amitriptyline and imipramine a lower dose was used during continuation treatment than that to which the patients had responded during acute treatment. These doses were effective with amitriptyline although not apparently with imipramine. There is also evidence from Montgomery and colleagues' (1993) study of continuation treatment with citalopram that a lower dose may be effective in continuation treatment than is required for acute treatment. In Montgomery and colleagues' (1992) acute study preceding the continuation treatment study which used two doses, 40 mg citalopram was shown to be effective in acute depression whereas 20 mg was not significantly better than placebo. However in the six-month continuation treatment study which followed, 20 mg citalopram was effective in relapse prevention.

In prophylactic treatment the balance points to the need for full doses of antidepressants. For example a one-year study of maprotiline (Rouillon *et al.*, 1989) which compared two doses directly, found that the lower dose was significantly less effective than the higher dose (75 mg). The study of imipramine of Frank *et al.* (1990) found that patients with higher drug plasma concentrations appeared to have a better outcome. In a subsequent small study in which higher and lower doses of imipramine were compared there was an advantage for the higher dose (Frank *et al.*, 1993).

On the basis of the information currently available it appears that the maxim "the dose that gets you well keeps you well" represents sound advice.

LENGTH OF TREATMENT

It appears from the studies of the Pittsburgh group that if a patient successfully completes prophylactic treatment for one year, maintaining treatment is likely to sustain efficacy for at least a further four years with a rather low rate of further recurrence (Kupfer *et al.*, 1992). In other words, the prophylactic studies produce the most important data in the first one year of a prophylactic study. It is therefore unnecessary to conduct studies with a duration longer than one year to establish that a drug is effective in prophylaxis, provided of course that the full dose continues to be taken. Discontinuing treatment with imipramine after three years revealed the same risk of recurrence of depression as was observed at the start of the study. Prophylactic or maintenance treatment therefore can be seen to suppress the risk of recurrence only as long as the treatment is taken. The underlying risk of recurrence persists and it is therefore likely that the prophylactic treatment will need to be taken indefinitely. If patients do discontinue treatment, as they are prone to do, they should be warned that all the evidence points to the fact that the underlying risk of recurrence is high and they will need to be followed up very closely. There is unfortunately also a suggestion that when a further episode appears treatment may not be as effective as it was during the prolonged, uninterrupted prophylaxis. There are pressing reasons for patients with recurrent depression with a high recurrence rate to be encouraged to persevere with prophylactic treatment to maintain the quality of life of long periods of remission.

REFERENCES

Anderson IM and Tomenson BM (1995) Treatment discontinuation with selective serotonin reuptake inhibitors compared with tricyclic antidepressants: a meta-analysis. *BMJ* **310**, 1433–1438.

Angst J (1992) How recurrent and predictable is depressive illness? In: Montgomery SA and Rouillon F (eds), *Long-term Treatment of Depression*, pp 1–14, Wiley, Chichester.

Damluji NF and Ferguson JM (1988) Paradoxical worsening of depressive symptomatology caused by antidepressants. *J Clin Psychopharmacol* **8**, 347–349.

Doogan DP and Caillard V (1992) Sertraline in the prevention of depression. *Br J Psychiatry* **160**, 217–222.

Frank E, Kupfer DJ, Perel JM, Cornes C, Jarrett DB, Mallinger AG, Thase ME, McEachran AB and Grochocinski VJ (1990) Three-year outcomes for maintenance therapies in recurrent depression. *Arch Gen Psychiatry* **47**, 1093–1099.

Frank E, Kupfer DJ, Perel JM, Cornes C, Mallinger AG, Thase ME, McEachran AB and Grochocinski VJ (1993) Comparison of full-dose versus half-dose pharmacotherapy in the maintenance treatment of recurrent depression. *J Affect Disord* **27**, 139–145.

Georgotas A, McCue RE and Cooper TB (1989) A placebo controlled comparison of nortriptyline and phenelzine in maintenance therapy of elderly depressed patients. *Arch Gen Psychiatry* **46**, 783–786.

Greenhouse JB, Stangl D, Kupfer DJ and Prien RF (1991) Methodological issues in maintenance therapy clinical trials. *Arch Gen Psychiatry* **48**, 313–318.

Johnson DAW (1981) Depression: treatment compliance in general practice. *Acta Psychiatr Scand* **63 S290**, 447–453.

Keller MB, Lavori PW, Klerman GL, Andreasen NC, Endicott J, Coryell WS, Fawcett J, Rice JP and Hirschfeld RMA (1986) Low levels and lack of predictors of somatotherapy and psychotherapy received by depressed patients. *Arch Gen Psychiatry* **43**, 458–466.

Klerman GL, Dimascio A, Weissman A, Prusoff B and Paykel ES (1974) Treatment of depression by drugs and psychotherapy. *Am J Psychiatry* **131**, 186–191.

Kupfer DJ, Frank E, Perel JM, Cornes C, Mallinger AG, Thase ME, McEachran AB and Grochocinski VJ (1992) Five-year outcome for maintenance therapies in recurrent depression. *Arch Gen Psychiatry* **49**, 769–773.

Lee AS and Murray AM (1988) The long term outcome of Maudsley depressives. *Br J Psychiatry* **153**, 741–751.

Mindham RHS, Howland C and Shepherd M (1973) An evaluation of continuation therapy with tricyclic antidepressants in depressive illness. *Psychol Med* **3**, 5–17.

Montgomery SA, Dufour H, Brion S, Gailledreau J, Lequeille X, Ferrey G, Moron P, Parant-Lucena N, Singer L, Danion JM, Beuzen JN and Pierredoin MA (1988) The prophylactic efficacy of fluoxetine in unipolar depression. *Br J Psychiatry* **153 (suppl 3)**, 69–76.

Montgomery SA, Bebbington PE, Cowen P, Deakin W, Freeling P, Hallstrom C, Katona C, King D, Leonard B, Levine S, Phanjoo A, Peet M and Thompson C (1993a) Guidelines for treating depressive illness with antidepressants. *J Psychopharmacol* **7**, 19–23.

Montgomery SA, Racagni G, Coppen A, Bunney WE, Carlsson P, De Montigny C, Giurgea C, Hansen B, Holsboer F, Judd LL, Langer SZ, Leber P, Mendlewicz J, Post R and Shibuja T (1993b) Impact of neuropharmacology in the 1990s—strategies for the therapy of depressive illness. *Eur Neuropsychopharmacol* **3**, 153–156.

Montgomery SA, Henry J, McDonald G, Dinan T, Lader M, Hindmarch I, Clare A and Nutt D (1994) Selective serotonin reuptake inhibitors: meta-analysis of discontinuation rates. *Int Clin Psychopharmacol* **9**, 47–53.

Montgomery SA (1995) Selective serotonin reuptake inhibitors in the acute treatment of depression. In: Bloom FE and Kupfer DJ (eds), *Psychopharmacology the Fourth Generation of Progress*, pp 1043–1051, Raven Press, New York.

Montgomery SA, Doogan DP and Burnside R (1991) The influence of different relapse criteria on the assessment of long-term efficacy of sertraline. *Int Clin Psychopharmacol* **6, Suppl 2**, 37–46.

Montgomery SA and Dunbar GC (1993) Paroxetine is better than placebo in relapse prevention and the prophylaxis of recurrent depression. *Int Clin Psychopharmacol* **8**, 189–195.

Montgomery SA and Kasper S (1995) Comparison of compliance between serotonin reuptake inhibitors and tricyclic antidepressants: a meta-analysis. *Int Clin Psychopharmacol* **9 S4**, 33–40.

Montgomery SA, Rasmussen JGC, Lyby K, Connor P and Tanghoj P (1992) Dose response relationship of citalopram 20 mg, citalopram 40 mg, and placebo in the treatment of moderate and severe depression. *Int Clin Psychopharmacol* **6 S5**, 65–70.

Montgomery SA, Rasmussen JGC and Tanghoj P (1993c) A 24 week study of 20 mg citalopram, 40 mg citalopram and placebo in the prevention of relapse of major depression. *Int Clin Psychopharmacol* **8**, 181–188.

Prien RF, Kupfer DJ, Manskey PA, Small JG, Tuasou VB, Voss C and Johnson WE (1984) Drug therapy in the prevention of recurrences in unipolar and bipolar affective disorders: Report of the NIMH Collaborative Study Group comparing lithium carbonate, imipramine and a lithium carbonate-imipramine carbonate combination. *Arch Gen Psychiatry* **41**, 1096–1104.

Prien RF, Klett CJ and Caffey EM (1973) Lithium carbonate and imipramine in the prevention of affective episodes. *Arch Gen Psychiatry* **29**, 420–425.

Robert P and Montgomery SA (1995) Citalopram in doses of 20 mg to 60 mg are effective in relapse prevention: a placebo controlled 6 months study. *Int Clin Psychopharmacol* **10** (S1), 29–35.

Rouillon F, Phillips R, Serrurier D, Ansarte E and Gerard MJ (1989) Rechutes de depression unipolaire et efficacite de la maprotiline. *L'Encephale* **15**, 527–534.

Seager CP and Bird RL (1962) Imipramine with electrical treatment in depression: a controlled trial. *J Ment Sci* **108**, 704–707.

Song F, Freemantle NS, House TA, Watson P and Long A (1993) Selective serotonin reuptake inhibitors: meta-analysis of efficacy and acceptability. *BMJ* **306**, 683–687.

Stein M, Rickels K and Weise CC (1980) Maintenance therapy with amitriptyline: a controlled trial. *Am J Psychiatry* **137**, 370–371.

WHO Mental Health Collaborating Centres (1995) Pharmacotherapy of depressive disorders. A consensus statement. *J Affect Disord* **17**, 197–198.

7

Serotonin specific re-uptake inhibitors in obsessive–compulsive disorder and related disorders

Dan J. Stein and Eric Hollander

INTRODUCTION

In recent years important advances have been made in our understanding and treatment of obsessive–compulsive disorder (OCD). Two findings have been particularly significant in propelling this research. First, OCD was shown to be much more common than previously estimated, with a lifetime prevalence of 2–3% in the United States (Karno *et al.*, 1988) as well as in many other parts of the world (Weissman, 1993). Previous underestimation of the prevalence of OCD may in part have been a result of patients hiding their symptoms from families and professionals. Second, OCD was found to respond to clomipramine, a predominantly serotonergic tricyclic antidepressant, but not to desipramine, a predominantly noradrenergic re-uptake inhibitor (Zohar and Insel, 1987; Leonard *et al.*, 1989). This finding differentiates OCD from disorders such as depression, which responds to both serotonergic and noradrenergic tricyclics.

Neurobiological research on OCD has therefore paid particular attention to the role of serotonin in OCD. A subset of OCD patients may have increased levels of the serotonin metabolite 5-hydroxyindoleacetic acid (5-HIAA) in the cerebrospinal fluid (Zohar and Insel, 1987), and these levels may decrease during effective treatment with a serotonergic tricyclic (Thoren *et al.*, 1980). Pharmacological challenge with

Selective Serotonin Re-uptake Inhibitors: Advances in Basic Research and Clinical Practice, Second Edition, Edited by J.P. Feighner and W.F. Boyer
© 1996 John Wiley & Sons Ltd

the serotonin agonist, m-chlorophenylpiperazine (m-CPP) may exacerbate symptoms in a subgroup of OCD patients, and may also demonstrate neuroendocrine blunting in OCD patients compared to healthy controls (Zohar et al., 1987; Hollander et al., 1992a). These behavioural and neuroendocrine phenomena are no longer seen after treatment with clomipramine (Zohar et al., 1988). When selective serotonin re-uptake inhibitors (SSRIs) became available, it was an obvious next step to employ them in the treatment of OCD.

In this chapter we focus not only on SSRIs in the treatment of OCD, but also on their use in disorders that may be related to OCD. Advances in OCD have in turn led to increased attention to disorders with similar phenomenology and neurobiology, and to the emergence of a concept of an OCD spectrum of disorders (Jenike, 1989; Hollander, 1993; Stein and Hollander, 1993). Such disorders may include body dysmorphic disorder, self-injurious behaviour, kleptomania, compulsive shopping, pathological gambling, certain eating disorders, certain sexual disorders, depersonalization disorder, and obsessive–compulsive personality disorder (OCPD). SSRIs have successfully been used in several of these possibly related disorders.

OBSESSIVE–COMPULSIVE DISORDER

Obsessive–compulsive disorder is characterized by the presence of obsessions or compulsions (American Psychiatric Association, 1994). Obsessions are defined as recurrent and persistent thoughts, impulses, or images that are experienced, at some time during the disturbance, as intrusive and inappropriate and that cause marked anxiety or distress. In addition, these thoughts, impulses, or images are not simply the person's excessive worries about real-life problems, the person attempts to ignore or suppress or neutralize them, and the person recognizes them to be a product of his or her own mind (American Psychiatric Association, 1994).

Compulsions, on the other hand, are repetitive behaviours or mental acts that the person feels driven to perform in response to an obsession, or according to rules that must be performed rigidly. In addition, these behaviours or mental acts are aimed at preventing or reducing distress, or preventing some dreaded event or situation—but they are not connected in a realistic way with what they are designed to neutralize or prevent, or are clearly excessive. In order for the diagnosis of OCD to be given to an adult, the DSM IV specifies that at some point during the course of the disorder, the person has recognized that the obsessions or compulsions are excessive or unreasonable (American Psychiatric Association, 1994).

Several open and controlled studies have focused on the use of SSRIs in adults with OCD (Table 1). Published studies include work on fluoxetine, fluvoxamine, sertraline, zimeldine, paroxetine and citalopram. In addition, several studies of SSRIs in children and adolescents have been undertaken (Riddle et al., 1992; Apter et al., 1994). In general, the SSRIs appear to be both effective and safe for the treatment of OCD. The published trials also provide evidence that supports the clinical rule-of-thumb

Table 1. Selected studies of SSRIs in the treatment of OCD.

Study	n	t (wk)	Drug	Dosage (max mg)	Design	Effect size*
Fontaine and Chouinard, 1986	7	9	Fluoxetine	80	Open	—
Jenike et al, 1989	61	12	Fluoxetine	80	Open	—
Levine et al, 1989	44	12	Fluoxetine	80	Open	—
Leibowitz et al, 1989	34	12	Fluoxetine	80	Open	—
Kim and Dysken, 1990	12	12	Fluoxetine	40	Open	—
Pigott et al, 1990	11	10	Fluoxetine	80	Medication control	—
Montgomery et al, 1993	52	8	Fluoxetine	20	Placebo control	0.24
Montgomery et al, 1993	52	8	Fluoxetine	40	Placebo control	0.17
Montgomery et al, 1993	54	8	Fluoxetine	60	Placebo control	0.40
Tollefson et al, 1994	87	13	Fluoxetine	20	Placebo control	0.63
Tollefson et al, 1994	89	13	Fluoxetine	40	Placebo control	0.73
Tollefson et al, 1994	90	13	Fluoxetine	60	Placebo control	0.91
Goodman et al, 1990b	21	8	Fluvoxamine	300	Medication control	—
Tamimi et al, 1991	9	12	Fluvoxamine	300	Medication control	—
Perse et al, 1987	16	8	Fluvoxamine	300	Placebo control	0.44
Goodman et al, 1989a	21	6	Fluvoxamine	300	Placebo control	1.23
Jenike et al, 1990a	18	10	Fluvoxamine	300	Placebo control	0.39
Wheadon et al, 1993	259	12	Paroxetine	60	Placebo control	—
Dunbar et al, 1995	53	52	Paroxetine	60	Placebo control	—
Zohar, 1994	201	12	Paroxetine	60	Placebo control	—
Chouinard et al, 1990	43	8	Sertraline	200	Placebo control	0.53**
Fontaine et al, 1985	9	6	Zimeldine	500	Open	—

*Effect size calculated in comparison with placebo using Y-BOCS.
**Effect size calculated from the data of Jenike et al. (1990c).

in OCD; namely that patients require relatively high doses for relatively long periods of time before a medication trial can be considered adequate (Montgomery *et al.*, 1993; Tollefson *et al.*, 1994).

The question next arises of which SSRI is most effective in OCD. It may be possible, for example, to compare the effect sizes of different agents using the techniques of meta-analysis. Nevertheless, a number of confounding factors limit such cross-trial comparisons. First, while several recent studies have been of adequate duration, a number of studies have been of shorter duration. Second, studies have used a range of different SSRI doses. Finally, studies have employed a variety of different measures of symptomatic improvement, with use of the current "gold-standard" in the field, the Yale–Brown Obsessive–Compulsive Scale (Y–BOCS) (Goodman *et al.*, 1989b) limited to recent trials.

In placebo controlled trials, effect size may be calculated as the ratio of the difference between scores of the active and control groups at the end of the study and the standard deviation of the control group at the end of the study. It turns out that the mean effect size for placebo controlled clomipramine trials (Table 2) is significantly higher than that for placebo controlled fluoxetine trials (Stein *et al.*, unpublished analysis). However, this calculation involves particularly few studies, so further compromising its outcome. Indeed, head-to-head comparison of fluoxetine and clomipramine indicates that fluoxetine may be useful in some patients who are refractory to clomipramine, and vice versa (Pigott *et al.*, 1990). Similarly, there are insufficient placebo controlled trials to compare validly the efficacy of SSRIs with other antidepressants or other psychotropics, despite the well-known studies showing that clomipramine is more effective than desipramine in OCD (Table 2).

On the other hand, the finding that the effect size of clomipramine may be higher than that of fluoxetine, and demonstration of the efficacy of a range of antidepressants in OCD, is consistent with the possibility that a range of neurotransmitters other than serotonin are involved in OCD (Goodman *et al.*, 1989b). Indeed, Jenike *et al.* (1990a) have suggested that the more selective the SSRI, the less effective it is in OCD. In addition, there may also be a role for such agents as the MAOIs in the pharmacotherapy of OCD (Vallejo *et al.*, 1992).

It may be countered, however, that SSRIs are more tolerable than clomipramine in the treatment of OCD. Although OCD patients on SSRIs and clomipramine do not necessarily differ in dropout rate during clinical trials (Montgomery *et al.*, 1993), patients on SSRIs appear to have fewer adverse effects (Jenike *et al.*, 1990b). The SSRIs are therefore a valuable first-line treatment option for OCD, particularly in patient populations where anticholinergic effects are of concern. SSRIs should be used at relatively high doses for relatively long durations if the treatment trial is to be considered adequate. Dunbar *et al.* (1995) reported on 104 patients with OCD treated up to one year in a double-blind comparison with placebo. Paroxetine was significantly superior to placebo in relapse prevention. A comparison against clomipramine and placebo (Zohar, 1994) showed similar efficacy between paroxetine and clomipramine but paroxetine was better tolerated as indicated by the lower

Table 2. Selected studies of other medications in the treatment of OCD.

Study	N	t (wk)	Drug	Dosage (max mg)	Design	Effect size*
Insel et al., 1983	12	6	Clomipramine	300	Medication control	—
Zohar and Insel, 1987	10	6	Clomipramine	300	Medication control	—
Pigott et al., 1990	11	10	Clomipramine	250	Medication control	—
Pato et al., 1991	9	6	Clomipramine	250	Medication control	—
Tamimi et al., 1991	11	12	Clomipramine	300	Medication control	—
Hewlett et al., 1992	24	6	Clomipramine	250	Medication control	—
Vallejo et al., 1992	14	12	Clomipramine	225	Medication control	—
DeVaugh-Geiss et al., 1991	118	10	Clomipramine	300	Placebo control	1.41
DeVaugh-Geiss et al., 1991	134	10	Clomipramine	300	Placebo control	1.88
Joffe and Swinson, 1990	17	8	Tranylcypromine	80	Open	—
Fogelson and Bystritsky, 1991	19	12	Imipramine	max	Open	—
Insel et al., 1983	11	6	Clorgyline	30	Medication control	—
Zohar and Insel, 1987	10	6	Desipramine	300	Medication control	—
Goodman et al., 1990b	19	8	Desipramine	300	Medication control	—
Vallejo et al., 1992	12	12	Phenelzine	75	Medication control	—
Pigott et al., 1992	13	10	Trazodone	300	Placebo control	—
Jenike and Baer, 1988	14	8	Buspirone	60	Open	—
Khanna, 1988	7	12	Carbamazepine	1000	Open	—
Hermesh et al., 1990	9	6	Trazodone	500	Open	—
Pato et al., 1991	9	6	Buspirone	60	Medication control	—
Hewlett et al., 1992	20	6	Clonazepam	10	Medication control	—
Hewlett et al., 1992	22	6	Clonidine	1	Medication control	—

*Effect size calculated in comparison with placebo using Y-BOCS.

number of dropouts due to adverse effects. A fixed dose study of paroxetine 20, 40 and 50 mg (Wheadon *et al*, 1993) indicated that 40 mg is the minimum effective dose in OCD..

If a serotonin re-uptake inhibitor proves ineffective despite an adequate trial, another, perhaps less selective, serotonin re-uptake inhibitor should be considered. Patients who show only partial response to an SSRI may benefit from augmentation with serotonergic medications such as clonazepam (Hewlett *et al.*, 1992) or dopaminergic agents such as pimozide (particularly when tics are also present) (McDougal *et al.*, 1994). A trial of an MAOI should be considered when patients fail to respond to several trials of serotonin re-uptake inhibitors. Finally, cognitive–behaviour therapy may also play an important role in augmenting pharmacotherapy. Future research will hopefully provide more information on the neurobiology (Hollander *et al.*, 1993) and pharmacotherapy of the subset of OCD patients who currently remain refractory to treatment.

BODY DYSMORPHIC DISORDER AND HYPOCHONDRIASIS

Both body dysmorphic disorder (BDD) and hypochondriasis (HYP) are characterized by repetitive thoughts and behaviours relating to the body. In BDD, thoughts concern the imagined ugliness of particular body features, and behaviours include repetitive mirror checking or surgical procedures (Phillips, 1991). In HYP, thoughts concern imagined medical illness, and behaviours include repetitive physician consultations (Fallon *et al.*, 1991). As in OCD, there is increasing evidence for the prevalence of these disorders. More than one-third of OCD patients may have BDD concerns (Simeon *et al.*, unpublished data), and HYP may be present in 4–9% of medical patients (Kellner *et al.*, 1983/84).

In a series of case reports, Hollander *et al.* (1989a) found that BDD responded to selective serotonin re-uptake inhibitors (SSRIs) but not to standard tricyclics. This series has subsequently been expanded to include over 40 patients treated openly in clinical practice (Hollander *et al.*, 1993). Other investigators have reported similar findings on retrospective review of the treatment of BDD patients (Phillips *et al.*, 1993). In addition, this group found that preferential response to SSRIs occurs irrespective of whether BDD symptoms are delusional or not (McElroy *et al.*, 1993).

Fallon *et al.* (1993) reported that open label treatment of HYP patients with high-dose fluoxetine for 12 weeks resulted in significant reduction in hypochondriacal concerns. HYP may, however, also respond to other antidepressants such as imipramine (Wesner and Noyes, 1991). In patients with delusional concerns about illness, the use of SSRIs has been less well studied than that of neuroleptics (Munro and Chmara, 1982). While controlled trials of the SSRIs in both BDD and HYP are needed, these agents offer hope for patients suffering from these disorders.

NEUROLOGICAL AND DEVELOPMENTAL DISORDERS

Perhaps the first evidence that OCD had a neurobiological basis was provided by the influenza epidemic earlier this century. Patients who developed the sequela of encephalitis lethargica sometimes had both involuntary movements, presumably on the basis of basal ganglia pathology, and also obsessive–compulsive symptoms (Von Economo, 1931). More recent work has shown that OCD is seen in neurological conditions with basal ganglia pathology, including Tourette's syndrome (Hollander *et al.*, 1989b), Sydenham's chorea (Swedo *et al.*, 1989a), and Huntington's disease (Cummings and Cunningham, 1992). Conversely, studies of comorbid tics in OCD (Pitman *et al.*, 1987), neurological soft signs (Hollander *et al.*, 1990a), and brain imaging scans (Insel, 1992) have provided evidence for basal ganglia involvement in OCD.

There is some evidence that in neurological disorders with obsessive–compulsive symptoms, SSRIs are also useful. In Tourette's syndrome, SSRIs have proven useful for comorbid OCD symptoms in open label studies (Riddle *et al.*, 1990; Como and Kurlan, 1991), but not in a small double-blind study (Kurlan *et al.*, 1993). Tics themselves may not, however, respond to antidepressants, including clomipramine and desipramine (Caine *et al.*, 1979). Instead, treatment of tics typically involves the use of agents, such as neuroleptics or clonidine, that act on neurotransmitters other than serotonin (Shapiro *et al.*, 1988). The use of SSRIs for OCD symptoms in other movement disorders such as Sydenham's chorea has not been well studied. Currently, involuntary movements in this disorder are treated with neuroleptics or valproate (Shannon and Fenichel, 1990; Daoud *et al.*, 1990).

SSRIs may have a role in developmental disorders with obsessive–compulsive features. In a 10-week double-blind cross-over trial, at dosages up to 250 mg, autism was found to respond preferentially to clomipramine in comparison to desipramine (Gordon *et al.*, 1992). Clomipramine was superior to desipramine on ratings of repetitive and compulsive behaviours, as well as for core autistic symptoms. This finding supports open studies indicating efficacy for SSRIs in autism (Cook *et al.*, 1992). In contrast, in a small group of autistic patients, imipramine has been reported to worsen symptoms in some subjects (Campbell *et al.*, 1971). The usefulness of other psychotropics, such as neuroleptics or fenfluramine, in autism remains open to debate (Ornitz, 1985; Aman and Kern, 1989).

TRICHOTILLOMANIA AND COMPULSIVE SELF-INJURIOUS BEHAVIOUR

Trichotillomania (TTM) is characterized by repetitive hair-pulling. Although this symptom is redolent of OCD rituals, there are typically no preceding obsessions. In addition, whereas OCD compulsions often vary over time, in TTM there may be no compulsions other than hair-pulling. While both TTM and OCD commonly have onset in childhood or adolescence, TTM is more often seen in females (Christenson *et al.*, 1991a).

Swedo and colleagues (Swedo *et al.*, 1989b; Swedo, 1993) treated 22 TTM patients with consecutive, randomly assigned, five-week trials of clomipramine and desipramine. Dosages of medication were increased as tolerated to 250 mg a day. For each of three scales of TTM symptoms, clomipramine was significantly more effective than desipramine. Although anxiety and depression also responded more to clomipramine than desipramine, reduction in these symptoms was not clinically significant.

Research on SSRIs for TTM has provided contrasting results. Winchel *et al.* (1992) gave fluoxetine (up to 80 mg/day) to 12 TTM patients in an open 16-week trial. Compared with baseline scores, severity scores on a TTM symptom scale decreased by 34%. On average, response onset occurred at about four weeks. Koran *et al.* (1992) also found that open-label fluoxetine was effective for TTM. However, Christenson *et al.* (1991b) conducted an 18-week placebo controlled, double-blind cross-over trial of fluoxetine (up to 80 mg/day) in 21 TTM patients, and found no significant effects of active drug.

In addition to this negative finding, there is some anecdotal evidence that response to serotonin re-uptake inhibitors in TTM is lost with time (Pollard *et al.*, 1991). Furthermore, treatment of TTM with agents other than serotonergic antidepressants, including lithium, may be effective (Christenson *et al.*, 1991c). Finally, augmentation of serotonin re-uptake inhibitors with agents that act on other neurotransmitters, such as dopamine, may be necessary to maintain initial treatment response (Stein and Hollander, 1992a). Thus, while SSRIs may be a useful treatment option in TTM, other psychotropics may also prove important.

TTM has been viewed as a "compulsive" form of self-injurious behaviour, in contrast to "impulsive" self-injurious behaviours, such as skin-cutting, which are typically seen in disorders such as borderline personality disorder (Favazza and Simeon, 1995). Other compulsive self-injurious behaviours may include skin-picking and nail-biting. An immediate question is whether such behaviours also respond to SSRIs.

Skin-picking has anecdotally been reported to respond to SSRIs (Stout, 1990; Stein *et al.*, 1993). Controlled trials of SSRIs have shown efficacy for self-mutilation symptoms in some populations (Markovitz *et al.*, 1993). Furthermore, in a double-blind, cross-over trial, severe nail-biting was found to respond preferentially to clomipramine compared with desipramine (Leonard *et al.*, 1991). Although other agents, such as opiate antagonists, may also be useful in the treatment of self-injurious behaviours, studies of such drugs have often been flawed (Winchel and Stanley, 1992).

Repetitive self-injurious behaviour is also seen in metabolic disorders such as Lesch–Nyhan syndrome, and in congenital disorders such as Prader–Willi syndrome (Stein *et al.*, 1994a). There is some evidence for the efficacy of clomipramine or SSRIs for self-injurious behaviours in such disorders, although other agents may also be useful (Yaryura-Tobias and Neziroglu, 1984; Stein *et al.*, 1994a). More detailed understanding of the neurobiology of these disorders may ultimately shed light on the pathogenesis of other kinds of repetitive behaviours.

IMPULSE CONTROL DISORDERS

Trichotillomania is classified as an impulse control disorder in DSM-IV. Indeed, although the disorder has many compulsive features, it has also certain impulsive characteristics (Stein *et al.*, 1992a). Similarly, other disorders that may fall under the rubric of impulse control disorders, such as kleptomania, compulsive shopping, pathological gambling, non-paraphilic sexual addictions, and certain eating disorders, may also have both compulsive and impulsive symptomatology.

Relatively little work has, however, been done on the pharmacotherapy of such disorders. There are anecdotal reports of kleptomania (McElroy *et al.*, 1991a) and compulsive shopping (McElroy *et al.*, 1991b) responding to various antidepressants. A recent case report suggests that pathological gambling may respond to clomipramine (Hollander *et al.*, 1992b). Controlled trials of SSRIs in these impulse control disorders will hopefully provide positive information about their treatment.

The term "non-paraphilic sexual addictions" has been used to refer to sexual interests and behaviours (e.g. compulsive masturbation) that are culturally acceptable but have a frequency or intensity that interferes with the capacity for sexual intimacy (Kafka, 1991). Open trials of antidepressants including the SSRIs indicate some efficacy for the treatment of such symptoms (Kafka, 1991; Kafka and Prentky, 1992; Stein *et al.*, 1992b). Single case reports have also suggested that certain paraphilias respond preferentially to serotonin re-uptake inhibitors (Zohar *et al.*, 1994). However, in a double-blind cross-over comparison of clomipramine and desipramine in paraphilias, there was no preferential response to the serotonergic agent (Kruesi *et al.*, 1992).

It can perhaps be posited that anorexia nervosa is a "compulsive" eating disorder, whereas bulimia nervosa is an "impulsive" eating disorder. This distinction may be made on the basis of phenomenology of the two disorders, and is supported by some neurobiological data, such as increased CSF 5-HIAA in anorexia in contrast to decreased 5-HIAA in bulimia (Hsu *et al.*, 1993). Both disorders, and bulimia in particular, may show improvement with SSRIs (Wood, 1993). Other antidepressants have, however, also been used in the treatment of these disorders (Walsh and Devlin, 1992).

DEPERSONALIZATION DISORDER

Depersonalization is characterized by repetitive alteration in the perception or experience of the self or body and its relation to the world. Serotonin re-uptake blockers have been reported effective in a small series of patients (Hollander *et al.*, 1990b). Further work is, however, necessary to determine the selective efficacy of these agents, and to ascertain that improvement is not simply a result of anti-anxiety or anti-depressive effects.

OBSESSIVE–COMPULSIVE PERSONALITY DISORDER

Psychoanalytic thought has long viewed OCD as on a spectrum with obsessive–compulsive personality disorder (OCPD). In this view, patients with OCPD have a predisposition toward the development of OCD. Modern studies of personality disorders in OCD have not, however, provided evidence for such a sequence of events (Stein and Hollander, 1994). Only a relatively small percentage of OCD patients have OCPD, and this disorder does not necessarily predispose to the development of OCD.

Nevertheless, there may be some evidence for serotonergic involvement in OCPD. We compared prolactin response to fenfluramine in patients with OCPD and patients with other personality disorders and normal controls. OCPD patients had significantly blunted prolactin responses compared with the two other groups (Stein *et al.*, unpublished data). In addition, there are anecdotal reports of patients with OCPD responding to SSRIs. Controlled studies should be undertaken in this area.

DELUSIONAL OCD

Some patients with OCD have so little insight into their symptoms that they appear psychotic (Insel and Akiskal, 1986; Eisen and Rasmussen, 1993). Whether or not such patients respond as well to SSRIs as do other OCD patients requires further study. OCD patients with schizotypal personality disorder reportedly have a worse response to serotonergic agents (Baer *et al.*, 1992).

OCD symptoms are sometimes seen in schizophrenia. There are reports that such symptoms improve with serotonin re-uptake inhibitors (Zohar *et al.*, 1993), and are exacerbated by clozapine (Baker *et al.*, 1992). The pathophysiology and clinical significance of such symptoms may well be a rewarding area for further study.

ANIMAL MODELS

A comprehensive discussion of the pharmacotherapy of OCD-related disorders requires some discussion of animal analogues of OCD. While grooming behaviour in animals can be modulated by different pharmacological interventions, the animal behaviours that appear most analogous to OCD and related disorders are those seen in companion animals with disorders of grooming (Rapoport *et al.*, 1992).

Dogs often develop a condition known as acral lick dermatitis, characterized by repetitive licking and chewing of distal extremities. This disorder has been reported to respond to clomipramine (Goldberger and Rapoport, 1991) and fluoxetine (Stein *et al.*, 1992c). In an elegant series of controlled studies, Rapoport *et al* (1992) found that for OCD, clomipramine was more effective than desipramine, that fluoxetine was more effective than fenfluramine, and that sertraline was more effective than placebo. The pharmacotherapeutic overlap with OCD is dramatic. Other research has also shown that acral lick dermatitis responds to opioid antagonists (Dodman *et al.*, 1988), perhaps suggesting that further work on the opiate system in OCD is necessary.

In cats, a similar disorder is known as psychogenic alopecia. Although this disorder has received less attention than OCD, there is some evidence that it responds to dopamine blockers (Willemse *et al.*, 1994). Response of psychogenic alopecia to SSRIs requires further study—such naturalistic animal models may prove useful for psychiatric research (Stein *et al.*, 1994b).

Animal work may, for example, prove important in providing the concept of an OCD spectrum with a valid basis in neurobiology. OCD and related disorders may involve the pathological release of fixed action patterns which are hard-wired in subcortical brain nuclei. This hypothesis complements evidence that points to an important role for the basal ganglia in the mediation of OCD symptoms (Wise and Rapoport, 1989). As might be expected from the effect of SSRIs on abnormal grooming behaviours, serotonergic neurones project to the basal ganglia, where they may exert an important modulating role. A better understanding of the neurochemistry and neuroanatomy of pathological grooming behaviours may ultimately shed light on OCD and related disorders.

CONCLUSIONS

As a clinical and research heuristic, the notion of an obsessive–compulsive spectrum of disorders is extremely valuable. In the clinic it reminds the practitioner to inquire about a range of symptoms which are often seen in the same patient, it provides a useful explanatory model to inform patients' understanding of their illness, and it suggests particular kinds of specific interventions (both pharmacotherapeutic and psychotherapeutic). For the researcher, the notion of this spectrum leads to study of similarities and dissimilarities of disorders not otherwise juxtaposed. In addition, it fosters the application of biological methods that are used in OCD (e.g. pharmacological challenge paradigms) to these disorders. Finally, it leads to important pharmacotherapy dissection studies in various disorders with strategies that have proven useful in OCD (e.g. clomipramine versus desipramine) (Table 3).

However, a heuristic should not be confused with the complexities of real phenomena. From a clinical point of view, it may be suggested that more general complaints are better conceptualized as part of the human condition, rather than as specific diseases. A certain level of obsessive–compulsive behaviour may play a useful role in ordinary life. Ruminations, for example, range from intrusive symptoms through to repetitive phenomena that may be an important component of problem-solving (Martin and Tessar, 1991). Even if such repetitive phenomena are mediated by the serotonergic system, it does not therefore follow that serotonergic agents are clinically indicated. At present, while there is good evidence

Table 3. Pharmacotherapy of OCD and related disorders.

Disorder	CMI > DMI	Open-label SSRIs	Open-label Other	Double-blind SSRIs	Double-blind Other
OCD	+	+	-/+	+	-/+
BDD	?	+	-	?	?
HYP	?	+	+?	?	?
OCD in Tourette's	?	+	?	-	?
Autism	+	+	-/+	?	-/+
TTM	+	+	+/+	-	-/+
Compulsive SIB	+	+	-/+	+	?
Sexual impulsivity	-	+	+	?	?
Depersonalization	?	+	?	?	?
OCPD	?	?	?	?	?
OCD in schizophrenia	?	+	+	+	?
Acral lick dermatitis	+	+	+	+	-

for the value of SSRIs in symptoms that are markedly similar to OCD symptoms (e.g. BDD), there is less evidence for the value of such medications in more distantly related and perhaps less impairing phenomena (e.g. OCPD).

From a research viewpoint, caution should be made not to overextend the concept of a spectrum (Rasmussen, 1994). Reports that obsessive–compulsive symptoms in depression respond to serotonin re-uptake blockers, for example, although consistent with the idea that OCD and depression have features in common, cannot simply be taken to imply that depression and OCD are closely related syndromes. This is not merely a theoretical concern; the Freudian concept of OCD as a neurotic spectrum disorder may well have led to neglect of a number of features of the illness. In particular, it should be remembered that OCD is itself a heterogeneous disorder, and it is likely that there is also variance in the range of related disorders. Unitary notions of a phenomenological spectrum may result in neglect of this variation. Similarly, too much of a focus on the notion of a biological spectrum mediated by serotonergic function may lead to a downplay of other paradigms (Stein and Hollander, 1992b) and variables, aetiological and therapeutic, that researchers should be paying attention to when studying OCD and the various disorders discussed in this review.

ACKNOWLEDGEMENT

Dr Stein is funded by a grant from the Medical Research Council of South Africa and the Lundbeck Fellowship Award.

REFERENCES

Amen MG and Kern RA (1989) Review of fenfluramine in the treatment of the developmental disabilities. *J Am Acad Adolesc Psychiatry* **28**, 549–565.

American Psychiatric Association (1994) *The Diagnostic and Statistical Manual of Mental Disorders*, Fourth Edition. American Psychiatric Press, Washington, DC.

Apter A, Ratzoni G, King RA, Weizman A, Iancu I, Binder M and Riddle MA (1994) Fluvoxamine open-label treatment of adolescent inpatients with obsessive–compulsive disorder or depression. *J Am Acad Child Adolesc Psychiatry* **33**, 342–348.

Baer L, Jenike MA, Black DW, Treece C, Rosenfeld R and Greist J (1992) Effects of axis II diagnoses on treatment outcome with clomipramine in 55 patients with obsessive–compulsive disorder. *Arch Gen Psychiatry* **49**, 862–866.

Baker RW, Chengappa KN, Baird JW, Steingard S, Christ MA and Schooler NR (1992) Emergence of obsessive compulsive symptoms during treatment with clozapine. *J Clin Psychiatry* **53**, 439–442.

Caine ED, Polinsky RJ, Ebert MH, *et al.* (1979) Trial of clomipramine and desipramine for Gilles de la Tourette syndrome. *Ann Neurol* **6**, 305–306.

Campbell M, Fish B, Shapiro T, *et al.* (1971) Imipramine in preschool autistic and schizophrenic children. *J Autism Child Schizo* **1**, 267–282.

Chouinard G, Goodman W, Greist J, *et al.* (1990) Results of a double-blind placebo controlled trial of a new serotonin reuptake inhibitor, sertraline, in the treatment of obsessive–compulsive disorder. *Psychopharmacol Bull* **26**, 279–284.

Christenson GA, Mackenzie TB and Mitchell JE (1991a) Characteristics of 60 adult chronic hair pullers. *Am J Psychiatry* **148**, 365–370.

Christenson GA, Mackenzie TB, Mitchell JE, *et al.* (1991b) A placebo-controlled, double-blind crossover study of fluoxetine in trichotillomania. *Am J Psychiatry* **148**, 1566–1571.

Christenson GA, Popkin MK, Mackenzie TB, *et al.* (1991c) Lithium treatment of chronic hair pulling. *J Clin Psychiatry* **52**, 116–120.

Como PG and Kurlan R (1991) An open-label trial of fluoxetine for obsessive–compulsive disorder in Gilles de la Tourette's syndrome. *Neurology* **41**, 872–874.

Cook EH, Rowlett R, Jaselskis C and Leventhal BL (1992) Fluoxetine treatment of children and adolescents with autistic disorder and mental retardation. *J Am Acad Child Adolesc Psychiatry* **31**, 739–745.

Cummings JL and Cunningham K (1992) Obsessive–compulsive disorder in Huntington's disease. *Biol Psychiatry* **31**, 263–270.

Daoud AS, Zaki M, Shakir R, *et al.* (1990) Effectiveness of sodium valproate in the treatment of Sydenham's chorea. *Neurology* **40**, 1140–1141.

DeVeaugh-Geiss J, Katz R, Landau P, *et al.* (1991) Clomipramine in the treatment of patients with obsessive–compulsive disorder: the clomipramine collaborative study group. *Arch Gen Psychiatry* **48**, 730–738.

Dodman NH, Shuster L, White SD, Court M, Parker D and Dixon R (1988) Use of narcotic agonists to modify stereotypic self-licking, self-chewing, and scratching behavior in dogs. *J Am Vet Med Assoc* **193**, 815–819.

Dunbar GC, Steiner M, Bushnell WD, Gergel I, Wheadon DE (1995) Long term treatment and prevention of obsessive compulsive disorder with paroxetine. *Eur Neuropsychopharmacol* **5**, 372.

Eisen JL and Rasmussen SA (1993) Obsessive–compulsive disorder with psychotic features. *J Clin Psychiatry* **54**, 373–379.

Fallon BA, Javitch J and Liebowitz MR (1991) Hypochondriasis and OCD. Overlaps in diagnosis and treatment. *J Clin Psychiatry* **52**, 457–460.

Fallon BA, Liebowitz MR, Salman E, *et al.* (1993) Fluoxetine for hypochondriacal patients without major depression. *J Clin Psychopharmacol* **13**, 438–441.

Favazza A, Simeon D (1995) Self-mutilation, in Hollander E, Stein DJ (eds), *Impulsivity and Aggression*. New York: John Wiley.

Fogelson DL and Bystritsky A (1991) Imipramine in the treatment of obsessive–compulsive disorder with and without major depression. *Ann Clin Psychiatry* **3**, 233–237.

Fontaine R and Chouinard G (1986) Fluoxetine in the treatment of obsessive–compulsive disorder. *Prog Neuropsychopharmacol Biol Psychiatry* **9**, 605–608.

Fontaine R, Chouinard G and Iny L (1985) An open clinical trial of zimeldine in the treatment of obsessive–compulsive disorder. *Curr Ther Res* **37**, 326–332.

Goldberger E and Rapoport JL (1991) Canine acral lick dermatitis: Response to anti-obsessional drug clomipramine. *J Am Anim Hosp Assoc* **22**, 179–182.

Goodman, WK, Price LH, Rasmussen SA, *et al.* (1989a) Efficacy of fluvoxamine in obsessive–compulsive disorder: a double-blind comparison with placebo. *Arch Gen Psychiatry* **46**, 36–44.

Goodman WK, Price LH, Rasmussen SA, *et al.* (1989b) The Yale-Brown Obsessive Compulsive Scale. I. Development, use, and reliability. *Arch Gen Psychiatry* **46**, 1006–1011.

Goodman WK, McDougle CJ, Price LH, *et al.* (1990a) Beyond the serotonin hypothesis: a role for dopamine in some forms of obsessive–compulsive disorder? *J Clin Psychiatry* **51 (suppl)**, 36–43.

Goodman WK, Price LH, Delgado PL, *et al.* (1990b) Specificity of serotonin reuptake inhibitors in the treatment of obsessive–compulsive disorder: comparison of fluvoxamine and desipramine. *Arch Gen Psychiatry* **47**, 577–585.

Gordon CT, Rapoport JL, Hamburger SD, *et al.* (1992) Differential response of seven subjects with autistic disorder to clomipramine and desipramine. *Am J Psychiatry* **149**, 363–366.

Hermesh H, Aizenberg D and Munitz H (1990) Trazodone treatment in clomipramine-resistant OCD. *Clin Neuropharmacol* **13**, 322–328.

Hewlett WA, Vinogradov S and Agras WS (1992) Clomipramine, clonazepam, and clonidine treatment of obsessive–compulsive disorder. *J Clin Psychopharmacol* **12**, 420–430.

Hollander E (1993) *Obsessive–Compulsive Related Disorders.* American Psychiatric Press, Washington, DC.

Hollander E, Liebowitz MR, Winchel R, *et al.* (1989a) Treatment of body dysmorphic disorder with serotonin reuptake blockers. *Am J Psychiatry* **146**, 768–770.

Hollander E, Liebowitz MR and DeCaria C (1989b) Conceptual and methodological issues in studies of obsessive–compulsive and Tourette's Disorders, *Psychiatric Developments* **4**, 267–296.

Hollander E, Schiffman E, Cohen B, *et al.* (1990a) Signs of central nervous system dysfunction in obsessive–compulsive disorder. *Arch Gen Psychiatry* **47**, 27–32.

Hollander E, Liebowitz MR, DeCaria CM, *et al.* (1990b) Treatment of depersonalization with serotonin reuptake blockers. *J Clin Psychopharmacol* **10**, 200–203.

Hollander E, DeCaria C, Nitescu A, *et al.* (1992a) Serotonergic function in obsessive–compulsive disorder: Behavioral and neuroendocrine responses to oral m-CPP and fenfluramine in patients and healthy volunteers. *Arch Gen Psychiatry* **49**, 21–28.

Hollander E, Frenkel M, DeCaria C, Trungold S and Stein DJ (1992b) Treatment of pathological gambling with clomipramine (let). *Am J Psychiatry* **149**, 710–711.

Hollander E, Stein DJ, DeCaria CM, Saoud JB, Klein DF and Liebowitz MR (1993) A pilot study of biological predictors of treatment outcome in obsessive–compulsive disorder. *Biol Psychiatry* **33**, 747–749.

Hsu LK, Kaye W and Weltzin T (1993) Are the eating disorders related to obsessive–compulsive disorder? *Int J Eating Disord* **14**, 305–318.

Insel TR (1992) Toward a neuroanatomy of obsessive–compulsive disorder. *Arch Gen Psychiatry* **49**, 739–744.

Insel TR and Akiskal HS (1986) Obsessive–compulsive disorder with psychotic features: A phenomenological analysis. *Am J Psychiatry* **143**, 1527–1533.

Insel TR, Murphy DL, Cohen RM, *et al.* (1983) Obsessive–compulsive disorder: A double-blind trial of clomipramine and clorgyline. *Arch Gen Psychiatry* **40**, 605–612.

Jenike MA (1989) Obsessive–compulsive related disorders: a hidden epidemic. *N Engl J Med* **321**, 539–541.

Jenike MA and Baer L (1988) An open trial of buspirone in obsessive–compulsive disorder. *Am J Psychiatry* **145**, 1285–1286.

Jenike MA, Buttolph L, Baer L, *et al.* (1989) Open trial of fluoxetine in obsessive–compulsive disorder. *Am J Psychiatry* **146**, 909–911.

Jenike MA, Hyman S, Baer L, *et al.* (1990a) A controlled trial of fluvoxamine in obsessive–compulsive disorder: Implications for a serotonergic theory. *Am J Psychiatry* **147**, 1209–1215.

Jenike MA, Baer L and Greist J (1990b) Clomipramine versus fluoxetine in obsessive–compulsive disorder: A retrospective comparison of side effects and efficacy. *J Clin Psychopharmacol* **10**, 122–124.

Jenike MA, Baer L, Summergrad P, *et al.* (1990c) Sertraline in obsessive–compulsive disorder: A double-blind comparison with placebo. *Am J Psychiatry* **147**, 923–928.

Joffe RT and Swinson RP (1990) Tranylcypromine in primary obsessive–compulsive disorder. *J Anxiety Disord* **4**, 365–367.

Kafka MP (1991) Successful antidepressant treatment of nonparaphilic sexual addictions and paraphilias in men. *J Clin Psychiatry* **52**, 60–65.

Kafka MP and Prentky R (1992) Fluoxetine treatment of nonparaphilic sexual addictions and paraphilias in men. *J Clin Psychiatry* **53**, 351–358.

Karno M, Golding JM, Sorenson SB, *et al.* (1988) The epidemiology of obsessive–compulsive disorder in five US communities. *Arch Gen Psychiatry* **45**, 1094–1099.

Kellner R, Abbott P, Pathak D, *et al.* (1983/4) Hypochondriacal beliefs and attitudes in family practices and psychiatric patients. *Int J Psychiatry Med* **13**, 127–139.

Khanna S (1988) Carbamezapine in obsessive–compulsive disorder. *Biol Psychiatry* **5**, 478–481.

Kim SW and Dysken MW (1990) Open fixed dose trial of fluoxetine in the treatment of obsessive–compulsive disorder. *Drug Development Research* **19**, 315–319.

Koran LM, Ringold A and Hewlett W (1992) Fluoxetine for trichotillomania: An open clinical trial. *Psychopharmacol Bull* **28**, 145–149.

Kruesi MJP, Fine S, Valladares L, Phillips RA and Rapoport JL (1992) Paraphilias: A double-blind crossover comparison of clomipramine versus desipramine. *Arch Sex Behav* **21**, 587–593.

Kurlan R, Como PG, Deeley C, McDermott M and McDermott MP (1993) A pilot controlled study of fluoxetine for obsessive–compulsive symptoms in children with Tourette's syndrome. *Clin Neuropharmacol* **16**, 167–172.

Leibowitz MR, Hollander E, Schneier F, *et al.* (1989) Fluoxetine treatment of obsessive–compulsive disorder: an open clinical trial. *J Clin Psychopharmacol* **9**, 423–427.

Leonard HL, Swedo SE, Rapoport JL, Koby EV, Lenane MC, Cheslow DC and Hamburger SD (1989) Treatment of obsessive–compulsive disorder with clomipramine and desipramine in children and adolescents: a double-blind crossover comparison. *Arch Gen Psychiatry* **46**, 1088–1092.

Leonard HL, Lenane MC, Swedo SE, *et al.* (1991) A double-blind comparison of clomipramine and desipramine treatment of severe onychophagia (nail biting). *Arch Gen Psychiatry* **48**, 821–827.

Levine R, Hoffman JS, Knepple ED, *et al.* (1989) Long-term fluoxetine treatment of a large number of obsessive–compulsive patients. *J Clin Psychopharmacol* **9**, 281–283.

Martin LL and Tesser A (1991) Toward a motivational and structural theory of ruminative thought. In: Uleman JS and Bargh JA (eds), *Unintended Thought.* Guilford Press, New York.

McDougle CJ, Goodman WK, Leckman JF, *et al.* (1994) Haloperidol addition in fluvoxamine-refractory obsessive-compulsive disorder: A double-blind placebo-controlled study in patients with and without tics. *Arch Gen Psychiatry* **51**, 302–308.

McElroy SL, Pope HG Jr, Hudson JI, Keck PE Jr and White KL (1991a) Kleptomania: a report of 20 cases. *Am J Psychiatry* **48**, 652–657.

McElroy SL, Satlin A, Pope HG, *et al.* (1991b) Treatment of compulsive shopping with antidepressants: a report of 3 cases. *Ann Clin Psychiatry* **3**, 199–204.

McElroy SL, Phillips KA, Keck PE Jr, Hudson JI and Pope HG Jr (1993) Body dysmorphic disorder: does it have a psychotic subtype? *J Clin Psychiatry* **54**, 389–395.

Markovitz PJ, Calabrese JR, Schulz SC, Meltzer HY (1991) Fluoxetine in the treatment of borderline and schizotypal personality disorders. *Am J Psychiatry* **148**, 1064–1067

Montgomery SA, McIntyre A, Osterheider M, *et al.* (1993) A double-blind, placebo-controlled study of fluoxetine in patients with DSM-III-R obsessive–compulsive disorder. *Eur Neuropsychopharmacol* **3**, 143–152.

Munro A and Chmara J (1982) Monosymptomatic hypochondriacal psychosis: A diagnostic checklist based on 50 cases of the disorder. *Can J Psychiatry* **27**, 374–376.

Ornitz E (1985) Should autistic children be treated with haloperidol? *Am J Psychiatry* **142**, 883–884.

Pato MT, Pigott TA, Hill JA, *et al.* (1991) Controlled comparison of buspirone and clomipramine in obsessive–compulsive disorder. *Am J Psychiatry* **148**, 127–129.

Perse TL, Greist JH and Jefferson JW (1987) Fluvoxamine treatment of obsessive–compulsive disorder. *Am J Psychiatry* **144**, 1543–1548.

Phillips KA (1991) Body dysmorphic disorder: the distress of imagined ugliness. *Am J Psychiatry* **148**, 1138–1149.

Phillips KA, McElroy SL, Keck PE Jr, *et al.* (1993) Body dysmorphic disorder: 30 cases of imagined ugliness. *Am J Psychiatry* **150**, 302–308.

Pigott TA, Pato MT, Bernstein SE, *et al.* (1990) Controlled comparisons of clomipramine and fluoxetine in the treatment of obsessive–compulsive disorder. *Arch Gen Psychiatry* **47**, 926–932.

Pigott TA, L'Heureux F, Rubenstein CS, *et al.* (1992) A double-blind, placebo controlled study of trazodone in patients with OCD. *J Clin Psychopharmacol* **12**, 156–162.

Pitman, RK, Green RC, Jenike MA, *et al.* (1987) Clinical comparison of Tourette's disorder and obsessive–compulsive disorder. *Am J Psychiatry* **144**, 1166–1171.

Pollard CA, Ibe IO, Krojanker DN, *et al.* (1991) Clomipramine treatment of trichotillomania: a follow-up report on four cases. *J Clin Psychiatry* **52**, 128–130.

Rapoport JL, Ryland DH and Kriete M (1992) Drug treatment of canine acral lick. An animal model of obsessive–compulsive disorder. *Arch Gen Psychiatry* **48**, 517–521.

Rasmussen SA (1994) Obsessive–compulsive spectrum disorders. *J Clin Psychiatry* **55**, 89–91.

Riddle MA, Hardin MT, King R, Scahill L and Woolston JL (1990) Fluoxetine treatment of children and adolescents with Tourette's and obsessive–compulsive disorders: preliminary clinical experience. *J Am Acad Child Adolesc Psychiatry* **29**, 45–48.

Riddle MA, Scahill L, King RA, Hardin MT, Anderson GM, Ort SI, Smith JC, Leckman JF and Cohen DJ (1992) Double-blind, crossover trial of fluoxetine and placebo in children and adolescents with obsessive–compulsive disorder. *J Am Acad Child Adolesc Psychiatry* **31**, 1062–1069.

Shannon KM and Fenichel GM (1990) Pimozide treatment of Sydenham's chorea. *Neurology* **40**, 186.

Shapiro AK, Shapiro ES, Young JG and Feinberg TE (1988) *Gilles de la Tourette Syndrome*, Second Edition. Raven Press, New York.

Stein DJ and Hollander E (1992a) Low-dose pimozide augmentation of serotonin reuptake blockers in the treatment of trichotillomania. *J Clin Psychiatry* **53**, 123–126.

Stein DJ and Hollander E (1992b) Cognitive science and obsessive–compulsive disorder. In: Stein DJ and Young JE (eds), *Cognitive Science and Clinical Disorders*. Academic Press, San Diego, CA.

Stein DJ and Hollander E (1993) The spectrum of obsessive–compulsive related disorders. In: Hollander E (ed), *Obsessive–Compulsive Related Disorders*. American Psychiatric Press, Washington, DC.

Stein DJ and Hollander E (1994) Personality disorders and obsessive–compulsive disorder. In: Hollander E, Johar Z, Marazzati D and Olivier B (eds), *Current Concepts in Obsessive–Compulsive Disorder*. John Wiley, New York.

Stein DJ, Hollander E, Mullen L, Trungold S, Cohen L and DeCaria CM (1992a) Compulsive and impulsive symptoms and traits in the obsessive–compulsive related disorders. *Biol Psychiatry* **31**, 267A.

Stein DJ, Hollander E, Anthony D, Schneier FR, Fallon BA, Liebowitz MR and Klein DF (1992b) Serotonergic medications for sexual obsessions, sexual addictions, and paraphilias. *J Clin Psychiatry* **53**, 267–271.

Stein DJ, Shoulberg N, Helton K and Hollander E (1992c) The neuroethological model of obsessive–compulsive disorder. *Compr Psychiatry* **33**, 274–281.

Stein DJ, Hutt C, Spitz J and Hollander E (1993) Compulsive picking and obsessive–compulsive disorder. *Psychosomatics* **34**, 177–181.

Stein DJ, Keating J, Zar HJ and Hollander E (1994a) A survey of the phenomenology and pharmacotherapy of compulsive and impulsive symptoms in Prader-Willi syndrome. *J Neuropsychiatry Clin Neurosci* **6**, 23–29.

Stein DJ, Dodman NH, Borchelt P and Hollander E (1994b) Behavioral disorders in veterinary practice: Relevance to psychiatry. *Compr Psychiatry* **35**, 275–285.

Stout RJ (1990) Fluoxetine for the treatment of compulsive facial picking. *Am J Psychiatry* **147**, 370.

Swedo SE, Rapoport JL, Cheslow DL, *et al.* (1989a) High prevalence of obsessive–compulsive symptoms in patients with Sydenham's chorea. *Am J Psychiatry* **146**, 246–249.

Swedo SE, Leonard HL, Rapoport JL, *et al.* (1989b) A double-blind comparison of clomipramine and desipramine in the treatment of trichotillomania (hair pulling). *N Engl J Med* **321**, 497–501.

Swedo SE (1993) Is trichotillomania an obsessive–compulsive spectrum disorder? In: Hollander E (ed), *Obsessive–Compulsive Related Disorders.* American Psychiatric Press, Washington, DC.

Tamimi RR, Mavissakalian MR, Jones B, *et al.* (1991) Clomipramine versus fluvoxamine in obsessive–compulsive disorder. *Ann Clin Psychiatry* **3**, 275–279.

Thoren P, Asberg M, Bertilsson L, *et al.* (1980) Clomipramine treatment of obsessive–compulsive disorder. II. Biochemical aspects. *Arch Gen Psychiatry* **37**, 1289–1294.

Tollefson GD, Rampey AH, Potvin JH, *et al.* (1994) A multicenter investigation of fixed-dose fluoxetine in the treatment of obsessive–compulsive disorder. *Arch Gen Psychiatry* **51**, 559–567.

Vallejo J, Olivares J, Marcos T, *et al.* (1992) Clomipramine versus phenelzine in obsessive–compulsive disorder: a controlled clinical trial. *Br J Psychiatry* **161**, 665–670.

von Economo C (1931) *Encephalitis Lethargica: Its Sequelae and Treatment.* Oxford University Press, London.

Walsh BT and Devlin MJ (1992) The pharmacologic treatment of eating disorders. *Psychiatr Clin North Am* **15**, 149–160.

Weissman MM (1993) The epidemiology of obsessive–compulsive disorder. Presented at the First International Conference on Obsessive–Compulsive Disorder, Capri, Italy.

Wesner RB and Noyes R (1991) Imipramine an effective treatment for illness phobia. *J Affect Disord* **22**, 43–48.

Wheadon DE, Bushnell WD, Steiner M (1993) *A fixed dose comparison of 20, 40 or 60 mg paroxetine to placebo in the treatment of obsessive compulsive disorder.* Presented at American College of Neuropsychopharmacology 32nd Annual Meeting.

Willemse T, Mudde M, Josephy M and Spruijt BM (1994) The effect of haloperidol and naloxone on excessive grooming behavior of cats. *Eur Neuropsychopharmacol* **4**, 39–45.

Winchel RM and Stanley M (1991) Self-injurious behavior: a review of the behavior and biology of self-mutilation. *Am J Psychiatry* **148**, 306–317.

Winchel RM, Jones JS, Stanley B, *et al.* (1992) Clinical characteristics of trichotillomania and its response to fluoxetine. *J Clin Psychiatry* **53**, 304–308.

Wise SP and Rapoport JL (1989) Obsessive–compulsive disorder: Is it basal ganglia dysfunction? In: Rapoport JL (ed), *Obsessive–Compulsive Disorders in Children and Adolescents.* American Psychiatric Press, Washington, DC.

Wood A (1991) Pharmacotherapy of bulimia nervosa – experience with fluoxetine. *Int Clin Psychopharmacology* **8**, 295–299.

Yaryura-Tobias JA and Neziroglu FA (1984) *Obsessive–Compulsive Disorders: Pathogenesis–Diagnosis–Treatment.* Marcel Dekker, New York.

Zohar J (1994) A double-blind study to assess the efficacy and tolerance of paroxetine compared with clomipramine and placebo in the treatment of obsessive compulsive disorder. Presented at the 7th AEP Congress, Sept 94, Copenhagen.

Zohar J and Insel T (1987) Obsessive–compulsive disorder: Psychobiological approaches to diagnosis, treatment, and pathophysiology. *Biol Psychiatry* **22**, 667–687.

Zohar J, Mueller EA, Insel TR, *et al* (1987) Serotonergic responsivity in obsessive–compulsive disorder: Comparison of patients and healthy controls. *Arch Gen Psychiatry* **44**, 946–951.

Zohar J, Insel TR, Zohar-Kadouch RC, *et al.* (1988) Serotonergic responsivity in obsessive–compulsive disorder: Effects of chronic clomipramine treatment. *Arch Gen Psychiatry* **45**, 167–172.

Zohar J, Kaplan Z and Benjamin J (1993) Clomipramine treatment of obsessive–compulsive symptomatology in schizophrenic patients. *J Clin Psychiatry* **54**, 385–388.

Zohar J, Kaplan Z and Benjamin J (1994) Compulsive exhibitionism successfully treated with fluvoxamine: a controlled case study. *J Clin Psychiatry* **55**, 86–88.

8

Selective serotonin re-uptake inhibitors in panic disorder

James C. Ballenger

INTRODUCTION

Traditionally, the medications used for the treatment of panic disorder have been from three classes: (1) the tricyclic antidepressants (TCAs), (2) the monoamine oxidase inhibitors (MAOIs), and (3) the benzodiazepines (BZs). However, more recently the selective serotonin re-uptake inhibitors (SSRIs), a relatively new class of drugs with demonstrated efficacy in the treatment of depression, have received considerable attention for this indication. This chapter focuses on the SSRIs and their use in panic disorder, beginning with a brief description of their proposed mechanism of action. A more extensive review of the literature follows which focuses on the clinical studies conducted to date with the various SSRIs in panic disorder patients, and will include information on efficacy, dosing, and side-effects.

SEROTONIN IN PSYCHIATRIC ILLNESS

Long considered to be directly involved in the development of affective illness, more recently evidence has accumulated that implicates the serotonin (5-HT) system in anxiety disorders as well (Pecknold, 1990). The demonstrated link between anxiety and depression and their frequent co-occurrence (Dealy *et al.*, 1981; Leckman *et al.*,

Selective Serotonin Re-uptake Inhibitors: Advances in Basic Research and Clinical Practice, Second Edition, Edited by J.P. Feighner and W.F. Boyer
© 1996 John Wiley & Sons Ltd

1983; Lesser *et al.*, 1988; Van Valkenberg *et al.*, 1984) lend further support to the potential role of 5-HT in anxiety. The MAOIs and TCAs have been proven to be effective in the treatment of both depression and panic disorder and share common pharmacological effects with the SSRIs including action on the serotonin (5-HT) system. Based on clinical evidence and research data that demonstrate the effectiveness of the SSRIs in the treatment of major depression (Boyer and Feighner, 1991), investigation of the effects of the SSRIs in the treatment of other conditions, including anxiety, was a logical extension of their original use.

ROLE OF 5-HT IN ANXIETY

Animal studies

The role of the 5-HT system in anxiety has been investigated, and both overactivity and underactivity of serotonin (5-HT) activity have been suggested (Humble and Wisdedt, 1992). A number of animal studies using stimulation, electrolytic lesions, and 5-HT synthesis inhibitors such as parachlorophenylalanine (PCPA) provide strong support for the role of serotonin in anxiety-related behaviours. In one study, investigators demonstrated that electrical stimulation of the median raphe nucleus caused behavioural inhibition, an anxiety equivalent. Rats that were trained to depress a lever using a schedule of water reinforcement exhibited behaviours associated with fear and/or anxiety, including suppression of lever pressing, defecation, teeth chattering, and crouching when they received electric tail shock. However, when PCPA was administered to rats in this experiment, these effects were reversed (Graeff and Filho, 1978). Similar findings have been demonstrated by other investigators who have also shown PCPA to be effective in relieving anxiety in animals using both conflict and social paradigms (Pecknold, 1990). Administration of 5-hydroxytryptophan, a 5-HT precursor, has been shown to antagonize the anxiolytic effects of PCPA (File and Hyde, 1977; Geller and Blum, 1970; Robichaud and Sledge, 1969; Stein *et al.*, 1973; Stevens and Fechter, 1969; Tennen, 1967). In another study using electric shock, behavioural inhibition was reversed by injecting 5-HT into the dorsal raphe (Thiebot *et al.*, 1982). However, the results of other investigators working with PCPA and the punishment paradigm have been less conclusive (Blakey and Parker, 1973; Cook and Sepinwall, 1975).

Investigators found that lesions of the 5-HTergic pathways produced anxiolytic effects in animals during conflict situations (Pelham *et al.*, 1975; Thiebot *et al.*, 1984; Tye *et al.*, 1979). Other studies however have not replicated these findings (Commissaris *et al.*, 1981; Thiebot *et al.*, 1982). Similar to the effects produced by BZ administration, suppression of 5-HT transmission reduces the anxiety demonstrated by animals involved in punishment situations (Geller and Blum, 1970; Graeff and Schoenfeld, 1970; Robichaud and Sledge, 1969; Sepinwall and Cook, 1980; Stein *et al.*, 1975, 1977; Thiebot *et al.*, 1983; Tye *et al.*, 1977).

Although these studies provide somewhat conflicting evidence, they strongly support 5-HT involvement in anxiety.

Laboratory induction of panic

Laboratory studies in which panic is induced by various agents, including yohimbine, sodium lactate, and isoproterenol (Gorman *et al.*, 1985, 1989; Murphy and Pigott, 1990), have further supported the theory that anxiety disorders may be correlated with an abnormality in brain serotonin function. Administration of sodium lactate induces panic attacks in panic disorder patients, but only infrequently in control subjects (Fink *et al.*, 1970; Liebowitz *et al.*, 1984, 1986; Pitts and McClure, 1967; Rifkin *et al.*, 1981). Providing further support for the serotonin hypothesis are studies that have demonstrated that imipramine, a TCA with proven action on the serotonin system, antagonizes panic if given prior to lactate administration (Klerman *et al.*, 1993). Studies by Gorman *et al.* (1984) demonstrated that administration of CO_2 frequently causes panic attacks in PD subjects, but similar to lactate, rarely in normal controls. Both lactate and CO_2 have been linked to the serotonin system because of their ability to increase the cerebral 5-HT re-uptake ratio (Lingjaerde, 1977, 1985).

Provocation studies with MCPP, a serotonin agonist, induced panic attacks in panic disorder patients but not in control subjects or depressed patients (Kahn *et al.*, 1988). Other investigators (Charney *et al.*, 1987) were able to extend these results to normal controls by using higher doses of MCPP. Comparable results were obtained when fenfluramine was studied under circumstances (Targum and Marshall, 1989).

The role of serotonin in regulating respiration has been studied (Armijo and Florez, 1974), and it has been demonstrated that a deficit in serotonin can result in hyperventilation (Olson *et al.*, 1979), while excess serotonin can reduce respiratory function (Lundberg *et al.*, 1980). Symptoms associated with anxiety frequently include respiratory difficulties, such as feelings of choking, hyperventilation, and inability to control the rate of breathing, further implicating the role of serotonin in panic disorder patients (Gorman and Papp, 1990). In the early 1950s, Cohen and White (1951) used 4% CO_2 to induce panic attacks in panic disorder patients. Although not actively pursued for a significant period of time, this line of investigation has gained renewed enthusiasm over the past decade. Similar to other provocation studies, Gorman and colleagues were able to induce panic through inhalation of CO_2 in panic disorder patients, but not in normal controls (Gorman *et al.*, 1984). Klein has recently theorized that respiratory symptoms should predict a better response to imipramine than benzodiazepines (Klein, 1993), a result observed in the large multinational panic disorder trial (Briggs *et al.*, 1993).

Finally, the correlation of untreated panic and suicide attempts (Weissman *et al.*, 1989) lends further support to this theory since suicide has been associated with decreased serotonin (Asberg *et al.*, 1987).

CLINICAL PROFILE OF THE SSRIs AND CLOMIPRAMINE IN PANIC DISORDER

Medications classified as SSRIs include fluoxetine, fluvoxamine, zimelidine, citalopram, sertraline, and paroxetine (Asberg and Martensson, 1993). Clomipramine, a tricyclic antidepressant, is also included in discussion of the SSRIs because its principal action appears to be on the serotonin system, and it has been extensively studied.

Clomipramine

A number of both open and controlled studies have demonstrated that clomipramine is effective for the treatment of panic disorder. In an early open study, Gloger *et al.* (1981) administered clomipramine to 20 patients with either panic disorder or agoraphobia with panic attacks. Medication was initiated at 25 mg/day and increased over a 7–10 day period to a maximum dose of 75–100 mg/day, based on the specific response of each patient. Forty-five percent of the patients, however, required less than 50 mg/day of clomipramine. In addition to clomipramine, panic disorder patients received psychotherapy. After initial improvement in panic attacks, agoraphobic patients received encouragement to confront their avoidant behaviours. During the first two weeks of treatment, 40% of the patients experienced an exacerbation of symptoms that required adjustments in dosage. Improvement began 10–14 days after medication was initiated, and by the end of the eight-week study, 75% of the patients were completely asymptomatic, with no panic attacks. In addition, 85% of the clomipramine-treated patients were improved to the point of having only mild (or no) symptoms that did not interfere with functioning as demonstrated by scores of two or less on disability ratings. Of the remaining five patients, three were significantly improved and experienced only mild symptoms related to panic attacks, while only two had minimal improvement (Gloger *et al.*, 1981). Other investigators achieved similar results with clomipramine in this patient population as well (Caetano, 1985; Pecknold *et al.*, 1982).

A subsequent study by Gloger *et al.* (1989) utilizing lower doses of clomipramine produced positive results, with 13 of the 17 patients becoming completely panic free and the remaining four reporting significant decreases in panic attacks. Self- and therapist ratings on the Global Clinical Improvement Scale showed that eight of the 17 patients had achieved "marked improvement" and the remaining nine had "no symptoms" by the conclusion of the study. Mean daily dose was 45 mg, with eight of the 17 patients receiving less than 25 mg/day. Five of the 17 patients experienced an initial exacerbation in symptoms; however, this was not severe enough to warrant study termination. This investigation provided more conclusive results for a specific drug effect since psychotherapy was not included in this protocol (Gloger *et al.*, 1989).

An effort was made by Johnston *et al.* (1988) to correct methodological problems associated with many of the early studies conducted with clomipramine, including mixed patient samples, few control groups, addition of behavioural management techniques, and lack of consistency in measures used to assess agoraphobic symptoms. Ninety-four agoraphobic women were entered in this eight-week, placebo controlled, double-blind study; of the 94 women, 70 completed the trial. Subjects were assigned to either placebo or clomipramine, 25 mg/day, with gradual increases to a maximum daily dose of 300 mg. This study demonstrated that clomipramine was significantly superior to placebo in reducing panic attacks and phobic and depressive symptoms (Johnston *et al.*, 1988).

Two studies were designed specifically to test the serotonin hypothesis of panic disorder. In the first study, clomipramine was compared to 5-hydroxytryptophan and placebo in an eight-week trial. Fifty-five anxiety disorder patients initially entered the study, with 10 drop-outs. Forty-five patients completed the study, with 15 in each treatment group. Diagnoses included: 30 agoraphobia with panic attacks, seven generalized anxiety disorder, five panic disorder, and three obsessive–compulsive disorder. Both clomipramine and 5-HTP were initiated at 25 mg/day and were increased gradually to a maximum daily dosage of 150 mg, as tolerated, over a two week period. Patients assigned to the 5-HTP group also received 150 mg/day of carbidopa. Clomipramine was significantly more effective, with 11 of the clomipramine patients achieving significant improvement and almost complete resolution of panic attacks compared to five of the 5-HTP and only one of the placebo patients. In addition, clomipramine was highly effective in improving and/or resolving depressive symptoms associated with anxiety disorders, whereas 5-HTP had little effect on depression (Kahn *et al.*, 1987).

In the second study, Den Boer *et al.* enrolled 58 anxiety disorder patients in a six-week study designed to compare clomipramine and fluvoxamine. Completing the study were 35 females and 15 males who were diagnosed according to DSM III criteria with the following disorders: 38 agoraphobia with panic attacks, six obsessive–compulsive disorder, five generalized anxiety disorder, and one agoraphobia without panic attacks. Following a two-week washout period, 26 patients were enrolled in the clomipramine group as 25 mg/day and 24 in the fluvoxamine group at 50 mg/day. Dosages were gradually increased over a two-week period to maximum doses of 150 mg clomipramine or 100 mg fluvoxamine. Clomipramine and fluvoxamine were determined to be approximately equally effective by the end of the study with 15 of the 26 clomipramine and 14 of the 24 fluvoxamine patients achieving almost complete resolution of all anxiety and depression symptoms. However, results obtained from the Symptom Check List (SCL-90) showed that clomipramine was more effective than fluvoxamine on both anxiety and depression measures (Den Boer *et al.*, 1987). Other studies utilizing comparable doses of clomipramine and fluvoxamine have demonstrated both drugs to be equally effective (Dick and Ferrer, 1983; Klok *et al.*, 1981). The differences observed in the

Den Boer study may be accounted for by the fact that clomipramine was administered at higher doses than fluvoxamine (150 mg/day versus 100 mg/day).

An open trial comparing clomipramine, at a mean daily dose of 128 mg, and imipramine, mean daily dose of 144 mg, was conducted in 59 panic disorder patients. This study found both drugs to be approximately equally effective on measures including reduction in panic attacks and improvement in phobic avoidance, anxiety, and depression. However, clomipramine's efficacy was demonstrated earlier, and was evident by the end of the second week (Cassano *et al.*, 1988).

Modigh *et al.* (1992) conducted a recent comparison of clomipramine, imipramine, and placebo. A total of 57 patients suffering from panic disorder, with or without agoraphobia, completed this 12-week drug trial with 10 subjects assigned to placebo, 25 to imipramine, and 22 to clomipramine. Both active drugs were administered at initial doses of 25 mg/day, with 25 mg increases every three days as indicated and tolerated, to a maximum daily dose of 250 mg. In addition to medication, supportive and educative therapy was provided throughout the study and patients with agoraphobia were encouraged to practise exposure therapy. Although both clomipramine and imipramine were effective in reducing the number of panic attacks and in decreasing anxiety symptoms between attacks, clomipramine demonstrated significantly superior results to both imipramine and placebo on all major outcome measures by study conclusion. Significant reduction in number of panic attacks was seen by the end of the fourth week in the clomipramine group, but not until after the eighth week in the imipramine-treated patients. By the end of the 12-week trial, the clomipramine group achieved complete cessation of full panic attacks, with reduction from six to zero. The clomipramine group also had significantly fewer total number of panic attacks (full plus mild) at study conclusion than the imipramine or placebo groups. Hamilton Anxiety scores were also significantly lower for the clomipramine than for the imipramine patients by study completion. Low doses of benzodiazepines (diazepam, 5 mg or less three times a day) were allowed in all groups throughout the trial, and at study entry BZs were used by approximately 56% of the imipramine group, 68% of the clomipramine group, and 70% of the placebo group. However, by the end of the study approximately 44% of the imipramine and 40% of the placebo patients compared to 32% of the clomipramine patients were still taking BZs. In addition, none of the 22 clomipramine compared to four of the 29 imipramine and seven of the 17 placebo patients stopped participating in the study (Modigh *et al.*, 1992). Finally, most of the clomipramine patients who were maintained on lower doses (i.e. 10 or 25 mg/day) of the drug and followed 1–2 years post-study, remained free from panic symptomatology (Westberg P., Eriksson F., Modigh K., unpublished data). There are very few studies that actually demonstrate superiority of one active drug over another, making this trial a potentially important one.

Lofepramine, a recently developed tricyclic antidepressant with fewer anticholinergic side-effects than traditional TCAs and low risk for overdose, was compared to clomipramine and placebo in a six-week acute trial (Fahy *et al.*, 1992), with a continuation phase to 24 weeks. Subjects included 79 outpatients with panic disorder with or without agoraphobia, as defined by DSM III R criteria. Patients were randomly assigned to drug or placebo after a 7–10 day drug washout. Clomipramine was administered initially at 50 mg/day with increases to a maximum of 100 mg/day. Lofepramine patients received initial doses of 70 mg/day with titration of dose to a maximum of 140 mg/day. Both medications were increased upward over a two-week period. Patients in both active medication groups were gradually tapered beginning at the end of the twelfth week during the continuation phase of the study. Subjects receiving placebo were reassigned at six weeks to either lofepramine or clomipramine, with dosages increased over a two-week period as described earlier. In addition to medication, subjects were provided with behaviour therapy at baseline and at 1–8 weeks on an alternating every-other week basis. Of the 79 original subjects, nine clomipramine patients stopped participating in the study within the first three weeks. Seven of the nine dropped out because of medication side-effects. There were two dropouts in each of the other two groups; however, none of these was attributed to the medication. An additional two subjects failed to complete the trial choosing to drop out after four weeks; one in the clomipramine group and one in the placebo group. Evaluable subjects included 24 in the lofepramine and placebo groups and 18 in the clomipramine group. Fifty-five of the 64 participated throughout the follow-up phase. At the end of the six-week acute study, clomipramine was slightly more effective than both lofepramine and placebo, although 67% of the patients in both active drug groups had no panic attacks, compared to 42% of the placebo group. Clomipramine also afforded rapid relief with subjects showing improvement by the second week. Those subjects initially assigned to placebo showed improvement when reassigned to active drug during the continuation phase. At 24 weeks, 93% of the clomipramine subjects were completely recovered from panic attacks compared to 64% of the lofepramine and 60% of the placebo groups (Fahy *et al.*, 1992).

Biological assays for platelet aggregation to noradrenaline, platelet α_2-receptor density and lymphocyte β_2-receptor density and platelet aggregation to serotonin, ^{3}H-ketanserin binding to platelet 5-HT$_2$ receptors and ^{3}H-5-HT uptake into platelets were performed on blood samples collected from patients at baseline and at regular intervals throughout the study and were matched to a comparable group of control subjects. These assays were undertaken to determine hypothesized changes in serotonergic and/or noradrenergic function between panic disorder patients and controls at baseline and throughout the study (Butler *et al.*, 1992). This study confirmed that measures of both serotonergic and noradrenergic function in panic disorder patients differ from normals, but further demonstrated that these differences were not altered in patients for whom treatment was effective. These investigators have planned a long-term follow-up study of these patients, 12–18 months post-study treatment, to determine if these disturbances are maintained or if they normalize somewhat in patients who remain asymptomatic for extended periods of time (Butler *et al.*, 1992).

Clomipramine was used in a recent study to treat agoraphobic inpatients who had not responded to behavioural therapy. Enrolled in the 12-week placebo cross-over study were 18 patients with panic disorder and agoraphobia who received clomipramine at maximum doses of 150 mg/day for three weeks, accompanied by supportive psychotherapy provided to help the patient deal with initial side-effects associated with clomipramine treatment. This study ensured that all patients, at some point during the trial, were treated with clomipramine for an adequate period to determine efficacy. In this study patients had improvement in symptoms on most measures for the period they received clomipramine compared to the period when they received placebo (Hoffart et al., 1993). These investigators are now conducting a two-year maintenance study to determine if long-term treatment with clomipramine is successful in maintaining initial treatment gains and further extending them to clinically significant levels and whether long-term treatment with clomipramine can prevent relapse in these patients (Hoffart et al., 1993).

A recent study compared the efficacy of clomipramine administered in conjunction with dixyrazine versus clomipramine and placebo in panic disorder patients, with or without agoraphobia. The investigators had observed that dixyrazine administered with imipramine had a greater antidepressant effect than imipramine alone (Feet et al., 1987), leading them subsequently to question whether the combination of clomipramine and dixyrazine would produce similar results. Of the 45 patients who entered the 12-week study, 16 dropped out; however analyses were based on intention-to-treat, and therefore include the entire 45 patients. The group treated with dixyrazine and clomipramine ($N = 21$) demonstrated significantly greater improvement than those patients treated with clomipramine alone ($N = 24$). Although both treatment groups had decreases in panic attacks and in scores on the Hamilton Anxiety panic disorder subscale, the decreases/improvements were much greater in the dixyrazine + clomipramine group. Evaluation of endpoint data on the patient's global evaluation of improvement for each of the 45 subjects initially enrolled in the study revealed the following: in the clomipramine + dixyrazine group, 16 (76%) were "considerably improved", three were improved, one was unchanged, and one was worse. The patients in the clomipramine + placebo group fared as follows: nine (38%) were "considerably improved", nine were improved, two were unchanged, and four were worse. There are issues related to the conduct of this study which make the results somewhat tentative, including the concomitant use of benzodiazepines, albeit at extremely low doses (less than 5 mg/day of either diazepam or oxazepam). However, these findings clearly warrant further study to confirm not only the increased efficacy of this combination, but also, as pointed out by the study investigators, to determine whether dixyrazine is an effective antipanic agent when administered alone (Feet and Gotestam, 1994).

Another recent study with clomipramine was conducted with 30 panic disorder, 35 depression, and nine panic disorder plus depression patients utilizing a combination of clomipramine and cognitive therapy. Patients were instructed to discontinue clomipramine at the end of the six-month treatment period, with subsequent follow-up one month later. Of the total sample, 72% were able to complete the entire six-month treatment period; only four patients remained in the study for less than one month. For those patients maintained in treatment for longer than one month, 81.4% had fair–good results. Following discontinuation of clomipramine, 30% of patients suffered a relapse within two months (Timmerman and Delta, 1994).

Fluoxetine

The first of the "true" SSRIs to be utilized extensively in panic disorder was fluoxetine. Gorman *et al.* (1987) enrolled 20 panic disorder patients in this study and administered placebo for a period of one week. Four of the patients responded to placebo during this period with complete cessation of panic attacks and were subsequently dropped from the study. The remaining 16 patients were entered in an 18-week open trial of fluoxetine, initiated at 10 mg/day, and increased by 10 mg/week to a maximum daily dose of 80 mg. The effects of fluoxetine in reducing panic attacks were seen in most patients at about six weeks. Seven of the subjects were considered responsive, defined as no panic attacks for at least four consecutive weeks. Of the nine nonresponders, eight discontinued the medication because of side-effects. Seven of the eight terminated study participation because of hyperstimulation associated with fluoxetine, i.e. increased agitation, insomnia, restlessness, jitteriness, and gastrointestinal symptoms.

Because of the high doses utilized that presumably led to the high dropout rate, the investigators involved in the previous trial studied the efficacy and tolerability of fluoxetine utilizing lower initial doses and more gradual medication increases (Schneier *et al.*, 1990). Studied in this trial were 25 outpatients suffering from panic disorder, with or without agoraphobia. Treatment of fluoxetine for most patients was initiated at 5 mg/day, and was gradually increased every seven days as tolerated and as indicated to achieve clinically significant results. Seventy-six percent of the patients (19 of 25) exhibited moderate to marked improvement in symptomatology. Of the remaining six patients, two had little improvement and four stopped participating in the study because of side-effects. Of the 25 study patients, 22 had been treated previously with other anti-anxiety medications. Thirteen of the 22 were responsive to these medications, but suffered from adverse side-effects. When treated with fluoxetine, 12 of the 13 achieved a moderate to marked response. The remaining nine patients had unsatisfactory previous responses to medication trials; of these, four had a moderate to marked response to fluoxetine. The extremely positive results are somewhat compromised due to concomitant BZ use by 19 of the 25 patients prior to and throughout the study. However, the investigators attribute the better tolerance in this study to lower doses and more gradual increases (Schneier *et al.*, 1990).

In an open trial, fluoxetine was administered in a mean dose of 20 mg/day, to 30 patients with panic disorder with agoraphobia. One-third of the patients dropped out of the eight-week study due to exacerbation of anxiety or ineffectiveness of the drug. Approximately half (48%) of the total sample had complete resolution of panic attacks, as well as significant reduction in anxiety and phobic avoidance. The remaining 19% of patients were unresponsive to fluoxetine (Pecknold and Luthe, 1991).

The use of fluoxetine in the treatment of refractory panic disorder was examined in two case reports. The first patient was unresponsive to inpatient hospitalization, behaviour therapy, psychoanalysis, and drug treatment with imipramine and clonazepam. The patient had responded to 75 mg/day of phenelzine but experienced an unacceptable weight gain of 22.75 kg. The patient began treatment with fluoxetine, 20 mg/day, increased within one week to 80 mg/day. Minor improvement was experienced during the first two weeks of treatment, but significant improvement was not seen until nine weeks when the patient experienced only one situational and one spontaneous panic attack a day, compared to her pretreatment frequency of 100 spontaneous attacks a day. This patient maintained treatment gains over a two-year period, but was unable to reduce or discontinue fluoxetine without exacerbation of symptoms. The second patient had been treated unsuccessfully with behaviour therapy, psychotherapy, imipramine, phenelzine, and alprazolam. She began treatment at 20 mg/day of fluoxetine with increases to 80 mg/day. Significant improvement was seen in both depressive symptoms and panic attacks by the third week of treatment. When fluoxetine was discontinued, symptoms returned. Subsequent treatment with fluoxetine was successful in maintaining treatment gains for the next 28 months (Solyom et al., 1991).

Another group studied fluoxetine in lower doses in depressed patients, with and without panic disorder. Patients included 133 outpatients with major depression, 27 of whom had concomitant panic disorder. Fluoxetine treatment was initiated at 5 mg/day and was increased by 5 mg every two days to a maximum daily dose of 20 mg or a dose that was tolerable to the patient. Patients who could not tolerate increases were instructed to increase the medication as described above, but only to a level that was tolerable (2–20 mg/day). Thirteen of the 27 comorbid depressed plus panic patients were able to reach the full dose of 20 mg/day of fluoxetine, nine discontinued the drug because of inability to tolerate side-effects, even at lower doses, and five continued fluoxetine at doses lower than 20 mg/day. Of the patients in the depressed only group, 83 of the 106 reached the full dose of fluoxetine, 13 discontinued fluoxetine treatment, and 10 were maintained on doses lower than 20 mg/day of fluoxetine. Unfortunately, the results from this study are not broken down between comorbid depressed plus panic disorder patients versus depressed only patients; instead, findings are provided for the group as a whole. All of the 22 patients who were unable to tolerate fluoxetine at any dose were assessed at follow-up and were not considered to be clinically improved. The 96 patients who were able to complete the study on 20 mg of fluoxetine demonstrated clinically significant improvement, based on scores on the Clinical Global Improvement Scale. However, interestingly, the 15 patients considered to comprise the low-dose group were actually significantly more improved than the full-dose patients. The authors indicate that these findings may have important implications for the population treated with fluoxetine. Their study demonstrated that more of the mixed group were unable to tolerate fluoxetine, even at lower doses, than the depressed only group. As described above, the mixed group had a much higher percentage of dropouts, i.e. none discontinued medication (33% versus 12%). Perhaps equally interesting is the fact that the patients in the low dose group were considered more improved than those on the high dose (Louie *et al.*, 1993).

Fluoxetine was used to enhance the effects of low dose TCAs in 16 panic disorder patients. The investigators also hoped to minimize the development of side-effects related to higher doses of TCAs with this strategy. Patients were administered 20 mg fluoxetine and TCAs 25–50 mg. Fourteen of the 16 patients were significantly improved with only minor side-effects (Varia and Donnelly, 1991).

Fluvoxamine

A number of studies have shown fluvoxamine to be superior to placebo in the treatment of panic disorder. A total of 188 panic disorder patients were entered in a large placebo controlled trial of fluvoxamine. Completing the study were 58 fluvoxamine and 63 placebo patients. Fluvoxamine was administered in doses up to 150 mg/day for two weeks, followed by doses in the range 100–300 mg/day for the next six weeks. At the end of the eight-week study, approximately 64% of the fluvoxamine patients compared to approximately 40% of the placebo patients were panic free. Fluvoxamine exerted its antipanic efficacy early on, with reduction in panic attacks as early as the first and second weeks of treatment. In addition, ratings on the Clinical Anxiety Scale demonstrated that 64% of the fluvoxamine versus 42% of the placebo patients were responsive (Woods *et al.*, 1994).

Fifty panic disorder patients were entered in an eight-week trial comparing fluvoxamine and placebo, with 25 patients assigned to each group. Patients were placed on placebo for a period of three weeks, and then placed on either placebo or fluvoxamine in 50 mg capsules. Both placebo and fluvoxamine were increased after three days to two capsules/day (100 mg fluvoxamine) for a period of five days, and then increased to three capsules/day for six days. Dosing was flexible from this point on, to a maximum of six capsules (300 mg/fluvoxamine). Dropouts included six patients in the fluvoxamine group, four due to side-effects and two no-shows, and seven placebo patients. Of the remaining 37 completers, only 36 were evaluable, evenly divided between fluvoxamine and placebo. This study utilized medication only, without supportive psychotherapy or behavioural therapy. Mean daily dose for fluvoxamine at the end of the eight-week study was 206.8 mg. The patients in the fluvoxamine group began to experience relief from panic attacks as early as the third week. However, relief from general anxiety and depressive symptoms did not occur until about the sixth week of fluvoxamine treatment. At the end of the study, 61% of the fluvoxamine group were completely free of panic attacks, compared to 22% of those patients who received placebo. Severity of remaining panic attacks, however, did not appear to be affected by fluvoxamine (Hoehn-Saric *et al.*, 1993).

A group of 117 panic disorder patients completed an eight-week multicentre double-blind, placebo controlled trial with fluvoxamine. Of the 117 patients, 56 were assigned to fluvoxamine and 61 to placebo. Fluvoxamine was demonstrated to be significantly superior to placebo on a number of measures including reduction of panic attacks, and measures of phobic avoidance and generalized anxiety, again with improvements beginning as early as the third week (Hoehn-Saric *et al.*, 1994).

These same investigators conducted a trial to determine if the efficacy of fluvoxamine is maintained during long-term treatment (Holland *et al.*, 1994). Seventy-three panic disorder patients were chosen to participate in this study, following completion of two double-blind, eight-week protocols. Thirty-one patients who had been treated with placebo were switched to fluvoxamine and the remaining 42 were maintained on fluvoxamine. Assessment was conducted on both groups every three months, up to one year from study entry. Improvement achieved following three months of active treatment with fluvoxamine was maintained throughout the 12-month study, and fluvoxamine was well tolerated during long-term treatment (Holland *et al.*, 1994).

Fluvoxamine was compared to cognitive therapy in an eight-week, placebo controlled study (Black *et al.*, 1993a). Of the 75 original patients, only 55 completed the study. Dropouts included four in the fluvoxamine group, nine in the cognitive therapy group, and seven in the placebo group. Interestingly, only two of the four fluvoxamine dropouts discontinued study participation because of adverse side-effects. Fluvoxamine was initiated at 50 mg/day and was increased to a maximum daily dose of 300 mg. By the eighth week, mean daily dose was 230 mg. Results demonstrated that fluvoxamine was superior to both cognitive therapy and placebo. By the end of the study, 90% of the fluvoxamine group achieved moderate to marked improvement and 81% were completely free of panic attacks, compared to 50% and 53% in the cognitive therapy group, and 39% and 29% in the placebo group. At study conclusion, ratings in work and social disability for the fluvoxamine patients indicated that 95% rated themselves three or better, defined as "minor interference with normal work or social activities", compared to 32% at baseline. Of the remaining patients, 75% of the cognitive therapy group and 61% of the placebo group rated themselves three or better, compared to 28% and 32% at study entry. Fluvoxamine also exerted its beneficial effects earlier than cognitive therapy (Black *et al.*, 1993a).

As described earlier, fluvoxamine was compared to clomipramine in a study of 50 panic disorder patients (Den Boer *et al.*, 1987). Although the effects of clomipramine were demonstrated earlier and were somewhat greater than those with fluvoxamine, both drugs were effective, and patients in both groups experienced decreased depression and anxiety. By study completion, 15 of the 26 clomipramine and 14 of the 24 fluvoxamine treated patients were completely free from symptoms (Den Boer *et al.*, 1987).

Another study conducted by Den Boer and colleagues (Den Boer and Westenberg, 1988) compared fluvoxamine, a specific 5-HT re-uptake blocker, with maprotiline, a specific norepinephrine re-uptake blocker. Forty-seven panic disorder patients entered the six-week, double-blind trial, with three dropouts in the first week of the study. There were 20 subjects assigned to the fluvoxamine group and 24 to the maprotiline group; both drugs were administered at doses averaging 150 mg/day. There was a significant decrease in panic attacks in the patients treated with fluvoxamine, but no decrease in the maprotiline-treated patients. In addition, the fluvoxamine-treated patients experienced decreases in anxiety and depressive symptoms. Maprotiline exerted a slight effect on depression but none on anxiety. At the end of the study, half of the fluvoxamine patients had improved substantially, while only five of the 24 (21%) maprotiline patients achieved this level of improvement. Twelve of the 24 maprotiline patients were placed on fluvoxamine after the six-week study, and most responded favourably. All of the fluvoxamine patients continued medication treatment for an additional three months, with continued clinical improvement. The trial provides further support for a serotonin abnormality in panic disorder patients (Den Boer and Westenberg, 1988).

To further examine the question of whether there is 5-HT$_2$ postsynaptic hyperactivity in panic disorder, investigators conducted an eight-week comparison of fluvoxamine and ritanserin in panic disorder patients (Den Boer and Westenberg, 1990; Westenberg and Den Boer, 1989). It was hypothesized that because ritanserin blocks the postsynaptic 5-HT$_2$ receptors, it might have a more rapid onset of action than fluvoxamine. This was not confirmed, however. Sixty panic disorder patients were entered in this study, with one dropout. Treatment was conducted with 150 mg fluvoxamine ($N = 20$), 20 mg ritanserin ($N = 20$), or placebo ($N = 19$). In addition to the treatment component, blood samples were drawn at several points during the study in order to conduct various biological assays. Measurement of plasma levels of β-endorphin, cortisol, 5-hydroxyindoleacetic acid, and MHPG revealed no group differences or changes from baseline and throughout the treatment period. Clinical results showed that 15 (75%) of the fluvoxamine treated patients compared to only two (10%) of the ritanserin group and one (5%) of the placebo group experienced a greater than 50% decrease on the HAM-A. Significant improvement was seen with fluvoxamine beginning in the fourth week and continued throughout the study with significant reduction in number of panic attacks and significant improvement in avoidance, anxiety, and depressive symptoms.

Fluvoxamine and lorazepam were compared in a group of patients diagnosed with mixed anxiety and depression. Entered into this six-week study were 112 patients; 56 assigned to fluvoxamine and 56 to lorazepam. Ten subjects dropped out of the fluvoxamine group, six due to adverse side-effects; there were five dropouts in the lorazepam group with four because of side-effects. Medication was initiated as follows: fluvoxamine 50 mg/day to a maximum daily dose of 300 mg; lorazepam 1 mg/day to a maximum of 6 mg/day. No other medications were allowed in this study. Both fluvoxamine and lorazepam were well tolerated and were extremely effective in reducing anxiety and depression, as early as the first week. At the completion of the study, 80% of the fluvoxamine group and 82% of the lorazepam group were considered to be responders, defined as much or very much improved. Improvement was cumulative and continued throughout the six weeks of the study. The only difference between the drugs demonstrated in this study was that fluvoxamine exerted its effects on depression slightly earlier than lorazepam. Additionally, in a subset of elderly patients, anxiety response was seen earlier with lorazepam, but there was less effect on depression (Laws *et al.*, 1990).

Black *et al.* (1993b) treated 14 panic disorder patients for eight months with fluvoxamine at doses up to 300 mg/day. At the end of this treatment period, fluvoxamine was abruptly discontinued, and patients were to remain medication free for two weeks. At the time that fluvoxamine was discontinued, mean daily dose was 236 mg and all patients were panic free. On the fifth day, one of the 14 patients experienced return of full blown panic disorder sufficient to warrant medication treatment, and this patient was discontinued from the study. On the whole, post-discontinuation patients developed a cluster of symptoms that appeared to be unrelated to their original illness. Symptoms began to emerge within 24 hours of medication discontinuation, peaked at about the fifth day, and then began gradually to decrease in severity. Symptoms reported by patients included dizziness, nausea, difficulty with coordination, headache, and irritability, all suggestive of a withdrawal syndrome. Despite study limitations, the authors indicate that more controlled investigation is warranted to confirm the presence of a withdrawal syndrome, separate and distinct from the recurrence of the patient's panic disorder (Black *et al.*, 1993b).

In direct contrast to Black's study, data were collected from 70 panic disorder patients following completion of two multicentre, placebo controlled trials with fluvoxamine, which did not demonstrate the presence of a withdrawal syndrome with fluvoxamine. Of the 70 patients, 26 actually participated in the entire study; the remaining 44 had discontinued participation prior to study conclusion. Forty-one of the patients had received fluvoxamine, at doses of 100–300 mg/day, and the remaining 29 had received placebo. For most patients (67%), data was collected 1–2 weeks after medication discontinuation. Neither rebound nor recurrence occurred at a higher frequency for the fluvoxamine patients than for the placebo patients. None of the patients in either group experienced a withdrawal syndrome (Holland, 1994). Obviously, further study is required to resolve this issue.

A recent study was conducted in Canada using a combination of moclobemide and fluvoxamine or moclobemide and sertraline in treatment refractory patients. Eleven patients were studied; six diagnosed with major depression, three with panic disorder, one with dysthymic disorder, and one with obsessive–compulsive disorder. Entry criteria required that each patient must have been treated at least twice previously and were considered to be treatment "failures" each time. Results with combined treatment in all patients were positive; seven experienced marked improvement and one experienced complete remission of symptoms (Joffe and

Bakish, 1994). These findings are interesting in that previous combination trials with earlier MAOIs were problematic, primarily due to side-effects and dietary and medication restrictions. Moclobemide, one of the new reversible MAOIs, does not have the same limitations as the earlier MAOIs. Although these results are clearly preliminary, they offer a potential treatment alternative for patients who are unresponsive to more traditional treatments.

One investigation explored the potential of SSRIs to induce or increase depression in panic disorder patients. From a sample of 230 patients with panic disorder and agoraphobia, 80 were identified as having been treated with fluvoxamine, mean daily dose of 100 mg. Of the 80, seven experienced depressive symptoms although anxiety was significantly improved. Five of the seven were then placed on fluoxetine, mean daily dose 20 mg, and all experienced depression. Even after the medications were increased, fluvoxamine to 183 mg and fluoxetine to 40 mg, the depression experienced by these patients failed to improve, and in four actually worsened (Fux *et al.*, 1993). Depression is very common in panic patients and therefore it cannot be proven that the SSRIs "caused" these depressive symptoms. However, the potential for development of depression in panic patients treated with SSRIs (and other medications) should be followed closely.

Zimelidine

Several studies have investigated the effects of zimelidine in panic disorder. In an open study of seven agoraphobic patients, Evans and Moore (1981) administered zimelidine at doses up to 300 mg/day. Marked improvement in symptoms was experienced by five of the seven patients. In another open trial, seven of the 13 patients studied responded positively (Koczkas *et al.*, 1981). A later study compared zimelidine to imipramine and placebo in a group of 44 panic disorder patients. Medication was initiated at doses of 50 mg/day and gradually increased to a maximum of 150 mg/day. Study results indicated that zimelidine was more effective than either imipramine or placebo (Evans *et al.*, 1986). With these promising findings, it is unfortunate that zimelidine has been withdrawn from the market because of its association with the rare but serious development of Guillain–Barré syndrome (Coplan *et al.*, 1992; Nilsson, 1983).

Citalopram

There are only a few small studies with citalopram in panic disorders (Hyttel, 1989). In the trial by Humble and colleagues (Humble *et al.*, 1989; Humble and Wistedt, 1992), it was shown during both acute and maintenance treatment to be well tolerated with a high degree of efficacy. Twenty panic disorder patients with and without agoraphobia were enrolled in an eight-week open study with citalopram, initiated at 5 mg/day and gradually increased to 20 mg/day where the dose was maintained during the third and fourth weeks. If needed to attain clinically significant results, the medication was further increased to a maximum dose of 60 mg/day, with maintenance at this dose through the seventh and eighth weeks. Patients were maintained during the 15-month extension on a flexible dose regimen. The mean dose of citalopram at the end of the eight-week acute study was 41 mg/day and at the end of the extension phase 38 mg/day. Three subjects dropped out of the study; however, only one of the three discontinued study participation due to side-effects. Subjects received no behavioural therapy or psychotherapy during study participation. Participants were allowed to continue taking BZs at doses that had not inhibited panic attacks, and if needed to deal with insomnia. There was a significant reduction in anxiety symptoms and panic attacks early in the study, with significant relief seen by the end of the second week. By the end of the acute study, four patients had complete resolution of panic attacks; another six experienced minor situational panic attacks. Five of the 16 subjects enrolled in the 15-month maintenance study dropped out, with two attributing discontinuation to medication side-effects. Initial treatment gains were generally extended during the maintenance phase (Humble *et al.*, 1989; Humble and Wistedt, 1992).

Paroxetine

Studies in animals indicate that paroxetine is effective in decreasing anxiety behaviours (Lightowler *et al.*, 1992). Male rats were treated for 21 days with paroxetine and placed in an unfamiliar environment, under bright light. The paroxetine treated rats were compared to a group of rats acutely treated with chlordiazepoxide, and increased social behaviour, an indicator of anxiolytic action, was observed in both groups (Lightowler *et al.*, 1992).

A Danish multicentre placebo controlled study compared paroxetine with placebo, all patients receiving cognitive therapy (Oehrberg *et al.*, 1995). In this study, 60 panic disorder patients (DSM-IIIR) were assigned to paroxetine and 60 to placebo. Subjects were maintained on active medication for 12 weeks, following a three-week placebo period. Paroxetine was initiated at 10 mg/day and increased to a maximum of 60 mg/day according to the patient's response and tolerability. Eighty-two percent of the paroxetine treated patients were considered responsive (fifty percent greater reduction in the frequency of attacks). Paroxetine plus cognitive therapy was found to be significantly more effective than placebo plus cognitive therapy, with greater reduction in panic attacks.

Lecrubier *et al.* (1994) compared paroxetine to clomipramine in 368 patients with panic disorder. After nine weeks of therapy 76.1% of the paroxetine patients had a 50% or more reduction in the total numbers of panic attacks compared to 64.5% of clomipramine patients, and 60% of placebo patients. Paroxetine was found to be significantly better than clomipramine in the second three-week period ($p = 0.08$)

and better than placebo in the third and fourth week periods ($p = 0.01$). There was no statistically significant difference between paroxetine and placebo groups with respect to emergent adverse events. Significantly more patients on clomipramine experienced adverse events compared to those on paroxetine ($p = 0.002$).

In summary, the study showed that paroxetine was significantly more effective than placebo in the treatment of patients with panic disorder and equally as effective as clomipramine. In some variables paroxetine had an earlier ameliorative effect. A nine-month extension of this study (Dunbar and Judge, 1995) demonstrated that both paroxetine and clomipramine were effective at maintaining and indeed improving efficacy with continued use. In the paroxetine O group over 70% of patients had become free of panic attacks at endpoint. Paroxetine was also better tolerated than clomipramine as indicated by fewer patient dropouts due to adverse effects. 7% vs 19% for paroxetine and clomipramine respectively.

Steiner *et al.* (1995) reported a 10-week study of 278 patients (DSM-IIIR) receiving fixed dose of paroxetine 10, 20 of 40 mg or placebo. Patients on the higher doses were titrated to these doses. After 10 weeks, at 40 mg, there was a significant difference between paroxetine and placebo.

Sertraline

A fixed dose, placebo controlled, multicentre study of sertraline was undertaken in 320 panic disorder patients, with or without agoraphobia. Following a two-week placebo washout, patients were assigned to placebo or sertraline 50 mg. The sertraline group was further divided into 50 mg, 100 mg, or 200 mg, and doses were increased as tolerated to those fixed doses. Patients were treated for a total of 12 weeks, with the number of panic attacks significantly decreased in the 100 mg, 200 mg, and pooled groups. In addition, significant improvement was demonstrated by the 50 mg, 100 mg, and pooled sertraline groups in anticipatory anxiety. There were no dropouts in the placebo group compared to 22% of the sertraline group. Side-effects observed most frequently in the sertraline-treated patients included dry mouth, sexual dysfunction (failure to ejaculate), nervousness, and agitation (Gorman and Wolkow, 1994).

DOSAGE

The dosage range for each of the SSRIs has been described in detail in the preceding sections. What has been demonstrated repeatedly and what requires particular emphasis is the need for careful clinical monitoring especially of the more activating SSRIs, e.g. fluoxetine. Because of the importance of initial side-effects, particularly hyperstimulation, it is recommended that fluoxetine be prescribed at beginning doses of 2.5–5.0 mg/day. Subsequent increases should be undertaken slowly, in increments of 2.5–5.0 mg every week or two as tolerated. One group has reported good results by initiating fluoxetine treatment at 2 mg/day in those individuals who have a history of hyperstimulatory reactions to medicines (Roy-Byrne and Wingerson, 1992). Initial increases are undertaken slowly and if tolerated, subsequent increases can be made more rapidly. This group reported that a total of 5 mg/day of fluoxetine has produced good results in a small number of patients who could not tolerate side-effects with a number of medications including the BZs and MAOIs. In this subset of patients, fluoxetine was initiated at 1 mg/day with gradual increases to 5 mg/day (Roy-Byrne and Wingerson, 1992). A number of investigators have found that fluoxetine in doses between 20 and 40 mg/day provided clinically significant results (Lyle *et al.*, 1989; Roy-Byrne and Wingerson, 1992).

In the studies described in this chapter, clomipramine was utilized at doses ranging from less than 25 mg/day to 300 mg/day. It has been found that doses as low as 10–30 mg/day, however, are adequate for significantly reducing or totally resolving panic attacks in a subset of patients (Walker and Ashcroft, 1989). The study described earlier by Gloger and colleagues found that 45% of their patients responded to clomipramine at doses less than 50 mg/day (Gloger *et al.*, 1981), and in a subsequent study, half of their subjects responded to clomipramine at less than 25 mg/day (Gloger *et al.*, 1989).

The clinician is advised to monitor the patient's progress closely for development of side-effects so that the dosage can be adjusted as needed to maintain compliance. Of interest is the finding by some investigators that patients who have the most difficulty with hyperstimulation respond to low doses of fluoxetine (Coplan *et al.*, 1992). The clinician should also keep in mind that PD patients are often exquisitely sensitive to substances such as caffeine, alcohol and medications, and should discuss the implications that use of these substances may have for the patient, i.e. enhanced panic-like symptoms.

Fluvoxamine has been demonstrated to be effective when compared at doses of 50, 100, and 150 mg/day. Similar results were produced by all three doses (J.A. Den Boer, unpublished communication, 1992). There were, however, more side-effects at the higher doses.

All the clinical studies with paroxetine described in this chapter utilized doses of 10 mg for a few days, then increased as needed to a maximum dose of 60 mg daily (Oehrberg *et al.*, 1995; Steiner *et al.*, 1995; Dunbar and Judge, 1995). Initial exacerbation of anxiety was not a feature of patients treated with paroxetine. The sertraline study by Gorman and Wolkow (1994) compared 50 mg, 100 mg, and 200 mg/day. Although higher doses, i.e. 100 mg and 200 mg/day, were needed for reduction in panic attacks, the lower dose was effective in decreasing anticipatory anxiety (Gorman and Wolkow, 1994).

SIDE-EFFECTS

The SSRIs do not typically cause weight gain, have significantly less anticholinergic side-effects, and do not affect blood pressure (Gorman, 1994). The SSRIs seem to have a relatively rapid onset of action, with improvement beginning as early as the second week in many studies. Their beneficial effects are exerted on both anxiety and depression, with complete resolution of panic attacks in many patients. Unlike the MAOIs, the SSRIs do not require dietary restrictions.

REFERENCES

Armijo JA, Florez J (1974) The influence of increased brain 5-hydroxytryptamine upon the respiratory activity of cats. *Neuropharmacology* **13**, 977–986.

Asberg M, Schalling D, Traskman-Bendz L and Wagner A (1987) Psychobiology of suicide, impulsivity, and related phenomena. In: Meltzer HY (ed) *Psychopharmacology: The Third Generation of Progress.* pp 655–668, Raven Press, New York.

Asberg M and Martensson B (1993) Serotonin selective antidepressant drugs: past, present, future. *Clin Neuropharmacol* **S3**, S32–S44.

Black DW, Wesner R, Bowers W, *et al.* (1993a) A comparison of fluvoxamine, cognitive therapy, and placebo in the treatment of panic disorder. *Arch Gen Psychiatry* **50**, 44–50.

Black DW, Wesner R and Gabel J (1993b) The abrupt discontinuation of fluvoxamine in patients with panic disorder. *J Clin Psychiatry* **54(4)**, 146–149.

Blakey TA and Parker LF (1973) Effects of parachlorophenylalanine on experimentally induced conflict behavior. *Pharmacol Biochem Behav* **1**, 600–613.

Boyer WF and Feighner JP (1991) The efficacy of selective serotonin reuptake inhibitors in depression. In: Feighner JP and Boyer WF (eds) *Selective Serotonin Re-uptake Inhibitors.* pp 89–108, Wiley, Chichester.

Briggs AC, Stretch DD and Brandon S (1993) Subtyping of panic disorder by symptom profile. *Br J Psychiatry* **163**, 201–209.

Butler J, O'Halloran A and Leonard BE (1992) The Galway Study of Panic Disorder II. Changes in some peripheral markers of noradrenergic and serotonergic function in DSM III-R panic disorder. *J Affect Disord* **26**, 89–100.

Caetano D (1985) Treatment for panic disorder with clomipramine (Anafranil): an open study of 22 cases. *J Bras Psiquiatr* **34**, 123–132.

Cassano GB, Petracca A, Perugi G, Nisita C, Musetti L, Mengali F and McNair DM (1988) Clomipramine for panic disorder: I. The first 10 weeks of a long-term comparison with imipramine. *J Affect Disord* **14**, 123–127.

Charney DS, Woods SW, Goodman WK and Heninger GR (1987) Serotonin function in anxiety. II. Effects of the serotonin agonist MCPP in panic disorder patients and healthy subjects. *Psychopharmacology* **92**, 14–24.

Cohen ME and White PD (1951) Life situations, emotions and neurocirculatory asthenia. *Psychosom Med* **13**, 335–357.

Commissaris RL, Lyness WH and Rech RH (1981) The effects of d-lysergic acid diethylamide (LSD), 2,5-dimethoxy-4-methylamphetamine (DOM), pentobarbital, and methaqualone on punished responding in control and 5,7-dihydroxytryptamine-treated rats. *Pharmacol Biochem Behav* **14**, 617–623.

Cook L and Sepinwall J (1975) Behaviour analysis of the effects of mechanisms of action of benzodiazepines. In: Costa E and Greengard P (eds) *Mechanism of Action of Benzodiazepines.* pp 1–28, Raven Press, New York.

Coplan JD, Gorman JM and Klein DF (1992) Serotonin related functions in panic-anxiety: A critical overview. *Neuropsychopharmacology* **6(3)**, 189–200.

Dealy RS, Ishiki DM, Avery DH, Wilson LG and Dumes DL (1981) Secondary depression in anxiety disorders. *Compr Psychiatry* **22**, 612–618.

Den-Boer JA and Westenberg HG (1988) Effect of a serotonin and noradrenaline uptake inhibitor in panic disorder: a double-blind comparative study with fluvoxamine and maprotiline. *Int Clin Psychopharmacol* **3**, 59–74.

Den Boer JA and Westenberg HGM (1990) Serotonin function in panic disorder: a double blind placebo controlled study with fluvoxamine and ritanserin. *Psychopharmacology* **102**, 85–94.

Den Boer JA, Westenberg HGM, Kamerbeek WDJ, Verhoeven WMA and Kahn RS (1987) Effect of serotonin uptake inhibitors in anxiety disorders; a double-blind comparison of clorimipramine and fluvoxamine. *Int Clin Psychopharmacol* **2**, 21–32.

Dick P and Ferrer E (1983) A double-blind comparative study of the clinical efficacy of fluvoxamine and chlorimipramine. *Br J Clin Pharmacol* **15(S3)**, 419S–425S.

Dunbar GC and Judge R (1995) Long term evaluation of paroxetine, clomipramine and placebo in panic disorder. *Eur Neuropsychopharmacology* **5**, 361.

Evans L, Kenardy J, Schneider P and Hoey H (1986) Effect of a selective serotonin uptake inhibitor in agoraphobia with panic attacks: A double blind comparison of zimelidine, imipramine and placebo. *Acta Psychiatr Scand* **73**, 49–53.

Evans L and Moore G (1981) The treatment of phobic anxiety by zimelidine. *Acta Psychiatr Scand* **63**, 342–345.

Fahy TJ, O'Rourke DO, Brophy J, Schazmann W and Sciascia S (1992) The Galway Study of Panic Disorder I. Clomipramine and lofepramine in DSM III-R panic disorder: A placebo controlled trial. *J Affect Disord* **25**, 63–76.

Feet PO, Larsen S, Lillevold PE, Liden A, Holm V and Robak OH (1987) Comparison of the serum levels in primary nonagitated depressed outpatients treated with imipramine in combination with placebo, diazepam or dixyrazine. *Acta Psychiatr Scand* **75**, 435–440.

Feet PO and Gotestam KG (1994) Increased antipanic efficacy in combined treatment with clomipraine and dixyrazine. *Acta Psychiatr Scand* **89**, 230–234.

File SE and Hyde JRG (1977) The effects of p-chlorophenylalanine and ethanolamine-O-sulphate in an animal test of anxiety. *J Pharmacol* **29**, 735–738.

Fink M, Taylor MA and Volavka J (1970) Anxiety precipitated by lactate (letter). *N Engl J Med* **281**, 1129.

Fux M, Taub M and Zohar J (1993) Emergence of depressive symptoms during treatment for panic disorder with specific 5-hydroxytryptophan reuptake inhibitors. *Acta Psychiatr Scand* **88**, 235–237.

Geller I and Blum K 91970) The effects of 5-HTP on parachlorophenylalanine (pCPA) attenuation of "conflict" behaviour in the rat. *Eur J Pharmacol* **9**, 319–324.

Gloger S, Grunhaus L, Birmacher B and Troudarf T (1981) Treatment of spontaneous panic attacks with clomipramine. *Am J Psychiatry* **138**, 1215–1217.

Gloger S, Grunhaus L, Gladic D, O'Ryan F, Cohen L and Codner S (1989) Panic attacks and agoraphobia: Low dose clomipramine treatment. *J Clin Psychopharmacol* **9**, 28–32.

Gorman JM (1994) New and experimental pharmacological treatments for panic disorder. In: Wolfe BE and Maser JD (eds), *Treatment of Panic Disorder: A Consensus Development Conference.* pp 83–90, American Psychiatric Press, Washington, DC.

Gorman JM, Askanazi J, Liebowitz MR, *et al.* (1984) Response to hyperventilation in a group of patients with panic disorder. *Am J Psychiatry* **141**, 857–861.

Gorman JM and Papp LA (1990) Respiratory physiology of panic. In: Ballenger JC (ed), *Neurobiology of Panic Disorder.* pp 187–203, Alan R. Liss, New York.

Gorman JM, Liebowitz MR, Fyer AJ, *et al.* (1985) Lactate infusions in obsessive–compulsive disorder. *Am J Psychiatry* **142**, 864–866.

Gorman JM, Liebowitz MR, Fyer AJ, *et al.* (1987) An open trial of fluoxetine in the treatment of panic attacks. *J Clin Psychopharmacol* **7**, 329–332.

Gorman JM, Liebowitz MR, Fyer AJ, *et al.* (1989) A neuroanatomical hypothesis for panic disorder. *Am J Psychiatry* **146**, 148–161.

Gorman J and Wolkow R (1994) Sertraline as a treatment for panic disorder. *Neuropsychopharmacology* **10(3S, part 2)**, 197S.

Graeff NG and Filho NGS (1978) Behavioural inhibition induced by electrical stimulation of the median raphe nucleus of the rat. *Physiol Behav* **21**, 477–484.

Graeff FG and Schoenfeld RI (1970) Tryptamine mechanisms in punished and nonpunished behaviour. *J Pharmacol Exp Ther* **173**, 277–283.

Hoehn-Saric R, Fawcett J, Munjack DJ and Roy-Byrne PP (1994) A multicentre, double-blind, placebo-controlled study of fluvoxamine in the treatment of panic disorder. Presented at the Annual Meeting of the College of International Neuropsychopharmacology, Washington, DC.

Hoehn-Saric R, McLeod DR and Hipsley PA (1993) Effect of fluvoxamine on panic disorder. *J Clin Psychopharmacol* **13(5)**, 321–326.

Hoffart A, Due-Madsen J, Lande B, Gude T, Bille H and Torgersen S (1993) Clomipramine in the treatment of agoraphobic inpatients resistant to behavioral therapy. *J Clin Psychiatry* **54(12)**, 481–487.

Holland RL (1994) Fluvoxamine in panic disorder: after discontinuation? Presented at the Annual Meeting of the International College of Neuropsychopharmacology, Washington, DC.

Holland RL, Fawcett J, Hoehn-Saric R, Munjack DJ and Roy-Byrne PP (1994) Long-term treatment of panic disorder with fluvoxamine in outpatients who had completed double-blind studies. *Neuropsychopharmacology* **10 (3S, part 2)**, 102S.

Humble M, Koczkas C and Wistedt B (1989) Serotonin and anxiety: an open study of citalopram in panic disorder; In: Stefanis CN, Soldatos CR and Rabavilas AD (eds), *Psychiatry Today: VIII World Congress os Psychiatry Abstracts.* p 151, Elsevier, New York.

Humble M and Wistedt B (1992) Serotonin, panic disorder and agoraphobia: Short-term and long-term efficacy of citalopram in panic disorders. *Int Clin Psychopharmacol* **6(5S)**, 21–39.

Hyttel J (1989) Citalopram: the pharmacological characteristics of the most selective inhibitor of serotonin uptake. In: Montgomery SA (ed), *Citalopram: The New Antidepressant from Lundbeck Research.* pp 11–21, Excerpta Medica, Amsterdam.

Joffe RT and Bakish D (1994) Combined SSRI-moclobemide treatment of psychiatric illness. *J Clin Psychiatry* **55(1)**, 24–25.

Johnston DG, Troyer IE and Whitsett SF (1988) Clomipramine treatment of agoraphobic women. An eight week controlled trial. *Arch Gen Psychiatry* **45**, 453–459.

Judge and Dunbar (1995) *Paroxetine, Clomipramine and Placebo in the Treatment of Panic.* Presented at the ECNP Congress, 1–4 October, Venice.

Kahn RS, Asnis GM, Wetzler S and van Praag HM (1988) Neuroendocrine evidence for serotonin receptor hypersensitivity in panic disorder. *Psychopharmacology* **96**, 360–364.

Kahn RS, Westenberg HGM, Verhoeven WMA, Gispen-De Wied CC and Kamerbeek WDJ (1987) Effect of a serotonin precursor and uptake inhibitor in anxiety disorders: a double-blind comparison of 5-hydroxytryptophan, clomipramine and placebo. *Int Clin Psychopharmacol* **2**, 33–45.

Klein DF (1993) False suffocation alarms, spontaneous panics, and related conditions: An integrative hypothesis. *Arch Gen Psychiatry* **50**, 306–317.

Klerman GL, Hirschfeld RMA, Weissman MM, Pelicier Y, Ballenger JC, Costa e Silva JA, Judd LL and Keller MB (eds) (1993) *Panic Anxiety and its Treatments: A Task Force Report of the*

World Psychiatric Association. p 47, American Psychiatric Press, Washington, DC.

Klok CJ, Brouwer GH, Van Praag HM and Doogan D (1981) Fluvoxamine and clomipramine in depressed patients: A double-blind clinical study. *Acta Psychiatr Scand* **64**, 1–11.

Koczkas S, Holmberg G and Wedin L (1981) A pilot study of the effect of 5-HT uptake inhibitor, zimelidine, on phobic anxiety. *Acta Psychiatr Scand* **64**, 1–11.

Laws D, Ashford JJ and Anstee JA 91990) A multicentre double-blind comparative trial of fluvoxamine versus lorazepam in mixed anxiety and depression treated in general practice. *Acta Psychiatr Scand* **81**, 185–189.

Leckman JF, Weissman MM, Merikangas KR *et al.* (1983) Panic disorder increases risk of major depression, alcoholism, panic, and phobic disorders in affectively ill families. *Arch Gen Psychiatry* **40**, 1055–1060.

Lecrubier Y (1994) A double-blind placebo controlled comparison of paroxetine and clomipramine in 368 patients with panic disorders. Presented at AEP Meeting, Copenhagen (Study 187).

Lesser IM, Rubin RT, Pecknold JC, Rifkin A, Swinson RP, Ballenger JC, Burrows GD, Dupont FL and Noyes R (1988) Secondary depression in panic disorder and agoraphobia. I. Frequency, severity, and relationship to panic and phobic symptomatology. *Arch Gen Psychiatry* **45**, 437–443.

Liebowitz MR, Fyer AJ, Gorman JM, *et al.* (1984) Lactate provocation of panic attacks. I: Clinical and behavioral findings. *Arch Gen Psychiatry* **41**, 764–770.

Liebowitz MR, Gorman JM, Fyer A, Dillon D, Levitt M and Klein DF (1986) Possible mechanisms for lactate's induction of panic. *Am J Psychiatry* **143**, 495–502.

Lightowler S, Williamson IJR, Kennett GA, Fears R and Tulloch IF (1991) Paroxetine, a new selective serotonin reuptake inhibitor, has anxiolytic activity in the rat social interaction model of anxiety. In: Feighner JP and Boyer WP (eds), *Selective Serotonin Reuptake Inhibitors.* pp 109–117, Wiley-Liss, New York, also presented at the Annual Meeting of the American College of Neuropsychopharmacology, 1992, p 16.

Lingjaerde O (1977) Platelet uptake and storage of serotonin. In: Essman WB (ed), *Serotonin in Health and Disease, Vol IV.* pp 139–199, Spectrum Publications, New York.

Lingjaerde O (1985) Lactate-induced panic attacks: possible involvement of serotonin reuptake stimulation. *Acta Psychiatr Scand* **72**, 206–208.

Louie AK, Lewis TB and Lannon RA (1993) Use of low-dose fluoxetine in major depression and panic disorder. *J Clin Psychiatry* **54(11)**, 435–438.

Lundberg DBA, Mueller RA and Breese GR (1980) An evaluation of the mechanism by which serotonergic activation depresses respiration. *J Pharmacol Exp Ther* **212**, 397–404.

Lyle A, Walker LG and Ashcroft GW (In preparation) Fluoxetine in the treatment of panic attacks: an open trial, (cited in Walker L, Ashcroft G (1989) Pharmacological approaches to the treatment of panic. In: Baker R (ed), *Panic Disorder: Theory Research and Therapy.* p 313, John Wiley, New York.)

Modigh K, Westberg P and Eriksson E (1992) Superiority of clomipramine over imipramine in the treatment of panic disorder: A placebo-controlled trial. *J Clin Psychopharmacol* **12(4)**, 251–261.

Murphy DL and Pigott TA (1990) A comparative examination of a role for serotonin in obsessive–compulsive disorder, panic disorder, and anxiety. *J Clin Psychiatry* **51 (4S)**, 53–58.

Nilsson BS (1983) Adverse reactions in connection with zimelidine treatment: A review. *Acta Psychiatr Scand (Suppl)* **308**, 115–119.

Oehrberg S, *et al* (1995) Paroxetine in the treatment of panic disorder, a randomised double blind placebo controlled study. *Br J Psychiatry* **167**, 374–379.

Olson EB, Dempsey JA and McCrimmon DR (1979) Serotonin and the control of ventilation in awake rats. *J Clin Invest* **64**, 689–693.

Pecknold JC (1990) Serotonin abnormalities in panic disorder. In: Ballenger JC (ed),

Neurobiology of Panic Disorder. pp 121–142, Wiley-Liss, New York.

Pecknold JC and Luthe L (1991) Efficacy of fluoxetine in panic disorder. *Biol Psychiatry* **29**, 240S.

Pecknold JC, McClure DJ, Appeltauer L, *et al.* (1982) Does tryptophan potentiate clomipramine in the treatment of agoraphobic and social phobic patients? *Br J Psychiatry* **140**, 484–490.

Pelham RW, Osterberg AC, Thibault L and Tanikella (1975) Interactions between plasma corticosterone and anxiolytic drugs of conflict behaviour in rates. Paper presented at 4th International Congress Social Psychoneuroendocrinology, Aspen, Colorado.

Pitts FN and McClure JN (1967) Lactate metabolism in anxiety neurosis. *N Engl J Med* **277**, 1328–1336.

Rifkin A, Klein DF, Dillon D and Levitt M (1981) Blockade by imipramine or desipramine of panic induced by sodium lactate. *Am J Psychiatry* **138**, 676.

Robichaud RC and Sledge KL (1969) The effects of p-chlorophenylalanine on experimentally induced conflict in the rat. *Life Sci* **8**, 965–969.

Roy-Byrne PP and Wingerson D (1992) Pharmacotherapy of anxiety disorder. In: Tasman A and Riba MB (eds), *Review of Psychiatry, Vol. 11.* pp 260–284, American Psychiatric Press, Washington, DC.

Schneier FR, Liebowitz MR, Davies SO, Fairbanks J, Hollander E, Campeas R and Klein DF (1990) Fluoxetine in panic disorder. *J Clin Psychopharmacol* **10(2)**, 119–121.

Sepinwall J and Cook K (1980) Mechanism of action of the benzodiazepines—Behavioural aspect. *Fed Proc* **39**, 3024–3031.

Solyom L, Solyom C and Ledwidge B (1991) Fluoxetine in panic disorder. *Can J Psychiatry* **36**, 378–380.

Stein L, Belluzzi JD and Wise CD (1975) Effects of benzodiazepines on central serotonergic mechanisms. In: Costa E and Grengard P (eds), *Mechanism of Action of Benzodiazepines.* pp 29–44, Raven Press, New York.

Stein L, Belluzzi JD and Wise CD 91977) Benzodiazepines: behavioural and neurochemical mechanisms. *Am J Psychiatry* **134**, 665–669.

Stein L, Wise CD and Berger BD (1973) Antianxiety action of benzodiazepines: decrease in activity of serotonin neurons in the punishment systems. In: Garattini S, Mussini E and Randall LO (eds), *The Benzodiazepines.* pp 299–326, Raven Press, New York.

Steiner M, Oakes R, Gergel IP, Burnham DB, Wheadon DE (1995) A fixed dose study of paroxetine and placebo in the treatment of panic disorder. Presented at the 148th APA, Miami (NR 355).

Stevens DA and Fechter LD (1969) The effects of p-chlorophenylalanine, a depletor of brain serotonin, on behaviour. II. Retardation of passive avoidance learning. *Life Sci* **8**, 370–385.

Targum SD and Marshall LE (1989) Fenfluramine provocation of anxiety in patients with panic disorder. *Psychiatry Res* **28**, 295–306.

Tennen SS (1967) The effects of p-chlorophenylalanine, a serotonin depletor, on avoidance acquisition, pain sensitivity, and related behaviour in the rat. *Psychopharmacologica* **10**, 204–219.

Thiebot MH, Hamon M and Soubrie P (1982) Attenuation of induced anxiety in rats by chlordiazepoxide: role of raphe dorsalis benzodiazepine binding sites and serotonergic neurones. *Neuroscience* **7**, 2287–2294.

Thiebot MH, Hamon M and Soubrie P (1983) The involvement of nigral serotonin innervation in the control of punishment-induced behavioural inhibition in rats. *Pharmacol Biochem Behav* **19**, 225–229.

Thiebot MH, Hamon M and Soubrie P (1984) Serotonergic neurones and anxiety-related behaviour in rats. In: Zarifian E and Trimble MR (eds), *Psychopharmacology of the Limbic System.* pp 164–174, Wiley, New York.

Timmerman L and Delta PZ (1994) Combined treatment with clomipramine and cognitive therapy in panic disorder and depression. *Neuropsychopharmacology* **10(3S, part 2)**, 218S.

Tye NC, Everitt BJ and Iversen SD (1977) 5-Hydroxytryptamine and punishment. *Nature* **268**, 741–743.

Tye NC, Iversen SD and Green AR (1979) The effects of benzodiazepines and serotonergic manipulations on punished responding. *Neuropharmacology* **18**, 689–695.

Van Valkenburg C, Akiskal HS, Puzantain V *et al.* (1984) Anxious depression, clinical family history and naturalistic outcome—Comparison with panic and major depressive disorders. *J Affect Disord* **6**, 67–82.

Varia IM and Donnelly DL (1991) Fluoxetine augments tricyclics in panic disorder. New Research Program and Abstracts, American Psychiatric Association Annual Meeting, NR 368, p 136.

Walker L and Ashcroft G (1989) Pharmacological approaches to the treatment of panic. In: Baker R (ed), *Panic Disorder: Theory Research and Therapy.* pp 301–314, John Wiley, New York.

Weissman MM, Klerman GL, Markowitz JS and Ouellette R (1989) Suicidal ideation and suicide attempts in panic disorder and attacks. *N Engl J Med* **321**, 1209–1214.

Westenberg HGM and den Boer JA (1989) Serotonin-influencing drugs in the treatment of panic disorder. *Psychopathology* **22(S1)**, 68–77.

Woods S, Black D,. Brown S *et al.* (1994) Fluvoxamine in the treatment of panic disorder in outpatients: A double-blind, placebo-controlled study. Presented at the Annual Meeting of the College of International Neuropsychopharmacology, Washington, DC.

9

Treating depression in older people

Cornelius L.E. Katona

INTRODUCTION

Depression in old age is common and disabling, yet it remains both underdetected and undertreated. It carries a high risk of recurrence and a considerable risk of suicide. Although a wide variety of management options (including psychological approaches as well as drug and other physical treatments) are available, there is little evidence that either clinical practice or patient outcome have improved substantially in recent years.

A practical understanding of the principles of treatment of depression in elderly patients requires some knowledge of the features that distinguish such patients from their younger counterparts. In order to provide such a background, this chapter reviews the clinical presentation and diagnosis of depression in old age, its epidemiology and its prognosis, before focusing on treatment in general and the use of drugs in particular.

THE CLINICAL FEATURES OF DEPRESSION IN OLD AGE

The presentation of depression in old age may be less obvious and straightforward than in younger patients, due both to the pathoplastic effects of ageing and the different characteristics of birth cohorts as they age. This provides some explanation for its underdetection, although failure by patients to acknowledge their own depression (or to be aware of its potential for treatment) may also be important.

Selective Serotonin Re-uptake Inhibitors: Advances in Basic Research and Clinical Practice, Second Edition, Edited by J.P. Feighner and W.F. Boyer
© 1996 John Wiley & Sons Ltd

Presentations in which hypochondriacal complaints are more prominent than overtly depressed mood are common.

The classic paper by Brown *et al.* (1984) examined 31 patients with depression of first onset after the age of 50 and compared them with two other groups: younger depressed patients and patients of similar age but with a past history of depression earlier in life. Regardless of age of first onset, older patients had greater initial insomnia, agitation and hypochondriasis but less depersonalization, suicidal intent and loss of libido. The late first onset group showed less guilt but had more somatic anxiety, anorexia and hypochondriasis than subjects of similar age with earlier first onset.

Shulman (1989) emphasizes that, in old age, depression more often presents with "neurotic" complaints such as generalized anxiety, subjective nervousness and irritability, than with overt sadness. The distraught, "importuning" elderly depressed patient may present a particularly difficult challenge to the tolerance as well as the diagnostic skills of the clinician. Similarly, Blazer (1994) has highlighted the frequent absence of reporting of depressed mood by the elderly who otherwise seem to be depressed by measurable objective criteria of other symptoms and outcome. This may be as a result of alexithymia (the inability of patients to verbalize or fantasize affective experience) or of rigid defence mechanisms. Wood *et al.* (1990) have stressed the importance of "affective flattening" characterized by unchanging facial expressions, decreased spontaneous movements, paucity of expressive gestures, poor eye contact, emotional non-reactivity, and lack of vocal inflection in severely ill elderly depressed patients.

Shulman (1989) suggests that because of these less obvious presentations of depression in old age, appropriate screening instruments validated in an elderly population are essential to avoid underdetection and undertreatment of depression in old age. The Geriatric Depression Scale (GDS; Yesavage *et al.*, 1983), a rating scale designed specifically for use in old age and appropriate for both self and interviewer-aided completion, may be particularly useful for such screening. The GDS has been extensively validated (Katona, 1994b) and appears to retain its validity in the physically ill elderly (Ramsay *et al.*, 1991). Its acceptability in a primary care context has also been demonstrated (D'Ath *et al.*, 1994).

Subtypes of depression in old age

Conventional diagnostic subtypings of depression may not be appropriate in elderly patients. In particular the "endogenous/non-endogenous" distinction is less reliable in older depressed subjects (Gallagher-Thompson *et al.*, 1992). A much higher proportion of older patients are classified as "endogenous" than would be the case for depression earlier in adult life (Burvill *et al.*, 1989). The "severe–mild" distinction may also be less informative in older depressed subjects: Kivela *et al.* (1989) found that elderly subjects identified in a community survey as having dysthymia (chronic *mild* depression) according to the criteria of DSM III (American Psychiatric Association, 1980) turned out to have depressions of similar severity to the much smaller number with "major" depression. The concept of "minor" depression in old age has recently been reviewed by Tannock and Katona (1995).

EPIDEMIOLOGY OF DEPRESSION IN THE ELDERLY

Estimates of the prevalence of depression in the elderly have varied widely, reflecting differences in sample selection, screening instruments and caseness criteria. Studies using interview schedules designed for elderly subjects suggest a community prevalence (for depression sufficiently severe not to be out of place in a psychiatric outpatient clinic) of about 15% (Livingston and Hinchliffe, 1993). If standardized diagnostic systems such as DSM III are used, many more subjects fulfil criteria for "dysthymia" than for "major depression". Snowdon (1990) has criticized studies using DSM criteria, suggesting that depression is systematically underdiagnosed with a corresponding excess of misdiagnosed anxiety states and subthreshold cases of depression.

As in younger subjects, there is a higher prevalence in women than in men. No consistent relationship with age has been found, at least until age 85. A recent review by Blazer (1994) reports that some studies find an apparent increase in the prevalence of depression in extreme old age, but emphasizes that even this disappears when allowance is made for the confounding effect of concurrent physical illness.

Depression as identified in community surveys is hardly ever treated. Livingston *et al.* (1990) found that only 13% of the survey subjects they identified as depressed were being treated with antidepressants. Copeland *et al.* (1992) reported an even lower treatment rate of 4%.

Studies using samples drawn in specific rather than general community settings usually produce higher prevalence rates. Mann *et al.* (1984) reported a prevalence of 38% in those residents of elderly people's homes in London who were not too severely demented to permit depressive symptoms to be rated. Similar findings have been reported from the United States (Parmelee *et al.*, 1989).

Elderly primary care attenders also appear to have higher prevalence rates for depression; Macdonald (1986) reported a prevalence rate of 31% and observed that, as in community studies, most elderly primary care attenders identified in surveys as depressed are not currently receiving treatment. A recent study by Mullan *et al.* (1994) found that, of elderly primary care attenders identified as depressed by GDS screening, only 20% had a diagnosis of depression recorded in their casenotes and only 14% were receiving treatment for it.

DEPRESSION AND PHYSICAL ILLNESS IN THE ELDERLY

Depression is consistently reported as commoner in physically ill than in healthy elderly subjects. Kennedy *et al.* (1990) found that 30% of community elderly subjects with four or more medical conditions were depressed compared with only 5% of those with no medical illnesses. Similarly, Evans and Katona (1993) found a prevalence of depression in elderly primary care attenders with poor physical health double that in the physically healthy.

Studies specifically examining depressive symptoms and caseness in the physically ill elderly reach similar conclusions. Kitchell *et al.* (1982) found major depression in 45% of an elderly sample of acute medical and neurological patients free of dementia. Koenig *et al.* (1991) found that although only 11.5% of consecutive elderly male medical admissions had major depression, a further 23% had significant depressive symptoms.

The main predictors of depression in the physically ill elderly appear to be positive psychiatric history (Koenig *et al.*, 1991) and severity of the physical illness itself (Rapp *et al.*, 1988).

DEPRESSION IN PEOPLE WITH DEMENTIA

Wragg and Jeste (1989) have reviewed several studies examining depressive symptoms and signs in people with established Alzheimer's disease. The median prevalence of depressed mood was 41% and that of depressive disorder 19%; most studies suggested a higher prevalence of depression than in non-demented controls. Patients with dementia who develop depression may become behaviourally more disturbed and lose daily living skills. Greenwald *et al.* (1989) noted an improvement in cognitive function as well as depressive symptoms when such patients were treated with imipramine. Depression may be difficult to assess in patients with severe dementia because of their loss of verbal skills. A number of rating scales, such as the Cornell Scale (Alexopoulos *et al.*, 1988) and the Depressive Signs Scale (Katona and Aldridge, 1985) have been devised to overcome this problem.

SUICIDE AND DEPRESSION IN OLD AGE

Suicide rates in most countries are highest in the elderly (despite recent increases in suicide rate in young men) and the relationship between depression and suicide is particularly close in the elderly. Barraclough (1971) found clear-cut evidence of depressive illness in 26 of 30 consecutive elderly suicides. Most had had recent contact with their primary care physician, the predominant current symptoms being insomnia, weight loss and hypochondriasis. There was a significant association with chronic physical illness compared with matched controls dying by natural causes. Depression is also commoner in elderly suicide attempters than in their younger counterparts, with reported rates of depression of between 57% (Upadhyaya *et al.*, 1989) and 93% (Pierce, 1987).

Simon (1989) has noted that suicide in elderly American men is almost invariably associated with depressive illness which is often not overt but obscured by coexistent physical illness. The elderly patient who "gives up" or "turns his face to the wall" represents a particular clinical trap. Depression should be considered before such behaviour is regarded as rational. Conwell and Caine (1991) state that "suicide in the absence of treatable affective illness is uncommon in the old . . . to the extent that clinical depressive illness precludes rational decision making, the proportion of rational self-inflicted deaths does not increase with age".

THE PROGNOSIS OF DEPRESSION IN OLD AGE

Depression in old age is associated with high chronicity and a considerable risk of relapse even after recovery. Cole (1990) has systematically reviewed 10 follow-up studies, the combined results showing that although 60% remained well or had relapses with recovery, about 25% developed chronic depression. Cole's review also shows that, although the short-term prognosis may be relatively good, longer follow-up reveals high relapse rates. In those studies lasting two years or less, 44% of subjects were well at follow-up, but in studies with longer follow-up, that figure fell to 27%, with the relapse rate going up from 16% to 34%. Katona (1994c) has reviewed a further six more recent studies from which a similar consensus view emerged. It should however be emphasized that the prognosis of depression does not necessarily become worse with increasing age. Meats *et al.* (1991) and Brodaty *et al.* (1993) have both compared outcome between elderly and younger cohorts of depressed patients and found old age to be associated with a relatively favourable prognosis.

Several studies find that depressed elderly patients have a mortality rate approximately double that found in age- and sex-matched community subjects. At least some of the excess appears to be related directly to the depression since it remains apparent after allowance is made for concurrent physical illness (Murphy *et al.*, 1988).

Several factors have been identified as of prognostic significance within depression in old age. Notable among these are the positive effects of appropriate treatment (reviewed below) and poor physical health. Kennedy *et al.* (1991) reported that worsening physical health was the most powerful predictor of persisting depression, and physical recovery of its remission. Family health status may be a further outcome predictor. A recent paper by Hinrichsen and Hernandez (1993) found that poor physical health in the carers of elderly depressed subjects was associated with non-remission of the depression.

GENERAL PRINCIPLES OF MANAGEMENT OF DEPRESSION IN OLD AGE

Although drug treatment is often the option of first choice in elderly depressed patients and represents the main focus of this chapter, psychological approaches and electroconvulsive therapy (ECT) should not be neglected.

Psychological approaches to depression in the elderly have received relatively little formal evaluation, although efficacy has been demonstrated for psychodynamic, behavioural and particularly cognitive approaches. Steuer *et al.* (1984) demonstrated similar efficacy in elderly depressed patients allocated randomly to behavioural, cognitive and psychodynamic individual therapy and similar conclusions are reached in the review by Morris and Morris (1991). As in younger patients, psychological and physical treatments are probably synergistic, although this has not been adequately demonstrated.

The use of ECT in the elderly is reviewed by Benbow (1989). Its safety profile is surprisingly good, and there is evidence of a broad spectrum of clinical responsiveness. Mulsant *et al.* (1991) carried out a meta-analysis of 1025 elderly patients receiving ECT in 14 separate studies and reported a favourable outcome in 83%, with 62% showing a complete response. This is at least as good an acute response as can be expected in younger patients. Elderly patients treated with ECT also appear to have a very good long-term prognosis, with 59% well at three years (Godber *et al.*, 1987), and most of the remainder (29%) having only mild residual symptoms. ECT is an important treatment option in elderly patients unresponsive to antidepressants, and those with very severe illnesses. It may be life-saving in patients who are acutely suicidal and those who, in the context of depressive retardation or stupor, have stopped eating and drinking.

DRUG TREATMENT OF DEPRESSION IN OLD AGE

In general, the same principles of antidepressant drug treatment apply as for younger patients. There are however a number of particular problems in treating older patients, relating mainly to age-related changes in drug handling and in cognitive function, which need to be considered when planning the treatment of individual patients.

Antidepressant drugs currently in use include well-established tricyclic antidepressants (TCAs) and monoamine oxidase inhibitors (MAOIs), as well as a relatively newly introduced TCA (lofepramine), an important group of selective serotonin re-uptake inhibitors (SSRIs), and a novel MAOI, moclobemide. The evidence regarding the efficacy and tolerability of each of these groups will be discussed in turn, concentrating on the newer drugs and on the question of whether their advantages in elderly patients might be sufficient to outweigh their higher cost.

The efficacy of TCAs and MAOIs in the depressed elderly

There have been surprisingly few placebo controlled trials of TCAs or MAOIs against placebo in patents over the age of 60. The reviews by Gerson *et al.* (1988) and Rockwell *et al.* (1988) identified only one placebo controlled evaluation of amitriptyline (Branconnier *et al.*, 1982), three of imipramine (Gerner *et al.*, 1980;

Meredith *et al.*, 1984; Wakelin, 1986) and none of desipramine or trimipramine. The MAOIs iproniazid (Shapiro *et al.*, 1960) and phenelzine (Georgotas *et al.*, 1986) have each been subjected to one placebo controlled study. Three studies (Georgotas *et al.*, 1987; Katz *et al.*, 1990; Lipsey *et al.*, 1984) have evaluated nortriptyline (which, as discussed above, may be particularly well tolerated by elderly subjects) against placebo in elderly patients. One of these (Katz *et al.*, 1990), however, was performed in a residential care setting, and another (Lipsey *et al.*, 1984) in stroke patients.

Although all the placebo-controlled studies found the active compound to be superior, it must be remembered that most of the elderly patients met with in routine clinical practice would not qualify for such clinical trials. The majority of elderly patients with significant depression fulfil DSM criteria for dysthymia rather than major depressive episode (Kivela *et al.*, 1988). However, most trials specify major depression as an entry criterion. Equally important, as pointed out by Salzman (1993), virtually no antidepressant trials have examined a very old (aged 80 +) sample since such patients, while remaining an important treatment target in clinical practice, almost invariably fulfil one or more of the exclusion criteria for drug trials.

A further problem with evaluative studies of antidepressants in the elderly is that the outcome measures used, like the inclusion criteria, are geared towards a younger population. This is exemplified in the most widely used scale for measuring depressive severity, the Hamilton Depression Rating Scale (HDRS; Hamilton, 1960). The HDRS contains several somatic items whose presence in elderly patients may reflect the coexistence of physical disease rather than the depression being assessed. It is thus unlikely that the relationship between change in scale score and true antidepressant response will be the same as in younger patients. Less age-related distortion in results would be seen if more appropriate response scales were used. Such scales include measures of clinical global impression (CGI); scales specifically designed to measure change in elderly depressed subjects like the GDS; or less somatically weighted scales such as the Montgomery Asberg Depression Rating Scale (Montgomery and Asberg, 1979).

The side-effects of TCAs and MAOIs in the elderly

Elderly patients are particularly likely to suffer side-effects when taking TCAs or MAOIs and are more vulnerable to serious adverse consequences as a result. The TCA side-effects of particular relevance in the elderly are summarized in Table 1. Perhaps most important is the fact that elderly patients are more vulnerable to accidents (Ray, 1992) and to falls (Campbell, 1991). Careful epidemiological data from the US relating antidepressant use and car-accident related injuries in people aged 65–84 found that use of cyclic antidepressants was associated with a doubling in the risk of crash involvement (Ray, 1992). TCAs and MAOIs both block

Table 1. Side-effects of tricyclic antidepressants of particular relevance in older patients.

Anticholinergic
  Confusion
  Urinary retention
  Precipitation/worsening of glaucoma
  Blurring of vision

Antihistaminic
  Sedation

Antiadrenergic
  Postural hypotension
  Dizziness
  Falls

α_1-adrenergic receptors and thereby exacerbate postural hypotension, which is often present anyway in view of the gradual blunting of baroreceptor reflexes in old age (Woodhouse, 1992). Falls may then result, with increased risk of long-bone fractures due to age-related osteoporosis. Many TCAs are powerfully sedating, reflecting an antihistaminic effect and, even in the absence of overt sedation, cognitive function is more likely in elderly patients to be impaired by antidepressants with powerful anticholinergic effects (Moskowitz and Burns, 1986). Both sedation and cognitive impairment are likely to enhance the risk of falls and accidents in elderly patients taking TCAs or MAOIs.

Since most tricyclics are extensively protein bound, age-related decreases in protein synthesis can increase free plasma drug levels. Reduced creatinine clearance and hepatic blood flow may also contribute to increased blood levels of tricyclics by delaying their excretion. These pharmacokinetic changes also increase the potential of antidepressants to cause side-effects. Inter-individual variability in blood levels of tricyclics and their active metabolites is however considerable in elderly as well as in younger subjects. Thus, in the absence of routinely available plasma level monitoring (and with the exception of nortriptyline for which plasma levels should remain within a "therapeutic window"), titration to maximum tolerated dose may be as necessary in elderly as in younger subjects, although the average dose required will be smaller.

Despite the need to monitor its levels closely, nortriptyline has been found to be relatively free of the problems associated with other tricyclics in elderly subjects. An open study of nortriptyline in elderly and younger depressed patients (Kanba *et al.*, 1992) found no difference in likelihood of adverse effects between older and younger subjects and, surprisingly, no age-related increase in blood level achieved for a given dose. In keeping with this, Miller *et al.* (1991) found that only five out of a series of 45 elderly depressed subjects given nortriptyline in an open trial were unable to tolerate it. In most subjects in this trial, side-effects decreased in tandem with depressive symptoms. No nortriptyline-associated increase in orthostatic hypotension was seen.

Practical aspects of treating older patients with TCAs and MAOIs

Compliance is often problematic with these drugs, both because of troublesome side-effects and because many involve taking several tablets two or even three times a day. Age-related increases in vulnerability to other diseases and likelihood of receiving other treatments make elderly patients more vulnerable to drug–drug and drug–disease interactions. There is some evidence that tricyclic antidepressants may take a surprisingly long time to be effective in elderly patients, with useful effects sometimes only emerging in the seventh and eighth week of treatment (Georgotas *et al.*, 1989b). The combination of side-effect vulnerability and these practical issues may go some way towards explaining why primary care physicians, as reported by Macdonald (1986) and by Mullan *et al.* (1994), seem reluctant to undertake antidepressant treatment in elderly patients.

Profile of the "ideal antidepressant" for the elderly

TCAs and MAOIs are clearly far from being "ideal" antidepressants for elderly patients. A theoretical "ideal" drug would show unchanged pharmacokinetics in elderly subjects, be free of interactions with other drugs commonly used in the elderly, and be safely administered even to frail patients with concomitant physical disease. Furthermore, such a drug would have a simple once daily dosage regimen and have proven clinical trial efficacy against established comparator drugs and placebo. Further requirements would include good side-effect profile, rapid onset of antidepressant action and demonstrable efficacy in preventing relapse as well as in alleviating depression acutely. Efficacy would be evident in intention-to-treat (ITT) analyses, which allow for dropout rates, as well as in trial completers (COMPs). Such trials should be of epidemiologically representative samples and use clinically valid measures of antidepressant response.

Short-term studies of newer antidepressants in the elderly

This section will examine available evidence for the tolerability and acute efficacy of newer antidepressants in comparison with longer-established comparators and where possible placebo, seeking to establish whether they represent any significant progress towards an ideal antidepressant for elderly patients. In particular, evidence will be reviewed for the novel tricyclic lofepramine, five SSRIs (fluvoxamine, fluoxetine, paroxetine, sertraline and citalopram), and one "new generation" MAOI (moclobemide). All have received some evaluation in elderly patients and are available in at least some.European countries.

Lofepramine
Lofepramine has a conventional tricyclic structure but *in vitro* studies and trials in non-elderly subjects suggest that it is relatively free of anticholinergic side-effects

(Sjogren, 1980). The effects of single doses of lofepramine (70–140 mg) have been compared with 50 mg amitriptyline and placebo in drug-free healthy elderly volunteers. The side-effect profile of lofepramine did not differ significantly from that of placebo. In contrast, amitriptyline was associated with more frequent subjective side-effects than either lofepramine or placebo. Amitriptyline significantly reduced standing diastolic blood pressure in comparison with lofepramine; salivary volume (an objective measure of dry mouth) was less in subjects treated with amitriptyline in comparison with either placebo or lofepramine. In contrast with amitriptyline, which impaired performance on choice reaction time, lofepramine was associated with significantly better choice reaction time than placebo (Ghose and Sedman, 1987). The same group (Ghose and Spragg, 1989) examined the pharmacokinetics of single doses of lofepramine and amitriptyline in healthy drug-free elderly subjects. They found the elimination half-life of lofepramine to be 2.5 hours (compared with 31 hours for amitriptyline), but noted considerable inter-individual variation in peak plasma lofepramine concentrations. These studies suggest that lofepramine has unchanged pharmacokinetics compared with younger subjects despite its very extensive (99%) protein binding (Sjogren, 1980). On this basis, it should be well tolerated by elderly people.

Two published studies have examined the efficacy of lofepramine in elderly depressed patients: against amitriptyline (Jessel et al., 1981), and against dothiepin (Fairbairn et al., 1989). Both studies were small (20/19 and 30/32 respectively) but had high completer rates. COMP analyses only were provided, and lofepramine was found to be significantly more effective than amitriptyline (72% response rate versus 47%) and as effective as dothiepin. Analysis of side-effects showed no difference from amitriptyline but less dry mouth and drowsiness than dothiepin.

Although lofepramine thus appears to be a reasonably effective antidepressant for elderly people, these results must be viewed with some caution. In particular there are no placebo controlled data and no ITT analyses; doses of both lofepramine and the comparators were relatively low (with no reporting of plasma levels); and total numbers of subjects included were small. There are also no long-term data on the efficacy of lofepramine in preventing relapse.

SSRIs

In general, SSRIs are well tolerated by older subjects and most studies suggest (as is also the case for younger patients) similar efficacy and time course of action to TCAs. In general, SSRIs are free of anticholinergic effects and cardiotoxicity, and do not cause postural hypotension. The main side-effects seen are headache and nausea. A recent study (Mullan et al., 1994) suggests that a higher proportion of elderly patients are fit to take SSRIs, reflecting their relatively few contraindications. Evidence in younger patients suggests that they may be more rapidly effective in reducing suicidal thoughts (Muijen et al., 1988). This may be of particular importance in the elderly, in whom the suicide rate is relatively high and the link with depression closer than earlier in life.

Fluvoxamine This drug is chemically and pharmacologically distinct from tricyclic antidepressants and is a potent and selective inhibitor of serotonin re-uptake. Animal studies show it to be free of MAO-inhibiting and anticholinergic effects and to have negligible effects on noradrenaline re-uptake (Classen *et al.*, 1977). It is rapidly absorbed, has no active metabolites, is excreted via the kidneys, and its plasma half-life of about 15 hours is unaffected by age (Benfield and Ward, 1986). While its adverse effect profile is similar to that of other SSRIs, nausea may be particularly prominent, especially at a high dose (Wagner *et al.*, 1992).

There have been three double-blind controlled comparisons between fluvoxamine and standard antidepressants in elderly patients. Only one of these (Wakelin, 1986) incorporated a placebo group (which only contained 12 subjects). Patients in this study were too young (age range 60–71) to make it representative of older depressed patients. Dropout rates were relatively high in both the fluvoxamine and comparator (imipramine) groups (17/33 and 13/29), and the study only lasted four weeks. Clear superiority of both active drugs over placebo was demonstrated for completers. It should be noted, however, that the superiority was much less striking in the ITT analysis.

The studies by Rahman *et al.* (1991) and Phanjoo *et al.* (1991) compared fluvoxamine with dothiepin and mianserin respectively. Neither had a placebo group, both were relatively small (26 and 25 entrants to each study arm) and both had similarly high dropout rates to those in the Wakelin (1986) study. Rahman *et al.* (1991) and Phanjoo *et al.* (1991) did however examine a more truly elderly sample (ages ranging up to 87), had a more adequate duration of treatment (six weeks), and used appropriate outcome measures (MADRS and CGI). Both studies found fluvoxamine to be as effective as the comparator drugs. Rahman *et al.* (1991) also provided adequate information about response rates, which at 64% for fluvoxamine and 60% for dothiepin are similar to those reported in studies in younger patients. Surprisingly, side-effect profiles were similar for fluvoxamine and comparators in all the studies although Wakelin (1986) found fluvoxamine to give rise to significantly less dry mouth than imipramine.

In the context of controlled clinical trials, fluvoxamine thus appears to be reasonably effective and well tolerated. Comparison against placebo is however very limited both by small numbers and high dropout rates, and there are no published data addressing the question of the drug's efficacy in relapse prevention.

Fluoxetine Like the other SSRIs currently available, fluoxetine has a novel pharmacological structure and is relatively free of cardiovascular, anticholinergic, antihistaminic and hypotensive effects (Feighner, 1983). It is metabolized in the liver and may interfere with the breakdown of other drugs, in particular causing increased plasma concentrations and toxicity of concurrently administered tricyclic antidepressants. The possibility has been raised of fluoxetine precipitating atrial fibrillation or sinus bradycardia in elderly patients (Buff *et al.*, 1991). A serious fluoxetine/MAOI interaction has also been noted (Feighner *et al.*, 1990), involving hypothermia and confusion and resulting in a number of deaths. It is now recommended that a minimum period of five weeks be left between stopping fluoxetine and starting an MAOI. Lucas and Osborne (1986) have examined the pharmacokinetics of fluoxetine and its major active metabolite norfluoxetine in elderly depressed patients and found no age-related alteration in the time course of their elimination. The elimination half-lives are however extremely long (2–3 days for fluoxetine and 7–9 days for norfluoxetine).

There has been one published study of fluoxetine (at the currently recommended dose of 20 mg/day) against placebo (Tollefson and Holman, 1993). The sample examined was very large (over 250 subjects in each study arm). Despite this the trend towards a larger change in HDRS score in the fluoxetine treated group failed to reach statistical significance, and although significantly more fluoxetine patients were classified as responders, response rate was low in both groups (35% versus 27%). Dropout rate was low and similar for fluoxetine and placebo.

In addition to this, three controlled comparisons between fluoxetine and established antidepressants have been published (Feighner and Cohn, 1985; Altamura et al., 1989; Falk et al., 1989). In the largest ($N = 78/79$) of these (Feighner and Cohn, 1985), with doxepin as comparator, relatively high doses of both drugs were used, with adequate treatment duration and the CGI as main outcome measure. The dropout rate was very high, approaching 50% in the fluoxetine group and exceeding it in the doxepin group. Despite this, reasonable ITT response rates (approaching 50%) were seen; these did not differ between the two drugs. No formal comparisons were made of emergent side-effects, but adverse experiences were the reason for dropout in 32% of fluoxetine patients and 43% of doxepin patients. Anticholinergic side-effects were more prominent in the doxepin group, and nausea, anxiety and insomnia with fluoxetine.

The much smaller ($N = 13/15$) study by Altamura et al. (1989) involved relatively young subjects (mean age 68.5 years), had a short treatment period of five weeks and used a fairly low dose of comparator drug (amitriptyline 75 mg). Drop out rates were low. In a COMP analysis the two drugs were equivalent in efficacy but amitriptyline appeared to have a faster onset of action. This presumably reflected the ability of amitriptyline to relieve anxiety and initial insomnia, since the superiority was not apparent for biological symptoms. Severity and frequency of side-effects tended to be lower in the fluoxetine group, the difference reaching statistical significance for dry mouth. Amitriptyline treated patients (unlike those on fluoxetine) showed significant weight gain during the trial.

Falk et al. (1989) compared fluoxetine and trazodone in variable dose for six weeks of active treatment. Unfortunately, only 10/14 patients on fluoxetine and 3/13 on trazodone completed the study. These numbers are clearly insufficient for very meaningful statistical evaluation of efficacy, although significantly fewer dropouts and more responders were found in the fluoxetine group. The only statistically significant differences in side-effects were more frequent constipation on trazodone and more insomnia on fluoxetine.

On the basis of these studies, fluoxetine appears to have a different side-effect profile to tricyclic antidepressants and to be comparable with them in efficacy. Unlike other SSRIs, fluoxetine has been fully evaluated against placebo. Evidence for its superiority over placebo is however surprisingly modest given the statistical power of so large a sample.

Paroxetine   This drug is a highly selective serotonin re-uptake inhibitor which is rapidly absorbed and extensively (95%) protein bound, with a complex metabolic pathway of oxidation, methylation and conjugation prior to excretion in the urine. The plasma half-life is approximately 24 hours but varies widely with some evidence of increased plasma half-life in the elderly (Kaye *et al.*, 1989).

Six controlled comparisons with established antidepressants in elderly patients have been published. Dunner *et al.* (1992), comparing paroxetine with doxepin, had a large sample size ($N = 136/135$) with a mean age of 68. Both drugs were administered in relatively high doses over six weeks and were found to be equivalent in efficacy, although paroxetine had a larger effect than doxepin on the physician-rated clinical global impression and on the depressed mood item of the HDRS. Dorman (1992), in a small study comparing paroxetine with a relatively low dose of mianserin in an elderly sample again undefined by mean age, found paroxetine to be superior. This finding must be viewed with some caution since only COMP analysis was reported and, although the response rate in the paroxetine group (48%) was reasonable, that in the mianserin group (18%) was very low. Hutchinson *et al.* (1991) compared paroxetine with amitriptyline in a fairly large ($N = 58/32$) although relatively young (mean age 72) elderly group over six weeks. Dropout rates were reasonably low and, in a COMP only analysis, the two drugs were found to be equally effective. Guillibert *et al.* (1989) compared the efficacy of paroxetine (20–30 mg) with clomipramine (up to 75 mg) in a six-week trial in 79 patients aged 60 and over. Both groups improved significantly with no apparent difference in efficacy (overall response rates of 65% for paroxetine and 72% for clomipramine) or in withdrawal rate.

All four of the above studies showed a tendency for more anticholinergic side-effects with comparator drugs than paroxetine. Dunner *et al.* (1992) reported significantly more frequent dry mouth, somnolence, headache, confusion and constipation with doxepin, but more diarrhoea and nausea with paroxetine. Similarly, Hutchinson *et al.* (1991) reported that anticholinergic effects overall were more frequent with amitriptyline than paroxetine, and Guillibert *et al.* (1989) found more tremor and somnolence with clomipramine than with paroxetine.

There have been two comparisons between paroxetine and another SSRI, fluoxetine. Schone and Ludwig (1993) found no difference in tolerability between the drugs; paroxetine was however associated with significantly more rapid response and greater cognitive improvement. Some but not all of the measures of the response at the end of the trial also significantly favoured paroxetine.

Paroxetine thus appears to be of at least equal efficacy to comparator drugs with some suggestion of superiority. The overall response rate to paroxetine was not however particularly high. Its side-effect profile in elderly patients closely resembles that which would be predicted from *in vitro* studies and data from younger patients. These conclusions would of course be much strengthened by placebo controlled trial data. Dunbar (1995) performed meta-analysis of 10 geriatric studies involving 387 patients on paroxetine and 349 patients on active controls (110 amitryptiline, 109 clomipramine, 102 doxepin, 28 mianserin). Paroxetine was consistently superior to the active controls for both efficacy and safety.

Sertraline   This drug is a specific serotonin re-uptake inhibitor unrelated chemically to other SSRIs and relatively free of anticholinergic, antihistaminic and adverse cardiovascular side-effects, which desensitizes 5-HT$_2$ receptors directly as well as inhibiting 5-HT re-uptake (Doogan and Caillard, 1988). It has been suggested that, unlike other SSRIs, sertraline has negligible effects on the P450 cytochrome system and is thus much less likely to inhibit the metabolism of concurrently administered drugs broken down through P450 pathways (Preskorn, 1993). Recent data, however, suggest that this is not the case, since sertraline inhibits the IID6 P450 isoenzyme for approximately the same extent as paroxetine and fluoxetine in vitro (Crewe *et al.*, 1992) and significantly inhibits desipramine metabolism in man (Barros and Asnis, 1993; Zussman *et al.*, 1995). Pharmacokinetic studies (Invicta, data on file) suggest that in elderly volunteers, the pharmacokinetics of sertraline are similar to those in younger subjects. Its major metabolite, desmethylsertraline, is however found in high concentrations in elderly subjects. The plasma half-life of sertraline in these elderly volunteers was 21.6 hours and that of desmethylsertraline 83.7 hours. Three out of 20 volunteers in an open study had to discontinue sertraline because of side-effects such as nausea, insomnia and dizziness. Comparison of the effects of sertraline and mianserin on psychomotor performance in elderly volunteers showed sertraline (at doses up to 200 mg daily) to have a generally neutral psychomotor profile (Hindmarch *et al.*, 1990) with significant improvement in vigilance compared with placebo (Hindmarch and Bhatti, 1988).

The only published controlled study of sertraline in elderly patients is a comparison with amitriptyline (Cohn *et al.*, 1990). This study used a relatively large (161/80) sample but did not include a placebo group; the mean age was relatively low. The completer rate in both sertraline and amitriptyline groups was less than 50%. The COMP analysis showed equivalent efficacy, although the ITT analysis indicated some superiority for amitriptyline in magnitude of HDRS change. The latter finding may be due, at least in part, to greater responsiveness of the anxiety and sleep items of this scale to the more sedating antidepressant. Rate of side-effect related withdrawal was similar (28% on sertraline subjects and 35% on amitriptyline); anticholinergic side-effects were significantly commoner on amitriptyline and gastrointestinal ones on sertraline. There was also a modest but statistically significant difference in weight change between the groups, amitriptyline being associated with weight gain and sertraline with weight loss.

Sertraline thus appears reasonably well tolerated by elderly patients. However, the high withdrawal rate and lack of placebo control limit the confidence that can be placed in these results.

Citalopram This is a highly specific inhibitor of 5-HT re-uptake. It is metabolized rapidly by oxidation and demethylation and has been shown to be an effective antidepressant in younger adults and to have significantly fewer side-effects (particularly those involving anticholinergic mechanisms) than tricyclics (Luo and Richardson, 1993). In the only controlled trial to date in elderly depressed subjects, Nyth *et al.* (1992) report on a six-week study of citalopram against placebo in 149 subjects aged 65 and over. Of the subjects 74% fulfilled DSM criteria for major depression, although 20% had a concomitant diagnosis of dementia. Global improvement was greater in the citalopram treated subjects but the change in HDRS scores did not differ significantly between them. On the MADRS, the results favoured citalopram in the total sample, but there were no significant differences when the analysis was restricted to subjects with major depression. Citalopram was well tolerated but was associated with significantly more side-effects than placebo. The findings illustrate the importance of having a placebo group, but provide only modest support for the use of citalopram in the elderly.

Moclobemide

Moclobemide, a benzamide derivative, is a recently introduced, short-acting, reversible, selective inhibitor of MAO-A (Da Prada *et al.*, 1989). There are no dietary restrictions except a recommendation to avoid very excessive consumption of tyramine-containing foods. The pharmacokinetics of moclobemide are very similar in younger and elderly subjects (Maguire *et al.*, 1991). Pooled clinical trial data show it to be as effective and, unlike its tricyclic comparators, as well tolerated in elderly as in younger depressed subjects (Angst and Stabl, 1992).

Three small clinical trials in elderly subjects have been published to date; each involves only COMP analyses and none contains a placebo group. De Vanna *et al.* (1990), in a brief report from two studies, found moclobemide to be as effective as both mianserin ($N = 40/40$) and maprotiline ($N = 20/19$). Tiller *et al.* (1990), using a sequential analysis design, also found no significant difference in efficacy between moclobemide ($N = 20$) and mianserin ($N = 19$). However, a recent trial against nortriptyline and placebo in 109 elderly depressed patients found that although nortriptyline was superior to placebo, moclobemide was not (Nair *et al.*, 1995).

The published data currently available is clearly inadequate to form definite conclusions about the use of moclobemide in elderly depressed patients.

How strong is the case for using newer antidepressants in elderly patients?

All the antidepressant drugs reviewed above appear to be effective in 50–60% of depressed elderly patients. This suggests that there is no clear difference in efficacy between them and their tricyclic predecessors. Placebo controlled data provide some measure of reassurance as far as fluoxetine and citalopram are concerned, although in both cases the overall results against placebo are less clear-cut than might have been expected. For the other drugs reviewed, the lack of evidence for superiority over placebo remains a major problem. No single drug can be claimed to be clearly superior to the others on the basis of the evidence reviewed above, although paroxetine may claim a slight edge in terms of numbers of patients studied and some suggestion of superiority over a variety of comparator drugs including another SSRI.

The new generation of antidepressant drugs probably do represent a modest step forward in the treatment of depression in elderly patients and may reasonably be seen as drugs of first choice. Their advantage lies not in greater clinical trial efficacy but in the fact that they have fewer contraindications and a less disabling side-effect profile which may enable a high proportion of the many depressed elderly patients in the real world who would not be eligible for entry into controlled clinical trials to be treated effectively (Mullan *et al.*, 1994). A further area which has as yet remained unexplored in the elderly is critical cost–benefit appraisal (Maynard, 1993) which is necessary to discover whether using newer, and much more expensive, antidepressants in an elderly population can be justified by their more favourable compliance and adverse effect profile.

TREATMENT OF DEPRESSION IN ELDERLY PATIENTS WITH CONCURRENT OTHER ILLNESS

Therapeutic nihilism is a particular trap in elderly medical patients with coexisting depression. Clinicians should be alert to contraindications to antidepressants and to the development of side-effects. According to Katz *et al.* (1990), risk of such drug side-effects is greater in the frail elderly, necessitating the use of lower (and perhaps therapeutically inadequate) doses of TCAs. Particular care is also needed due to the danger of toxic effects in overdose (Montgomery, 1990).

The clinical challenge of controlled trials of antidepressant treatment in this population is considerable. This is epitomized in the report by Koenig *et al.* (1989), who attempted a trial of nortriptyline against placebo in elderly patients admitted to the medical wards of a Veterans' Administration hospital. Although 964 were evaluated, only 773 were cognitively well enough preserved to allow GDS screening. Eighty-one scored positive for depression, and 63 of them were further evaluated by a psychiatrist. Forty-one were found to have DSM III Major Depressive Episode, but 14 of them had already been treated with antidepressants, 15 had medical contraindications to their use and five refused. Of seven subjects randomized, four dropped out. All of three completed the study (two on placebo and one on nortriptyline) and all improved! A number of small trials have however been successfully completed. Lipsey *et al.* (1984) have demonstrated the efficacy of nortriptyline in the treatment of post-stroke depression in a double-blind study of 34 patients with a mean age around 60. Patients who were successfully treated had serum nortriptyline levels in the conventional therapeutic range. It should be noted however that only 14 patients were on active treatment, and three of these developed antidepressant-related acute confusional states. Reding *et al.* (1986) reported that trazodone showed a non-significant trend towards benefit when compared with placebo in stroke patients. Their findings are however difficult to interpret since not all subjects entered into the trial were clinically depressed and the main outcome measure was change in level of dependency rather than alleviation of depression. Schifano *et al.* (1990) compared the efficacy of mianserin and maprotiline in 48 elderly physically ill subjects with major depression or (in four cases) dysthymia. Thirty-five completed the trial, with mianserin showing significant superiority in terms of GDS scores. Only 40% of subjects in each group, however, were improved or very much improved on the CGI.

Despite the relative lack of controlled-trial evidence demonstrating the efficacy of specific treatments for depression in physically ill elderly patients, such treatment is nonetheless often necessary in clinical practice. Close links between the geriatrician and the psychiatrist are important to ensure that the possibility of comorbid depression is considered in the initial assessment and subsequent care of elderly patients admitted to acute or chronic hospital beds. Treatment should be considered particularly in patients with prominent neurovegetative symptoms (particularly retardation, poor appetite and poor food and fluid intake) unexplained by their physical condition. Other "pointers" to initiate treatment of depression include the expression of suicidal thoughts or intent, and depressive symptoms that are persistent, intense, or impair social functioning. Patients who become depressed while undergoing medical treatment may become intolerant of levels of pain or disability that they were previously able to withstand without complaint. The possibility of depression should also be considered in patients whose medical problems fail to respond to apparently appropriate and effective treatment.

Systematic trials of antidepressants with better side-effect profiles and fewer medical contraindications are clearly needed in this population who, from the point of view of the pharmaceutical companies involved, represent a considerable potential market. Fogel and Kroessler (1987) suggest that MAOIs may be a safe option among elderly depressed patients and, indeed, that many elderly patients who do not respond to tricylics will respond favourably to one of the MAOIs. Despite the relatively high risk of toxicity it carries in the frail elderly, lithium augmentation (which is discussed in the next section) has been specifically reported to be beneficial in physically ill elderly patients with refractory depression (Kushnir, 1986).

Similar considerations apply for depression in patients with concurrent dementia. Imipramine has been shown to be effective (Greenwald *et al.*, 1989). On theoretical grounds, however, TCAs with their powerful anticholinergic effects, might be expected to carry considerable risk of cognitive and behavioural retardation, particularly where pre-treatment cognitive deficits are already severe. In this context, newer and cognitively neutral or enhancing antidepressants, such as the SSRIs and moclobemide, may carry a considerable advantage. The study of Nyth *et al* (1992) bears out the potential benefits of SSRIs in depression within dementia, although the patients were not well enough characterized for firm conclusions to be drawn. A further treatment option that has fallen into undeserved disrepute is the use of psychostimulants such as methylphenidate. A recent review by Arcand and Hottin (1993) observes that between 1957 and 1980 as many as five placebo controlled studies of methylphenidate in patients with dementia and depression were published. Although patient characterization was poor, it remains striking that the methylphenidate was well tolerated and, in all but one of the studies, was superior to placebo.

PHARMACOLOGICAL STRATEGIES FOR REFRACTORY DEPRESSION IN OLD AGE

As has been discussed above, antidepressant drugs offer no guarantee of response in elderly patients, any more than is the case for depression in younger subjects. In patients failing to respond, full review including assessment of the appropriateness and adequacy (in terms of dosage, duration and compliance) of any treatment trial should be undertaken. The use of electroconvulsive therapy and of specific psychological approaches should also be considered.

Several drug combination treatments (such as tricyclic–MAOI combinations, the addition of tri-iodothyronine and the co-administration of tricyclic antidepressants and neuroleptics) have been proposed and to a limited extent evaluated in younger patients (Katona, 1994a). These treatment manoeuvres have however received no evaluation in elderly subjects and are in any case likely to be relatively hazardous.

Georgotas *et al* (1983) have however noted that 65% of elderly patients failing to respond to tricyclic antidepressants recovered during an open trial of phenelzine. Another treatment option is the addition of lithium, which is probably the best evaluated pharmacological strategy in younger antidepressant-resistant patients (Austin *et al*, 1991). Kushnir (1986) reported the benefit of lithium augmentation in a small open series of five elderly physically ill patients. In a retrospective analysis of a consecutive series of elderly depressed patients, Finch and Katona (1989) demonstrated a clinically useful response to lithium augmentation in six out of nine patients, with maintained benefit for up to 18 months. Similar acute responses have been noted by Lafferman *et al* (1988) with seven out of 14 subjects showing complete remission and a further three a partial response. A larger retrospective series by Bekker *et al* (1990) reported complete response to lithium augmentation in 15/43, with symptomatic improvement in another 15. Lithium augmentation thus appears the best documented pharmacological option for refractory depression in old age. It must however be borne in mind that placebo controlled evaluation in the elderly is as yet lacking. Furthermore, as discussed in detail elsewhere in this volume, neurological side-effects to lithium are common in the elderly and lithium augmentation must therefore be carried out cautiously. Since lithium toxicity may occur at relatively low serum levels in the elderly, initial doses of lithium should be low (100–200 mg/day) with gradual dosage titration to achieve blood levels within a downward-adjusted therapeutic range (0.4–0.8 mmol/l).

CONTINUATION TREATMENT

The value of prophylactic antidepressant treatment in preventing relapse has been very inadequately evaluated in elderly subjects. The most recent study published (Old Age Depression Interest Group, 1993) has provided fairly definitive evidence. In 69 patients whose depression had responded to antidepressants and who were subsequently allocated randomly to receive dothiepin (75 mg/day) or placebo over a two-year period, survival analysis showed relative risk of relapse to be two and a half times greater in the placebo group. It must be noted that the dose of dothiepin used was relatively small.

Placebo controlled evidence over a shorter (one-year) period is provided by Georgotas *et al.* (1989a), who carried out a placebo controlled evaluation of maintenance nortriptyline and phenelzine in elderly depressed patients who had responded to antidepressants. Patients on phenelzine had a much lower (13.3%) relapse rate than those on either nortriptyline (53.8%) or placebo (65.2%). The latter two groups did not differ significantly. This study clearly establishes the potential prophylactic usefulness of phenelzine in initial phenelzine responders. The lack of prophylactic efficacy of nortriptyline may in the authors' view be due to the accumulation of its metabolite 10-hydroxynortriptyline which increases with age and may interfere with the antidepressant effect of the parent compound. In this context it should be noted that a recent small study by Reynolds *et al.* (1992) showed nortriptyline to be superior to placebo in preventing relapse over a 16-week period.

Some of the SSRI studies reviewed earlier in this chapter provide evidence (although without the benefit of a placebo comparison) for their efficacy, and that of their tricyclic comparators, in relapse prevention. Feighner and Cohn (1985) showed very low relapse rate over 48 weeks in the continuation phase of their comparison between fluoxetine and doxepin, with no difference emerging between the two drugs. Similar results are available for a 16-week continuation phase study of the sertraline versus amitriptyline study (Invicta, data on file).

These studies suggest that TCAs and SSRIs are similarly effective in relapse prevention in old age. It must however be borne in mind that the long-term use of TCAs may become increasingly hazardous in older patients who are likely to become physically more frail as they age. More specifically, the possibility has been raised on the basis of animal studies (Glassman and Roose, 1994) that the quinidine-like effects of TCAs may provoke cardiac dysrhythmias in the context of acute myocardial ischaemia. This raises the spectre that these drugs may increase the acute mortality following myocardial infarction, to which older patients are relatively prone. The option of using newer and safer drugs for prophylaxis is attractive despite the fact that there is no evidence from the very limited controlled trial data to date to confirm their superiority.

The prophylactic effectiveness of lithium in preventing depressive relapse has been established in a substantial cohort of elderly patients examined retrospectively by Abou-Saleh and Coppen (1983). The prophylactic efficacy of lithium probably extends to patients initially refractory to treatment; Katona and Finch (1990) demonstrated that lithium augmentation in elderly depressed patients was associated with a good outcome for up to 18 months.

Overall, the limited available evidence suggests quite strongly that even in mild to moderate depression, treatment should be continued for at least 6–12 months and preferably for two years after clinical recovery. In patients relapsing despite continuation treatment, lithium may be useful.

CONCLUSIONS

The grounds for therapeutic optimism in managing older depressed patients are considerable, despite the particular challenges to be met in treating such a relatively vulnerable group. Antidepressant drugs must, in elderly as in younger patients, be seen as only a part of a holistic approach. Particular care is necessary in patients with concurrent physical illness. Even though antidepressant drugs have been relatively rigorously evaluated and found to be effective in the more severely ill patients and under controlled conditions, their utility in the milder depressions encountered in primary care has yet to be properly evaluated. Although newer antidepressants have not been shown to have an overwhelming advantage, their relative safety and the lack of cognitive impairment associated with their use may justify their use as first-choice drugs in an elderly population. Even in apparently treatment-resistant cases, the response to more aggressive treatment approaches can be gratifying and not necessarily associated with excessive hazard. The high risk of recurrence of depression in old age can be significantly reduced by continued prophylactic drug treatment.

REFERENCES

Abou-Saleh MT and Coppen A (1983) The prognosis of depression in old age: the case for lithium therapy. *Br J Psychiatry* **143**, 527–528.

Alexopoulos GS, Abrams RC, Young RC and Shamoian CA (1988) Cornell Scale for Depression in Dementia. *Bio Psychiatry* **23**, 271–284.

Altamura AC, Percudani M, Guercetti G and Invernizzi G (1989) Efficacy and tolerability of fluoxetine in the elderly: a double-blind study versus amitriptyline. *Int Clin Psychopharmacol* **4**, 103–106.

American Psychiatric Association (1980) *Diagnostic and Statistical Manual of Mental Disorders* (3rd edition). American Psychiatric Association, Washington, DC.

American Psychiatric Association (1987) *Diagnostic and Statistical Manual of Mental Disorders* (3rd edition, revised). American Psychiatric Association, Washington, DC.

Angst J and Stabl M (1992) Efficacy of moclobemide in different patient groups: a meta-analysis of studies. *Psychopharmacology* **106**, S109–S113.

Arcand M and Hottin P (1993) Le traitement de la depression chez les personnes ages. *Le Medicin de Famille Canadien* **39**, 2420–2425.

Austin M-PV, Souza FGM and Goodwin GM (1991) Lithium augmentation in antidepressant-resistant patients. A quantitative analysis. *Br J Psychiatry* **159**, 510–514.

Barraclough BM (1971) Suicide in the elderly. In: Kay DWK and Walk A (eds), *Recent Developments in Psychogeriatrics.* pp 87–97, Headley Bros, Ashford.

Barros J and Asnis G (1993) An interaction of sertraline and desipramine. *Am J Psychiatry* **150**, 1751.

Bekker FM, van Marwijk HWJ, Nolen WA, *et al.* (1990) Lithium bij de behandeling van depressieve bejaarden. *Ned Tijdschr Geneeeskd* **134**, 442–445.

Benbow SM (1989) The role of electroconvulsive therapy in the treatment of depressive illness in old age. *Br J Psychiatry* **155**, 147–152.

Benfield P and Ward A (1986) Fluvoxamine: a review of its pharmacodynamic and pharmacokinetic properties, and therapeutic efficacy in depressive illness. *Drugs* **32**, 313–334.

Blazer DG (1994) Is depression more frequent in late life? An honest look at the evidence. *Am J Geriatr Psychiatry* **2**, 193–199.

Branconnier RJ, Cole JO, Ghasvinian S *et al.* (1982) Treating the depressed elderly patient: the comparative behavioural pharmacology of mianserin and amitriptyline. In: Costa E and Racagni G (eds), *Typical and Atypical Antidepressants: Clinical Practice.* Raven Press, New York.

Brodaty H, Harris L, Peters K, *et al.* (1993) Prognosis of depression in the elderly. A comparison with younger patients. *Br J Psychiatry* **163**, 589–596.

Brown RP, Sweeney J, Loutsch E, *et al.* (1984) Involutional melancholia revisited. *Am J Psychiatry* **137**, 439–444.

Buff DD, Brenner R, Kirtane SS and Gilboa R (1991) Dysrhythmia associated with fluoxetine treatment in an elderly patient with cardiac disease. *J Clin Psychiatry* **52**, 174–176.

Burvill PW, Hall WD, Stampfer HG and Emmerson JP (1989) A comparison of early-onset and late-onset depressive illness in the community. *Br J Psychiatry* **155**, 673–679.

Campbell AJ (1991) Drug treatment as a cause of falls in old age: a review of offending agents. *Drugs and Aging* **1**, 289–302.

Classen V, Davies JE, Hertting G, *et al.* (1977) Fluvoxamine: a specific 5-hydroxytryptamine uptake inhibitor. *Br J Pharmacol* **60**, 505–516.

Cohn CK, Shrivastava R, Mendels J, *et al.* (1990) Double-blind, multicenter comparison of sertraline and amitriptyline in elderly depressed patients. *J Clin Psychiatry* **51**, 28–33.

Cole MG (1990) The prognosis of depression in the elderly. *Can Med Assoc J* **142**, 633–639.

Conwell Y and Caine ED (1991) Rational suicide and the right to die: reality and myth. *N Engl J Med* **325**, 1100–1103.

Copeland JR, Davidson IA, Dewey ME, *et al.* (1992) Alzheimer's disease, other dementias, depression and pseudodementia: prevalence, incidence and three-year outcome in Liverpool. *Br J Psychiatry* **161**, 230–239.

Crewe HK, Leonard MS, Tucker GT, *et al.* (1992) The effect of selective serotonin re-uptake inhibitors on cytochrome P450 2D6 (CYP 2D6) activity in human liver microsomes. *Br J Clin Pharmacol* **34**, 262–265.

Da Prada M, Kettler R, Keller HH, *et al.* (1989) Neurochemical profile of moclobemide, a short-acting and reversible inhibitor of monoamine oxidase type A. *J Pharmacol Exp Ther* **248**, 400–413, W:G7.

D'Ath P, Katona P, Mullan M, et al (1994) Screening, detection and management of depression in elderly primary care attenders. 1: The Acceptability and Performance of the 15 item Geriatric Depression Scale (GDS15) and The Development of Short Versions. Family Practice 11, 260–266.

de Vanna M, Kummer J, Agnoli A, et al (1990) Moclobemide compared with second-generation antidepressants in elderly people. Acta Psychiatr Scand (Suppl) 360, 64–66.

Doogan DP and Caillard V (1988) Sertraline: a new antidepressant. J Clin Psychiatry 49, 46–51.

Dorman T (1992) Sleep and paroxetine: a comparison with mianserin in elderly depressed patients. J Clin Psychiatry 53 (Suppl), 53–58.

Dunbar GC (1995) Paroxetine in the elderly: a comparative metanalysis against standard antidepressant pharmacotherapy. Pharmacology 51, 137–144.

Dunner DL, Cohn JB, Walshe T, et al (1992) Two combined, multicenter double-blind studies of paroxetine and doxepin in geriatric patients with major depression. J Clin Psychiatry 52 (2, Suppl), 57–60.

Evans S and Katona CLE (1993) Prevalence of depressive symptoms in elderly primary care attenders. Dementia 4, 327–333.

Fairbairn AF, George K and Dorman T (1989) Lofepramine versus dothiepin in the treatment of depression in elderly patients. Br J Clin Pract 43, 55–60.

Falk WE, Rosenbaum JE, Otto MW, et al (1989) Fluoxetine versus trazodone in depressed geriatric patients. J Geriatr Psychiatry Neurol 2, 208–214.

Feighner JP, Boyer WF, Tyler DL and Heborsky RJ (1990) Fluoxetine and MAOIs: adverse interactions. J Clin Psychiatry 51, 222–225.

Feighner JP and Cohn JB (1985) Double-blind comparative trials of fluoxetine and doxepin in geriatric patients with major depressive disorder. J Clin Psychiatry 46, 20–25.

Feighner JP (1983) The new generation of antidepressants. J Clin Psychiatry 44, 49–55.

Finch EJL and Katona CLE (1989) Lithium augmentation of refractory depression in old age. Int J Geriatr Psychiatry 4, 41–46.

Fogel BS and Kroessler D (1987) Treating late-life depression on a medical-psychiatric unit. Hosp Community Psychiatry 38, 829–831.

Gallagher-Thompson D, Futterman A, Hanley-Paterson P, et al (1992) Endogenous depression in the elderly: prevalence and agreement among measures. J Consult Clin Psychol 60, 300–303.

Georgotas A, McCue RE, Friedman E, et al (1987) The response of depressive symptoms to nortriptyline, phenelzine and placebo. Br J Psychiatry 151, 102–106.

Georgotas A, Friedman E, McCarthy M, et al (1983) Resistant geriatric depressions and therapeutic response to monoamine oxidase inhibitors. Biol Psychiatry 18, 195–205.

Georgotas A, McCue RE and Cooper TB (1989a) A placebo-controlled comparison of nortriptyline and phenelzine in maintenance therapy of elderly depressed patients. Arch Gen Psychiatry 46, 783–785.

Georgotas A, McCue RE, Cooper TB, et al (1989b) Factors affecting the delay of anti-depressant effect in responders to nortriptyline and phenelzine. Psychiatry Res 28, 1–9.

Georgotas A, McCue RE, Hapworth W, et al (1986) Comparative efficacy and safety of MAOIs versus TCAs in treating depression in the elderly. Biol Psychiatry 21, 1155–1166.

Gerner R, Estabrook W, Steuer J, et al (1980) Treatment of geriatric depression with trazodone, imipramine and placebo: a double-blind study. J Clin Psychiatry 41, 216–220.

Gerson SC, Plotkin DA and Jarvik LF (1988) Antidepressant drug studies 1946 to 1986: empirical evidence for aging patients. J Clin Psychopharmacol 8, 311–322.

Ghose K and Sedman E (1987) A double-blind comparison of the pharmacodynamic effects of single doses of lofepramine, amitriptyline and placebo in elderly subjects. Eur J Clin Pharmacol 33, 505–509.

Ghose K and Spragg BP (1989) Pharmacokinetics of lofepramine and amitriptyline in elderly healthy subjects. *Int Clin Psychopharmacol* **4**, 201–215.

Glassman AH and Roose SP (1994) Risks of antidepressants in the elderly: tricyclic antidepressants and arrhythmia—revising risks. *Gerontology* **40 (S1)**, 15–20.

Godber C, Rosenvinge H, Wilkinson D, *et al.* (1987) Depression in old age: prognosis after ECT. *Int J Geriatr Psychiatry* **2**, 19–24.

Greenwald BS, Kramer-Ginsberg E, Marin DB, *et al.* (1989) Dementia with coexistent major depression. *Am J Psychiatry* **146**, 1472–1478.

Guillibert E, Pelicier Y, Archembault JC, Chabannes JP, Clerk G, Desvilles M, Guibert M, Pagot R, Poisat JL and Thobie Y (1989) A double-blind, multicentre study of paroxetine versus clomipramine in depressed elderly patients. *Acta Psychiatr Scand* **80 (Suppl. 350)**, 132–134.

Hamilton M (1960) A rating scale for depression. *J Neurol Neurosurg Psychiatry* **23**, 56–62.

Hindmarch I and Bhatti JZ (1988) Psychopharmacological effects of sertraline in normal healthy volunteers. *Eur J Clin Pharmacol* **35**, 221–223.

Hindmarch I, Shillingford J and Shillingford C (1990) The effects of sertraline on psychomotor performance in elderly volunteers. *J Clin Psychiatry* **51**, 34–36.

Hinrichsen G and Hernandez NA (1993) Factors associated with recovery from and relapse into major depressive disorder in the elderly. *Am J Psychiatry* **150**, 1820–1825.

Hutchinson DR, Tong S, Moon CAL, *et al.* (1991) A double-blind study in general practice to compare the efficacy and tolerability of paroxetine and amitriptyline in depressed elderly patients. *Br J Clin Res* **2**, 43–47.

Jessel H-J, Jessel I and Wegener G (1981) Therapy for depressive elderly patients: lofepramine and amitriptyline tested under double-blind conditions. *ZFA* **57**, 784–787.

Kanba S, Matsumoto K, Nibuya M, *et al.* (1992) Nortriptyline response in elderly depressed patients. *Prog Neuropsychopharmacol Biol Psychiatry* **16**, 301–309.

Katona CLE (1994a) Refractory Depression. In: Sensky T, Montgomery S and Katona C (eds), *Psychiatry in Europe*. Gaskell Press, London.

Katona CLE (1994b) Screening for depression: the Geriatric Depression Scale. In: Philp I (ed), *Assessing Elderly Patients*. Farrand Press, London.

Katona CLE (1994c) The prognosis of depression in old age. In: Katona CLE (ed) *Depression in Old Age*. John Wiley, Chichester.

Katona CLE and Aldridge CR (1985) The dexamethasone suppression test and depressive signs in dementia. *J Affect Disord* **8**, 83–89.

Katona CLE and Finch EJL (1990) Lithium augmentation for refractory depression in old age. In: Amsterdam J (ed) *Refractory Depression*. Raven Press, New York.

Katz IR, Simpson GM, Curlik SM, *et al.* (1990) Pharmacologic treatment of major depression for elderly patients in residential care settings. *J Clin Psychiatry* **51 (7, Suppl)**, 41–47.

Kaye CM, Haddock RE, Langley PF, *et al.* (1989) A review of the metabolism and pharmacokinetics of paroxetine in man. *Acta Psychiatr Scand* **80**, 60–75.

Kennedy GJ, Kelman HR and Thomas C (1990) The emergence of depressive symptoms in late life: the importance of declining health and increasing disability. *J Community Health* **15**, 93–104.

Kennedy GJ, Kelman HR and Thomas C (1991) Persistence and remission of depressive symptoms in late life. *Am J Psychiatry* **148**, 174–178.

Kitchell MA, Barnes RF, Veith RC, *et al.* (1982) Screening for depression in hospitalized geriatric medical patients. *J Am Geriatr Soc* **30**, 174–177.

Kivela SL, Pahkala K and Eronen A (1989) Depressive symptoms and signs that differentiate major and atypical depression from dysthymic disorder in elderly Finns. *Int J Geriatr Psychiatry* **4**, 79–85.

Kivela S-L, Pahkala K and Laippala P (1988) Prevalence of depression in an elderly population in Finland. *Acta Psychiatr Scand* **78**, 401–413.

Koenig HG, Meador KG, Shelp F, *et al.* (1991) Major depressive disorder in hospitalized medically ill patients: an examination of young and elderly male veterans. *J Am Geriatr Soc* **39**, 881–890.

Koenig HG, Goli V, Shelp F, *et al.* (1989) Antidepressant use in elderly medical inpatients: lessons from an attempted clinical trial. *J Gen Intern Med* **4**, 498–505.

Kushnir SL (1986) Lithium-antidepressant combinations in the treatment of depressed physically ill geriatric patients. *Am J Psychiatry* **143**, 378–379.

Lafferman J, Solomon K and Ruskin P (1988) Lithium augmentation for treatment-resistant depression in the elderly. *J Geriatr Psychiatry* **1**, 49–52.

Lipsey JR, Robinson RG, Pearlson GD, *et al.* (1984) Nortriptyline treatment of post-stroke depression: a double-blind study. *Lancet* **i**, 297–300.

Livingston G and Hinchcliffe AC (1993) The epidemiology of psychiatric disorders in the elderly. *Int Rev Psychiatry* **5**, 317–326.

Livingston G, Thomas A, Graham N, *et al.* (1990) The Gospel Oak Project: The use of health and social services by dependent elderly people in the community. *Health Trends* **2**, 70–73.

Lucas RA and Osborne DJ (1986) The disposition of fluoxetine and norfluoxetine in elderly patients with depressive illness compared to younger subjects. *Proceedings of 16th CINP Congress,* Puerto Rico.

Luo H and Richardson JS (1993) A pharmacological comparison of citalopram, a bicyclic serotonin selective uptake inhibitor, with traditional tricyclic antidepressants. *Int Clin Psychopharmacol* **8**, 3–12.

Macdonald AJD (1986) Do general practitioners "miss" depression in elderly patients? *BMJ* **292**, 1365–1367.

Maguire K, Pereira A and Tiller J (1991) Moclobemide pharmacokinetics in depressed patients: lack of age effect. *Hum Psychopharmacol* **6**, 249–252.

Mann AH, Graham N and Ashby D (1984) Psychiatric illness in residential homes for the elderly: a survey in one London borough. *Age Ageing* **13**, 257–265.

Maynard A (1993) Cost management: the economist's viewpoint. *Br J Psychiatry* **163 (Suppl 20)**, 7–13.

Meats P, Timol M and Jolley D (1991) Prognosis of depression in the elderly. *Br J Psychiatry* **159**, 549–553.

Meredith CH, Feighner JP and Hendrickson G (1984) A double-blind comparative valuation of the efficacy and safety of nomifensine, imipramine and placebo in depressed geriatric outpatients. *J Clin Psychiatry* **45**, 73–77.

Miller MD, Pollock BG, Rifai AH, *et al.* (1991) Longitudinal analysis of nortriptyline side effects in elderly depressed patients. *J Geriatr Psychiatry Neurol* **4**, 226–230.

Montgomery SA and Asberg M (1979) A new depression scale designed to be sensitive to change. *Br J Psychiatry* **134**, 382–389.

Montgomery SA (1990) Depression in the elderly: pharmacokinetics of antidepressants and death from overdose. *Int Clin Psychopharmacol* **Suppl 3**, 67–76.

Morris RG and Morris LW (1991) Cognitive and behavioural approaches with the depressed elderly. *Int J Geriatr Psychiatry* **6**, 407–413.

Moskowitz H and Burns MM (1986) Cognitive performance in geriatric subjects after acute treatment with antidepressants. *Neuropsychobiology* **15**, 38.

Muijen M, Roy D, Silverstone T, *et al.* (1988) A comparative clinical trial of fluoxetine, mianserin and placebo with depressed out-patients. *Acta Psychiatr Scand* **78**, 384–390.

Mullan E, Katona P, D'Ath P and Katona C (1994) Screening, detection and management of depression in elderly primary care attenders. 2. Detection and Fitness for Treatment: a Case Record Study. *Family Practice* **11**, 267–270.

Mulsant BH, Rosen J, Thornton JE and Zubenko GS (1991) A prospective naturalistic study of electroconvulsive therapy in late-life depression. *J Geriatr Psychiatry Neurol* **4**, 3–13.

Murphy E, Smith R, Lindesay J and Slattery J (1988) Increased mortality rates in late-life depression. *Br J Psychiatry* **152**, 347–353.

Nair NP, Amin M, Holm P, *et al.* (1995) Moclobemide and nortriptyline in elderly depressed patients. A randomised, multicentre trial against placebo. *J Affect Disord* **33**, 1–9.

Nyth Al, Gottfries CG, Lyby K. A controlled multicenter clinical study of citalopram and placebo in elderly depressed patients with and without concomitant dementia. *Acta Psychiatr Scand* **86**, 138–145.

Old Age Depression Interest Group (1993) How long should the elderly take antidepressants? A double-blind placebo-controlled study of continuation/prophylaxis therapy with dothiepin. *Br J Psychiatry* **162**, 175–182.

Parmelee PA, Katz IR and Lawton MP (1989) Depression among institutionalised aged: assessment and prevalence estimation. *J Gerontol* **44**, M22–M29.

Phanjoo AL, Wonnacott S, and Hodgson A (1991) Double-blind comparative multicentre study of fluvoxamine and mianserin in the treatment of major depressive episode in elderly people. *Acta Psychiatr Scand* **83**, 476–479.

Pierce D (1987) Deliberate self-harm in the elderly. *Int J Geriatr Psychiatry* **2**, 105–110.

Preskorn SH (1993) Recent pharmacologic advances in antidepressant therapy for the elderly. *Am J Med* **94** **(Suppl. 5A)**, 2S–11S.

Rahman MK, Akhtar MJ, Savla NC, *et al.* (1991) A double-blind, randomised comparison of fluvoxamine with dothiepin in the treatment of depression in elderly patients. *Br J Clin Pract* **45**, 255–258.

Ramsay R, Wright P, Katz A, Beilawska C and Katona C (1991) The detection of psychiatric morbidity and its effects on outcome in acute elderly medical admissions. *Int J Geriatr Psychiatry* **6**, 861–866.

Rapp SR, Parisi SA and Walsh DA (1988) Psychological dysfunction and physical health among elderly medical inpatients. *J Consult Clin Psychol* **56**, 851–855.

Ray WA (1992) Psychotropic drugs and injuries among the elderly: a review. *J Clin Psychopharmacol* **12**, 386–396.

Reding MJ, Orto LA, Winter SW, *et al.* (1986) Antidepressant therapy after stroke: a double-blind trial. *Arch Neurol* **43**, 763–765.

Reynolds CF, Frank E, Perel JM, *et al.* (1992) Combined pharmacotherapy and psychotherapy in the acute and continuation treatment of elderly patients with recurrent major depression. A preliminary report. *Am J Psychiatry* **149**, 1687–1692.

Rockwell E, Lam RW and Zisook S (1988) Antidepressant drug studies in the elderly. *Psychiatr Clin North Am* **11**, 215–233.

Romanoski AJ, Folstein MF, Nestadt G, *et al.* (1992) The epidemiology of psychiatrist-ascertained depression and DSM III depressive disorders: results from the Eastern Baltimore Mental Health Survey Clinical Reappraisal. *Psychol Med* **22**, 629–655.

Salzman C (1993) Pharmacologic treatment of depression in the elderly. *J Clin Psychiatry* **54** **(2, Suppl)**, 23–28.

Schifano F, Garbin A, Renesto V, *et al.* (1990) A double-blind comparison of mianserin and maprotiline in depressed medically ill elderly people. *Acta Psychiatr Scand* **81**, 289–294.

Schone W and Ludwig M (1993) A double-blind study of paroxetine compared with fluoxetine in geriatric patients with major depression. *J Clin Psychopharmacol* **13** **(Suppl. 2)**, 34S–39S.

Shapiro AK, Dussik KT, Tolentino JC, *et al.* (1960) A "browsing" double blind study of iproniazid in geriatric patients. *Dis Nerv System* **21**, 286–287.

Shulman K (1989) Conceptual problems in the assessment of depression in old age. *Psychiatr J Univ Ottawa* **14**, 364–371.

Sifneos PE (1973) The prevalence of alexithymia characteristics in psychosomatic patients. *Psychother Psychosom* **22**, 255–262.

Simon RI (1989) Silent suicide in the elderly. *Bull Am Acad Psychiatry Law* **17**, 83–95.

Sjogren C (1980) The pharmacological profile of lofepramine: a new antidepressant drug. *Neuropharmacology* **19**, 1213–1214.

Snowdon J (1990) The prevalence of depression in old age. *Int J Geriatr Psychiatry* **5**, 141–144.

Steuer JL, Mintz J, Hammen CL, *et al.* (1984) Cognitive behavioural and psychodynamic group psychotherapy in treatment of geriatric depression. *J Consult Clin Psychol* **52**, 180–189.

Syversen S (1992) A controlled multicenter clinical study of citalopram and placebo in elderly depressed patients with and without concomitant dementia. *Acta Psychiatr Scand* **86**, 138–145.

Tannock C and Katona C (1995) Minor depression in the aged: Concepts, prevalence and optimal management. *Drugs Aging* **6**, 278–292.

Tiller J, Maguire K and Davies B (1990) A sequential double-blind controlled study of moclobemide and mianserin in elderly depressed patients. *Int J Geriatr Psychiatry* **5**, 199–204.

Tollefson GD and Holman SL (1993) Analysis of the Hamilton Depression Rating Scale factors from a double-blind, placebo-controlled trial of fluoxetine in geriatric major depression. *Int Clin Pharmacol* **8**, 253–259.

Upadhyaya AK, Warburton H and Jenkins JC (1989) Psychiatric correlates of non-fatal deliberate self harm in the elderly: a pilot study. *J Clin Exp Gerontol* **11**, 131–143.

Wagner W, Plekkenpol B, Gray TE, Vlaskamp H and Essers H (1992) Review of fluvoxamine safety database. *Drugs* **43 (Suppl. 2)**, 48–54.

Wakelin JS (1986) Fluvoxamine in the treatment of the older depressed patient: double-blind placebo-controlled data. *Int Clin Psychopharmacol* **1**, 221–230.

Wood KA, Nissenbaum H and Livingston M (1990) Affective flattening in elderly patients. *Age Aging* **19**, 253–256.

Woodhouse K (1992) The pharmacology of major tranquillisers in the elderly. In: Katona C and Levy R (eds) *Delusions and Hallucinations in Old Age.* Gaskell, London.

Wragg RE and Jeste DV (1989) Overview of depression and psychosis in Alzheimer's disease. *Am J Psychiatry* **146**, 577–586.

Yesavage JA, Brink TL, Rose TL and Lum O (1983) Development and validation of a geriatric depression screening scale: a preliminary report. *J Psychiatr Res* **17**, 37–49.

Zussman BD, Davie CC, Fowles SE, Kumar R, Lang U, Wargenau M and Sourgens H (1995) Sertraline, like other SSRIs is a significant inhibitor of desipramine metabolism in vivo. *Br J Clin Pharmacol* **39**, 550–551.

10

Treating depression in adolescent patients

Graham J. Emslie

INTRODUCTION

Depression is a major cause of morbidity and mortality in the adolescent age group (Fleming and Offord, 1990). School failure and school dropout are common outcomes for the depressed adolescent (Weinberg and Emslie, 1988a) and suicide remains one of the leading causes of death in adolescents (Brent, 1987; Pfeffer *et al.*, 1991; Rao *et al.*, 1993). The age of onset of depression is decreasing with succeeding decades (Kovacs and Gatsonis, 1994) with the result that many individuals will experience their first episodes of depression during their adolescent years. Puberty also marks a substantial rise in the prevalence of depression, particularly in females, the sex ratio moving more towards the adult pattern of females predominating.

However, research in the treatment of depression in adolescents, while increasing, lags far behind the work of adults. It cannot be assumed that information from adults can be extrapolated to adolescents. Differences between adolescents and adults are evident in phenomenology, pathophysiology and treatment (McCracken, 1992; Cantwell, 1992).

For many adolescents, depression continues to be a problem for many years. Poznanski *et al.* (1976) report that 50% of a sample of depressed adolescent outpatients were depressed when contacted 6.5 years later. Eastgate and Gilmour (1984) recontacted 19 of 36 adolescent inpatients with depression 7–8 years later.

Selective Serotonin Re-uptake Inhibitors: Advances in Basic Research and Clinical Practice, Second Edition, Edited by J.P. Feighner and W.F. Boyer
© 1996 John Wiley & Sons Ltd

Forty-two percent ($N = 8$) were psychiatrically ill, 21% with major depression. The chronicity of the problem is evident even in depressed adolescents ascertained from community samples. Fleming *et al.* (1993) report on a group of depressed adolescents identified from a community sample. When reinterviewed two to four years later, 31% reported depression within the past six months.

Since depression tends to be an episodic condition, not only overall outcome but also the course of depressive symptoms over the intervening period is of particular interest. Remission or recovery rates have been studied in different populations of children and adolescents. In a study of 42 child outpatients with major depressive disorder (MDD), Kovacs *et al.* (1984a) found that 59% had recovered (asymptomatic for two months) by one year, 92% had recovered by 18 months. Strober *et al.* (1993) found that 81% of 58 adolescent inpatients with MDD had recovered by one year and 98% by two years from the time of admission, with the average time to recovery being 27.5 weeks from admission. They also reported that 28% of those with psychotic depression had developed their first manic episodes over this two-year follow up. Both these studies are similar to McCauley *et al.*'s. (1993) report of 65 depressed children and adolescents, predominantly outpatients. McCauley found that 80% had recovered by one year.

However, once recovered, depressed children and adolescents have a high rate of relapse of their depression. In Kovacs *et al.*'s. (1984b) study of depressed children with MDD, there was a cumulative rate of 72% for a new episode of depression within five years. Asarnow *et al.* (1988) reported rehospitalization in 45% of inpatients with MDD within two years. Within McCauley's sample of depressed children and adolescents (McCauley *et al.*, 1993), 54% experienced another major depressive episode within three years.

It appears that depression in adolescents continues, by and large, into adult depressive conditions. That is, many depressed adolescents become depressed adults. Kandel and Davies (1986) describe poor adult outcomes in a large group of adolescents identified as having depressive symptoms on a self-report scale. However, it is not possible from this study to determine whether the outcome was specific to the depression. Harrington *et al.* (1990) in a follow-up study of 80 depressed and 80 nondepressed adolescent outpatients showed that, as adults, depressive disorders were more common in the group who were depressed adolescents.

Given the significant morbidity and mortality associated with depression and longitudinal course of the disorder, it is essential that specific and effective treatments be available for depressed adolescents. However, research in the treatment of depression in adolescents, while increasing, lags far behind the similar work in adults. This is particularly true in the psychopharmacology of adolescent depression where randomized controlled trials (RCTs) have failed so far to show any antidepressant to be consistently more effective than placebo. This lack of clear responsiveness in adolescents to antidepressants has led to substantial debate, which centres around four issues.

1. Are the populations studied to date atypical, i.e. do they contain a high proportion of potential bipolar patents or "treatment resistant" subjects? Different studies have reported both high and low overall response rates.
2. Are adolescents more responsive to placebo as a group or is this a reflection of them not having "true" depression?
3. Are the numbers of patients studied just too few, especially in comparison with adults, and, therefore these are just chance findings?
4. Finally, are adolescents not responsive because the disorder is different in this age group, or they have unique developmental characteristics which make antidepressants ineffective (e.g. hormonal differences, receptor density differences, etc.)?

This chapter attempts to address these issues in the treatment of adolescent depression by reviewing the phenomenology of the disorder, reviewing published studies of treatment, and reporting on our and others' clinical experience with serotonin specific re-uptake inhibitors (SSRIs).

DIAGNOSIS

Failure to identify depression in adolescents doing poorly still remains a major reason for inappropriate or under-treatment. Currently, DSM III R or DSM IV (APA, 1987, 1994) criteria for affective disorders are used for diagnoses in adolescents. The ability to diagnose depression in this age group is influenced by understanding the developmental differences in the way symptoms present and the process for eliciting symptoms in this age group.

Symptoms

Depressed mood in major depressive disorder must be present most of the day, nearly every day by either subjective report or by observation. The mood disturbance in adolescents can be manifest primarily by irritability. The subjective feeling that they get "mad more easily" is often reported. The persistence of the mood disturbance is often hard to elicit in adolescence, where mood is often more labile, possibly because, cognitively, they have a more "here and now" orientation. Total anhedonia occurs less frequently in adolescents but they often note significant changes in their interest in activities.

Other differences in depressive symptoms include less pronounced appetite, weight changes and sleep disturbance. Initial insomnia is common but is often interpreted by the adolescent as just wanting to stay up late, but on questioning, they cannot get to sleep earlier even if they try. Difficulty waking on school days is problematic for many adolescents. Psychomotor agitation or retardation is less often reported or observed. This may be because the expectations about the activity level in this age group are unclear. Fatigue is often described as boredom, and worthlessness and guilt are often externalized so the adolescent perceives others as being mean to them as opposed to expressing their own feelings of guilt or worthlessness. Decreased concentration most often shows up as a significant change in school performance with a drop in grades. Suicidal ideation and attempts are common presenting problems for this age group.

Table 1 lists the number of positive symptoms reported by 100 consecutive children and adolescents who met DSM III R criteria for major depressive disorder (MDD). The sample was taken from subjects evaluated for entry into a double-blind study of fluoxetine. The subjects met MDD criteria on three separate interviews over a three-week period and the items are taken from the depressive items on the Kiddie Schedule for Affective Disorders and Schizophrenia (KSADS) (Chambers *et al.*, 1985) and are a consensus of the three separate interviews. The 4% who did not have depressed mood as a persistent disturbance had irritable mood. The commonest symptoms were decreased concentration, insomnia, fatigue, and loss of interest. Less common were guilt, psychomotor agitation or retardation and hypersomnia. Thirty-six percent report suicidal ideation or attempts and an additional 27% report suicidal thoughts without plans. There is little difference between those aged 12 and under ($N = 56$) and those aged 13 and over ($N = 44$). Anhedonia, loss of interest, fatigue, hypersomnia, and appetite changes were all more common in adolescents. Psychomotor agitation is reported most by younger males, and adolescent females more commonly reported guilt, hypersomnia and decreased appetite and weight. The psychomotor agitation in younger males might be associated with their frequency of comorbid Attention Deficit Hyperactivity Disorder (ADHD).

Clinical evaluation

The diagnosis of depression is based on clinical interview using established criteria for depression. Adjunctive criteria developed specifically for this age group can be helpful (Weinberg *et al.*, 1973; Petti, 1978, 1985; Poznanski *et al.*, 1985, 1986). The interviews of adolescents are conducted utilizing a semistructured format with both parent and child separately. Usually the adolescent is interviewed first. On occasion, information is obtained from teachers and peers. Both adolescents and their parents must be interviewed, as parent or adolescent report alone is not sufficient. While parents are important sources of information regarding the behavioural manifestations of psychiatric symptoms and temporal course of illness, adolescents are more able to report subjective symptoms and some vegetative symptoms such as sleep disturbance.

While the diagnosis of depression in adolescents is best made by clinical interview, self-report measures can be useful as screening instruments and are useful in detecting and monitoring symptoms in the clinical setting. Frequently used

Table 1. Frequency of criteria symptoms.

Kiddie SADS items	Age 12 and under N = 56		Age 13 and older N = 44		Total N (%)
	Male, n = 32 n (%)	Female, n = 24 n (%)	Male, n = 20 n (%)	Female, n = 24 n (%)	
Depressed mood	30 (93.8)	23 (95.8)	20 (100)	23 (95.8)	96 (96)
Irritability	25 (78.1)	18 (75)	17 (85)	23 (95.8)	83 (83)
Reactivity of mood	19 (59.4)	16 (66.7)	12 (60)	14 (58.3)	61 (61)
Diurnal mood variation	6 (18.8)	4 (16.7)	4 (20)	6 (25)	20 (20)
Guilt	14 (43.8)	8 (33.3)	6 (30)	12 (50)	40 (40)
Anhedonia	19 (59.4)	13 (54.2)	14 (70)	18 (75)	63 (63)
Loss of interest	23 (71.9)	16 (66.7)	16 (80)	23 (95.8)	78 (78)
Fatigue	24 (75)	20 (83.3)	19 (95)	24 (100)	87 (87)
Decreased concentration	31 (96.9)	22 (91.7)	19 (95)	24 (100)	96 (96)
Psychomotor agitation	16 (50)	7 (29.2)	6 (30)	5 (20.8)	34 (34)
Psychomotor retardation	10 (31.3)	7 (29.2)	10 (50)	9 (37.5)	36 (36)
Hypersomnia	3 (9.4)	1 (4.2)	2 (10)	8 (33.3)	14 (14)
Insomnia	22 (68.8)	21 (87.5)	17 (85)	15 (62.5)	75 (75)
Change in appetite	10 (31.3)	10 (41.7)	9 (45)	17 (70.8)	46 (46)
Change in weight	5 (15.6)	8 (33.3)	7 (35)	12 (50)	32 (32)
Suicidical behaviour (>3)	21 (65.5)	15 (62.5)	13 (65)	14 (58.3)	63 (63)

self-report measures for adolescents are the Beck Depression Inventory (BDI) (Beck *et al.*, 1961; Emslie *et al.*, 1989), and the Weinberg Screening Affective Scale (WSAS) (Emslie *et al.*, 1989; Weinberg and Emslie, 1988b). Confirmation of a diagnosis of depression, however, requires a diagnostic interview by a clinician who is able to recognize the sometimes subtle signs and symptoms of a depressive illness.

No evaluation of children and adolescents with affective disorders would be complete without a detailed biological family history, including both first-, second- and third-degree relatives. The offspring of adults with affective illness show a high rate of depression and bipolar disorder (Akiskal *et al.*, 1985). Conversely, adolescents with major depressive disorder have high familial ratings of depression, alcoholism, anxiety, and other psychiatric diagnoses in first- and second-degree relatives (Weinberg *et al.*, 1973; Brumback *et al.*, 1977; Biederman *et al.*, 1991). It is expected that children and adolescents with MDD will have a positive family history of mood disorders in 50–80% of cases, depending on whether first- or second-degree relatives are evaluated and depending on criteria used (i.e. treated or untreated; definite versus possible). In evaluating family history, it is preferable to interview both parents of the patient, even if the mother appears to know the father's family history.

Concurrent diagnosis

Most children and adolescents who meet the criteria for depression also present symptoms which fulfil criteria for other diagnostic categories (Biederman *et al.*, 1991). In a recent epidemiological study, concurrent diagnoses were found in almost 50% of children and adolescent subjects who met criteria for psychiatric disorders (Bird *et al.*, 1988). In this study, a high rate of comorbidity was found among the four diagnostic domains utilized from DSM III (affective, conduct/ oppositional, attention deficit disorder (ADD), anxiety). In those with affective disorder, 24% also manifested conduct/oppositional disorders, 17% ADD, and 17% anxiety disorder. Kovacs *et al.* (1988) found the second most common diagnosis in children with affective illness to be conduct disorder.

In a previously mentioned sample of 100 consecutive MDDs, only 19% met criteria for MDD alone (Table 2). Comorbid dysthymic disorder and anxiety disorders were the next most common at 42% and 44% respectively.

Whether the high rate of comorbidity in children and adolescents is due to the lack of well-developed exclusionary criteria in this age group or represents true comorbid disorders is unclear. Further clarification of this issue is under way from prospective studies.

Evaluation of a patient for depression must include a systematic medical evaluation. Depression can be induced by head trauma, viral postencephalitic recovery periods, or medical illnesses such as hyperthyroidism or systemic disseminated lupus. Additionally, depression can be induced by various drugs

Table 2. Comorbid diagnosis.

Comorbid diagnosis	Age 12 and under N = 56		Age 13 and older N = 44		Total, N = 100 n (%)
	Male, n (%)	Female, n (%)	Male, n (%)	Female, n (%)	
MDD only	5 (15.6)	5 (20.8)	4 (20)	5 (20.8)	19 (19)
Dysthymic disorder	13 (40.6)	11 (45.8)	10 (50)	8 (33.3)	42 (42)
Attention deficit disorder	14 (43.8)	7 (29.2)	7 (35)	4 (16.7)	32 (32)
Oppositional/conduct disorder	12 (37.5)	5 (20.8)	9 (45)	4 (16.7)	30 (30)
Anxiety disorders	13 (40.6)	11 (45.8)	5 (25)	15 (62.5)	44 (44)
Others	5 (15.6)	1 (4.2)	0	4 (16.7)	10 (10)
Additional diagnosis					
1	7 (21.9)	8 (33.3)	7 (29.2)	6 (25)	28 (28)
2	8 (25)	6 (25)	4 (20)	8 (33.3)	26 (26)
3	10 (31.3)	3 (12.5)	4 (20)	3 (12.5)	20 (20)
4	2 (6.3)	2 (8.3)	1 (4.2)	2 (8.3)	7 (7)

used to treat medical conditions or other psychiatric conditions such as ADHD. The benzodiazepines, stimulants, antihypertensives, and anticonvulsants are notable for heightening the dysphoric mood symptoms of depression. Additionally, the use of nonprescribed drugs or alcohol should always be assessed. Routine physical examination should include examination for "soft" neurological signs, with appropriate neurological referral as indicated.

PSYCHOPHARMACOLOGY OF ADOLESCENT DEPRESSION

The efficacy of antidepressant treatment for MDD in adults is well established (Baldessarini, 1989; Quitkin *et al.*, 1984), and has recently been reviewed extensively in the Clinical Practice Guidelines (Depression Guideline Panel, 1993). No one antidepressant is clearly more effective than another except probably the MAOIs with atypical depression (Quitkin *et al.*, 1990).

The current state of antidepressant treatment in adolescents is very unclear, as mentioned above. The failure of any randomized controlled trial to show any differences between drug and placebo is causing substantial controversy. However, antidepressants continue to be prescribed widely in this age group, primarily based on adult data, similarity of clinical picture, and clinical experiences.

The possible reasons for differences between adults and adolescents have been reviewed (Kutcher *et al.*, 1994; Ryan, 1990). Ryan (1990) noted that medications studied to date had been primarily noradrenergic or were metabolized quickly to a noradrenergic metabolite. It has been suggested that the noradrenergic system does not develop fully until early adulthood (Black *et al.*, 1971; Goldman-Rakic and Brown, 1982) suggesting that serotonergic agents may be more effective in this age group. Ryan also suggested that high levels of hormones during puberty decrease the effectiveness of tricyclic antidepressants. Several reports have commented on design issues (Conners, 1992; Jensen *et al.*, 1992, Strober *et al.*, 1992), small sample size, differences in definitions of response, comorbidity, and length of treatment (Ambrosini *et al.*, 1989). A primary concern is whether the populations studied are sufficiently homogeneous to allow a study of the effectiveness of medication. The concerns are that either the populations studied are abnormally treatment resistant (incipient bipolar, atypical depressives, substantial comorbidity), or overly treatment responsive (not "true" depressives).

Tricyclic antidepressants

In Ambrosini *et al.*'s (1993) review of antidepressant treatment of adolescents, he identified four open design studies and four placebo controlled studies with a total of 228 adolescents. Sixty-six subjects were on placebo across these studies, and 162 on antidepressants. The studies utilized amitriptyline, imipramine, desipramine, nortriptyline, and fluoxetine. Overall 80 out of 162 (49%) responded to antidepressants, compared to 28 out of 66 (42%) on placebo. Since then, a report has been published on an expanded sample of the desipramine study (Kutcher *et al.*, 1994) and preliminary data have been presented but have not been published on ongoing double-blind studies reviewed by Jensen *et al.* (1992).

The first double-blind study in adolescents with TCAs was by Kramer and Feiguine (1981). This study was with 20 adolescent inpatients, and amitriptyline was used at 200 mg/day. The measures used included the Psychiatric Rating Scale (PRS), Minnesota Multiphasic Personality Inventory (MMPI), and Depression Adjective Check-list (DACL). At the end of the six weeks, all subjects had improved and there was no difference between active and placebo groups except in the DACL, which was significantly lower in the active group. All subjects received intensive inpatient treatment in addition to medication. In Geller *et al.*'s (1990) study of nortriptyline, 52 subjects were enrolled and 35 randomized, of whom four dropped out. Only one active subject responded and four placebo subjects in spite of a mean amitriptyline level for the active group of 91.1 $\pm$ 18.3 ng/ml. Response was defined as a CDRS (Children's Depression Rating Scale) of < 25, and K-SADS-P depressive items score of two or less, except concentration. Kutcher *et al.* (1994) recently reported on a double-blind study of desipramine in adolescents. This was an extension of the earlier report by Boulos *et al.* (1991). They studied 60 adolescents with up to 200 mg of desipramine versus placebo. Eighteen dropped out before six weeks, of those, 13 were on active treatment. Forty percent (15 out of 42) of the entire group responded to treatment (50% or greater drop in Hamilton Depression Rating Scale), 48% were on active treatment and 35% on placebo. Jensen *et al.* (1992), in their review, report on three incomplete studies, which to date have been negative.

Two open studies of imipramine in inpatients ($N = 34$), (Strober *et al.*, 1990) and predominantly outpatients ($N = 39$) (Ryan *et al.*, 1986), have been reported with response rates of 30% and 44% respectively.

The apparent lack of effectiveness has led to suggestions of longer trials (Ambrosini *et al.*, 1989), larger samples, and the use of augmentative strategies including lithium (Ryan *et al.*, 1988a; Strober *et al.*, 1992) and MAOIs (Ryan *et al.*, 1988b). Additionally, there has been increased interest in SSRIs. The lack of apparent effectiveness of more noradrenergic antidepressants is a factor as well as the side-effect profile.

Selective serotonin re-uptake inhibitors (SSRIs)

There are published reports of the use of both fluoxetine and paroxetine in adolescent depression. Two multicentre studies of paroxetine have just been initiated. Early reports on fluoxetine were encouraging. Boulos *et al.* (1992) reported on 15 adolescents and young adults (aged 16–24) who had failed to respond to prior treatment with tricyclics. Sixty-four percent showed a therapeutic response over a 6–7 week trial. In a chart review of 31 hospitalized children and adolescents treated with fluoxetine, Jain et al. (1992) reported 74% showed improvement, with 54% being "much" to "very much" improved on the Clinical Global Impression Scale (CGI). Simeon et al. (1990) reported on 40 adolescents in a double-blind placebo controlled study of fluoxetine. Fifteen subjects in each group completed the study. Approximately two thirds of the subjects showed mild to moderate improvement with both fluoxetine and placebo. The dosage of fluoxetine was fairly high with subjects receiving 60 mg per day by the second week of the study.

Rodriguez-Ramos et al. (1995) studied paroxetine in 25 depressed adolescents aged 13–17; 76% had significant improvement with minimal side-effects. Only two patients discontinued because of side-effects. The dosage was 20 to 40 mg per day.

Side-effects
In all three of the above reports, the commonest side-effects from fluoxetine were nausea, decreased appetite, irritability, restlessness and insomnia.

Whether it is more common with SSRIs than TCAs is unclear, but mania is a reported side-effect of treatment with fluoxetine. Venkataraman et al. (1992) reported on five depressed adolescents who developed mania while being treated with fluoxetine. Single cases are reported by Achamallach and Decker (1991) and Rosenberg et al. (1992). In the above study reported by Jain et al. (1992), 28% of cases discontinued treatment because of increased irritability and hypomanic-like symptoms. One patient of Boulos et al.'s (1992) study of 15 subjects, became manic.

The presence of treatment-induced mania in this age group may reflect the fact that, as adolescents are relatively early in their potential course of illness, many would have developed bipolar illness with time. A concern is that early treatment might induce bipolar cycling in individuals who would not otherwise do so (Geller et al., 1993).

Hypomanic symptoms are also present but pose a diagnostic challenge in adolescents who have substantial comorbid symptomatology. Two major confounding factors are development of a frontal lobe-type disinhibition syndrome, and akathisia. Walkup (1994) reviewed the information available from adults in this area and suggested that they could be a factor in suicidal behaviour seen in the course of treatment. Hoehn-Saric et al. (1990, 1991) reported on frontal lobe syndrome in obsessive–compulsive disorder (OCD) treated with fluoxetine and fluvoxamine, describing symptoms including apathy and indifference. They report that prior to treatment a patient with OCD had elevated frontal region cerebral blood flow on SPECT scanning, and after treatment on fluoxetine 100 mg per day for four months there was a decrease in frontal lobe blood flow. Stuss and Benson (1986) report on frontal lobe dysfunction being characterized by apathy, decreased ability to self monitor and disinhibition. Riddle et al. (1991) report on behavioural side-effects during fluoxetine treatment in children and adolescents. They present information on 24 children and adolescents treated with fluoxetine for OCD and depression. Fifty percent developed behavioural side-effects characterized by motor restlessness, sleep disturbance, social disinhibition, or a subjective sense of excitation. The symptoms diminished with discontinuation or reduction of dosage. King *et al.* (1991) have also reported on the emergence of self-destructive behaviour in children and adolescents treated with fluoxetine for OCD.

In our ongoing study of fluoxetine, one particular case illustrates this diagnostic dilemma. The patient was an adolescent female who presented with severe depression of three months' duration. In the course of her episode, she had intense suicidal ideation with a well-thought-out plan. Her premorbid personality was fairly rigid. She had been an excellent student and reported little comorbid symptomatology. After a three-week evaluation period, and one week single blind placebo run-in, she remained very depressed. Her suicidal ideation diminished in response to support and the positive feeling that the problem was identified and she was going to feel better. Two weeks after randomization, she was evaluated and her depressive symptoms were minimal and she appeared slightly euphoric. Three days later, after a misunderstanding with a boyfriend, she came home and impulsively took pills (cold medicines, etc) in her medicine cabinet. She told her parents and was hospitalized. She denied suicidal ideation after the attempt and the behaviour was seen as out of character for her. Obviously, the exact interpretation of this incident is open to many theories but it raises questions of attempting to disentangle mild hypomania from a frontal lobe disinhibition, leading to uncharacteristic behaviour.

To further confound the clinical picture, there have been several reports in the adult literature on the development of akathisia in subjects treated with fluoxetine (Lipinski *et al.*, 1989; Hamilton and Opler, 1992; Rothschild and Locke, 1991). In adolescents, this can be an increase in motor restlessness and a worsening of an underlying attention deficit disorder. Riddle *et al.* (1991) report that three children with ADHD showed an exacerbation of symptoms on fluoxetine. The symptoms of hyperactivity, restlessness, and impulsivity may be particularly difficult to discriminate from common psychopathological symptoms seen in this age group.

Insomnia is another side-effect commonly seen in treatment with fluoxetine in adolescents. Again, this is particularly difficult to evaluate in depressed adolescents who often report insomnia prior to treatment. However, some patients report feeling their depression has improved but they remain tired during the day, often with either initial insomnia or the feeling that they have not slept well, if they have slept. Several studies in adults have reported that fluoxetine disrupts sleep, resulting in decreased sleep efficiency, increased stage 1 sleep and nocturnal wakefulness (Hendrickse *et al.*, 1994; Cooper, 1988). Also, fluoxetine has been shown to produce unusual eye movements in non-rapid eye movement (NREM) sleep (Keck *et al.*, 1991; Schenck *et al.*, 1992). Dorsey *et al.* (1992) also found increased myoclonic activity during NREM sleep and Ellison and Stanziani (1993) report on the development of nocturnal bruxism in four patients on fluoxetine and sertraline. Whether an adolescent's complaints of excessive daytime tiredness and apathy during treatment is a result of residual depression, normal adolescence, disrupted night-time sleep or frontal lobe apathy poses a potential diagnostic challenge.

The above side-effects are discussed primarily in relation to fluoxetine, whether the same is true of other SSRIs is unknown. Overall, the incidence of side-effects as a cause of treatment discontinuation with fluoxetine and SSRIs is fewer than with TCAs. The ability to tolerate treatment can often be a major factor in an adolescent's compliance with treatment. Adolescents appear to equate taking medication as a sign that they are continually "sick", independent of whether their symptoms have remitted or not. They are often, therefore, intolerant of side-effects and discontinue treatment.

PSYCHOTHERAPY OF ADOLESCENT DEPRESSION

Empirical investigations of the efficacy of psychotherapies for the treatment of depression in adolescents is limited. While a limited number of controlled clinical trials with group psychotherapy have been published, there are no controlled clinical trials with individual psychotherapies published, although some are on-going (Mufson, 1994; Birmaher, 1994).

Cognitive behavioural therapy in groups has been compared to waiting list controls (Reynolds and Coats, 1986; Kahn et al., 1990; Lewinsohn et al., 1990) and has been found to be more effective in improving depressive symptoms. Clark and Lewinsohn (1994) recently reported on cognitive behavioural group therapy using an educational approach based on the manual *Coping with Depression Course for Adolescents* (CWS-A) (Clark et al., 1990). The adolescents are diagnosed by structured interview and are assigned to one of three treatment conditions: adolescents only, adolescent and parent, and waiting list. Treatment sessions provide education on developing relaxation skills, increasing pleasant events, controlling negative or irrational thinking, improving social communication and conflict resolution. The parent group presents the same information as well as coping skills focused on family problems. Both treatment groups improved significantly compared to waiting list controls. At the end of treatment, 50% of the treatment groups still met criteria for depression compared with 95% in the waiting list controls. There was a trend for more improvement in the adolescent and parents group as opposed to the adolescent only group but this was not statistically significant. Improvement was maintained on 24-month follow up.

Individual psychotherapy for depression has been strongly influenced by the early work in adults primarily focusing on cognitive therapy and interpersonal therapy. Modification of these therapies for adolescents have been published in treatment manuals (Mufson et al., 1993; Wilkes et al., 1994). Cognitive behavioural and family models are also being evaluated (Birmaher, 1994).

Mufson et al. (1994) report on the use of IPT-A with 14 adolescent patients, diagnosed with depression using K-SADS, self-report and clinician-report measures. Assessments were done at intake and weeks zero, two, four, eight and 12. Adolescents were all treated by the same clinician and demonstrated significant improvement in depressive symptoms and symptoms of psychological and physical distress. At the end of treatment, none of the subjects met criteria for any depressive disorder. A randomized controlled clinical trial is currently under way to evaluate the effectiveness of this treatment modality (Mufson, 1994).

Wilkes and Rush (1988) discussed the adaptation of the traditional cognitive therapy approach used with adults for the treatment of adolescents. Belsher *et al.* (1995) reports on cognitive therapy, using this manual, in the treatment of 18 subjects, aged 14–17, diagnosed with depression. Subjects were treated for 12 sessions, and at the end of treatment, 86% of the subjects had remitted based on clinician ratings and 73% based on self-report. These gains were maintained up to five months post-therapy. Comorbidity with ADHD and schizoid personality predicted poor response to treatment.

Birmaher (1994) reported on a psychotherapy comparison study in which subjects, diagnosed with K-SADS for depression, were randomly assigned to either cognitive-behavioural therapy (CBT), systems-based family therapy (SBFT), or nondirective, supportive therapy (NST). All three treatment modalities demonstrated similar rates of efficacy, with 72.7% remission in CBT, 56.2% remission in SBFT, and 61.1% in NST. The differences between groups were not statistically significant. Comorbidity with anxiety predicted poor response to treatment.

Belsher and Wilkes (1994) identify 10 key principles of adolescent cognitive therapy (see Table 3). Many of these are applicable to any form of psychotherapy with depressed adolescents. The development of a therapeutic alliance with the adolescent is central to effective treatment. This requires an understanding that the adolescent developmentally will be more "self"-centred. The alliance is developed by incorporating the adolescent into an investigation of his or her problems and maintaining an objective stance. This is often difficult as the family and other social influences compete for attention. Technically, more of the therapy is conducted in the "here and now", examining situations in the session which are the most emotionally charged at the time. Often more abstract ideas will have to be made more concrete for the adolescent. Adolescents more often think in "black and

Table 3. Key principles of adolescent cognitive therapy. (Reproduced from Belsher and Wilkes, 1994 with permission.)

Acknowledge the adolescent's narcissism
Adopt a mode of collaborative empiricism
Adopt an objective stance
Include members of the social system
Chase the affect
Use socratic questioning
Challenge the binary motif
Avoid blame
Operationalize the abstract
Model for the adolescent

white" terms and this has to be examined through collaborative questioning without appearing to say that thinking this way is wrong.

The recent development of manuals for both cognitive therapy and interpersonal therapy and cognitive behavioural therapy for adolescents with depression are an important first step in evaluating the efficacy of individual therapy with depressed adolescents.

CONCLUSION

While the treatment of adolescent depression is an important exciting and developing area of study, there remain more questions than answers. Even the area of diagnosis continues with substantial controversy.

Treatment for an individual adolescent will most often be multimodal incorporating medication, individual therapy, family therapy, and social interventions. Of debate is whether psychosocial treatments need to be implemented prior to starting treatment with antidepressants. While some adolescents will respond to psychosocial interventions alone, the decision about treatment remains dependent on a thorough multimodal evaluation of each adolescent's situation. While arguments continue of the appropriateness of medication for depressed adolescents, it is likely that the majority of depression continues to go unrecognized and undertreated.

Acknowledgement
This work was supported by Charles E. and Sarah M. Seay and grant MH 39188 from the National Institute of Mental Health, Bethesda, MD. The manuscript could not have been submitted without the secretarial assistance of Melody Brummett.

REFERENCES

Achmallah NS and Decker DH (1991) Mania induced by fluoxetine in an adolescent patient. *Am J Psychiatry* **148**, 1404.
Akiskal HS, Down J, Jordan P, *et al.* (1985) Affective disorders in referred children and younger siblings of manic-depressives. *Arch Gen Psychiatry* **42**, 996–1003.
Ambrosini PJ, Bianchi MD, Rabinovich H, *et al.* (1993) Antidepressant treatment in children and adolescents I. Affective disorder. *J Am Acad Child Adolesc Psychiatry* **1**, 1–6.
Ambrosini PJ, Metz C, Bianchi M, *et al.* (1989) Open nortriptyline treatment over 10 weeks in depressed adolescent outpatients. *Proc Am Acad Child Adolesc Psychiatry* **5**, 59.
American Psychiatric Association (1987) *Diagnostic and Statistical Manual of Mental Disorders, Third Edition—Revised.* American Psychiatric Association, Washington, DC.
American Psychiatric Association (1994) *Diagnostic and Statistical Manual of Mental Disorders, Fourth Edition.* American Psychiatric Association, Washington, DC.
Asarnow JR, Goldstein MJ, Carlson GA, *et al.* (1988) Childhood-onset depressive disorders: A follow-up study of rates of rehospitalization and out-of-home placement among child psychiatric inpatients. *J Affect Disord* **15**, 245–253.
Baldessarini RJ (1989) Current status of antidepressants: Clinical pharmacology and therapy. *J Clin Psychiatry* **50**, 117–126.

Beck AT, Ward CH, Mendelson M, *et al.* (1961) An inventory for measuring depression. *Arch Gen Psychiatry* **4**, 561–571.

Belsher G and Wilkes TCR (1994) Ten key principles of adolescent cognitive therapy. In: Wilkes TCR, *et al.* (eds) *Cognitive Therapy for Depressed Adolescents*, pp 22–44, Guilford Press, New York.

Belsher G, Wilkes TCR and Rush AJ (1995) An open multi-site pilot study of cognitive therapy for depressed adolescents. *J Psychother Pract Research* **4**, 52–66.

Biederman J, Farone SV, Keenan K, *et al.* (1991) Evidence of familial association between attention deficit disorder and major affective disorders. *Arch Gen Psychiatry* **48**, 633–642.

Bird HR, Canino G, Rubio-Stipec M, *et al.* (1988) Estimates of the prevalence of childhood maladjustment in a community survey in Puerto Rico. *Arch Gen Psychiatry* **45**, 1120–1126.

Birmaher B (1994) *CBT with suicidal youth*. Presented at the Annual Child and Adolescent Depression Consortium Meeting, Providence, Rhode Island.

Black IB, Hendry IA and Iversen LL (1971) Trans-synaptic regulation of growth and development of adrenergic neurons in a mouse sympathetic ganglion. *Brain Res* **24**, 229–240.

Boulos C, Kutcher S, Gardner D, *et al.* (1992) An open naturalistic trial of fluoxetine in adolescents and young adults with treatment resistant major depression. *J Child Adolesc Psychopharmacol* **2**, 103–111.

Boulos C, Kutcher S, Marton P, *et al.* (1991) Response to desipramine treatment in adolescent major depression. *Psychopharmacol Bull* **27**, 59–65.

Brent DA (1987) Correlates of medical lethality of suicide attempts in children and adolescents. *J Am Acad Child Adolesc Psychiatry* **26**, 87–89.

Brumback RA, Dietz-Schmidt SA and Weinberg WA (1977) Depression in children referred to an Educational Diagnostic Center: Diagnosis and treatment and analysis of criteria and literature review. *Dis Nerv System* **38**, 529–535.

Cantwell DP (1992) Clinical phenomenology and nosology. *Child and Adolescent Psychiatric Clinics of North America* **1 (1)**, 1–12.

Chambers WJ, Puig-Antich J, Hirsch M, *et al.* (1985) The assessment of affective disorders in children and adolescents by semi-structured interview. *Arch Gen Psychiatry* **42**, 697–702.

Clark GN, Lewinsohn PM and Hops H (1990) *Adolescent Coping with Depression Course: Leaders Manual for Adolescent Groups*. Castalia, Eugene, Oregon.

Clarke GH (1994) *Cognitive-Behavioral Therapy in Adolescents*. Presented at the Annual Child and Adolescent Depressive Consortium Meeting, Providence, Rhode Island.

Conners K (1992) Methodology of antidepressant drug trials for treating depression in adolescents. *J Child Adolesc Psychopharmacol* **2**, 11–22.

Cooper GL (1988) The safety of fluoxetine—an update. *Br J Psychiatry* **153**, 77–86.

Depression Guideline Panel (1993) *Depression in Primary Care: Vol 2. Treatment of major depression. Clinical Practice Guideline, Number 5*. Department of Health and Human Services, Agency for Health Care Policy and Research. AHCPR Publications No 93-0551, Rockville, MD.

Dorsey CM, Cunningham SL, Lukos SE, *et al.* (1992) Fluoxetine-induced eye movements during non-REM sleep. *Sleep Res* **21**, 55.

Eastgate J and Gilmour L (1984) Long-term outcome of depressed children: A follow-up study. *Dev Med Child Neurol* **26**, 68–72.

Ellison JM and Stanziani P (1993) SSRI-associated nocturnal bruxism in four patients. *J Clin Psychiatry* **54**, 432–434.

Emslie GJ, Weinberg WA, Rush AJ, *et al.* (1989) Depressive symptoms by self-report in adolescents: Phase I of the development of a questionnaire for depression by self-report. *J Child Neurol* **3**, 114–121.

Fleming JE, Boyle MH and Offord DR (1993) The outcome of adolescent depression in the Ontario Child Health: Study follow-up. *J Am Acad Child Adolesc Psychiatry* **32**, 28–33.

Fleming JE and Offord DR (1990) Epidemiology of childhood depressive disorders: A critical review. *J Am Acad Child Adolesc Psychiatry* **29**, 571–580.

Geller B, Cooper TB, Graham DL, *et al.* (1990) A double-blind placebo-controlled study of nortriptyline in depressed adolescents using a "fixed plasma level" design. *Psychopharmacol Bull* **26**, 85–90.

Geller B, Fox LW and Fletcher M (1993) Effect of tricyclic antidepressants on switching to mania and on the onset of bipolarity in depressed 6- to 12-year-olds. *J Am Acad Child Adolesc Psychiatry* **32**, 43.

Goldman-Rakic P and Brown RM (1982) Postnatal development of monoamine content and synthesis in the cerebral cortex of rhesus monkeys. *Dev Brain Res* **4**, 339–349.

Hamilton MS and Opler LA (1992) Akathisia, suicidality, and fluoxetine. *J Clin Psychiatry* **53 (11)**, 401–406.

Harrington R, Fudge H, Rutter M, *et al.* (1990) Adult outcomes of childhood and adolescent depression. *Arch Gen Psychiatry* **47**, 465–473.

Hendrickse WA, Roffwarg HP, Grannemann BD, *et al.* (1994) The effects of fluoxetine on the polysomnogram of depressed outpatients: A pilot study. *Neuropsychopharmacology* **10**, 85–91.

Hoehn-Saric R, Harris GJ, Pearlson GD, *et al.* (1991) A fluoxetine-induced frontal lobe syndrome in an obsessive–compulsive patient. *J Clin Psychiatry* **52**, 131–133.

Hoehn-Saric R, Lipsey JR and McLeod DR (1990) Apathy and indifference on fluvoxamine and fluoxetine. *J Clin Psychopharmacol* **10**, 343–345.

Jain U, Birmaher B, Garcia M, *et al.* (1992) Fluoxetine in children and adolescents with mood disorders: A chart review of efficacy and adverse effects. *J Child Adolesc Psychopharmacol* **4**, 259–261.

Jensen PS, Ryan ND and Prien R (1992) Psychopharmacology of child and adolescent major depression: Present status and future direction. *J Child Adolesc Psychopharmacol* **2**, 31–48.

Kahn JS, Kehle TJ, Jenson WR, *et al.* (1990) Comparison of cognitive or cognitive-behavioral, relaxation, self modeling interventions for depression among middle school students. *School Psychol Rev* **19**, 196–211.

Kandel DB and Davies M (1986) Adult sequela of adolescent depressive symptoms. *Arch Gen Psychiatry* **43**, 255–262.

Keck PE, Hudson JI, Dorsey CM, *et al.* (1991) Effect of fluoxetine on sleep. *Biol Psychiatry* **29**, 618.

King RA, Riddle MA, Chappell PB, *et al.* (1991) Emergence of self-destructive phenomena in children and adolescents during fluoxetine treatment. *J Am Acad Child Adolesc Psychiatry* **30 (2)**, 179–186.

Kovacs M, Feinberg TL, Crouse-Novak MA, *et al.* (1984a) Depressive disorders in childhood. I. A longitudinal prospective study of characteristics and recovery. *Arch Gen Psychiatry* **41**, 229–237.

Kovacs M, Feinberg TL, Crouse-Novak MA, *et al.* (1984b) Depressive disorders in childhood. II. A longitudinal study for the risk of subsequent major depression. *Arch Gen Psychiatry* **41**, 643–649.

Kovacs M and Gatsonois C (1994) Secular trends in age at onset of major depressive disorder in a clinical sample of children. *J Psychiatr Res* **28 (3)**, 319–329.

Kovacs M, Paulauskas S, Gatsonis C, *et al.* (1988) Depressive disorders in childhood: III. A longitudinal study of comorbidity with and risk for conduct disorders. *J Affect Disord* **15**, 205–217.

Kramer A and Feiguine R (1981) Clinical effects of amitriptyline in adolescent depression: A pilot study. *J Am Acad Child Psychiatry* **20**, 636–644.

Kutcher S, Boulos C, Ward B, *et al.* (1994) Response to desipramine treatment in adolescent depression: A fixed dose, placebo controlled trial. *J Am Acad Child Adolesc Psychiatry* **35**

(5), 686–694.

Lewinsohn PM, Clark GN, Hops H, *et al.* (1990) Cognitive behavioral treatment for depressed adolescents. *Behav Res Ther* **21**, 285–401.

Lipinski JF Jr, Mallya G, Zimmerman P, *et al.* (1989) Fluoxetine-induced akathisia: Clinical and theoretical implications. *J Clin Psychiatry* **50**, 339–342.

McCauley E, Myers K, Mitchell J, *et al.* (1993) Depression in young people: Initial presentation and clinical course. *J Am Acad Child Adolesc Psychiatry* **32**, 714.

McCracken JT (1992) The epidemiology of child and adolescent mood disorders. *Child and Adolescent Psychiatric Clinics of North America* **1 (1)**, 53–72.

Moreau D, Mufson L, Weissman MM, *et al.* (1991) Interpersonal psychotherapy for adolescent depression: Description of modification and preliminary applications. *J Am Acad Child Adolesc Psychiatry* **30**, 642–661.

Mufson L (1994) *Interpersonal therapy—adolescents.* Presented at the Annual Child and Adolescent Depression Consortium Meeting. Providence, Rhode Island.

Mufson L, Moreau D, Weissman MM, *et al.* (1993) *Interpersonal Psychotherapy for Depressed Adolescents.* Guilford Press, New York.

Mufson L, Moreau D, Weissman MM, *et al.* (1994) Modification of interpersonal psychotherapy with depressed adolescents (IPT-A): Phase I and II studies. *J Am Acad Child Adolesc Psychiatry* **33**, 695–705.

Petti TA (1978) Depression in hospitalized child psychiatry patients: Approaches to measuring depression. *J Am Acad Child Adolesc Psychiatry* **17**, 49–59.

Petti TA (1985) The bellevue index of depression (BID). *Psychopharmacol Bull* **21**, 959–968.

Pfeffer CR, Klerman GL, Hurt SW, *et al.* (1991) Suicidal children grow up: Demographic and clinical risk factors for adolescent suicide attempts. *J Am Acad Child Adolesc Psychiatry* **30**, 609–616.

Poznanski EO, Grossman JA, Buchsbaum Y, *et al.* (1986) Preliminary studies of the reliability and validity of the children's depression rating scale. *J Am Acad Child Psychiatry* **23**, 191–197.

Poznanski EO, Krahenbuhl V and Zrull JP (1976) Childhood depression: A longitudinal perspective. *J Am Acad Child Psychiatry* **15**, 491–501.

Poznanski EO, Mokros HB, Grossman J, *et al.* (1985) Diagnostic criteria in childhood depression. *Br J Psychiatry* **142**, 1168–1173.

Quitkin FM, McGrath PJ, Steward JW, *et al.* (1990) Atypical depression, panic attacks, response to imipramine and phenelzine: A replication. *Arch Gen Psychiatry* **47**, 935–941.

Quitkin F, Rabkin J, Ross D, *et al.* (1984) Identification of true drug response to antidepressants: Use of pattern analysis. *Arch Gen Psychiatry* **41**, 782–786.

Rao U, Weissman MM, Martin JA, *et al.* (1993) Childhood depression and risk of suicide: A preliminary report of a longitudinal study. *J Am Acad Child Adolesc Psychiatry* **32**, 21–27.

Reynolds WM and Coats KI (1986) A comparison of cognitive-behavioral therapy and relaxation training for the treatment of depression in adolescents. *J Consult Clin Psychol* **5**, 653–660.

Riddle MA, King RA, Hardin MT, *et al.* (1991) Behavioral side effects of fluoxetine in children and adolescents. *J Child Adolesc Psychopharmacol* **1 (3)**, 193–198.

Rodriguez-Ramos P, *et al.* (1995) *Preliminary Study with Paroxetine in Adolescents with Depressive Disorder.* Presented at the ECNP Congress, 1–4 October, Venice.

Rosenberg DR, Johnson K and Sahl R (1992) Evolving mania in an adolescent treated with low dose fluoxetine. *J Child Adolesc Psychopharmacol* **2**, 299–306.

Rothschild AJ and Locke CA (1991) Re-exposure to fluoxetine after serious suicide attempts by three patients: The role of akathisia. *J Clin Psychiatry* **52**, 491–493.

Ryan N (1990) Pharmacotherapy of adolescent major depression: Beyond TCA's. *Psychopharmacol Bull* **26**, 75–90.

Ryan N, Puig-Antich J, Cooper T, et al. (1986) Imipramine in adolescent major depression: Plasma levels and clinical response. Acta Psychiatr Scand 73, 275–288.

Ryan ND, Meyer V, Dachille S, et al. (1988a) Lithium antidepressant augmentation in TCA refractory depression in adolescents. J Am Acad Child Adolesc Psychiatry 27, 371–376.

Ryan ND, Puig-Antich J, Rabinovich H, et al. (1988b) MAOs in adolescent major depression unresponsive to tricyclic antidepressants. J Am Acad Child Adolesc Psychiatry 27, 755–758.

Schenck CH, Mahowald MW, Kim SW, et al. (1992) Prominent eye movements during NREM sleep and REM sleep behavior disorder associated with fluoxetine treatment of depression and obsessive–compulsive disorder. Sleep 15, 226–235.

Simeon JG, Dinicola VF, Ferguson HB, et al. (1990) Adolescent depression: A placebo-controlled fluoxetine study and follow-up. Prog Neuropsychopharmacol Biol Psychiatry 14, 791–795.

Strober M (1992) The pharmacotherapy of depressive illness in adolescence III. Diagnostic and conceptual issues in studies of tricyclic antidepressants. J Child Adolesc Psychopharmacol 2, 23–29.

Strober M, Freeman R and Rigali J (1990) The pharmacotherapy of depressive illness in adolescence: An open label trial of imipramine. Psychopharmacol Bull 26, 80–84.

Strober M, Freeman R, Rigali J, et al. (1992) The pharmacotherapy of depressive illness in adolescence: II. Effects of lithium augmentation in nonresponders to imipramine. J Am Acad Child Adolesc Psychiatry 31, 16–20.

Strober M, Lampert C, Schmidt S, et al. (1993) The course of major depressive disorder in adolescents: I. Recovery and risk of manic switching in a follow-up of psychotic and nonpsychotic subtypes. J Am Acad Child Adolesc Psychiatry 32, 34–42.

Stuss DT and Benson DF (1986) The Frontal Lobes. pp 121–138, Raven Press, New York.

Venkataraman S, Naylor MW and King CA (1992) Mania associated with fluoxetine treatment in adolescents. J Am Acad Child Adolesc Psychiatry 31, 276–281.

Walkup JT (1994) A differential diagnosis of the adverse behavioral effects of fluoxetine. Newsletter American Acad Child & Adolescent Psychiatry 25 (3), 28–30

Weinberg WA and Emslie GJ (1988a) Adolescents and school problems: Depression, suicide and learning disorders. In: Feldman RA and Stiffman AR (eds) Advances in Adolescent Mental Health, III: Depression and Suicide. pp 181–205, JAI, Greenwich, Conn.

Weinberg WA and Emslie GJ (1988b) Weinberg screening affective scales (WSAS and WSAS-SF). J Child Neurol 3, 294–296.

Weinberg WA, Rutman A, Sullivan L, et al. (1973) Depression in children referred to an educational diagnostic center: Diagnosis and treatment. J Pediatr 83, 1065–1073.

Wilkes TCR and Rush AJ (1988) Adaptations of cognitive therapy for depressed adolescents. J Am Acad Child Adolesc Psychiatry 27, 381–386

Wilkes TCR, Belsher G, Rush AJ, et al. (1994) Cognitive Therapy for Depressed Adolescents. Guilford Press, New York.

11

Efficacy of selective serotonin re-uptake inhibitors in the treatment of dysthymia

David L. Dunner

The purpose of this chapter is to discuss the treatment of dysthymia with particular emphasis on the use of newer agents, selective serotonin re-uptake inhibitors (SSRIs). Dysthymia is an interesting mood disorder. The concept of a mild chronic depression predates DSM III (APA, 1980) and the subsequent revisions of this nomenclature. Dysthymia as a disorder was delineated from unipolar mood disorders in DSM III and the intent in DSM III was to define a condition which was milder in severity than major depression. In DSM III the condition was termed "dysthymic disorder or depressive neurosis". The criteria for DSM III were similar to the current DSM IV (APA, 1994) criteria except a 13-question check-list was employed with a requirement of three symptoms being positive to establish the diagnosis. Symptoms needed to be present more days than not for a two-year or greater period. In DSM III R (APA, 1987), the term used was "dysthymia (or depressive neurosis)" and the symptom criteria included two of six symptoms. Early or late onset (age 21) was to be identified. In ICD 10 (1992), dysthymia requires three symptoms from an 11-item list.

DIAGNOSIS

There was considerable discussion about the criteria for dysthymia for DSM IV (1994). A field trial was undertaken using DSM III R criteria for including subjects

Selective Serotonin Re-uptake Inhibitors: Advances in Basic Research and Clinical Practice, Second Edition, Edited by J.P. Feighner and W.F. Boyer
© 1996 John Wiley & Sons Ltd

(Keller *et al.*, 1995). A listing of other symptoms frequently found in dysthymic patients was compiled. The proposed symptom list resulting from this research was a grouping of nine items which essentially deleted the more vegetative symptoms from the DSM III R list and included more cognitive symptoms. (DSM IV Draft Criteria, 1993). However, the work group on mood disorders for DSM IV felt the data were premature to allow dysthymia to be redefined in this manner and therefore the DSM IV criteria are the same as DSM III R. The appendix to DSM IV lists these proposed criteria for further research study. Interestingly, in DSM IV the term used is "dysthymic disorder" and "depressive neurosis" is dropped. The early and late onset provision is maintained.

In general, two types of dysthymic disorder can be envisioned. The more common form is sporadic depression, the patient having more depressed days than not without sustained euthymia (2 months or more) and without sustained uninterrupted depressive symptoms (i.e. 2 weeks or more). About 85% of patients with dysthymia have sporadic depression. The other form is less common and is characterized by chronic symptoms every day but with too few persistent symptoms to meet criteria for major depression, i.e. individuals do not have five of the nine symptoms which characterize major depression nearly every day but could have up to four of nine symptoms.

Importantly, the differential diagnosis lies with major depression on the one hand and cyclothymic disorder and "depressive personality" on the other. For cyclothymic disorder the diagnosis is made if the mood goes from depressed to hypomanic, the hypomanic episodes are brief, and the depressions last less than two weeks. Thus, patients who have highs and lows would be termed cyclothymic, whereas patients whose mood alternates from depressed to normal in a sporadic fashion would be termed dysthymic. Criteria for a proposed category "depressive personality" are included in the appendix in DSM IV (1994). These criteria include five of seven symptoms (with considerable overlap in these symptoms with the cognitive symptoms derived from the field trial noted above). The differential from major depression is a complicated one. Major depressive disorder is the most frequent complication of dysthymia and patients who have both major depression and a dysthymic pattern have been termed "double depression" (Keller and Shapiro, 1982). Chronic major depression is differentiated from dysthymia by the number of symptoms present nearly every day, or by the sporadic nature of these symptoms in dysthymia. Another point of differential diagnosis is major depressive episode with incomplete recovery. Some patients with major depression will only partially recover from symptoms and instead of full return to normal mood will have a dysthymic pattern at the termination of their major depressive syndrome. Dysthymia is not diagnosed in the two-year period after partial recovery from a major depressive episode.

In terms of prevalence studies, the ECA data suggest that dysthymia is a disorder of considerable prevalence with lifetime prevalence rates ranging from 1–2.3% in men and 2.3–4.8% in women (Weissman *et al.*, 1988). The mean lifetime rate for dysthymia is 3.1%. A site-by-site comparison showed differences with highest rates in

Los Angeles (4.2%) as compared to Baltimore (2.1%). The rates tended to diminish after the age of 65. Dysthymia was frequently comorbid with other disorders. The more frequent complicating psychiatric disorders were major depression, panic disorder, any anxiety disorders, and substance abuse.

In a study from our centre, we determined that major depression was the most likely comorbid disorder with dysthymic disorder and that dysthymic disorder, a chronic sporadic depression, differed considerably from uncomplicated generalized anxiety disorder (GAD) on several variables (Shores *et al.*, 1992). The pure dysthymia group (dysthymia with no comorbid disorder) differed from the pure GAD group on total Hamilton Anxiety (HAM-A) and Hamilton Depression (HAM-D) (Hamilton, 1959, 1960) scores as well as profiles of somatic anxiety within the HAM-A scores, which were higher for GAD than dysthymic patients. Furthermore on the HAM-D, 40% of the individual items were significantly different with high ratings for dysthymic patients on depressed mood, guilt, psychomotor retardation, impairment of work and activities, and diurnal variation. Family history also showed more depression in relatives of dysthymic patients and more anxiety disorders in relatives of GAD patients.

In summary dysthymic disorder is a prevalent chronic depressive illness with either sporadic symptoms or relatively few daily symptoms, with generally lower mean ratings for depression than patients with major depression, and indeed frequently complicated by major depression. Very early (childhood onset) of dysthymic disorder is noted to be complicated with major depressive episodes and, at times, bipolar disorder (Kovacs *et al.*, 1994).

TREATMENT

At the time of publication of DSM III (1980), dysthymia was thought to be a disorder which should be preferentially treated with psychotherapy. However, Akiskal *et al.* (1980) (Akiskal, 1981) showed that dysthymic patients whose illness was complicated by major depressive episodes demonstrated biological factors in common with "endogenously" depressed patients. These factors include non-suppression of cortisol in response to dexamethasone administration and shortened REM (rapid eye movement) latency. These studies encouraged investigators to attempt to treat dysthymia with antidepressant medication. Indeed there are now several studies demonstrating efficacy of antidepressants in dysthymic patients (Kivella and Lehomaki, 1987; Vallejo *et al.*, 1987; Defrance *et al.*, 1988; Kocsis *et al.*, 1988; Waring *et al.*, 1988; Kocsis, 1989; Bersani *et al.*, 1991; Howland, 1991; Rosenthal *et al.*, 1992; Bakish *et al.*, 1993; Harrison and Stewart, 1993; Hellerstein *et al.*, 1993; Keller *et al.*, 1993; Dunner and Schmaling, 1994; Lapierre, 1994; Lee *et al.*, 1994; Marin *et al.*, 1994; Nobler *et al.*, 1994; Ravindran *et al.*, 1994a).

There are, however, a number of problems peculiar to the study of antidepressants in dysthymic patients. Most dysthymic patients have a milder depression with mean

HAM-D scores in the 16–20 point range as compared to patients with major depression, where mean HAM-Ds are more typically in the 20–25 point range. Thus, it may be more difficult to show an effect of treatment since patients begin at a lower rating. Furthermore, the HAM-D may not be an optimal rating scale for the assessment of degree of depression in dysthymia since dysthymia may be less characterized by the vegetative symptoms emphasized in the HAM-D than by "psychological" symptoms (Hellerstein et al., 1994).

In our studies of treatment resistant patients, we have noted certain personality effects (as measured by the tridimensional; personality questionnaire) (Cloninger et al., 1991). We hypothesized that these effects were the result of patients being chronically depressed (Nelsen and Dunner, 1993). Dysthymic patients by definition are chronically depressed and such personality factors as a result of the chronicity of their illness may make change more difficult to detect.

Studies of treatment effects in major depressive disorder are of interest in regard to dysthymia. For example, the collaborative project on psychotherapy of depression assigned depressed patients to treatment with imipramine, cognitive psychotherapy, interpersonal psychotherapy, or a control group (Elkin et al., 1989). Patients with major depression who had mild severity of illness tended to have side-effects to modest doses of imipramine, which was generally used successfully in more moderately depressed patients. This suggests that patients with mild depression (and dysthymia is a mild depression) may be more prone to side-effects of traditional tricyclic medication as compared to patients with moderate depression.

Additionally, it is not clear that all investigators who study dysthymic patients are including similar cohorts. Dysthymia may be a complicating type of depression for some patients who have other antecedent primary diagnoses. Thus the Washington University criteria (Feighner et al., 1972) proposed that patients could be classified as primary or secondary based on which illness occurred first. Patients whose dysthymic-type illness is a complication of prior substance abuse, alcoholism or other psychiatric disorders such as panic disorder, may not have the same course of illness as patients who have a primary dysthymic condition, meaning that their illness began and continues as chronic sporadic depression. Furthermore, it is possible that different criteria sets (DSM III R and ICD 10 for example) could identify dissimilar patients as dysthymic.

It is sometimes difficult for treatment centres to recruit large numbers of dysthymic patients for research. This would seem to be logical since dysthymia, although a prevalent condition, is "a way of life" for many patients and there is no particular reason for them to recognize that they have a mood disorder that might respond to treatment.

The duration of studies for dysthymia may have considerable bearing on the treatment outcome. For example, we studied a serotonin medication (ritanserin) in a six-week study which failed to show outcome for dysthymic patients as compared to placebo (Dunner, personal communication). Since dysthymia is a chronic disorder, longer treatment trials might be better than shorter ones. Thus, optimal treatment trials of dysthymic patients might involve very careful attention to diagnostic issues, use of rating scales in addition to the HAM-D so that psychological symptoms might also be assessed, treatment duration somewhat longer than usual, and careful attention to dose titration to avoid side-effects.

Many treatments have been reported to be effective for dysthymia including imipramine, amitriptyline, doxepin, desipramine, trazodone, ritanserin, sulpiride, phenelzine, amineptine, and moclobemide. Only recently have the selective serotonin re-uptake inhibitors (SSRIs) been studied in dysthymic patients (Table 1). Rosenthal *et al.* (1992) reported positive results using fluoxetine versus trazodone in an open-label five-month study of 20 dysthymic patients. Patients had a mean HAM-D at entry of 14 points with ranges from seven to 21 points and were randomized to fluoxetine or trazodone. Fluoxetine was begun at 20 mg/day. After six weeks, if there was inadequate response, fluoxetine could be increased to a maximum dose of 60 mg/day. Trazodone was started at 50 mg/day and increased to a maximum of 350 mg/day, with dose increments every three days. Patients who could not tolerate the initial medication because of side-effects were crossed over to the comparator medication. Doses at three months were about 31 mg of fluoxetine and about 240 mg of trazodone. The results indicated that most of the patients completed 12 weeks of medication and initial assignment of medication. At three months, six of nine fluoxetine completers had responded and four of five trazodone completers had responded, using improvement on HAM-D and global impressions as outcome. The conclusions from this study were that both medications were well tolerated and effective.

Hellerstein *et al.* (1993) studied 35 patients who met criteria for dysthymia and who were assigned to a double-blind eight-week trial of fluoxetine or placebo. The dose of fluoxetine could be varied and the mean dose was about 33 mg and ranged from 20 mg every other day to 60 mg/day. Thirty-two of the 35 patients completed the eight-week study. Their mean HAM-D score was about 19 points at baseline. At the end of the study, 10 of the 16 fluoxetine-treated, and three of 16 placebo patients were defined as responders using improvement on HAM-D and clinical global impressions as criteria. This difference was significant. Only one subject discontinued treatment because of side-effects although side-effects were noted in several patients. The conclusions were that fluoxetine was well tolerated by dysthymic patients and significantly more patients responded to fluoxetine. Placebo response in this study was relatively low. One interesting finding from their study was that no significant differences were found using the Cornell Dysthymia Scale (Hellerstein *et al.*, 1994).

Ravindran *et al.* (1994a, b), recently reported a study of fluoxetine treatment in dysthymia patients who also had measurements of platelet monoamine oxidase (MAO) activity and plasma cortisol levels. Fifty-two dysthymic patients were treated with fluoxetine 20–60 mg for six weeks. Of these patients 73% responded according to a revised HAM-D. Overall, patients had a low rate of dexamethasone nonsuppression (7%). Responders to treatment had a higher mean pretreatment dexamethasone

Table 1. SSRIs in the treatment of dysthymia.

Authors	Year	Drug	Patients N	Initial HAM-D	Duration	Type of study	Outcome
Rosenthal et al.	1992	Fluoxetine vs Trazodone	12 8	13.8	3 months 5 months	Open with crossover	Six of nine fluoxetine completers and four of five trazodone completers respond at three months
Hellerstein et al.	1993	Fluoxetine vs placebo	19 16	19	8 weeks	Randomized, double-blind	16 completers in each group; 10 fluoxetine and three placebo-treated patients responded
Ravindran et al.	1994	Fluoxetine	52	18	6 weeks	Open treatment	73.1% responded; biological correlates of response noted
Nobler et al.	1994	Fluoxetine	21 (elderly)	14	13 weeks	Single-blind	75% of 12 completers responded
Dunner and Schmaling	1994	Fluoxetine vs cognitive therapy	18 13	16 15	16 weeks	Randomized with blind assessments	Significant decrease in HAM-D and BDI with fluoxetine at weeks eight and 16; significant decrease in BDI and HAM-D at weeks eight and 16 with cognitive therapy
Lee et al.	1994	Sertraline vs amitriptyline	16 13	23* 24*	6 weeks	Randomized, double-blind	85% sertraline and 100% amitriptyline patients responded

*Includes data from patients with major depression.

cortisol response and lower pretreatment platelet MAO activity than non-responders. The authors hypothesized that low platelet MAO activity may be a biological marker for a subtype of dysthymia. In a companion paper, these authors also noted that responders had lower urinary 5-hydroxyindoleacetic acid (5-HIAA) levels prior to treatment as compared to non-responders (Ravindran *et al.*, 1994c).

Our study is still ongoing and only preliminary results have been reported (Dunner and Schmaling, 1994). Thirty-one patients with dysthymia were randomly assigned to fluoxetine 20 mg (fixed dose) or weekly cognitive psychotherapy. Although the treatments were not blinded, the assessments were. HAM-D scores were assessed at baseline and at weeks eight and 16. The mean HAM-D at entry was about 15 points. The results of this study showed significant improvement for fluoxetine considering both the HAM-D and the Beck Depression Inventory (BDI) (Beck *et al.*, 1979) at weeks eight and 16. Significant improvement for cognitive therapy was also found at weeks eight and 16 with the BDI and the HAM-D. In general, fluoxetine was well tolerated. Three patients initially assigned to fluoxetine dropped out of treatment because they wished to have cognitive therapy. These results suggest that fluoxetine and cognitive psychotherapy may both be effective for the treatment of dysthymia.

Nobler *et al.* (1994) recently reported a pilot study of fluoxetine treatment in 21 elderly depressives (mean age about 68 years) utilizing a single-blind design with doses from 20 to 40 mg. The mean baseline HAM-D score was about 14 points and after seven weeks of fluoxetine this had dropped to about eight points, and at 13 weeks to about seven points. These results suggested that fluoxetine is a safe and effective treatment in elderly dysthymic patients.

Treatment studies of the newer SSRIs, sertraline and paroxetine, are in progress with controlled studies under way for both antidepressants. Lee *et al.* (1994) recently reported a comparison of sertraline and amitriptyline over a six-week period in patients with dysthymia or major depression. Twenty-nine of these patients were diagnosed as having dysthymia. All of the amitriptyline-treated and 85% of the sertraline-treated patients responded.

Psychotherapy has also been shown to be effective not only in our study but also in a report by Waring *et al.* (1988). They administered cognitive marital therapy to dysthymic patients who were also treated with doxepin or placebo. Their preliminary data suggested a positive effect for the combined therapy. McCullough (1991) reported improvement in 10 dysthymic patients treated with cognitive therapy. Paykel (1994) recently reviewed the role of psychotherapy for milder depressions.

In general the SSRIs are better tolerated than the tricyclic antidepressants and thus may be better choices for dysthymic patients. Side-effects associated with tricyclic antidepressants are robust and reflect the broad receptor effects of these compounds (Richelson, 1993). Tricyclic side-effects related to muscarinic receptor blockade include dry mouth, blurred vision, tachycardia, constipation, sweating, and urinary retention. Histaminergic blockade can result in sedation and weight gain, and alpha-adrenergic effects include blood pressure changes. Tricyclic antidepressants can be lethal in overdose. In contrast, SSRIs are more limited in their receptor effects resulting in more limited side-effects. SSRI side-effects typically include nausea, diarrhoea, and sexual dysfunction. SSRIs are considered safe in overdose situations.

Since dysthymia is a chronic form of depression, chronic or long-term treatment would seem to be indicated. Montgomery *et al.* (1994) have shown better rates of compliance with treatment (and equal efficacy) for SSRIs compared with tricyclic antidepressant treatment for major depression. This meta-analysis of treatment outcome studies supports the use of SSRIs as initial treatment for depression, since noncompliance with treatment can result in increased morbidity and mortality from depression (and thus greater economic burden).

Our view of the treatment of dysthymia is that SSRIs should be used as a first-line treatment, that treatment should be continued for longer rather than shorter periods, and that combined pharmacotherapy and psychotherapy may be optimal. We use SSRIs initially because their lower side-effect profile is likely to result in enhanced compliance, particularly in instances where long-term pharmacotherapy may be indicated. Longer half-life compounds (fluoxetine) may be preferable to shorter half-life compounds for long-term treatment on hypothetical grounds. Direct comparison studies of various SSRIs in dysthymic patients would be of interest.

We encourage the combined use of pharmacotherapy with those psychotherapies which have been studied in depression, namely cognitive therapy and interpersonal psychotherapy (Elkin *et al.*, 1989). Although there are no data to support greater efficacy for combined treatment, the suggestion of personality effects resulting from chronic (treatment resistant) depression suggests the possible need for combined therapy—the medication to reduce depressive symptoms, and the psychotherapy to repair self-esteem and interpersonal processes.

In summary, dysthymia is a depressive disorder shown to respond to a variety of treatments for depression, including psychotherapy and a variety of antidepressant pharmacotherapies. The use of SSRIs, particularly fluoxetine, is supported by research studies of treatment effects in dysthymia. Studies of other SSRIs in dysthymia are ongoing and these results should considerably add to our knowledge of dysthymia and its response to treatment.

REFERENCES

Akiskal HS, Rosenthal TL, Haykal RF, Lewis H, Rosenthal RH and Scott-Strauss A (1980) Characterological depressions: Clinical and sleep EEG findings separating "subaffective dysthymias" from "character spectrum disorders". *Arch Gen Psychiatry* **37**, 777–783.
Akiskal HS (1981) Subaffective disorders: Dysthymic, cyclothymic and bipolar II disorders in the "borderline" realm. *Psychiatr Clin North Am* **4**, 25–46.
Bakish D, Lapierre YD, Weinstein R, Klein J, Wiens A, Jones B, Horn E, Browne M, Bourget D, Blanchard A, Thibaudeau C, Waddell C and Raine D (1993) Ritanserin, imipramine, and placebo in the treatment of dysthymic disorder. *J Clin Psychopharmocol* **13**, 409–414.
Beck AT, Rush AJ, Shaw BF and Emery G (1979) *Cognitive Therapy of Depression*. Guilford,

New York.

Bersani G, Pozzi F, Marini S, Grisoini A, Pasini A and Ciani N (1991) 5-HT$_2$ receptor antagonism in dysthymic disorder: A double-blind placebo-controlled study with ritanserin. *Acta Psychiatr Scand* **8-3**, 244–248.

Cloninger CR, Svrakic DM and Przybeck TR (1991) The Tridimensional Personality Questionnaire: US normative data. *Psychol Rep* **69**, 1047–1057.

Defrance R, Marey C and Kamoun A (1988) Antidepressant and anxiolytic activities of tianeptine: An overview of clinical trials. *Clin Neuropharmacol* **11**, S74–S82.

APA (1980) *Diagnostic and Statistical Manual of Mental Disorders—Third Edition.* American Psychiatric Assn, Washington, DC.

APA (1987) *Diagnostic and Statistical Manual of Mental Disorders—Third editions, revised.* American Psychiatric Assn, Washington, DC.

APA (1994) *Diagnostic and Statistical Manual of Mental Disorders—Fourth Edition.* American Psychiatric Assn, Washington, DC.

Dunner DL and Schmaling KB (1994) Treatment of dysthymia: Fluoxetine versus cognitive therapy. Presented at the XIXth Collegium Internationale Neuro-Psychopharmacologicum Congress, Washington, DC, June 27 – July 1. *Neuropsychopharmacology* **10, (Number 35/Part 2)**, 234S.

Elkin I, Shea TM, Watkins JT, Imber SD, Sotsky SM, Collins JF, Glass DR, Pilkonis PA, Leber WR, Docherty JP, Fiester SJ and Parloff MB (1989) The National Institute of Mental Health Treatment of Depression Collaborative Research Program: General effectiveness of treatments. *Arch Gen Psychiatry* **46**, 971–932.

Feighner JP, Robins E, Guze SB, Woodruff RA, Jr., Winokur G and Munoz R (1972) Diagnostic criteria for use in psychiatric research. *Arch Gen Psychiatry* **26**, 57–63.

Hamilton M (1959) The assessment of anxiety by rating. *Br J Med Psychol* **32**, 50–56.

Hamilton M (1960) A rating scale for depression. *J Neurol Neurosurg Psychiatry* **23**, 56–62.

Harrison WM and Stewart JW (1993) Pharmacotherapy of dysthymia, *Psychiatric Annals* **23**, 638–648.

Hellerstein DJ, Samstag LW, Little S and Yanowitch P (1994) *Dysthymia: Assessing Symptoms and Treatment Response with the Cornell Dysthymia Rating Scale.* Presented at the Annual Meeting, American Psychiatric Assn., Philadelphia, PA, May 21–26 (New Research Program and Abstracts, p 111).

Hellerstein DJ, Yanowitch P, Rosenthal J Samstag LW, Maurer M, Kasch K, Burrows L, Poster M, Cantillon M and Winston A (1993) A randomized double-blind study of fluoxetine versus placebo in the treatment of dysthymia. *Am J Psychiatry* **150**, 1169–1175.

Howland RH (1991) Pharmacotherapy of dysthymia: a review. *J Clin Psychopharmacol* **11**, 83–92.

Keller MB, Klein DN, Hirschfeld RMA, Kocsis JH, McCullough JP, Miller I, First MB, Holzer CPIII, Keitner GI, Marin DB and Shea T (1995) Results of the DSM-IV mood disorders field trial. *Amer J Psychiatry* **152**, 843–849

Keller MB, Baker LA and Russell CW (1993) Classification and treatment of dysthymia. In: Dunner DL (ed) *Current Psychiatric Therapy,* pp 210–214. W. B. Saunders Co., Philadelphia, PA.

Keller MB and Shapiro RW (1982) "Double depression": Superimposition of acute depressive episodes on chronic depressive disorders. *Am J Psychiatry* **139**, 438–442.

Kivella SL and Lehomaki E (1987) Sulpiride and placebo in depressed elderly outpatients: A double-blind study. *Int J Geriatr Psychiatry* **2**, 255–260.

Kocsis JH (1989) Dysthymic disorder. In: Karasu B (ed) *Treatment of Psychiatric Disorders,* American Psychiatric Assn., Washington, DC.

Kocsis JH, Frances AJ, Voss C, Mann JJ, Mason BJ and Sweeney J (1988) Imipramine treatment for chronic depression. *Arch Gen Psychiatry* **45**, 253–257.

Kovacs M, Akiskal HS, Gatsonis C and Parrone PL (1994) Childhood-onset dysthymic disorder. *Arch Gen Psychiatry* **51**, 365–374.

Lapierre YD (1994) Pharmacological therapy of dysthymia. *Acta Psychiatr Scand* **89 (Suppl 383)**, 42–48.

Lee HS, Kim SH, Suh KY and Kwak DI (1994) Efficacy of sertraline in dysthymia. Presented at the XIXth Collegium International Neuro-Psychopharmacologicum Congress, Washington, DC, June 27 – July 1. *Neuropsychopharmacology* **10 (Number 3S/Part 2)**, 222S.

Marin DB, Kocsis JH, Frances AJ and Parides M (1994) Desipramine for the treatment of "pure" dysthymia versus "double" depression. *Am J Psychiatry* **151**, 1079–1080.

McCullough JP (1991) Psychotherapy for dysthymia: A naturalistic study of ten patients. *J Nerv Ment Dis* **179**, 734–740.

Montgomery SA, Henry J, McDonald G, Dinan T, Lader M, Hindmarch I, Clare A and Nutt D (1994) Selective serotonin reuptake inhibitors: meta-analysis of discontinuation rates. *Int Clin Psychopharmacol* **9**, 47–53.

Nelsen MR and Dunner DL (1993) Treatment resistance in unipolar depression and other disorders. *Psychiatr Clin North Am* **16**, 541–566.

Nobler MS, Devanand DP, Singer TM, Roose SP and Sackheim HA (1994) *Fluoxetine Treatment for Elderly Patients with Dysthymic Disorders: A Pilot Study.* Presented at the Annual meeting, American Psychiatric Assn., Philadelphia, PA, May 21–26. (New Research Program and Abstracts, p 91).

Paykel ES (1994) Psychological therapies. *Acta Psychiatr Scand* **89 (Suppl 383)**, 35–41.

Ravindran AV, Bialik RJ and Lapierre YD (1994a). Therapeutic efficacy of specific serotonin reuptake inhibitors (SSRIs) in dysthymia. *Can J Psychiatry* **39**, 21–26.

Ravindran AV, Bialik RJ and Lapierre YD (1994b) Primary early onset dysthymia, biochemical correlates of the therapeutic response to fluoxetine: I. Platelet monoamine oxidase and the dexamethasone suppression test. *J Affect Disord* **31**, 111–117.

Ravindran AV, Bialik RJ, Brown GM and Lapierre YD (1994c) Primary early onset dysthymia, biochemical correlates of the therapeutic response to fluoxetine: II. Urinary metabolites of serotonin, norepinephrine, epinephrine and melatonin. *J Affect Disord* **31**, 119–123.

Richelson, E (1993) Treatment of acute depression. *Psychiatr Clin North Am* **16**, 461–478.

Rosenthal J, Hemlock C, Hellerstein DJ, Yanowitch P, Kasch K, Schupak C, Samstag L and Winston A (1992) A preliminary study of serotonergic antidepressants in treatment of dysthymia. *Prog Neuropsychopharmacol Biol Psychiatry* **16**, 933–941.

Shores MM, Glubin T, Cowley DS, Dager SR, Roy-Byrne PP and Dunner DL (1992) The relationship between anxiety and depression: A clinical comparison of generalized anxiety disorder, dysthymic disorder, panic disorder, and major depressive disorder. *Compr Psychiatry* **33**, 237–244.

Vallejo J, Gasto C, Catalan R and Salamero M (1987) Double-blind study of imipramine versus phenelzine in melancholias and dysthymic disorders. *Br J Psychiatry* **151**, 639–642.

Waring EM, Chamberlaine CH, McCrank EW, Stalker CA, Carver C, Fry R and Barnes S (1988) Dysthymia: A randomized study of cognitive marital therapy and antidepressants. *Can J Psychiatry* **33**, 96–99.

Weissman MM, Leaf PJ, Bruce ML and Florio L (1988) The epidemiology of dysthymia in five communities: Rates, risks comorbidity and treatment. *Am J Psychiatry* **145**, 815–819.

World Health Organization (1992) The ICD-10 classification of mental and behavioural disorders—clinical descriptions and diagnostic guidelines. WHO, Geneva.

12

Depression and comorbidity

Robert J. Boland and Martin B. Keller

INTRODUCTION

> When the matter is divers and confused, how should it otherwise be, but that the species should be divers and confused? . . . It is a hard matter, I confess, to distinguish [the difference species of melancholy] . . . to express their several causes, symptoms, cures, being that they are so often confounded amongst themselves, having such affinity, that they can scarce be discerned by the most accurate physicians; and so often intermixed with other diseases, that the best experienced have been plunged.

As Robert Burton demonstrates in his *Anatomy of Melancholy* (1652), the idea of comorbidity is nothing new. Even Kraepelin, who was dedicated to discovering the "single morbid process" underlying a group of disorders, acknowledged that:

> When in the course of manic-depressive insanity arteriosclerotic changes* are added or, what also occasionally happens, fairly severe senile changes, psychic states of weakness may be developed, which obliterate the original morbid picture. I have repeatedly seen patients, who had suffered from a series of attacks without any injury to their psychic capacities worth mentioning, become demented in advanced age. . . . As we know cases enough of the opposite kind, in which manic-depressive patients suffer no kind of psychic loss at all in spite of advanced age, we must possibly always connect the appearance of a definite dementia of that kind with the addition of a fresh, more or less, independent disease.

> (Kraepelin, 1921)

Thus, even at the advent of modern psychiatry's nosology, the role of comorbidity was understood. In the above discussion, Kraepelin dramatically articulates the

---

* Adhering to contemporary theories, Kraepelin attributed progressive degenerative dementias of the Alzheimer's type to a vascular cause.

Selective Serotonin Re-uptake Inhibitors: Advances in Basic Research and Clinical Practice, Second Edition, Edited by J.P. Feighner and W.F. Boyer
© 1996 John Wiley & Sons Ltd

principle that will often be repeated in this chapter: that comorbid illnesses can fundamentally alter the presentation of a mood disorder. We will concentrate on major depression, and its relationship with various comorbid disorders.

We have only begun to gather useful information about the effect of comorbid depression in the last two decades, and insight into the aetiology and meaning of such comorbidity is even more recent. Despite Kraepelin's pioneering efforts to develop objective diagnostic criteria, the succeeding generation largely abandoned this approach in favour of diagnoses that were based on hypothetical aetiologies. As such, early studies are flawed by the lack of valid and reliable diagnostic criteria. With the introduction of DSM III's phenomenological approach (American Psychiatric Association, 1980), and the use of validated research diagnostic criteria (Spitzer *et al.*, 1985), a consistent approach to the diagnosis of major depression, and other psychiatric illnesses, became available. With the availability of these tools, we could begin to explore the ramifications and meaning of comorbid depression.

In reviewing the literature, we will find various approaches to understanding comorbid depression. Epidemiological studies reveal the high prevalence of comorbidity in the population. Such studies define the scope and seriousness of the problem; however, they are generally cross-sectional, and can tell us little about the course of comorbid depression. A number of longitudinal studies now exist, however, that have taken into account the role of comorbidity. These studies primarily involve clinical samples—patients in treatment—and may contain certain biases. People seeking treatment are likely to be more severely ill than other people. Similarly, having multiple disorders can increase the likelihood of seeking treatment for at least one of the disorders (Berkson, 1946). Thus, studies using clinical samples are likely to overestimate the prevalence of comorbidity. Through such longitudinal clinical studies, however, we are able to follow the course of a disease. We can begin to understand the effect of a comorbid illness on the course of major depression, and in turn, how major depression can influence another illness. From a preventive stance, we can learn how comorbid illnesses alter the risk for developing depression, and vice versa.

Beyond the epidemiological and clinical implications of comorbidity, investigators are beginning to unravel the nature of the relationship between depression and other disorders. Does one illness "cause" another, or is it caused by it? It is usually assumed that the temporal relationship of two illnesses implies a primary and secondary relationship, thus, longitudinal data can help us to answer these questions. But what is the nature of such a cause? To answer this question properly, we would have to understand better the underlying mechanisms of depression. Often, we assume "indirect mechanism"—reactions to stress, such as a chronic disorder—can make one susceptible to other disorders. Additionally, the presence of one disorder may "directly" produce another disorder, perhaps through a physiological mechanism; for example, depressive symptoms can result directly from the toxic effects of alcohol. However, it is also possible that neither illness causes the other, but rather that they share a common aetiology. In disorders that are familial in transmission—as is major depression and many other psychiatric disorders—we can probe these relationships through familial and twin studies.

By looking at the phenotypic expression of two disorders across generations, we can examine their pattern of inheritance. It may be that two disorders will be inherited by a person only if there is a family history of *both* disorders—the two disorders, thus, are inherited independently. If the comorbid form of a disorder is inherited only when one forebear also had the *comorbid* disorder—that is, if the two disorders "cosegregate"—this implies that the comorbid form is different from the "pure" form of either disorder alone. It is possible, however, that one can inherit either of two disorders, or both, although the forebear had only *one* of the disorders. In the last case, a common aetiological factor must be responsible for the expression of more than one disorder. When such a common aetiological factor is genetic this is called "pleiotropy", in which the same gene or genes can influence the expression of more than one trait (Kendler, 1993). A common aetiological factor can also be environmental: parenting style, social, ethnic or economic factors can also be common to a group of progeny. Other environmental factors, such as a particular event or trauma, can be unique to an individual, and not transmitted to succeeding generations.

Family studies can determine if there is a pattern of inheritance, and what that pattern is. They cannot distinguish, however, among genetic and common environmental factors, as both may be "passed on" to the next generation. Twin studies, however, can distinguish these different possibilities. When twin studies and family studies are combined, powerful analyses can test different models of inheritance. Most notable in this regard are the population-based Swedish (Kendler *et al.*, 1992d) and Virginia (Kendler *et al.*, 1992a) twin studies. The latter study involved structured personal interviews on 2163 female twins who were part of the Virginia Twin Register. They also studied first-degree relatives of these twins. Using these data, they were able to test complex models that compare the relative effects of genetic, common and unique environmental factors.

This chapter explores the comorbidity of depression in several ways. First, it looks at the overall problem of comorbid depression. The bulk of the chapter presents a more detailed look at comorbid depression, and how it relates to certain disorders. Finally, the chapter briefly surveys the problem in specific populations: children, the elderly, and the medically ill.

THE PROBLEM OF COMORBIDITY

Almost two decades ago, it became clear that progress in treating mental illnesses required better information on the prevalence of such disorders in the community (The President's Commission on Mental Health and Illness, 1978). Obtaining such data was not really possible until valid standardized instruments were developed for assessing mental illness in the community. The Diagnostic Interview Schedule

(Robins *et al.*, 1981) was designed to meet this need, and this enabled the implementation of the Epidemiologic Catchment Area (ECA) study (Robins *et al.*, 1991). The ECA study interviewed more than 20 000 participants in five communities. The information from this study continues to be our primary source for prevalence data on psychiatric illness in the United States.

The ECA study contained a number of surprises. One of these was the high rate of comorbid psychiatric disorders in the community. Of those subjects with at least one psychiatric disorder, over 60% had two or more disorders (Robins *et al.*, 1991). Psychiatric comorbidity was also associated with a high utilization of medical services (Helzer and Pryzbeck, 1988).

The ECA study measured prevalence and incidence. A subsequent study, the National Comorbidity Survey (NCS) (Kessler *et al.*, 1994), looked also at the risk factors and consequences of psychiatric disorders. More than 8000 participants representing a national sample were surveyed with a modified form of the Diagnostic Interview Schedule, incorporating the conversion to DSM III R (American Psychiatric Association, 1987). The investigators found that almost half of the subjects had at least one lifetime psychiatric disorder, and almost one third had suffered from a disorder in the past year. The most common lifetime disorder was major depression, which had a prevalence of 13% in men and 21% in women.

The NCS paid particular attention to comorbid disorders. As with the ECA study, this study found that the majority of subjects with a psychiatric disorder had more than one disorder. Only 21% of the subjects had a single disorder—13% had two, and 14% had three or more (Kessler *et al.*, 1994). Of the lifetime psychiatric disorders found in the sample, almost 80% were comorbid psychiatric disorders. This comorbid group included the majority of those with recent (12 month) disorders and those with more severe disorders. The study concludes that "the major burden of psychiatric disorder . . . is concentrated in a group of highly comorbid people" (Kessler *et al.*, 1994).

Thus, comorbid psychiatric disorders appear to be the rule rather than the exception. This appears particularly true for major depression. In the NCS, 394 subjects had current major depression. Of this group, 56% had a comorbid psychiatric disorder in addition to the depression. An examination of demographic risk factors for "pure" versus comorbid depression also provided surprising results. A number of generally held risk factors for major depression—younger age, poorer education and income, for example—were only associated with the comorbid form of major depression. Alternatively, "nonblack race/ethnicity" was primarily associated with the "pure" form of major depression (Blazer *et al.*, 1994).

The NCS was cross-sectional in design. Thus, it cannot give prospective data about comorbidity's effect on the outcome of a disorder. Some longitudinal research into the outcome of depression has looked at the effect of comorbidity. Akiskal and colleagues (1981) found that patients with an incomplete recovery from a major depressive disorder tended to have comorbid alcohol dependence, sedative dependence and incapacitating medical disorders. Levitt and colleagues (1991) found that patients with chronic depression had more comorbid disorders, particularly anxiety, than did patients with non-chronic major depression. Similarly, Keitner and colleagues (1992) found comorbidity to be one of the most important factors that predicted one-year outcome of patients originally hospitalized for major depression.

One of the longest and most comprehensive studies of the course of depression is the ongoing National Institute of Mental Health Collaborative Study of the Psychobiology of Depression (CDS) (Keller *et al.*, 1992). In this study, a prior history of a non-affective psychiatric disorder predicted a slower time to recovery from an episode of major depression (Keller *et al.*, 1984). This study also collected data on specific comorbid disorders; where relevant, this data will be discussed in the following sections of this chapter. Dysthymia can also be comorbid with depression ('double-depression'). See chapter 11 for more details.

ANXIETY DISORDERS

Among the various disorders that commonly occur with depression, none has received as much attention as the anxiety disorders. Anxiety is so frequently comorbid with depression that some question whether the two can really be considered distinct disorders at all. Regardless of the true relation between the disorders, the combination of anxiety and depression complicates the prognosis of either. Some particular diagnoses will be considered.

Panic disorder

There is a high comorbidity between major depression and panic disorder. This has been documented in a number of settings, including clinical (Barlow *et al.*, 1986) and community samples (Angst *et al.*, 1990; Boyd *et al.*, 1984). Panic attacks may occur in as many as one-third of patients with depression (Coryell *et al.*, 1988; Grunhaus, 1988). Boyd and colleagues (1984), using ECA data, determined that an individual with DSM III-defined major depression has an almost 19-fold chance of also meeting the criteria for panic disorder. Such a high relationship remains true for subtypes of depression: for example, Halle and Dilsaver (1993) found a high (24%) rate of panic disorder in patients with seasonal depression. The relationship is also stable across different ethnic groups: Horwath and colleagues (1993), using data from the ECA study, found similar rates of major depression among both African Americans and whites with panic disorder (Horwath *et al.*, 1993). The reverse relation seems to be true as well—patients with panic disorder have, roughly, a 50% chance of also having a history of major depression (Noyes *et al.*, 1990).

Numerous studies have documented the detrimental effect of such comorbidity. Patients with panic disorder and depression tend to have more severe symptoms (Breier *et al.*, 1984; Lesser *et al.*, 1988) and worse outcomes (Van Valkenburg *et al.*, 1984; Nutzinger and Zapotcszky, 1985) than patients with either disorder alone.

They may also respond less well to either drug or behavioural therapy (Reich *et al.*, 1987; Zitrin *et al.*, 1980). Noyes and colleagues (1990) conducted a three-year naturalistic follow-up of patients treated for panic disorder. The panic disorder patients with depression tended to be ill longer, to have more severe anxiety symptoms, and more frequent panic attacks than the "pure" panic disorder group. They also had a worse outcome. These results are complicated in that the comorbid group also had a higher rate of other comorbid illnesses as well (particularly personality disorders). Albus and Scheibe (1993) however, showed similar results in a healthier group recruited from nonpsychiatric settings. Although Albus and Scheibe's subjects had a better outcome than that described by Noyes' subjects, the group with comorbid depression and panic disorder had a relatively poor outcome.

The relationship between major depression and panic disorder has been clarified by a number of important family and twin studies. Early family studies are somewhat contradictory—this most likely relates to methodological differences in subject selection and case definition. For example, Crowe and colleagues (1983), found that the risk for major depression among first-degree relatives of panic disorder patients did not differ significantly from controls. Their cases were selected from an anxiety disorders clinic, and lacked a comparison group with depression but not panic disorder. On the other hand, Leckman and colleagues (1983) found that subjects had a greater risk of developing panic disorder if their first-degree relatives had both panic disorder and depression. Leckman and colleagues studied subjects in a depression research clinic, thus, they lacked a group with panic disorder alone. Weissman and colleagues (1993) addressed these issues of patient selection by recruiting patients and relatives from *both* anxiety and depression specialty treatment sites. Their data supported a model of independent transmission of panic disorder and major depression, as relatives of subjects with panic disorder alone had a higher risk of panic disorder, but not major depression. Similarly, relatives of probands with early onset major depression alone had a higher risk of major depression, but not panic disorder. Comorbidity of major depression and panic disorder occurred in relatives regardless of the initial disorder in the proband, suggesting that comorbid panic with depression is not a distinct disorder. The comorbid form did occur at a rate greater than would be predicted by chance, however, suggesting that having either panic disorder or depression does predispose to the other disorder. As this was a familial study, the mechanism of such a predisposition could not be determined.

Kendler and colleagues (1994), examining the Virginia twin cohort, also report that comorbidity in one twin with panic disorder and depression increased the risk for major depression in the other twin.

Generalized anxiety disorder

Brawner-Mintzer and colleagues (1993) reported that 42% of patients recruited for a study on generalized anxiety disorder (GAD) also had a lifetime history of major depression. In the Harvard/Brown Anxiety Disorders Research Program—which is studying the treatment of anxiety disorders—one-quarter of the subjects with GAD also had major depression at the time of intake (Massion *et al.*, 1993). Although some investigators have reported a much lower rate of comorbidity (Brown and Barlow, 1992) the majority of studies support the findings of high comorbidity between the two disorders (Noyes *et al.*, 1992; Boyd *et al.*, 1984; Angst *et al.*, 1990).

Outcome studies have also investigated the implications of comorbidity. Ormel (1993), for example, observed 201 primary care patients with psychiatric symptoms for three years. They found that patients with symptoms of both anxiety and depression were more disabled at follow-up than patients with depression alone.

The relationship between GAD and major depression appears to be familial. Two studies (Angst *et al.*, 1990; Weissman *et al.*, 1984) found such a relationship. One notable exception, however, was a controlled study by Noyes and colleagues (1987) which did not find a familial relationship.

Kendler and colleagues have conducted the most thorough examination of the relationship between major depression and GAD. In two twin studies, one from Australia (Kendler *et al.*, 1987) and one using the Virginia Twin Registry (Kendler *et al.*, 1992b), the authors' findings suggest that anxiety and depression share a common genetic origin—a type of "nonspecific distress". The Australian study used only self-report data; it is consistent, however, with the more rigorous Virginia study. Both studies agree that there seems to be genetic transmission of a "neurobiological diathesis" common to both GAD and major depression. Common (familial) environmental factors played little role in the aetiology of the two disorders. Unique (individual specific) environmental factors, however, appeared to be solely responsible for determining whether the disorder manifested itself as GAD or depression.

The idea of GAD and major depression as two variants of a basic disorder is consistent with other lines of research. For example, pharmacological studies have usually shown that antidepressants are useful in the treatment of GAD (Rickels *et al.*, 1993).

The high rate of comorbidity between GAD and other disorders (such as depression and other anxiety disorders), and the evidence of common origin has led many to question the validity of GAD. It has been suggested that GAD might be better imagined as a feature of other illnesses. It is possible, for example, that GAD is better thought of as part of the symptom complex of major depression, rather than as a comorbid disorder. Despite this, there are many people with GAD alone, and GAD frequently precedes the onset of other disorders.

Mixed anxiety–depression

Further confusing the relationship between anxiety and depression is the observation that there are a number of cases in which both anxiety and depression are present, but do not meet the threshold for any clinical diagnosis. In the DSM IV field trials

(Zinbarg *et al.*, 1994) found that such "subthreshold" cases were common, particularly in primary care settings. Although these cases did not meet strict criteria for either anxiety or depressive diagnoses, they still caused substantial impairment.

Observations of this common overlap of anxiety and depressive symptoms (Fawcett and Cravitz, 1988; Paykel, 1971; Van Valkenburg *et al.*, 1984) led to the addition of "mixed anxiety–depression" to the appendix of DSM IV (American Psychiatric Association, 1994; Brown *et al.*, 1994). The presence of this apparently common syndrome may predict a poorer course of illness (Fawcett *et al.*, 1988; Coryell *et al.*, 1988). It is not clear, however, whether such poor outcomes are simply due to the greater severity of illness in this group. Joffe and colleagues (1993) found poor outcomes to be related to the increased functional and symptomatic severity found among anxious–depressed patients; Clayton and colleagues (1991) found the delayed treatment response to be independent of illness severity. The introduction of anxiety–depression to the official nomenclature may help clarify these apparent discrepancies.

Agoraphobia, simple phobia and social phobia

Kendler and colleagues (1992c) found relatively low rates of comorbidity between simple phobias and major depression. In comparison, the rate of comorbidity between agoraphobia and major depression was high. This relationship between agoraphobia and depression is often seen, as in the ECA study (Eaton and Keyl, 1990), and may relate more to the frequent comorbidity of agoraphobia and panic disorder. In Kendler's study (Kendler *et al.*, 1992c), simple phobias showed a pattern of early onset, low heritability and low rates of comorbidity. Agoraphobia showed the opposite pattern, and social phobias occupied a position intermediate between the other two disorders.

Other studies report a high rate of comorbidity between social phobias and depression in both clinical (de Ruiter *et al.*, 1989) and epidemiological (Schneier *et al.*, 1992) samples, leading some authors to suggest that social phobias may be a risk factor for developing other psychiatric disorders (Schneier *et al.*, 1992).

Posttraumatic stress disorder

Posttraumatic stress disorder (PTSD) also has a high rate of comorbidity with other psychiatric disorders (Davidson *et al.*, 1985). In the ECA study, there was a high risk of dysthymia among subjects with PTSD (Helzer *et al.*, 1987). Two studies of war zone veterans, the Vietnam Experience Study (Centers for Disease and Control and Prevention, 1988) and the National Vietnam Veterans Readjustment Study (Kulka *et al.*, 1988) described similarly high rates of anxiety and depression in veterans exposed to high war zone stress. In the Vietnam Experience Study, 66% of veterans with PTSD had a lifetime prevalence of anxiety or depression.

This high rate of comorbidity occurs in civilian victims as well. For example, North and colleagues (1994) interviewed the survivors of a mass shooting. Not surprisingly, PTSD was the most common psychiatric disorder found among these survivors. Of those with PTSD, 35% of the women and 25% of the men also had comorbid major depression.

The combination of PTSD and substance abuse may pose a particular threat: Brady and colleagues (1994) compared two groups of women in treatment for their substance abuse—one group with, and one without, PTSD. They found that the PTSD group was at greater risk for comorbid mood disorders. The PTSD group with depression was more severely ill, and was more likely not to comply with treatment.

Clinical samples of PTSD cases predictably find greater comorbidity. Sierles and colleagues (1983) investigated a group of hospitalized veterans—almost all of whom had PTSD—and found that nearly three-quarters had a history of depression. Davidson and colleagues (1990b), in their sample of veterans with PTSD, found a 59% rate of lifetime depression.

Depression can complicate the course of PTSD: Davidson and colleagues (1990a) investigated the treatment of PTSD with amitriptyline, and found recovery rates to be lower in patients with comorbid major depression than in those with PTSD alone. The PTSD group with comorbid depression also had other comorbid psychiatric disorders as well, which no doubt added to the worsened outcome.

Despite the alarming rate of comorbid depression in PTSD, and its deleterious effect on outcome, little information is available about the relationship of the two disorders. It would be interesting to know, for example, which disease usually occurs first. One can make a plausible hypothesis for either disorder being predominant. Suffering from PTSD could cause a depression; alternatively, depression could increase the risk of developing PTSD in a stressful situation. It is also possible that the precipitant trauma is independently responsible for both illnesses.

Davidson and colleagues (1990b) report that depressive symptoms tended to occur *after* the development of PTSD. This sequence was also seen by Mellman and colleagues (1992), who investigated combat veterans exposed to extreme stress (such as having been a prisoner of war). Both PTSD and depression were very common in this group, and veterans with active substance abuse (a typical confounder in such studies) were excluded from the investigation. In this group, PTSD usually occurred acutely—within six months of the trauma, with an average age of onset of 23. Major depression, on the other hand, occurred later, with an average onset of 30 years.

Depression, thus, may be secondary to PTSD. It is interesting that such a finding is consistent with physiological studies of PTSD. For example, in a study by Yehuda and colleagues (1993), the authors found that patients with PTSD had an exaggerated suppression response to dexamethasone, as opposed to the nonsuppression seen with depression. Such a "supersuppression" response was seen in PTSD patients regardless of whether or not they had comorbid depression.

Obsessive–compulsive disorder

Obsessive–compulsive disorder (OCD) also shows high rates of comorbidity with depression. Calvocoressi and colleagues (1993) reported that among OCD patients on a neuroscience unit, 43% had comorbid depression. In a study of adolescent OCD, the rates of comorbid major depression and dysthymia in this group were 45% and 29% respectively (Valleni-Basile *et al.*, 1994). Depression may often be secondary to OCD: Black and colleagues (1992) excluded subjects in which depression preceded their OCD, and still found that three-quarters of their subjects with OCD had a history of major depression.

This frequent association between OCD and depressive disorders has led some to question whether OCD would be better categorized as a depressive disorder (Tynes *et al.*, 1990; Rasmussen and Tsuang, 1984). The high degree of comorbidity between other anxiety disorders and depression would argue against singling out OCD for such a categorical change. As we have seen for GAD, however, the relationship between depression and anxiety is quite complex and may reflect common aetiological underpinnings.

SUBSTANCE ABUSE

Few clinicians would be surprised at the high rate of comorbidity found between substance abuse and depression. The ECA study found that about 13% of subjects with substance abuse or dependence will also have a lifetime diagnosis of a mood disorder (Regier *et al.*, 1990). Of those with a lifetime history of major depression, 27% also had a lifetime diagnosis of substance abuse or dependence. Helzer and colleagues (1990), using methodology similar to the ECA study but comparing international population surveys, found that major depression was 1.3–2.1 times as likely to be diagnosed in alcoholics than in nonalcoholics.

These rates dramatically increase in clinical settings. In the ECA study, 55% of subjects with substance abuse who had sought treatment also had a comorbid mental disorder—over twice as many as those not seeking treatment (Regier *et al.*, 1990). Ross and colleagues (1988) found that, in a large sample of patients seeking substance abuse treatment, 23% also had major depression and 13% had dysthymia. In a survey of all patients with alcoholism who sought treatment at a Veterans' Administration hospital over a one-month period, Blow and colleagues (1992) found mood disorders to be the most common comorbid diagnosis. Most notable in their study was that,while the prevalence for most disorders peaked at an early age and then diminished, mood disorder rates increased with age and remained stable across older age groups. A later Veterans' Administration survey by Walker and colleagues (1994) found that veterans with substance abuse (mainly alcohol and cocaine-related disorders) had 2.6 times the risk for depression as veterans free of substance abuse.

Alcoholism

Alcoholism can adversely affect the course of major depression. Akiskal and colleagues (1981) found that alcohol and sedative–hypnotic dependence predicted a chronic course of depression. Mueller and colleagues (1994), using data from the CDS cohort, compared subjects with major depression and alcoholism against those with major depression alone, for up to 10 years of follow-up. The authors found that subjects who currently suffered from alcoholism were only half as likely as those without alcoholism to recover from their episode of major depression.

A number of theories have been offered to explain the relationship between the two disorders. Khantzian (1985) has interpreted comorbid substance abuse as a type of "self-medication" for depression. This remains a popular doctrine among many clinicians; nevertheless, most of the evidence for this hypothesis is based on clinical and case studies. There is, however, indirect evidence for self-medication found in an analysis of ECA data by Burke and colleagues (1994) who found that adolescents with an early onset mood disorder were more likely to develop a subsequent substance use disorder. Overall, support for this hypothesis has been mixed, as have treatment strategies based on it. A study by Leibenluft and colleagues (1993) may help to clarify some of these discrepancies. They found that alcoholics reported drinking in response to depressive *symptoms*, rather than because of major depression *per se.*

Winokur (1979), observing the familial relationship between alcohol and depression in women, has suggested that substance abuse should be considered part of a depressive spectrum. More recent data indicates the opposite—that the depressive symptoms seen in acute alcoholism are a direct result of the alcohol abuse. The latter hypothesis is strongly supported by the observations of Brown and colleagues (Brown and Schuckit, 1988; Brown *et al.*, 1995) who studied depressed male veterans in alcohol treatment. They found that, after four weeks of abstinence, the symptoms of depression resolved without any specific antidepressant treatment.

Finally, there is good data to support genetic arguments. Kendler and colleagues (1993a), using the Virginia twin sample, determined that the substantial comorbidity between major depression and alcoholism in their female twins primarily resulted from genetic factors influencing the risk of both disorders. They did not, however, agree with Winokur that major depression and alcoholism are manifestations of the same disorder—in their model the two disorders appeared to have both common and separate genetic factors that independently influenced the liability to either disorder.

The simultaneous support of different theories underscores the heterogeneity of alcoholism. For instance, Zucker (1987), in his developmental model of alcoholism, described "negative-affect alcoholism". This syndrome is found primarily in women, for which alcohol serves as a mood regulator. Zucker compared this type to other categories, such as "antisocial alcoholism" and "developmentally cumulative alcoholism", in which the alcohol dependence exists independently of other psychiatric disorders (Babor *et al.*, 1992). In a similar manner, Babor and colleagues

(1992) identified two subtypes of alcoholism, designated types "A" and "B". Type A alcoholism is less severe, has less psychopathology, and has a later onset than type B alcoholism, which has earlier onset, greater familial risk factors and greater psychopathology. In their sample of patients in alcohol treatment, males with type B alcoholism had twice as many depressive symptoms as males with type A alcoholism; this difference was sufficient to distinguish the two groups. The female groups, however, could not be distinguished by the degree of depressive symptoms, as they all were very depressed (Babor *et al.*, 1992).

There are other variations on these schemes. Common to many of these is the role of gender. Wilcox and Yates (1993), for example, examined a cohort in treatment for their substance abuse and found that women had a higher rate of depressive symptoms, whereas men had higher rates of sociopathy—a finding that is common among many different subtypes.

Nicotine dependence

A relationship between nicotine dependence and depression has been seen in both epidemiological and clinical samples (Brown *et al.*, 1993). Hughes found that a clinical sample of depressed outpatients were twice as likely to smoke as the general population (Hughes *et al.*, 1986). Glassman reported that, of patients presenting for smoking cessation, 60% had a lifetime history of major depression. In Glassman's study, smokers with a history of major depression had twice the failure rate as smokers without such a history—even if they were not depressed at the time of smoking cessation (Glassman *et al.*, 1988). Thus, the presence of depression among smokers may play a large interfering role for those who attempt smoking cessation. This finding may be particularly significant in male smokers (Covey *et al.*, 1993).

These findings are also seen in community samples. The Centers for Disease Control and Prevention found higher measures of depressive symptoms in smokers than in non-smokers (Anda *et al.*, 1990). Other community samples (Glassman, 1993; Breslau *et al.*, 1991; Zimmerman *et al.*, 1991) have shown similar results. The St. Louis cohort of the ECA study collected data on both smoking and depression, and showed more than double the rate (6.6% versus 2.9%) of major depression in people who smoke (Glassman *et al.*, 1990). Conversely, individuals in the study with a lifetime history of major depression were more likely to have smoked in their lifetime (76% versus 52% in those without depression). The effect on smoking cessation was also replicated—smokers with major depression were less likely to have successfully quit smoking (14% versus 28% in those without depression).

Depression's interference with smoking cessation may have important treatment implications. Covey and colleagues have shown that smokers with a history of major depression experience more severe withdrawal than those without such a history (Covey *et al.*, 1990). In some cases, smoking cessation may even precipitate an episode of major depression (Glassman, 1993). Preliminary evidence from open trials suggests that antidepressants may benefit such patients (Nunes *et al.*, 1993; Glassman *et al.*, 1989). Also, Hall and colleagues (1992), using nicotine gum for smoking cessation, demonstrated that smokers with a history of major depression were more likely to benefit if adjunctive cognitive behavioural treatment was added to the regimen.

As with alcoholism, one can imagine a variety of theories to explain the relationship between smoking and depression, with either disorder causing the other. Kendler and colleagues (1993d), however, using the Virginia twin sample, found that, in their group of women, the best fitting model supported a non-causal relationship. As with alcoholism, the comorbidity between nicotine dependence and depression appears to depend on familial factors, probably genetic, which predispose to both disorders.

Other substance abuse

Although less data exist, the association between depression and substance abuse presumably exists for other substances as well. There appears to be a high rate of depression associated with cocaine abuse in both community (Regier *et al.*, 1990), and clinical settings (Ziedonis, 1992). Carroll and Rounsaville (1992) found high rates of lifetime depression among both treatment-seeking and community dwelling cocaine abusers, although the rate of current major depression was significantly higher in the treatment-seeking population. The combination of cocaine dependence and depression is likely to be a predictor of poor outcome. In a study on a dual diagnosis unit, Wolpe and colleagues (1993) found that patients with cocaine dependence and any depressive diagnosis were the most likely to be noncompliant with follow-up care. Similarly, patients on methadone maintenance who are depressed tend to have a worse outcome (Rounsaville *et al.*, 1985).

SCHIZOPHRENIA AND THE PSYCHOSES

An approach to understanding the comorbidity among the psychotic illnesses and mood disorders can be confused by diagnostic intricacies. Psychotic depression, on the one hand, and schizoaffective disorder on the other, inherently overlap in symptomatology. Despite this fact, Kraepelin's view of schizophrenia and depression as distinct entities remains the predominant conceptual approach. The majority of research in this area, therefore, is of a phenomenological type, and assumes *a priori* this distinction. Such research focuses on the significance of concurrent psychosis and depression. A newer body of research, however, has begun to question the presumed discontinuity of the two disorders.

Clearly, psychotic features adversely influence the course of major depression, both by increasing the risk of recurrence, and by increasing the risk of suicide

246   R.J. Boland and M.B. Keller

(Glassman and Roose, 1981). The presence of psychotic features also influences the choice of treatment, as psychotic depression is more likely to respond to a combination of an antipsychotic agent and an antidepressant (Spiker *et al.*, 1985), or electroconvulsive therapy (Kantor and Glassman, 1977), than to antidepressants alone.

The effect of depressive symptoms on the course of a psychotic illness is less clear. The literature on schizophrenia varies in its assessment of the influence of depressive symptoms. This likely relates to such factors as the stage of illness: depression appears to have a negative connotation in the chronic schizophrenic patient (Johnson, 1988), whereas it has long been considered a positive prognostic indicator in the patient with acute psychosis (Vaillant, 1964). Many factors confuse the findings in these studies. Strakowski and colleagues (1993), for instance, found that patients admitted to a psychiatric hospital with a first onset affective psychosis were more likely than nonaffective first-time psychotic patients to have a comorbid substance abuse as well. Thus, the presence of depression may be only one among several mitigating variables. The effects of other factors—such as long term antipsychotic treatment—further complicate the pictures.

Koreen and colleagues (1993) address some of these potentially confounding variables by looking at the presence of depressive symptoms in first-episode schizophrenia. They found that depressive symptoms in a population of psychotic men and women did not predict outcome. Interestingly, the depressive symptoms improved along with the improvement in psychosis, and did not require specific treatment. This finding suggests that the depressive symptoms in this group may be a part of the core psychosis, rather than a separate illness.

Thus, the issue of whether each disorder is primary or secondary is of paramount importance. If this is the case, then schizoaffective disorder, in which the relative importance of psychotic and mood symptoms are approximately equivalent, should show a degree of morbidity in between schizophrenia and the mood disorders. Such a position for schizoaffective disorders appears to be the case. Coryell and colleagues (1990, 1984), using data from the CDS cohort, compared subjects with schizoaffective depression and major depression with psychotic features. In a two-year (Coryell *et al.*, 1984), and then five-year (Coryell *et al.*, 1990) follow-up, the schizoaffective group had a worse outcome, with more hospitalizations, more persistent depressive symptoms, and a higher likelihood of chronic delusions. Coryell and colleagues also divided the schizoaffective group into "mainly affective" and "mainly schizophrenic" subtypes. The "mainly affective" schizoaffective group fared better than the "mainly schizophrenic" group—they found no difference in outcome between the "mainly affective" schizoaffective group and the psychotically depressed group at two-year follow-up. By five-year follow-up, however, there was a greater difference among the groups. The "mainly schizophrenic" group had the worst outcome, the "mainly affective" schizoaffective group a somewhat better outcome, and the psychotically depressed group had the best outcome (Coryell *et al.*, 1990).

Modern studies generally support the independence of schizophrenia and major depression (Tsuang *et al.*, 1980; Kendler *et al.*, 1985; Coryell and Zimmerman, 1988;

Baron *et al.*, 1982; Frangos *et al.*, 1985; Maj, 1989). Some studies, however, have questioned this distinction. Gershon and colleagues (1988), for example, saw an increase in depression among relatives of schizophrenic subjects. Several recent studies describe similar findings. Taylor and colleagues (1993) found a higher rate of mood disorders (unipolar and bipolar illness combined) in relatives of schizophrenic probands than in control subjects. Maier and colleagues (1993) also found an increased risk for unipolar depression among first-degree relatives of schizophrenic patients. This risk was independent of the depressive subtype, the diagnostic criteria, and the order of disease onset. The presence or absence of a history of depression in the probands also did not affect this observation.

Although these studies argue for a more complex relationship between the two disorders, other contemporary studies disagree. Kendler and colleagues (1993b), looking at a rural community sample in Ireland, did not find an increased risk for mood disorders among subjects with schizophrenia.

Few twin studies exist to clarify this issue. Some older data support a genetic predisposition towards mood disorders in siblings of subjects with schizophrenia (Slater and Shields, 1953). However, such studies predate the contemporary nomenclature, and attempts to analyse them with modern criteria have yielded different interpretations (Farmer *et al.*, 1987).

The issue seems somewhat clearer with schizoaffective disorder. In a manner analogous to outcome assessment, one expects schizoaffective subjects to show a higher familial loading for mood disorders than in schizophrenia, but less so than in "pure" depression. Although results from individual studies are not always significant, the trend overall seems to suggest that this is the case (Coryell *et al.*, 1990). In the aforementioned study by Kendler and colleagues (1993b), there was no relationship between schizophrenia and the mood disorders. However, in relatives of subjects with schizoaffective disorder, there was an increased likelihood of having a mood disorder. This relationship was true even when conservative criteria for schizoaffective disorder were used.

SOMATOFORM ILLNESSES

Hypochondriasis

Hypochondriasis is generally divided into "primary" and "secondary" conditions. In primary hypochondriasis, either no other psychiatric disorder exists, or the hypochondriasis is thought to be independent of any other psychiatric disorders. Secondary hypochondriasis is a syndrome rather than an autonomous disorder. The designation "secondary" implies that it occurs as a part of a "primary" disorder. Few longitudinal studies exist, however, that examine the validity of this distinction.

Clinical studies reveal a considerable overlap between hypochondriasis and other psychiatric disorders, including the anxiety disorders (particularly panic and phobic disorders), somatization disorder and depression (Barsky *et al.*, 1992). The overlap between hypochondriasis and depression is not surprising—somatic preoccupations can be the presenting feature of a depressive disorder (Lesse, 1983). The question thus remains whether hypochondriasis comorbid with depression is really a discrete disorder.

The degree of overlap between depression and hypochondriasis is particularly dependent on the setting studied. Patients with primary hypochondriasis are more likely to be found in medical settings, as they rarely perceive their complaints to have a psychiatric basis. Patients with secondary hypochondriasis are seen more in psychiatric settings, seeking treatment of the comorbid psychiatric disorder (Barsky *et al.*, 1992). In a chart review of psychiatric inpatients, 82% of those with secondary hypochondriasis were also depressed (Kenyon, 1964). Fava and colleagues (1992) found that depressed medical and surgical inpatients were more hypochondriacal than non-depressed patients, and their depression scores correlated highly with their level of "disease conviction". Barsky and colleagues (1986) reported that depressive symptoms predicted one-third of the variance among a group of medical inpatients. More recently, Barsky and colleagues (1992) compared patients with hypochondriasis seen at a general medical clinic with a control group from the same setting. They found that, compared with the control group, the hypochondriacal patients had an eight-fold risk for dysthymia and a seven-fold risk for major depression. Many patients also reported having "double depression" (both dysthymia and major depression). Only somatization and anxiety disorders were more common. Unfortunately, cross-sectional studies cannot resolve questions of aetiology between the two disorders. They are, however, very useful in clarifying the high degree of overlap between these disorders.

Somatization disorder

Somatization disorder is also common in depression (Smith, 1994). This has been shown in a variety of settings. In clinical settings, figures as high as 90% comorbidity between somatization disorder and depression are reported (Morrison and Herbstein, 1988). In a primary care setting, Brown and colleagues (1990) found that more than half of patients with somatization disorder also had major depression. Again, although there is a clear overlap of disorders, much work needs to be done to understand the relationship between somatization disorder and depression.

EATING DISORDERS

Eating disorders, particularly anorexia nervosa, are frequently associated with major depression (Hendren, 1983; Toner *et al.*, 1988; Laessle *et al.*, 1987; Halmi *et al.*, 1991). Estimates of the prevalence of depression in anorexia nervosa differ depending on the setting and other methodological issues. Halmi and colleagues

(1991) found that 68% of patients with anorexia nervosa had a lifetime history of major depression, compared with 21% of controls. This was a surprisingly high figure: for example, Toner and colleagues (1988) had found a prevalence rate of 36% in their sample of patients with anorexia nervosa, and Laessle and colleagues (1987) found a rate of 38% in their sample. The older age and higher morbidity of Halmi's group (half of their patients had been hospitalized before entering the study) may explain these differences. One previous study (Gershon *et al.*, 1984) found a comparable rate (54%), using a similar age group. Although the specific rates may vary, the high comorbidity between anorexia nervosa and major depression seems apparent.

This high comorbidity seems to be true for other eating disorders as well. In obese patients with binge eating disorder (a disorder that now appears in the appendix of DSM IV), several investigators have found high levels of major depression (Yanovski *et al.*, 1993).

The effect of depression on the course of eating disorders is complicated. Halmi's group (1991) found that the presence of a lifetime diagnosis of major depression did not predict outcome in their patients with anorexia nervosa. They did find, however, that patients with current major depression were less likely to have recovered. They also found a trend towards more severe depression in subjects with both anorexia nervosa and bulimia than for those with anorexia nervosa alone. This association between depression and a possible subtype of anorexia nervosa was suggested previously by Strober (1981).

First-degree relatives of persons with anorexia nervosa are at high risk for developing depression (Cantwell *et al.*, 1977; Gershon *et al.*, 1984; Winokur *et al.*, 1980). Winokur and colleagues (1980), for example, found that 36% of the mothers of patients with anorexia nervosa had a history of major depression. Analogous to the discussions on anxiety and substance abuse, these high correlations inevitably raise the question of whether anorexia nervosa is really a variant of depression (Cantwell *et al.*, 1977). This question is reinforced by the success of antidepressants in treating eating disorders—particularly bulimia nervosa (Fluoxetine Bulimia Nervosa Collaborative Study Group, 1992). Some studies, however, have not found a significant correlation between anorexia nervosa and depression in relatives (Halmi *et al.*, 1991), and it appears that the effectiveness of antidepressants in anorexia nervosa is independent of depressive symptoms (Fluoxetine Bulimia Nervosa Collaborative Study Group, 1992). Thus, it is not at all clear whether eating disorders should be regarded as a *forme fruste* of depression.

PERSONALITY DISORDERS

Both clinicians and investigators have reported a high rate of comorbidity between personality disorders and major depression. Reported rates range from 30% to almost 90% (Shea *et al.*, 1992; Charney *et al.*, 1981; Pilkonis and Frank, 1988; Pfohl *et* al., 1987; Shea et al., 1987; Friedman et al., 1983). Community samples show similar rates of comorbidity (Zimmerman and Coryell, 1989).

As one might expect, the personality disorders most often seen in inpatient psychiatric samples are those of the "dramatic" (cluster B: histrionic, narcissistic, borderline, and antisocial personality disorders) type, as the impulsive behaviours associated with these personality disorders are likely to lead to hospitalization (Pfohl et al., 1984). Outpatient samples are more likely to show "cluster C" or "anxious–fearful" types (avoidant, dependent, obsessive–compulsive and passive–aggressive personality disorders) (Shea et al., 1987). Thus, studies on personality disorders will largely depend on the setting studied.

It is generally believed that depressed patients with a comorbid personality disorder are less likely to respond to somatic treatments. Few controlled studies have tested this belief; naturalistic studies, however, tend to support this assumption (Shea et al., 1992; Shea, 1993). Some studies also suggest that depressed patients with borderline personality features may preferentially respond to monoamine oxidase inhibitors (Liebowitz et al., 1988). It appears that depressed patients with a comorbid personality disorder also respond poorly to psychosocial treatments, (Shea et al., 1992)—with the possible exception of cognitive therapy (Shea et al., 1990).

This poor response to treatment may, in part, reflect a greater severity of illness that results from the combination of major depression and a personality disorder (Charney et al., 1981; Pilkonis and Frank, 1988; Shea et al., 1987; Black et al., 1988). The CDS (Shea et al., 1990) demonstrated that, although patients with a personality disorder did improve with psychotherapy, they were less likely than groups without a personality disorder to recover fully from a depressive episode. Recently, Diguer and colleagues (1993) found that depressed outpatients with a comorbid personality disorder were more severely depressed at the beginning and end of therapy than were the depressed patients without a personality disorder. Dulit and colleagues (1994) investigated self-mutilatory behaviour among inpatients with borderline personality disorder. They found that the group who self-mutilated were more likely to have a diagnosis of major depression than the 'non-mutilators".

Studies on the relationship between personality disorders, particularly borderline personality disorder, and suicide are mixed. This may reflect the difficulties inherent in doing studies on a complicated population. A number of investigators have reported a relationship between comorbid borderline personality disorder, depression, and an increased risk of suicide (McGlashan, 1986; Stone, 1989; Fyer et al., 1988; Friedman et al., 1983; Crumly, 1979). Others, however, have not found such a relationship (Shearer et al., 1988; Paris et al., 1989; Kullgren, 1988; Kjelsberg et al., 1991). A recent study by Soloff and colleagues (1994) may explain some of these differences. Investigating suicide attempts associated with borderline personality disorder, they found that although major depression did not predict suicide attempts, the presence of depressive symptoms did predict suicide attempts.

Thus, the presence of a depressive mood may be more important than the depressive diagnosis per se. This may relate to methodological and nosological difficulties, as will be discussed below. It is interesting, however, that a similar argument was made by Leibenluft and colleagues (1993) for the relationship between alcohol abuse and depression.

It is possible that the reported comorbidities represent an artifact. Individuals suffering from a major depressive episode may overestimate their own personality pathology. Nosological issues are equally important—the definition of the two disorders may so overlap as to make discrimination between the Axis I and Axis II disorder complicated.

If the comorbidity of the two disorders is a real phenomenon, one can imagine causality occurring in either direction. Individuals with personality disorders may be at a higher risk for depression; however, individuals with depression, particularly chronic or recurrent types, may be more likely to develop personality disorders.

Alternatively, depression and personality disorders can be imagined as different manifestations of more basic characteristics. Some investigators have found it helpful to look at "personality dimensions", or certain features of a personality. Fava and colleagues (1993) identified a group of depressed outpatients who were prone to anger attacks. This group scored higher on measures of both state and trait hostility, and were more likely to suffer from concomitant anxiety and somatic symptoms. When assessed for personality disorders, the group with anger attacks were more likely to suffer from cluster B-type personality disorders. There was a trend towards a male predominance of this syndrome.

Kendler and colleagues (1993c) looked at two dimensions of personality. Using Eysenck's construct (Eysenck and Eysenck, 1975), they examined the relationship between major depression, "neuroticism" and "extraversion" in their Virginia twin sample. They found no relationship between extraversion and major depression. They did find, however, a strong association between neuroticism and both lifetime and one-year prevalence of major depression. Overall, the estimated correlation between neuroticism and the liability for major depression was largely due to shared genetic risk factors. Shared environmental risk factors played a much smaller role, and the direct effect of major depression on neuroticism was negligible. Their best fitting model suggested that neuroticism had no direct effect on major depression. Thus, at least for neuroticism, the effect of personality on major depression appears to be mediated through common genetic and environmental risk factors.

Thus, attempting to understand the relationship between the personality disorders and depression typifies the difficulties characteristic of investigations into comorbidity.

COMORBIDITY IN SPECIFIC PATIENT POPULATIONS

Children

Although a full review of comorbidity in child psychiatry is beyond our scope, it is worth noting that many studies report links between childhood depression and a number of common non-mood childhood psychiatric disorders. In a review of this subject, Angold and Costello (1993) suggest that the presence of depression in a child or adolescent strongly increases the chance of another psychiatric disorder, often by 20-fold, and up to 100-fold in some studies. Conduct disorders and anxiety disorders were the most common comorbid illnesses; attention deficit disorder (ADD) also seemed to be associated with depression. The reverse relationship seemed true as well: with the possible exception of ADD, the risk of depression was higher in children who had the aforementioned disorders.

Angold and Costello note significant methodological limitations in the data they reviewed; however, more recent studies generally confirm their conclusions. For example, Jensen and colleagues (1993) found that, in a clinical sample of 47 children with ADD, 10 also had a diagnosis of depression alone, and eight had a diagnosis of both depression and anxiety.

Clearly, we need more sophisticated familial studies to unravel the nature of the association between the disorders. The available data is probably most robust for the association between ADD and major depression. Biederman and colleagues (1991) investigated first-degree relatives of children and adolescents with ADD. About a third of the ADD group also had a mood disorder (mostly major depression). They found that relatives of patients with ADD had a significantly higher risk for both ADD and mood disorders than did control subjects. The risk for either disorder was independent of the presence of a depression in the proband group, and the two disorders did not cosegregate in families.

These data suggest that ADD and mood disorders share a common familial aetiology, manifesting in some children as ADD alone, and in others as ADD with a comorbid mood disorder. Although such a study cannot directly determine what would account for the different manifestations of illness, the implication would appear to be that nonfamilial, hence environmental, influences play the greatest role in determining how the illness will manifest itself. Biederman and colleagues (1992) later replicated their finding in a different group of psychiatric and paediatric referrals. To our knowledge, these fascinating findings have yet to be applied to a community sample.

The elderly

It is usually believed that comorbid psychiatric illnesses play a smaller role in late-life depression. Medical comorbidity, on the other hand, is thought to play a much larger role (Caine *et al.*, 1993). A few comorbid psychiatric illnesses associated with late-life depression are considered below. Comorbid medical illnesses will be discussed separately.

Dementia and depression
Reports of the prevalence of depression in Alzheimer's disease have differed greatly. This is due to varying methodology, both in sample selection size and assessment

tools (Wragg and Jeste, 1989). Recently, Migliorelli and colleagues (1995) reported a series of patients with probable Alzheimer's disease attending a neurology outpatient service. Using structured interviews, they found that 23% of their patients met criteria for major depression and 28% were dysthymic.

Reactive mechanisms are often invoked to explain the prevalence of depression in dementia. It is therefore interesting that Migliorelli and colleagues (1995) report that, in their sample, demented patients with dysthymia had significantly less anosognosia (denial of disease) than other patients. This relationship was not true for major depression. Thus, this study suggests that dysthymia may be a reaction to the awareness of disease, whereas major depression may relate to direct effects of the dementing process on the brain.

Such a relationship is suggested for other dementias as well. For example, it is thought that major depression may occasionally precede choreiform movements in individuals eventually diagnosed with Huntington's disease (Baxter *et al.*, 1992). Most reports, however, have been retrospective. In a prospective study, Baxter and colleagues (1992) examined first-degree relatives of individuals with Huntington's disease, and rated them as to their likely risk for also developing the disease. They failed to find a difference in the rate of major depression across their groups, although the aggregate prevalence of major depression was higher than the normal population. They did find a higher rate of subjective anger/hostility in the group considered most likely to develop Huntington's disease (and who were blind to their risk status).

Comorbid anxiety and depression in the elderly
Less research is available about anxiety and comorbid depression in the elderly. Alexopoulos (1991) found that 38% of their population of depressed geriatric psychiatric patients also suffered from an anxiety disorder. Ben-Arie and colleagues (1987) reported that, for patients diagnosed with depression, 26% also had GAD, and 5.3% had panic attacks. In a study using both nursing home residents and elderly patients living in the community, Parmelee and colleagues (1993) found that 80% of the anxious respondents were also depressed. The reverse was not true, only 15% of those with possible major depression also had a possible comorbid anxiety disorder.

There findings suggest that, in the elderly, symptoms of anxiety may be part of a depressive disorder, rather than a distinct anxiety disorder. This interpretation is consistent with that of Blazer and colleagues (1991), who found such a high correlation between anxiety and depression (in elderly patients previously hospitalized for depression), they concluded that anxiety and depression may be so intertwined as to be indistinguishable. Blazer and colleagues hypothesized that many episodes of anxiety in the elderly may represent incomplete recoveries from depression. Colenda and Smith (1993), however, using a random sample of elderly primary care patients, argue that they were able to separate anxiety from depression using several psychosocial, clinical and environmental variables. They did, however, identify a distinct group of patients who had mixed anxiety–depression. This mixed group was associated with more stressful life events, less social support, and a poorer perception of health. They also tended to use more benzodiazepines.

Whether the mixture of anxiety and depression represents a unique disorder, or whether it reflects diagnostic difficulties, there remain important implications for treatment in this population. As alluded to by Colenda and Smith (1993), elderly patients with both anxiety and depression are more likely to be treated with tranquillizers than with antidepressants (Ben-Arie *et al.*, 1987; Lindesay, 1991). Thus, clinicians may be mistakenly treating secondary symptoms rather than an underlying disorder.

Depression and personality disorders in the elderly
Most studies report low rates of comorbid personality disorders in elderly psychiatric patients (Mezzich *et al.*, 1987; Casey and Schrodt, 1989). The rate of comorbid personality disorders increases somewhat when elderly depressed patients are evaluated (Abrams *et al.*, 1987; Fogel and Westlake, 1990; Kunik *et al.*, 1993; Thompson *et al.*, 1988). Recently, Kunik and colleagues (1994) examined over 500 elderly psychiatric inpatients and found that, whereas the rate of personality disorders was low (6%) in patients with DSM III R organic mental disorders, the rate was much higher (24%) in patients with major depression. It is possible that this discrepancy may allude to a causal relationship between personality disorders and depression. It is more likely, however, that the difference was due to difficulties in assessing personality disorders in patients with dementia. Among the depressed group with a comorbid personality disorder, Kunik and colleagues found "personality disorder not otherwise specified" to be the most common personality disorder. This fact raises questions about the applicability of the personality disorder criteria to the elderly. Dependent personality disorder was the next most common diagnosis, and there were no diagnoses of borderline personality disorder. The presence or absence of a personality disorder in this group did not influence the response to treatment.

Thus, although comorbid personality disorders may be relatively common in the elderly depressed patient, the significance of such comorbidity is still not clear. Part of the difficultly may relate to nosological problems in applying the current personality disorder diagnoses to the elderly.

Depression in the medically ill

As already observed, the subject of depression in the medically ill deserves, and has received, separate volumes, and this will comprise a brief survey of the subject.

It is estimated that 2–4% of persons in the community, 5–10% of primary care patients, and 10–14% of medical inpatients suffer from major depression (US Department of Health and Human Services, 1993; Katon and Schulberg, 1991). Unfortunately, depression is often unrecognized and untreated in the medical population (US Department of Health and Human Services, 1993; Gerber *et al.*, 1989; Pérez-Stable *et al.*, 1990; Lipowski, 1992). Such inadequate treatment may in part reflect the obsolete view that depressive symptoms with a clear cause are not the same as "clinical depression". In addition, the standard psychiatric nosology may not adequately encompass a number of "subclinical depressions" that can still produce significant impairment in the medical population (Von Korff *et al.*, 1987; Barret *et al.*, 1988).

Regardless of the reason, the neglect of depression in the medical population constitutes a serious health risk (US Department of Health and Human Services, 1993; Keller *et al.*, 1984). Available data suggest that comorbid medical illnesses can worsen the course of major depression (Moos, 1990; Shea *et al.*, 1990; Keitner *et al.*, 1991). The importance of depression in medical illness is well documented in the large-scale Medical Outcomes Study (Wells *et al.*, 1989), which studied more than 22 000 patients receiving care from 523 clinicians. The study focused on five specific diseases: myocardial infarction, congestive heart failure, hypertension, diabetes, and depression. The MOS found an additive effect on patients' functioning when depression and other chronic medical illnesses were combined, suggesting a worse course for the medically comorbid depressed patients (Wells *et al.*, 1989). In a two-year follow-up, they found that certain medical disorders predicted a worse course of depression. The most adverse association was between myocardial infarction and depression: depressed patients with a history of myocardial infarction had more frequent spells and worse symptoms of depression during the period of follow-up. There was no significant effect found, however, for either diabetes or hypertension. This lack of an effect may be due to the varied severity of illness in those two disorders; whereas a myocardial infarction is almost always serious, there are great variations of impairment in both hypertension and diabetes.

Issues of the aetiology of comorbidity take on a different connotation when considering depression and comorbid medical illnesses. Whereas, in other cases we are dealing with two diseases of unknown aetiology, here the aetiology of at least one of the disorders is usually known. The question then becomes whether knowing the pathology of the medical disorder helps to clarify the unknown pathology of depression, or is the depression simply an indirect "reaction" to the medical disease. Such questions have been asked at least since the early part of this century (Goldstein, 1939). Also relevant is the question asked by many physicians—whether they should treat a depression that seems a reaction to a medical illness. Isn't it natural, for example, that a patient would be depressed about having cancer? Such questions represent a type of reasoning that is akin to the "endogenous" versus "exogenous" distinctions of depression, distinctions that have been largely abandoned in the past decade.

Exogenous and endogenous distinctions were relinquished largely because of the realization that the identification of a "precipitating event" was both common in depression, and unrelated to issues of severity and outcome (Goldberg, 1993). Often, the precipitating event is a type of loss. The loss of one's health, and the loss of one's illusion of immortality can be comparable to the loss of a loved one. Thus, to observe that a comorbid depression is a reaction to a medical illness does not devalue that depression, but instead implies that the disorder is no different from the "classic" type of major depression.

There are, however, a few examples of illnesses that seem to cause depression directly. Most convincing is the association reported between damage to the left frontal cortex and subcortex and the onset of a depressive episode. Destruction of the noradrenergic fibres that ascend to the cortex through the left frontal pole may be responsible for this phenomenon, which is seen in about 25% of patients suffering a left hemisphere cerebrovascular accident (Robinson and Starkstein, 1990). The hypothesis of a direct effect on mood is supported by the observation that non-vascular forms of injury to this area are also associated with depression (Fedoroff *et al.*, 1992).

Although the data are less robust for other neurological lesions, a number are also associated with depression. Right-sided parietal lesions, epilepsy (particularly with temporal foci), and disorders causing subcortical damage (for example, Parkinson's and Huntington's disease) may all cause depressive episodes, possibly through direct damage to the brain (Salloway and Duffy, 1993).

Some peripheral conditions, such as endocrine disorders, have been similarly implicated. Such illnesses should be distinguished from medical illnesses that can "mimic" depression through the production of depression-like symptoms. For example, both cancer and HIV can directly cause symptoms such as fatigue and anorexia without producing the dysphoria one would associate with depression. Differentiation between these can be a challenge, as both cancer and HIV infection are also associated with "real" depression, presumably in the form of the aforementioned "reaction" to illness, although there may be direct causative mechanisms as well.

REFERENCES

Abrams RC, Alexopoulos GS, Young RC (1987) Geriatric depression and DSM-III-R personality disorder criteria. *J Am Geriatr Soc* **35**, 383–386.

Akiskal HS, King D, Rosenthal TL, Robinson D and Scott-Strauss A (1981) Chronic depression, part I: clinical and familial characteristics in 137 probands. *J Affect Disord* **3**, 297–315.

Albus M and Scheibe G (1993) Outcome of panic disorder with or without concomitant depression: a 2-year prospective follow-up study. *Am J Psychiatry* **150**, 1878–1880.

Alexopoulos GS (1991) Anxiety and depression in the elderly. In: Salzman C and Lebowitz BD (eds) *Anxiety in the Elderly: Treatment and Research*, pp 63–77. Springer, New York.

American Psychiatric Association (1980) *Diagnostic and Statistical Manual of Mental Disorders*, Third Edition. American Psychiatric Association, Washington, DC.

American Psychiatric Association (1987) *Diagnostic and Statistical Manual of Mental Disorders*, Third Edition, Revised. American Psychiatric Association, Washington, DC.

American Psychiatric Association (1994) *Diagnostic and Statistical Manual of Mental Disorders*, Fourth Edition. American Psychiatric Association, Washington, DC.

Anda RF, Williamson DF, Escobedo LG, Mast EE, Giovino GA and Remington PL (1990) Depression and the dynamics of smoking: a national perspective. *JAMA* **264**, 1541–1545.

Angold A and Costello EJ (1993) Depressive comorbidity in children and adolescents: empirical, theoretical, and methodological issues. *Am J Psychiatry* **150**, 1779–1791.

Angst J, Vollrath M, Merikangas KR and Ernst C (1990) Comorbidity of anxiety and depression in the Zurich cohort study of young adults. In: Maser JD and Cloninger CR (eds) *Comorbidity of Mood and Anxiety Disorders*, pp 123–138. American Psychiatric Press Inc., Washington, DC.

Babor TF, Hoffmann M, Delboca FK, Hesselbrock V, Meyer RE, Dolinsky ZS and Rounsaville B (1992) Types of alcoholics, I: evidence for an empirically derived typology based on indicators of vulnerability and severity. *Arch Gen Psychiatry* **49**, 599–608.

Barlow DH, DiNardo PA, Vermilyea BB, Vermilyea J and Blanchard EB (1986) Comorbidity and depression among the anxiety disorders: issues in diagnosis and clarification. *J Nerv Ment Dis* **174**, 63–72.

Baron M, Gruen R, Asnis L and Kane J (1982) Schizoaffective illness, schizophrenia and affective disorders: morbidity, risk and genetic transmission. *Acta Psychiatr Scand* **65**, 253–262.

Barret JE, Barret JA, Oxman TE and Gerber PD (1988) The prevalence of psychiatric disorders in a primary care practice. *Arch Gen Psychiatry* **45**, 1100–1106.

Barsky AJ, Wyshak G and Klerman GL (1986) Hypochondriasis: an evaluation of the DSM-III criterion in medical outpatients, *Arch Gen Psychiatry* **43**, 493–500.

Barsky AJ, Wyshak G and Klerman GL (1992) Psychiatric co-morbidity in DSM-III-R hypochondriasis. *Arch Gen Psychiatry* **49**, 101–108.

Baxter LR, Mazziotta JC, Pahl JJ, Grafton ST, St. George-Hyslop P, Haines JL, Gusella JF, Szuba MP, Selin CE, Guze B and Phelps ME (1992) Psychiatric, genetic, and positron emission tomographic evaluation of persons at risk for Huntington's disease. *Arch Gen Psychiatry* **49**, 148–154.

Ben-Arie O, Swartz L and Dickman BJ (1987) Depression in the elderly living in the community: its presentation and features. *Br J Psychiatry* **150**, 169–174.

Berkson J (1946) Limitations of the application of four-fold tables to hospital data. *Biometric Bull* **2**, 47–53.

Biederman J, Faraone SV, Keenan K, Benjamin J, Krifcher B, Moore C, Sprich-Buckminster S, Ugaglia K, Jellinek MS, Steingard R, Spencer T, Norman D, Kolodny R, Kraus I, Perrin J, Keller MB and Tsuang MT (1992) Further evidence for family-genetic risk factors in attention deficit hyperactivity disorder: patterns of comorbidity in probands and relatives in psychiatrically and pediatrically referred samples. *Arch Gen Psychiatry* **49**, 728–738.

Biederman J, Faraone SV, Keenan K and Tsuang MT (1991) Evidence of familial association between attention deficit disorder and major affective disorders. *Arch Gen Psychiatry* **48**, 633–642.

Black DW, Bell S, Hulbert J and Nasrallah A (1988) The importance of axis II in patients with major depression: a controlled study. *J Affect Disord* **14**, 115–122.

Black DW, Noyes R, Goldstein RB and Blum N (1992) A family study of obsessive–compulsive disorder. *Arch Gen Psychiatry* **49**, 362–368.

Blazer D, George LK and Hughes D (1991) The epidemiology of anxiety disorders: an age comparison. In: Salzman C and Lebowitz BD (eds) *Anxiety in the Elderly: Treatment and Research*, pp 17–30. Springer, New York.

Blazer DG, Kessler RC, McGonagle KA and Swartz MS (1994) The prevalence and distribution of major depression in a national community sample: The national comorbidity survey. *Am J Psychiatry* **151**, 979–986.

Blow FC, Cook CAL, Booth BM, Falcon SP and Friedman MJ (1992) Age-related psychiatric comorbidities and level of functioning in alcoholic veterans seeking outpatient treatment. *Hosp Community Psychiatry* **43**, 990–995.

Boyd JH, Burke JD Jr, Gruenberg E, Holzer CE III, Rae DS, George LK, Karno M, Stolzman R, McEvoy L and Nestadt G (1984) Exclusion criteria of DSM-III: a study of co-occurrence and hierarchy-free syndromes. *Arch Gen Psychiatry* **41**, 983–989.

Brady KT, Killeen T, Saladin ME, Dansky B and Becker S (1994) Comorbid substance abuse and posttraumatic stress disorder. *Am J Addict* **3**, 160–164.

Brawner-Mintzer O, Lydiard B, Emmanuel N, Payeur R, Johnson M, Roberts J, Jarrel MP and Ballenger JC (1993) Psychiatric comorbidity in patients with generalized anxiety disorder. *Am J Psychiatry* **150**, 1216–1218.

Breier A, Charney DS and Heninger GR (1984) Major depression in patients with agoraphobia and panic disorder. *Arch Gen Psychiatry* **41**, 1129–1135.

Breslau N, Kilbey MM and Andreski P (1991) Nicotine dependence, major depression, and anxiety in young adults. *Arch Gen Psychiatry* **48**, 1069–1074.

Brown FW, Golding JM and Smith GR (1990) Psychiatric comorbidity in primary care somatization disorder. *Psychosom Med* **52**, 445–451.

Brown RA, Goldstein MG, Niaura R, Emmons KM and Abrams DB (1993) Nicotine dependence: assessment and management. In: Stoudemire A and Fogel BS (eds) *Psychiatric Care of the Medical Patient.* Oxford Press, New York.

Brown SA, Inaba RK, Gillin JC, Schuckit MA, Stewart ME and Irwin MR (1995) Alcoholism and affective disorder: clinical course of depressive symptoms. *Am J Psychiatry* **152**, 45–52.

Brown SA and Schuckit MA (1988) Changes in depression among abstinent alcoholics. *J Stud Alcohol* **49**, 412–417.

Brown TA and Barlow DH (1992) Comorbidity among anxiety disorders: implications for treatment and DSM-IV. *J Consult Clin Psychol* **60**, 835–844.

Brown TA, Barlow DH and Liebowitz MR (1994) The empirical basis of generalized anxiety disorder. *Am J Psychiatry* **151**, 1272–1280.

Burke JD, Burke KC and Rae DS (1994) Increased rates of drug abuse and dependence after onset of mood or anxiety disorders in adolescence. *Hosp Community Psychiatry* **45**, 451–455.

Burton, R (1652) *The Anatomy of Melancholy.* The Classics of Psychiatry and Behavioral Medicine Library, Birmingham AL, 1988.

Caine ED, Lyness JM and King DA (1993) Reconsidering depression in the elderly. *Am J Geriatr Psychiatry* **1**, 4–20.

Calvocoressi L, McDougle CI, Wasylink S, Goodman WK, Trufan SJ and Price LH (1993) Inpatient treatment of patients with severe obsessive–compulsive disorder. *Hosp Community Psychiatry* **44**, 1150–1154.

Cantwell DP, Sturzenberg S and Burroughs J (1977) Anorexia nervosa: an affective disorder? *Arch Gen Psychiatry* **34**, 1087–1093.

Carroll KM and Rounsaville BJ (1992) Contrast of treatment-seeking and untreated cocaine abusers. *Arch Gen Psychiatry* **49**, 464–471.

Casey DA and Schrodt CJ (1989) Axis II diagnoses in geriatric inpatients. *J Geriatr Psychiatry Neurol* **2**, 87–88.

Centers for Disease and Control and Prevention (1988) Health status of Vietnam veterans, 1: psychosocial characteristics: the Centers for Disease Control Vietnam Experience Study. *JAMA* **259**, 2701–2707.

Charney DS, Nelson JC and Quinlan DM (1981) Personality traits and disorder in depression. *Am J Psychiatry* **138**, 1601–1604.

Clayton PJ, Grove WM, Coryell W, Keller M, Hirschfeld R and Fawcett J (1991) Follow-up and family study of anxious depression. *Am J Psychiatry* **148**, 1512–1517.

Colenda CC and Smith SL (1993) Multivariate modelling of anxiety and depression in community-dwelling elderly persons. *Am J Geriatr Psychiatry* **1**, 327–338.

Coryell W, Endicott J, Andreasen NC, Keller MB, Clayton PJ, Hirschfeld RM, Scheftner WA and Winokur G (1988) Depression and panic attacks: the significance of overlap as reflected in follow-up and family study data. *Am J Psychiatry* **145**, 293–300.

Coryell W, Keller M, Lavori P and Endicott J (1990) Affective syndromes, psychotic features, and prognosis. *Arch Gen Psychiatry* **47**, 651–657.

Coryell W, Lavori P, Endicott J, Keller M and VanEerdewegh M (1984) Outcome in schizo-affective, psychotic and nonpsychotic depression. *Arch Gen Psychiatry* **41**, 787–791.

Coryell W and Zimmerman M (1988) The heritability of schizophrenia and schizoaffective disorder. *Arch Gen Psychiatry* **45**, 323–327.

Covey LS, Glassman AH and Stetner F (1990) Depression and depressive symptoms in smoking cessation. *Compr Psychiatry* **31**, 350–354.

Covey LS, Glassman AH, Stetner F and Becker J (1993) Effect of history of alcoholism or major depression on smoking cessation. *Am J Psychiatry* **150**, 1546–1547.

Crowe RR, Noyes R, Pauls DL and Slymen D (1983) A family study of panic disorder. *Arch Gen Psychiatry* **40**, 1065–1069.

Crumly FE (1979) Adolescent suicide attempts. *JAMA* **241**, 2404–2407.

Davidson J, Kudler H, Smith R, Mahorney SL, Lipper S, Hammett E, Saunders WB and Cavenar JO (1990a) Treatment of posttraumatic stress disorder with amitriptyline and placebo. *Arch Gen Psychiatry* **47**, 259–266.

Davidson JRT, Kudler HS, Saunders WB and Smith RD (1990b) Symptom and morbidity patterns in World War II and Vietnam veterans with post-traumatic stress disorder. *Compr Psychiatry* **31**, 1662–1170.

Davidson JRT, Swartz M, Stork M, Krishnan KRR and Hammett E (1985) A diagnostic and family study of post-traumatic stress disorder. *Am J Psychiatry* **142**, 90–93.

de Ruiter C, Ryken H, Garssen B, van Schaik A and Kraaimaat F (1989) Comorbidity among the anxiety disorders. *J Anxiety Disord* **3**, 57–68.

Diguer L, Barber JP and Luborsky L (1993) Three concomitants: personality disorders, psychiatric severity, and outcome of dynamic psychotherapy of major depression. *Am J Psychiatry* **150**, 1246–1248.

Dulit RA, Fyer MR, Leon AC, Brodsky BS and Frances AJ (1994) Clinical correlates of self-mutilation in borderline personality disorder. *Am J Psychiatry* **151**, 1305–1311.

Eaton WW and Keyl PM (1990) Risk factors for the onset of diagnostic interview schedule/DSM-III agoraphobia in a prospective population-based study. *Arch Gen Psychiatry* **47**, 819–824.

Eysenck HJ and Eysenck SBG (1975) *Manual of the Eysenck Personality Questionnaire.* Hodder & Stoughton, London.

Farmer AE, McGuffin P and Gottesman II (1987) Twin concordance for DSM-III schizophrenia: scrutinizing the validity of the definition. *Arch Gen Psychiatry* **44**, 634–641.

Fava GA, Pilowsky I, Pierfedenci A, Bernardi M and Pathak D (1992) Depression and illness behavior in a general hospital: a prevalence study. *Psychother Psychosom* **38**, 141–153.

Fava M, Rosenbaum JF, Pava JA, McCarthy MK, Steingard RJ and Bouffides E (1993) Anger attacks in unipolar depression, I: clinical correlates and response to fluoxetine treatment. *Am J Psychiatry* **150**, 1158–1163.

Fawcett J and Cravitz HM (1988) Anxiety syndromes and their relationship to depressive illness. *J Clin Psychiatry* **44**, 8–11.

Fedoroff JP, Starkstein SE, Forrester AW, Geisler FH, Jorge RE, Arndt SV and Robinson RG (1992) Depression in patients with acute traumatic brain injury. *Am J Psychiatry* **149**, 918–923.

Fluoxetine Bulimia Nervosa Collaborative Study Group (1992) Fluoxetine in the treatment of bulimia nervosa. A multicenter placebo-controlled double-blind trial. *Arch Gen Psychiatry* **49**, 139–147.

Fogel BS and Westlake R (1990) Personality disorder diagnoses and age in inpatients with major depression. *J Clin Psychiatry* **51**, 232–235.

Frangos E, Althanassenas G, Tsitourides S, Katsanou M and Alexandrakou P (1985)

Prevalence of DSM-III schizophrenia among the first-degree relatives of schizophrenic probands. *Acta Psychiatr Scand* **72**, 382–386.

Friedman RC, Aronoff MS, Clarkin JF, Corn R and Hurt SW (1983) History of suicidal behavior in depressed borderline inpatients. *Am J Psychiatry* **140**, 1023–1026.

Fyer MR, Frances AJ, Sullivan T, Hurt SW and Clarkin J (1988) Suicide attempts in patients with borderline personality disorder. *Am J Psychiatry* **145**, 737–739.

Gerber PD, Barrett J, Barrett J, Manheimer E, Whiting R and Smith R (1989) Recognition of depression by internists in primary care: a comparison of internist and "gold standard" psychiatric assessments. *J Gen Intern Med* **4**, 7–13.

Gershon ES, DeLisi Le, Hamovit J, Nurnberger JI, Maxwell ME, Schreiber J, Dauphinais D, Dingman CW II and Guroff JJ (1988) A controlled family study of chronic psychoses. *Arch Gen Psychiatry* **45**, 328–336.

Gershon E, Schreiber J, Hamovit J, Dibble E, Kaye W, Nurnberger GJ, Anderson A and Ebert M (1984) Clinical findings in patients with anorexia nervosa and affective illness in their relatives. *Am J Psychiatry* **149**, 1419–1422.

Glassman AH (1993) Cigarette smoking: implications for psychiatric illness. *Am J Psychiatry* **150**, 546–553.

Glassman AH, Covey LS and Stetner F (1989) Smoking cessation, depression, and antidepressants. In: *New Research Program and Abstracts*, 142nd Annual Meeting of the American Psychiatric Association, Washington, DC.

Glassman AH, Helzer JE, Covey LS, Cottler LB, Stetner F, Tipp JE and Johnson J (1990) Smoking, smoking cessation, and major depression. *JAMA* **264**, 1546–1549.

Glassman AH and Roose SP (1981) Delusional depression. *Arch Gen Psychiatry* **38**, 424–427.

Glassman AH, Stetner F, Walsh Raizman PS, Fleiss JL, Cooper TB and Covey LS (1988) Heavy smokers, smoking cessation, and clonidine: results of a double-blind, randomized trial. *JAMA* **259**, 2863–2866.

Goldberg RJ (1993) Depression in medical patients. *RI Med J* **76**, 391–396.

Goldstein K (1939) *The Organism: A Holistic Approach to Biology Derived from Pathological Data in Man.* American Books, New York, NY.

Grunhaus L (1988) Clinical and psychobiological characteristics of simultaneous panic disorder and major depression. *Am J Psychiatry* **145**, 1214–1221.

Hall SM, Munoz R and Reus V (1992) Depression and smoking treatment: a clinical trial of an affect regulation treatment. *NIDA Res Monogr* **119**, 326.

Halle MT and Dilsaver SC (1993) Comorbid panic disorder in patients with winter depression. *Am J Psychiatry* **150**, 1108–1110.

Halmi KA, Eckert E, Marchi P, Sampugnaro V, Apple R and Cohen J (1991) Comorbidity of psychiatric diagnoses in anorexia nervosa. *Arch Gen Psychiatry* **48**, 712–718.

Helzer JE, Canino GJ, Yeh E, Cland RC, Lee CK, Hwu H and Newman S (1990) Alcoholism—North America and Asia: A comparison of population surveys with the diagnostic interview schedule. *Arch Gen Psychiatry* **47**, 313–319.

Helzer JE and Pryzbeck TR (1988) The co-occurrence of alcoholism with other psychiatric disorders in the general population and its impact on treatment. *J Stud Alcohol* **49**, 219–224.

Helzer JE, Robins LN and McElroy L (1987) Post-traumatic stress disorder in the general population: findings of the Epidemiologic Catchment Area Survey. *N Engl J Med* **317**, 1630–1634.

Hendren R (1983) Depression in anorexia nervosa. *J Am Acad Child Psychiatry* **22**, 59–62.

Horwath E, Johnson J and Hornig CD (1993) Epidemiology of panic disorder in African-Americans. *Am J Psychiatry* **150**, 465–469.

Hughes JR, Hatsukami DK, Mitchell JE and Dahlgren LA (1986) Prevalence of smoking among psychiatric outpatients. *Am J Psychiatry* **143**, 993–997.

Jensen PS, Shervette RE, Xenakis SN and Richters J (1993) Anxiety and depressive disorders in attention deficit disorder with hyperactivity: new findings. *Am J Psychiatry* **150**, 1203–1209.

Joffe RT, Bagby RM and Levitt A (1993) Anxious and nonanxious depression. *Am J Psychiatry* **150**, 1257–1258.

Johnson DAW (1988) Significance of depression in the prediction of relapse in chronic schizophrenia. *Br J Psychiatry* **152**, 320–323.

Kantor SJ and Glassman AH (1977) Delusional depression: natural history and response to treatment. *Br J Psychiatry* **131**, 351–360.

Katon W and Schulberg H (1991) Epidemiology of depression in primary care. *Gen Hosp Psychiatry* **14**, 237–247.

Keitner GI, Ryan CE, Miller IW, Kohn R and Epstein NB (1991) 12-month outcome of patients with major depression and comorbid psychiatric or medical illness (compound depression). *Am J Psychiatry* **148**, 345–350.

Keitner GI, Ryan CE, Miller IW and Norman WH (1992) Recovery and major depression: Factors associated with twelve-month outcome. *Am J Psychiatry* **149**, 93–99.

Keller MB, Klerman GL, Lavori PW, Coryell W, Endicott J and Taylor J (1984) Long-term outcome of episodes of major depression: clinical and public health significance. *JAMA* **252**, 788–792.

Keller MB, Lavori PW, Mueller TI, Endicott J, Coryell W, Hirschfeld RM and Shea T (1992) Time to recovery, chronicity, and levels of psychopathology in major depression: a 5-year prospective follow-up of 431 subjects. *Arch Gen Psychiatry* **49**, 809–816.

Kendler KS (1993) Twin Studies of psychiatric illness: current status and future directions. *Arch Gen Psychiatry* **50**, 905–915.

Kendler KS, Gruenberg AM and Tsuang MT (1985) Psychiatric illness in first-degree relatives of schizophrenic and surgical control patients: a family study using DSM-III criteria. *Arch Gen Psychiatry* **42**, 770–779.

Kendler KS, Heath AC, Martin NG and Eaves LJ (1987) Symptoms of anxiety and symptoms of depression: same genes, different environments? *Arch Gen Psychiatry* **44**, 451–457.

Kendler KS, Heath AC, Neale MC, Kessler RC and Eaves LJ (1993a) Alcoholism and major depression in women: a twin study of the causes of comorbidity. *Arch Gen Psychiatry* **50**, 690–698.

Kendler KS, McGuire M, Gruenberg AM, O'Hare A, Spellman M and Walsh D (1993b) The Roscommon family study. IV. Affective illness, anxiety disorders, and alcoholism in relatives. *Arch Gen Psychiatry* **50**, 952–960.

Kendler KS, Neale MC, Kessler RC, Heath AC and Eaves LJ (1994) The clinical characteristics of major depression as indices of the familial risk to illness. *Br J Psychiatry* **165**, 66–72.

Kendler KS, Neale MC, Kessler RC, Heath AC and Eaves LJ (1992a) A population-based twin study of major depression in women: the impact of varying definitions of illness. *Arch Gen Psychiatry* **49**, 257–266.

Kendler KS, Neale MC, Kessler RC, Heath AC and Eaves LJ (1992b) Major depression and generalized anxiety disorder: same genes, (partly) different environments? *Arch Gen Psychiatry* **49**, 716–722.

Kendler KS, Neale MC, Kessler RC, Heath AC and Eaves LJ (1992c) The genetic epidemiology of phobias in women: the interrelationship of agoraphobia, social phobia, situational phobia, and simple phobia. *Arch Gen Psychiatry* **49**, 273–281.

Kendler KS, Neale MC, MacLean CJ, Heath AC, Eaves LJ and Kessler RC (1993d) Smoking and major depression: a causal analysis. *Arch Gen Psychiatry* **50**, 36–43.

Kendler KS, Neale MC, Kessler RC, Heath AC and Eaves LJ (1993c) A longitudinal twin study of personality and major depression in women. *Arch Gen Psychiatry* **50**, 853–862.

Kendler KS, Pederson N, Johnson L, Neale MC and Mathe AA (1992d) A pilot Swedish twin study of affective illness, including hospital- and population-ascertained subsamples. *Arch Gen Psychiatry* **50**, 699–706.

Kenyon FE (1964) Hypochondriasis: a clinical study. *Br J Psychiatry* **110**, 478–488.

Kessler RC, McGonagle KA, Zhao S, Nelson CB, Hughes M, Eshleman S, Wittchen H and Kendler KS (1994) Lifetime and 12-month prevalence of DSM-III-R psychiatric disorders in the United States: results from the National Comorbidity Survey (NCS). *Arch Gen Psychiatry* **51**, 8–19.

Khantzian EJ (1985) The self-medication hypothesis of addictive disorders: focus on heroin and cocaine dependence. *Am J Psychiatry* **142**, 1259–1264.

Kjelsberg E, Eikeseth PH and Dahl AA (1991) Suicide in borderline patients: predictive factors. *Acta Psychiatr Scand* **84**, 283–287.

Koreen AR, Siris SG, Chakos M, Alvir J, Mayerhoff D and Lieberman J (1993) Depression in first-episode schizophrenia. *Am J Psychiatry* **150**, 752–757.

Kraepelin E (1921) *Manic Depressive Insanity.* (Barclay RM, trans) E & S Livingstone, Edinburgh.

Kulka R, Schlenger W, Fairbank J, Hough R, Jordan BK, Marmar C and Weiss D (1988) *Executive Summary: Contractual Report of Findings from the National Vietnam Veterans Readjustment Study.* Research Triangle Park, NC, Research Triangle Institute.

Kullgren G (1988) Factors associated with completed suicide in borderline personality disorder. *J Nerv Ment Dis* **176**, 40–44.

Kunik ME, Mulsant BH, Rifai AH, Sweet RA, Pasternak RE, Rosen J and Zubenko GS (1993) Personality disorders in elderly inpatients with major depression. *Am J Geriatr Psychiatry* **1**, 38–45.

Kunik ME, Mulsant BH, Rifai AH, Sweet RA, Pasternak R and Zubenko GS (1994) Diagnostic rate of comorbid personality disorder in elderly psychiatric inpatients. *Am J Psychiatry* **151**, 603–605.

Laessle R, Kittl S, Fitcher M, Wittchen L and Pirke K (1987) Major affective disorder in anorexia nervosa and bulimia. *Br J Psychiatry* **151**, 785–789.

Leckman JF, Weissman MM, Merikangas KR, Pauls DL and Prusoff BA (1983) Panic disorder and major depression: increased risk of depression, alcoholism, panic and phobic disorders in families of depressed probands with panic disorder. *Arch Gen Psychiatry* **40**, 1055–1060.

Leibenluft E, Fiero PL, Bartko JJ, Moul DE and Rosenthal NE (1993) Depressive symptoms and the self-reported use of alcohol, caffeine, and carbohydrates in normal volunteers and four groups of psychiatric outpatients. *Am J Psychiatry* **150**, 294–301.

Lesse S (1993) The masked depression syndrome—results of a seventeen-year clinical study. *Am J Psychother* **37**, 456–475.

Lesser IM, Rubin RT, Pecknold JC, Rifkin A, Swinson RP, Lydiard RB, Burrows GD, Noyes R and DuPont RL (1988) Secondary depression in panic disorder and agoraphobia, I: frequency, severity and response to treatment. *Arch Gen Psychiatry* **45**, 437–443.

Levitt AJ, Joffe RT and MacDonald C (1991) Life course of depressive illness and characteristics of current episode in patients with double depression. *J Nerv Ment Dis* **179**, 678–682.

Liebowitz MF, Quitkin FM, Stewart JW, McGrath PJ, Harrison WM, Markowitz JS, Rabkin JG, Tricamo E, Goetz DM and Klein DF (1988) Antidepressant specificity in atypical depression. *Arch Gen Psychiatry* **45**, 129–137.

Lindesay J (1991) Phobic disorders in the elderly. *Br J Psychiatry* **159**, 531–541.

Lipowski ZJ (1992) Is the education of primary care physicians adequate? *Gen Hosp Psychiatry* **14**, 361–362.

Maier W, Lichtermann D, Minges J, Hallmayer J, Heun R, Benkert O and Levinson D (1993) Continuity and discontinuity of affective disorders and schizophrenia. *Arch Gen Psychiatry* **50**, 871–883.

Maj M (1989) A family study of two subgroups of schizoaffective patients. *Br J Psychiatry* **154**, 640–643.

Massion AO, Warshaw MG and Keller MD (1993) Quality of life and psychiatric morbidity in panic disorder and generalized anxiety disorder. *Am J Psychiatry* **150**, 600–607.

McGlashan TH (1986) The Chestnut Lodge Follow-Up Study III: long-term outcome of borderline personalities. *Arch Gen Psychiatry* **43**, 2–30.

Mellman TA, Randolph CA, Brawman-Mintzer O, Flores LP and Milanes FJ (1992) Phenomenology and course of psychiatric disorders associated with combat-related posttraumatic stress disorder. *Am J Psychiatry* **149**, 1568–1574.

Mezzich JE, Fabrega H, Coffman GA and Glavin YW (1987) Comprehensively diagnosing geriatric patients. *Compr Psychiatry* **28**, 68–76.

Migliorelli R, Teson A, Sabe L, Petracchi M, Leiguarda R and Starkstein SE (1995) Prevalence and correlates of dysthymia and major depression among patients with Alzheimer's disease. *Am J Psychiatry* **152**, 37–55.

Moos RH (1990) Depressed outpatients' life contexts, amount of treatment, and treatment outcome. *J Nerv Ment Dis* **178**, 105–112.

Morrison J and Herbstein J (1988) Secondary affective disorder in women with somatization disorder. *Compr Psychiatry* **29**, 433–440.

Mueller TI, Lavori PW, Keller MB, Swartz A, Warshaw M, Hasin D, Coryell W, Endicott J, Rice J and Akiskal H (1994) Prognostic effect of the variable course of alcoholism on the 10-year course of depression. *Am J Psychiatry* **151**, 701–706.

North CS, Smith EM and Spitznagel EL (1994) Posttraumatic stress disorder in survivors of a mass shooting. *Am J Psychiatry* **151**, 82–88.

Noyes R, Clarkson C, Crowe RR, Yates WR and McChesney CM (1987) A family study of generalized anxiety disorder. *Am J Psychiatry* **144**, 1019–1024.

Noyes R Jr, Reich J, Christiansen J, Suelzer M, Pfohl B and Coryell WA (1990) Outcome of panic disorder: relationship of diagnostic subtypes and comorbidity. *Arch Gen Psychiatry* **47**, 809–818.

Noyes R, Woodman C, Garvey MJ, Cook BL, Suelzer M, Clancy J and Anderson DJ (1992) Generalized anxiety disorder vs panic disorder: distinguishing characteristics and patterns of comorbidity. *J Nerv Ment Dis* **180**, 369–379.

Nunes EV, McGrath PJ, Quitkin FM, Stewart JP, Harrison W, Tricamo E and Ocepek-Welikson K (1993) Imipramine treatment of alcoholism with comorbid depression. *Am J Psychiatry* **150**, 963–965.

Nutzinger DO and Zapotcszky HG (1985) The influence of depression on the outcome of cardiac phobia (panic disorder). *Psychopathology* **18**, 155–162.

Ormel J, Oldehinkel T, Brilman E, Brink W (1993) Outcome of depression and anxiety in primary care: a three-wave, $3\frac{1}{2}$-year study of psychopathology and disability. *Arch Gen Psychiatry* **50**, 759–766.

Paris J, Nowlis D and Brown R (1989) Predictors of suicide in borderline personality disorder. *Can J Psychiatry* **34**, 8–9.

Parmelee PA, Katz IR and Lawton MP (1993) Anxiety and its association with depression among institutionalized elderly. *Am J Geriatr Psychiatry* **1**, 46–58.

Paykel ES (1971) Classification of depressed patients: a cluster analysis derived grouping. *Br J Psychiatry* **118**, 275–288.

Pérez-Stable EJ, Miranda J and Ying Y (1990) Depression in medical outpatients. *Arch Intern Med* **150**, 1083–1088.

Pfohl B, Coryell W, Zimmerman M and Stangl D (1987) Prognostic validity of self-report and interview measures of personality disorder in depressed patients. *J Clin Psychiatry* **48**, 468–472.

Pfohl B, Stargl D and Zimmerman M (1984) The implications of DSM-III personality disorders for patients with major depression. *J Affect Disord* **7**, 309–318.

Pilkonis PA and Frank E (1988) Personality pathology in recurrent depressions: nature, prevalence, and relationship to treatment response. *Am J Psychiatry* **145**, 435–441.

The President's Commission on Mental Health and Illness (1978) Report to the President From the President's Commission on Mental Health, V.1. US Government Printing Office; Stock No. 040-000-00390-8, Washington, DC.

Rasmussen SA and Tsuang MT (1984) The epidemiology of obsessive–compulsive disorder. *J Clin Psychiatry* **45**, 450–457.

Regier DA, Farmer ME, Rae DS, Locke BZ, Keith SJ, Judd LL and Goodwin FK (1990) Comorbidity of mental disorders with alcohol and other drug abuse: results from the Epidemiologic Catchment Area (ECA) Study. *JAMA* **264**, 2511–2518.

Reich J, Noyes R Jr and Troughton E (1987) Dependent personality disorder associated with phobic avoidance in patients with panic disorder. *Am J Psychiatry* **144**, 323–326.

Rickels K, Downing R, Schweizer E and Hassman H (1993) Antidepressants for the treatment of generalized anxiety disorder: a placebo-controlled comparison of imipramine, trazodone, and diazepam. *Arch Gen Psychiatry* **50**, 884–895.

Robins LN, Helzer JE, Croiughan JL and Ratcliff KS (1981) National Institute of Mental Health Diagnostic Interview Schedule: its history, characteristics and validity. *Arch Gen Psychiatry* **38**, 381–389.

Robins LN, Locke BZ and Regier DA (1991) An overview of psychiatric disorders in America. In: Robins LN and Regier DA (eds) *Psychiatric Disorders in America: The Epidemiological Catchment Area Study*, pp 328–366. Free Press, New York.

Robinson RG and Starkstein SE (1990) Current research in affective disorders following stroke. *J Neuropsychiatry* **2**, 1–14.

Ross HE, Glaser FB and Germanson T (1988) The prevalence of psychiatric disorders in patients with alcohol and other drug problems. *Arch Gen Psychiatry* **45**, 1023–1031.

Rounsaville BJ, Kosten TR, Weissman MM, *et al.* (1985) *Evaluating and Treating Depressive Disorders in Opiate Addicts.* DHHS pub (ADM) 85–1406. National Institute of Mental Health, Rockville, Md.

Salloway S and Duffy J (1993) Neuropsychiatric aspects of depression. *RI Med* **76**, 425–430.

Schneier FR, Johnson J, Hornig CD, Liebowitz MR and Weissman MM (1992) Social phobia: comorbidity and morbidity in an epidemiologic sample. *Arch Gen Psychiatry* **49**, 282–288.

Shea MMT (1993) Personality disorders and depression: an overview of issues and findings. *RI Med* **76**, 405–408.

Shea MT, Glass D, Pilkonis PA, Watkins J and Docherty JP (1987) Frequency and implications of personality disorder in a sample of outpatients. *J Pers Disord* **1**, 27–42.

Shea MT, Pilkonis PA, Beckham E, Collins FJ, Eldin I, Sotsky S and Docherty JF (1990) Personality disorders and treatment outcome in the NIMH Treatment of Depression, Collaborative Research Program. *Am J Psychiatry* **147**, 711–718.

Shea MT, Widiger TA and Klein MH (1992) Co-morbidity of personality disorders and depression: implications for treatment. *J Consult Clin Psychol* **60**, 857–868.

Shearer SL, Peters CP, Quaytman MS and Wadman BE (1988) Intent and lethality of suicide attempts among female borderline inpatients. *Am J Psychiatry* **145**, 1424–1427.

Sierles FS, Chen J-J, McFarland RE and Taylor MA (1983) Posttraumatic stress disorder and concurrent psychiatric illness: a preliminary report. *Am J Psychiatry* **140**, 1177–1179.

Slater E and Shields J (1953) *Psychotic and Neurotic Illnesses in Twins: Medical Research Council Special Report Series Number 278.* Her Majesty's Stationary Office, London.

Smith GR (1994) The course of somatization and its effects on utilization of health care resources. *Psychosomatics* **35**, 263–267.

Soloff PH, Lis JA, Kelly T, Cornelius J and Ulrich R (1994) Risk factors for suicidal behavior in borderline personality disorder. *Am J Psychiatry* **151**, 1316–1323.

Spiker DG, Weiss JC, Dealy RS, Griffin SJ, Hanin I, Neil JF, Perel JM, Rossi AJ and Soloff PH (1985) The pharmacological treatment of delusional depression. *Am J Psychiatry* **142**, 430–436.

Spitzer RL, Endicott J and Robins E (1985) *Research Diagnostic Criteria for a Selected Group of Functional Disorders* (2nd ed.). Biometrics Research Division, New York State Psychiatric Institute, New York.

Stone MH (1989) The course of borderline personality disorder. In: Tasman A, Hales RE and Frances AJ (eds) *American Psychiatric Press Review of Psychiatry*, Vol 8. American Psychiatric Press, Washington, DC.

Strakowski SM, Tohen M, Stoll AL, Faedda GL, Mayer PV, Kolbrener ML and Goodwin DC (1993) Comorbidity in psychosis at first hospitalization. *Am J Psychiatry* **150**, 752–757.

Strober M (1981) The significance of bulimia in juvenile anorexia nervosa: an exploration of possible etiologic factors. *Int J Eating Disord* **1**, 28–43.

Taylor MA, Berenbaum SA, Jampala VC and Cloninger CR (1993) Are schizophrenia and affective disorder related? Preliminary data from a family study. *Am J Psychiatry* **150**, 278–285.

Thompson LW, Gallagher D and Czirr R (1988) Personality disorder and outcome in the treatment of late-life depression. *J Geriatr Psychiatry* **21**, 133–146.

Toner B, Garfinkel P and Garner D (1988) Affective and anxiety disorders in the long-term follow-up of anorexia nervosa. *Int J Psychiatry Med* **18**, 357–364.

Tsuang MT, Winokur G and Crowe RR (1980) Morbidity risks of schizophrenia and affective disorders among first degree relatives of patients with schizophrenia, mania, depression and surgical conditions. *Br J Psychiatry* **137**, 497–504.

Tynes LL, White K and Steketee GS (1990) Toward a new nosology of obsessive–compulsive disorder. *Compr Psychiatry* **31**, 465–480.

US Department of Health and Human Services (1993) *Depression in Primary Care*. AHCPR Publication No. 93-0550.

Vaillant GE (1964) Prospective prediction of schizophrenic remission. *Arch Gen Psychiatry* **11**, 509–518.

Valleni-Basile LA, Garrison CZ, Jackson KL, Waller JL, Mckeown RE, Addy CL and Cuffe SP (1994) Frequency of obsessive–compulsive disorder in a community sample of young adolescents. *J Am Acad Child Adolesc Psychiatry* **33**, 782–791.

Van Valkenburg C, Akiskal HS, Puzantian V and Rosenthal T (1984) Anxious depressions: clinical, family history and naturalistic outcome: comparisons with panic and major depressive disorders. *J Affect Disord* **6**, 67–82.

Von Korff M, Shapiro S, Burke JD, Teitlebaum M, Skinner EA, German P, Turner RW, Klein L and Burns B (1987) Anxiety and depression in a primary care clinic: comparison of Diagnostic Interview Schedule, General Health Questionnaire, and practitioner assessments. *Arch Gen Psychiatry* **44**, 152–156.

Walker RD, Howard MO, Lambert MD and Suchinsky R (1994) Psychiatric and medical comorbidities of veterans with substance use disorders. *Hosp Community Psychiatry* **45**, 232–237.

Weissman MM, Gershon ES, Kidd KK, Prusoff BA, Leckman JF, Dibble E, Hamovit J, Thompson WD, Pauls DL and Guroff JJ (1984) Psychiatric disorders in the relatives of probands with affective disorders: the Yale University National Institute of Mental Health Collaborative Study. *Arch Gen Psychiatry* **41**, 13–21.

Weissman MM, Wickramaratne P, Adams PB, Lish JD, Horwath E, Charney D, Woods SW, Leeman E and Frosch E (1993) The relationship between panic disorder and major depression: a new family study. *Arch Gen Psychiatry* **50**, 767–780.

Wells KB, Stewart A, Hays RD, Burnam A, Rogers W, Daniel M, Berry S, Greenfield S and Ware J (1989) The functioning and well-being of depressed patients—results of the Medical Outcome study. *JAMA* **262**, 914–919.

Wilcox JA and Yates WR (1993) Gender and psychiatric comorbidity in substance-abusing individuals. *Am J Addict* **2**, 3.

Winokur A, March V and Mendels J (1980) Primary affective disorder in relatives of patients with anorexia nervosa. *Am J Psychiatry* **137**, 695–698.

Winokur G (1979) Unipolar depression: is it divisible into autonomous subtypes? *Arch Gen Psychiatry* **36**, 47–52.

Wolpe PR, Gorton G, Serota R and Sanford B (1993) Predicting compliance of dual diagnosis inpatients with aftercare treatment. *Hosp Community Psychiatry* **44**, 45–48.

Wragg RE and Jeste DV (1989) Overview of depression and psychosis in Alzheimer's Disease. *Am J Psychiatry* **146**, 577–587.

Yanovski SZ, Nelson JE, Dubbert BK and Spitzer RL (1993) Association of binge eating disorder and psychiatric comorbidity in obese subjects. *Am J Psychiatry* **150**, 1472–1479.

Yehuda R, Southwick SM, Krystal JH, Bremner D, Charney DS and Mason JW (1993) Enhanced suppression of cortisol following dexamethasone administration in posttraumatic stress disorder. *Am J Psychiatry* **150**, 83–86.

Ziedonis DM (1992) Comorbid psychopathology and cocaine addiction. In: Kosten TR and Kleber HD (eds) *Clinicians' Guide to Cocaine Addiction: Theory, Research, and Treatment.* Guilford Press, New York.

Zimmerman M and Coryell W (1989) DSM-III personality disorder diagnoses in a non-patient sample. *Arch Gen Psychiatry* **46**, 682–689.

Zimmerman M, Coryell WH and Black DW (1991) Cigarette smoking and psychiatric illness. In: *CME Syllabus and Scientific Proceedings in Summary Form*, 144th Annual Meeting of the American Psychiatric Association. Washington, DC.

Zinbarg RE, Barlow DH, Liebowitz M, Street L, Broadhead E, Katon W, Roy-Byrne P, Lepine J-P, Teherani M, Richards J, Brantley PJ and Kraemer H (1994) The DSM-IV field trial for mixed anxiety-depression. *Am J Psychiatry* **151**, 1153–1162.

Zitrin CM, Klein DF and Woerner MG (1980) Treatment of agoraphobia with group exposure *in vivo* and imipramine. *Arch Gen Psychiatry* **37**, 63–72.

Zucker RA (1987) The four alcoholisms: a developmental account of the etiologic process. In: Rivers PC (ed) *Alcohol and Addictive Behavior.* University of Nebraska Press, Lincoln NE.

13

Other uses of the selective serotonin re-uptake inhibitors in psychiatry

William F. Boyer and John P. Feighner

INTRODUCTION

Since the first edition of this book there has been considerable interest in exploring conditions other than depression for which SSRIs may be helpful. This chapter will review the evidence for the efficacy of SSRIs in some of these disorders. One or two of the SSRIs, usually fluoxetine and fluvoxamine, have been most often studied in each of these areas. From a scientific perspective one must withhold judgement about the other SSRIs until proper studies have been done. However from a clinical perspective it has usually been the case that if one SSRI has been effective for a certain condition then the others are too, with few exceptions. We will attempt to point out the times when this rule does not hold. Some of the efficacy data are clearly much better established than others, but the broad scope of these conditions is likely to be of interest to both clinicians and basic scientists.

BULIMIA

Fluoxetine

Fluoxetine has been the best studied SSRI for bulimia and has an indication for this disorder. The Fluoxetine Bulimia Nervosa Study Group performed an eight-week

Selective Serotonin Re-uptake Inhibitors: Advances in Basic Research and Clinical Practice, Second Edition, Edited by J.P. Feighner and W.F. Boyer
© 1996 John Wiley & Sons Ltd

trial of fluoxetine 60 or 20 mg/day and placebo in 387 outpatients with bulimia nervosa (Fluoxetine Bulimia Nervosa Study Group, 1992). The higher fluoxetine dose showed the largest, and significant, drug–placebo difference in reducing bingeing and vomiting; 20 mg/day was intermediate. Side-effects were more frequent with fluoxetine than placebo but the data suggest that these were generally mild as there was no significant difference in the number of patients who discontinued due to side-effects in the three groups.

Goldstein and Wilson (1994) examined whether response to fluoxetine in bulimia was associated with baseline depression. They retrospectively analysed efficacy, adjusting for baseline depression scores. Interestingly, patients without depression tended to improve *more* than those with depressive comorbidity. For non-depressed patients 20 mg/day was as effective as 60 mg/day. Fluoxetine 60 mg was effective in reducing binge-eating ($p < 0.001$) and vomiting ($p < 0.001$) independent of baseline depression scores. This suggests that the effect of the higher fluoxetine dosage may have been to override the negative effect of depression on outcome, perhaps by relieving the depression.

Opioid antagonists have also been reported to be helpful in anorexia nervosa and bulimia (Maltazzi *et al.*, 1994). Bandechhi (1994) treated a sample of 94 bulimic patients with placebo, fluoxetine (60 mg/day), naltrexone (50 mg/day) or fluoxetine plus naltrexone. The percentage of patients who showed significant improvement on standard rating scales was placebo 8%, naltrexone 11%, fluoxetine 31%, and fluoxetine plus naltrexone 81%. If these findings are replicated, combined SSRI–opioid antagonist treatment of bulimia may be an important option.

Fluvoxamine

Ayuso-Gutierrez and colleagues (1994) reported an open trial of fluvoxamine 50–150 mg/day in 20 patients with bulimia nervosa. Fluvoxamine was associated with significant improvement in binge eating and was well tolerated.

Gardiner and colleagues (1993) conducted a small pilot study of fluvoxamine in non-vomiting binge-eating female patients and women with bulimia nervosa. Ten non-vomiting subjects and six with bulimia nervosa were treated on an open basis with 100–200 mg daily. Five non-vomiting patients and three with bulimia nervosa completed the study. Non-vomiters showed a significant reduction in number of binges, scores on eating disorder scales, weight, and anxiety. Those with bulimia nervosa had a significant reduction in hunger and a reduction in depression which tended towards significance.

Hudson and colleagues (1994) performed a nine-week, double-blind trial of fluvoxamine (50–300 mg/day) versus placebo in 67 patients with binge-eating disorder. Subjects treated with fluvoxamine showed a significantly greater clinical global improvement ($p < 0.05$) and greater decrease in binge eating than those treated with placebo (75% versus 45%, $p < 0.05$).

Other SSRIs

There are case reports of the successful use of sertraline in bulimia (Robert and Lydiard, 1993; Durran, 1994; Eppel, 1994; Kramer, 1994). In one of these the patient had previously failed to respond to fluoxetine (Kramer, 1994). Information concerning the use of other SSRIs in this disorder is lacking.

Comment

The risks and benefits of antidepressant treatment of bulimia are still unclear. Russel and colleagues (1994) reported that bulimic patients relapsed following cessation of fluoxetine treatment. Fluoxetine has been reported to induce anorexia in a bulimic patient (Vaz and Salcedo, 1994) and to have been abused by an anorexic patient for its appetite-reducing properties (Wilcox, 1987). That these reports concerned fluoxetine is most likely due to its wide use rather than any special problems of the particular drug in treating bulimia.

The efficacy of antidepressants in bulimia may depend more on dose than the particular drug used. Boyer and Feighner (1994) performed a meta-analysis of placebo-controlled, non-cross-over studies of antidepressants in bulimia. Thirteen studies which included 936 patients were identified. Antidepressants included imipramine, amitriptyline, desipramine, trazodone, phenelzine, isocarboxazide, bupropion and fluoxetine. There were no significant differences between effect sizes based on type of antidepressant (i.e. SSRI versus TCA, TCA versus MAOI, serotonergic versus noradrenergic). Antidepressants as a whole were very significantly superior to placebo for both bingeing ($p = 0.7 \times 10^{-10}$) and vomiting ($p = 0.3 \times 10^{-9}$). There was a highly significant relationship between dose and reduction of bingeing ($p = 0.0004$) but only a marginal relationship between dose and reduction in vomiting ($p = 0.1$). Approximately two-thirds of the maximum recommended dose appeared necessary for a significant reduction. This dose-response pattern persisted if the fluoxetine studies were excluded. The fact that relatively high doses are required suggests that antidepressants may work by a different mechanism in bulimia than depression. The significant dose-response relationship for bingeing but not vomiting may reflect the smaller number of studies which presented results on reduction in vomiting, or that different mechanisms produce bingeing and vomiting.

ANOREXIA NERVOSA

Little has been written about the use of SSRIs in anorexia nervosa. Indeed the weight loss frequently associated with SSRIs might seem to make them relatively contraindicated. However two case series suggest that fluoxetine may have some benefit in achieving or maintaining weight gain in anorexia nervosa (Gwirtsman *et* al., 1990; Kaye et al., 1991). Positive response does not seem related to baseline depression. Indeed, in one series patients who were depressed at baseline improved less than those who were not (Kaye et al., 1991).

PANIC DISORDER

Paroxetine

There is considerable evidence from controlled studies to suggest that paroxetine is effective and well tolerated in the treatment of panic disorder. In one 12-week study, paroxetine (20–60 mg) plus cognitive was significantly superior to placebo plus cognitive therapy in alleviating panic attacks (Oehrberg et al., 1995). Steiner and colleagues (1995) reported a second, large placebo controlled study in which the paroxetine dosing schedule was fixed at 10, 20 or 40 mg per day. After 10 weeks, patients given 40 mg per day experienced significantly greater reduction in their panic attacks than placebo patients. Paroxetine has also been compared to clomipramine for panic disorder (Lecrubier et al., 1994) in a 12-week double blind placebo controlled study involving 368 patients. In this study the effect of paroxetine and clomipramine was similar, though paroxetine appeared to have an earlier onset of action. In a nine-month extension of this study (Dunbar and Judge, 1995) continued use with paroxetine and clomipramine further improved the outcome with over 70% of patients becoming full panic attack free. These studies also indicated that paroxetine was better tolerated than clomipramine as indicated by the lower number of patients who dropped out due to adverse effects. Please refer to chapter 8 for more details.

Fluvoxamine

Fluvoxamine blocks experimentally induced panic attacks (Goddard et al., 1993; Megen et al., 1994). It was highly superior to placebo in reducing the frequency of severity of panic attacks in an eight-week multicentre trial of fluvoxamine and placebo in 188 patients (Woods et al., 1994). Similar results have been reported in smaller double-blind comparisons (Hoehn-Saric et al., 1993, 1994). Complementary studies have shown that fluvoxamine is more effective than cognitive therapy and at least as effective as imipramine in panic disorder (Black et al., 1993a; Bakish et al., 1993; Servant et al., 1990).

Holland and colleagues (1994) followed 73 panic disorder patients treated openly with fluvoxamine for one year. They noted continued improvement in the Clinical Anxiety Scale and Clinical Global Impressions score during the follow-up period. While Black and colleagues (1993b) reported that withdrawal symptoms were common in panic patients after abrupt discontinuation of fluvoxamine, the absence of a placebo group did not control for the psychological effect of abruptly stopping pill-taking. Holland (1994) found no evidence of withdrawal reactions when fluvoxamine was discontinued.

Other SSRIs

Available evidence for other SSRIs suggests they also reduce panic attacks. A preliminary analysis of the first 191 patients to be enrolled in a placebo controlled 12-week multicentre fixed-dose study of sertraline showed a significant reduction in the frequency of panic attacks (Gorman and Wolkow, 1994). The results suggested that the best results may be obtained with a sertraline dose of 100 mg a day or more.

Given the widespread use of fluoxetine for panic disorder, surprisingly little data have been presented. Several open-label studies and reports have suggested that fluoxetine may be helpful in panic disorder (Gorman *et al.*, 1987; Brady *et al.*, 1989; Schneier *et al.*, 1990; Solyom *et al.*, 1991). Clark and Jacob (1994) reported results of a small double-blind, placebo controlled study of 20 patients in which fluoxetine was significantly superior to placebo. Panic disorder is covered in greater detail in Chapter 8.

OBSESSIVE–COMPULSIVE DISORDER

The literature is clear that antidepressants which potently inhibit serotonin uptake are superior to other antidepressants in the treatment of obsessive–compulsive disorder (OCD) (Dunbar *et al.*, 1995). This was shown, for example, in a meta-analysis of clomipramine, fluvoxamine and sertraline in comparison to either placebo or traditional TCAs and MAOIs in OCD. The high potency selective serotonin re-uptake inhibitors were clearly superior to both placebo and the standard antidepressants ($p = 1 \times 10^{-13}$) (Davis *et al.*, 1990).

Fluvoxamine

Fluvoxamine has been well studied in OCD. It was significantly superior to placebo in a 10-week multicentre trial of fluvoxamine versus placebo in 160 patients with DSM III R OCD. Forty-two percent of fluvoxamine-treated patients rated themselves as much or very much improved at endpoint compared to only 13.3% of placebo-treated patients (Rasmussen *et al.*, 1992).

Fluvoxamine has also been compared to clomipramine, the standard pharmacological treatment for OCD, in a 10-week study of 66 OCD patients. There were no significant differences in the mean reduction in total Yale–Brown Obsessive–Compulsive Scale (Y-BOCS) score at any time-point in the intent-to-treat population. A mean reduction of 8.6 (33%) was seen in the fluvoxamine group and 7.8 (31%) in the clomipramine group (Freeman *et al.*, 1994).

Other SSRIs

Three hundred forty-eight patients with DSM III R OCD were randomized to receive either 20, 40 or 60 mg/day of paroxetine or placebo in a 12-week, fixed-dose, multicentre study. Endpoint analysis of change in Y-BOCS total score revealed statistically significant improvement for the two higher paroxetine dose groups compared to placebo (Steiner *et al.*, 1994).

Similar research programmes were conducted for fluoxetine and sertraline. Fixed doses of 20, 40 or 60 mg/day of fluoxetine were compared to placebo in two randomized double-blind 13-week trials. A total of 355 outpatients with OCD were studied. All doses of fluoxetine were significantly superior to placebo on the Y-BOCS total score and other efficacy measures. A trend suggested greater efficacy at 60 mg/day (Tollefson *et al.*, 1994). Sertraline was studied in two large OCD trials ($N = 412$), one of which utilized fixed doses. The results of both suggested that sertraline was effective in reducing OCD symptoms (Chouinard, 1992). Paroxetine has also been studied and shown to be efficacious in OCD; results are described in more detail in chapter 7. Clinical and basic science aspects of the use of SSRIs in OCD are described further in Chapter 7.

WEIGHT LOSS

Goldstein and colleagues (1994) reported results of a 52-week double-blind multicentre trial of fluoxetine and placebo in 458 obese outpatients. Fluoxetine (60 mg/day) resulted in statistically significantly greater mean weight loss than placebo up to week 28. There was no treatment difference at 52 weeks. The authors felt that the wider spacing of follow-up intervals toward the end of the trial may have contributed to the lack of effect at one year. Patients who were more obese at baseline tended to lose more weight.

Levine and colleagues (1989) reported results of 655 non-depressed patients who were given fluoxetine, 10, 20, 40 or 60 mg/day, once a day for eight weeks. The highest dose was associated with the greatest weight loss, lower doses with less. There was no difference in any of the fluoxetine-treated groups and the placebo group in dropout rates, but there were dose-dependent increases in complaints of somnolence, asthenia and sweating.

Wise (1992) reviewed weight loss in fluoxetine studies. In studies that used a fluoxetine dose of 60 mg/day the mean weight loss was approximately 0.5 kg/week. Longer-term studies have shown maximum weight loss to occur at 12–20 weeks of therapy.

Ferguson and Feighner (1987) found that fluoxetine (average 65 mg/day) produced significantly more weight loss than placebo and somewhat more weight loss than benzphetamine among 150 non-depressed obese outpatients in an eight-week study. Marcus and colleagues (1990) conducted a one-year study of fluoxetine and behaviour therapy in weight loss. They reported that patients treated with 60 mg/day of fluoxetine in addition to behaviour therapy lost more weight than those treated with behaviour therapy plus placebo.

Maintenance of weight loss is a problem with the SSRIs, as it is with other weight-loss strategies. Darga and coworkers (1991) compared diet plus either fluoxetine or placebo in the treatment of 45 non-depressed and obese patients. The fluoxetine-treated patients lost significantly more weight, but had a tendency to regain it. At the end of one year there were no significant differences between the fluoxetine and placebo groups.

Obese diabetics

Data from a number of centres in a multicentre investigation of fluoxetine in obese diabetic patients have been published (Gray *et al.*, 1992a, b; Kutnowski *et al.*, 1992; OKane *et al.*, 1994). These were briefly summarized by Goldstein and colleagues (1992). The design was a randomized, 36-week double-blind trial and compared placebo ($N = 139$) with fluoxetine, ($N = 139$) in obese patients (body mass index $> 99 \text{ kg/m}^2$) with non-insulin dependent diabetes mellitus. Patients were instructed on caloric consumption monthly, but there was no behavioural or exercise counselling. At endpoint there were significant reductions in weight, fasting blood glucose, and glycosolated haemoglobin. Dosage of hypoglycaemic agents was also reduced, although not significantly.

Other SSRIs

De-Zwaan and colleagues (1989) studied 62 obese female outpatients with current or past DSM III major depression, randomly assigned to fluvoxamine + diet, fluvoxamine + behaviour therapy, placebo + behaviour therapy, placebo + diet in a 12-week study. Interim results based on 48 patients show a significant weight loss (5.9 kg) overall, with no significant differences between groups. Abell and colleagues (1986) found that depressed women with refractory obesity lost more weight with fluvoxamine (100–200 mg/day) than with placebo, although the difference was not statistically significant. Fernstrom and colleagues (1988) reported a patient in whom fluvoxamine appeared to increase metabolic rate and promote weight loss.

Feighner and Rosenblatt (1989) found significantly more weight loss with sertraline, 50–200 mg/day, than placebo in 150 non-depressed obese outpatients. Clark and Rosenblatt (1989) treated 80 obese diabetic patients with sertraline or placebo in double-blind fashion. Sertraline (150 mg/day) was associated with significantly more weight loss than placebo (2.9 versus 0.76 kg).

Paroxetine tends often to be weight neutral than the other SSRIs (Rasmussen, 1991). Therefore one would expect that it would not be especially helpful in promoting weight loss in non-depressed obese subjects.

ALCOHOLISM

Fluvoxamine

Fluvoxamine is the only SSRI which has been studied in double-blind fashion for alcoholism. Block and colleagues (1994) conducted a placebo controlled, double-blind, multicentre study of fluvoxamine in non-depressed alcoholics. After a two-week, single-blind placebo run-in, 108 patients who met DSM III R criteria for alcohol dependence or abuse were treated and followed up for a period of three months. Assessments included biological measures (gamma-glutamyl transferase and mean corpuscular volume), clinician's assessment of drinking, and a patient diary of alcohol use performed at days 15, 30, 60 and 90. Fluvoxamine was found to be superior to placebo, both clinically and statistically, at days 60 and 90, with trends evident as early as day 15. This was most apparent in the number of patients achieving abstinence, the proportion of days of heavy drinking, and percent reduction in alcohol consumption. However, Kranzler and colleagues (1993) reported that the usefulness of fluvoxamine in alcoholism treatment may be limited by side-effects. This is certainly an area which merits further study.

Fluoxetine

The published studies of fluoxetine in alcoholism are open-label and do not exclude patients with concomitant depression. Borup and Unden (1994) reported a 70% rate of "good clinical outcome" in a study of fluoxetine plus disulfiram in 188 alcoholics with comorbid major depression or panic disorder.

Cornelius and colleagues (1993) treated 12 patients with alcohol dependence and DSM III R major depression with 20–40 mg per day of fluoxetine for eight weeks. All 12 patients reported prominent suicidal ideation upon admission to the hospital; six had made serious suicide attempts shortly before admission. Statistically significant improvements were noted on measures of depression and post-discharge alcohol consumption. No paradoxical increases in suicidality were noted.

Sertraline

O'Brien (1994) studied a group of 22 alcoholics with a history of long-term drinking, multiple relapses, treatment failures, and symptoms of prolonged depression. Half were started on sertraline early in therapy for alcoholism (within four days after last drink) and the other half served as controls. The study was not blinded and placebo was not administered to the controls. Both groups were followed daily while inpatients and weekly after discharge. Sixty percent of sertraline treated subjects versus 25% of controls reported improvement in appetite, sleep patterns, mood swings and reduction in intensity of dysphoric symptoms within two weeks. One-third demonstrated improvement within seven days. No patient experienced side-effects sufficiently severe to warrant discontinuation of the medication. Twenty-two percent reported continued and sustained improvement and abstinence in follow-up to three months.

Citalopram

Naranjo and colleagues (1994) conducted trials of several agents in "moderately" dependent alcoholics. They found that both citalopram and fluoxetine decreased the desire to drink and alcohol intake compared to placebo. Citalopram seemed somewhat more potent to the investigators in this regard.

DRUG ABUSE

Evidence from animal studies suggests that fluoxetine may antagonize the reinforcing properties of cocaine (Richardson and Roberts, 1991). However most of the published data concerning SSRI use in cocaine dependence is anecdotal. More positive results in reducing cocaine consumption have been in patients who are dependent on both opiates and cocaine (e.g. in a methadone maintenance programme) than in patients dependent on cocaine alone (Pollack and Rosenbaum, 1991; Batki *et al.*, 1992, 1993a). The addition of fluoxetine to a counselling programme for primary cocaine addicts appeared to have no added benefit in the one study which examined this issue (Covi *et al.*, 1992). The reason that SSRIs may be helpful in cocaine plus opiate dependence but not cocaine dependence alone may be related to significantly higher rates of depression in the former group (Batki *et al.*, 1993b).

It is important to note that there may be significant clinical differences between the SSRIs in this population. It has been reported that fluvoxamine increases plasma

Table 1. Fluoxetine versus placebo in heroin addicts.

Group	A	B	C
High Buss–Durkee scores	guilt, resentment	assault, irritability	—
Age of onset	late	early	late
Legal problems	+	+ +	—
Drugs other than heroin	alcohol	alcohol, cocaine	heroin
Prolactin response to fenfluramine	↓↓	↓	normal
Response to fluoxetine	+ +	+	not different to placebo

levels of methadone, but fluoxetine does not (Batki *et al.*, 1993a; Bertschy *et al.*, 1994a, b). Patients on methadone may even have opiate withdrawal symptoms after discontinuing fluvoxamine (Bertschy *et al.*, 1994a).

Gerra and colleagues (1994) analysed the efficacy of fluoxetine against placebo in a sample of 98 heroin addicts divided according to history and results on the Buss–Durkee Hostility scale (see Table 1). The investigators found fluoxetine to be superior to placebo in group A and in patients in group B who had lower levels of post-fenfluramine prolactin.

SOCIAL PHOBIA

Positive experience with sertraline, paroxetine and fluoxetine in social phobia has been presented. Katzelnick and colleagues (1994) found that sertraline was significantly superior to placebo in a double-blind cross-over study of 12 socially phobic patients treated in a 12-week trial. Several open studies support this finding (Czepowicz *et al.*, 1994; Martins *et al.*, 1994; Munjack, 1994; Van Ameringen *et al.*, 1994).

Mancini (1995) reported moderate or marked improvement with 15 of 18 patients with social phobia treated with paroxetine in a 12-week open-label trial. Case series (Sheehan, 1984; Van-Ameringen *et al.*, 1993) and case reports (Sternbach, 1990; Schneier *et al.*, 1992) also suggest that fluoxetine may be effective in social phobia. Avoidant personality disorder is very closely related to generalized social phobia and a case series suggests that fluoxetine may be helpful (Deltito and Stam, 1989).

HYPOCHONDRIASIS

Fallon and colleagues have published or presented several positive reports of the use of fluoxetine for hypochondriasis. These investigators used doses of fluoxetine typically employed for obsessive–compulsive disorder (average 40–60 mg/day) because of phenomenological similarities between the two disorders (Fallon *et al.*, 1991, 1993; Brown, 1992). Viswanathan and Paradis (1991) reported on the successful use of fluoxetine with a hypochondriacal patient whose illness centred on the belief she had cancer. Similarly, Brophy described a patient with hypochondriacal "psychosis" who responded to paroxetine (Wagstaff and McTavish, 1994).

PERSONALITY DISORDERS

Most of the data concerning the use of SSRIs in personality disorders involve fluoxetine. Salzman has conducted two similar placebo controlled studies in borderline personality disorder. In both studies fluoxetine was significantly superior to placebo in reducing anger. This effect was independent of improvement in depression (Salzman *et al.*, 1992; Salzman, 1994). In an open trial Norden (1989) reported that eight out of 12 patients with borderline personality disorder improved to a significant degree with fluoxetine. Most of these patients continued to be much or very much improved when followed up after 1–2 years. All but one patient discontinued fluoxetine against advice at some point. The usual result was deterioration within a few days with prompt recovery upon reinstatement (Norden, 1991). Other open studies or case reports have supported the efficacy of fluoxetine in reducing the impulsivity and anger associated with borderline personality disorder (Coccaro *et al.*, 1990; Cornelius *et al.*, 1990; Markovitz *et al.*, 1991; Hull *et al.*, 1993).

Kavoussi and colleagues (1994) found that sertraline was associated with decreased irritability and impulsive aggression in an open trial of 11 patients with at least one personality disorder. Fava and colleagues reported that fluoxetine was helpful in reducing anger attacks in depressed outpatients (Faua *et al.*, 1993). The presence of anger attacks were significantly associated with the presence of a Cluster B personality disorder (i.e. borderline, narcissistic, antisocial, histrionic).

PROBLEMATIC SEXUAL BEHAVIOURS

Several reports have appeared of the successful treatment of a variety of problematic sexual behaviours with SSRIs. These behaviours appear to share the quality of obsessive preoccupation and/or compulsive activity. Zohar and colleagues (1994b) reported a case of compulsive exhibitionism which was successfully treated with fluvoxamine. After stabilization, identical-looking desipramine or placebo pills were substituted in single-blind fashion and were associated with relapse.

Kafka and Prentky (1992) reported a series of 20 men who sought treatment for paraphilias or nonparaphilic sexual addiction. Fluoxetine treatment was associated with statistically significant improvement in the 16 men who completed this four-week trial. Nineteen of these 20 men met DSM III R criteria for dysthymia and 11 met criteria for current major depression.

Perilstein and colleagues (1991) reported three other cases of paraphilias responsive to fluoxetine. Other behaviours which have been successfully treated include cross-dressing, compulsive exhibitionism and paraphilic coercive disorder (rape) (Jorgensen, 1990; Kafka, 1991; Zohar *et al.*, 1994a).

Wing and colleagues (1994) described the case of a 37-year-old Chinese man who suffered from narcolepsy and morbid jealousy which were precipitated by head injury. Fluoxetine 20 mg/day reduced his narcoleptic symptoms and morbid jealousy but not his sleepiness. On defaulting treatment, the patient's symptoms and marital problem recurred. Gross (1991) described the dramatic response of another case of pathological jealousy to fluoxetine.

POSTTRAUMATIC STRESS DISORDER

Nagy and colleagues (1993) treated 27 veterans with PTSD with fluoxetine in a 10-week open trial. The dose started at 20 mg/day and increased to 80 mg/day depending on response and side-effects. Appreciable improvement tended to occur after six weeks, which suggested that high doses or a longer duration might be required. Positive results with fluoxetine were also reported in a smaller open study (Davidson et al., 1991) and a case report (March, 1992).

Den Boer and colleagues (1992) conducted an open trial of fluvoxamine in combat-related PTSD. Twenty-four Dutch World War II resistance fighters participated. Although improvement was noted in a number of areas, quantitative improvement was "modest".

Kline and colleagues (1993) reported an open trial of sertraline in 19 combat veterans with PTSD and comorbid major depression. All of the subjects had failed a previous trial of another antidepressant. Twelve patients were "much improved" as measured on the Clinical Global Impressions scale. Symptoms which improved included dysphoria, irritability, and social volatility but not insomnia.

LATE LUTEAL PHASE DYSPHORIC DISORDER

Fluoxetine

Most of the reported experience with SSRI treatment of late luteal phase dysphoric (LLPD) disorder (premenstrual syndrome) has been with fluoxetine. The most powerful demonstration of its potential in this condition was a multi-centre double-blind placebo controlled trial. Subjects were recruited at seven Canadian university-affiliated women's health clinics. All had regular menstrual cycles, were medication-free, and had no current or recent medical or psychiatric illness. The diagnosis of severe DSM III R LLPD was established prospectively over at least two menstrual cycles. Phase 1 of the study was a single-blind, placebo-only, two menstrual-cycles period, which allowed the elimination of placebo responders. Placebo non-responders were then entered into Phase 2 in which subjects were randomly assigned to placebo, fluoxetine 20 mg/day or 60 mg/day for six consecutive menstrual cycles. The primary outcome measures were Visual Analogue Scales (VAS) for tension, irritability and dysphoria during the late luteal phase. A total of 313 women were randomized into Phase 2 of the trial; 180 women completed the required six cycles of the study. Improvement in VAS scores at each cycle was significantly higher and clinically relevant in those receiving fluoxetine 20 mg or 60 mg versus placebo ($p < 0.01$) and this improvement was maintained through cycle six. There was no significant difference between the two doses of fluoxetine in terms of efficacy, but more side-effects were seen with the higher dose (Menkes et al., 1993; Steiner, 1994).

Two relatively small (total $N = 24$) placebo-controlled cross-over trials of fluoxetine 20 mg/day in LLPD have been reported. Active treatment in both trials was both statistically and clinically highly significant (Wood *et al.*, 1992; Menkes *et al.*, 1993).

One study examined the efficacy and tolerability of fluoxetine for the long-term treatment of LLPD. Pearlstein and Stone followed 64 women for an average of 18.6 months. Fluoxetine dosage was titrated according to clinical response and side-effects. Fifty-seven percent of patients remained on 20 mg/day and most of the rest took 40 mg/day. All patients who continued medication achieved a complete or partial remission. Fluoxetine retained its efficacy during the follow-up period (Pearlstein and Stone, 1994).

Although there has been a single case report of fluoxetine's efficacy in once-a-month administration (Daamen and Brown, 1992), treatment generally needs to be on a continuous basis. Symptoms tend to recur after discontinuing medication but remit when therapy is reinstituted (Vaughn and Leff, 1985; Elks, 1993; Pearlstein *et al.*, 1993).

Other SSRIs

Comparatively little has been presented concerning other SSRIs in LLPD. Freeman and Rickels (1994) have reported success in the open treatment of LLPD with sertraline in 16 patients. Yonkers and colleagues (1994) conducted an open trial of paroxetine for LLPD. Data from the first 10 patients to be entered showed significant symptomatic relief with paroxetine. Eriksson and colleagues (1994, 1995) found paroxetine to be significantly more effective than both placebo and maprotiline, a selective norepinephrine re-uptake inhibitor. This strongly suggests that effects on serotonin neurotransmission are crucial for treatment of this disorder.

PREMATURE EJACULATION

Both sertraline and paroxetine have been studied in double-blind, placebo controlled trials for premature ejaculation. Mendels and Camera randomized 52 non-depressed males into double-blind treatment with sertraline or placebo. Sertraline dose was titrated from 50 to 200 mg, depending upon clinical response. Treatment was associated with statistically and clinically significant improvement (Mendels and Camera, 1994) in 17 patients. Paroxetine was also associated with significantly greater improvement than placebo in another study (Waldinger *et al.*, 1994).

An early report of the efficacy of SSRIs in premature ejaculation was given by Crenshaw and Wiesner (1992). Forty-six males were treated for premature ejaculation with fluoxetine, 20–60 mg/day. All of the subjects initially reported less than 30 seconds of intercourse before ejaculation, which increased to over five minutes in all cases. Lee and colleagues (1994) treated 11 male patients with fluoxetine, 20–60 mg/day, for premature ejaculation with significant improvement again being seen. Power-Smith (1994) reported several cases of beneficial sexual side-effects of fluoxetine in men with erectile impotence and premature ejaculation. The beneficial effects seemed to be independent of antidepressant activity.

PAIN

Diabetic neuropathy

Diabetic neuropathy is a common, painful complication of diabetes. Sindrup and colleagues (1990) conducted two double-blind, controlled studies of SSRIs in this condition. In the first, the investigators compared imipramine, paroxetine and placebo. Both active drugs were superior to placebo, although paroxetine was somewhat less effective than imipramine. Paroxetine was better tolerated, as shown by the fact that five imipramine patients versus none on paroxetine dropped out due to side-effects. The investigators also noted that the patients who did not respond to paroxetine had low plasma levels of the drug. In a subsequent open study the same group confirmed that analgesic response to paroxetine in diabetic neuropathy was associated with higher plasma levels (Sindrup et al., 1991).

Sindrup and colleagues (1992) also treated 15 diabetic neuropathy patients with citalopram in a double-blind placebo controlled cross-over study. The dosage, 40 mg/day, was relatively high compared to the average dose for depression. Citalopram significantly relieved the pain compared to placebo. There was no relationship between drug plasma level and improvement, which may have been due to relatively few patients with low plasma levels. The authors commented that citalopram, like paroxetine, may be somewhat less effective than standard tricyclic antidepressants but better tolerated.

Max and colleagues (1992) published a paper in which they compared results with amitriptyline, desipramine, fluoxetine and placebo in 57 patients with diabetic neuropathy. The data were compiled from two double-blind studies of a cross-over comparison of amitriptyline (a serotonin and norepinephrine uptake inhibitor) versus desipramine (a relatively pure norepinephrine uptake inhibitor), and a separate cross-over study of fluoxetine and placebo. Patients were randomized both to studies and treatments. Response rates to the first treatment received were compared. Amitriptyline was associated with moderate or greater relief in 74% of patients, compared to 61% for desipramine, 48% for fluoxetine and 41% for placebo. The differences in response between amitriptyline and desipramine and between fluoxetine and placebo were not statistically significant, but both amitriptyline and desipramine were superior to placebo. Fluoxetine reduced pain only in depressed patients, in contrast to amitriptyline and desipramine. This may explain an earlier report by Theesen and March (1989) of a patient with diabetic neuropathy and major depression, both of which responded to fluoxetine.

Headache

Although headache is listed as a possible side-effect of SSRIs, these drugs may be beneficial for some headache sufferers. Since early reports of the use of fluoxetine in headache appeared promising (Diamond and Freitag, 1989) Sandrini and colleagues (1991) systematically compared fluoxetine 20 mg/day and amitriptyline 50 mg/day in 38 depressed chronic headache patients. Depression was operationally defined as a Hamilton Depression score greater than 18. Both drugs were superior to placebo and not significantly different from each other. Manna and colleagues (1994) found similar efficacy of fluvoxamine and mianserin in chronic tension headaches.

Langemark and Olesen (1994) compared paroxetine and sulpiride, a dopamine antagonist, in a cross-over study of chronic tension headache. The results were not dramatic with either drug. Neither was associated with an average improvement of more than one point on a five-point global scale. Sulpiride appeared to be slightly superior.

Adly and colleagues (1992) conducted an eight-week placebo controlled double-blind trial of fluoxetine in the prophylaxis of migraine headaches. Fluoxetine caused a significant reduction in headache scores starting with the third and fourth weeks of treatment; there was no significant change with placebo. Depression scores did not differ between groups before treatment, and interestingly, did not significantly change with either treatment.

Fibromyalgia

An early case report suggested that fluoxetine may have some value in the treatment of fibromyalgia (Geller, 1989). However Cortet and colleagues (1992) reported essentially negative results with fluoxetine in a three-month open trial in 23 patients. It is interesting, however, that 57% of the patients felt that treatment was effective.

Conclusions

Overall, the pain literature suggests that SSRIs may have some benefit in pain, especially in patients who cannot tolerate conventional therapies. They may also deserve consideration in patients who have not responded to standard treatments. Hirsch and colleagues (1994) treated 52 such patients with 20–60 mg/day of fluoxetine. Sixty-five percent reported a significant reduction in pain.

DISCUSSION

An important theoretical question is how one class of medication could be helpful for such a disparate group of disorders. Part of this dilemma is artifactual: it is relatively common for patients with one disorder, for example borderline personality disorder, to present with features of other disorders. In this case the SSRI may be treating a feature of an associated disorder and contributing only indirectly to improvement in another.

Another hypothesis is one put forward by Apter and others (1990) that abnormal serotonin function affects behaviour in ways that cross traditional nosological boundaries. For example, disturbed serotonin function may be related to depressed mood, anxiety, impulsivity, and aggression. Many of the conditions for which the SSRIs are helpful have varying degrees of these features. The implication of this theory is that traditional nosological boundaries may need to be re-examined in light of this biochemical and pharmacological data.

A related possibility is that abnormalities in serotonin function may only begin a pathological process, the ultimate form of which is shaped by the social environment, intrapsychic factors or other biological conditions. This is reminiscent of earlier psychodynamic formulations regarding symptom "choice".

Another hypothesis is that SSRIs may have a therapeutic effect which is unrelated to the aetiology of the disorder. There are many illnesses in which effective treatments do not act on the cause of the illness. For example, diuretics are helpful for hypertension although high blood pressure is rarely caused by water or salt retention. Insulin is used in type II diabetes even though the pathology lies in sub-sensitivity to insulin rather than lack of insulin. Histamine-1 receptor blockers and antacids are mainstays of therapy for gastrointestinal ulcers although ulcers are not caused by an excess of histamine and only rarely by excessive acid production. Selective serotonin re-uptake inhibition may not be the crucial factor in the treatment of these disorders. Many of the conditions covered in this chapter have been reported on occasion to respond to other classes of antidepressants. It may be that the improved tolerability of SSRIs allows more patients to be treated, hence more reports appear of the efficacy of SSRIs in these disorders. These speculations on the apparently broad range of indications for the SSRIs are also of course not mutually exclusive.

REFERENCES

Abell CA, Farquhar DL, Galloway SM, Steven F, Philip ARE and Munro JF (1986) Placebo controlled double-blind trial of fluvoxamine maleate in the obese. *J Psychosom Res* **30**, 143–146.

Adly C, Straumanis J and Chesson A (1992) Fluoxetine prophylaxis of migraine. *Headache* **32**, 101–104.

Apter A, Van-Praag HM, Plutchik R, Sevy S, Korn M and Brown S-L (1990) Interrelationship among anxiety, aggression, impulsivity, and mood: A serotonergically linked cluster? *Psychiatry Res* **32**, 191–199.

Ayuso-Gutierrez JL, Palazon M and Ayuso-Mateos JL (1994) Open trial of fluvoxamine in the treatment of bulimia nervosa. *Int J Eating Disord* **15**, 245–249.

Bakish D, Filteau Marie-J, Charbonneau Y, Fraser G, West Dixy-L and Hooper C (1993) *A Double-blind, Placebo-controlled Trial Comparing Fluvoxamine and Imipramine in the Treatment of Panic Disorder with or without Agoraphobia.* Presented at the CINP Regional Workshop, Current Therapeutical Approaches in Panic and Other Anxiety Disorders, Monte Carlo, Nov 20–22 1993.

Bandecchi A (1994) *Drug—Addiction Without Drug: A Model for Treatment of Eating Disorders.* Presented at the XIX CINP Meeting, Washington, DC, 1994.

Batki SL, Manfredi LB, Jacob P and Jones RT (1993a) Fluoxetine for cocaine dependence in methadone maintenance: quantitative plasma and urine cocaine/benzoylecgonine concentrations. *J Clin Psychopharmacol* **13**, 243–250.

Batki SL, Manfredi L, Jones RT, Goldberger L and Murphy JM (1992) *Fluoxetine for Cocaine Abuse: Psychiatric Factors.* Presented at the American Psychiatric Association Annual Meeting, Washington, DC, 1992.

Batki SL, Wasburn AM, Manfredi LB, Herbst MD, Murphy J and Jones RT (1993b) *Fluoxetine for Cocaine Abuse: Depression and Antisocial Personality Disorder.* Presented at the American Psychiatric Association Annual Meeting, San Francisco, 1993.

Bertschy G, Baumann P, Eap CB and Baettig D (1994a) Probable metabolic interaction between methadone and fluvoxamine in addict patients. *Ther Drug Monit* **16**, 42–45.

Bertschy G, Eap CB and Baumann P (1994b) *Methadone Plasma Levels After Fluvoxamine or Fluoxetine Addition.* Presented at the XIX CINP Meeting, Washington, DC, 1994.

Black DW, Wesner R, Bowers W and Gabel J (1993a) A comparison of fluvoxamine, cognitive therapy, and placebo in the treatment of panic disorder. *Arch Gen Psychiatry* **50**, 44–50.

Black DW, Wesner R and Gabel J (1993b) The abrupt discontinuation of fluvoxamine in patients with panic disorder. *J Clin Psychiatry* **54**, 146–149.

Block BA, Holland RL and Ades J (1994) *Recidivist Alcoholics: A Double-blind, A Placebo-controlled Study of Fluvoxamine.* Presented at the XIX CINP Meeting, Washington, DC, 1994.

Borup C and Unden M (1994) Combined fluoxetine and disulfiram treatment of alcoholism with comorbid affective disorders. A naturalistic outcome study, including quality of life measurements. *Eur Psychiatry* **9**, 83–89.

Boyer W and Feighner JP (1994) *Antidepressant Dose-response Relationship in Bulimia.* Presented at the XIX CINP Meeting, Washington, DC, 1994.

Brady K, Zarzar M and Lydiard RB (1989) Fluoxetine in panic disorder patients with imipramine-associated weight gain. *J Clin Psychopharmacol* **9**, 66–67.

Brophy JJ (1994) Monosymptomatic hypochondriacal psychosis treated with paroxetine: A case report. *Ir J Psychol Med* **11(1)**, 21–22.

Brown WA (1992) *Those Intolerant to One Selective Serotonin Reuptake Inhibitor May Tolerate Another.* Presented at the American Psychiatric Association Annual Meeting, Washington, DC, 1992.

Chouinard G (1992) Sertraline in the treatment of obsessive–compulsive disorder: two double-blind, placebo-controlled studies. *Int Clin Psychopharmacol* **7 (Suppl 2)**, 37–41.

Clark C and Rosenblatt S (1980) *A Multicenter Study of Sertraline in the Treatment of Diabetic Obesity.* Paper presented at Progress in the Treatment of Simple and Complicated Obesity, Lisbon, 19 September, 1989.

Clark DB and Jacob RG (1994) *A Double-blind Placebo-controlled Pilot Study of Fluoxetine for Panic Disorder.* Presented at the American Psychiatric Association Annual Meeting, Philadelphia, 1994.

Coccaro EF, Astill JL, Herbert JL and Schut AG (1990) Fluoxetine treatment of impulsive aggression in DSM-III-R personality disorder patients. *J Clin Psychopharmacol* **10**, 373–375.

Cornelius JR, Salloum IM, Cornelius MD, Perel JM, Thase ME, Ehler JG, *et al.* (1993) Fluoxetine trial in suicidal depressed alcoholics. *Psychopharmacol Bull* **29**, 195–199.

Cornelius JR, Soloff PH, Perel JM and Ulrich RF (1990) Fluoxetine trial in borderline personality disorder. *Psychopharmacol Bull* **26**, 151–154.

Cortet B, Houvenagel E, Forzy G, Vincent G and Delcambre B (1992) Evaluation of the effectiveness of serotonin (fluoxetine hydrochloride) treatment. Open study in fibromyalgia. *Rev Rhum Mal Osteoartic* **59**, 497–500.

Covi L, Hess JM, Haertzen CA and Jaffe JJ (1992) *Fluoxetine and Counselling in Cocaine Abuse.* Presented at the American Psychiatric Association Annual Meeting, Washington, DC, 1992.

Crenshaw RT and Wiesner MG (1992) *Treatment of Premature Ejaculation with Prozac.* Presented at the American Psychiatric Association Annual Meeting, Washington, DC, 1992.

Czepowicz VD, Johnson MR, Emmanuel NP, Lydiard RB and Ballenger JC (1994) *Sertraline in Social Phobia.* Presented at the American Psychiatric Association Annual Meeting, Philadelphia, 1994.

Daamen MJ and Brown WA (1992) Single-dose fluoxetine in management of premenstrual syndrome [letter]. *J Clin Psychiatry* **53**, 210–211.

Darga LL, Carroll-Michals L, Botsford SJ and Lucas CP (1991) Fluoxetine's effect on weight loss in obese subjects. *Am J Clin Nutr* **54**, 321–325.

Davidson J, Roth S and Newman E (1991) Fluoxetine in post-traumatic stress disorder. *J Traumatic Stress* **4**, 419–425.

Davis JM, Israni T, Holland D and Janicak PG (1990) A meta-analysis of the efficacy of drugs for obsessive–compulsive disease. *17th CINP Congress Abstracts* **1**, 159.

Deltito JA and Stam M (1989) Psychopharmacological treatment of avoidant personality disorder. *Compr Psychiatry* **30**, 498–504.

Den Boer M, Op-den-Velde W, Falger PJ, Hovens JE, De-Groen JH and Van-Duijn H (1992) Fluvoxamine treatment for chronic PTSD: a pilot study. *Psychother Psychosom* **57**, 158–163.

De-Zwaan M, Schonbeck G, Nutzinger D, Cayiroglu S, Macura R, Bugnar A, *et al.* (1989) Fluvoxamine and behavior therapy in the treatment of depressed obese. *Pharmacopsychiatry* **22**, 223.

Diamond S and Freitag FG (1989) The use of fluoxetine in the treatment of headache. *Clin J Pain* **5**, 200–201.

Dunbar GC and Judge (1995) *Long Term Evaluation of Paroxetine, Clomipramine and Placebo in Panic.* Presented at the ECNP Congress, 1–4 October, Venice.

Durran K (1994) Personal Communication, 11 December 1994.

Elks ML (1993) Open trial of fluoxetine therapy for premenstrual syndrome. *S Afr Med J* **86**, 503–507.

Eppel A (1994) Personal Communication, 11 December 1994.

Eriksson E, Sundblad C, Wikander I, Modigh K, Hedberg M and Andersch B (1995) *Importance of Serotonin and Androgens for Premenstrual Dysphoria.* Presented at the XIX CINP Meeting, Washington, DC, 1994.

Eriksson E, *et al.* (1995) The serotonin reuptake inhibitor paroxetine is superior to the noradrenaline reuptake inhibitor maprotiline in the treatment of premenstrual syndrome. *Neuropsychopharmacology* **12**, 167–176.

Fallon BA, Liebowitz MR, Salman E, Schneier FR, Jusino C, Hollander E, *et al.* (1993) Fluoxetine for hypochondriacal patients without major depression. *J Clin Psychopharmacol* **13**, 438–441.

Fallon BA, Liebowitz MR, Schneier F, Campeas R, Salman E and Davies SO (1991) *An open Trial of Fluoxetine for Hypochondriasis.* Presented at the American Psychiatric Association Annual Meeting, New Orleans, 1991.

Fava M, Rosenbaum JF, Pava JA, McCarthy MK, Steingard RJ, Bouffides E (1994) Anger attacks in unipolar depression. Part 1: Clinical correlates and response to fluoxetine treatment. *Am J Psychiatry* **150** (8, Aug), 1158–1163.

Feighner JP and Rosenblatt S (1989) *A Double-blind Placebo-controlled Study of Sertraline in the Treatment of Obesity.* Paper presented at Progress in the Treatment of Simple and Complicated Obesity, Lisbon, 19 September 1989.

Ferguson JM and Feighner JP (1987) Fluoxetine-induced weight loss in overweight non-depressed humans. *Int J Obes* **11 (Suppl 3)**, 163–170.

Fernstrom MH, Massoudi M and Kupfer DJ (1988) Fluvoxamine and weight loss. *Biol Psychiatry* **24**, 948–949.

Fluoxetine Bulimia Nervosa Study Group (1992) Fluoxetine in the treatment of bulimia nervosa. A multicenter, placebo-controlled, double-blind trial. *Arch Gen Psychiatry* **49**, 139–147.

Freeman CP, Trimble MR, Deakin JF, Stokes TM and Ashford JJ (1994) Fluvoxamine versus clomipramine in the treatment of obsessive–compulsive disorder: a multicenter, randomized, double-blind, parallel group comparison. *J Clin Psychiatry* **55**, 301–305.

Freeman EW and Rickels K (1994) *Serotonergic Drugs and Progesterone in PMS.* Presented at the XIX CINP Meeting, Washington, DC, 1994.

Gardiner HM, Freeman CP, Jesinger DK and Collins SA (1993) Fluvoxamine: an open pilot study in moderately obese female patients suffering from atypical eating disorders and episodes of bingeing. *Int J Obes* **17**, 301–305.

Geller SA (1989) Treatment of fibrositis with fluoxetine hydrochloride (Prozac). *Am J Med* **87**, 594–595.

Gerra G, Fertonani G, Zaimovic A, Tagliavini P, Riva M, Maestri D, *et al.* (1994) *Hostility in Substance Abusers Subtypes: Fluoxetine and Naltrexone Treatment.* Presented at the XIX CINP Meeting, Washington, DC, 1994.

Goddard AW, Woods SW, Sholomskas DE, Goodman WK, Charney DS and Heninger GR (1993) Effects of the serotonin reuptake inhibitor fluvoxamine in yohimbine-induced anxiety in panic disorder. *Psychiatry Res* **48**, 119–133.

Goldstein DJ, Rampey AH, Potvin JH and Fludzinski LA (1992) Fluoxetine in obese patients with non-insulin dependent diabetes mellitus. *Clin Res* **40**, 240A.

Goldstein DJ, Rampey AH Jr, Enas GG, Potvin JH, Fludzinski LA and Levine LR (1994) Fluoxetine: A randomized clinical trial in the treatment of obesity. *Int J Obes* **18**, 129–135.

Goldstein DJ and Wilson MG (1994) Fluoxetine efficacy in bulimia nervosa is independent of baseline depression. Presented at the XIX CINP Meeting, Washington, DC, 1994.

Gorman JM, Liebowitz MR, Fyer AJ, Goetz D, Campeas RB, Fyer MR, *et al.* (1987) An open trial of fluoxetine in the treatment of panic attacks (published erratum appears in *J Clin Psychopharmacol* 1988 **8(1)**, 13). *J Clin Psychopharmacol* **7**, 329–332.

Gorman J and Wolkow R (1994) *Sertraline as a Treatment for Panic Disorder.* Presented at the XIX CINP Meeting, Washington, DC, 1994.

Gray DS, Fujioka K, Devine W and Bray GA (1992a) Fluoxetine treatment of the obese diabetic. *Int J Obes* **16**, 193–198.

Gray DS, Fujioka K, Devine W and Bray GA (1992b) A randomized double-blind clinical trial of fluoxetine in obese diabetics. *Int J Obes* **16(Suppl 4)**, S67–72.

Gross MD (1991) Treatment of pathological jealousy by fluoxetine. *Am J Psychiatry* **48**, 683–684.

Gwirtsman HE, Guze BH, Yager J and Gainsley B (1990) Fluoxetine treatment of anorexia nervosa: an open clinical trial. *J Clin Psychiatry* **51**, 378–382.

Hirsch AR, Goodman JA and Malzer RL (1994) Fluoxetine hydrochloride in the treatment of chronic pain syndromes. *Headache Q* **4**, 350–351.

Hoehn-Saric R, Fawcett J, Munjack DJ and Roy-Byrne PP (1994) *A Multicentre, Double-blind, Placebo-controlled Study of Fluvoxamine in the Treatment of Panic Disorder.* Presented at the XIX CINP Meeting, Washington, DC, 1994.

Hoehn-Saric R, McLeod DR and Hipsley PA (1993) Effect of fluvoxamine on panic disorder. *J Clin Psychopharmacol* **13**, 321–326.

Holland RL (1994) *Fluvoxamine in Panic Disorder: After Discontinuation?* Presented at the XIX CINP Meeting, Washington, DC, 1994.

Holland RL, Fawcett, J, Hoehn-Saric R, Munjack DJ and Roy-Byrne PP (1994) *Long-term Treatment of Panic Disorder with Fluvoxamine in Outpatients Who Had Completed Double-blind Studies.* Presented at the XIX CINP Meeting, Washington, DC, 1994.

Hudson J, McElroy SL, Raymond NC, Crow S, Keck PE and Jonas JM (1994) *Fluvoxamine Treatment of Binge Eating Disorder: A Multicenter, Placebo-controlled Trial.* Presented at the American Psychiatric Association Annual Meeting, Philadelphia, 1994.

Hull JW, Clarkin JF and Alexopoulos GS (1993) Time series analysis of intervention effects. Fluoxetine therapy as a case illustration. *J Nerv Ment Dis* **181**, 48–53.

Jorgensen VT (1990) Cross-dressing successfully treated with fluoxetine. *NY State J Med* **90**, 566–567.

Kafka MP (1991) Successful treatment of paraphilic coercive disorder (a rapist) with fluoxetine hydrochloride. *Br J Psychiatry* **158**, 844–847.

Kafka MP and Prentky R (1992) Fluoxetine treatment of nonparaphilic sexual addictions and paraphilias in men. *J Clin Psychiatry* **53**, 351–358.

Katzelnick DJ, Greist JH, Jefferson JW and Kobak KA (1994) *Sertraline in Social Phobia: A Controlled Pilot Study.* Presented at the XIX CINP Meeting, Washington, DC, 1994.

Kavoussi RJ, Liu J and Coccaro EF (1994) An open trial of sertraline in personality disordered patients with impulsive aggression. *J Clin Psychiatry* **55**, 137–141.

Kaye WH, Weltzin TE, Hsu LKG and Bulik CM (1991) An open trial of fluoxetine in patients with anorexia nervosa. *J Clin Psychiatry* **52**, 464–471.

Kline NA, Dow BM, Brown SA and Matloff JL (1993) *Sertraline for PTSD with Comorbid Major Depression.* Presented at the American Psychiatric Association Annual Meeting, San Francisco, 1993.

Kramer J, Personal Communication, 11 December 1994.

Kranzler HR, Del-Boca F, Korner P and Brown J (1993) Adverse effects limit the usefulness of fluvoxamine for the treatment of alcoholism. *J Subst Abuse Treat* **10**, 283–287.

Kutnowski M, Daubresse JC, Friedman H, Kolanowski J, Krzentowski G, Scheen A, *et al.* (1992) Fluoxetine therapy in obese diabetic and glucose intolerant patients. *Int J Obes* **16 (Suppl 4)**, S63–66.

Langemark M and Olesen J (1994) Sulpiride and paroxetine in the treatment of chronic tension-type headache. An explanatory double-blind trial. *Headache* **34**, 20–24.

Lecrubier Y (1994) Paroxetine and clomipramine in the treatment of panic disorder. Presented at the Association for European Psychopharmacology Meeting, Copenhagen.

Lee HS, Song DH, Rhee HS, Jeon JY, Kee SW and Choi HK (1994) *An Open Trial of Fluoxetine in the Treatment of Premature Ejaculation.* Presented at the XIX CINP Meeting, Washington, DC, 1994.

Levine LR, Enas GG, Thompson WL, Byyny RL, Dauer AD, Kirby RD, *et al.* (1989) Use of fluoxetine, a selective serotonin-uptake inhibitor, in the treatment of obesity: a dose-response study. *Int J Obes* **13**, 635–645.

Maltazzi MA, Kinzie J and Luby ED (1994) Abstract No. 435. *Naltrexone in the Treatment of Anorexia and Bulimia Nervosa.* Presented at the Society for Biological Psychiatry Annual Meeting, Philadelphia, 1994.

Mancini CL (1995) *An Open Trial of Paroxetine in Social Phobia.* Presented at the American Psychiatric Association Annual Meeting, Miami, Fl, 1995.

Manna V, Bolino F and Di-Cicco L (1994) Chronic tension-type headache, mood depression and serotonin: therapeutic effects of fluvoxamine and mianserine. *Headache* **34**, 44–49.

March JS (1992) Fluoxetine and fluvoxamine in PTSD. *Psychiatry* **149**, 413.

Marcus MD, Wing RR, Ewing L, Kern E, McDermott M and Gooding W (1990) A double-blind, placebo-controlled trial of fluoxetine plus behavior modification in the treatment of obese binge-eaters and non-binge-eaters. *Am J Psychiatry* **147**, 876–881.

Markovitz PJ, Calabrese JR, Schulz SC and Meltzer HY (1991) Fluoxetine in the treatment of borderline and schizotypal personality disorders. *Am J Psychiatry* **148**, 1064–1067.

Martins EA, Pigott TA, Bernstein S, Doyle BB, Smolka VM and Dubbert B (1994) *Sertraline Pharmacotherapy in Patients with Social Phobia.* Presented at the American Psychiatric Association Annual Meeting, Philadelphia, 1994.

Max MB, Lynch SA, Muir J, Shoaf SE, Smoller B and Dubner R (1992) Effects of desipramine, amitriptyline, and fluoxetine on pain in diabetic neuropathy. *N Engl J Med* **326**, 1250–1256.

Megen H van, Westenberg H and Boer J den (1994) *Effect of the Selective Serotonin Reuptake Inhibitor (SSRI) Fluvoxamine on CCK-4 Induced Panic Attacks.* Presented at the XIX CINP Meeting, Washington, DC, 1994.

Meudels J, Camera A (1994) Sertraline treatment for premature ejaculation. Presented at the XIX CINP meeting, Washington, DC.

Menkes DB, Taghavi E, Mason PA and Howard RC (1993) Fluoxetine's spectrum of action in premenstrual syndrome. *Int Clin Psychopharmacol* **8**, 95–102.

Munjack D (1994) *Zoloft (Sertraline) in the Treatment of Social Phobia.* Presented at the XIX CINP Meeting, Washington, DC, 1994.

Nagy LM, Morgan CA, Southwick SM and Charney DS (1993) Open prospective trial of fluoxetine for posttraumatic stress disorder. *J Clin Psychopharmacol* **13**, 107–113.

Naranjo CA, Bremner KE and Poulos CX (1994) *Research Strategies to Assess Pharmacotherapies for Alcoholism.* Presented at the XIX CINP Meeting, Washington, DC, 1994. Norden MJ (1989) Fluoxetine in borderline personality disorder. *Prog Neuropsychopharmacol Biol Psychiatry* **13**, 885–893.

Norden MJ (1989) Fluoxetine in borderline personality disorder. *Prog Neuropsychopharmacol Biol Psychiatry* **13**, 885–893.

Norden MJ (1991) *Borderline Patients on Maintenance Fluoxetine.* Presented at the American Psychiatric Association Annual Meeting, New Orleans, 1991.

O'Brien K (1994) *Depression Seen During Alcohol Detoxification: Early Intervention with Sertraline.* Presented at the XIX CINP Meeting, Washington, DC, 1994.

Oehrberg *et al.* (1995) Paroxetine in the treatment of panic disorder, a randomised double blind placebo controlled study. *Br J Psychiatry* **187**, 374–379.

O'Kane M, Wiles PG and Wales JK (1994) Fluoxetine in the treatment of obese Type 2 diabetic patients. *Diabetic Med* **11**, 105–110.

Pearlstein TB, Stone AB (1994) Long-term treatment of late luteal phase dysphoric disorder. *J Clin Psychiatry* **55**(8, Aug), 332–335.

Perilstein RD, Lipper S and Friedman LJ (1991) Three cases of paraphilias responsive to fluoxetine treatment. *J Clin Psychiatry* **52**, 169–170.

Pollack MH and Rosenbaum JF (1991) Fluoxetine treatment of cocaine abuse in heroin addicts. *J Clin Psychiatry* **52**, 31–33.

Power-Smith P (1994) Beneficial sexual side-effects from fluoxetine. *Br J Psychiatry* **164**, 249–250.

Rasmussen JGC (1991) *Comparative Effects of Selective Serotonin Uptake Inhibitors Paroxetine and Fluoxetine on Food Intake in Rats and Effect of Paroxetine on Body Weight in Depressed Patients.* Presented at the American Psychiatric Association Annual Meeting, New Orleans, 1991.

Rasmussen SA, Griest JH, Jenike MA and Robinson DG (1992) *A Multicenter Trial of Fluvoxamine in OCD.* Presented at the American Psychiatric Association Annual Meeting, Washington, DC, 1992.

Richardson NR and Roberts DC (1991) Fluoxetine pretreatment reduces breaking points on a progressive ratio schedule reinforced by intravenous cocaine self-administration in the rat. *Life Sci* **49**, 833–840.

Ringold AL (1994) Paroxetine efficacy in social phobia. *J Clin Psychiatry* **55**, 363–364.

Robert JM and Lydiard RB (1993) Sertraline in the treatment of bulimia nervosa. *Am J Psychiatry* **150**, 1753.

Russell J, Beumont P, Touyz S, Buckley K, Lowinger K and Talbot P (1994) *Fluoxetine and the Management of Bulimia Nervosa.* Presented at the XIX CINP Meeting, Washington, DC, 1994.

Salzman C (1994) *Effect of Fluoxetine on Anger in Borderline Personality Disorder.* Presented at the XIX CINP Meeting, Washington, DC, 1994.

Salzman C, Schatzberg AF, Miyawaki E, Albanese M, Wolfson A and Looper J (1992) *Fluoxetine in BPD.* Presented at the American Psychiatric Association Annual Meeting, Washington, DC, 1992.

Sandrini G, Ruiz L, Patruno G, Bussone G, Verri AP and Nappi G (1991) Antalgic and antidepressant activities of fluoxetine in daily chronic headache. *Cephalalgia* **11 (11 Suppl)**, 280–281.

Schneier FR, Chin SJ, Hollander E and Liebowitz MR (1992) Fluoxetine in social phobia. *J Clin Psychopharmacol* **12**, 62–64.

Schneier FR, Liebowitz MR, Davies SO, Fairbanks J, Hollander E, Campeas R, et al. (1990) Fluoxetine in panic disorder. *J Clin Psychopharmacol* **10**, 119–121.

Servant D, Bailly D, Le-Seach H and Parquet PJ (1990) Obsessive–compulsive symptoms associated with panic disorder. Predictive factor of a good therapeutic response to fluvoxamine. *Encephale* **16**, 359–362.

Sheehan DV (1984) Delineation of anxiety and phobic disorders responsive to monoamine oxidase inhibitors: implications for classification. *J Clin Psychiatry* **45 (7 Pt 2)**, 29–36.

Sindrup SH, Bjerre U, Dejgaard A, Brosen K, Aaes-Jorgensen T and Gram LF (1992) The selective serotonin reuptake inhibitor citalopram relieves the symptoms of diabetic neuropathy. *Clin Pharmacol Ther*, **52**, 547–552.

Sindrup SH, Gram LF, Brsen K, Eshj O and Mogensen EF (1990) The selective serotonin reuptake inhibitor paroxetine is effective in the treatment of diabetic neuropathy symptoms. *Pain* **42**, 135–144.

Sindrup SH, Grodum E, Gram LF and Beck-Nielsen H (1991) Concentration-response relationship in paroxetine treatment of diabetic neuropathy symptoms: A patient-blinded dose-escalation study. *Ther Drug Monit* **13**, 408–414.

Solyom L, Solyom C and Ledwidge B (1991) Fluoxetine in panic disorder. *Can J Psychiatry* **36**, 378–380.

Steiner M (1994) *Fluoxetine in the Treatment of LLPDD: A Multicentre, Placebo-controlled, Double-blind Trial.* Presented at the XIX CINP Meeting, Washington, DC, 1994.

Steiner M, Oakes R, Gergel IP, Burnham DB and Wheadon DE (1995) *A Fixed Dose Study of Paroxetine and Placebo in the Treatment of Panic Disorder.* Presented at the American Psychiatric Association Annual Meeting, Miami FL, 1995.

Steiner M, Oakes R, Gergel IP and Wheadon DE (1994) *Predictors of Response to Paroxetine Therapy in OCD.* Presented at the American Psychiatric Association Annual Meeting, Philadelphia, 1994.

Sternbach H (1990) Fluoxetine treatment of social phobia. *J Clin Psychopharmacol* **10**, 230–231.

Theesen KA and Marsh WR (1989) Relief of diabetic neuropathy with fluoxetine. *DICP* **23**, 572–574.

Tollefson GD, Rampey AH Jr, Potvin JH, Jenike MA, Rush AJ, Dominguez RA, et al. (1994) A multicenter investigation of fixed-dose fluoxetine in the treatment of obsessive–compulsive disorder. *Arch Gen Psychiatry* **51**, 559–567.

Van-Ameringen M, Mancini C and Streiner DL (1993) Fluoxetine efficacy in social phobia. *J Clin Psychiatry* **54**, 27–32.

Van Ameringen M, Mancini C and Streiner D (1994) Sertraline in social phobia. *J Affect Disord* **31**, 141–145.

Vaz FJ and Salcedo MS (1994) Fluoxetine-induced anorexia in a bulimic patient with antecedents of anorexia nervosa (2). *J Clin Psychiatry* **55**, 118–119.

Viswanathan R and Paradis C (1991) Treatment of cancer phobia with fluoxetine. *Am J Psychiatry* **148**, 1090.

Wagstaff AJ and McTavish D (1994) Tacrine. A review of its pharmacodynamic and pharmacokinetic properties, and therapeutic efficacy in Alzheimer's disease. *Drugs Aging* **4**, 510–540.

Waldinger MD, Hengeveld MW and Zwinderman AH (1994) Paroxetine treatment of premature ejaculation: a double-blind, randomized, placebo-controlled study. *Am J Psychiatry* **151**, 1377–1379.

Wilcox JA (1987) Abuse of fluoxetine by a patient with anorexia nervosa. *Am J Psychiatry* **144**, 1100.

Wing YK, Lee S, Chiu HFK, Ho CKW and Chen CN (1994) A patient with coexisting narcolepsy and morbid jealousy showing favourable response to fluoxetine. *Postgrad Med J* **70**, 34–36.

Wise SD (1992) Clinical studies with fluoxetine in obesity. *Am J Clin Nutr* **55**, 181S–184S.

Wood SH, Mortola JF, Chan YF, Moossazadeh F and Yen SS (1992) Treatment of premenstrual syndrome with fluoxetine: a double-blind, placebo-controlled, crossover study. *Obstet Gynecol* **80(3 Pt 1)**, 339–344.

Woods S, Black D, Brown S, Asnis G, Potkin S, Hameedi F, *et al.* (1994) *Fluvoxamine in the Treatment of Panic Disorder in Outpatients: A Double-blind, Placebo-controlled Study.* Presented at the XIX CINP Meeting, Washington, DC, 1994.

Yonkers KA, Williams AS, Novak K and Rush AJ (1994) *Paroxetine for the Treatment of Premenstrual Dysphoric Disorder.* Presented at the XIX CINP Meeting, Washington, DC, 1994.

Zohar J, Kaplan Z and Benjamin J (1994a) Compulsive exhibitionism successfully treated with fluvoxamine: A controlled case study. *J Clin Psychiatry* **55**, 86–88.

Zohar J, Kaplan Z, Benjamin J and Rasmussen SA (1994b) Compulsive exhibitionism successfully treated with fluvoxamine: A controlled case study. *J Clin Psychiatry* **55**, 86–91.

14

Safety and tolerability of selective serotonin re-uptake inhibitors

William F. Boyer and John P. Feighner

One of the major reasons for the SSRIs' importance is their improved side-effect profile compared to tricyclic antidepressants (TCAs) and monoamine oxidase inhibitors (MAOIs). This chapter reviews topics related to the acceptability of SSRIs compared to first generation antidepressants and specific safety issues pertaining to the SSRIs. It is not the intention to review exhaustively all adverse events which may be related to SSRIs. Instead those issues which are most common and/or important will be highlighted. Management of side-effects is covered in Chapter 15.

PATIENT DROP-OUT RATES

A gross measure of the tolerability of one drug compared to another is the proportion of people who stop taking each due to side-effects. Montgomery and colleagues (1994) published a meta-analysis of 42 published controlled SSRI studies which examined this question. They found that significantly fewer patients on SSRIs compared to TCAs discontinued their medication due to side-effects (14.9% versus 19%, $p < 0.01$). This is consistent with both another meta-analysis by Song *et al.* (1993) which found a strong trend for SSRIs to be associated with fewer side-effect related dropouts (15.4% versus 18.8% on TCAs, $p = 0.06$) and with clinical trial data from the Feighner Research Institute (1994) (SSRI drop-outs due to adverse effects, 14%; TCA drop-outs, 21%; $p = 0.015$). All of these studies employed more

Selective Serotonin Re-uptake Inhibitors: Advances in Basic Research and Clinical Practice, Second Edition, Edited by J.P. Feighner and W.F. Boyer
© 1996 John Wiley & Sons Ltd

conservative two-tailed tests of significance, which implies that there is equal reason to think that SSRIs might be associated with significantly *more* side-effect related dropouts than TCAs. If one-tailed tests are used the *p* levels would be half of those reported. Furthermore, naturalistic studies indicate that patients prescribed a second-generation antidepressant, which includes SSRIs, are significantly more likely than those given a TCA to have their initial prescriptions refilled (Katon *et al.*, 1992).

SSRIs and TCAs differ, as groups, in patient acceptability. Marked differences between the SSRIs themselves are not apparent. Direct comparative studies of fluoxetine and paroxetine (Shrivastava *et al.*, 1993; Tignol, 1992; De Wilde *et al.*, 1993; Garcia-Barriga, 1994; Geretsegger *et al.*, 1994; Schone and Ludwig, 1993) and fluoxetine and sertraline (Schone and Ludwig, 1993; Martindale and Bennie, 1993) have not shown any consistent and clinically meaningful differences in the frequency of specific adverse events.

COMMON SIDE-EFFECTS

Gastrointestinal

The most common side-effect associated with SSRI therapy is nausea. Figure 1 illustrates data from 94 published studies of over 5000 patients treated with fluvoxamine, fluoxetine, paroxetine or sertraline (Ottervanger, 1994). The figure shows two important points, that the incidence of nausea is approximately the same for all four antidepressants (25–30%) and that the incidence of severe nausea, as reflected by patients who discontinued the antidepressant for that reason, was relatively low.

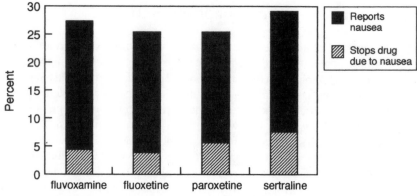

Figure 1. Compiled incidence of nausea for four SSRIs.

Weight loss

Fluoxetine and sertraline are often associated with weight loss, especially in higher doses (fluoxetine $\geqslant 60$ mg/day, sertraline $\geqslant 150$ mg/day). Fluvoxamine, paroxetine and citalopram tend to be more weight-neutral, although the effect of higher doses of these agents on weight has not been systematically studied (Abell *et al.*, 1986; Wilde *et al.*, 1993; Lyby *et al.*, 1988). The absolute amount of weight loss usually depends on the initial degree of obesity, which suggests that weight loss in normal weight individuals should not be a clinically significant problem. However Brymer and Winograd (1992) found that depressed, medically ill patients over age 75 experienced significantly more weight loss than similar patients, aged 61–75. The frequency and clinical significance of this occurrence remains to be determined.

Other gastrointestinal side-effects include diarrhoea, constipation, dyspepsia, vomiting, abdominal pain, anorexia, dry mouth, flatulence, taste change, increased appetite and increased weight. Diarrhoea may be somewhat more common with sertraline, and dry mouth and constipation may occur slightly more often with paroxetine. In general there is little difference between the SSRIs in the incidence of these side-effects.

Headache

The second most commonly reported side-effect of SSRIs is often headache. However the incidence of headache reported with SSRIs is only slightly more than that reported with placebo. This is illustrated in Figure 2, which shows data compiled from US package insert data for fluoxetine, sertraline and paroxetine. In some individuals SSRIs significantly reduce the frequency of headache (Adly *et al.*, 1992; Diamond and Freitag, 1989; Sandrini *et al.*, 1991; Manna *et al.*, 1994).

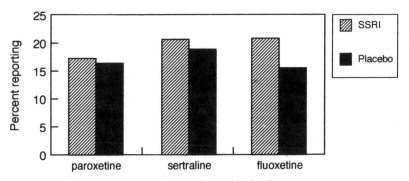

Figure 2. Incidence of headaches on active drug and placebo.

Sexual

Perhaps the most troublesome side-effects of SSRI treatment are sexual side-effects, which usually are diminished libido and delayed orgasm or complete anorgasmia. Sexual side-effects tend to be dose-related but generally do not significantly improve over time.

As shown in Figure 3 the frequency of sexual side-effects of SSRIs in published reports are not dramatically different between SSRIs and amitriptyline or imipramine. The frequency of sexual side-effects is also much less than that associated with clomipramine and phenelzine (Monteiro *et al.*, 1987 Kelly *et al.*, 1994; Harrison *et al.*, 1986). Unusual sexual side-effects associated with SSRIs include increased libido, sexual preoccupation, spontaneous orgasm and priapism (Balon, 1994; Mendelson and Franko, 1994).

The reputation of SSRIs as causing sexual side-effects may be due to at least two factors. One is that these side-effects, like many, tend to occur on a continuum. This means that the harder they are sought the more often they will be found. If a drug has a reputation as causing side effect "X" then more clinicians will look for X and find it. An increase in the publicity surrounding sexual side-effects means that more patients are aware of the potential for such adverse reactions and will be more likely to report them. The other reason is that because SSRI-treated patients generally do not have the sedation, dry mouth, weight gain, etc. of TCAs to tolerate they are more likely to notice and complain of the side-effects they do have.

Insomnia

Insomnia is both commonly associated with SSRI therapy and a primary symptom of depression. Like other antidepressants, SSRIs tend to increase rapid eye movement

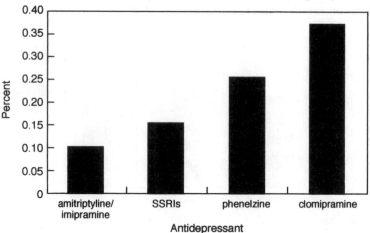

Figure 3. Reported incidence of adverse effect of antidepressants on ejaculation/orgasm.

(REM) latency and reduce REM sleep (Oswald and Adam, 1986; Staner *et al.*, 1992; von-Bardeleben *et al.*, 1989; Nicholson and Pascoe, 1988; Kerkhofs *et al.*, 1990; Winokur *et al.*, 1992; Kupfer *et al.*, 1991). Comparative studies of SSRIs and TCAs suggest the latter may sometimes have more beneficial effects on sleep continuity (Nicholson and Pascoe, 1988; Kerkhofs *et al.*, 1990; Kupfer *et al.*, 1991). It may be that TCAs, by virtue of their sedative, anticholinergic and antihistaminergic side-effects, may have a primary hypnotic effect which SSRIs lack. However SSRIs also tend to improve sleep in depressed patients. Saterlee and colleagues (1994) investigated changes in depression and sleep disturbance among 89 patients with DSM III R major depression. Both depression and sleep were rated on the Hamilton Depression Rating Scale (HAMD). Fluoxetine-treated patients tended to have greater improvement on HAMD sleep items and were less likely to experience worsening of their sleep disturbance during the first week of treatment than patients given placebo.

Anxiety/agitation

"Anxiety" subsumes a number of related terms, including anxiety, agitation and jitteriness. There is also an overlap in some cases with akathisia. It is important to distinguish between anxiety as a side-effect and anxiety as a symptom of depression. Data clearly shows that antidepressant therapy, including SSRIs, decreases anxiety associated with depression (Dunbar and Fuell, 1992; Tollefson *et al.*, 1994; Moon *et al.*, 1994). However, some patients experience an increase in anxiety within the first few weeks of SSRI therapy, which typically resolves within a few weeks. Baseline anxiety or agitation does not appear to predict this side-effect, but panic attacks may (Dunbar and Fuell, 1994; Tollefson *et al.*, 1994). There are also reports of panic attacks which appeared *de novo* following the start of fluoxetine or sertraline therapy (Zinner, 1994; Altshuler, 1994).

SOME LESS COMMON SIDE-EFFECTS

Extrapyramidal side-effects (EPS)

EPS are a rare but dramatic side-effect of SSRI treatment. They have taken several forms. Parkinsonian symptoms have worsened or appeared during fluoxetine therapy (Chouinard and Sultan, 1992; Bouchard *et al.*, 1989) or following the addition of fluoxetine to carbamazepine (Keppel-Hesselink *et al.*, 1992; Touw *et al.*, 1992; Jansen and Kolling, 1992). Akathisia has been reported with fluoxetine (Lipinski *et al.*, 1989; Friedman, 1990; Wirshing *et al.*, 1991; Bertschy and Vandel, 1993; Maany and Dhopesh, 1990), fluvoxamine (Ansseau *et al.*, 1991) and sertraline (Opler, 1994; Klee and Kronig, 1993; Settle, 1993; LaPorta, 1993). Akathisia is postulated to provoke suicidal ideation in some patients (Wirshing *et al.*, 1991; Rothschild and Locke, 1991; Teicher *et al.*, 1993; Hamilton and Opler, 1992; Wirshing *et al.*, 1992). Dystonias have also been reported with fluoxetine (Meltzer *et al.*, 1979; Reccoppa *et al.*, 1990; Dave, 1994; Rio *et al.*, 1992; Black and Uhde, 1992; Coulter and Pillans, 1995), fluvoxamine (Rovei *et al.*, 1983) and paroxetine (Berk, 1993). Dyskinesias have been described with fluoxetine (Coulter and Pillans, 1995; Stein, 1991; Budman and Bruun, 1991; Mander *et al.*, 1994; Madi *et al.*, 1994; Fallon and Liebowitz, 1991) and fluvoxamine (Arya and Szabadi, 1993). In at least one instance the dyskinesia was described as persistent (Budman and Bruun, 1991).

Given these case reports one might expect SSRIs routinely to worsen EPS when given to patients with schizophrenia. In fact this does not always occur. Paroxetine, 20 mg/day, did not worsen EPS in 40 schizophrenics taking neuroleptics (Chiaie *et al.*, 1994). In a series of eight schizophrenic patients fluoxetine was associated with a 20% increase in haloperidol levels. EPS scores did not increase in these patients (Goff *et al.*, 1991). In another series of nine patients fluoxetine raised haloperidol levels an average of 45% and some of these patients experienced worse EPS (Ames *et al.*, 1993). Given this limited information it appears that the mechanism of increased EPS in psychotic patients may be interference with the antipsychotic's metabolism, which may be manageable by reduction of the antipsychotic dose. In many of the case reports involving patients with affective disorders the patient was not receiving an antipsychotic, so the mechanism of increased EPS must be different and may require the SSRI to be stopped. In fact there must be more than one mechanism involved as illustrated by a case report of EPS occurring after fluoxetine was *discontinued* (Stoukides and Stoukides, 1991).

Beasley and Potvin (1993) evaluated adverse event data from a fixed-dose study comparing placebo and fluoxetine, 5, 20 and 40 mg/day, in the treatment of major depression disorder ($N = 363$) and the pooled data from two fixed-dose studies comparing placebo and fluoxetine, 20, 40 and 60 mg/day, in the treatment of major depression disorder ($N = 746$). The adverse events "nervousness", "anxiety", "agitation" and "insomnia" were considered indicative of activation; "somnolence" and "asthenia" were considered indicative of sedation. Activation and sedation were both statistically significant treatment-emergent phenomena ($p \leqslant 0.05$), but dose-effect relationships differed. Activation rates were relatively stable between 5 mg/day and 40 mg/day, but they increased at 60 mg/day. Sedation rates increased linearly up to 40 mg/day, and then were comparable at 40 mg/day and 60 mg/day. Discontinuations due to either phenomenon were uncommon. The temporal patterns of first occurrences and persistence of activation and sedation differed. First occurrences of activation peaked early and declined over time at all doses. First occurrences of sedation also peaked early at all doses, but there may have been greater variability in first occurrences of sedation over time in patients receiving lower doses. The persistent occurrences of sedation may decline less over time than the persistent occurrences of activation.

Bleeding problems

Several groups have reported patients who developed easy bruising or increased bleeding tendencies while undergoing treatment with fluoxetine or fluvoxamine (Humphries *et al.*, 1990; Ottervanger *et al.*, 1993; Eisenhauer and Jermain, 1993; Yaryura-Tobias *et al.*, 1991). An increased bleeding tendency was reported with paroxetine administered by itself (Ottervanger *et al.*, 1994) and when co-administered with warfarin (Bannister *et al.*, 1989). Stanford and Patton (1993) found increased skin haematoma formation in newborn rats whose mothers had been treated with fluoxetine. They recommended caution with prolonged fluoxetine treatment during pregnancy. The mechanism of this effect is thought to involve inhibition of platelet serotonin uptake. Bleeding time may or may not be increased, but platelet aggregation tests may be abnormal (Alderman *et al.*, 1992). Although problems with increased bleeding have not been published for sertraline, fluvoxamine or citalopram, it would be premature to conclude that these medications are free of this adverse effect.

Bradycardia

Tricyclic antidepressants characteristically increase the pulse rate through both noradrenergic uptake blockade and inhibition of the vagus nerve's inhibitory effect. Para-chloroamphetamine, an indirect serotonin agonist, causes bradycardia and hypotension in laboratory rats (Robertson *et al.*, 1988). Clinically significant SSRI-induced bradycardia may be more common in the elderly and those with known cardiac disease (Buff *et al.*, 1991; Ahmed and Zaheeruddin, 1991; Masquelier *et al.*, 1993; Hussein and Kaufman, 1994). However middle-aged patients have also been reported to experience this adverse effect (Feder, 1991; Ellison *et al.*, 1990). Most of these reports have concerned fluoxetine, which is probably a function of its widespread use rather than any special toxicity. Fluvoxamine has been linked with bradycardia when taken in overdose (Garnier *et al.*, 1993; Langlois and Paquette, 1994) and symptomatic bradycardia was reported in trials of citalopram (Dufour *et al.*, 1987) and sertraline (Fisch and Knoebel, 1992).

There is a disease entity of vagally mediated position-sensitive hypotension and bradycardia. Grubb and colleagues (1993, 1994) have reported that both fluoxetine and sertraline are helpful in patients with this syndrome who are unresponsive to standard therapy.

Hyponatremia

Hyponatremia and/or SIADH has been reported with fluoxetine (Hwang and Magraw, 1989; Cohen *et al.*, 1990; Ahmed *et al.*, 1993; Blacksten and Birt, 1993; Ten-Holt *et al.*, 1994; Schillinger *et al.*, 1994), fluvoxamine (Ball, 1993; Baliga and

McHardy, 1993; Scrimali *et al.*, 1994), sertraline (Doshi and Borison, 1994; Crews *et al.*, 1993; Llorente *et al.*, 1994) and paroxetine (Lisi, 1993). The elderly may be especially at risk (Llorente *et al.*, 1994; Gommans and Edwards, 1990; Vrtovsnik *et al.*, 1992, 1993; Jeandel *et al.*, 1993; Vishwanath *et al.*, 1991; Marik *et al.*, 1990; Staab *et al.*, 1990; Van-Iperen *et al.*, 1994). Hyponatremia resolves upon cessation of the SSRI.

DRUG INTERACTIONS

Alcohol

Considerable research indicates that SSRIs do not interact with alcohol in any clinically meaningful way (Allen and Lader, 1989; Schaffler, 1986, 1989; Lemberger *et al.*, 1985; Lader *et al.*, 1986; McClelland and Raptopoulos, 1985; Hindmarch and Harrison, 1988; Cooper *et al.*, 1989; Hindmarch *et al.*, 1990; Kerr *et al.*, 1992; van-Harten *et al.*, 1992). The psychomotor impairment caused by alcohol may, in some situations, be antagonized by SSRIs (Schaffler, 1986; McClelland and Raptopoulos, 1985).

The serotonin syndrome

The most serious drug interaction involving the SSRIs is the serotonin syndrome. Sternbach (1991) suggested the following criteria for diagnosis of the serotonin syndrome:

1. Coincident with the addition of or increase in a known serotonergic agent to an established medication regimen, at least three of the following clinical features are present:

   • mental status changes (confusion, hypomania)
   • agitation
   • myoclonus
   • hyperreflexia
   • diaphoresis
   • shivering
   • tremor
   • diarrhoea
   • incoordination
   • fever

2. Other aetiologies (e.g. infectious, metabolic, substance abuse or withdrawal) have been ruled out.
3. A neuroleptic had not been started or increased in dosage prior to the onset of the signs and symptoms listed above.

The serotonin syndrome ranges in severity from very mild to lethal. Most reported cases have involved use of an SSRI in conjunction with or in close temporal proximity to phenelzine or tranylcypromine therapy (Graham and Ilett, 1988; Feighner *et al.*, 1990; Beasley *et al.*, 1993; Graber *et al.*, 1994; Bhatara and Bandettini, 1993). However, none of the MAOIs should be considered safe when used with an SSRI. The serotonin syndrome has been reported in conjunction with sertraline plus isocarboxazid (Brannan *et al.*, 1994). Joffe and Bakish (1994) reported good results in the treatment of 11 patients with resistant depression when they combined fluvoxamine or sertraline with moclobemide. However, a fatal interaction has been reported between citalopram and moclobemide (Neuvonen *et al.*, 1994). Similarly, Waters (1994) reported no serious or unusual side-effects in 23 patients who received fluoxetine plus selegiline but the serotonin syndrome has been reported with this combination as well (Suchowersky and de Vries, 1990 Montastruc *et al.*, 1993; Jermain *et al.*, 1992).

In general, SSRIs and MAOIs should not be used concurrently. When switching from an SSRI to MAOI there should be sufficient time for the SSRI to "wash out" before the MAOI is started. For fluoxetine five weeks is recommended, but for sertraline, paroxetine, fluvoxamine and citalopram two weeks is sufficient. Clinicians should still hold a high index of suspicion, as there has been a reported case of the serotonin syndrome which occurred six weeks after fluoxetine was discontinued (Coplan and Gorman, 1993).

The serotonin syndrome has also been reported with the combination of lithium and either fluoxetine (Muly *et al.*, 1993; Archer *et al.*, 1985) or fluvoxamine (Ohman and Spigset, 1993), and fluoxetine plus carbamazepine (Dursun *et al.*, 1993; Gernaat *et al.*, 1991; Touw *et al.*, 1992; Keppel-Hesselink, 1992). A probable case was also reported when pentazocine was given to a patient being treated with fluoxetine (Hansen *et al.*, 1990). Fluoxetine plus L-tryptophan has also been implicated (Steiner and Fontaine, 1986). These drug combinations should not be considered contraindicated in the appropriate patient. The clinician should however bear these reports in mind when evaluating patient reports of adverse effects.

The serotonin syndrome is not limited to drug combinations involving the SSRIs. Clomipramine, which is a potent non-selective serotonin re-uptake inhibitor, has frequently been implicated (Neuvonen *et al.*, 1994; Spigset *et al.*, 1993; Kojima *et al.*, 1993). In one series 10 of 38 depressed inpatients treated with TCAs had symptoms of the serotonin syndrome, tremor plus myoclonus, diaphoresis, and shivering (Lejoyeux *et al.*, 1993). One of us (WB) has seen a case which involved the concomitant use of phenelzine and desipramine.

The serotonin syndrome is most commonly treated supportively. There are also case reports of its successful treatment with drugs which antagonize serotonin's effects, such as cyproheptadine (Lappin and Auchincloss, 1994), methysergide (Sandyk, 1986) and inderal (Guze and Baxter, 1986). Cyproheptadine and methysergide also attenuate the serotonin syndrome in laboratory animals (Marley and Wozniak, 1984).

Interactions with mood-stabilizer medications

Studies of lithium combined with sertraline, fluvoxamine, paroxetine or citalopram have shown no pharmacokinetic interactions (Stellamans, 1991; Souche *et al.*, 1991; Andersen *et al.*, 1991; Hendrickx and Floris, 1991). Other investigators have found no interaction between carbamazepine and paroxetine, fluoxetine or fluvoxamine (Andersen *et al.*, 1991; Spina *et al.*, 1993) or between paroxetine and either valproate or phenytoin (Andersen *et al.*, 1991). Most of these studies were performed with small samples and some with healthy volunteers. Clinical experience shows that interactions may sometimes occur.

The SSRIs have been reported to raise blood levels of both anticonvulsants and lithium in some individuals. Increased phenytoin levels have been described with the administration of fluoxetine plus phenytoin (Woods *et al.*, 1994; Darley, 1994; Jalil, 1992). Similarly, increased carbamazepine levels with toxic symptoms have been reported with the combination of fluvoxamine, sertraline or fluoxetine and carbamazepine (Martinelli *et al.*, 1993; Pearson, 1990; Fritz *et al.*, 1991; Joblin and Ghose, 1994; Joblin, 1994; Lane, 1994). Fluoxetine appeared to raise blood levels of valproic acid in another case report (Sovner and Davis, 1991). Fluvoxamine raises plasma methadone levels (Bertschy *et al.*, 1994a) although fluoxetine many not (Bertschy *et al.*, 1994b). Fluoxetine has been reported to potentiate the effects of calcium channel blockers (Sternbach, 1991b). Fluoxetine or fluvoxamine given in conjunction with lithium may raise serum lithium levels and/or produce toxic reactions in some individuals (Salama and Shafey, 1989a, b; Noveske *et al.*, 1989; Evans and Marwick, 1990; Sacristan *et al.*, 1991; Wright and Seth, 1992; Hadley and Cason, 1989).

Other interactions

There is a potential interaction between SSRIs and drugs metabolized through the cytochrome P450 enzyme system. These include tricyclic antidepressants, antipsychotics and type 1c antiarrhythmics (propafenone, flecainide, ecainide), beta-blockers, benzodiazepines, phenobarbital and cimetidine. The hepatic mechanisms involved in these drug interactions are discussed in detail in Chapter 4.

Because SSRIs are tightly protein-bound there is the potential for an interaction with other such medications, such as digoxin and warfarin. These interactions might result in higher unbound fractions of the SSRI, digoxin or warfarin, or both. A case of fluoxetine–warfarin interaction has been reported (Woolfrey *et al.*, 1993).

Both neurotoxicity and severe bradycardia have been reported with the concomitant administration of paroxetine or fluoxetine with pimozide (Ahmed *et al.*, 1993; Darley, 1994, Horrigan and Barnhill, 1994; Hansen-Grant *et al.*, 1993). Increased theophylline levels with signs of toxicity have been reported with the combination of fluvoxamine and theophylline (Sperber, 1991). Visual hallucinations have been reported after combining fluoxetine and dextromethorphan (Achamallah, 1992).

Preventing drug interactions

Given the long list of interactions just discussed, there is the danger of losing track of the fact that serious drug–drug interactions are much less of a problem with SSRIs than they were with either TCAs or MAOIs. Most of the interactions presented in this chapter, when they occur, do so because of inhibition of the metabolism of the non-SSRI. The most important principle in the safe use of SSRIs with other medications is to be aware of this possibility. If the non-SSRI is started first, addition of the SSRI may produce increased blood levels of the non-SSRI which may result in increased side-effects. Dosage reduction of the non-SSRI may be appropriate. If the non-SSRI is added after the SSRI the patient may not need a standard dose of the second agent or may experience side-effects of the non-SSRI at what appears to be a low dosage.

OTHER SAFETY TOPICS

Drug–disease interactions

A drug–disease interaction occurs when a drug exacerbates a particular illness. Most of these are actually drug–drug interactions. SSRIs have often been found to be helpful adjuncts in the treatment of schizophrenia (Goff *et al.*, 1990; Goldman and Janecek, 1990; Bacher and Ruskin, 1991; Silver and Nassar, 1992) although a minority of patients experience worsening symptoms (Bacher and Ruskin, 1991; Lindenmayer *et al.*, 1990; Rocco and De-Leo, 1992). SSRIs may theoretically aggravate a primary coagulopathy through their action on blood platelets. To our knowledge this has not been reported. Patients with sick sinus syndrome may be more at risk of developing symptomatic bradycardia from the slight lowering of pulse rate associated with SSRI treatment (Hussein and Kaufman, 1994).

Suicide

The media preoccupation with the alleged link between fluoxetine and suicide was an unfortunate footnote in the history of psychiatry, especially because much of the impetus came from a fringe religious organization with an anti-psychiatry agenda (Thomas, 1991; Behar, 1991). Several large-scale reviews of clinical trial data have shown that fluoxetine and other SSRIs are not associated with increases in suicidality (Beasley *et al.*, 1991, 1992; Wheadon *et al.*, 1992; Montgomery, 1989, 1991; Mewett, 1991; Kasper and Moeller, 1992; Henry *et al.*, 1992; Montgomery *et al.*, 1995). Data from clinical practice suggests that overdose attempts may be somewhat more likely with more noradrenergic compounds such as desipramine (Kapur *et al.*, 1992) (Figure 4). Rouillon and colleagues (1989) reported significantly more suicide attempts among patients treated with maprotiline, a relatively pure norepinephrine

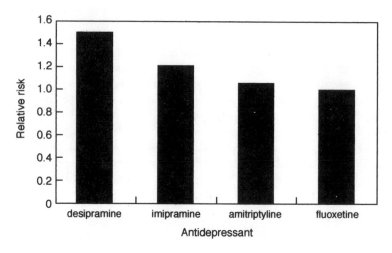

Figure 4. Relative risk of overdose among antidepressants.

uptake inhibitor, than patients who received placebo. These data are not strong enough to suggest that adrenergic antidepressants should be avoided in potentially suicidal patients, but they clearly do not support any *increased* risk of suicide with SSRIs.

Toxicity in overdose

One of the main advantages of SSRIs over first-generation antidepressants is their greatly reduced toxicity in overdose. Figure 5 illustrates findings from 87 overdose cases in which fluoxetine was the only drug taken. As can be seen, nearly half of all patients showed no symptoms at all. There is no evidence that SSRIs contribute to the lethality of other drugs taken in a mixed overdose, with the possible exception of prolonging TCA clearance (Rosenstein *et al.*, 1991).

Other SSRIs are associated with a similarly benign overdose experience (Boyer and Blumhardt, 1992; Doogan, 1991). Garnier and colleagues (1993) examined 299 cases of fluvoxamine overdose. The symptoms included drowsiness, tremor, nausea, vomiting, abdominal pain, bradycardia and anticholinergic effects. Seizures occurred in a few cases after doses of 1500 mg or more. Sinus bradycardia was noted with doses of less than 1000 mg, but was always moderate and required no treatment. Conduction abnormalities were rare.

Pregnancy

There is little data concerning the safety of SSRIs during pregnancy. In one series of 128 pregnancies women treated with fluoxetine or tricyclic antidepressants during

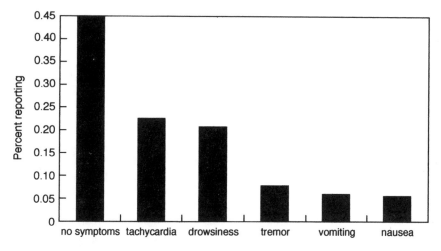

Figure 5. Frequency of side-effects with fluoxetine overdose (*n* = 87). Reproduced from Borys *et al.*, 1992 with permission.

the first trimester did not show an increased rate of fetal malformation but may have had an increased rate of spontaneous abortion (13.5% fluoxetine, 12.2% TCAs, 6.8% no teratogen exposure) (Pastuszak *et al.*, 1993). Seifritz and colleagues (1993) reported a case in which citalopram appeared to have no detrimental effect during the first trimester. Until more information is available it would be most prudent to avoid SSRI treatment, especially during the first trimester of pregnancy.

Withdrawal syndrome

Most of the cases of possible SSRI withdrawal symptoms have involved paroxetine. However withdrawal symptoms have been reported with all SSRIs as well as TCAs. A long list of symptoms has been reported with SSRIs, primarily nausea, vomiting, diarrhoea, vertigo and light-headedness (Barr *et al.*, 1994; Keuthen *et al.*, 1994). Sertraline withdrawal was associated with fatigue, abdominal cramps, memory impairment, insomnia, headache and sore eyes (Louie *et al.*, 1994). Hypomania and irritability was attributed to fluvoxamine withdrawal in one patient (Szabadi, 1992). Ellison (1994) reported that approximately 5% of patients withdrawn from fluoxetine, sertraline or paroxetine experience very brief episodes of disorientation and confusion with "shock-like" feelings for up to several weeks following discontinuation. Abrupt discontinuation of fluoxetine was blamed for the onset of pain in a patient with thalamic lesions (Lauterbach, 1994).

It seems unlikely that all of these disparate symptoms represent true withdrawal phenomena. The paroxetine-treated patients developed symptoms 1–10 days following drug discontinuation, which is not consistent with paroxetine's half-life of approximately 24 hours. Also contrary to expectation, more sleep disturbance was found in patients withdrawn from low-dose paroxetine (20 mg/day) than high-dose paroxetine (40 mg/day) (23% versus 11%) (Stoker and Eric, 1993). Withdrawal symptoms have not been reported in placebo controlled studies. None of the reports of withdrawal symptoms comes from placebo controlled studies, which is necessary to control for the effect of pill withdrawal. Clearly more data is needed to ascertain the nature and frequency of SSRI withdrawal symptoms.

CONCLUDING REMARKS

It is important to step back from the data presented in this chapter to appreciate some overall conclusions concerning the safety and tolerability of SSRIs. First, the SSRIs are, on average, much better tolerated than first generation antidepressants. Common side-effects such as nausea tend to be transient and prompt few patients to discontinue treatment. While less common side-effects do occur their frequency and clinical significance are uncertain. Because suicide is an ever-present possibility in depressive illness the greatly reduced toxicity of the SSRIs if taken in overdose is a major advantage. Clinically significant drug interactions are uncommon and tend to involve concomitant psychotropic medication, such as MAOIs (the serotonin syndrome), tricyclics or neuroleptics (elevated blood levels). The improved safety profile of SSRIs compared to first-generation antidepressants is one of the major reasons that this class of medication is so important.

REFERENCES

Abell CA, Farquhar DL, Galloway SM, Steven F, Philip AE and Munro JF (1986) Placebo controlled double-blind trial of fluvoxamine maleate in the obese. *J Psychosom Res* **30**, 143–146.

Achamallah NS (1992) Visual hallucinations after combining fluoxetine and dextromethorphan [letter]. *Am J Psychiatry* **149**, 1406.

Adly C, Straumanis J and Chesson A (1992) Fluoxetine prophylaxis of migraine. *Headache* **32**, 101–104.

Ahmed I, Dagincourt PG, Miller LG and Shader RI (1993) Possible interaction between fluoxetine and pimozide causing sinus bradycardia. *Can J Psychiatry* **38**, 62–63.

Ahmed SH and Zaheeruddin (1991) Early experience with fluoxetine. *J Pak Med Assoc* **41**, 275–277.

Alderman CP, Moritz CK and Ben-Tovim DI (1992) Abnormal platelet aggregation associated with fluoxetine therapy. *Ann Pharmacother* **26**, 1517–1519.

Allen D and Lader M (1989) Interactions of alcohol with amitriptyline, fluoxetine and placebo in normal subjects. *Int Clin Psychopharmacol* **4 (Suppl 1)**, 7–14.

Altshuler LL (1994) Fluoxetine-associated panic attacks. *J Clin Psychopharmacol* **14**, 433–434.

Ames D, Wirshing WC, Marder SR, Yuwiler A and Brammer GL (1993) Fluoxetine in haloperidol-stabilized schizophrenics. Presented at the American Psychiatric Association annual meeting, San Francisco, CA.

Andersen BB, Mikkelsen M, Vesterager A, Dam M, Kristensen HB and Pedersen B (1991) No influence of the antidepressant paroxetine on carbamazepine, valproate and phenytoin. *Epilepsy Res* **10**, 201–204.

Ansseau M, von-Frenckell R, Gerard MA, Mertens C, De-Wilde J and Botte L (1991) Interest of a loading dose of milnacipran in endogenous depressive inpatients. Comparison with the standard regimen and with fluvoxamine. *Eur Neuropsychopharmacol* **1**, 113–121.

Archer T, Tandberg B, Renyi L and Ross SB (1985) Antagonism of 5-methoxy-N, N-dimethyltryptamine-induced changes in postdecapitation convulsions in rats by repeated treatment with drugs enhancing 5-hydroxytryptamine neurotransmission. *J Pharm Pharmacol* **37**, 648–650.

Arya DK and Szabadi E (1993) Dyskinesia associated with fluvoxamine [letter]. *J Clin Psychopharmacol* **13**, 365–366.

Bacher NM and Ruskin P (1991) Addition of fluoxetine to treatment of schizophrenic patients. *Am J Psychiatry* **148**, 274–275.

Baliga RR and McHardy KC (1993) Syndrome of inappropriate antidiuretic hormone secretion due to fluvoxamine therapy [published erratum appears in *Br J Clin Pract* (1993) **47 (3)**:119]. *Br J Clin Pract* **47**, 62–63.

Ball CJ (1993) Fluvoxamine and SIADH [letter]. *Br J Clin Pract* **47**, 227.

Balon R (1994) Sexual obsessions associated with fluoxetine. *J Clin Psychiatry* **55**, 496.

Bannister SJ, Houser VP, Hulse JD, Kisicki JC and Rasmussen JGC (1989) Evaluation of the potential for interactions of paroxetine with diazepam, cimetidine, warfarin and digoxin. *Acta Psychiatr Scand* **80 (Suppl 350)**, 102–106.

Barr LC, Goodman WK and Price LH (1994) Physical symptoms associated with paroxetine discontinuation. *Am J Psychiatry* **151**, 289.

Beasley CM, Dornseif BE, Bosomworth JC, Sayler ME, Rampey AH and Heilegstein JH (1991) Fluoxetine and suicide: a meta-analysis of controlled trials of treatment for depression. *BMJ* **303**, 685–692.

Beasley CM Jr and Potvin JH (1993) Fluoxetine: activating and sedating effects. *Int Clin Psychopharmacol* **8**, 271–275.

Beasley CM Jr, Potvin JH, Masica DN, Wheadon DE, Bornseif BE and Genduso LA (1992) Fluoxetine: no association with suicidality in obsessive–compulsive disorder. *J Affect Disord* **24**, 1–10.

Beasley CM Jr, Masica DN, Heiligenstein JH, Wheadon DE and Zerbe RL (1993) Possible monoamine oxidase inhibitor-serotonin uptake inhibitor interaction: fluoxetine clinical data and preclinical findings. *J Clin Psychopharmacol* **13**, 312–320.

Behar R (1991) The thriving cult of greed and power: Ruined lives, lost fortunes, federal crimes. *Time* **137**, 50–58.

Berk M (1993) Paroxetine induces dystonia and parkinsonism in obsessive–compulsive disorder: 2. *Hum Psychopharmacol* **8**, 444–445.

Bertschy G, Baumann P, Eap CB and Baettig D (1994a) Probable metabolic interaction between methadone and fluvoxamine in addict patients. *Ther Drug Monit* **16**, 42–45.

Bertschy G, Eap CB and Baumann P (1994b) *Methadone Plasma Levels After Fluvoxamine or Fluoxetine Addition*. Presented at the XIX CINP Meeting, Washington, DC, 1994.

Bertschy G and Vandel S (1993) Fluoxetine-related indifference and akathisia. A case report [letter]. *Therapie* **48**, 158–159.

Bhatara VS and Bandettini FC (1993) Possible interaction between sertraline and tranylcypromine. *Clin Pharm* **12**, 222–225.

Black B and Uhde TW (1992) Acute dystonia and fluoxetine [letter; comment]. *J Clin Psychiatry* **53**, 327.

Blacksten JV and Birt JA (1993) Syndrome of inappropriate secretion of antidiuretic hormone secondary to fluoxetine. *Ann Pharmacother* **27**, 723–724.

Borys DJ, Setzer SC, Ling LJ, Reisdorf JJ, Day LC and Krenzelok EP (1992) Acute fluoxetine overdose: a report of 234 cases. *Am J Emerg Med* **10**, 115–120.

Bouchard RH, Pourcher E and Vincent P (1989) Fluoxetine and extrapyramidal side effects [letter]. *Am J Psychiatry* **146**, 1352–1353.

Boyer WF and Blumhardt CL (1992) The safety profile of paroxetine. *J Clin Psychiatry* **53** **(Suppl 6)**, 1–6.

Brannan SK, Talley BJ and Bowden CL (1994) Sertraline and isocarboxazid cause a serotonin syndrome. *J Clin Psychopharmacol* **14**, 144–145.

Brymer C and Winograd CH (1992) Fluoxetine in elderly patients: is there cause for concern? *J Am Geriatr Soc* **40**, 902–905.

Budman CL and Bruun RD (1991) Persistent dyskinesia in a patient receiving fluoxetine [letter]. *Am J Psychiatry* **148**, 1403.

Buff DD, Brenner R, Kirtane SS and Gilboa R (1991) Dysrhythmia associated with fluoxetine treatment in an elderly patient with cardiac disease. *J Clin Psychiatry* **52**, 174–176.

Chiaie RD, Brunetti G, Parise P, Riccio L and Pancheri P (1994) *Efficacy of Add-on Paroxetine Treatment on Negative Symptoms of Chronic Schizophrenia.* Presented at the XIX CINP Meeting, Washington, DC, 1994.

Chouinard G and Sultan S (1992) A case of Parkinson's disease exacerbated by fluoxetine. *Hum Psychopharmacol* **7**, 63–66.

Cohen BJ, Mahelsky M and Adler L (1990) More cases of SIADH with fluoxetine. *Am J Psychiatry* **147**, 948–949.

Cooper SM, Jackson D, Loudon JM, McClelland GR and Raptopoulos P (1989) The psychomotor effects of paroxetine alone and in combination with haloperidol, amylobarbitone, oxazepam, or alcohol. *Acta Psychiatr Scand* **80** **(Suppl 350)**, 53–55.

Coplan JD and Gorman JM (1993) Detectable levels of fluoxetine metabolites after discontinuation: an unexpected serotonin syndrome [letter]. *Am J Psychiatry* **150**, 837.

Coulter DM and Pillans PI (1995) Fluoxetine and extrapyramidal side effects. *Am J Psychiatry* **152**, 122–125.

Crews JR, Potts NL, Schreiber J and Lipper S (1993) Hyponatremia in a patient treated with sertraline [letter]. *Am J Psychiatry* **150**, 1564.

Darley J (1994) Interaction between phenytoin and fluoxetine. *Seizure* **3**, 151–152.

Dave M (1994) Fluoxetine-associated dystonia. *Am J Psychiatry* **151**, 149.

De-Wilde J, Spiers R, Mertens C, Bartholome F, Schotte G and Leyman S (1993) A double-blind, comparative, multicentre study comparing paroxetine with fluoxetine in depressed patients. *Acta Psychiatr Scand* **87**, 141–145.

Diamond S and Freitag FG (1989) The use of fluoxetine in the treatment of headache. *Clin J Pain* **5**, 200–201.

Doogan DP (1991) Toleration and safety of sertraline: experience worldwide. *Int Clin Psychopharmacol* **6** **(Suppl 2)**, 47–56.

Doshi D and Borison R (1994) Association of transient SIADH with sertraline. *Am J Psychiatry* **151**, 779–780.

Dufour H, Bouchacourt M, Thermoz P, Viala A, Phak-Rop P and Gouezo F (1987) Citalopram—a highly selective 5-HT uptake inhibitor—in the treatment of depressed patients. *Int Clin Psychopharmacol* **2**, 225–237.

Dunbar GC and Fuell DL (1992) The anti-anxiety and anti-agitation effects of paroxetine in depressed patients. *Int Clin Psychopharmacol* **6** **(Suppl 4)**, 81–90.

Dursun SM, Mathew VM and Reveley MA (1993) Toxic serotonin syndrome after fluoxetine plus carbamazepine [letter]. *Lancet* **342**, 442–443.

Eisenhauer G and Jermain DM (1993) Fluoxetine and tics in an adolescent. *Ann Pharmacother* **27**, 725–726.

Ellison JM (1994) SSRI withdrawal buzz. *J Clin Psychiatry* **55**, 544–545.

Ellison JM, Milofsky JE and Ely E (1990) Fluoxetine-induced bradycardia and syncope in two patients. *J Clin Psychiatry* **51**, 385–386.

Evans M and Marwick P (1990) Fluvoxamine and lithium: an unusual interaction. *Br J Psychiatry* **156**, 286.

Fallon BA and Liebowitz MR (1991) Fluoxetine and extrapyramidal symptoms in CNS lupus [letter]. *J Clin Psychopharmacol* **11**, 147–148.

Feder R (1991) Bradycardia and syncope induced by fluoxetine [letter]. *J Clin Psychiatry* **52**, 139.

Feighner Research Institute (1994) Data on file.

Feighner JP, Boyer WF, Tyler DL and Neborsky RJ (1990) Adverse consequences of fluoxetine-MAOI combination therapy. *J Clin Psychiatry* **51**, 222–225.

Fisch C and Knoebel SB (1992) Electrocardiographic findings in sertraline depression trials. *Drug Invest* **4**, 305–312.

Friedman EH (1990) Fluoxetine-induced akathisia in male OCD patients. *J Clin Psychiatry* **51**, 212.

Fritze J, Unsorg B and Lanczik M (1991) Interaction between carbamazepine and fluvoxamine. *Acta Psychiatr Scand* **84**, 583–584.

Garcia-Barriga AOC (1994) *A Double-blind Study With Paroxetine vs Fluoxetine in Depressive Patients.* Presented at the Society for Biological Psychiatry Annual Meeting, Washington, DC, 1994.

Garnier R, Azoyan P, Chataigner D, Taboulet P, Dellattre D and Efthymiou ML (1993) Acute fluvoxamine poisoning. *J Int Med Res* **21**, 197–208.

Geretsegger C, Bohmer F and Ludwig M (1994) Paroxetine in the elderly depressed patient: Randomized comparison with fluoxetine of efficacy, cognitive and behavioural effects. *Int Clin Psychopharmacol* **9**, 25–29.

Gernaat HB, Van-de-Woude J and Touw DJ (1991) Fluoxetine and parkinsonism in patients taking carbamazepine [letter]. *Am J Psychiatry* **148**, 1604–1605.

Goff DC, Brotman AW, Waites M and McCormick S (1990) Trial of fluoxetine added to neuroleptics for treatment-resistant schizophrenic patients. *Am J Psychiatry* **147**, 492–494.

Goff DC, Midha KK, Brotman AW, Waites M and Baldessarini RJ (1991) Elevation of plasma concentrations of haloperidol after the addition of fluoxetine. *Am J Psychiatry* **148**, 790–792.

Goldman MB and Janecek HM (1990) Adjunctive fluoxetine improves global function in chronic schizophrenia. *J Neuropsychiatry Clin Neurosci* **2**, 429–431.

Gommans JH and Edwards RA (1990) Fluoxetine and hyponatremia. *N Z Med J* **103**, 106.

Graber MA, Hoehns TB and Perry PJ (1994) Sertraline–phenelzine drug interaction: a serotonin syndrome reaction. *Ann Pharmacoth* **28**, 732–735.

Graham PM and Ilett KF (1988) Danger of MAOI therapy after fluoxetine withdrawal. *Lancet* **2**, 1255–1256.

Grubb BP, Samoil D, Kosinski D, Kip K and Brewster P (1994) Use of sertraline hydrochloride in the treatment of refractory neurocardiogenic syncope in children and adolescents. *J Am Coll Cardiology* **24**, 490–494.

Grubb BP, Wolfe DA, Samoil D, Temesy-Armos P, Hahn H and Elliott L (1993) Usefulness of fluoxetine hydrochloride for prevention of resistant upright tilt induced syncope. *PACE* **16** **(3 Pt 1)**, 458–464.

Guze BH and Baxter LR (1986) The serotonin syndrome: a case report. *J Clin Psychopharmacol* **6**, 119–120.

Hadley A and Cason MP (1989) Mania resulting from lithium-fluoxetine combination [letter]. *Am J Psychiatry* **146**, 1637–1638.

Hamilton MS and Opler LA (1992) Akathisia, suicidality, and fluoxetine. *J Clin Psychiatry* **53**, 401–406.

Hansen TE, Dieter K and Keepers GA (1990) Interaction of fluoxetine and pentazocine [letter]. *Am J Psychiatry* **147**, 949–950.

Hansen-Grant S, Silk KR and Guthrie S (1993) Fluoxetine–pimozide interaction [letter]. *Am J Psychiatry* **150**, 1751–1752.

Harrison WM, Rabkin JG, Ehrhardt AA, Stewart JW, McGrath PJ and Ross D (1986) Effects of antidepressant medication on sexual function: a controlled study. *J Clin Psychopharmacol* **6**, 144–149.

Hendrickx B and Floris M (1991) A controlled pilot study of the combination of fluvoxamine and lithium. *Curr Ther Res Clin Exp* **49**, 106–110.

Henry EW, Chandler LP, Burnside R, Doogan DP and Salsburg D (1992) Evaluation of suicidality in the sertraline, placebo, and active control groups in the sertraline depression program. *Clin Neuropharmacol* **15 (Suppl B)**, 82.

Hindmarch I and Harrison C 91988) The effects of paroxetine and other antidepressants in combination with alcohol in psychomotor activity related to car driving. *Hum Psychopharmacol* **3**, 13–20.

Hindmarch I, Shillingford J and Shillingford C (1990) The effects of sertraline on psychomotor performance in elderly volunteers. *J Clin Psychiatry* **51 (Suppl B)**, 34–36.

Horrigan JP and Barnhill LJ (1994) Paroxetine–pimozide drug interaction. *J Am Acad Child Adolesc Psychiatry* **33**, 1060–1061.

Humphries JE, Wheby MS and VandenBerg SR (1990) Fluoxetine and the bleeding time. *Arch Pathol Lab Med* **114**, 727–728.

Hussein S and Kaufman BM (1994) Bradycardia associated with fluoxetine in an elderly patient with sick sinus syndrome (4). *Postgrad Med J* **70**, 56.

Hwang AS and Magraw RM (1989) Syndrome of inappropriate secretion of antidiuretic hormone due to fluoxetine. *Am J Psychiatry* **146**, 399.

Jalil P (1992) Toxic reaction following the combined administration of fluoxetine and phenytoin: two case reports [letter]. *J Neurol Neurosurg Psychiatry* **55**, 412–413.

Jansen EN and Kolling P (1992) Parkinsonism following addition of fluoxetine to treatment with neuroleptics or carbamazepine [letter]. *Ned Tijdschr Geneeskd* **136**, 755–756.

Jeandel C, Jouanny P, Herbeuval F, Mallie JP, Trechot P and Royer RJ (1993) Severe hyponatremia caused by inappropriate antidiuretic hormone secretion syndrome induced by fluoxetine [letter]. *Therapie* **48**, 487–489.

Jermain DM, Hughes PL and Follender AB (1992) Potential fluoxetine-selegiline interaction [letter]. *Ann Pharmacother* **26**, 1300.

Joblin M (1994) Possible interaction of sertraline with carbamazepine [letter]. *N Z Med J* **107**, 43.

Joblin M and Ghose K (1994) Possible interaction of sertraline with carbamazepine. *N Z Med J* **107**, 43.

Joffe RT and Bakish D (1994) Combined SSRI-moclobemide treatment of psychiatric illness. *J Clin Psychiatry* **55**, 24–25.

Kapur S, Mieczkowski T and Mann JJ (1992) Antidepressant medications and the relative risk of suicide attempt and suicide. *JAMA* **268**, 3441–3445.

Kasper S and Moeller HJ (1992) Serotonin re-uptake inhibitors and suicidality. *Clin Neuropharmacol* **15 (1 Suppl B)**, 36.

Katon W, von-Korff M, Lin E, Bush T and Ormel J (1992) Adequacy and duration of antidepressant treatment in primary care. *Med Care* **30**, 67–76.

Kelly A, Moriarty J and George M (1994) *Fluvoxamine vs Clomipramine in OCD: A Multi-center Randomized, Double-blind Study.* Presented at the XIX CINP Meeting, Washington, DC, 1994.

Keppel-Hesselink JM (1992) Parkinsonism following addition of fluoxetine to treatment with neuroleptics or carbamazepine [letter]. *Ned Tijdschr Geneeskd* **136**, 754–755.

Keppel-Hesselink JM, Touw DJ, Gernaat HBPE, Van-De-Woude J, Jansen ENH and Kolling P (1992) Parkinsonism following addition of fluoxetine to the treatment with neuroleptics or carbamazepine. *Ned Tijdschr Geneeskd* **136**, 754–756.

Kerkhofs M, Rielaert C, de-Maertelaer V, Linkowski P, Czarka M and Mendlewicz J (1990) Fluoxetine in major depression: efficacy, safety and effects on sleep polygraphic variables. *Int Clin Psychopharmacol* **5**, 253–260.

Kerr JS, Fairweather DB, Mahendran R and Hindmarch I (1992) The effects of paroxetine, alone and in combination with alcohol on psychomotor performance and cognitive function in the elderly. *Int Clin Psychopharmacol* **7**, 101–108.

Keuthen NJ, Cyr P, Ricciardi JA, Minichiello WE, Buttolph ML and Jenike MA (1994) Medication withdrawal symptoms in obsessive–compulsive disorder patients treated with paroxetine. *J Clin Psychopharmacol* **14**, 206–207.

Klee B and Kronig MH (1992) Case report of probable sertraline-induced akathisia. *Am J Psychiatry* **150**, 986–987.

Kojima H, Terao T and Yoshimura R (1993) Serotonin syndrome during clomipramine and lithium treatment [letter]. *Am J Psychiatry* **150**, 1897.

Kupfer DJ, Perel JM, Pollock BG, Nathan RS, Grochocinski VJ and Wilson MJ (1991) Fluvoxamine versus desipramine: comparative polysomnographic effects. *Biol Psychiatry* **29**, 23–40.

Lader M, Melhuish A, Frcka G, Fredricson-Over K and Christensen V (1986) The effects of citalopram in single and repeated doses and with alcohol on physiological and psychological measures in healthy subjects. *Eur J Clin Pharmacol* **31**, 183–190.

Lane RM (1994) Carbamazepine and sertraline. *Magnetic Resonance in Medicine* **107**, 209.

Langlois RP and Paquette D (1994) Sustained bradycardia during fluvoxamine and buspirone intoxication. *Can J Psychiatry* **39**, 126–127.

LaPorta LD (1993) Sertraline-induced akathisia. *J Clin Psychopharmacol* **13**, 219–220.

Lappin RI and Auchincloss EL (1994) Treatment of the serotonin syndrome with cyproheptadine. *N Engl J Med* **331**, 1021–1022.

Lauterbach EC (1994) Fluoxetine withdrawal and thalamic pain. *Neurology* **44**, 983–984.

Lejoyeux M, Rouillon F, Leon E and Ades J (1994) *Prospective Evaluation of the Serotonin Syndrome in Depressed Patients Treated with Tricyclic Antidepressants.* Presented at the XIX CINP Meeting, Washington, DC, 1994.

Lemberger L, Rowe H, Bergstrom RF, Farid KZ and Enas GG (1985) Effect of fluoxetine on psychomotor performance, physiologic response, and kinetics of ethanol. *Clin Pharmacol Ther* **37**, 658–664.

Lindenmayer JP, Vakharia M and Kanofsky D (1990) Fluoxetine in chronic schizophrenia. *J Clin Psychopharmacol* **10**, 76.

Lipinski JR Jr, Mallya G, Zimmerman P and Pope HG Jr (1989) Fluoxetine-induced akathisia: clinical and theoretical implications. *J Clin Psychiatry* **50**, 339–342.

Lisi DM (1993) Comment: paroxetine-associated hyponatremia [letter]. *Ann Pharmacother* **27**, 1547–1548.

Llorente MD, Gorelick M and Silverman MA (1994) Sertraline as a cause of inappropriate antidiuretic hormone secretion. *J Clin Psychiatry* **55**, 543–544.

Louie AK, Lannon RA and Ajari LJ (1994) Withdrawal reaction after sertraline discontinuation. *Am J Psychiatry* **151**, 450–451.

Lyby K, Elsborg L, Hopfner-Petersen HE and Skovlund E (1988) *Long-term Safety of Citalopram.* Presented at the XVIth CINP Congress, Munich, 1988.

Maany I and Dhopesh V (1990) Akathisia and fluoxetine [letter; comment]. *J Clin Psychiatry* **51**, 210–212.

Madi L, O'Brien AAJ and Fennell J (1994) Status epilepticus secondary to fluoxetine: 3. *Postgrad Med J* **70**, 383–384.

Mander A, McCausland M, Workman B, Flamer H and Christophidis N (1994) Fluoxetine induced dyskinesia. *Aust NZ J Psychiatry* **28**, 328–330.

Manna V, Bolino F and Di-Cicco L (1994) Chronic tension-type headache, mood depression and serotonin: therapeutic effects of fluvoxamine and mianserine. *Headache* **34**, 44–49.

Marik PE, van-Heerden W and Steenkamp V (1990) Fluoxetine-induced syndrome of inappropriate antidiuretic hormone excretion [letter]. *S Afr Med J* **78**, 760–761.

Marley E and Wozniak KM (1984) Interactions of a non-selective monoamine oxidase inhibitor, phenelzine, with inhibitors of 5-hydroxytryptamine, dopamine or noradrenaline re-uptake. *J Psychiatr Res* **18**, 173–189.

Martindale JJ and Bennie E (1993) *Double-blind Study of Sertraline and Fluoxetine in Outpatients with Major Depression.* Presented at the American Psychiatric Association Annual Meeting, San Francisco, CA, 1993.

Martinelli V, Bocchetta A, Palmas AM and Del-Zompo M (1993) An interaction between carbamazepine and fluvoxamine. *Br J Clin Pharmacol* **36**, 615–616.

Masquelier I, Saint-Jean O, Bourdioil MC, Boiffin A and Bouchon JP (1993) Bradycardia and hypothermia in an elderly patient receiving fluoxetine [letter]. *Presse Med* **22**, 553.

McClelland GR and Raptopoulos P (1985) Psychomotor effects of paroxetine and amitriptyline, alone and in combination with ethanol. *Br J Clin Pharmacol* **19**, 578.

Meltzer HY, Young M, Metz J, Fang VS, Schyve PM and Arora RC (1979) Extrapyramidal side effects and increased serum prolactin following fluoxetine, a new antidepressant. *J Neural Transm* **45**, 165–175.

Mendelson WB and Franko T (1994) Priapism with sertraline and lithium. *J Clin Psychopharmacol* **14**, 434–435.

Mewett S (1991) *Suicidal Thoughts and Behavior with Paroxetine.* New Research Program and Abstracts, American Psychiatric Association Annual Meeting, New Orleans, 1991.

Montastruc JL, Chamontin B, Senard JM, Tran MA, Rascol O and Llau ME (1993) Pseudophaeochromocytoma in parkinsonian patient treated with fluoxetine plus selegiline [letter]. *Lancet* **341**, 55.

Monteiro WO, Noshiryani HF, Marks IM and Lelliott PT (1987) Anorgasmia from clomipramine in obsessive–compulsive disorder: A controlled trial. *Br J Psychiatry* **151**, 107–112.

Montgomery SA (1989) Fluoxetine in the treatment of anxiety, agitation and suicidal thoughts. In: Stefanis CN, Soldatos CR and Rabavilas AD (eds) *Psychiatry Today:* VIII World Congress of Psychiatry Abstracts. p 335, Elsevier, New York.

Montgomery SA (1991) Clinical significance of 5-HT uptake inhibitors. *Hum Psychopharmacol* **6**, S3–7.

Montgomery SA, Dunner DL and Dunbar GC (1995) Reduction of suicidal thoughts with paroxetine in comparison with reference antidepressants and placebo. *Eur Neuro-psychopharmacol* **5**, 5–13.

Montgomery SA, Henry J, McDonald G, Dinan T, Lader M and Hindmarch I (1994) Selective serotonin reuptake inhibitors: meta-analysis of discontinuation rates. *Int Clin Psychopharmacol* **9**, 47–53.

Moon CAL, Jago LW, Wood K and Doogan DP (1994) A double-blind comparison of sertraline and clomipramine in the treatment of major depressive disorder and associated anxiety in general practice. *J Psychopharmacol* **8**, 171–176.

Muly EC, McDonald W, Steffens D and Book S (1993) Serotonin syndrome produced by a combination of fluoxetine and lithium [letter]. *Am J Psychiatry* **150**, 1565.

Neuvonen PJ, Pohjola SS, Tacke U and Vuori E (1994) Five fatal cases of serotonin syndrome after moclobemide-citalopram or moclobemide-clomipramine overdoses. *Lancet* **342**, 1419.

Nicholson AN and Pascoe PA (1988) Studies on the modulation of the sleep-wakefulness continuum in man by fluoxetine, a 5-HT uptake inhibitor. *Neuropharmacology* **27**, 597–602.

Noveske FG, Hahn KR and Flynn RJ (1989) Possible toxicity of combined fluoxetine and lithium. *Am J Psychiatry* **146**, 1515.

Ohman R and Spigset O (1993) Serotonin syndrome induced by fluvoxamine-lithium interaction [letter]. *Pharmacopsychiatry* **26**, 263–264.

Opler LA (1994) Sertraline and akathisia. *Am J Psychiatry* **151**, 620–621.

Oswald I and Adam K (1986) Effects of paroxetine on human sleep. *Br J Clin Pharmacol* **22**, 97–99.

Ottervanger EA (1994) *SSRI Treatment-emergent Nausea*. Presented at the XIX CINP Meeting, Washington, DC, 1994.

Ottervanger JP, Stricker BHC, Huls J and Weeda JN (1994) Bleeding attributed to the intake of paroxetine (5). *Am J Psychiatry* **151**, 781–782.

Ottervanger JP, van-den-Bemt PM, de-Koning GH and Stricker BH (1993) Risk of haemorrhage with the use of fluoxetine (Prozac) or fluvoxamine (Fevarin). *Ned Tijdschr Geneeskd* **137**, 259–261.

Pastuszak A, Schick-Boschetto B, Zuber C, Feldkamp M, Pinelli M and Sihn S (1993) Pregnancy outcome following first-trimester exposure to fluoxetine (Prozac). *JAMA* **269**, 2246–2248.

Pearson HJ (1990) Interaction of fluoxetine with carbamazepine. *J Clin Psychiatry* **51**, 126.

Reccoppa L, Welch WA and Ware MR (1990) Acute dystonia and fluoxetine [letter]. *J Clin Psychiatry* **51**, 487.

Rio J, Molins A, Viguera ML and Codina A (1992) Acute dystonia caused by fluoxetine [letter]. *Med Clin (Barc)* **99**, 436–437.

Robertson DW, Jones ND, Swartzendruber JK, Yang KS and Wong DT (1988) Molecular structure of fluoxetine hydrochloride, a highly selective serotonin-uptake inhibitor. *J Med Chem* **31**, 185–189.

Rocco PL and De-Leo D (1992) Fluvoxamine-induced acute exacerbation in residual schizophrenia [letter]. *Pharmacopsychiatry* **25**, 245.

Rosenstein DL, Takshita J and Nelson JC (1991) Fluoxetine-induced elevation and prolongation of tricyclic levels in overdose [letter]. *Am J Psychiatry* **148**, 807.

Rothschild AJ and Locke CA (1991) Reexposure to fluoxetine after serious suicide attempts by three patients: the tole of akathisia. *J Clin Psychiatry* **52**, 491–493.

Rouillon F, Phillips R, Serrurier D, Ansart E and Gerard MJ (1989) Rechutes de depression unipolaire et efficacite del la maprotiline. *L'Encephale* **15**, 527–534.

Rovei V, Chanoine F, Strolin-Benedetti M, Zini R and Tillement JP (1983) Plasma protein binding of the reversible type A MAO inhibitor cimoxatone (MD 780515). *Biochem Pharmacol* **32**, 2303–2308.

Sacristan JA, Iglesias C, Arellano F and Lequerica J (1991) Absence seizures induced by lithium: possible interaction with fluoxetine [letter]. *Am J Psychiatry* **148**, 146–147.

Salama AA and Shafey M (1989a) A case of lithium toxicity induced by combined fluoxetine and lithium carbonate. *Am J Psychiatry* **146**, 278.

Salama AA and Shafey M (1989b) A case of severe lithium toxicity induced by combined fluoxetine and lithium carbonate [letter]. *Am J Psychiatry* **146**, 146–278.

Sandrini G, Ruiz L, Patruno G, Bussone G, Verri AP and Nappi G (1991) Antalgic and antidepressant activities of fluoxetine in daily chronic headache. *Cephalalgia* **11 (11 Suppl)**, 280–281.

Sandyk R (1986) L-dopa induced "serotonin syndrome" in a parkinsonism patient on bromocriptine. *J Clin Psychopharmacol* **6**, 194–195.

Satterlee WG, Faries DE, Heiligenstein JH and Tollefson GD (1994) *Effects of Fluoxetine on Symptoms of Insomnia in Depressed Patients*. Presented at the American Psychiatric Association Annual Meeting, Philadelphia, PA, 1994.

Schaffler K (1986) Study on performance and alcohol interaction with the antidepressant fluoxetine—a selective serotonin reuptake inhibitor—using computer assisted psycho-physiological methodology. *Br J Clin Pract* **40**, 28–33.

Schaffler K (1989) Study on performance and alcohol interaction with the antidepressant fluoxetine. *Int Clin Psychopharmacol* **4 (Suppl 1)**, 15–20.

Schillinger F, Mathieu Y, Ferrer M, Montagnac R and Milcent T (1994) Fluoxetine-induced hyponatremia. *Sem Hop* **70**, 815–818.

Schone W and Ludwig M (1993) A double-blind study of paroxetine compared with fluoxetine in geriatric patients with major depression. *J Clin Psychopharmacol* **13 (6 Suppl 2)**, 34S–39S.

Scrimali T, Grimali L, Corriere A, Grasso F and Flavia-Frisone M (1994) Fluoxetine in the pharmacological treatment of bulimia nervosa. *Riv Psichiatr* **29**, 171–177.

Seifritz E, Holsboer-Trachsler E, Haberthur F, Hemmeter U and Poldinger W (1993) Unrecognized pregnancy during citalopram treatment [letter]. *Am J Psychiatry* **150**, 1428–1429.

Settle EC Jr (1993) Akathisia and sertraline [letter]. *J Clin Psychiatry* **54**, 321.

Shrivastava RK, Shrivastava S and Overweg N (1993) *Efficacy Trial: Paroxetine and Fluoxetine in Depression.* Presented at the American Psychiatric Association Annual Meeting, San Francisco, CA, 1993.

Silver H and Nassar A (1992) Fluvoxamine improves negative symptoms in treated chronic schizophrenia: an add-on double-blind, placebo-controlled study. *Biol Psychiatry* **31**, 698–704.

Song F, Fremantle N and Sheldon TA (1993) Selective serotonin reuptake inhibitors: meta-analysis off efficacy and acceptability. *BMJ* **306**, 683–687.

Souche A, Montaldi S, Uehlinger C, Kasas A, Reymond MJ and Reymond P (1991) Traitement de la depression resistante par l'association citalopram-lithium. Methodologie d'une etude multicentrique en double aveugle et resultats preliminaires. *L'Encephale* **17**, 213–219.

Sovner R and Davis JM (1991) A potential drug interaction between fluoxetine and valproic acid [letter]. *J Clin Psychopharmacol* **11**, 389.

Sperber AD (1991) Toxic interaction between fluvoxamine and sustained release theophylline in an 11-year-old boy. *Drug Safety* **6**, 460–462.

Spigset O, Mjorndal T and Lovheim O (1993) Serotonin syndrome caused by a moclobemide-clomipramine interaction. *BMJ* **306**, 248.

Spina E, Avenoso A, Pollicino AM, Caputi AP, Fazio A and Pisani F 91993) Carbamazepine coadministration with fluoxetine or fluvoxamine. *Ther Drug Monit* **15**, 247–250.

Staab JP, Yerkes SA, Cheney EM and Clayton AH (1990) Transient SIADH associated with fluoxetine [letter]. *Am J Psychiatry* **147**, 1569–1570.

Staner L, Mendlewicz J, Kerkhofs M, Detroux D, Bouillon E and de la Fuente JR (1992) *Effects of Paroxetine on Sleep EEG.* New Research Program and Abstracts, American Psychiatric Association Annual Meeting, Washington, DC, 1992.

Stanford MS and Patton JH (1993) *In utero* exposure to fluoxetine HCl increases hematoma frequency at birth. *Pharmacol Biochem Behav* **45**, 959–962.

Stein MH (1991) Tardive dyskinesia in a patient taking haloperidol and fluoxetine. *Am J Psychiatry* **148**, 683.

Steiner W and Fontaine R (1986) Toxic reaction following the combined administration of fluoxetine and L-tryptophan: five case reports. *Biol Psychiatry* **21**, 1067–1071.

Stellamans G (1991) *A Study to Investigate the Efficacy, Adverse Events, Safety, and Pharmacokinetic Effects of Coadministration of Paroxetine and Lithium.* New Research Program and Abstracts, American Psychiatric Association Annual Meeting, New Orleans, 1991.

Sternbach H (1991a) The serotonin syndrome. *Am J Psychiatry* **148**, 705–713.

Sternbach H (1991b) Fluoxetine-associated potentiation of calcium-channel blockers [letter]. *J Clin Psychopharmacol* **11**, 390–391.

Stoker DMJ and Eric PL (1993) *A Comparison of Withdrawal Effects Following Discontinuation of Paroxetine and Imipramine.* Presented at the American Psychiatric Association Annual Meeting, San Francisco, CA, 1993.

Stoukides JA and Stoukides CA (1991) Extrapyramidal symptoms upon discontinuation of fluoxetine [letter]. *Am J Psychiatry* **148**, 1263.

Suchowersky O and de Vries JD (1990) Interaction of fluoxetine selegiline. *Can J Psychiatry* **35**, 571–572.

Szabadi E (1992) Fluvoxamine withdrawal syndrome. *Br J Psychiatry* **160**, 283–284.

Teicher MH, Glod CA and Cole JO (1993) Antidepressant drugs and the emergence of suicidal tendencies. *Drug Safety* **8**, 186–212.

Ten-Holt WL, Klaassen CH and Schrijver G (1994) Severe hyponatremia, possibly due to inappropriate antidiuretic hormone secretion, during use of the antidepressant fluoxetine. *Ned Tijdschr Geneeskd* **138**, 1181–1183.

Thomas P (1991) Sad attack: Prozac and violent behavior. *Harvard Health Letter* **16**, 1.

Tignol J (1992) A double-blind, randomised, multicenter study comparing paroxetine 20 mg daily versus fluoxetine 20 mg daily in the treatment of adults with major depression. *Clin Neuropharmacol* **15 (1 Suppl B)**, 177.

Tollefson GD, Homan SL, Sayler ME and Potvin JH (1994) Fluoxetine, placebo, and tricyclic antidepressants in major depression with and without anxious features. *J Clin Psychiatry* **55**, 50–59.

Touw DJ, Gernaat HB and van-der-Woude J (1992) Parkinsonism following addition of fluoxetine to the treatment with neuroleptics or carbamazepine. *Ned Tijdschr Geneeskd* **136**, 332–334.

van-Harten J, Stevens LA, Raghoebar M, Holland RL, Wesnes K and Cournot A (1992) Fluvoxamine does not interact with alcohol or potentiate alcohol-related impairment of cognitive function. *Clin Pharmacol Ther* **52**, 427–435.

Van-Iperen CE, Grootjans-Geerts I and Bartelink AKM (1994) Severe hyponatremia possibly caused by inadequate antidiuretic-hormone secretion due to use of antidepressive fluoxetine: 2. *Ned Tijdschr Geneeskd* **138**, 1881.

Vishwanath BM, Navalgund AA, Cusano W and Navalgund KA (1991) Fluoxetine as a cause of SIADH [letter]. *Am J Psychiatry* **148**, 542–543.

von Bardeleben U, Steiger A, Gerken A and Holsboer F (1989) Effects of fluoxetine upon pharmacoendocrine and sleep-EEG parameters in normal controls. *Int Clin Psychopharmacol* **4 (Suppl 1)**, 1–5.

Vrtovsnik F, Bridoux F, Caron J, Hazzan M, Lemaitre V and Vanhille P (1993) Hyponatremia caused by inappropriate antidiuretic hormone secretion syndrome during treatment with fluoxetine [letter]. *Therapie* **48**, 513.

Vrtovsnik F, Bridoux F, Hazzan M, Lemaitre V, Mounier-Vehier C and Vanhille P (1992) Fluoxetine-induced hyponatremia due to inappropriate secretion of antidiuretic hormone. Two observations. *Rev Med Interne* **13 (3 Suppl)**, S115.

Waters CH (1994) Fluoxetine and selegiline—lack of significant interactions. *Can J Neurol Sci* **21**, 259–261.

Wheadon DE, Rampey AH Jr, Thompson VL, Potvin JH, Masica DN and Beasley CM Jr (1992) Lack of association between fluoxetine and suicidality in bulimia nervosa. *J Clin Psychiatry* **53**, 235–241.

Wilde MI, Plosker GL and Benfield P (1993) Fluvoxamine. An update review of its pharmacology, and therapeutic use in depressive illness. *Drugs* **46**, 895–924.

Winokur A, Sewitch DE, Biniaur IV and Phillips JL (1992) Effects of sertraline on sleep architecture in patients with major depression. *Clin Neuropharmacol* **15 (1 Suppl B)**, 84.

Wirshing WC, Rosenberg J, Van Putten T and Marder SR (1991) *Fluoxetine and Suicidality: A Consequence of Akathisia*. New Research Program and Abstracts, American Psychiatric Association Annual Meeting, New Orleans, 1991.

Wirshing WC, Van-Putten T, Rosenberg J, Marder S, Ames D and Hicks-Gray T (1992) Fluoxetine, akathisia, and suicidality: is there a causal connection? *Arch Gen Psychiatry* **49**, 580–581.

Woods DJ, Coulter DM and Pillans P (1994) Interaction of phenytoin and fluoxetine. *Magnetic Resonance in Medicine* **107**, 19.
Woolfrey S, Gammack NS, Dewar MS and Brown PJ (1993) Fluoxetine–warfarin interaction. *BMJ* **307**, 241.
Wright P and Seth R (1992) Lithium toxicity, hypomania and leucocytosis with fluoxetine. *Ir J Psychol Med* **9**, 59–60.
Yaryura-Tobias JA, Kirschen H, Ninan P and Mosberg HJ (1994) Fluoxetine and bleeding in obsessive–compulsive disorder [letter]. *Am J Psychiatry* **148**, 949.
Zinner SH (1994) Panic attacks precipitated by sertraline. *Am J Psychiatry* **151**, 147–148.
(1993) Dystonia and withdrawal symptoms with paroxetine (Seroxat). *Curr Probl Pharmacovigilance* **19**, 1.

15

Practical use of the selective serotonin re-uptake inhibitors

William F. Boyer and John P. Feighner

The purpose of this chapter is to supplement the scholarly content of the other chapters with material directed to those who use SSRIs clinically. Clinicians are often faced with patients and situations which go beyond data from double-blind clinical trials.

This chapter discusses in this light some of the more common issues facing clinicians who treat patients with SSRIs. Relevant literature is cited where it is available and what we hope are reasonable recommendations are made.

MANAGING SIDE-EFFECTS

Insomnia

SSRI-induced insomnia tends to be both time-limited and dose-dependent. If it is not too severe, patients should be encouraged to continue therapy until it subsides. If this is not possible, a conservative first step is temporary dose reduction.

Regular hypnotic agents may be used in conjunction with SSRIs. SSRI therapy may prolong the half-life of some benzodiazepines, such as alprazolam and diazepam, although the clinical significance of this is unclear. Our experience with other hypnotics, including antihistamines, chloral hydrate and zolpidem suggests there is no contraindication to their use with an SSRI. Zopiclone has also been used in this context (Patten, 1995; Swinson, 1995).

Selective Serotonin Re-uptake Inhibitors: Advances in Basic Research and Clinical Practice, Second Edition, Edited by J.P. Feighner and W.F. Boyer

Trazodone is commonly used as an adjunctive agent to treat SSRI-associated insomnia. The published accounts of its usefulness are mixed, however. Metz and Shader (1990) reported that five of 16 patients given 25–75 mg of trazodone for fluoxetine-induced insomnia had to stop the medication because of excessive sedation. Nierenberg and colleagues (1992) presented a series of eight fluoxetine treated patients who received trazodone either for sleep or to potentiate its antidepressant effect. Three patients experienced improvements in both sleep and depression. The other five either had no improvement or had intolerable side-effects. The same investigators later reported a somewhat more positive double-blind crossover trial of trazodone or placebo given to 17 patients who had insomnia while taking fluoxetine or bupropion. Of the 15 completers, 67% experienced improvement with trazodone compared to 14% with placebo (Nierenberg *et al.*, 1994). Amitriptyline, doxepin, and trimipramine are sedating antidepressants which we have sometimes found helpful in the treatment of insomnia and which may provide an additional antidepressant effect. Mianserin can also be used for this purpose (Tenck, 1995).

Anxiety

It is important to distinguish between anxiety as a symptom of depression and anxiety as a side-effect of its treatment. Data clearly indicate that SSRI therapy is associated with reduction in anxiety, sometimes by as early as one week. The presence of anxiety prior to treatment may actually predict preferential response to an SSRI.

Some patients develop anxiety as a side-effect of SSRI therapy. Pretreatment ratings of anxiety do not predict who will become anxious, but patients with panic attacks are prone to exacerbation of panic. These patients are optimally treated with initial prescription of a very low dose of SSRI accompanied by slow dose titration (Giesecke, 1990). In our experience, paroxetine appears less likely to be associated with anxiety, although it may occur with this agent as well.

Anxiety which appears during the course of SSRI treatment may also be related to akathisia. Dose reduction, every-other-day therapy for a few days, propranolol and/or benzodiazepines may be helpful for this (Fleischhacker, 1991). A very small number of patients may develop anxiety or agitation accompanied by such intense dysphoria that further treatment with the SSRI is simply unwise.

The only published study of SSRI-induced anxiety to date is by Amsterdam and colleagues (1994). These investigators conducted a prospective study of the efficacy of adjunctive alprazolam therapy for fluoxetine-induced jitteriness symptoms. Fifty-four subjects with major depression were treated with fluoxetine 20 mg daily. Subjects experiencing an increase in jitteriness symptoms within two weeks of starting fluoxetine were given adjunctive alprazolam 0.5–4.0 mg daily for two weeks followed by a two-week taper period. Eighteen of 54 (33.3%) patients experienced jitteriness symptoms during fluoxetine treatment. There was a statistically significant reduction in the severity and number of jitteriness symptoms with adjunctive alprazolam. Moreover, in most cases jitteriness symptoms did not reappear during the alprazolam taper period or after alprazolam was discontinued.

Lethargy

Lethargy may sometimes occur with SSRIs or it may be a part of the initial constellation of symptoms and not respond fully to antidepressant treatment (Ahmed and Zaheeruddin, 1991). Lethargy may occasionally improve with dose reduction but frequently may require an adjunctive stimulant (amphetamine, methylphenidate, pemoline) or other dopamine agonists such as amantadine or bromocriptine (Goldberg, 1995a; Yee, 1995).

Sexual

Sexual side-effects are commonly associated with SSRI treatment. The most frequent include decreased libido and delay in or inability to achieve orgasm. These side-effects may occasionally improve with time but usually do not.

Sexual side-effects tend to be dose-related. Some patients may improve with SSRI dose reduction and time. It has also been found that drug holidays (such as weekend breaks from medication) can be helpful in the case of paroxetine, but not fluoxetine, due to the long half life of the latter agent (Rothschild), 1995). A number of adjunctive treatments have been reported to be at least occasionally helpful in reversing SSRI-associated sexual dysfunction. In one series eight of nine patients reported improvement with yohimbine, although five patients experienced side-effects that led to discontinuation in two cases (Jacobsen, 1992). Buspirone was reported to benefit 11 out of 16 patients in another series, although baseline irritability recurred in several patients (Norden, 1995). Cyproheptadine may also be effective, but it is commonly sedating and there have been reports of loss of SSRI therapeutic effect with this agent as well (McCormick *et al.*, 1990; Feder, 1991; Goldbloom and Kennedy, 1991; Cohen, 1992; Arnott and Nutt, 1994; Katz and Rosenthal, 1994). Amantadine 100 mg b.i.d. successfully reversed anorgasmia in five of seven patients in one series (Hollander *et al.*, 1992). No side-effects were noted. Switching SSRI therapy to bupropion may be a tactic for patients with intractable sexual dysfunction (Walker *et al.*, 1993). Labbate and Pollack (1994) reported a case of using adjunctive bupropion to treat fluoxetine-induced sexual dysfunction in a 50-year-old man with a history of recurrent major depression. One of us (JPF) has used methylphenidate, 10–30 mg/day, to treat SSRI associated sexual side-effects in three patients.

Nausea

Modification of dose schedule may be of some value in combating SSRI-induced nausea. Siddiqui and colleagues (1985) found that patients experienced fewer side-effects and there were fewer patients who could not tolerate medication when their total daily fluvoxamine dose was given at night. Taking the medication with food may also be of some value, although the absorption of sertraline is increased in the presence of food.

A low dose of the 5-HT$_4$ antagonist cisapride (5 mg b.i.d.) produced rapid relief from SSRI-associated nausea in eight patients (Bergeron and Blier, 1994). Good results have also been reported with cyproheptadine 2 mg t.i.d. although larger doses may be sedating and antagonize the SSRIs' therapeutic effects as previously noted.

Diarrhoea

Acidophilus has been reported to be helpful for diarrhoea associated with sertraline (Kline and Koppes, 1994). Acidophilus bacilli may be found in yogurt, specially marked cartons of milk, or in capsules in health food stores.

MANAGING PARTIAL OR NON-RESPONSE

Depression

The first questions to be addressed in managing the partial or non-responder is how long should it take to see a response? The "conventional wisdom" is that a six to eight week trial may be required. However we have published data compiled from antidepressant trials at the Feighner Research Institute which suggest that few patients who have not shown some measurable improvement by the third or fourth week suddenly respond by week six (Boyer and Feighner, 1994). Patients who have been chronically depressed for over a year may sometimes take longer for improvement to be seen.

It has been noted that patients who initially respond well to fluoxetine may lose some of their improvement after the first weeks (Ahmed and Zaheeruddin, 1991; Cain, 1992). This corresponds to the time when norfluoxetine plasma levels, which may be associated with poorer response, reach steady state (Montgomery et al., 1990). Although Keck and McElroy (1992) found no relationship between fluoxetine or norfluoxetine plasma levels and sedation, they did find that the ratio of fluoxetine to norfluoxetine was less than one in patients with sedation and greater than one in patients without sedation.

The literature does not provide clear guidance for what to do in this situation. Possibly the most relevant paper was by Cain (1992), in which the author reported a series of 23 patients treated with fluoxetine, 20 mg/day. Four of these patients did not maintain their improvement for six weeks. These patients were treated by being withdrawn from fluoxetine for two weeks and then resuming fluoxetine, 20 mg every other day. All four patients responded to this intervention.

A study by Fava and colleagues (1994) dealt with patients who do not respond or respond only partially to acute fluoxetine treatment. Although this is not the same situation the findings are possibly relevant. In this trial patients were randomly assigned to dosage increase to 40 mg/day or adjunctive treatment with desipramine or lithium. The most effective intervention turned out to be the dosage increase. The same group also reported their experience with 18 patients who lost their response to 20 mg/day of fluoxetine during maintenance therapy. The investigators increased the fluoxetine dose to 40 mg/day. Thirteen patients responded fully, three partially and three dropped out due to side-effects (Fava *et al.*, 1995).

These three studies suggest that either dosage increase or decrease may be helpful. In practice we generally try to ascertain whether the loss of acute response is related to SSRI side-effects, such as lethargy or apathy, or due to continuation of baseline symptoms. This requires good initial assessment and documentation of symptoms. If the patient appears to be having side-effects we generally decrease the dose, or if the patient appears to be having continued depressive symptoms (more often the case) we increase the dose.

Lithium augmentation

Lithium augmentation is arguably the most commonly cited method of managing treatment-resistant depression. A number of open and controlled studies indicate that lithium augmentation of SSRIs is also a viable technique.

In one of the first such reports, Pope and colleagues (1988) reported that five depressed patients who had shown no improvement with trials of antidepressants from several chemical families, including fluoxetine, responded when adjunctive lithium was administered.

Katona and colleagues (1993) compared lithium augmentation to placebo in a six-week, double-blind trial of 62 outpatients who had failed to respond to a trial of either fluoxetine or lofepramine (a relatively selective norepinephrine uptake inhibitor). The chance of responding was significantly greater among patients taking adjunctive lithium than those given placebo (52% versus 33%). Patients with therapeutic lithium levels were the most likely to respond. There was no difference in response rates between the fluoxetine–lithium and fluoxetine–lofepramine combinations. Ontiveros and colleagues (1991) reported results of a similar open study in which lithium was added to either fluoxetine or desipramine treatment of 60 patients whose depression was described as resistant. These investigators found that more fluoxetine-treated patients responded during the first week of adjunctive lithium therapy, but that there were fewer relapsers among those patients who responded to lithium plus desipramine. Other reports of successful lithium augmentation of fluoxetine, sertraline or citalopram have been published (Fontaine *et al.*, 1991; Howland, 1991; Souche *et al.*, 1991; Goodnick, 1992; Dinan, 1993).

However the published data of lithium augmentation of SSRIs is not uniformly positive. Flint and Rifat (1994) reported only a 24% response to lithium augmentation among 32 elderly depressed patients who received adjunctive lithium.

Tricyclic antidepressant (TCA) augmentation
The combination of an SSRI and a TCA may be of benefit for some patients. Much of the published data concerns use of desipramine, a norepinephrine uptake inhibitor. The combination of fluoxetine and desipramine in one study appeared to provide earlier relief of depression than desipramine alone (Nelson *et al.*, 1991). Weilburg and associates (1991) reported a 65% response rate when low doses of desipramine (10–50 mg/day) were added to the regimen of fluoxetine in non-responders. TCA plasma levels obtained in a subsample of these patients were higher than would be expected for that dose of TCA used alone, but none of the levels was in the toxic range. Others have reported successful use of fluoxetine plus either desipramine or clomipramine in resistant depression (Eisen, 1989; Rosenzweig and Amsterdam, 1992).

It is difficult to know to what extent the usefulness of a TCA–SSRI combination is due to pharmacodynamic or pharmacokinetic effects, since SSRIs may raise TCA blood levels by decreasing TCA metabolism. It does seem clear that simple metabolic effects are not always responsible for the effectiveness of this combination. Baettig and colleagues (1993) reported the case of a patient who had citalopram added to her regimen of amitriptyline 75 mg/day. There was no effect on serum TCA levels, but the patient responded clinically.

Lithium versus TCA augmentation
A study by Fava and colleagues (1994) has already been mentioned but merits elaboration. In this study the investigators compared three strategies for managing depression resistant to fluoxetine. Forty-one patients who had failed to respond to eight weeks of fluoxetine were randomly assigned to four weeks of increased fluoxetine dose (40–60 mg/day), desipramine (25–50 mg/day) or lithium (300–600 mg/day). Patients treated with a higher dose of fluoxetine did best. Patients who had partially responded to fluoxetine before entering the trial also did well with lithium augmentation. This study suggests that a reasonable first step for an SSRI-treated patient who does not fully respond is to increase the dose. The next step would be to add lithium if the patient had partially responded, or switch to another antidepressant if not.

Other augmentation techniques
Several other augmentation techniques have been described. Joffe and Schuller (1993) reported that 17 of 25 patients who had failed to respond to fluoxetine or fluvoxamine responded to a three-week trial of buspirone augmentation. It is interesting that while buspirone appears to have antidepressant properties in its own right (Feighner and Boyer, 1990: Rickels *et al.*, 1991), it has also been reported to block the antidepressant effect of fluoxetine in some patients (Proulx and Fontaine, 1991). The clinician should be aware of this possibility if using buspirone augmentation.

Medicines such as buspirone have mixed agonist/antagonist activity at 5-HT_{1A} receptors. Pindolol, a beta-blocker, is also a 5-HT_{1A} antagonist. Artigas and associates

(1994) reported that pindolol was associated with clinically significant improvement in seven patients with resistant depression when it was added to their antidepressant regimen. Five of these patients were taking an SSRI, either paroxetine or fluvoxamine. At least one attempt to replicate these findings has not been successful (Goldberg, 1995a).

The combination of an SSRI with thyroid, amphetamine, or magnesium pemoline (a stimulant) has also been reported to convert some patients to full responders (Linet, 1989; Metz and Shader, 1991; Gupta *et al.*, 1992; Joffe, 1992; Rabkin *et al.*, 1994). There is no clear relationship between the efficacy of these interventions and the presence of target symptoms such as hypothyroidism or fatigue.

Small and colleagues (1994) published an interesting retrospective finding which may be relevant to SSRI augmentation strategies. They found that elderly women who were taking oestrogen replacement therapy at the time they entered a fluoxetine trial ($N = 72$) responded significantly better than those who were not ($N = 295$). The relevance of this for clinical practice is uncertain because the patients were not randomized to oestrogen replacement. Experience with oestrogen augmentation of TCAs has not been promising (Zohar *et al.*, 1985).

Little has been written about the augmentation of SSRIs with anticonvulsants such as carbamazepine or valproic acid (Corrigan, 1992). Our own experience and that of some other practitioners suggest that these agents are definitely helpful for mood stabilization and possibly for antidepressant augmentation in both bipolar patients and some who display prominent mood instability or lability suggestive of Axis II pathology (Coccaro and Kavoussi, 1991; Gitlin, 1993; Goldberg, 1995b).

Obsessive–compulsive disorder (OCD)

Lithium augmentation
In contrast to depression, there has been little written about adjunctive lithium use with SSRIs for treatment-resistant OCD. Rueg reported successful lithium augmentation in the open-label treatment of four OCD patients (Ruegg, *et al.*, 1992). However McDougle and colleagues (1991) reported very disappointing results in two series of patients ($N = 20$) and ($N = 10$). The response rates were 18% and 0%, respectively.

TCA augmentation
The combination of fluoxetine and clomipramine may be of benefit in resistant cases of OCD (Simeon *et al.*, 1990). Browne and colleagues (1993) reported four such cases. In two, neither drug individually was of benefit. In the other two the patient responded partially to clomipramine, and more fully when fluoxetine was added.

Desipramine successfully augmented SSRIs for 23 patients who partially responded to SSRIs. Three of 10 patients treated with desipramine but none of the 13 patients treated with placebo had a greater than 25% reduction in OCD score (Psychiatry *et al.*, 1994).

Buspirone augmentation
McDougle and colleagues (1993) found that the addition of buspirone was not significantly better than placebo for three OCD patients who were refractory to fluvoxamine therapy. However, in another study buspirone (up to 30 mg/day) produced improvement among 12 OCD patients who had, at best, a partial response to 10 week of fluoxetine therapy (Markovitz *et al.*, 1989). Similar results have been reported by others (Alessi and Bos, 1991; Jenike *et al.*, 1991).

Clomipramine is a potent serotonin re-uptake inhibitor, but because of the activity of its major metabolite, is not selective. Therefore it is relevant that four of 14 OCD patients who had responded only partially to clomipramine improved an additional average of 25% when buspirone was added to their regimen in a placebo controlled trial. However, overall results were not dramatically positive (Pigott *et al.*, 1992).

Other augmentation strategies
McDougle and colleagues (1994) found that haloperidol augmentation of fluvoxamine was significantly more effective than placebo for 34 OCD patients who were refractory to fluvoxamine alone. However the benefit of haloperidol appeared to be confined to patients with comorbid tic disorders.

Hollander and colleagues (1990) found that fenfluramine, a serotonin releaser and re-uptake inhibitor, was of some benefit in a series of seven OCD patients who had responded only partially to SSRIs or clomipramine. The combination of fluoxetine and trazodone was effective in the treatment of OCD in a single patient who had been refractory to multiple other medications (Swerdlow and Andia, 1989).

Panic disorder

Very little has been written about the use of adjunctive medication for patients with panic disorder who are treated with an SSRI. Tiffon and colleagues (1994) reported a series of seven panic disorder patients who had responded incompletely to either fluoxetine or a TCA. Those taking fluoxetine had a TCA added to their regimen and vice versa. All seven patients improved. In another study 14 of 16 patients who had responded incompletely to fluoxetine, 20 mg/day, had a significant improvement when 25–50 mg/day of a TCA was added to their regimen (Varia and Donnelly, 1991). We frequently use adjunctive benzodiazepines with good success in the treatment of panic disorder. Augmentation with lithium or valproic acid has also been effective in some patients.

SUMMARY

Although the SSRIs represent a significant advance in the pharmacological treatment of depression they are not without side-effects. We have reviewed some of the more common of these. Most, with the notable exception of sexual dysfunction, improve with time. Others may require dose reduction or treatment with adjunctive medication. Some of these adjunctive treatments carry the risk of antagonizing the SSRI's therapeutic effects.

Some patients do not respond fully to SSRIs or may lose their response. Many times, these patients may improve with an increased dose or with adjunctive therapy. We have seen that the same augmenting strategies have been tried, with varying success, for patients with depression, OCD and panic disorder.

The optimum clinical use of SSRIs continues to evolve. By combining the observations in this chapter with his or her own experience, it is hoped that the clinician can achieve the maximum benefits for his or her patients with minimum risk.

REFERENCES

Ahmed SH and Zaheeruddin (1991) Early experience with fluoxetine. *Pak Med Assoc* **41**, 275–277.

Alessi N and Bos T (1991) Buspirone augmentation of fluoxetine in a depressed child with obsessive–compulsive disorder. *Am J Psychiatry* **148**, 1605–1606.

Amsterdam JD, Hornig-Rohan M and Maislin G (1994) *Efficacy of alprazolam in selective serotonin reuptake inhibitor-induced jitteriness.* Presented at the American Psychiatric Association Annual Meeting, Philadelphia, PA.

Arnott S and Nutt D (1994) Successful treatment of fluvoxamine-induced anorgasmia by cyproheptadine. *Br J Psychiatry* **164**, 838–839.

Artigas F, Perez V and Alvarez E (1994) Pindolol induces a rapid improvement of depressed patients treated with serotonin reuptake inhibitors. *Arch Gen Psychiatry* **51**, 248–251.

Baettig D, Bondolfi G, Montaldi S, Amey M and Baumann P (1993) Tricyclic antidepressant plasma levels after augmentation with citalopram: a case study. *Eur J Clin Pharmacol* **44**, 403–405.

Bergeron R and Blier P (1994) Cisapride for the treatment of nausea produced by selective serotonin reuptake inhibitors. *Am J Psychiatry* **151**, 1084–1086.

Boyer WF and Feighner JP (1994) Clinical significance of early non-response in depressed patients. *Depression* **2**, 32–35.

Browne M, Horn E and Jones TT (1993) The benefits of clomipramide–fluoxetine combination in obsessive–compulsive disorder. *Can J Psychiatry* **38**, 242–243.

Cain JW (1992) Poor response to fluoxetine: underlying depression, serotonergic over-stimulation, or a "therapeutic window"? *J Clin Psychiatry* **53**, 272–277.

Coccaro EF and Kavoussi RJ (1991) Biological and pharmacological aspects of borderline personality disorder. *Hosp Community Psychiatry* **42**, 1029–1033.

Cohen AJ (1992) Fluoxetine-induced yawning and anorgasmia reversed by cyproheptadine treatment. *J Clin Psychiatry* **53**, 174.

Corrigan FM (1992) Sodium valproate augmentation of fluoxetine or fluvoxamine effects. *Biol Psychiatry* **31**, 1178–1179.

Dinan TG (1993) Lithium augmentation in sertraline-resistant depression: a preliminary dose-response study. *Acta Psychiatr Scand* **88**, 300–301.

Eisen A (1989) Fluoxetine and desipramine: a strategy for augmenting antidepressant response. *Pharmacopsychiatry* **22**, 272–273.

Fava M, Rappe SM, Pave JA, *et al.* (1995) Relapse in patients on long-term fluoxetine treatment: response to increased fluoxetine dose. *J Clin Psychiatry* **56**, 52–55.

Fava M, Rosenbaum JF, McGrath PJ, Stewart JW, Amsterdam JD and Quitkin FM (1994) Lithium and tricyclic augmentation of fluoxetine treatment for resistant major depression: a double-blind, controlled study. *Am J Psychiatry* **151**, 1372–1374.

Feder R (1991) Reversal of antidepressant activity of fluoxetine by cyproheptadine in three patients. *J Clin Psychiatry* **52**, 163–164.

Feighner JP and Boyer WF (1990) Buspirone in the treatment of depression. *Drug Ther* August (Suppl), 9–16.

Fleischhacker WW (1991) Propanolol for fluoxetine-induced akathisia. *Biol Psychiatry* **30**, 531–532.

Flint AJ and Rifat SL (1994) A prospective study of lithium augmentation in antidepressant-resistant geriatric depression. *J Clin Psychopharmacol* **14**, 353–356.

Fontaine R, Ontiveros A, Elie R and Vezina M (1991) Lithium carbonate augmentation of desipramine and fluoxetine in refractory depression. *Biol Psychiatry* **29**, 946–948.

Giesecke ME (1990) Overcoming hypersensitivity to fluoxetine in a patient with panic disorder. *Am J Psychiatry* **147**, 532–533.

Gitlin MJ (1993) Pharmacotherapy of personality disorders: conceptual framework and clinical strategies. *J Clin Psychopharmacol* **13**, 343–353.

Goldberg I (1995a) Personal communication. 20 Feb 1995.

Goldberg I (1995b) Personal communication. 24 Jan 1995.

Goldbloom DS and Kennedy SH (1991) Adverse interaction of fluoxetine and cyproheptadine in two patients with bulimia nervosa. *J Clin Psychiatry* **52**, 261–262.

Goodnick PJ (1992) Adjunctive lithium treatment with bupropion and fluoxetine: A naturalistic report. *Lithium* **3**, 74–76.

Gupta S, Ghaly N and Dewan M (1992) Augmenting fluoxetine with dextroamphetamine to treat refractory depression. *Hosp Community Psychiatry* **43**, 281–283.

Hollander E, Cohen L, DeCaria C, Stein DJ, Trungold Apter S and Islam M (1992) Fluoxetine and depersonalization syndrome. *Psychosomatics* **33**, 361–362.

Hollander E, DeCaria CM, Schneier FR, Schneier HA, Liebowitz MR and Klein DF (1990) Fenfluramine augmentation of serotonin reuptake blockade antiobsessional treatment. *J Clin Psychiatry* **51**, 119–123.

Howland RH (1991) Lithium augmentation of fluoxetine in the treatment of OCD and major depression: a case report. *Can J Psychiatry* **36**, 154–155.

Jacobsen FM (1992) Fluoxetine-induced sexual dysfunction and an open trial of yohimbine. *J Clin Psychiatry* **53**, 119–122.

Jenike MA, Baer L and Buttolph L (1991) Buspirone augmentation of fluoxetine in patients with obsessive–compulsive disorder. *J Clin Psychiatry* **52**, 13–14.

Joffe RT (1992) Triiodothyronine potentiation of fluoxetine in depressed patients. *Can J Psychiatry* **37**, 48–50.

Joffe RT and Schuller DR (1993) An open study of buspirone augmentation of serotonin reuptake inhibitors in refractory depression. *J Clin Psychiatry* **54**, 269–271.

Katona CL, Robertson MM, Abou-Saleh MT, Nairac BL, Edwards DR, Lock T, *et al.* (1993) Placebo-controlled trial of lithium augmentation of fluoxetine and lofepramine. *Int Clin Psychopharmacol* **8**, 323.

Katz RJ and Rosenthal M (1994) Adverse interaction of cyproheptadine with serotonergic antidepressants. *J Clin Psychiatry* **55**, 314–315.

Keck PE Jr and McElroy SL (1992) Ratio of plasma fluoxetine to norfluoxetine concentrations and associated sedation. *J Clin Psychiatry* **53**, 127–129.

Kline MD and Koppes S (1994) Acidophilus for sertraline-induced diarrhea. *Am J Psychiatry* **151**, 1521–1522.

Labbate LA and Pollack MH (1994) Treatment of fluoxetine-induced sexual dysfunction with bupropion: A case report. *Ann Clin Psychiatry* **6**, 13–15.

Linet LS (1989) Treatment of a refractory depression with a combination of fluoxetine and d-amphetamine. *Am J Psychiatry* **146**, 803–804.

Markovitz PJ, Stagno SJ and Calabrese JR (1989) Buspirone augmentation of fluoxetine in obsessive–compulsive disorder. *Biol Psychiatry (Suppl)* **25**, 186A.

McCormick S, Olin J and Brotman AW (1990) Reversal of fluoxetine-induced anorgasmia by cyproheptadine in two patients. *J Clin Psychiatry* **51**, 383–384.

McDougle CJ, Goodman WK, Leckman JF, Holzer JC, Barr LC, McCance-Katz E, *et al.* (1993) Limited therapeutic effect of addition of buspirone in fluvoxamine-refractory obsessive–compulsive disorder. *Am J Psychiatry* **150**, 647–649.

McDougle CJ, Goodman WK, Leckman JF, Lee NC, Heninger GR and Price LH (1994) Haloperidol addition in fluvoxamine-refractory obsessive–compulsive disorder: A double-blind, placebo-controlled study in patients with and without tics. *Arch Gen Psychiatry* **51**, 302–308.

McDougle CJ, Price LH, Goodman WK, Charney DS and Heninger GR (1991) A controlled trial of lithium augmentation in fluvoxamine-refractory obsessive–compulsive disorder: lack of efficacy. *J Clin Psychopharmacol* **11**, 175–184.

Metz A and Shader RI (1990) Adverse interactions encountered when using trazodone to treat insomnia associated with fluoxetine. *Int Clin Psychopharmacol* **5**, 191–194.

Metz A and Shader RI (1991) Combination of fluoxetine with pemoline in the treatment of major depressive disorder. *Int Clin Psychopharmacol* **6**, 93–96.

Montgomery SA, Baldwin D, Shah A, Green M, Fineberg N and Montgomery D (1990) Plasma-level response relationship with fluoxetine and zimelidine. *Clin Neuropharmacol* **13 (Suppl 1)**, S71–75.

Nelson JC, Mazure CM, Bowers MB and Jatlow PI (1991) A preliminary, open study of the combination of fluoxetine and desipramine for rapid treatment of major depression. *Arch Gen Psychiatry* **48**, 303–307.

Nierenberg AA, Adler LA, Peselow E, Zomberg G and Rosenthal M (1994) Trazodone for antidepressant-associated insomnia. *Am J Psychiatry* **151**, 1069–1072.

Nierenberg AA, Cole JO and Glass L (1992) Possible trazodone potentiation of fluoxetine: a case series. *J Clin Psychiatry* **53**, 83–85.

Norden MJ (1995) Buspirone treatment of sexual dysfunction associated with selective serotonin reuptake inhibitors. *Depression* **2**, 109–112.

Ontiveros A, Fontaine R and Elie R (1991) Refractory depression: the addition of lithium to fluoxetine or desipramine. *Acta Psychiatr Scand* **83**, 188–192.

Patten S (1995) Personal communication. 25 Feb 1995.

Pigott TA, L'Heureux F, Hill JL, Bihari K, Bernstein SE and Murphy DL (1992) A double-blind study of adjuvant buspirone hydrochloride in clomipramine-treated patients with obsessive–compulsive disorder. *J Clin Psychopharmacol* **12**, 11–18.

Pope HG Jr, McElroy SL and Nixon RA (1988) Possible synergism between fluoxetine and lithium in refractory depression. *Am J Psychiatry* **145**, 1292–1294.

Proulx J and Fontaine R (1991) Buspirone prevents the antidepressant effect of fluoxetine. *Biol Psychiatry (Suppl)* **29**, 129A.

Psychiatry LCB, Goodman WK, Anand A and Price LH (1994) *Desipramine augmentation of selective serotonin reuptake inhibitor treatment of refractory OCD patients.* Presented at the American Psychiatric Association Annual Meeting, Philadelphia, PA.

Rabkin JG, Rabkin R and Wagner G (1994) Effects of fluoxetine on mood and immune status in depressed patients with HIV illness. *J Clin Psychiatry* **55**, 92–97.

Rickels K, Amsterdam JD, Clary C, Puzzuoli G and Schweizer E (1991) Buspirone in major depression: A controlled study. *J Clin Psychiatry* **52**, 34–38.

Rosenzweig MH and Amsterdam JD (1992) *Clomipramine augmentation in resistant depression.* Presented at the American Psychiatric Association Annual Meeting, Washington, DC.

Rothschild AJ (1995) Selective serotonin re-uptake inhibitor induced sexual dysfunction: Efficacy of a drug holiday. *Am J Psychiatry* **152(10)**, 514–6.

Ruegg RG, Evans DL, Comer WS, Golden RN (1992) Lithium augments fluoxetine treatment of obsessive–compulsive disorder, *Lithium* **3(1)**, 69–71.

Siddiqui UA, Chakravarti SK and Jesinger DK (1985) The tolerance and antidepressive activity of fluvoxamine as a single dose compared to a twice daily dose. *Curr Med Res Opin* **9**, 681–690.

Simeon JG, Thatte S and Wiggins D (1990) Treatment of adolescent obsessive–compulsive disorder with a clomipramine–fluoxetine combination. *Psychopharmacol Bull* **26**, 285–290.

Small GW, Schneider LS, Holman S, Brystritsky A, Meyers BS and Nemeroff CB (1994) *Estrogen plus fluoxetine for geriatric depression.* Presented at the American Psychiatric Association Annual Meeting, Philadelphia, PA.

Souche A, Montaldi S, Uehlinger C, Kasas A, Reymond MJ, Reymond P, *et al.* (1991) Treatment of resistant depression with the citalopram-lithium combination. Methodology of a doubleblind multicenter study and preliminary results. *Encephale* **17**, 213–219.

Swerdlow NR and Andia AM (1989) Trazodone–fluoxetine combination for treatment of obsessive–compulsive disorder. *Am J Psychiatry* **146**, 1637.

Swinson R (1995) Personal communication. 26 Feb 1995.

Tenck C (195) Personal communication. 19 Feb 1995.

Tiffon L, Coplan JD, Papp LA and Gorman JM (1994) Augmentation strategies with tricyclic or fluoxetine treatment in seven partially responsive panic disorder patients. *J Clin Psychiatry* **55**, 66–69.

Varia IM and Donnelly CL (1991) *Fluoxetine augments tricyclics in panic disorder.* Presented at the American Psychiatric Association Annual Meeting, New Orleans.

Walker PW, Cole JO, Gardner EA, Hughes AR, Johnston JA, Batey SR, *et al.* (1993) Improvement in fluoxetine-associated sexual dysfunction in patients switched to bupropion. *J Clin Psychiatry* **54**, 459–465.

Weilburg JB, Rosenbaum JF, Meltzer-Brody S and Shushtari J (1991) Tricyclic augmentation of fluoxetine. *Ann Clin Psychiatry* **3**, 209–213.

Yee W (1995) Personal communication. 24 Feb 1995.

Zohar J, Shapira B, Oppenheim G, Ayd FJ and Belmaker RH (1985) Addition of estrogen to imipramine in female-resistant depressives. *Psychopharmacol Bull* **21**, 705–706.

16

Depression in the workplace: An economic perspective

Paul E. Greenberg, Ronald C. Kessler, Tara L. Nells,
Stan N. Finkelstein and Ernst R. Berndt

INTRODUCTION

In recent years, the use of economic tools has increasingly been incorporated into the mainstream of mental health analyses (e.g. Frank and Manning, 1992). Research investigations have examined behavioural responses to economic incentives related to mental health care, as well as the effects of mental health status on a variety of economic outcomes (McGuire, 1992). In many instances, these lines of investigation have focused on cost-related issues. For example, cost-of-illness, cost-effectiveness, cost-benefit, and cost-utility models have been used to estimate the magnitude of resources expended on mental health disorders, and to assess the relative merits of alternative interventions (e.g. Rice *et al.*, 1990; Sturm and Wells, 1995; Kamlet *et al.*, 1992).

Initially, the primary focus of these types of analyses was on direct treatment costs alone, with a particular emphasis on out-of-pocket resource utilization. Economic researchers have examined the cost tradeoffs between short-term and long-term care, those among inpatient, outpatient and pharmaceutical therapies, as well as those among comorbid illnesses (Wilde and Whittington, 1995). In addition, questions concerning cost offsets between the medical and mental health sectors have occupied substantial attention, and have offered insights into the manner in

Selective Serotonin Re-uptake Inhibitors: Advances in Basic Research and Clinical Practice, Second Edition, Edited by J.P. Feighner and W.F. Boyer
© 1996 John Wiley & Sons Ltd

which direct costs accrue with alternative levels and types of treatment (Mumford *et al.*, 1994).

With the direct economic implications of mental health disorders being systematically analysed and better documented, more recent investigations have concentrated on indirect cost categories. As the nexus of decision-making authority has been shifting to payers in recent years, employers have become much more significant participants in the health care sector. This trend has created a growing need to document the magnitude of mental health costs that accrue in the workplace. (Although indirect mortality costs arising from premature death are of relevance to assessments of lost societal resources due to illness, from an economic perspective, morbidity costs are likely to have more immediate relevance to employers. The economic reality is that the workplace costs associated with lingering illness often substantially exceed those associated with premature death.)

One mental illness that has been analysed in great detail from the perspective of workplace costs is depression (see Jönsson and Rosenbaum (1993) for review). Recent economic research concerning the costs of depression has reached several important conclusions (Greenberg *et al.*, 1993a, 1993b). First, the economic burden of depression—estimated most recently to be almost $44 billion per year—is comparable to that of many catastrophic physical illnesses such as cancer, coronary heart disease, and AIDS, in terms of costs to society. Second, nearly three-quarters of the costs of depression are indirect. Third, employers bear more than half of all the costs that result from this illness, in terms of increased absenteeism of depressed employees as well as their reduced productivity while at work.

Many of the underlying characteristics of depression contribute to the high workplace costs that have been documented. For example, among the symptoms of this illness are poor concentration, indecisiveness, lack of self-confidence—or inflated self-confidence in the case of mania—and general fatigue, each of which tends to reduce an employee's productive capacity in the workplace. Furthermore, depression tends to affect people in their prime working years and has the potential, if not properly treated, to last for a significant period of a sufferer's lifetime. Thus, the general profile of this illness is consistent with substantial workplace costs.

Although it is now clear that depression exacts enormous costs in the workplace, precise estimates to the magnitude of these costs are critically dependent on the quality of the clinical data used in the underlying economic calculations, and the resulting assumptions that are required to generate reasonable results. This observation was expressed in the conclusion of Greenberg *et al.* (1993a) concerning their cost-of-illness analysis:

> . . . the cost estimates presented here are predicated on numerous assumptions concerning the prevalence, duration, treatment, and effects of depression. As clinical studies advance our understanding of affective illness, they will facilitate cost refinement that will improve our estimates of the economic burden of depression.

Recent epidemiological data based on the National Comorbidity Survey (NCS) allow the earlier cost model to be refined and updated. Whereas in the earlier analysis it was assumed that people who suffer from depression had equal labour force participation rates as their asymptomatic counterparts, the new prevalence data permit direct investigation of the burden of illness by employment status. In addition, new data from the National Institute of Mental Health (NIMH) permit more precise distinctions to be made concerning the proportion of treated and untreated sufferers of each type of depression.

This chapter incorporates these recent data into the cost-of-illness model described in Greenberg *et al.* (1993a). We refine our estimates of the cost of depression in the workplace, using the same prevalence-based, human capital approach, to estimate the 1990 workplace costs as has been previously reported. We focus solely on the workplace costs of depression because the methodology and content of the data used to estimate the other relevant cost categories has not been significantly changed since our previous work. We continue to focus on three types of affective disorders, major depression (MDE), bipolar disorder (BD) depression, and dysthymia (DYS).

Our methodology relies upon estimates from the medical and mental health literature concerning the average duration of episodes of depression, and distinguishes the portion of each episode spent away from work versus that at work. Absenteeism focuses on the number of days per episode that an individual suffering from depression is absent from the workplace due to symptoms of the illness. These costs are calculated by multiplying the daily market wage rate by the cumulative number of days lost. Explicit attention is also paid to the remaining episode days of depression that are spent in the workplace where some reduction in productive capacity is likely. From the employer's perspective, the costs of depression include the difference between the value of output produced by an asymptomatic worker compared with that produced by an employee who is incapacitated to some degree because of the effects of this illness. To isolate lost productivity due to depression, we calculate the potential contribution of sufferers while at work during depressive episodes, and apply an overall impairment percentage.

EPIDEMIOLOGICAL UNDERPINNINGS OF COST-OF-ILLNESS ANALYSIS

Methods

The National Comorbidity Survey (NCS) is the first nationally representative survey in the United States to study the prevalence, risk factors, and consequences of psychiatric morbidity and comorbidity. The survey included interviews with 8098 respondents aged 15–54, and was carried out between September 1990 and February 1992. Respondents were selected using probability methods from a multi-stage area sample of households nationwide. The response rate was 82.4%. Further details about the NCS sample design and field procedures are presented elsewhere (Kessler *et al.*, 1994).

The data reported in Table 1 have been weighted to adjust for variation in

Table 1. Representatives of NCS.

Characteristic	% of NCS sample (weighted)	US population (1989)
Sex		
Male	49.5	49.1
Female	50.5	50.9
Marital status		
Married/cohabitation	62.9	59.8
Separated/widowed/divorced	10.0	10.1
Never married	27.1	30.1
Age		
15–24	24.7	25.5
25–34	30.1	30.8
35–44	27.1	25.9
45–54	18.1	17.8
Race		
Black	11.5	11.9
Hispanic	9.7	8.6
Non-black, non-hispanic	78.8	79.5

within-household probabilities of selection and nonresponse bias, and have been post-stratified by means of an iterative procedure to approximate the national population distributions of the cross-classification of age, sex, race/ethnicity, marital status, education, living arrangements, region and urbanicity as defined by the 1989 US National Health Interview Survey (US Department of Health and Human Services, 1992). A more detailed description of the NCS sampling design is presented elsewhere (Kessler *et al.*, 1994). As shown in Table 1, the NCS data are representative of the total US population within the age range covered by the sample on a variety of social and demographic characteristics.

The diagnostic data in the NCS were coded using the criteria of DSM III R based on a modified version of the Composite International Diagnostic Interview (CIDI; World Health Organization, 1990a). This is a fully structured diagnostic interview, and was developed in a collaborative WHO/ADAMHA project to foster epidemiological and cross-cultural comparative research by producing diagnoses according to the definitions and criteria of both DSM III R (APA, 1987) and the Diagnostic Criteria for Research of the ICD-10 (World Health Organization, 1991).

Diagnoses were generated by the CIDI diagnostic programme (World Health Organization, 1990b). The DSM III R diagnoses in the core NCS include major depression, mania, dysthymia, posttraumatic stress disorder, panic disorder, agoraphobia, social phobia, simple phobia, generalized anxiety disorder, alcohol abuse, alcohol dependence, drug abuse, drug dependence, antisocial personality disorder, and non-affective psychosis. All the diagnoses presented here were defined with diagnostic hierarchy rules.

The reliability and validity of the diagnostic assessments in the CIDI have been examined in a series of international studies carried out as part of the WHO field trials of the CIDI. These field trials have documented good acceptance and cultural appropriateness of the CIDI (Cottler *et al.*, 1989; Wittchen *et al.*, 1990), excellent interrater reliability (Wittchen *et al.*, 1991; Cottler *et al.*, 1991) and good test–retest reliability (Wacker *et al.*, 1990; Wittchen *et al.*, 1990). Good validity of the CIDI has been documented with regard to concordance with clinical diagnoses (Semler, 1989; Spengler and Wittchen, 1988; Janca *et al.*, 1992; Leitmeyer, 1990), procedural validity compared to the present state examination (Semler, 1989; Farmer *et al.*, 1987, 1991), as well as with regard to specific issues such as the validity of the probe questions and assessments of comorbidity (Leitmeyer, 1990).

The NCS was designed to take the next step beyond the Epidemiologic Catchment Area (ECA) study which was the basis for the Greenberg *et al.* (1993a) cost-of-illness estimates. Several study design advances are noteworthy. First, the NCS diagnoses are based on DSM III R while the ECA study diagnoses are based on DSM III. Second, while the ECA was designed primarily to generate data on prevalence and incidence of psychiatric disorder, the NCS was designed to provide comprehensive data on risk factors as well. Third, because the ECA study design focused on institutional respondents and clinical reappraisals, it was necessary to conduct that study in a small number of regional samples. In contrast, the different goals established in undertaking the NCS made it possible to use a nationally representative sample. Fourth, a general procedure that was absent from the ECA was added in the NCS to address the problem of response bias. A systematic nonrespondent survey was administered in which a random subsample of initial nonresponders were offered a financial incentive to complete a screening form of the diagnostic interview. The results of this survey documented that initial nonresponders were more likely to have a history of psychiatric disorder than initially co-operative responders. A nonresponse adjustment weight was used to compensate for the downward bias in prevalence estimates introduced by this systematic nonresponse.

A number of factors may have contributed to the higher prevalence of major depression in the NCS (9.6%) as compared to the ECA study (2.7%). One possibility is that individuals in the NCS were younger, on average, and therefore the overall prevalence would be expected to be higher, given that the lowest prevalence for major depression were among the over-65 age group in the ECA sample (Regier *et al.*, 1988). A second possibility is that secular trends could also account for part of this difference, as the NCS was conducted approximately 10 years after the ECA study. Another explanation may be a methodological one; namely, that the CIDI is a more sensitive instrument than the DIS in community population studies. Along these lines, a modification made to the method of case ascertainment for major depression in the CIDI may have led to a higher proportion of true cases being reported in the NCS. Responders were given three chances to respond to a stem question for major depression (i.e. questions asked about episodes of feeling "sad, blue, or depressed", feeling "down in the dumps and gloomy", and "losing interest in things you usually enjoy") rather than one question in the DIS.

A final possibility is that this more detailed probing resulted in false positives in the NCS. In an effort to investigate this possibility, a brief CIDI/major depressive validation was performed in the NCS. Thirty responders—20 of whom reported a lifetime history of major depression according to the structured interview and 10 who gave a positive answer to a stem question for major depression but failed to meet DSM III R criteria—were re-interviewed. These validating re-interviews were performed by clinicians blind to the CIDI diagnosis, using the Structured Clinical Interview for DSM III R (SCID, Spitzer *et al.*, 1990). Fourteen of the 20 respondents, or 70%, who had a lifetime major depression according to the CIDI were classified as having lifetime major depression according to the SCID, while eight of the 10, or 80%, classified as non-cases in the interview were classified the same way by the SCID. These validation results are similar to those found for major depression according to the DIS in the ECA Study (Helzer *et al.*, 1985).

In contrast to the widely divergent results for major depression, the 12-month prevalences of bipolar disorder—1.3% in the NCS compared with 1.2% in the ECA—are quite similar in the two surveys. Although the ECA did not report 12-month prevalence data for dysthymia, the lifetime prevalence (3.2%) is quite similar to the lifetime rate of 2.8% reported in the NCS. The somewhat lower prevalence in the NCS is consistent with the fact that the DSM III R diagnostic system used to make NCS diagnoses defines dysthymia more narrowly than the DSM III criteria used in the ECA.

Discussion

The NCS data are categorized into three discrete employment groupings: (1) in the labour force/employed; (2) in the labour force/not employed; and (3) not in the labour force. Whereas Greenberg *et al* (1993a) assumed that the same employment rate applied to the depressed population as was found in the overall economy, the NCS provides estimates of the prevalence of depression by employment status. This permits refinement of the estimated costs associated with depression in the workplace.

Due to incomplete reporting of prevalence data from the ECA study, Greenberg *et al.* (1993a) applied gender distributions reported for depression generally to each sub-type of affective disorder. In contrast, the prevalence data based on the National Comorbidity Survey (NCS) are categorized by age, sex, type of disorder and employment status. This extensive detail enables us to refine the earlier estimates that had been based on interpolations of reported ECA results. Thus, unlike the earlier analysis, here we rely on observed prevalence totals broken out in several ways.

To obtain a complete matrix of one-year prevalence rates, several assumptions were made. The NCS survey population included persons 18–54 years old, whereas the ECA included attention to all adults. Therefore, the prevalence data for those aged 54 and over had to be extrapolated from alternative data sources. Prevalence rates for individuals in the 55–64 age category are assumed to be the same as those for individuals aged 45–54, as shown in Tables 1 and 2. In addition, the one-year prevalence rates for the 65 and older age group are based on the overall relationship between the earlier ECA and NCS findings, applied to this particular age group.

In addition to providing prevalence data on the three different affective disorders, the NCS data list two additional categories; sufferers of both MDE and DYS, and

Table 2. Morbidity of depression in 1990, by age, sex, and type of disorder. One-year prevalence rates of employed persons.

Age	Male One-year prevalence		Female One-year prevalence		Overall One-year prevalence	
	No. of cases	Rate (%)	No. of cases	Rate (%)	No. of cases	Rate (%)
All affective disorders						
Total	4 334 286	6.9	6 019 460	11.5	10 353 746	9.0
18–29	1 608 243	9.1	1 910 277	12.5	3 518 520	10.7
30–44	2 100 571	8.0	2 551 567	11.8	4 652 138	9.7
45–64	586 233	3.4	1 502 624	10.8	2 088 857	6.7
65+	39 239	2.0	54 992	3.8	94 231	2.7
Major depression						
Total	3 708 554	5.9	5 299 913	10.1	9 008 467	7.8
18–29	1 414 724	8.0	1 780 482	11.7	3 195 206	9.7
30–44	1 706 221	6.5	2 090 506	9.6	3 796 727	7.9
45–64	554 241	3.2	1 382 052	9.9	1 936 293	6.2
65+	33 369	1.7	46 873	3.2	80 241	2.3
Bipolar disorder						
Total	400 094	0.6	281 208	0.5	681 303	0.6
18–29	129 897	0.7	45 047	0.3	174 943	0.5
30–44	261 586	1.0	234 328	1.1	495 913	1.0
45–64	6053	0.0	0	0.0	6053	0.0
65+	2560	0.1	1834	0.1	4394	0.1
Dysthymia						
Total	225 638	0.4	438 339	0.8	663 977	0.6
18–29	63 623	0.4	84 749	0.6	148 371	0.5
30–44	132 765	0.5	226 734	1.0	359 498	0.7
45–64	25 940	0.2	120 572	0.9	146 512	0.5
65+	3311	0.2	6285	0.4	9596	0.3

Notes:
Prevalence rates are based on the National Comorbidity Survey.
Prevalence for 65+ age group is calculated by applying the average growth rate between the prevalence rates based on the Epidemiologic Catchment Area study as reported by Weissman *et al.*, 1991 and the NCS data for each respective category.
Number of cases are based on the 1990 labour force as reported by the Bureau of Labor Statistics.

sufferers of both MDE and BD. In our cost-of-illness analysis, these relatively small groups of individuals are divided equally between the appropriate disorders.

Since the goal of the analysis presented here is to estimate the workplace costs of depression, only those *employed* in the labour force are incorporated in our calculations. The number of people who suffer from the various forms of depression can be estimated by applying the detailed prevalence percentages to 1990 population totals. One-year prevalence of depression for employed persons, disaggregated by age and gender, as well as by type of affective illness, is reported in Table 2.

One new insight offered by the NCS data is that there are indeed a substantial number of *workers* who suffer from this illness. In a given year, 9% of the employed labour force—10.3 million workers—experience a depressive episode. The vast majority, over 9 million, of those workers who suffer from this form of mental illness each year experience major depression, while bipolar disorder and dysthymia each account for an additional 700 000 cases. Because its symptoms can at times be debilitating, a very large group of people thereby comprise the "working depressed" in any given year. With so many individuals included in this group, their health status can have significant effects on any given company or on the economy as a whole.

The number of working women who suffer from depression is almost 1.4 times that of working men. Although overall prevalences are even more heavily skewed towards women, the gender disparity of suffering individuals is mitigated by the fact that there are fewer employed women than there are employed men. The distribution of sufferers in the case of the other two categories of depression is somewhat different from that of major depression. Whereas twice as many working women compared with working men suffer from dysthymia, bipolar disorder actually affects more working men than working women.

Twelve-month prevalences for the working depressed fall from 10.7% for the youngest age group to 2.9% for the oldest. In addition, of all workers experiencing depression, almost 80% are below the age of 45. Since this illness has the potential to linger for many years if untreated or improperly treated, this age distribution suggests a clear mechanism by which substantial costs can accrue in the workplace.

As shown in Table 3, there is a markedly higher prevalence of depression within the unemployed group compared with the employed group. In a given year, over 20% of the unemployed labour force, or approximately 1.3 million people, has an episode of depression. Even if a causal link could be made between being depressed and being unemployed, it is not clear which direction such an effect would take. In many instances, the symptoms of depression may cause an individual to have difficulty finding or retaining a job, while in other cases, being laid off may trigger an episode of depression (Kessler *et al.*, 1987, 1989). It is noteworthy that the vast majority of these people—1.1 million—suffer from major depression. In addition, as with the employed population, the number of unemployed women who suffer from depression is almost 1.4 times that of unemployed men.

Table 4 completes the prevalence analysis by employment status, and reveals that

Table 3. Morbidity of depression in 1990, by age, sex, and type of disorder. One-year prevalence rates of unemployed persons.

Age	Male One-year prevalence		Female One-year prevalence		Overall One-year prevalence	
	No. of cases	Rate (%)	No. of cases	Rate (%)	No. of cases	Rate (%)
All affective disorders						
Total	537 687	15.2	755 556	26.6	1 293 243	20.3
18–29	267 429	16.8	405 349	31.0	672 778	23.2
30–44	204 442	16.9	265 019	25.7	469 461	21.0
45–64	62 953	9.4	81 354	17.9	144 307	12.8
65+	2863	4.7	3834	8.3	6697	6.3
Major depression						
Total	446 701	12.7	652 894	23.0	1 099 595	17.3
18–29	227 704	14.3	318 563	24.4	546 267	18.9
30–44	178 751	14.8	254 204	24.7	432 955	19.3
45–64	38 033	5.7	76 781	16.9	114 814	10.2
65+	2214	3.6	3346	7.3	5560	5.2
Bipolar disorder						
Total	17 844	0.6	80 414	2.8	98 258	1.5
18–29	11 918	0.8	75 537	5.8	87 455	3.0
30–44	5864	0.5	0	0.0	5864	0.3
45–64	0	0.0	4573	1.0	4573	0.4
65+	63	0.1	304	0.7	367	0.3
Dysthymia						
Total	73 142	2.1	22 248	0.9	95 390	1.5
18–29	27 808	1.8	11 249	0.9	39 056	1.3
30–44	19 828	1.6	10 815	1.1	30 643	1.4
45–64	24 920	3.7	0	0.0	24 920	2.2
65+	587	1.0	184	0.4	771	0.7

Notes:
Prevalence rates are based on the National Comorbidity Survey.
Prevalence for 65 + age group is calculated by applying the average growth rate between the prevalence rates based on the Epidemiologic Catchment Area study as reported by Weissman *et al.*, 1991 and the NCS data for each respective category.
Number of cases are based on the 1990 labour force as reported by the Bureau of Labor Statistics.

almost 10% of individuals who are not in the labour force suffer from depression. This is slightly higher than the prevalence rate reported among employed individuals, but less than half that found within the unemployed group. With 2.2 depressed women for every depressed man with this employment status, this gender distribution is particularly skewed. In addition, the prevalence distribution by age group is markedly different compared with the distribution for individuals within the labour force. Whereas approximately 80% of depressed individuals in the labour force are between the ages of 18 and 44, less than 50% of those not in the labour

Table 4. Morbidity of depression in 1990, by age, sex, and type of disorder. One-year prevalence rates of persons not in the labour force.

Age	Male One-year prevalence		Female One-year prevalence		Overall One-year prevalence	
	No. of cases	Rate (%)	No. of cases	Rate (%)	No. of cases	Rate (%)
All affective disorders						
Total	1 842 058	9.4	4 013 707	10.0	5 855 765	9.8
18–29	415 849	13.1	715 781	10.5	1 131 630	11.3
30–44	383 758	23.9	1 180 786	15.9	1 564 544	17.3
45–64	806 358	18.4	1 644 224	16.6	2 450 582	17.2
65 +	236 093	2.3	472 916	3.0	709 009	2.7
Major depression						
Total	1 227 786	6.3	3 257 428	8.1	4 485 214	7.5
18–29	377 468	11.9	651 823	9.6	1 029 291	10.3
30–44	297 437	18.6	1 041 455	14.0	1 338 891	14.8
45–64	390 039	8.9	1 199 759	12.1	1 589 798	11.1
65 +	162 843	1.6	364 391	2.3	527 234	2.0
Bipolar disorder						
Total	484 924	2.5	231 145	0.6	716 069	1.2
18–29	38 381	1.2	27 216	0.4	65 597	0.7
30–44	65 483	4.1	62 049	0.8	127 531	1.4
45–64	333 537	7.6	122 253	1.2	455 790	3.2
65 +	47 524	0.5	19 628	0.1	67 151	0.3
Dysthymia						
Total	129 347	0.7	525 134	1.3	654 482	1.1
18–29	0	0.0	36 742	0.5	36 742	0.4
30–44	20 839	1.3	77 282	1.0	98 121	1.1
45–64	82 782	1.9	322 212	3.3	404 994	2.8
65 +	25 726	0.2	88 898	0.6	114 624	0.4

Notes:
Prevalence rates are based on the National Comorbidity Survey.
Prevalence for 65 + age group is calculated by applying the average growth rate between the prevalence rates based on the Epidemiologic Catchment Area study as reported by Weissman *et al.*, 1991 and the NCS data for each respective category.
Number of cases are based on the 1990 labour force as reported by the Bureau of Labor Statistics.

force are within this age range. (See Figure 1 for a comparison of prevalence rates by employment status, gender and age groups.)

WORKPLACE COSTS

Reduction in productive capacity due to excess absenteeism

Methods

To estimate the amount of lost work time due to depression, we focus on those employees suffering from major depression or bipolar disorder, and recognize that

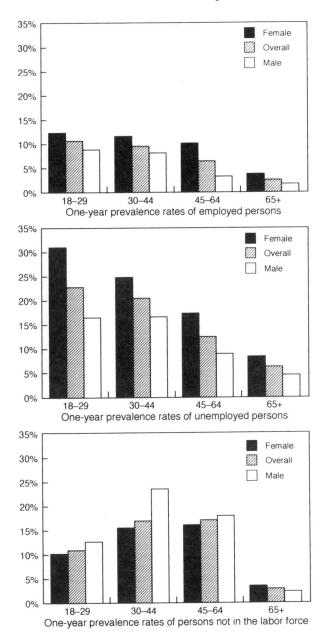

Figure 1. Depression in 1990 by age, sex and employment status. One-year prevalence rates. Prevalence rates are taken from Tables 2, 3 and 4.

the effects of the illness result in excess absentee days. However, unlike these forms of the illness, which are episodic in nature, dysthymia is a chronic condition that lasts at least two years. Dysthymia sufferers are not assumed to exhibit excess absenteeism due to their affective disorder. Instead, we consider the workplace cost associated with these individuals to accrue solely as a result of their impaired performance on the job. To the extent that dysthymia actually causes excess absenteeism from work, this assumption understates the workplace costs of affective illness. (This is because the costs associated with lost productive capacity are likely to be greater for an absentee day, in which the value of potential output of the entire day is lost, than for partial performance impairment while at work.)

At the outset, it is necessary to define the average duration of each episode, as well as the number of days per episode that the employee is unable to attend work in order to calculate the cumulative number of days lost from work in a given year due to depression. It is presupposed that these are dependent on whether or not treatment is sought. We assume that each episode of MDE or BP lasts an average of 12 weeks, or 84 days, for treated cases of depression, and 18 weeks, or 126 days, for untreated cases. These assumptions are consistent with those in Greenberg *et al.* (1993a), and are based on those described in Stoudemire *et al.* (1986). Evidence from the psychiatric literature suggests that these assumptions likely understate the actual average episode length (Keller *et al.*, 1982).

Whereas Stoudemire's assumptions regarding average episode duration for treated and untreated individuals reflected those suffering from major depression alone (Stoudmire *et al.*, 1986), the same assumptions are used in this analysis to estimate the costs associated with bipolar disorders well. Ongoing and future clinical research regarding average episode duration of bipolar sufferers is likely to result in possible refinements to this particular assumption.

Although neither the ECA nor the NCS reports data on average episode duration, a potential derivation is the ratio of the one-month prevalence rate to the 12-month prevalence rate multiplied by 12. Based on NCS data, this calculation implies an average episode length of approximately 21 weeks. This suggests that the 12-week and 18-week assumptions used here for the treated and untreated groups, respectively, are conservative.

It has been shown that persons suffering from MDE and BD tend to exhibit substantially more absentee days compared to asymptomatic individuals (Broadhead *et al.*, 1990). The underlying assumptions used in Greenberg *et al.* (1993a) are that treated patients spend an average of 16 days in the hospital during each episode of depression, while untreated sufferers spend twice as long—32 days—at home unable to work. It is assumed that treated patients lose an additional one quarter of each remaining day of the episode seeking outpatient treatment, and untreated individuals lose an additional third of each episode day. Together, these assumptions imply that treated patients are unable to attend work for as many as 33 days during a 12-week episode, and that untreated individuals are unable to attend work for as many as 60 days during an 18-weeks episode. Thus, treatment is expected to decrease an episode length by one-third. The resulting total number of lost days are shown in Tables 5 and 6.

Data on service utilization by type of mental disorder were recently collected by the NIMH and reported by Regier *et al.* (1993). As shown in Figure 2, the following treatment percentages are reported: bipolar disorders 61%; major depression 54%; and dysthymia 42%. The majority of treatment is received in either a specialist medical/mental health care facility or in the general medical sector.

These data are based on the ECA study, which was not the basis for the prevalence findings reported in Tables 2 – 4. But that earlier collection effort, which includes very specific detail on service utilization by type of depression is especially useful for our analysis. Although individuals may have obtained treatment from various sources, the percentages depicted in Figure 2 count each individual only once. Individuals treated in multiple settings were subtracted proportionally from each sector.

In comparison to the ECA service utilization data that is disorder specific, the NCS reports in Kessler *et al.* (1993) that the 12-month utilization rate of professional services for an individual suffering from any mental illness is approximately 20%. The NCS professional services category includes all mental health specialists, physicians, social workers, counsellors, nurses or other health professionals. This definition is most readily compared to the combination of specialty mental/addictive and general medical services in the ECA, for which the treatment rate is 37.8%.

Discussion

By combining data on the number of people who suffer from MDE and BD with assumptions concerning expected episode lengths and likely treatment percentages, we estimate that in 1990 almost 440 million days were lost as a result of these mental health disorders. Tables 7 and 8 show that this equates to over 1.2 million lost work years. To compute the total costs of excess absenteeism, the work years are converted to work weeks and are multiplied by median weekly wages, as reported by the Bureau of Labor Statistics, for each age and gender category. We conclude that approximately $24.5 billion per year was lost as a result of depression-related absenteeism.

Because it accounts for a relatively high share of total prevalence, the vast majority of these excess absenteeism costs are due to the effects of major depression. In addition, as shown in Tables 7 and 8, almost half the total cost associated with excess absenteeism is attributable to the 30–44 age group. Furthermore, although over 57% of all work weeks lost due to depression are attributable to women, they account for only 50% of all costs of excess absenteeism from work. This is because the lower median wages of women versus men result in a lower market valuation of their time lost from work.

Table 5. Morbidity of depression: Episode days lost by employed sufferers of major depression.

Age	No. of cases		Percentage of cases		Male One-year prevalence		Female One-year prevalence	
	Male	Female	Treated (%)	Untreated (%)	Treated	Untreated	Treated	Untreated
	[1]	[2]	[3]	[4]	[5] = [1] × [3]	[6] = [1] × [4]	[7] = [2] × [3]	[8] = [2] × [4]
Major depression								
Total	3 708 554	5 299 913	54	46	1 998 911	1 709 643	2 856 653	2 443 260
18–29	1 414 724	1 780 482	54	46	762 536	652 188	959 680	820 802
30–44	1 706 221	2 090 506	54	46	919 653	786 568	1 126 783	963 723
45–64	554 241	1 382 052	54	46	298 736	255 505	744 926	637 126
65+	33 369	46 873	54	46	17 986	15 383	25 264	21 608

Lost days from treated cases

Age	Average episode length (days)	Average hospital days	Average outpatient treatment days	Lost days per individual	Male Number of treated individuals	Male Episode days lost	Female Number of treated individuals	Female Episode days lost	Total Episode days lost by treated individuals
	[9]	[10]	[11] = ([9] − [10]) × 0.25	[12] = [10] + [11]	[13] = [5]	[14] = [12] × [13]	[15] = [7]	[16] = [12] × [15]	[17] = [14] + [16]
Total	84	16	17	33	1 998 911	65 964 048	2 856 653	94 269 546	160 233 594
18–29	84	16	17	33	762 536	25 163 690	959 680	31 669 433	56 833 123
30–44	84	16	17	33	919 653	30 348 553	1 126 783	37 183 829	67 532 382
45–64	84	16	17	33	298 736	9 858 278	744 926	24 582 556	34 440 835
65+	84	16	17	33	17 986	593 527	25 264	833 728	1 427 255

Lost days from untreated cases

Age	Average episode length (days) [18]	Average days at home unable to work [19]	Average additional lost days [20] = ([18] − [19]) × 0.3	Lost days per individual [21] = [19] + [20]	Male Number of untreated individuals [22] = [6]	Male Episode days lost [23] = [21] × [22]	Female Number of untreated individuals [24] = [8]	Female Episode days lost [25] = [21] × [24]	Total Episode days lost by untreated individuals [26] = [23] + [25]
Total	126	32	28.2	60.2	1 709 643	102 920 529	2 443 260	147 084 236	250 004 765
18–29	126	32	28.2	60.2	652 188	39 261 694	820 802	49 412 293	88 673 986
30–44	126	32	28.2	60.2	786 568	47 351 386	963 723	58 016 139	105 367 526
45–64	126	32	28.2	60.2	255 505	15 381 397	637 126	38 354 979	53 736 377
65+	126	32	28.2	60.2	15 383	926 052	21 608	1 300 825	2 226 877

Sources:

Average episode length, [9] and [18], Hospital days [10], Days at home unable to work [19], Outpatient treatment days [11], and Additional lost days [20] from Stoudemire *et al.*, 1986. Percentage of treated and untreated cases, [3] and [4], from Regier *et al.*, 1993.

Table 6. Morbidity of depression: Episode days lost by employed sufferers of bipolar disorder.

Age	No. of cases		Percentage of cases		Male One-year prevalence		Female One-year prevalence	
	Male	Female	Treated (%)	Untreated (%)	Treated	Untreated	Treated	Untreated
	[1]	[2]	[3]	[4]	[5] = [1] × [3]	[6] = [1] × [4]	[7] = [2] × [3]	[8] = [2] × [4]
Bipolar disorder								
Total	400 094	281 208	61	39	243 657	156 437	171 256	109 952
18–29	129 897	45 047	61	39	79 107	50 790	27 433	17 613
30–44	261 586	234 328	61	39	159 306	102 280	142 706	91 622
45–64	6053	0	61	39	3686	2367	0	0
65+	2560	1834	61	39	1559	1001	1117	717

Lost days from treated cases

Age	Average episode length (days)	Average hospital days	Average outpatients treatment days	Lost days per individual	Male		Female		Total
					Number of treated individuals	Episode days lost	Number of treated individuals	Episode days lost	Episode days lost by treated individuals
	[9]	[10]	[11] = ([9] − [10]) × 0.25 + [10]	[12] = [10] + [11]	[13] = [5]	[14] = [12] × [13]	[15] = [7]	[16] = [12] × [15]	[17] = [14] + [16]
Total	84	16	17	33	243 657	8 040 697	171 256	5 651 445	13 692 142
18–29	84	16	17	33	79 107	2 610 531	27 433	905 300	3 515 830
30–44	84	16	17	33	159 306	5 257 084	142 706	4 709 282	9 966 366
45–64	84	16	17	33	3686	121 638	0	0	121 638
65+	84	16	17	33	1559	51 444	1117	36 864	88.308

Lost days from untreated cases

					Male		Female		Total
Age	Average episode length (days [18]	Average days at home unable to work [19]	Average additional lost days [20] = (([18] − [19]) × 0.3 + [20]	Lost days per individual [21] = [19] + [20]	Number of untreated individuals [22] = [6]	Episode days lost [23] = [21] × [22]	Number of untreated individuals [24] = [8]	Episode days lost [25] = [21] × [24]	Episode days lost by untreated individuals [26] = [23] + [25]
Total	126	32	28.2	60.2	156 437	9 417 502	109 952	6 619 139	16 036 641
18–29	126	32	28.2	60.2	50 790	3 057 531	17 613	1 060 314	4 117 844
30–44	126	32	28.2	60.2	102 280	6 157 252	91 622	5 515 650	11 672 902
45–64	126	32	28.2	60.2	2367	142 466	0	0	142 466
65+	126	32	28.2	60.2	1001	60 253	717	43 176	103 429

Sources:

Average episode length, [9] and [18], Hospital days [10], Days at home unable to work [19], Outpatient treatment days [11], and Additional lost days [20] from Stoudemire *et al*, 1986. Percentage of treated and untreated cases, [3] and [4], from Regier *et al*, 1993.

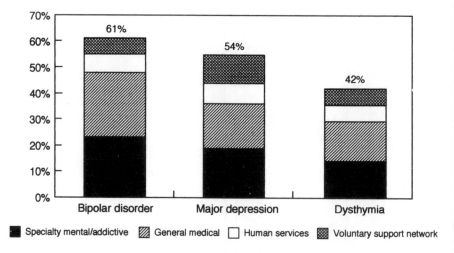

Figure 2. Percentage of individuals suffering from affective disorders receiving treatment. One-year utilization rates by type of disorder and service sector. Treatment data from Regier *et al.*, 1993. Although persons may have received treatment from different service sectors, the rates count each individual once. Multiple-sector treated individuals are subtracted in relative proportions from each sector.

Reduction in productive capacity while at work

Methods

A serious symptom of depression is its negative effect on productive capacity. This section of the analysis focuses on the days people attend work during episodes of depression, but are unable to achieve their usual performance. The total potential output of depressed individuals during these episode days spent at work is valued at 1990 median wage rates. By applying an overall impairment rate to the potential output, the costs associated with this forgone productive capacity are then calculated.

The same set of assumptions used to estimate lost days with respect to MDE and BD are employed to calculate the remaining episode days. More precisely, the remaining episode days are equal to the average episode length minus the excess absentee days, as presented in Tables 7 and 8. Tables 9 and 10 show the number of remaining episode days for MDE and BD sufferers.

To assess the economic costs of DYS at work, we assume that an untreated employee is impaired every working week, or 50 weeks of the year. Treatment of DYS is assumed to reduce the episode length by one-third, which is comparable to the assumption made for treated and untreated MDE and BD episodes. Thus, a treated DYS employee is presumed to be impaired approximately 33 working weeks per year. As noted above, specific service utilization data are available for DYS from Regier *et al.* (1993), and a 42% treatment rate is applied in Table 11.

Tables 12, 13, and 14 present estimates of the number of work weeks during which sufferers attend work, but at a reduced level of performance. As shown in these tables, over two million person-years of work time are characterized by impaired performance due to depression. The output that could be produced during this time is valued at the median wage for each age and gender category. Table 15 presents a summary of these findings by age, sex and type of disorder.

Discussion
We find that employees suffering from depression could potentially produce output valued at over $42 billion during their episodes if they could work at full capacity. As was the case with respect to absenteeism costs, the wage differential between men and women tends to equalize their relative potential contributions at $20.1 billion for men and $22.2 billion for women. Individuals suffering from MDE contribute almost 70% of the potential output. In addition, the 30–44 age group is responsible for $21.9 billion in potential output, or over 50% of the $42.3 billion total.

Of course, only a portion of this potential output is lost due to the inability of employees to work at full capacity during episodes of depression. The precise extent of workplace incapacitation due to this particular mental illness has not been systematically studied. We assume that depressed workers produce 20% less during an episode than they would in a non-depressed state. This estimate, used in Greenberg *et al.* (1993a), is based on empirical estimates of impairment percentages of workers suffering from any type of mental illness. Applying this impairment percentage to the $42.3 billion in potential output implies a productivity cost valued at approximately $8.5 billion. Preliminary analysis of the NCS suggests that the estimate of 20% work loss capacity is conservative and may underestimate the true impairment percentage by more than one-half. For example, if the impairment percentage were increased to 40%, the resulting productivity costs would approach $18 billion annually.

CONCLUSIONS

The purpose of this analysis has been to demonstrate the critical importance of underlying epidemiological and medical data used to develop informative economic estimates. In the case of the mental health sector, significant advances have recently been made in these underlying information sources. Thus, it is no surprise that economic analyses relying on earlier sources may be subject to substantial revision.

Greenberg *et al.* (1993a) estimated the annual costs to society associated with depression in the US at almost $44 billion, $24 billion (55%) of which arose in the workplace as a result of excess absenteeism and reduced productivity of depressed workers. In this analysis, we rely on more recent epidemiological and treatment data to refine the estimates of depression in the workplace. Our results suggest that depression is even more costly to employers than had been previously understood. As shown in Figure 3, we estimate that the costs of this illness in the workplace total

Table 7. Morbidity costs of depression: Reduction in productive capacity of employed major depression sufferers due to excess absenteeism.

Age	Lost labour force days	Lost labour force years	Average weeks worked per year	Lost work weeks	Median weekly wage ($)	Total cost ($)
	[1]	[2] = [1]/365	[3]	[4] = [2] × [3]	[5]	[6] = [4] × [5]
Male						
Total	168 884 577	462 697		23 134 874		11 063 788 740
18–29	64 425 383	176 508	50	8 825 395	376	3 318 348 507
30–44	77 699 939	212 877	50	10 643 827	535	5 694 447 611
45–64	25 239 676	69 150	50	3 457 490	569	1 967 311 717
65+	1 519 579	4163	50	208 161	402	83 680 905
Female						
Total	241 353 782	661 243		33 062 162		11 688 610 864
18–29	81 081 726	222 142	50	11 107 086	313	3 476 517 836
30–44	95 199 969	260 822	50	13 041 092	383	4 994 738 076
45–64	62 937 536	172 432	50	8 621 580	363	3 129 633 620
65+	2 134 552	5848	50	292 404	300	87 721 331

Sources:
Total lost days from Table 5.
Average weeks worked per year [3], and 1990 Median weekly wage [5], from the Bureau of Labor Statistics.

Table 8. Morbidity costs of depression: Reduction in productive capacity of employed bipolar disorder sufferers due to excess absenteeism.

Age	Lost labour force days [1]	Lost labour force years [2] = [1]/365	Average weeks worked per year [3]	Lost work weeks [4] = [2] × [3]	1990 Median weekly wage ($) [5]	Total cost ($) [6] = [4] × [5]
Male						
Total	17 458 199	47 831		2 391 534		1 155 210 730
18–29	5 668 062	15 529	50	776 447	376	291 944 012
30–44	11 414 336	31 272	50	1 563 608	535	836 530 075
45–64	264 104	724	50	36 179	569	20 585 658
65+	111 697	306	50	15 301	402	6 150 983
Female						
Total	12 270 584	33 618		1 680 902		624 027 074
18–29	1 965 613	5385	50	269 262	313	84 279 025
30–44	10 224 932	28 014	50	1 400 676	383	536 458 745
45–64	0	0	50	0	363	0
65+	80 040	219	50	10 964	300	3 289 304

Sources:
Total lost days [1] from Table 6.
Average weeks worked per year [3], and 1990 Median weekly wage [5], from the Bureau of Labor Statistics.

Table 9. Morbidity of depression: Remaining episode days of employed major depression sufferers.

Age	Average episode length (days)	Average hospital days	Average outpatient treatment days	Remaining episode days per individual	Male		Female		Total remaining episode days by treated individuals
					Number of treated individuals	Remaining episode days	Number of treated individuals	Remaining episode days	
	[1]	[2]	[3] = ([1] − [2]) × 0.25	[4] = [1] − ([2] + [3])	[5]	[6] = [4] × [5]	[7]	[8] = [4] × [7]	[9] = [6] + [8]
Total	84	16	17	51	1 998 911	101 944 438	2 856 653	145 689 299	247 633 737
18–29	84	16	17	51	762 536	38 889 338	959 680	48 943 670	87 833 008
30–44	84	16	17	51	919 653	46 902 309	1 126 783	57 465 918	104 368 227
45–64	84	16	17	51	298 736	15 235 521	744 926	37 991 223	53 226 745
65 +	84	16	17	51	17 986	917 269	25 264	1 288 488	2 205 757

Remaining episode days from untreated cases

Age	Average episode length (days) [10]	Average days at home unable to work [11]	Average additional lost days [12] = ([10] − [11]) × 0.3	Remaining episode days per individual [13] = [9] − ([11] + [12])	Male		Female		Total remaining episode days by untreated individuals [18] = [15] + [17]
					Number of untreated individuals [14]	Remaining episode days [15] = [13] × [14]	Number of untreated individuals [16]	Remaining episode days [17] = [13] × [16]	
Total	126	32	28.2	65.8	1 709 643	112 494 532	2 443 260	160 766 491	273 261 022
18–29	126	32	28.2	65.8	652 188	42 913 944	820 802	54 008 785	96 922 729
30–44	126	32	28.2	65.8	786 568	51 756 167	963 723	63 412 989	115 169 156
45–64	126	32	28.2	65.8	255 505	16 812 225	637 126	41 922 884	58 735 109
65+	126	32	28.2	65.8	15 383	1 012 196	21 608	1 421 832	2 434 028

Sources:
Average episode length, [1] and [10], Hospital days [2], Days at home unable to work [11], Outpatient treatment days [3], and Additional lost days [12] from Stoudemire *et al*, 1986.
Number of treated and untreated cases [5], [7], [14], and [16] from Table 5.

350

Table 10. Morbidity of depression: Remaining episode days of employed bipolar disorder sufferers.

Age	Average episode length (days)	Average hospital days	Average outpatient treatment days	Remaining episode days per individual	Remaining episode days from treated cases				
					Male		Female		
					Number of treated individuals	Remaining episode days	Number of treated individuals	Remaining episode days	Total remaining episode days by treated individuals
	[1]	[2]	[3] = (([1] − [2]) × 0.25	[4] = [1] − ([2] + [3])	[5]	[6] = [4] × [5]	[7]	[8] = [4] × [7]	[9] = [6] + [8]
Total	84	16	17	51	243 657	12 426 532	171 256	8 734 051	21 160 583
18–29	84	16	17	51	79 107	4 034 457	27 433	1 399 099	5 433 556
30–44	84	16	17	51	159 306	8 124 584	142 706	7 277 981	15 402 565
45–64	84	16	17	51	3686	187 986	0	0	187 986
65+	84	16	17	51	1559	79 505	1117	56 971	136 476

Remaining episode days from untreated cases

Age	Average episode length (days) [10]	Average days at home unable to work [11]	Average additional lost days [12] = ([10] − [11]) × 0.3	Remaining episode days per individual [13] = [9] − ([11]+[12])	Male		Female		Total remaining episode days by untreated individuals [18] = [15] + [17]
					Number of untreated individuals [14]	Remaining episode days [15] = [13] × [14]	Number of untreated individuals [16]	Remaining episode days [17] = [13] × [16]	
Total	126	32	28.2	65.8	156 437	10 293 548	109 952	7 234 873	17 528 422
18–29	126	32	28.2	65.8	50 790	3 341 952	17 613	1 158 947	4 500 900
30–44	126	32	28.2	65.8	102 280	6 730 019	91 622	6 028 734	12 758 753
45–64	126	32	28.2	65.8	2367	155 719	0	0	155 719
65+	126	32	28.2	65.8	1001	65 858	717	47 192	113 050

Sources:
Average episode length, [1] and [10], Hospital days [2], Days at home unable to work [11], Outpatient treatment days [3], and Additional lost days [12] from Stoudemire *et al.*, 1986.
Number of treated and untreated cases [5], [7], [14], and [16] from Table 6.

Table 11. Morbidity of depression: Episode days of employed dysthymia sufferers.

Age	No. of cases		Percentage of cases		Male One-year prevalence		Female One-year prevalence	
	Male	Female	Treated (%)	Untreated (%)	Treated	Untreated	Treated	Untreated
	[1]	[2]	[3]	[4]	[5] = [1] × [3]	[6] = [1] × [4]	[7] = [2] × [3]	[8] = [2] × [4]
Total	225 638	438 339	42	58	94 768	130 870	184 102	254 237
18–29	63 623	84 749	42	58	26 722	36 901	35 594	49 154
30–44	132 765	226 734	42	58	55 761	77 003	95 228	131 504
45–64	25 940	120 572	42	58	10 895	15 045	50 640	69 932
65 +	3311	6285	42	58	1391	1920	2640	3645

Employed persons' episode days suffering from dysthymia

Age	Episode days		Male		Female		Total	
	Treated	Untreated	Treated	Untreated	Treated	Untreated	Male	Female
	[9]	[10]	[11] = [5] × [9]	[12] = [6] × [10]	[13] = [7] × [9]	[14] = [8] × [10]	[15] = [11] + [12]	[16] = [13] + [14]
Total	233	350	22 112 489	45 804 442	42 957 242	88 982 859	67 916 931	131 940 101
18–29	233	350	6 235 034	12 915 428	8 305 353	17 203 946	19 150 463	25 509 299
30–44	233	350	13 010 921	26 951 194	22 219 898	46 026 931	39 962 115	68 246 829
45–64	233	350	2 542 071	5 265 719	11 816 090	24 476 187	7 807 790	36 292 277
65 +	233	350	324 463	672 101	615 901	1 275 796	996 564	1 891 697

Sources:
Number of cases [1] and [2] from Table 2.

353

Table 12. Morbidity costs of depression: Value of potential output of employed major depression sufferers during episodes of affective illness.

Age	Remaining episode days	Episode years	Average weeks worked per year	Suffering weeks while at work	1990 Median weekly wage ($)	Value of potential output ($)
	[1]	[2] = [1]/365	[3]	[4] = [2] × [3]	[5]	[6] = [4] × [5]
Male						
Total	214 438 970	587 504	50	29 375 201		14 048 100 176
18–29	81 803 283	224 119	50	11 205 929	376	4 213 429 354
30–44	98 658 476	270 297	50	13 514 860	535	7 230 449 927
45–64	32 047 746	87 802	50	4 390 102	569	2 497 968 167
65+	1 929 465	5286	50	264 310	402	106 252 728
Female						
Total	306 455 790	839 605	50	41 980 245		14 841 459 847
18–29	102 952 455	282 062	50	14 103 076	313	4 414 262 779
30–44	120 878 907	331 175	50	16 558 754	383	6 342 002 952
45–64	79 914 108	218 943	50	10 947 138	363	3 973 811 110
65+	2 710 320	7426	50	371 277	300	111 383 006

Sources:
Average weeks worked per year [3], and 1990 Median weekly wage [5], from the Bureau of Labor Statistics.

Table 13. Morbidity costs of depression: Value of potential output of employed bipolar disorder sufferers during episodes of affective illness.

Age	Remaining episode days	Episode years	Average weeks worked per year	Suffering weeks while at work	1990 Median weekly wage ($)	Value of potential output ($)
	[1]	[2] = [1]/365	[3]	[4] = [2] × [3]	[5]	[6] = [4] × [5]
Male						
Total	22 720 080	62 247	50	3 112 340		1 503 389 939
18–29	7 376 409	20 209	50	1 010 467	376	379 935 608
30–44	14 854 603	40 698	50	2 034 877	535	1 088 659 296
45–64	343 705	942	50	47 083	569	26 790 153
65+	145 362	398	50	19 913	402	8 004 883
Female						
Total	15 968 925	43 750	50	2 187 524		812 108 129
18–29	2 558 047	7008	50	350 417	313	109 680 628
30–44	13 306 715	36 457	50	1 822 838	383	698 146 805
45–64	0	0	50	0	363	0
65+	104 164	285	50	14 269	300	4 280 697

Sources:
Average weeks worked per year [3], and 1990 Median weekly wage [5], from the Bureau of Labor Statistics.

Table 14. Morbidity costs of depression: Value of potential output of employed dysthymia sufferers during episodes of affective illness.

Age	Remaining episode days	Episode years	Average weeks worked per year	Suffering weeks while at work	1990 Median weekly wage ($)	Value of potential output ($)
	[1]	[2] = [1]/365	[3]	[4] = [2] × [3]	[5]	[6] = [4] × [5]
Male						
Total	67 916 931	186 074	50	9 303 689		4 578 569 348
18–29	19 150 463	52 467	50	2 623 351	376	986 380 002
30–44	39 962 115	109 485	50	5 474 262	535	2 928 730 309
45–64	7 807 790	21 391	50	1 069 560	569	608 579 757
65+	996 564	2730	50	136 516	402	54 879 280
Female						
Total	131 940 101	361 480	50	18 073 986		6 556 787 883
18–29	25 509 299	69 888	50	3 494 424	313	1 093 754 853
30–44	68 246 829	186 978	50	9 348 881	383	3 580 621 284
45–64	36 292 277	99 431	50	4 971 545	363	1 804 670 778
65+	1 891 697	5183	50	259 137	300	77 740 968

Sources:
Average weeks worked per year [3], and 1990 Median weekly wage [5], from the Bureau of Labor Statistics.

Table 15. Summary of potential output by employed affective disorder sufferers. Estimates in billions of 1990 dollars.

| | Potential output in billions of 1990 dollars | | |
Age	Male	Female	Total workplace cost of depression
Major depression			
18–29	4.2	4.4	8.6
30–44	7.2	6.3	13.6
45–64	2.5	4.0	6.5
65+	0.1	0.1	0.2
Subtotal	14.0	14.8	28.9
Bipolar disorder			
18–29	0.4	0.1	0.5
30–44	1.1	0.7	1.8
45–64	0.0	0.0	0.0
65+	0.0	0.0	0.0
Subtotal	1.5	0.8	2.3
Dysthymia			
18–29	1.0	1.1	2.1
30–44	2.9	3.6	6.5
45–64	0.6	1.8	2.4
65+	0.1	0.1	0.1
Subtotal	4.6	6.6	11.1
Total potential output			
18–29	5.6	5.6	11.2
30–44	11.2	10.6	21.9
45–64	3.1	5.8	8.9
65+	0.2	0.2	0.4
Total	20.1	22.2	42.3

Notes: Columns and rows may not sum to totals reported due to rounding.

approximately $33 billion per year, the vast majority of which is due to the effects of major depression. In addition, this implies economic costs in the workplace that are approximately $9 billion more than had been suggested by previous estimates. Furthermore, it results in an estimate of aggregate depression-related costs to society of almost $53 billion in 1990, as opposed to the earlier estimate of $44 billion.

Table 16, as well as Figure 4 disaggregate total costs into various categories, such as age, sex, type of disorder, and source of reduction in productive capacity. We find that 78% of the total workplace costs are attributable to adult employees who are below the age of 45. In addition, absenteeism accounts for 74% of all workplace costs, while MDE contributes over 85% to this total.

Since it is assumed the workplace costs of depression depend critically on the

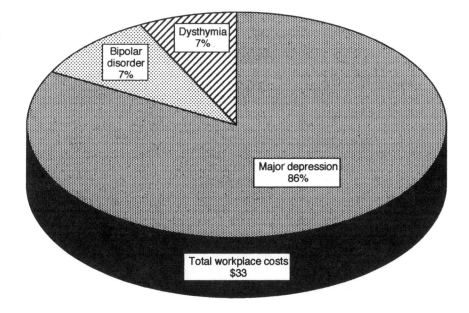

Figure 3. Total workplace costs of depression in billions of 1990 dollars.

definition of depression used and the epidemiological data relied upon, it is useful to compare cost estimates that utilize alternative underlying prevalences. Table 17 compares estimates based on the NCS with the results obtained in Greenberg *et al.* (1993a), which were based on the earlier ECA data. Each refinement of underlying economic and epidemiological data brings us closer to accurate measurements of depression-related costs. Furthermore, if a greater number of cases of depression were more accurately diagnosed and properly treated it has been suggested that the workplace costs of depression described in this analysis would decline. To examine this possibility, Table 18 also compares the $33 billion workplace cost estimate found here with estimates of workplace costs following an increase in the treatment rate of each disorder by 20 percentage points. As shown in the table, as the mix of treated-to-untreated individuals grows, workplace costs are reduced by over $3.4 billion, from $33 billion to $29.6 billion. At the same time, however, direct costs would likely rise as treatment is extended to an increasing share of the depressed workforce.

Further economic research must be undertaken to investigate the extent to which indirect costs fall in the workplace as direct costs rise. Prospective studies can be designed to explore these issues in a controlled experimental context. Alternatively, objective measures of impairment can be designed to examine the effects on workplace performance associated with suffering from a debilitating mental illness

Table 16. Workplace costs of depression by age and sex. Estimates in billions of 1990 dollars.

	Costs due to reduction in productive capacity ($)		
Age	Male	Female	Total workplace cost of depression
From excess absenteeism			
18–29	3.6	3.6	7.2
30–44	6.5	5.5	12.1
45–64	2.0	3.1	5.1
65+	0.1	0.1	0.2
Subtotal	12.2	12.3	24.5
While at work – impairment rate = 20%			
18–29	1.1	1.1	2.2
30–44	2.2	2.1	4.4
45–64	0.6	1.2	1.8
65+	0.03	0.04	0.1
Subtotal	4.0	4.4	8.5
Total workplace costs of depression			
18–29	4.7	4.7	9.4
30–44	8.8	7.7	16.4
45–64	2.6	4.3	6.9
65+	0.1	0.1	0.3
Total	16.2	16.8	33.0

Notes:
Columns may not sum to totals reported due to rounding.
Costs due to excess absenteeism are from Tables 7 and 8.
Costs due to reduction in productive capacity while at work are derived from Tables 12, 13 and 14.

such as depression. We are currently developing analyses in these and other research directions to gain further insight into the manner in which costs accrue in the workplace, and the extent to which they may be avoided through cost-effective interventions.

Unless we continue to sharpen the precision of our estimates of the costs of depression in the workplace, it will be difficult for employers to accept any recommendation whose premise is that expanded treatment programmes are justified on purely economic grounds. This challenge requires economists to work with mental health experts in devising increasingly effective techniques for measuring workplace costs, and in describing the economic implications of alternative treatment approaches.

Table 17. Summary of workplace costs of depression. Estimates in billions of 1990 dollars.

Treatment data:	NIMH Treatment rates	+20% NIMH Treatment rates*	2/3 Treated—1/3 Untreated Assumption
Source of epidemiological data:	NCS	NCS	ECA Wave I**
Costs due to reduction in productive capacity ($)			
From excess absenteeism	24.5	21.6	11.7
	(74.3%)	(73.0%)	(49.0%)
While at work	8.5	8.0	12.1
	(25.7%)	(27.0%)	(50.6%)
Total workplace costs of depression ($)	33.0	29.6	23.8
	(100.0%)	(100.0%)	(100.0%)

Notes:
*The percentage of treated individuals was increased by 20 percentage points and the percentage of untreated individuals was reduced by 20 percentage points.
**As presented in Greenberg, 1993a.
Figures in parentheses are percentage of total costs.

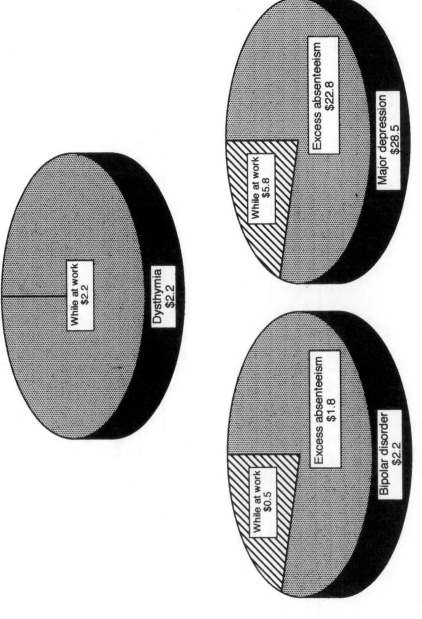

Figure 4. Total workplace costs of depression. Estimates in billions of 1990 dollars.

ABSTRACT

The purpose of this analysis is to update and refine existing workplace cost calculations associated with depression. Our analysis demonstrates the critical role of the underlying clinical data upon which economic estimates are made. We conclude that the annual workplace costs associated with depression are even larger than had been previously understood, totalling approximately $33 billion in 1990. This finding is $9 billion higher than our earlier estimate of the same workplace cost categories. The new results underscore the importance of incorporating workplace cost consideration formally in a variety of health outcomes research investigations, especially in analyses of mental health issues, to gain a clearer sense of the manner in which resource utilization is affected by health care decisions.

REFERENCES

American Psychiatric Association (1980) *Diagnostic and Statistical Manual of Mental Disorders—3rd edn.* American Psychiatric Association, Washington, DC.

American Psychiatric Association (1987) *Diagnostic and Statistical Manual of Mental Disorders—3rd edn, revised.* American Psychiatric Association, Washington, DC.

American Psychiatric Association (1994) *Diagnostic and Statistical Manual of Mental Disorders—4th edn.* American Psychiatric Association, Washington, DC.

Bartel A and Taubman P (1986) Some economic and demographic consequences of mental illness. *J Labor Econ* **4**, 243–256.

Blazer DG, Kessler RC, McGonagle KA and Swartz MS (1994) The prevalence and distribution of major depression in a national community sample: The National Comorbidity Survey. *Am J Psychiatry* **151**, 979–986.

Broadhead WE, Blazer DG, George LK and Tse CK (1990) Depression, disability days, and days lost from work in a prospective epidemiologic survey. *JAMA* **264**, 2524–2528.

Cottler LB, Robins LN and Helzer JE (1989) The reliability of the CIDI-SAM: A comprehensive substance abuse interview. *Br J Addict* **84**, 802–814.

Cottler LB, Robins LN, Grant B, Blaine J, Towle I, Wittchen H-U, Sartorius N, Burke J, Regier D, Helzer J and Janca A (1991) The CIDI-CORE substance abuse and dependence questions: Cross-cultural and nosological issues. *Br J Psychiatry* **159**, 653–658.

Eaton WW, Holzer CE, Von Korff M, *et al.* (1984) The design of the Epidemiologic Catchment Area Surveys: The control and measurement of error. *Arch Gen Psychiatry* **41**, 942–948.

Eisenberg L (1992) Treating depression and anxiety in primary care: Closing the gap between knowledge and practice. *N Engl J Med* **326**, 1080–1084.

Farmer AE, Jenkins PL, Katz R and Ryder L (1991) Comparison of CATEGO-derived ICD-8 and DSM-III classifications using the Composite International Diagnostic Interview in severely ill subjects. *Br J Psychiatry* **158**, 177–182.

Farmer AE, Katz R, McGuffin P and Bebbington P (1987) A comparison between the Present State Examination and the Composite International Diagnostic Interview. *Arch Gen Psychiatry* **44**, 1064–1068.

Frank R and Gertler P (1987) The effect of mental distress on income: Results from a community survey. *Working Paper Number 2433*, National Bureau of Economic Research.

Frank RG and Manning WG Jr (eds) (1992) *Economics and Mental Health.* The Johns Hopkins University Press, Baltimore, MD.

Greenberg PE, Stiglin LE, Finkelstein SN and Berndt ER (1993a) The economic burden of depression in 1990. *J Clin Psychiatry* **54**, 405–418.

Greenberg PE, Stiglin LE, Finkelstein SN and Berndt ER (1993b) Depression: A neglected major illness. *J Clin Psychiatry* **54**, 419–424.

Helzer JE, Robins LN, McEvoy LT and Spitznagel E (1985) A comparison of clinical and diagnostic interview schedule diagnoses. *Arch Gen Psychiatry* **42**, 657–666.

Janca A, Robins LN and Cottler LB (1992) Clinical observation of CIDI assessments: An analysis of the CIDI field trials—wave II at the St Louis site. *Br J Psychiatry* **160**, 815–818.

Janca A, Robins LN, Bucholz KK and Early TS (1992) Comparison of Composite International Diagnostic Interview and clinical DSM-III-R criteria checklist diagnoses. *Acta Psychiatr Scand* **85**, 440–443.

Jönsson B and Rosenbaum J (1993) *Perspectives in Psychiatry, Volume 4, Health Economics of Depression.* John Wiley & Sons, Chichester.

Kamlet MS, Wade M, Kupfer DJ, *et al.* (1992) Cost-utility analysis of maintenance treatment for recurrent depression: a theoretical framework and numerical illustration. In: Frank RG and Manning (eds) *Economics and Mental Health.* Johns Hopkins University Press, Baltimore, MD.

Keller MB, Shapiro RW, Lavori PW and Wolfe N (1982) Recovery in major depressive disorder: Analysis with the life table and regression models. *Arch Gen Psychiatry* **39**, 905–910.

Kessler RC, Turner JB and House JS (1987) Unemployment and health in a community sample. *J Health and Soc Behavior* **28**, 51–59.

Kessler RC, House JS and Turner JB (1989) Unemployment, reemployment and emotional functioning in a community sample. *Am Soc Rev* **54**, 648–657.

Kessler RC, McGonagle KA, Swartz, *et al.* (1993) Sex and depression in the National Comorbidity Survey I: Lifetime prevalence, chronicity and recurrence. *J Affect Disord* **29**, 85–96.

Kessler RC, McGonagle KA, Nelson CB, *et al.* (1993) Sex and depression in the National Comorbidity Survey II: Cohort effects. *J Affect Disord* **30**, 15–26.

Kessler RC, McGonagle KA, Zhoa S, *et al.* (1994) Lifetime and 12-month prevalence of DSM-III-R psychiatric disorders in the United States. *Arch Gen Psychiatry* **51**, 8–19.

Kessler RC, Mroczek DK and Belli RF (in press) Retrospective adult assessment of childhood psychopathology. In: Shaffer D and Richters J (eds) *Assessment in Child and Adolescent Psychopathology.* Guilford Press, New York, NY.

Klerman GL (1989) Depressive disorders: Further evidence for increased medical morbidity and impairment of social functioning. *Arch Gen Psychiatry* **46**, 856–858.

Leitmeyer P (ed) (1990) *Zur Symptomerfassung mit dem standarisierten Interview CIDI-C in der Allgemeinpraxis: Inaugural Dissertation zur Erlangung des medizinischen Doktorgrades fur klinische Medizin.* Universitat Mannheim, Mannheim, Germany.

Mandersheid RW and Sonnenschein MA (eds) (1990) *Mental Health, United States, 1990.* National Institute of Mental Health, Washington, DC.

McGuire TG (1992) Research on economics and mental health: The past and future prospects. In: Frank RG and Manning WG Jr (eds) *Economics and Mental Health.* The Johns Hopkins University Press, Baltimore, MD.

Mumford E, Schlesinger HJ, Glass GV, Patrick C and Cuerdon T (1984) A new look at evidence about reduced cost of medical utilization following mental health treatment. *Am J Psychiatry* **141**, 1145–1158.

Regier DA, Hirschfeld RMA, Goodwin FK, *et al.* (1988) The NIMH depression awareness, recognition, and treatment program: Structure, aims, and scientific bias. *Am J Psychiatry* **145**, 1351–1357.

Regier DA, Myers JK, Kramer M, *et al.* (1984) The NIMH Epidemiologic Catchment Area program: Historical context, major objectives, and study population characteristics. *Arch Gen Psychiatry* **41**, 934–941.

Regier DA, Narrow WE, Rae DS, *et al.* (1993) The de facto US mental and addictive disorders service system. *Arch Gen Psychiatry* **50**, 85–94.

Rice DP, Kelman S, Miller LS and Dunmeyer (1990) *The Economic Costs of Alcohol and Drug Abuse and Mental Illness: 1980.* Research Triangle Institute, Research Triangle Park, NC.

Semler G (1989) Reliabilitat und Validitat des Composite International Diagnostic Interview. *Inaugural-Dissertation zur Erlangung des akademischen Grades eines Doktors der Philosophie.* Mannheim Universitat, Mannheim, Germany.

Spengler P and Wittchen H-U (1988) Procedural validity of standardized symptom questions for the assessment of psychotic symptoms: A comparison of the DIS with two clinical methods. *Compr Psychiatry* **29**, 309–322.

Spitzer RL, Williams JBW, Gibbon M and First MB (1992) The structured clinical interview for DSM-III-R (SCID). I. History, rationale, and description. *Arch Gen Psychiatry* **49**, 624–629.

Stoudemire A, Frank R, Hedemark N, *et al.* (1986) The economic burden of depression. *Gen Hosp Psychiatry* **8**, 387–394.

Sturm R and Wells KB (1995) How can care for depression become more cost-effective? *JAMA* **273**, 51–58.

US Department of Health and Human Services (1992) *National Health Interview Survey: 1989* (computer file). National Center for Health Statistics, Hyattsville, MD.

Wacker HR, Battegay R, Mullejans R and Schlosser C (1990) Using the CIDI-C in the general population. In: Stefanis CN, Rabavilas AD and Soldatos CR (eds) *Psychiatry: A World Perspective.* Elsevier Science Publishers B, Amsterdam, New York, Oxford.

Weissman MM, Bruce ML, Leaf PJ, *et al.* (1991) Affective disorders. In Robins LN and Regier DA (eds) *Psychiatric disorders in America: The Epidemiologic Catchment Area Study.* The Free Press, New York.

Wells KB, Stewart A, Hays RD, *et al.* (1989) The functioning and well-being of depressed patients: Results from the Medical Outcomes Study. *JAMA* **262**, 914–919.

Wilde MI and Whittington R (1995) Paroxetine. A pharmoeconomic evaluation of its use in depression. *PharmoEconomics* **8**, 62–81.

Wittchen H-U, Robins LN, Cottler L, Sartorius N, Altamura AC, Andrew G, Dingemanns R, Droux A and Essau CA (1990) *Interrater Reliability of the Composite International Diagnostic Interview (CIDI)—Results of the Multicenter WHO/ADAMHA Field Trials (Wave I).* Excerpta Medica, Amsterdam, New York, Oxford.

Wittchen H-U, Robins LN, Cottler LB, Sartorisu N, Burke JD, Regier DA, and Participants in the Multicentre WHO/ADAMHA Field Trials (1991) Cross-cultural feasibility reliability and sources of variance in the Composite International Diagnostic Interview (CIDI). *Br J Psychiatry* **159**, 645–653.

World Health Organization (1990a) *Composite International Diagnostic Interview (CIDI) Version 10.* World Health Organization, Geneva, Switzerland.

World Health Organization (1990b) *International Classification of Diseases—10 Classification of Mental and Behavioral Disorders: Diagnostic Criteria for Research.* World Health Organization, Geneva, Switzerland.

World Health Organization (1991) Mental health and behavioral disorders (including disorders of psychological development). In *International Classification of Diseases—10th Revision.* World Health Organization, Geneva, Switzerland.

Index

Index compiled by Geoffrey Jones